BALTIC SEA

Tilsit
Niemen R.

Königsberg
Pregel R.
Gumbinnen

Danzig

Eylau
Rothenen
Friedland

Passarge R.
Bartenstein
Alle R.
Heilsberg

Elbing
Marienburg
EAST
Gutstadt

Colberg
Treptow

Saalfeld
Finkenstein
Osterode
Rosenberg
PRUSSIA

Greiffenberg

Riesenburg
Marienwerder

Freistadt
Deutsch–
Eylau

E
Stettin

P O M E R A N I A

Willenberg

Oder R.

Bromberg
Thorn

Golymin
Pultusk

Schwedt

Warthe R.

Vistula R.

P O L A N D

P R U S S I A

Posen

Warsaw

Kalisch

Bree R.
Neisse R.
Bobr R.

Beuthen
Glogau

Polkwitz
Katzbach R.
Bunzlau

Queis R.

S I L E S I A

Oder R.

Bautzen
Görlitz
Reichenbach
Marckersdorf
Waldau

Pleiswitz

chkirch
Bischofswerda
Koenigstein

L U S A T I A

RIESENGEB.

Elbe R.

Prague

B O H E M I A

Olmütz

Moldava R.

M O R A V I A

Brünn
Wischau
Austerlitz

Morova R.

Znaim

A U S T R I A

Hollabrunn

Dürrenstein
Krems

Wagram

Linz
Melk
Essling

Ens
Ips
Amstetten
Neumarkt
St. Pölten
Vienna

**CAMPAIGNS OF
1805, 1806, 1807, 1809, 1813**

0   25   50   75   100
STATUTE MILES

THE ANATOMY OF GLORY

BROWN UNIVERSITY BICENTENNIAL PUBLICATIONS

STUDIES IN THE FIELDS OF GENERAL SCHOLARSHIP

PLATE I

THE
ANATOMY OF
GLORY

Napoleon and his Guard

A STUDY IN LEADERSHIP

With illustrations and maps

Adapted from the French of

HENRY LACHOUQUE

by

ANNE S. K. BROWN

1962

BROWN UNIVERSITY PRESS

PROVIDENCE, RHODE ISLAND

LUND HUMPHRIES

LONDON

FIRST EDITION SPRING 1961

SECOND REVISED EDITION WINTER 1962

THIS ADAPTATION OF

Napoléon et la Garde Impériale

IS MADE WITH THE

GRACIOUS PERMISSION OF THE AUTHOR, COMMANDANT HENRY LACHOUQUE

AND OF THE PUBLISHERS, MM. BLOUD & GAY, PARIS

SPONSORED BY THE COMPANY OF MILITARY COLLECTORS AND HISTORIANS

LIBRARY OF CONGRESS CATALOG CARD NUMBER 62/11764

MADE AND PRINTED IN GREAT BRITAIN BY

PERCY LUND, HUMPHRIES AND CO. LTD, LONDON AND BRADFORD

COLOR BLOCKS BY BEISSNER AND CO., VIENNA

To J. N. B.
whom many, given the chance,
would follow to Elba . . .

CONTENTS

vii

PLATES

xi

MAPS AND PLANS

TRANSLATOR'S PREFACE

WHY, many will ask, this translation and condensation of a work available to all scholars, and to the many laymen who have a reading knowledge of French?

The answer is: because Commandant Lachouque's masterful history of Napoleon and his Guard answers many questions being asked today. For instance, what is leadership? What makes a military force effective? Is it necessary to be loved in order to be obeyed? What makes men do better than their best? Was Napoleon right or wrong? Was he good or bad?

In this book, which is essentially a diary of an organization that grew from a brigade of under two thousand men into a virtual army without losing its essential character, the technique of leadership, as well as its value, is clearly demonstrated. The Imperial Guard with Napoleon was a human fortress which no one but he could dominate, and no enemy could penetrate. Lightly armed and protected by no more than several layers of cloth, its strength was largely moral. Designed, built, and nurtured as a bodyguard for one man, who nevertheless symbolized a renascent nation, it owed and gave its ultimate loyalty to him.

Neither phrases nor philosophies could confuse the Guardsman; he was the Emperor's man. The Emperor did not have to be perfect to command his allegiance; but he had to be just, attentive, and grateful.

Napoleon never forgot these primary rules. Thus, when misfortune overtook him his Guard remained faithful. His departure for Elba is one of the most singular and inspiring examples of personal loyalty in all history.

Napoleon was loved by men from whom all other loves and loyalties had been systematically removed. The officers of the Guard, like General Desvaux, General Curial – indeed Napoleon himself – wrote their wives. Some, like Marshal Lefebvre, went to pieces at the death of a beloved son. But the soldiers mostly wrote their parents. And all seemed to be talking to themselves about the wars, about the Emperor.

The modern demagogic approach seemed to apply then as now, with a few notable exceptions. The pay in the Guard was good, exceptionally good for that day; so were the food, the beds, the clothes, the entertainments, the rewards and advancement, the medical care, the retirement benefits. But the hours were long, the discipline stringent, privacy and vacations virtually nonexistent, and the work monotonous, arduous, or lethal. In short, a career in the Guard led either to death or glory. You suffered, you died miserably but gloriously; or you lived in the certain knowledge that you were a man, a prince among men, and possibly a hero.

For your hard and glamorous master was a genius. He counted on you. If you did not fail him, you could safely put your life into his hands and profit from doing better than your best. Because you were the elect of the supreme mortal authority. Therefore, your self-respect was invincible and was matched by your prestige.

Viewed in the light of today, Napoleon's ideas for Europe were not as chimerical as they may have seemed to his contemporaries. A federated Europe, based upon the classical Roman Empire, might have recreated a *Pax Romana* that would have changed the course of (nineteenth – and) twentieth-century history and cleared its pages of much blood. A greatly magnified Switzerland on one side of the Atlantic, with a dynamic – if less heterogeneous – United States on the other, is a dream Western nations could pleasantly dally with amid today's alarms.

The problems of Asia Napoleon could not solve, though he realized in advance of his time that they were vast and dreadful. England's splendid isolation from a continent only a few miles off was but an adumbration of the isolation of the United States in 1920; though the historic British role of troubling continental waters in order to fish in them was then entering its last profitable phase. America and Africa intrigued and disillusioned Napoleon in turn. His hardheaded Latin commonsense ultimately eschewed the dream of empire beyond the range of his restless traveling coach.

With so many good ideas, then why did he fail? Because he was in a hurry. In the case of some geniuses and most dictators, motion eventually intoxicates. Once intoxicated, its initiator tries to make it perpetual. Napoleon's early dream of peace, of completion, eventually became a nightmare. In full swing, the man of action never really wants to stop; and when he must, he has forgotten how.

The reader will wonder whether it was in fact Russia, or whether it was not rather Spain that sowed the seeds of Napoleon's downfall. The Russian campaign was short and disastrous, but hardly fatal. The Spanish venture was poisonous from the outset; it was conceived in cupidity and carried out in absentia. The seeds of dissent and disillusion were sown in the Guard from 1807 on in that stark and impassioned land where each peasant was more effectively armed by his sense of injury than by a dozen arsenals Wellington deserves more credit for making the most of the opportunity to march against Napoleon's demoralized lieutenants than for his hard fought but conventional victory over the tired and bemused fox himself at Waterloo.

Napoleon was no ordinary genius. His intellect and energy, his universality and ubiquity, his infinite imagination mark him as a superman. But as a man, he had the ordinary range of faults and virtues: vain, arrogant, devious, impetuous, and often callous towards others, he was direct, solicitous, and magnanimous towards his soldiers. He had an unrivaled capacity for inspiring men to serve their best selves in serving him.

When welcoming his 'baby Guard', did he promise the *pupilles* a happy life, with ice cream – or its equivalent – on Sundays? No. He said: 'In admitting you to my Guard I assign you a duty that is hard to perform.' And then, by way of reward, he promised to make them 'worthy of their sires'.

This book is a free translation of a monumental work from which, with the author's permission, I have eliminated many names and details. In those passages dealing with the initial organization and many reorganizations of the Guard as its tasks increased, I have tried to preserve the details of its basic structure as Napoleon conceived it.

For this nucleus of elite soldiers was able 'by precept and example' to inspire raw recruits to brilliant performance. The Guard was ever changing. Its old members were continually being transferred at a higher rank to the army where their prestige, technique, and boundless faith in the Emperor served to inoculate the common clay of the Line. Conversely, the heroes and elite of the Line were constantly rewarded by admission to the Guard. Thus the Guard never staled, and this dynamic corps ultimately permeated the whole military structure of France, enabling the Emperor to perform miracles on the battlefield while conserving an incorruptible force which had earned its right to be trusted.

Commandant Lachouque has told the story, built around quotations from the letters and reports of the participants, in pithy soldier speech. This I have tried to render into colloquial English.

Above all, he has convinced us that battles are not decided by generals and logistics alone, but also by the performance of a nucleus of truly dedicated men.

Harbour Court
Newport, Rhode Island
31 October 1959

NOTE ON THE SECOND EDITION

Like most second editions, this one has profited handsomely from thousands of readers, throughout the world, of the first edition. Among these were scholars whose specialized knowledge has enabled us to make alterations and corrections, and critics who have suggested improvements. Thus, this edition has been printed on thinner paper, substantially reducing its bulk, and plate references have been added to the text to guide the reader to the particular scene or object described.

A complete general index, though desirable, would have added many pages to the book, increasing its size and cost beyond reason. Since Commandant Lachouque's narrative is essentially a diary set down in chronological sequence, the reader is urged to use the Table of Contents, Appendices 'A', 'B', and 'C' (giving dates of organization of Guard units, troop levies, and principal events) and the Index of Names to locate those passages in the text to which he wishes to refer quickly.

A.S.K.B.

November Night

Saint-Cloud, 19 *brumaire*, year VIII.[1] Midnight.

The Directory had just expired. In the Orangerie, denuded of its windowpanes, a few smoking lamps and four candles in sconces above the empty tribune shed a sepulchral light over the overturned benches, tattered hangings, bonnets shorn of plumes, torn cloaks, togas, badges – all vestiges of the parliamentary rout. People came and went, talking loud. It was the usual audience of great political events: elegantly dressed women exposing their persons to the maximum, foppish men, intriguers, generals, flunkeys, prophets of the future. Even the expelled deputies came running from neighboring cafés to answer the *huissiers'* summons, ready to rally to the new government. They discussed the day's events, congratulated one another, and saluted the dawn of a new day and the happy era about to commence.

The coup d'état had to be ratified, the semblance of an assembly convoked, an appeal to the nation drafted, the oath administered to the new Consuls . . . Oath to whom? To what? The Consulate was but a provisional government. The old constitution was dead and the new one yet to be born. Bah! They would take an oath to the Republic, to liberty, equality . . .

2 a.m. The drums beat the salute *'Aux Champs'*. A nervous little general, an unfrocked priest, and a former justice of the peace[2] could be discerned in the gloom. These men were the Consuls of the Republic. Behind them pressed the curious. The rustle of silks, the jingling of sabers, and the buzz of conversation drowned out the voice of ex-President Lucien Bonaparte as he read the oath; but the threefold response *'Je le iure!'* – 'I swear!' – was audible, greeted by perfunctory cries of *'Vive la République!'*

Outside in the chill November wind the soldiers shivered behind their stacked arms. There were about eight hundred, under the command of Adjutant General Blanchard. These old partisans of the Republic were revolutionists who had served under successive regimes as National Gendarmes, Grenadier-Gendarmes of the Convention, and Grenadiers of the National Representatives. They were now called Grenadiers of the Legislature. They wore blue coats with scarlet revers, black gaiters, and fur bonnets, and smoked the company pipe in succession while awaiting the outcome of the affair in which they had just taken part without understanding precisely what had happened.

Contradictory shouts of 'Outlaw!' 'Long live Bonaparte!' *'Vive la République!'* 'Every man for himself!' 'Down with the tyrant!' and 'Long live the conqueror of Italy and Egypt!' had been eclipsed when Generals Leclerc and Murat roared: 'Throw these people out!' indicating the members of the Assembly to the troops directly charged with their protection. And then the Assembly voted them a testimonial!

---

[1] 10 November, 1799

[2] Bonaparte, Sieyès, and Roger-Ducos. The two latter were soon replaced by Cambacérès and the elder Lebrun. – Ed.

Besides the Grenadiers of the Legislature there were grenadiers of the Guard of the Directory, one hundred foot dressed like the Line except that they wore bearskin bonnets with brass plaques. Flanking these were twenty musicians in hats and, drowsing behind them, their bridles over their arms, 100 horse grenadiers bundled up in their white cloaks.

All these soldiers, who now had nothing more to guard, were bound together by a common anxiety.

Suddenly Bonaparte appeared. He knew these veterans whom he had commanded four years before in *vendémiaire*[3] when he had cited the best for 'never having forgot for a moment that they were fighting Frenchmen possessed by madness rather than malice . . .'

'Grenadiers', he said, 'from now on the Guards of the Legislature and the Directory will be called the Guard of the Consuls. I have never wished to be a party man . . .'

This profession was interrupted by cries of '*Vive le général Bonaparte!*'

While his carriage proceeded at a good clip towards his house in the Rue Victoire, the grenadiers took the road to Paris singing the '*Ça ira!*' This cry of hope arising from the nascent revolution had later been parodied and associated with the Saturnalias of the Red Terror. But on this night, inaugurating the 'greatest government France has ever known', it was sung in the Jacobin version of 1793 by men satisfied with themselves and content with their new master. In the words of Albert Vandal, they were perhaps 'persuaded that they had saved the Republic and the Revolution . . .' One can be sure they were pleased to have 'deserved well of their country' while preserving their posts in an elite corps, with all its material and moral advantages.

It is the same under all regimes.

As for their thirty-year-old chief, who had seized power in an atmosphere laden with the wreckage of the Revolution, he had just performed the initial act of his political life as sovereign in creating an elite corps, a symbol of obedience, heroism, and devotion to France and to the Emperor, whose memory is imperishable and whose glory is eternal: the Imperial Guard.

---

[3] During the popular uprising against the Convention in 1795 Bonaparte was made military governor of Paris, and restored order. – Ed.

BOOK I

THE GUARD IS BORN

CHAPTER 1

The Ancestors

IN the distant past the chief was served by a mayor, or 'major', who guarded his door, and a constable who took charge of his stables, assisted by a marshal.

About A.D.1000 armed men guarded the outside of the palace while palatine 'officers' (since they held office) policed the interior.

In the Louvre, Philip Augustus was guarded by sergeants-at-arms renowned for their strength and bravery; hence the word 'noble' derived from *nobilis*, meaning renowned or known. Soldiers wearing rich hauberks and carrying bows, swords, or maces marched in the royal processions and accompanied the King to war.

More than three centuries later Francis I entered Milan accompanied by a *Grande Garde* of 200 mounted gentlemen, appointed to 'stand watch and guard at night' when the King was in camp and 'at all times during the day', followed by a *Petite Garde* composed of Scottish and French archers, *Cent-Suisse* (100 Swiss), *Gardes de la Porte*, and the provost of the palace. This latter personage, a direct descendant of the mayors of the palace, policed the King's lodging with 36 archers. Three hundred years later we shall meet these men again in the Jeu de Paume.[1]

As the military spirit – 'that spontaneous conjunction of patriotism, a taste for arms, and rumors of war' – developed in France, the Monarchy ensured to its institutions a certain continuity. Louis XIV united all guard corps into the *Maison du Roy*, or 'King's Household', which gave him prestige as well as cadres of officers for his army and a cavalry reserve in war. In addition to the ancient corps, the Gendarmes, Light-Horse (*Chevau-légers*), Musketeers, and Horse Grenadiers, selected from the finest soldiers in the army, provided the royal armies with a household brigade of 6,000 horse.

The infantry of the *Maison du Roy* was composed of the *Gardes françaises*, a smart, aggressive, and warlike troop, and the *Gardes suisses*, a model of discipline and fidelity.

'You cannot beat the *Maison du Roy*', said the Duke of Marlborough, 'you have to destroy it.' This feat was eventually performed by the French themselves.

Vigorous, ardent, and impulsive, the French amused themselves during the latter half of the eighteenth century by talking nonsense and paying court to the King of Prussia[2] who consistently defeated them. Louis XV recognized the danger but could not avert it.

Saint-Germain, war minister of the weak Louis XVI, regarded the *Maison du Roy* as both costly and obsolete and undertook to abolish it. Between 1776 and 1786 all the

[1] The Tennis Court, a building adjoining the palace of Versailles. – Ed.
[2] Frederick the Great.

cavalry corps were disbanded except the *Gardes du corps* which was reduced in strength. The *Gardes françaises* betrayed the king and was dissolved after the fall of the Bastille, followed by the *Gardes du corps* in 1791. Still King of France, though he no longer reigned, Louis was subsequently guarded by a troop called the 'Constitutional Guard' which was disbanded the following year. Less than three months later royalty was abolished. The Swiss Guard rushed forward at the Tuileries to die at the steps of the throne. The King was guillotined in January 1793.

The kings and their guards were dead. A thousand years of French monarchy fell into the abyss. All men were leveled. Nothing remained except a tradition – and one corps which was spared by its own defection.

This was the Provost Guard[3] of 140 officers and 79 men standing guard at the Salle des Menus Plaisirs[4] in Versailles during the sitting of the Estates-General in June of 1789. When the session was dissolved the Third Estate took refuge in the Jeu de Paume, where they performed the initial act of the Revolution. Sent to expel them, the Provost Guards offered them protection instead, thus winning the favor of the deputies who rechristened them 'Guards of the Assembly'. Several of them turned up later in the Guard of the Consuls.

Thus, through many incarnations, the eldest corps of the *Maison du Roy* bridged the gap between the Royal and Imperial Guards.

The Guards of the Assembly were replaced in 1791 by the National Gendarmes, though the roster was but little changed. The following year the Gendarmes were purged by Danton. Their successors, the 'Grenadier-Gendarmes', wore red epaulets and bearskin bonnets and were good republicans, expelling all their officers except a single lieutenant who prudently assumed the title of 'Citizen Villeminot' thereafter. Bernelle, who later made a career in the Imperial Guard, was elected captain. One lieutenant, Ponsard by name, reappeared as a major six years later and led the first battalion of the Grenadiers of the Legislature to Saint-Cloud on the day of the coup d'état. He ended as a general in 1813.

After the revolution in the Vendée, where many grenadier-gendarmes were killed and even more deserted, the corps was re-formed in 1794. Now coifed in the democratic hat, it guarded the doors of the Convention so poorly that it was replaced by a new corps recruited from the army.

The new Guard, called 'Grenadiers of the National Representatives' and later 'Grenadiers of the Legislature', was composed of old soldiers with good service records and experienced officers. But its members were soon contaminated by politics and their discipline destroyed. These 'Tricolor Guards' became in time a veritable Praetorian Guard.[5]

The corps was a body without a head, afflicted with all the ills of the regime. Citizen Villemenot reported: 'Certain grenadiers . . . cannot resist the temptations of a corrupt

---

[3] *Gardes de la Prévôté de l'Hôtel.*
[4] Literally 'Hall of the Small Pleasures'. – Ed.
[5] Roman cohort guarding the commanding general under the Republic, and later the emperor, whose lack of discipline and misuse of power became notorious. – *Ibid.*

city like Paris . . . It is impossible to keep them in barracks . . . They abuse and maltreat the citizens . . . Some have jobs in Paris and only show up for meals.' Villemenot was returned to the Line – probably for daring to tell the truth.

The corps numbered 1,200 men appointed by the Directory, and its grenadiers ranked with corporals of the Line. Their uniform was a blue coat faced with scarlet, worn with red epaulets, white waistcoat and breeches, and a fur bonnet whose plate bore a grenade and the device '*Garde du Corps législatif*' (see Plate 2).

Many of its officers and NCO's (noncommissioned officers) turned up later in the Consular and Imperial Guards, including Adjutant General Blanchard, a former constabulary guard; Ponsard, mentioned above; Captain Couloumy, nephew of the Convention's president; Chéry, a gunner in the La Fère artillery before Lieutenant Bonaparte's arrival; Bernelle, Faucon, and Flamand, future adjutant general of the Imperial Guard and baron of the Empire, etc., etc. These were seasoned campaigners, but the Revolution had spoiled them.

The grenadiers were no less spoiled. Some months before the coup d'état they sent a petition to the 'Fathers of the People' – as the Directors were called – protesting an order to wear full dress every day.

'Well, what next?' the petition ran. 'Is Liberty, then, to become an empty word? . . . Revoke therefore, Citizens, revoke this order to be always in full dress. Are waistcoats and breeches to become an apple of discord thrown into the Patriots' midst to divide them and strengthen the Royalists? Not in the accoutrements, but in the heart, lies the sanctuary of Republicanism . . .'

One imagines himself to be dreaming when he reads such drivel which, nevertheless, was solemnly transmitted to the Minister of War who refused the request with lengthy explanations and apologies.

In 1796 the Guard of the Directory was formed to escort the Directors 'in public ceremonies and parades'. Its recruiting standards were strict. Candidates had to be literate, over five-foot-ten, with a perfect conduct record, and must have participated in two campaigns. The army commanders were instructed to choose their best-qualified men and send them to the Directors for further scrutiny.

The infantry of the new Guard wore the grenadier uniform with buttons stamped with a Roman fasces and '*Garde du Directoire exécutif*' in abbreviated form, and red cuffs slashed and closed with a white flap. The cavalry uniform was similar, though the epaulets were replaced by red trefoil shoulder knots piped with white, and an aiguillette – the distinctive insignia of guard cavalry – worn on the right shoulder. White or buff leather breeches were worn with top boots and spurs, and white cloaks.

The twenty-five piece band was furnished by the Conservatoire and led by Guiardel, its first clarinet. The musicians wore plain blue coats with red turnover collars edged with white, and red turned-back cuffs trimmed with a gold musician's stripe. They wore no epaulets.

The corps contained a staff, two companies of grenadiers, and two of horse grenadiers. Lt. General Krieg was its commander. His aide-de-camp Dumoustier will be heard from later. Among the adjutants were Colonel Fuzy, former subaltern of the *Gardes françaises* who had led a volunteer corps in five campaigns, and Major[6] Oehler, a former royal drum major who had served in the Army of the Rhine and been wounded in the Vendée.

Major Dubois commanded the foot battalion. His ensign, Lemarois, came from the police legion. Captains Schobert from the 96th Demi-brigade, Auger from the horse grenadiers, and Lieutenant Vézu, son of the Ain deputy, all reappeared in the Guard of the Consuls.

Though most of the Guardsmen were good men the army commanders took advantage of the opportunity to rid themselves of some questionable characters. 'We have married troopers and soldiers living in concubinage', wrote Col. Jubé, 'and about thirty who should be expelled ... having done irreparable harm to many fine soldiers ...'

The Guard of the Directory did not increase the prestige of the government. Nevertheless, the '*Maison de la Directoire*', as it was quaintly termed in a decree of 1798, was in a satisfactory military state when Drum Major Sénot raised his baton at Saint-Cloud on the 19th *brumaire* (10 November) signaling his drummers to beat the Charge at the gates of the Orangerie.

That night the Guards of the Legislature and Directory were rechristened the Guard of the Consuls.

---

[6] The rank of major was called *chef de battalion* in the infantry, and *chef d'escadron* in the cavalry at this time; and the rank of colonel, *chef de brigade*. – Ed.

CHAPTER 2

The Guard of the Consuls

ON 28 November, eighteen days after the coup d'état, the Guard of the Consuls was officially created out of the Guards of the Directory and Legislature.

Bonaparte was in a hurry. He had seized power by a stroke of luck. Tired of disorder, revolution, ministerial crises, and corrupt politicians, the Parisians were indifferent. What did another change of government matter to them? A civic fête, speeches, singing . . . And the country would continue its headlong course towards the abyss.

The new Consul must regularize his position, repair the injustices, restore the currency, put the country's affairs in order, repel the invader, and avenge the nation's defeats with victories in the war that had been raging for the past eight years. For France, infatuated with 'la gloire', had been humiliated. It was a Titan's task.

Bonaparte purged the two corps of 'dangerous Robespierrists', overage officers, and men with unsavory reputations, and retained and flattered the rest. He had Grenadier Thomé, who had 'preserved him from the daggers on the 19th *brumaire*', rewarded by Josephine, and granted him a bonus of 600 francs.

On 2 December Citizen Murat, a lieutenant general,[1] was named commander in chief and inspector general of the new Guard.

Several weeks later Murat wrote the following:

'The First Consul[2] intends that the Guard shall be a model for the army. Admission will be restricted to men who have performed heroic actions, have been wounded, or have otherwise given proof . . . in several campaigns of their bravery, patriotism, discipline, and exemplary conduct.

'They must be not less than twenty-five, between 1·78 and 1·84 metres[3] in height, of robust constitution and exemplary conduct. They must have participated in three campaigns in the Wars of Liberty and know how to read and write.'

To prove that something had indeed changed, he added: 'The councils of administration of the several corps shall be held responsible for their choice of candidates.'

This was only a beginning.

The decree organizing the Guard of the Consuls was dated 13 *nivôse* year VIII (3 January 1800). A total complement of 2,089 men provided for a general staff, 50 musicians divided between infantry and cavalry, two battalions of grenadiers, a

---

[1] *Général de division.* Murat remained in this post only a few weeks.
[2] Bonaparte was named First Consul on 24 December 1799.
[3] Between five-foot-ten and six feet.

company of light infantry, two squadrons of light cavalry, a company of mounted chasseurs,[4] and one of light, or horse, artillery.

The decree established the pay for each grade and set up modest regimental funds for uniforms and equipment, to be reimbursed by deductions from the soldiers' pay. Later the infantry band was increased to fifty pieces, and a kettledrummer assigned to the horse Guard.

The new Guard was of modest size, but the current political and financial situation imposed caution. That the Guard's organization progressed smoothly was due to the popularity and prestige of the First Consul, and to his determination to reorganize the army which had been left in a shocking material and moral state by the old government.

The revolutionists had destroyed every vestige – real or imaginary – of the old regime except its uniform. Even while stamping out despotism and decapitating the king, the Parisians were seized with a sudden passion for traditional military dress, for joining the army, for discipline 'by free consent', and for practising marksmanship in the streets of the capital.

The painter David tried to persuade them to adopt new fashions and dress in the Roman style, but the kilts the of École de Mars[5] met with small success. The Jacobins clung to the historic dress of the *Gardes françaises* which, besides being of the national blue, white, and red, was, after all, the uniform worn by the stormers of the Bastille. Moreover, a long war had emptied the clothing magazines and had left no time to destroy all the trappings of Tyranny.

Consequently, peasants, bourgeois, and workmen, young and old, conscripts and volunteers, were rigged out in old-fashioned regimentals, usually outgrown as well, with pouchbelts too long and pantaloons of every hue, and were brigaded with veterans of America whose coats had not yet been dyed blue.[6] Rabid Jacobins and eager bourgeois were drilled in the rude craft of warfare alongside the king's troops turned republican, and bawled at by sergeants whose language had not changed one whit. These same men would presently be led to defeat, and later to victory, by chiefs chosen in many cases from the rank and file.

One might suppose that all vanity had been dispersed by the breeze of equality blowing through their ranks; but the national pride was at stake. The soldiers were disgusted with their clothes, with the faded liberty caps, the mangy bearskin bonnets, the ill-matched shoes. Such garments lowered their prestige (see Plate 7).

The commanders gradually grew aware of their own importance and adopted the epaulets, sashes, and plumes that they had envied the marquises in the old days. Hence Augureau was laced with gold from head to foot, and the most ardent Jacobins trailed swords which were veritable works of art.

[4] *Chasseurs à cheval.*
[5] In the Revolution the cadets of the Military School were dressed in short tunics with plumed cylindrical headdresses. – Ed.
[6] The royal army, with few exceptions, wore white uniforms. – *Ibid.*

Unconsciously the soldiers followed suit, relieving their squalor by the surprising – if typically French – expedient of adding bits of finery such as grenade and hunting horn insignia, epaulets and shoulder pieces to their ragged regimentals to distinguish their unit (which of course was the best in the demi-brigade!).

With the use of better cloth, real leather, gold lace, and plumes a new type of soldier appeared in the Consular army at the dawn of 1800. Of this army the Guard prided itself on being the criterion. Guardsmen ruined themselves for clothes and accoutrements. An officer thought nothing of spending 35 francs[7] for a bearskin bonnet and 18 for a pair of boots.

Workmen, peasants, ex-policemen, valets, clerks, and low characters with degrading occupations who were nonetheless brave and hardy, developed a sudden taste for soldiering and for those bits of lace and plumes that pleased the girls. They had come under the spell of the uniform and discovered the prestige of the sword which set them apart from men who wore neither. They strutted a bit, felt the first stirrings of esprit de corps, and performed prodigies of valor.

Under the vigorous thumb of Bonaparte who loved and understood them they pulled themselves together, repaired their tattered garments, and forgot their empty bellies. Now at last their records, their conduct under fire, their wounds and qualities counted for something. The ranks of an elite corps were opened to them – something like the old Royal Guard, they said, 'only now it belonged to this amazing little brat of a conqueror who cut you in on the glory, and claimed that nothing rated with him like performance.

Officers, NCO's, and soldiers of the new Guard of the Consuls, whose new blue, white, and red uniforms looked like those of the *Gardes françaises*, combed their queues and tied them just two inches below the base of the skull, shined their boots, chalked their crossbelts, cleaned their muskets, installed their plumes, polished their harness, and groomed their horses to appear before their commander Murat – that connoisseur of panache – in the Luxembourg gardens on 18 February, before submitting next day to a minute inspection in the Place de la Carrousel, under the gimlet eye of the First Consul who had just moved to the Tuileries.

Doubtless some had dirty hands, but all wore clean gloves. The great mystery of military dress, which every army must preserve and every nation honor if it hopes to survive, had performed a metamorphosis. The men had performed no miracles, to be sure. Here and there an ornament was missing from a skirt-flap or some other detail was wrong, but the garters were pulled tight and the queues aligned, and Paris proclaimed the parade '*impeccable*'.

There was Caffarelli, the adjutant general; an old Noailles dragoon, he once commanded the 9th Legion. Behind him, under bobbing tricolor plumes, marched the senior adjutants, Colonel Fuzy of the Guard of the Directory with Blanchard and Ponsard of the Legislature Grenadiers. Majors Dubois, Auger, and the good Oehler of the Guard of the Directory marched in the second file.

The sappers, who wore leather aprons, were greeted with applause. Drum Major Sénot, a captain in the Austrasie Regiment in the king's time, wore a blue coat with

[7] Approximately 14,000 francs ($40) in 1956.

9

white facings, laced with gold on collar, cuffs, and revers. His epaulets were gold, as was the binding of his hat with its tricolor plumes. With a silver-pommeled, silver-tipped baton he led twenty-four drummers, each a virtuoso (see Plate 25b).

The band followed – the old band of the Directory – still led by Guiardel, playing hymns and popular songs including *Dans la rue Chiffonnière* whose tune was borrowed by a soldier-poet for the stirring march the men sang later at Marengo and during the Empire to the words: '*On va leur percer le flanc.*'[8]

Colonel Frère, an ex-pharmacist, passed by at the head of the infantry. Leading the first grenadier battalion was Soulès, a compatriot of Lannes, flanked by Adjutant Lieutenant Flamand.

The troops filed past by company. These were professionals, no longer young, and some were scored with honorable scars. All wore blue coats with white revers and scarlet cuffs, white waistcoats and breeches, red epaulets, and bearskin bonnets. Their white leather saber- and pouchbelts were crossed over the breast.

Under the heavy headdresses adorned with gilt plaques and tasseled cords one saw the familiar faces of Captain Lemarois, former ensign of the Guard of the Directory; Charpentier of the *Gardes françaises*; Lieutenants Vézu and Carré. There were newcomers, too, such as Lajonquière of the 4th Demi-brigade, a hero of Arcole. But almost all the lieutenants and half the subalterns were from the old Guards.

Père Tortel, a veteran of fifty-three, commanded the second battalion whose subaltern adjutant Faucon came from the Guard of the Directory.

Six companies filed past, all commanded by old Guardsmen such as Chéry, Bernelle, and Captain Ragois. The latter had served in the horse chasseurs before joining the infantry in Italy; then in the Guides of Bonaparte whom he knew at Toulon. Wounded on the Mincio and at Arcole, Ragois had just arrived from Egypt.

The light infantry company had not yet been formed. The horse Guard's twenty-five musicians came from the infantry.

Colonel Bessières rode at the head of the cavalry. All the horse grenadiers of the Directory were present, including Major Oulié, Adjutant Dahlmann, and Captain Barbanègre from the guides.

The two squadrons were superb. Their dignified uniform would never change from the grenadier coat with orange aiguillette and shoulder knots. Their white leather breeches were tucked into high boots. Their fur caps were trimmed with orange cords and had no plates. Their horse furniture was blue, the housings and triple-tiered holsters trimmed with orange braid, and their white cloaks were neatly folded over the portmanteaux. Their standards were borne by old NCO's of the Guard of the Directory. Some of the lieutenants, like Auzoni, came from the guides; others, like Rossignol, from the Line (see Plate 28).

At first this corps was designated 'light cavalry', and later 'line cavalry'; but from this moment on it took the name 'horse grenadiers' in memory of the heroic giants of the *Maison du Roy*.

[8] Literally 'We shall pierce their flank'.

Next came the company of *chasseurs à cheval*, or mounted chasseurs, composed of guides from Egypt and led by the First Consul's stepson and aide-de-camp, Captain Eugène Beauharnais. There were 112 sunburned fellows, less precise in formation and movement than the grenadiers, but bold and dashing withal.

The light artillery, wearing blue and scarlet hussar uniforms, closed the parade. Captain Couin, twice wounded before he commanded them in Egypt, marched at their head. Dogureau and Digeon were second captains as they had been in the East. Chauveau and Dubuard (called Marin) were first lieutenants, and Berthier a second lieutenant. All of them had just returned from Egypt with Bonaparte.

Apart from several new faces and uniform changes, these were virtually the Tricolor Guards of the days before *brumaire*.

At thirty, an age when men normally start their careers, the First Consul showed himself a wise commander and an incomparable leader of men. Watching the parade of what he was pleased to call 'his Guard,' he thought perhaps that now he was master in place of the king he had once served. Nevertheless, he must proceed slowly and discreetly.

He leaned for support on this handful of veterans of obscure antecedents and doubtful pasts, some of whose officers could barely sign their names; yet they had served him in the wars and at the coup d'état. His knowledge of men was sufficiently profound to inspire their devotion; besides, he was prepared to grant them special favors.

Their pay – which interests soldiers in every age – was substantial. First, all arrears had been paid up. This considerable sum was much appreciated. Whereas a lieutenant general drew 12,000 francs, the commander in chief of the Guard drew 24,000, and so on down the line to the grenadiers who drew 240 francs in the Guard as against 128.10 in the army. This golden bridge was built by maintaining a separate pay office for the Guard.

As in the Directory, men were assimilated into the Guard one grade above their rank in the Line. The allotments for clothing, subsistence, harness, and fuel were all higher. The councils of administration of each corps passed on the purchases of cloth, wine, flour, and vinegar – a precious prerogative at that epoch. The inspector[9] verified the accounts, but the Guard ran its own administration and enjoyed complete autonomy.

If the War Ministry had cause to wonder at the word 'equality', what must the Maréchal de Ségur, that hero of the Seven Years' War and former minister of Louis XVI, have thought on being rendered honors by the Guard of the Consuls when he visited the Tuileries on 6 March? Ruined by the Revolution, he came to thank the young Corsican (whom he had appointed to the La Fère Artillery fifteen years before as a matter of routine) for granting him the pay of a lieutenant general.

Whatever their individual reactions, the new 'popular knighthood' presented arms without batting an eye.

Nevertheless, the discipline was not perfect. Bessières had to request the *chasseurs à cheval* to refrain from smoking their pipes 'while escorting the Council of State', as well as to salute generals and other officers. They should 'set an example in all things'.

[9] *Inspecteur aux revues*

In the face of pitched battles between the gunners of the Guard and the Line, Bessières wrote: 'A soldier of the Guard should realize that the troops of the Line are his comrades-in-arms'.

Punishment rained down on the heads of the horse grenadiers for 'frequenting low dives'. Ordener prescribed a 'uniform length of hair; the queue must be six inches long'. It was forbidden to leave quarters unarmed after ten o'clock. The prescribed dress was blue *surtouts*[10] with collars and black cravats. In this uniform the guard was mounted at Malmaison, but on *quintidi* and *décadi*[11] full dress was worn.

Whatever else it may have been, the Guard of the Consuls was a valuable political instrument, a fact that did not escape Bonaparte. But its military value and its conduct in the field remained to be demonstrated.

The first months of 1800 were filled with maneuvers and reviews. Boots were fitted by the master bootmakers. Leather strapping was added to the traveling overalls.

What was up?

---

[10] Undress tail coats without facings or revers (see Plate 29a). – Ed.
[11] Sundays being abolished by the revolutionary calendar, the 5th and 10th days were holidays. – *Ibid.*

CHAPTER 3

Marengo

ON 11 April 1800 Bessières led the Guard, equipped for war, to Corbeil. From there they left for Nyon. Here they found the First Consul determined to liberate Italy and consolidate his position at home by a decisive victory.

For a bonus of 500 francs for every cannon hoisted over the Italian Alps, the grenadiers harnessed themselves to the guns and hauled the artillery up to the monastery of St. Bernard. 'It took that little brat of a globe-trotter to put on such a performance!' the soldiers exclaimed. The horses and the cavalrymen in their heavy boots slipped and slid on their way up to the Hospice where each man drained a glass of wine provided by the monks.

It appeared they were going to the assistance of the Army of Italy which still lacked 45,000 of the 53,000 pairs of breeches it had requisitioned. In any case, the old-timers were not obliged to the Milanese who, whether from surprise or fright, neglected to throw flowers at them or cheer them.

Nevertheless, the '*Tondu*'[1] heard a Te Deum in the Cathedral and Grassini perform at La Scala, harangued the bishops, and held reviews at the Castello. But at 11 p.m. on 7 June Bourrienne[2] reported that Masséna, having exhausted his supply of bread concocted of starch, linseed, and cacao, had surrendered Genoa.

Alert, everybody!

On the 9th it rained on the road to Pavia. The army crossed the Po at San Cipriano. Up front Lannes covered himself with glory at Montebello, and the Guard, drenched to the bones, slept at Stradella. 'I have a wretched cold', Bonaparte wrote Josephine.

Where were the '*Kaiserliks*'[3] of Melas? Marching to Genoa? At Alessandra? . . . What did Desaix think?

Having made his escape from Egypt, Desaix had just arrived. The old-timers recognized his spare figure, his enormous moustache, his gentleness and calm. Bonaparte gave him two divisions, one of which (Boudet's) was sent to Novi to watch the road to Genoa, with orders to rally to the sound of gunfire wherever it occurred.

At the town hall in Voghera, across the flooding Staffora River, the Guard saw Austrian envoys arrive on the 12th with a flag of truce. They wanted peace?

No, only an exchange of prisoners.

---

[1] Literally 'Shorn One', the Guard's pet name for Napoleon. – Ed.
[2] Bonaparte's secretary.
[3] French nickname for the Austrian '*Kaiserliche und Königliche Armee*'. – Ed.

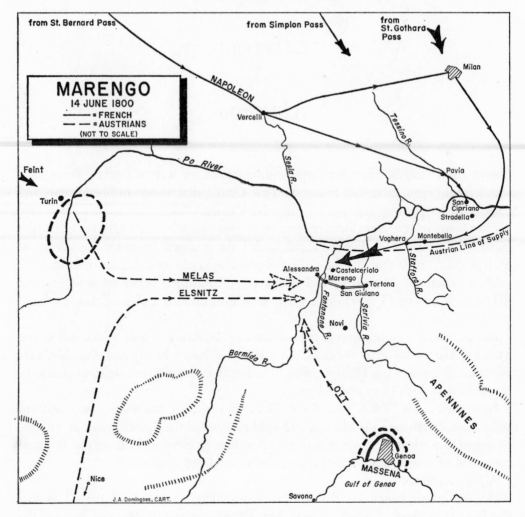

MARENGO

As First Consul, Bonaparte desired peace but the Coalition was not co-operative. He therefore raised a Reserve Army to supplement the Army of the Rhine under Moreau and the Army of Italy under Masséna. The Austrians under Melas defeated Masséna in Italy and besieged him in Genoa. Bonaparte led the Reserve Army in several columns across the Alps. He made a feint at Turin, concentrated his forces at Milan, then moved to cut Melas' line of supply. Deceived by the French feint from the west, the Austrians allowed themselves to be pushed up against the Alps.

In order to prevent their escape Bonaparte divided his forces. Melas attacked in superior numbers at Marengo on 14 June 1800 and drove the French back in disorder. Bonaparte recalled his detached forces under Desaix who attacked the pursuing Austrians. Finally, a co-ordinated attack by the French sealed the victory, though Desaix was killed.

Melas sued for peace because the French had cut him off from his bases of supply.

PLATE 2

PLATE 3

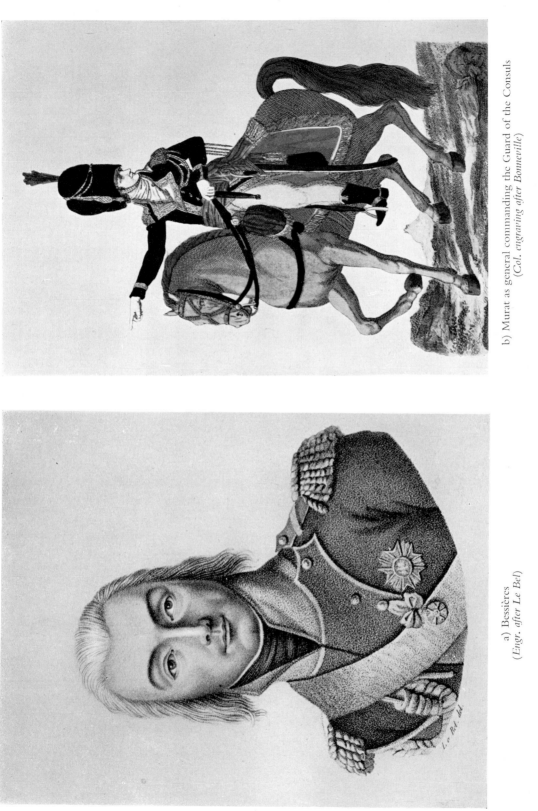

b) Murat as general commanding the Guard of the Consuls
(Col. engraving after Bonneville)

a) Bessières
(Engr. after Le Bel)

PLATE 4

Bonaparte as First Consul
(*From an original calligraphic drawing by Auvrest*)

PLATE 5

PLATE 6

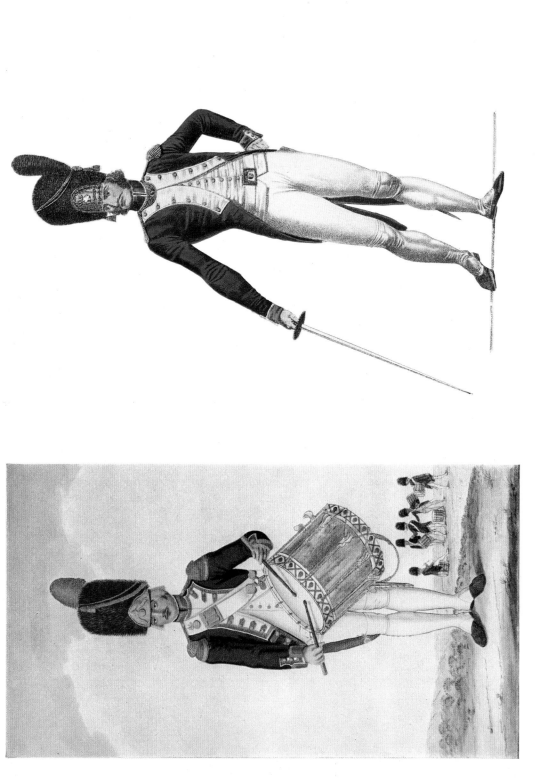

PLATE 7

PLATE 8

The crossing of the Great Saint-Bernard, 14 May 1800
(From a contemporary lithograph by Muller)

PLATE 9

Marengo
(From an original drawing by Martinet)

PLATE 10

PLATE II

a) Desaix
(*Engr. Monsaldi after Dutertre*)

b) Barbanègre
(*Engr. Réville after Couché*)

c) Daumesnil
(*Portrait by Riesener: Collection Baronne Fririon*)

d) Soulès
(*Engr. Réville*)

e) Caffarelli
(*Engr. Réville after Vauthier*)

PLATE 12

Grenadier Brabant at Marengo
(From a lithograph by G. Engelmann)

The 19th *Légère*[4] and the 70th Line Infantry passed on ahead. The army was posted on the Scrivia.

During the whole day of the 13th, under a drenching rain punctuated by claps of thunder, the horse grenadiers pivoted in the plain towards the Bormida, behind Bonaparte. No one had given the order to unroll their cloaks. At forty paces from the cavalry the 'little Corporal' was seen skirting Castelceriolo, walking along the Fontanone, visiting the village of Marengo, climbing to the top of the tower. He inspected the terrain, meditated, looked worried, gave orders . . .

The troops thought the Austrians had evacuated Alessandra whose cathedral and citadel they could make out in the distance. However, the cavalry pointed out two bridges, one of which had been thrown recently across the river before the town.

At the day's end the Guard set down their packs before the castle of Baron di Garofoli, a long pile of masonry crowned with a campanile, where the First Consul was lodging. Numb with cold and absolutely soaked, in mud up to their ankles, the grenadiers and chasseurs emptied the provision wagons of bread while Soulès and Bessières examined the terrain. Two leagues[5] and a half away, on the road from Tortona to Alessandra, was the village of Marengo where General Victor was encamped with Gardanne and Chambarlhac. Lannes was on his right. The ground between was dotted with copses.

Some deserters arrived, escorted by cavalry.

The men slept with one eye open in three farm houses in San Giuliano.

On 14 June they were 'awakened by a reveille of gunfire', according to Joseph Petit of the horse grenadiers. The Croats were massacring two pickets. Dawn was breaking; they had breakfast; it was the same menu as the night before – bread.

7 a.m. A general Austrian attack, from Lannes' right wing to Marengo and beyond, began. Some wounded passed. 'They are attacking in force.'

11 a.m. The First Consul mounted his horse and the escort followed him across the plain where a fusillade extended over a five-mile front. In the smoke and thunder of more than two hundred guns one could no longer distinguish anything. On the left, trumpets were sounding a charge; they belonged to the 2nd and 20th Cavalry of Kellermann. In the center, the Commander in Chief waited calmly under a hail of cannon balls. 'Keep your chins up!' shouted a sergeant of the horse grenadiers.

Retreating infantry passed along the road to Tortona; it seemed as if the whole French line were giving way . . . But no, here came the grenadiers and chasseurs of the Guard, drums beating, singing *On va leur percer le flanc* to the accompaniment of Guiardel's bandsmen, as well as the 19th *Légère* of General Monnier, with Bonaparte leading the lot. Nine hundred bearskin bonnets formed a square between Lannes and Carra Saint-Cyr and stopped the Lobkowitz Dragoons in their tracks. The horse grenadiers, with the light artillery in support, attacked a 'cloudful of cavalry in battle array' which was outflanking Murat and the dragoons of Champeaux. This would protect their retreat . . .

[4] Light infantry.
[5] A league is approximately 2½ miles. – Ed.

But the infantry of the Guard stood firm. Without artillery, it braced itself to sustain the shock from the Austrian center. Harassed, charged three times by enemy cavalry, fired on at a hundred paces by their infantry, this 'fortress of granite' surrounding the flag and the wounded ran out of cartridges. Whereupon Brabant, a grenadier of uncommon strength, took over an abandoned four-pounder and worked it alone for half an hour. Ensign Aune swept his comrades on. Then they retreated lest the enemy should reach their headquarters before them.

Bonaparte moved from one battalion to another, encouraging those in the upper vineyards who were defending the exit from San Giuliano. These were the last . . .

At four in the afternoon, on a front five miles wide, 6,000 infantry, a thousand cavalry, and six pieces of artillery were still fighting. The men were tortured by hunger and thirst; some officers were leaving the field. 'Bonaparte is risking death!'

If he should be killed . . .

But the Austrians would not break through. Rushed from Novi, the 9th *Légère* marching at the head of Boudet's division came up at the charge in close column formation and overwhelmed the Austrians on the road to Alessandra. On his own initiative, Kellermann hurled his 800 horsemen against the enemy left, forcing the Hungarian grenadiers to lay down their arms, while Bessières and Eugène Beauharnais rushed in with the horse grenadiers and the mounted chasseurs of the Guard.

'*Escadrons . . . en avant . . . marche!*[6] . . . *Au trot!*'

Cloaks slung diagonally across their shoulders, carrying their sabers high, the four hundred horsemen advanced at a slow trot because their horses were tired. Then: 'To the right by files!' followed by the double command: '*Au galop! . . . Chargez!*' they swooped down upon the Austrian cavalry trying to cover the retreat of its infantry and pursued it to the brink of a ditch where the enemy broke in disorder.

Schmitt, a trumpeter of the grenadiers, surrounded by enemies and called on to surrender, killed one. The others wounded him, smashing his trumpet over his haunch. But thanks to his horse, the hero succeeded in rejoining his squadron. Sergeant Lanceleur and Grenadiers Millet and Leroy each captured an enemy flag.

Now the whole army swept forward. The cavalry flogged the Austrians in their headlong flight towards Marengo, towards the bridges over the Bormida, towards Alessandra. Citizen Judas, a bassoon player in the foot Guard band, lost his instrument in the fray . . .

The victory was complete, but Desaix was dead.

Ten o'clock struck in the belfry at Marengo. The Guard returned to its headquarters at San Giuliano. The cavalrymen slept on their worn-out horses.

A carriage left for Milan under escort. In it lay Desaix, covered by his cloak.

On 17 June, having reviewed the troops at San Giuliano the night before, the First Consul departed for Milan, escorted by the *chasseurs à cheval*. He traveled the hundred kilometers without a pause.

Marengo was Bonaparte's first victory as head of the state. He had won it by precision and by stealth.

[6] Squadrons . . . forward . . . march!'

16

His Guard, employed as a reserve, had covered itself with glory. He and it, from now on inseparable, entered Milan together, this time under a rain of flowers to the strains of the Consular March.

On 6 July the Guard received its reward. Soulès and Marin won swords of honor; Sergeants Mirabel and Castanié and several corporals and gunners, gold grenades; Trumpet Major Krettly, a trumpet of honor. Barbanègre was promoted to major, Digeon to captain, Daumesnil to lieutenant. Aune, the bravest grenadier in the Army of Italy, a legendary hero as full of holes as a colander who possessed a sword of honor and was ensign of the grenadiers, felt the breeze of a ball which cut off the tails of his coat. His hat was perforated by bullets as well, yet he 'did not suffer the slightest scratch'. It was the first time he had ever been in battle without being wounded.

As a reward, he was married to the beautiful Mademoiselle de Montmorency. On the day of the wedding Beauharnais opened the ball and several officers came to wish him happiness, a wish not to be realized since he died of consumption in 1803. Later Bonaparte granted a pension of 500 francs to his widow and – a unique occurrence – published the name of Lieutenant Aune, promoted posthumously, on the roster of officers of the Legion of Honor on 14 June 1804.

Arriving from Liguria after twenty-nine days of forced marches, the dusty Guard entered Paris on 13 July. The capital was *en fête*. After a week of impatience bordering on sedition, a million Parisians honored Bonaparte and the heroes of Marengo. Ever since his furtive arrival on the 2nd, their idol had been surrounded by crowds consisting of the whole Faubourg Saint-Antoine and all the loafers in town. They had not yet heard him speak but they knew his every act. To be sure, he had said: 'I command and keep silent'. Now he could do anything. He wished the fête to be called the '*Fête de la Concorde*', or 'Festival of Peace', a name borne forever after by the Place of the Revolution that had just ended.

The pomp was strictly military. The grenadiers of the Guard, bronzed and crowned with glory, were the guests of honor. They presented arms in the Place Vendôme before the newborn column erected to the Brave and saluted the flags of the Republic unfurled for the occasion. To the thunder of cannon at the Invalides they escorted the Consuls to the church (called the 'Temple of Mars' at that epoch) where Méhul's '*Chant du 25 messidor*' (14 July) was sung. Then they proceeded to the place reserved for them on the Champ de Mars which was decked with flags.

The whole city was there to cheer them. The reception might have degenerated into a riot but for the intervention of the First Consul. From the balcony of the École Militaire he saluted the flags of the Army presented by Carnot, the Minister of War.

Twilight fell. Brushed and polished, the grenadiers forgot their fatigue in the arms of their girls while the orchestras played. During the banquet, at which Bonaparte presided, his piercing voice was heard in a toast 'to the 14th of July and the French people!'

Outside on the Pont de la Concorde there were fireworks. An allegorical statue of Victory was saluted with cries of '*Vive le Premier Consul!*' It was an unforgettable day.

In its barracks, the Guard dreamed.

In his office at the Tuileries, Bonaparte worked.

He worked like a madman: in the Council of the Consuls, in the Council of State, with his ministers. He set in order the administration, the finances, the courts, and the army; he called on his young friends at the École Polytechnique and his old comrades at the Invalides; he visited schools, hospitals, and barracks; he saw everything, read everything, signed everything. His acquaintance with men and affairs was well-nigh universal.

At the same time he charmed, and his charm derived from an informed will.

He was the idol of the Guard.

On 8 September he initialed a decree for 1800, strengthening the Guard. The war was not yet over, and it was important to reinforce the reserve of the army with an elite corps which, brilliantly garbed and grouped about him, would increase his prestige and assure his safety in the palace, in the streets, and on the battlefield.

The general staff assumed impressive proportions with a lieutenant general as commander in chief, a major general[7] under him, two senior staff officers with sixteen senior adjutants and aides, and even a professor of mathematics to instruct the artillery.

The infantry now had three battalions of 8 companies each, including two of grenadiers and one of chasseurs; the cavalry, three squadrons of 2 troops in the same proportion. A train of twelve guns was attached to the artillery as well as an artillery park and a train company. The teams and munitions must be complete, since the country was at war.

The pay remained unchanged. For the first time the conditions of admission to the Guard were specific. The height requirement was amended to 5 foot 10 inches for the grenadiers and artillery, and 5 foot 7 inches for the chasseurs.

There was the problem of uniforms. The wardrobe of a foot grenadier or chasseur was large and cost 258 francs (approximately 100,000 francs in 1956). It included a bearskin cap, two dress coats, two waistcoats, and two pairs of breeches; but only one pair of stockings and a single shirt! This last economy, which applied also to the cavalry, presented certain problems.

The mounted men drew three pairs of breeches and a luxurious outfit on the whole which cost 517 francs for a horse grenadier. A single hussar uniform of green dolman and scarlet pelisse of a *chasseur à cheval* cost 216 francs (see Plate 10).

The soldiers of the newly created train wore steel-blue uniforms piped with scarlet. They were the poor relations and remained substantially the 'wagoners' they were to begin with. They were issued a single coat, waistcoat, and pair of pantaloons, a pair of sheepskin breeches, a hat, a forage cap (or '*bonnet de police*') and one pair of boots worth 15 francs. The whole kit cost only 80 francs. And yet this stepchild was a veritable millionaire compared to his opposite number in the Line, who was still in the most frightful state of destitution.

The officers' uniforms were literally loaded with gold lace. The regulations anticipated an initial outlay of 1,500 francs for the staff, chasseurs, and artillery; 1,000 francs

[7] *Général de brigade*. See note at end of chapter.

for the cavalry, and 800 for the infantry. These figures are purely hypothetical, however, since luxury was the fashion of the day and military men have ever been slaves to fashion.

On 23 November Isabey and Carle Vernet exhibited their painting of the review of the First Consul called the *Revue de décadi* which impresses one with the richness of its costumes. In it generals and bedizened aides-de-camp surround Bonaparte who is calm and slightly stooped (he took Isabey to task for this) and wears his undress hat without plumes. The luxury of the Guard was overwhelming; it drove the crowds to frenzies of enthusiasm every *décadi*, and set the girls to dreaming (see Plate 15).

Lannes, the victor of Montebello, hero of Marengo, and a close friend of the First Consul, was now commander of the gilded phalanx. In the handsome quarters of its general staff he kept open house and dreamed of Caroline Bonaparte, of beautiful uniforms, rich fabrics, and towering plumes. He had just treated himself to a superb forage cap, artistically embroidered. Then he proceeded to order for his officers, trumpeters, and kettledrummers lavish green and gold waistbelts, sabretaches[8] fringed with gold, gold lace and epaulets, tall plumes, velvet saddles, and fur shabracks.[9]

Carried away by these fireworks, he found himself one fine morning saddled with a debt of 200,000 francs (some say 400,000) for the Guard of the Consuls. Fortunately, Augureau was on leave at his estate of La Houssaye where he always kept a well-filled money chest. Since he was a good comrade he ordered his attorney to set the finances of the Guard afloat again.

Bonaparte was not ignorant of the origin of these munificences. Lannes was relieved of his command and sent to Portugal to recoup his fortunes, while Augureau was shortly placed in command of the camp at Bayonne. Like Caesar's wife, the Guard must be above reproach.

[8] Literally 'sword pockets', ornamental pouches worn suspended from their sword-belts by light cavalry-men, etc. (see Plates 13, 14a). – Ed.

[9] Blanket or cushion of fur placed over the saddle by cavalrymen. The British Household Cavalry still use fur shabracks. – *Ibid.*

Note: Because of the deceptive similarity, the rank of *général de brigade* at this epoch is sometime trans-lated 'brigadier general', though in fact, at the fall of the Monarchy, the ranks of *lieutenant général* (3 stars) and *maréchal de camp* (2 stars) were changed by decree to *général de division* (3 stars) and *général de brigade* (2 stars) and the seldom conferred general rank of *brigadier* (one star) abolished. – *Ibid.*

CHAPTER 4

The Guides of Bonaparte

PEACE was signed with Austria on 9 February 1801; and with God, in the concordat of 15 July. England was still at war; however, negotiations with her were scheduled to start in October. Menou's capitulation at Alexandria on 2 September and the loss of Egypt were forgotten in the rejoicing over the soldiers' return from the East.

Now Bonaparte planned to complete his Guard with the guides who had fought under him in Italy and Egypt.

In 1792 the Assembly raised small detachments of guides to guard and escort the headquarters of each field army, dressing them in the hussar style. Augureau had a guide company, as did Brune, Moreau, Masséna, Macdonald, Bernadotte, and Murat. These companies were employed as small personal bodyguards and were handsomely dressed and appointed.

As commander in chief of the Army of Italy Bonaparte took over the guides he found at Albenga in 1796. These had been raised by Kellermann and consolidated with those of the Armies of the Pyrenees and the Alps. Though they fought with distinction at Mondovi and Lodi, they guarded the commander in chief poorly. After the battle of Borghetto, Bonaparte was lunching with Masséna and his aide Murat when they were surprised by Austrian cavalry. They escaped by climbing over a wall. Bonaparte lost one of his boots in the process.

After this episode Colonel Lannes was put in charge of guarding the headquarters with two battalions of grenadiers and 100 horse and foot guides. A week later Captain Bessières of the 22nd Chasseurs, a friend and compatriot of Murat, was given command of the 'Company of Guides of the Commander in Chief'. These were the ancestors of the *chasseurs à cheval* of the Imperial Guard who did not leave Napoleon until after Waterloo. Under the Empire the escorts of chasseurs were known as the 'service' or 'duty' squadrons and were sometimes still referred to as 'guides'.

The Guides of Bonaparte earned an illustrious reputation at Roveredo where Bessières and six troopers captured two guns, and again at Arcole where the victory was partly due to their black Lieutenant Domingo, nicknamed 'Hercules', and his trumpeters.

In 1796 the company numbered 136, and its major was granted 1,200 francs for a band. The guides are said to have worn green coats with scarlet collars and cuffs, green waistcoats, and red or green breeches, or overalls with leather strapping. Though this dress was prescribed, dress regulations were somewhat illusory in an army where soldiers filched their caps from the sutlers, and their boots and whatever passed for breeches from the dead.

However, the guides traditionally wore green, the color of meadows in spring, signifying youth and renewal. It was the Emperor's favorite color; hence he habitually wore the green undress uniform of the *chasseurs à cheval* of the Guard (see Plate 69).

During the Italian campaign, in which Bonaparte's cavalry was sadly deficient in both strength and morale, his crack troop was the guides. He kept them on the go day and night in the Po valley. He concerned himself with their pay, their bread, and their glory and earned their undying devotion.

They rode into Milan before this general with the 'pitiful countenance and exhausted demeanor' amid cheers which were perhaps not entirely spontaneous. With their standard flying from the Cathedral spire, they heard Archbishop Visconti hail this 'captain of beggars', who was a father to them, as an 'envoy from Heaven'. The inhabitants were struck by his 'unhealthy emaciation' and stooping carriage, his 'grey-blue eyes, lively and piercing', and his meditative air.

'They have seen nothing yet!' observed Marmont.

At the head of the troop rode Bessières who had left a surgeon's lancet to join the Constitutional Guard of the king. Outlawed for appearing at the Tuileries on the 10th of August,[1] he took refuge for three months with the Duc de la Rochefoucauld, then joined the 22nd Chasseurs who elected him their second lieutenant in 1793. He campaigned in Cerdaña, Catalonia, and led the charge of the 'tatterdemalions' at Le Boulou. He was a captain in the Army of Italy when the 'Puny One' came to take command. This 'intrepid and calm' cavalier commanded the guides after Borghetto.

Under him served Lieutenants Jean-Baptiste Barbanègre of the 22nd Chasseurs, later killed at Jena; Lallemand who was wounded as a general at Waterloo; and Daumesnil who, as commandant of the chasseurs at Wagram, lost a leg for which he made the enemy pay at Vincennes in 1814.

Among the troopers were Dahlmann, son of a trooper of the Dauphine Cavalry, and Michel, known as Desmichels. The former died a major general at Eylau; the latter, a colonel at Waterloo, lived to fight Abd-el-Kader in Algeria.

In addition to the mounted troop there was a company of foot guides which Bonaparte revived later in the foot chasseurs of the Guard.

Early in their career Bonaparte described his mounted guides as 'an elite company of two hundred daredevils, well-mounted and brave'; but when Bessières was sent to the Directory with eighteen flags they had captured at Rivoli his confidence in them increased.

When Bonaparte was appointed general in chief of the Army of the East in 1798 he sent for them. The mounted troop embarked with their horses and were joined in Egypt by about 400 foot. On 7 July 1799 their drummer Calla abandoned his bass drum to be first on the ramparts at Alexandria. Bessières was made colonel of the Regiment of Guides which included four companies of horse and three of foot, 60 horse gunners, 20 musicians, and three companies of native auxiliaries. The regiment served as the commander in chief's bodyguard as well as a reserve.

[1] The date of the storming of the Tuileries by the Paris mob after the return of the Royal Family to Paris in the summer of 1792. – Ed.

Crossing the desert, parched with thirst, the army reached the Pyramids. There the guides attacked the Mameluk horsemen who could cut a scarf in two in mid-air with their sharp scimitars. To reward their intrepidity Bonaparte presented to his guides the weapons captured in the camp of Murad Bey.

Later the guides' enthusiasm was somewhat dampened by the disillusion of conquest. Several were assassinated, and others were killed in the Cairo riots. However, they enjoyed dashing about after the commander in chief, and the bathing parties on the Nile, the watermelon feasts, band concerts, and donkey rides.

Wearing turbans and burnouses, most of the guides followed Bonaparte to Syria where forty were killed at the seige of Acre. There an artillery sergeant named Dubuard but called Marin, a charter member of the corps, was wounded. He had previously served as an artificer under Captain Bonaparte at Toulon. On 18 July the General brevetted him a sub-lieutenant with the following citation:

'Desiring to give Citizen Marin, sergeant in the Guides, a testimonial of the Government's satisfaction with his distinguished conduct at the battle of Aboukir, the General in chief appoints said Citizen "on the field" a sergeant in the Guard[2] with the rank of sub-lieutenant.'

Dear old Marin – he was neither distinguished nor particularly temperate. His last wound was a saber cut in the head during the Guard's retreat at Waterloo. By then the Emperor had made him a baron with an income of 12,000 francs which helped to pay his debts. He eventually died in bed in 1837.

Two hundred of the mounted troop left Egypt with their chief in August 1799, but did not reach Paris until after the coup d'état. The rest returned in 1802 under Colonel Dériot who had sustained no less than seventeen wounds at Heliopolis.

The guides were now incorporated in the Guard. The foot reinforced the battalion of foot chasseurs, while the mounted troop was turned over to the second squadron of *chasseurs à cheval*, created on 6 August.

On 25 May 1801 some odd if high-ranking personages arrived in Paris. Don Luis, Infante of Parma and nephew of Marie-Antoinette, and his consort the Infanta Maria Luisa, daughter of Charles IV of Spain, had come to thank the First Consul for giving them the crown of Etruria (Tuscany).

'The younger generation does not know what a king looks like', said Bonaparte. 'We shall show them one.'

The visit was a fiasco. The Queen was ugly, and so was the King who was grotesque to boot. Frightened and sickly, he was dragged from party to party at the houses of Talleyrand, Berthier, etc. and to the Comédie Française. By turns severe or giggling hysterically, he struck the grenadiers and chasseurs taking part in the commemoration of the battle of Marengo as so odd that they could not keep a straight face under arms. To make matters worse, the parade was being reviewed by Cardinal Consalvi who had come to sign the concordat with the Holy See.

During the reviews that season Bonaparte concluded that certain officers and soldiers of the Guard were too old, and others were unfit for active duty because of wounds.

[2] Guard of the Directory.

Some would eventually be pensioned and others retired to the Invalides; however, their present was precarious.

On 12 July he created a Company of Veterans of the Guard, drawing the same pay and allotments as the active Guard. This company was restricted to men 'who by reason of age or infirmity were unable to remain on active duty'.

In the course of a summer passed at Malmaison, where Josephine held a sort of miniature court, the First Consul was taking a walk with Berthier in the park of Saint-Cloud. They discussed many problems, including that of the crippled veterans. When Bonaparte observed that Malmaison was becoming too small for him, Berthier pointed to the Château of Saint-Cloud and suggested that he move there.

The château of the Duc d'Orléans?[3] So soon after *brumaire*? Was it not too soon?

The night brought its counsel. The Company of Veterans would be installed at Saint-Cloud. Père Tortel was placed in command.

The Guard Veteran, one of Bonaparte's cleverest creations, wore the grenadier uniform, but with scarlet revers and a hat in place of the 'beehive'.[4] The First Consul announced to this privileged character[5] the fact of his existence, and – a favor transcending all others – the fact that he still belonged to the Guard. In the Veterans Company he remained 'among his own people' (see Plate 14b).

Awakened by roll of drum and committed to a painless bi-weekly guard duty, without changing his habits the Veteran could look after his wounds and rheumatism, spin yarns about his campaigns, and sing the praises of Bonaparte until, at the end of his activity, he would be relieved for good and retired to the Invalides. We shall meet him again during the 'Hundred Days'.

Meanwhile, the Company of Veterans left Saint-Cloud for Meudon in 1802, leaving the active Guard to watch over the château to which Bonaparte moved upon being named First Consul for life. To compensate them for the move, each Veteran received ten days' pay plus a bonus of 240 francs.

---

[3] Brother of Louis XV. – Ed.
[4] Soldier slang for the bearskin bonnet. – *Ibid.*
[5] Members of the Company of Veterans in the Imperial Guard should not be confused with the many veterans on active service nor the Guardsmen who retired to civil life. – *Ibid.*

CHAPTER 5

'The Guard'

1802 was a wonderful year. During its course Bonaparte filled the French with the 'joy of revival' in response to their mystic faith in him. It was the year of the Code, of the general peace, of the institution of the Legion of Honor, and of Bonaparte's appointment to the consulate for life. During his rapid rise to power he had had his cipher 'NB' displayed here and there, replacing the outmoded liberty caps of the Revolution, which now only appeared at the top of the 'liberty trees'. Now he was pleased to change the name of the Guard of the Consuls to the 'Consular Guard', or simply 'The Guard'.

On 14 November he organized his palace in the style of a petty sovereign – but a sovereign no less – naming his aide-de-camp Duroc as governor. From now on Duroc took orders direct from the First Consul. He was given ten senior adjutants[1] to assist him, with several junior adjutants and aides. Four lieutenant generals of the Guard were to be 'in constant attendance on the Consuls for ten-day periods, in rotation.'

The Guard provided both inside and outside guards at the palace, and thus became intimately attached to the First Consul's daily life. This arrangement served to emphasize its official, rather than its purely military, status.

Generals Davout and Bessières commanded the infantry and cavalry. Later Songis became general of the artillery, and a general of engineers was projected. Up to this time the artillery had been too small to warrant a general in command, and the Guard had no engineers. However, the mere mention of the new posts on the organization table indicated that the First Consul intended to increase the Guard and make it into a miniature army embracing all branches of the service.

Engineer officers were appointed a few weeks later, followed by commissaries, a chief surgeon, and a librarian. In fact, nothing essential to administer, lodge, feed, care for, and instruct an independent corps was omitted.

Bonaparte outlined the organization as follows:

'The foot Guard shall be composed of two corps containing two battalions of grenadiers and two of chasseurs respectively, each commanded by a colonel under the orders of the general commanding the infantry of the Guard.'

Though these 'corps' contained but one regiment each, their designation as such indicated that their strength would eventually be increased.

---

[1] Colonels Fuzy and Tortel, Majors Dubois, Reynaud, Humbert, Auger, Clément, Ragois, Lefebvre, and Captain Dumoustier. Nearly all had served in the Guards of the Directory and Legislature.

Colonel Hulin was given command of the grenadiers. A veteran soldier of the Champagne, Navarre, and Touraine Regiments and of the Swiss Guards, he was later employed as a servant by the Marquis de Conflans, as director of a Geneva laundry, and was one of the authentic stormers of the Bastille. Then he had served a term in prison and a brilliant one at war. Bonaparte did not select him for his fine manners, but for his character, discipline, and fidelity to military duty.

The cadres showed little change. Lajonquière was promoted major, and Flamand captain and adjutant major. Sergeant Major Deleuze, who made his career in the grenadiers and ended up at Waterloo as the oldest captain in the regiment with the Legion of Honor and a pension of 1,800 francs, was made lieutenant.

The grenadiers were already a closed corps, homogeneous, sound, disciplined, proud of ranking at the top of the Guard, and of the respect in which they were held.

Colonel Soulès commanded the foot chasseurs, inaugurated 14 November 1801. A veteran of Italy, he had been wounded at Castiglione and Arcole and had won a sword of honor leading his grenadiers at Marengo.

The regiment had absorbed Captain Schobert's light infantry company, also the foot guides of Egypt in which Schobert and Captain Meunier – now a major – had served. Captains Jeanin, a future Waterloo general, and Barbanègre, defender of Huningue, were from the Army of Egypt, as well as Lieutenant Rignon, etc. etc. Malet, the old drum major of the guides, was commissioned subaltern, as were Sergeants Colomban of the chasseurs and Castanié of the grenadiers.

Prelier and Labusquette were brought from the Line, while certain other officers were appointed spontaneously like the nameless sentry in the following anecdote:

On 13 May 1803 a grenadier sentry at the Tuileries bridge presented arms to General Moreau who passed by in civilian dress. The post commander reprimanded the soldier and marched him off to prison. The Guard never rendered honors to civilians; moreover, Moreau was retired and was suspected of plotting against the First Consul. Bonaparte learned of the incident and sent for the grenadier.

'Why did you present arms to a general in civilian clothes?' he asked.

'Because I knew him', replied the soldier. 'I served under him, and I did it without thinking.'

So! The grenadier was doubtless a good soldier and a brave man; perhaps he was devoted to Moreau? Henceforth he should be devoted to Bonaparte who, with great acumen, appointed him a second lieutenant in the foot chasseurs.

The chasseurs were a younger corps than the grenadiers, and less homogeneous; but they were scrappier perhaps, gayer, livelier, and more supple.

The cavalry was increased. A third squadron was added to the horse grenadiers, commanded by Michel Ordener, former major in the 10th Chasseurs and hero of Lodi, whose wounds sustained in the army of the Helvetian Republic had become proverbial.[2] Rossignol was promoted captain, and Ligier lieutenant.

[2] In a single battle he received seven saber wounds, three bullet wounds, and one from a cannon ball.

Enormous on their magnificent horses, the horse grenadiers in their great boots were nicknamed 'big heels',[3] and sometimes called the 'gods' because of their austerity and haughty demeanor. They were totally lacking in imagination; nevertheless, Ordener took the precaution of forbidding 'any woman under forty to come in and make soup for them'.

The horse chasseurs were reinforced by 120 chasseurs and hussars from the Line and the mounted guides from Egypt. Colonel Eugène Beauharnais was their commander. Young, brave, and generous, he was loved dearly by Bonaparte. Majors Morland and Dahlmann came from the 11th Chasseurs and the guides respectively. Captains Daumesnil and Guyot were joined by many guides officers, including Desmichels and Rabusson. Sergeant Maziaux, a former guide, was shortly made subaltern.

The *chasseurs à cheval* of the Guard inherited the tradition of the guides. Able horsemen all, they were resourceful, versatile, full of life, and devoted body and soul to Bonaparte who indulged them in every way. They were bound to the foot chasseurs by common memories of Italy and Egypt where life had been rugged but colorful. Who knew the First Consul better than they?

The foot and horse grenadiers resembled one another in the high opinion they held of themselves and in their faith in their own superiority. Both 'big heels' and 'gaiter straps'[4] carried their heads high, wore their queues carefully powdered, and kept their legs stiff in marching or straight in the saddle, sure of the effect they were producing at parades or in battle. They knew the *Tondu* counted on them.

Lt. General Songis, a veteran of the king's artillery and a chevalier of Saint-Louis, commanded the artillery, which was built around artillerymen from Egypt, until he was obliged to retire for ill health. His aide Major Dogureau and the commander of the horse battery, Major Couin, were both from the Army of Egypt, as were Captains Digeon, Marin, Greiner, and Chauveau, and Sergeant Boisselier, all of whom had served under Songis at the seige of Acre.

The artillery train mustered 80 men and 120 horses. Between a gunner and a train soldier there was the same distinction as between master and coachman; nevertheless, in this instance, both wore the button of the Guard which was what counted.

The Hospice of the Gros-Caillou, reserved for the Guard, was run by an administrative council of officers and NCO's and a first class medical staff. Chief Physician Suë, whose son Eugène became a famous novelist, was professor of anatomy at the Faculty of Surgery. Chief Surgeon Larrey, renowned in the Army of Egypt for his talent and energy, was assisted by six surgeons. Chief Pharmacist Sureau had four assistants.

The cost of care was a daily charge of 2 francs; a burial fee of 7·50 francs represented the price of a 'coffin and shroud'. The First Consul reserved the right to appoint the medical staff as well as the company clerks of the Guard. Actually, the minister confined himself to receiving the lists of candidates for all Guard corps and

[3] *Gros talons.*
[4] *Sous-pieds de guêtre*, nickname of the grenadiers. – Ed.

forwarding them to the generals; but no grenadier or chasseur was admitted to the Guard without the approval of the First Consul.

On 26 June 1802 Bonaparte submitted a permanent schedule of recruitment for the Consular Guard. One man from each foot battalion of the Line and two from each cavalry and artillery regiment were to be named annually by the corps commanders on the 1st *fructador*.

The number of officers admitted was very small. Here is how one of them came to be appointed:

Captain Bigarré of the 14th Demi-brigade was taking the baths at Luxeuil in the spring of 1802. A former sailor, at twenty-five he had been wounded three times and had had his jaw shattered at Soleure.

Madame Bonaparte was at Plombières. Bigarré was sent to invite her to a ball arranged in his honor at Luxeuil. The wife of the First Consul was charming, talked to him during the reception, and took an interest in his career. Why did he not seek admission to the Guard of the Consuls?

'I replied', reported Bigarré, 'that I did not believe it easy for an officer of the Army of the Rhine to obtain such a favor.'

'Write to the First Consul, and you shall see that your request will be welcomed.'

On some beautiful pink writing-paper, Bigarré penned the following:

'Luxeuil, 7 *thermidor*, year X

'Citizen Consul: Though I never had the honor of serving under you in Italy or Egypt, if service rendered the Republic in the Armies of the West, Sambre-et-Meuse, and Rhine are not reprehensible in your eyes, permit me to ask the favor, now that we are at peace, of being allowed to watch over your person and the safety of the State in the Guard.

'I have the honor to be, with the most profound respect . . . etc. etc.'

Here is Bonaparte's reply, written by Davout:

'I write to advise you, Citizen Captain, that the First Consul is satisfied with your conduct. Wishing to reward your valuable services and give proof of his personal esteem, he has appointed you a captain of chasseurs in his Guard.'

This decision fitted in with Bonaparte's plan. Bigarré was a hothead; but this fault was usually appeased by army life. The survivors of Moreau's Army of the Rhine[5] had been infected with ideas hostile to the regime. The malcontents of the Consulate were just beginning to understand that service with the First Consul, whose popularity was considerable, involved certain material and moral advantages, and that military glory, citations, and admission to the Legion of Honor (created 19 May) could lead one day to the formation of a new aristocracy from which it would be inexpedient to find one's self excluded.

Naturally the Line was jealous of the Guard, and with reason. Bonaparte knew the French who tolerated an elite corps only on condition that they might belong to it.

After ten years of war he wished his soldiers to taste the delights of peace. Those privileged to be garrisoned in Paris were gilded by the rays of a rising sun, already hot.

[5] Most of them went to Santo-Domingo with Leclerc.

They danced, played, and attended receptions given by the charming Citizeness Bonaparte whom they now referred to as 'Madame'.

The First Consul received the generals and senior officers, but would no longer tolerate muddy boots, leather breeches, nor the language of the guardroom. He himself laid aside his uniform and began to wear a silk suit and buckled shoes.

Messieurs de Luçay, de Rémusat, and Didelot took charge of the etiquette of the palace, assisted by the aides Lemarois, Caffarelli, Caulincourt, Lauriston, Savary, Rapp, etc. Suddenly the Guardsmen began to watch their language. Officers and soldiers made a stab at fine manners. In the guardroom a dancing master instructed them in bowing and the figures of the quadrille.

The soldiers bought new linen and silk stockings. The Guard of 1802 set the tone. From a look at the roster one suspects that, though the habit does not make the monk, it goes far towards making the soldier.

It was now forbidden for a Guardsman to care for an officer's horse, or even hold its bridle. Hence officers were obliged to keep a servant whose livery was prescribed as a green stable jacket with a yellow collar, green waistcoat and trousers, and a green cloak. NCO's and trumpeters rated three grooms per company, dressed in green jerseys with yellow collars.

To make dandies out of boors, there was nothing so effective as coifing them with plumed bearskin bonnets and trimming their coats with gold lace. Having to wear gloves made the most rebellious characters wash their hands.

It was Bonaparte himself who had caused this metamorphosis. His note books review every fact concerning the officers and men of the Guard – the admissions, promotions, and punishments. Its generals reported to him daily every pertinent detail of the lives, difficulties, and desires of their men so that, aided by his phenomenal memory, he called the men by name at reviews and referred to their problems, promising them aid, promotion, or rewards, righting their wrongs and correcting their mistakes.

'Grenadier Gambin has killed himself for love', he wrote in an order of the day on 26 *floréal*. 'A soldier should know how to conquer grief . . . caused by the passions . . . It requires as much real courage to suffer anguish of soul with equanimity as to face the fire from a battery without flinching. Abandoning one's self to grief, killing one's self to get away from it, is like leaving a battlefield before one is vanquished.'

Bonaparte was the idol not only of the Guard but of Paris as well. Two years before, he had found this people beaten, embittered, resigned, doubting all things including himself and his future. However, on 18 April they turned out to line his route from the Tuileries to Notre-Dame and acclaim him as their 'savior'.

He was going to attend a service of thanksgiving for the Peace of Amiens and for the revival of religion in France. The Guard escorting the Consul's coach, drawn by eight horses, and those of the ambassadors and ministers, did not resemble the Praetorians of the Directory. The grenadiers looked rather too wooden, with even their moustaches aligned. The chasseurs looked more natural. The horse grenadiers seemed able to make even their horses march in step. The horse chasseurs on their nervous mounts were wearing their new hussar uniforms. The troop was led by Beauharnais. Their two crimson guidons were embroidered and fringed with gold (see Plate 10).

Amid deafening cries of '*Vive* Bonaparte!' the gold-spangled procession flowed through the Rue Saint-Honoré to the sound of trumpets in the spring sunshine.

He was a magician, this elect of the people. Here were grenadiers of the Guard escorting him to one of those '*capucinades*'[6] that only yesterday they had ridiculed and reviled. Paris now regarded the flags hanging from the vaulted ceiling of the Invalides church – newly restored to Christendom – the most beautiful sight in the world.

The horses of the coach were led by mounted Mameluks, fairly blazing with gold. Until then, the only Mameluk the Parisians had seen was Roustam, the First Consul's personal attendant. Where had the rest come from?

That is a long story.

[6] Revolutionary slang for religious services. – Ed.

CHAPTER 6

Savages and Sailors

THE evening of Marengo, mixing expediency with sentiment, Bonaparte adopted Desaix's two orphaned aides, Colonels Rapp and Savary.[1] He had watched them in Egypt and knew their qualities, though the two were quite different.

On 13 October 1801 Bonaparte ordered Jean Rapp, a superb soldier with twenty-two wounds, to organize a 'Squadron of Mameluks of the First Consul'.

The idea might not have occurred to him had he not received a letter from Colonel Barthélémy. This officer of Greek extraction was once engaged in recruiting irregulars for the general in chief. (Menou had appointed him to command those 'authentic head-hunters', the Regiment of Mameluks of the Republic.) He had just landed in France accompanied by his family, and a group of officers and troopers who had brought along their brothers, wives, and children – reminding one of General Lagrange's disembarkation at Toulon followed by his harem.

The moment Colonel Barthélémy landed, he wrote the First Consul that he and his *smala*[2] were devoted to his person to the death and awaited his orders. Presented with so touching an expression of collective fidelity, Bonaparte decided that a native troop of valiant and splendid cavaliers would help to reinforce the Guard squadrons, as well as his own prestige.

The sons of the desert were given an enthusiastic welcome by the Parisians who loved color and panache. The people of Paris were charmed by Roustam with his operatic costume. Without knowing a single fact of Mameluk history – which, Heaven knows, is complicated – or even the meaning of the word, they proceeded to decorate their apartments in the Egyptian style, dress '*à la Grecque*,' and wrap their heads in Mameluk turbans.

Once among the rather homesick newcomers in Marseilles, Rapp discovered some sober facts. Some Mameluks were too old for active service; others, accustomed to the freedom of the desert, refused to submit to the rigors of camp discipline, or plumb the mysteries of the Cavalry Drill Manual. Consequently in January 1802, after reading Rapp's report, Bonaparte decided to form a single squadron of 150 Mameluks 'organized like a squadron of hussars'.

Colonel Rapp had half a dozen officers and NCO's put at his disposal. A Mameluk must cost no more than a chasseur; therefore, since his oriental kit was elaborate and expensive, his pay had to be reduced.

[1] He did the same for the aides of Marshal Lannes and Generals La Harpe, d'Hautpoul, and Caulaincourt.
[2] Retinue of an Arab chieftain, sometimes used in French slang to mean 'circus'. – Ed.

PLATE 13

PLATE 14

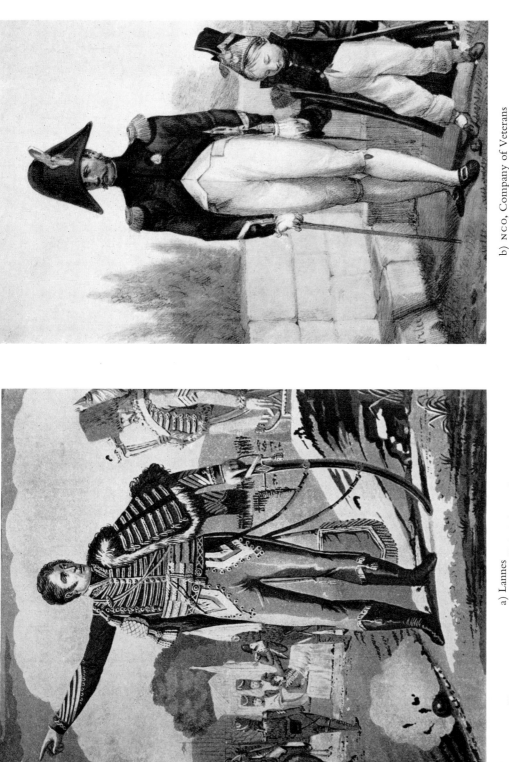

b) NCO, Company of Veterans
(From a lithograph by Charlet)

a) Lannes
(From a contemporary aquatint published chez Esbrard)

PLATE 15

LA REVUE DE QUINTIDI

(From an engraving by Pauquet after the painting by Isabey and Carle Vernet)

PLATE 16

PLATE 17

b) Duroc
(From a contemporary mezzotint)

a) Hulin
(From a contemporary colored engraving)

PLATE 18

a) Larrey
(*After Girodet: Collection Baron Larrey*)

b) Ordener
(*Contemp. lithograph: Bibliothèque Nationale*)

c) Chauveau
(*After miniature: Collection Mme. Leconte*)

d) Bigarré
(*Engr. Forestier*)

e) Davout
(*Lith. Delpech*)

PLATE 19

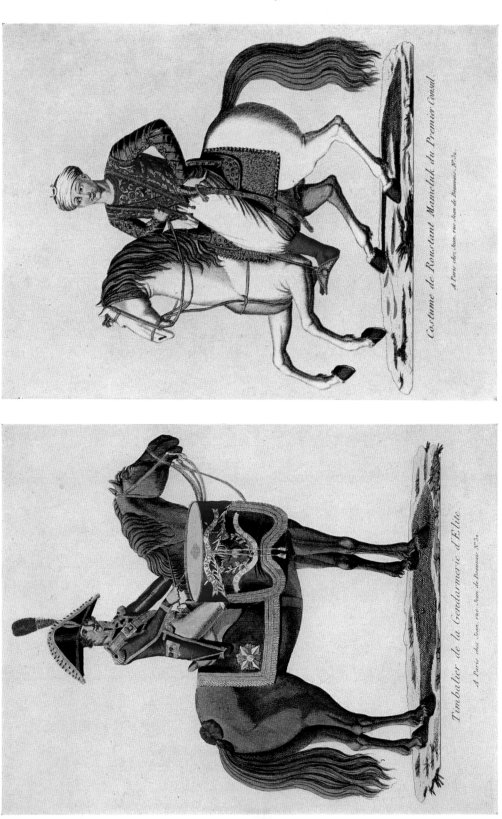

Costume de Roustant Mameluk du Premier Consul.

A Paris chez Jean, rue Jean de Beauvais, N°.32.

Timbalier de la Gendarmerie d'Elite.

A Paris chez Jean, rue Jean de Beauvais N°.32.

PLATE 20

a) Decrès
(*After portrait: Musée de Versailles*)

b) Baste
(*Contemp. engraving*)

c) Fouché
(*Engr. Velyn after Noireterre*)

d) Savary
(*Lith. Delpech*)

PLATE 21

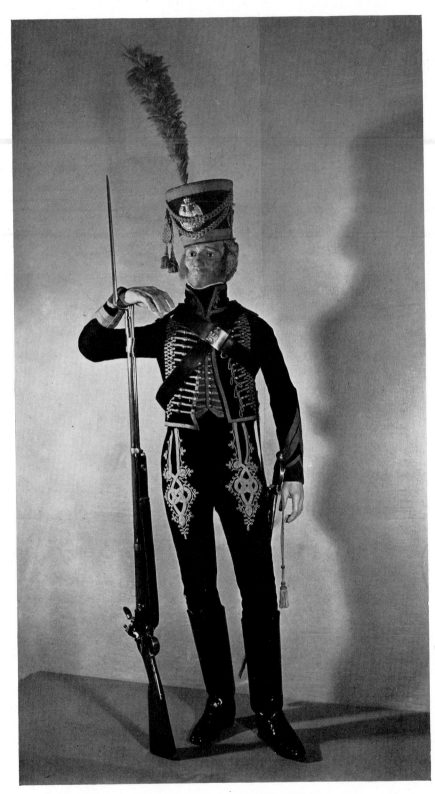

Quartermaster, marines of the Guard
(*Collection Raoul et Jean Brunon*)

PLATE 22

PLATE 23

'YOU HAVE MOST ESTIMABLE PARENTS.' A conscript treating Guard NCO's
(*From a lithograph by Hippolyte Bellangé*)

PLATE 24

Mameluk
(*From a lithograph by Charlet*)

'As a reward for their faithful service to the French Army', Bonaparte decreed, 'their turbans shall be green – the color of the Prophet.' The First Consul was mistaken; it was the *kaouk*[3] that should be green, while the turbans were, and would remain, white. On 15 April the error was corrected and the corps given definite status.

The staff was French. Captain Edouard de Colbert was put in charge of administration. Later he pursued his brilliant career as a swordsman to Quatre-Bras, Waterloo, and beyond to North Africa with the expedition to Constantine, and finally to the Arc de Triomphe, on which his name is inscribed today.

Delaître, future commanding general of the Cavalry School at Saumur, was quartermaster. A surgeon, veterinarian, and trumpet major were added, as well as master artisans who were clever at fashioning the short boots, the maroon *sarouals*,[4] short-sleeved jackets or *yeleks*, scarlet *fermlas*,[5] white *schalls* (turbans), gold-trimmed holsters, beaver belts, and Turkish harness. The master artisans, who were dressed as chasseurs, were real soldiers as well as experienced craftsmen. Their master saddler transferred later to the lancers and campaigned with them, and the master cobbler was wounded in the knee on the Berezina.

Each company numbered 4 officers, a French trooper, and 75 native horsemen, and was initially garrisoned at Melun. Each trooper was a veritable arsenal with a carbine, blunderbuss (soon abolished), two brace of pistols (one in his belt), a saber, dagger, mace, powder horn, and eventually a battle-axe and bayonet, all furnished by the Republic.

The table of organization granted a special favor. The old men, women, and children who had followed the Mameluks to France were formed into two companies and placed on the payroll. Fortunately, the number of dependents did not exceed thirty-six. The male children were to enter active service at sixteen.

The squadron was costly but magnificent – so much so that Bonaparte had to give the Mameluks a bonus over and above their allotment to pay for their kit. Since the uniforms of foreign troops on their soil, whether friends or foes, have always captivated the French, one can imagine what effect the Mameluks produced on the population. Besides the furniture and bibelots 'straight from Egypt' that 'one must have in one's house' – and such an obligation is no joke to a Parisian! – oriental fashions became the rage. Imitating Madame Bonaparte, the ladies doted on turbans, while every self-respecting officer – even in the light infantry – carried a Turkish scimitar.

Commanding Mameluks was somewhat ticklish. Warriors by nature, they were as independent as gazelles and brave to the point of folly, but also rather barbarous and often ferocious. Rapp was shortly relieved by Dupas, a future general whose memoirs are still preserved in the museum at Evian.

Soon the squadron began to shrink. By Christmas 1803 there were but 114 troopers left. Collisions were reported between the Mameluks and the citizens of Melun – and

[3] Bell-crowned visorless cap, around whose base the turban was wound (see Plate 173). – Ed.
[4] Loose Turkish trousers.
[5] Sleeveless overvests.

even Paris. Captain Delaître finally succeeded in bringing the company to order. Bonaparte loved his Mameluks well, but he wanted no adventurers in his Guard.

Desaix's second aide, Colonel Savary, had an aptitude for police work that Bonaparte admired. In July 1801 the First Consul organized an elite legion of gendarmes uniquely at his service to 'maintain public safety and police the government residences'.

The legion received official status in March 1802. With a large staff, two mounted squadrons, and two companies of foot, the unit numbered 608 including officers. It was recruited from the departmental gendarmes and restricted to men between twenty-five and forty who were five-foot-nine and veterans of four campaigns.

The gendarmes' uniform resembled that of the departmental gendarmes, though the hat was larger and bound with silver, the aiguillette was white rather than tricolored, and the buff belt was edged with white or silver braid (see Plate 22).

Jacquin, a former *Chasseur de Bretagne*, was appointed major and later commanded the corps. Severely wounded at Madrid in 1808, he retired as a major general and lived to the ripe age of eighty-two. Captains Henry and Dautancourt also ended as generals and succeeded in turn to the command of the corps.

Though the elite gendarmes did not officially belong to the Guard, a detachment was quartered at Rueil to guard Malmaison.

As Bonaparte ascended the throne step by step he employed his time on the landings very cleverly. He won men through their weaknesses. In June 1803 he granted the new corps the same pay as the horse grenadiers and – contrary to the rule in the departments – ordered it clothed and mounted at the state's expense. However, since the army feared gendarmes in general, he did not immediately admit them to the Guard.

On 15 August the result of the plebiscite electing Bonaparte Consul for life (by 3,568,883 yeas to 8,474 nays) was celebrated by a grand fête. There were receptions in the palace, and a Te Deum was sung in the metropolitan church over which a star shone during the evening. On a buttress of the Pont Neuf a statue of Peace – in plaster – was displayed. Both symbols were significant.

'Hero of the people . . . and object of a mystic faith', Bonaparte was also President of the Italian Republic and Mediator of Switzerland. He had 15,000 soldiers occupying Holland. Protestant Germany referred to him as the 'Most Christian Consul' and placed his portrait beside Frederick the Great's. Brune, his ambassador in Constantinople, arrived in the Golden Horn under escort by a naval squadron. Sebastiani toured the Mediterranean ports.

In the economic sphere France was producing more, buying less, exporting to Europe, and replenishing her gold reserve.

England was frightened. Her ambassador, Lord Whitworth, declared that his government would not evacuate Malta under the terms of the Treaty of Amiens until it was satisfied that France had no aggressive intentions.

On 16 March 1803 the First Consul questioned him in Josephine's salon.

It appeared that London was uneasy. The King had said that France was preparing further aggressions. He was mistaken. He claimed that there were differences between their two cabinets. The First Consul knew of none. True, the Treaty of Amiens had not yet been implemented . . . Were the English trying to intimidate the French by making warlike preparations? The French could be killed. But intimidated? Never!

On 16 May a message from the Throne to Parliament announced the rupture between the two countries. On the 18th the British schooner *Doris* shelled the French lugger *Affronteur* in the Bay of Audierne.

It was war – war for thirteen years.

The British navy was three times the size of the French, and in better shape. The French navy had been ruined by the Revolution and the disaster at Aboukir.[6] It would take ten years of peace to rebuild it, and the work had hardly begun. But the strength of their land forces was just the reverse.

Though skeptical of sailors, Bonaparte decided to invade England and to prepare the means forthwith. A formidable army was concentrated on the coasts. A large flotilla was under construction in the ports, the cities, on the Esplanade of the Invalides – everywhere. Departments, communes, and individuals contributed money and boats. The Liane basin and the ports of Etaples, Wimereux, and Ambleteuse were dredged.

In June 1803 Bonaparte left Boulogne for Paris to raise sailors.

Though he had just missed joining the navy himself on graduation from Brienne, he was suspicious of its conservatism and attachment to routine. He now sought a man capable of 'making seamen act and keeping them on the move'.

He chose Decrès, who was amenable but skeptical, believing neither in Bonaparte nor the navy. Bonaparte, as was his habit, relied principally upon Bonaparte and planned the operation himself. To transport men and equipment he required a fleet of lugger-rigged longboats mounting cannon, armed brigs, thirty-oared pinnaces rowed by two men to an oar, and some armed scows mounting 36-pounders. While he doubted whether soldiers could be made into sailors, he believed he could make sailors into soldiers – provided they were never referred to as such!

At Aboukir Nelson had returned 3,000 sailors he could not feed, retaining their officers. Bonaparte had formed 1,500 of these tars into a valuable legion which had shown remarkable endurance. He now decided to organize crews to man and defend the boats transporting him and his staff across the channel.

In September he created within the Consular Guard a battalion of 737 sailors containing five crews of five squads each, under a naval captain[7] assisted by a comman-der.[8] Within five days of receipt of the order each maritime prefect was to send his quota of sailors to the depot at Courbevoie. 'Selected for the honor of joining the entourage of the First Consul', the sailors must be robust, at least five-foot-ten, and have earned a reputation for good conduct and loyalty.

[6] The Battle of the Nile in which Nelson destroyed the French fleet. – Ed.
[7] *Capitaine de vaisseau.*
[8] *Capitaine de frégate.*

These sunburned tars with gold rings in their ears were nicknamed 'naval hussars' because of their uniform which consisted of a Hungarian jacket or 'dolman' and a plumed shako. Their officers were 'gilded like chalices' with lace and galloon. But these gaudy outfits were worn only ashore; aboard ship the marines of the Guard were dressed as sailors, which was poorly. They were paid the same as the cavalry of the Guard (see Plate 21).

Captain Daugier was distinguished and trustworthy but an indifferent seaman. He was rather lazy and lacked enthusiasm. Commander Baste, on the contrary, was a tough and energetic man but a surly chief. He succeeded eventually to the command of the corps and was killed at Brienne in 1814. Lieutenant Grivel was a magnificent seaman and a splendid officer who ended as a vice-admiral and died at ninety-two in 1869. Commander Roquebert, Lieutenants Bouvier-Destouches, de Saizieu, Gerdy, and Ensigns Barberi and Gérodias joined the battalion one by one.

The glittering grenadiers initiated the marines into the mysteries of the manual of arms at the Courbevoie barracks. The seamen paraded at the Tuileries 'with a serious and reflective air and a free, if rather unusual, gait', after which the crews were dispatched to various channel ports before being concentrated at Boulogne where Captain Daugier took command in May 1804.

Feudal Europe kept an anxious eye on the new France. While the victims of social injustice placed their hopes in Bonaparte, the privileged classes rallied round the kings who felt their thrones menaced. England had no army, but plenty of money to hire those of the kings.

Now ruler of the French and Italian Republics, Bonaparte knew this and dreamed of checkmating England by uniting the nations of Europe. He knew also that the first essential of success was strength.

CHAPTER 7

The Fledglings

THE French army of that day was the finest in the world, with seasoned generals, young officers, old soldiers, and a solid reserve. All it needed was a constant flow of matériel and cadres. The first was up to the War Ministry while the second was up to the Guard.

La Noue[1] in his *Discours militaires* proposed the creation of military academies so that the young would no longer have as their masters 'men who were often debauched . . .' The valiant Guébriant[2] was graduated from the school of La Flèche founded by Henri IV. Bonaparte's own youth was spent at the École Militaire founded in 1751. Now on 1 May 1802 he inserted the following into the Laws of Public Instruction:

'There shall be established . . . a Special Military School designed to teach the elements of war to a number of *lycée* graduates. This School shall have 500 pupils, formed into a battalion, who shall accustom themselves to military service and discipline.' Later he decreed that the school should be under the jurisdiction of the Ministry of War.

On 28 January the school was established at Fontainebleau, 'a ruin out of which something could possibly be made'. After the Emperor removed the original school to Saint-Cyr, Fontainebleau became a school for the Guard.

An historic source of officer cadres had been the cadet system. Bonaparte knew that the companies of *mousquetaires* had been 'the best military schools of their day', and that 'the sons of the most illustrious families had made their debut in carrying the pike and musket' in the *Régiment du Roy* personally commanded by Louis XIV. So in January 1804 Bonaparte created the '*vélites* of the Guard', employing a Roman term more acceptable than 'cadet' to republican sensibilities.

With his imperial future still uncertain, the First Consul showed considerable cunning in expounding the ideas of Napoleon I under the signature of Bonaparte.

'The corps of *vélites* shall be recruited from the annual conscriptions . . . If . . . there shall not be a sufficient number of candidates, qualified volunteers of eighteen may be accepted . . . The captains, lieutenants, and noncommissioned officers shall be furnished by the corps of grenadiers and chasseurs of the Guard . . .

'The pay of the (*vélite*-grenadiers and *vélite*-chasseurs) shall be the same as for the grenadiers and chasseurs of the Guard, except that an allowance of 200 francs, furnished by the parents, will be paid into the regimental fund to replace a similar dispersement by the Public Treasury.

[1] Famous Protestant captain of the Religious Wars, who captured Orléans in 1567. – Ed.
[2] Marshal of France who distinguished himself in the Low Countries in 1638–42. – *Ibid.*

'There shall be attached to each corps at government expense the requisite number of instructors in reading, writing, arithmetic, and military gymnastics. Instructors in mathematics and drawing shall be paid in part by the State and in part by those *vélites* wishing such instruction.

'*Vélites* distinguishing themselves by their conduct, learning, aptitude, bearing, and zeal may be admitted to the Guard of the Government before reaching the age and completing the years of service required for admission. They may also be selected . . . for company clerks and corporals in the Line, or for the Special Military School.'

At the end of 1803 Bonaparte wrote: 'The army is insufficient to recruit the Guard. It cannot even maintain it on a peace footing without stripping itself of a small number of extremely precious men.'

He therefore recruited the *vélites* from the conscripts of the reserve, without encroaching upon the Line's. By choosing sons of fairly affluent families he was able to provide Guard pay to the *vélites* without opening his purse.

What would the old soldiers say, who had to produce wounds and deeds of valor for admission to the Guard? Nothing, because the First Consul could not be wrong. No one dreamed of questioning his decisions.

Had he demanded physical qualifications alone, recruiting the new corps might have presented problems. However, the candidates had to have some education as well as parents 'in easy circumstances'. Here were the 'cadets' of Louis XIV on a popular scale. And since ambition and patriotism are often indistinguishable, applications were numerous.

The drawing master was a pupil of David. The fencing masters gave dancing lessons to the accompaniment of drums. Grenadiers and chasseurs taught the profession of arms without any deviation. Under the heavy hand of the Guard sergeants the *vélites* felt the weight of Davout's who drilled the grenadiers.

The novices were full of zeal. Many complained: 'They do not give us enough drill.' Patience, my lads, the future will bring you complete satisfaction! The old soldiers welcomed them and judged quickly which ones had fat purses. Their amiability and praise depended upon the *vélites'* generosity. 'What, you are already mounting guard? Usually you have to wait two months. You will go far. . . .'

Indeed they would go far . . . All the way to Poland, all the way to Spain. They would become acquainted with the finest profession in the world with its joys and hardships, its servitude and grandeur; with the pride of bearing arms, a privilege denied the common man, and of wearing a cap made from the hide of an animal, like the Gauls, or a shako of oriental origin which they spelled 'chacot'.

They soon learned the ambiguities of military language, in which the *prêt*, or pay, so eagerly awaited proved little more than '*prêté*', or loaned,[3] being as mysterious as the 'revenue' of the state that everybody talked about and no one ever saw. And the *ordinaire*, or mess, for which they shelled out 7 centimes of their pay each day in Paris, was most *ex*traordinary – and usually poor.

[3] As in all armies of that day, the soldier was docked a large part of his pay for the regimental funds (*masse*) to pay for his clothing, food, and equipment. – Ed.

This was a rude environment with a common bowl. To stick your spoon into it twice might lead to oaths and even duels. You came in contact with veterans of the revolutionary bands whose morals were doubtful and who were braggarts all.

Among the recruits was a young country squire, an aristocrat who felt displaced, distressed, and disappointed. His name was Thomas Robert Bugeaud. 'There are a great many boys here who do not come of good family, sons of peasants and workmen', he wrote his sister. 'There are a few who are quite well bred but in general this corps is not what you would suppose.'

He did his job nevertheless, carried his pack, bit off the top of his cartridges, won his corporal's stripes at Austerlitz, learned the meaning of military honor that no manual can teach, and became a marshal of France. Père Bugeaud, foul-mouthed as a grenadier, surly as a sergeant, was 'great in heart and character', according to Marshal Canrobert.

Little by little the *vélites* earned their stripes and epaulets of gold. *Sic itur ad astra.*[4]

1804 was still called 'year XII' from habit.[5] The act elevating General Bonaparte to the Imperial throne was dated '28 *floréal*' (18 May), a name of springtide which was full of promise.

France was in good order and well governed. The nation's life was intense in every domain. The notables of the electoral colleges fell into line with the national celebrities admitted to the Legion of Honor, and together they guarded the institutions of France.

The Guard, charged with protecting its creator, was preparing to change its name again. It was a privileged corps, luxuriously maintained, comfortably housed, faithful, disciplined, military, and war-wise. The men were well fed and their horses fat. A whole world separated the Guard from the Line.

While a major in the Guard drew 416 francs, his colleague in the Line drew 300. A *vélite* drew 34·80 francs, whereas an ordinary conscript drew 9·11. Substantial bonuses supplemented the monthly pay, and retirement pensions were 50 per cent higher. New bonuses were granted in August to NCO's promoted officers, traveling as escorts of the First Consul, and men participating in special maneuvers or guarding Malmaison and Saint-Cloud. The Guard had first priority of clothing, and allowances for housing and mounts. An officer might rate anywhere from two to twenty horses. The senior captain of each battalion was mounted. Even the commandant of the marines rated six horses.

No economies were practised that diminished the Guard's prestige. At the widow Chaillot's a cavalry guidon of red damask, embroidered and fringed, 'with inscription', cost 4,200 francs. A trumpet banner 'with six ells of gold silk cord' cost 850 francs, and a pair of green velvet drum aprons with sixty gold tassels, 9,000 (see Plates, 5, 32).

Amid such luxury Bonaparte appeared at reviews in the undress uniform of the *chasseurs à cheval* and his little black bicorne hat without any ornament. Over this occasionally, as at Marengo, he wore a blue greatcoat which was replaced by a grey

[4] Thus he journeys towards the stars.
[5] The Revolutionary calendar was abolished with the advent of the Empire in 1804. – Ed.

one at the Camp of Boulogne and never varied thereafter. Sometimes on Sunday he wore a grenadier uniform. The cleverness of this man, who understood men as well as the basis of his own prestige, was phenomenal.

A Guardsman rarely passed into the Line without a rise in rank. (The new rank of *major*, equivalent to lieutenant colonel, was instituted at this period.) Several Guard officers, including Meunier and Lajonquière, were sent to the Line as lieutenant colonels and colonels.

Guardsmen introduced into the Line the methods of service in the Guard as well as its spirit and discipline. Simultaneously they created vacancies in the Guard which were filled by men like Poret de Morvan, a veteran of Italy and Santo Domingo, who had led Leclerc's corps back to France after the latter's death.

Bonaparte assigned four of his best generals to the Guard: Davout, the most learned, to the grenadiers; Soult, the warrior, to the chasseurs; Bessières, the most loyal, to the cavalry; Mortier, the epic soldier of the Rhine, to the artillery and marines. All held the rank of 'colonel general'.

Ten thousand strong, the Guard was now a model for the army, a school of cadres, and a solid and homogeneous reserve capable of deciding the great battles ahead. It was conscious of its strength which it owed to its creator. It surrounded him and protected him. Immobile on their four-footed sentinels, or else galloping behind his coach, the troopers kept watch, forbidden to unroll their cloaks while serving as his escort. Bonaparte knew how to instill in them the military spirit that bred discipline, loyalty, and devotion; and upon this knowledge he founded his sovereignty.

There was no intermediary between Bonaparte and the Guard. On 4 August he wrote Berthier: 'I cannot conceive why you wish to deprive the major generals of their plumes and sashes, nor why you have changed the color of the aides-de-camp's uniform . . . As for the Guard of the Consuls, no one interferes with what may be – for good or ill – an improvement in its dress or welfare except me . . .'

In some respects the year of the coronation was a year of terror with Moreau arrested, the Duc d'Enghien shot, Cadoudal guillotined, and Pichegru found dead under mysterious circumstances.

Among the actors in these dramas were Caulaincourt, Bonaparte's aide-de-camp, and men well known in the Guard like Savary, Ordener, Hulin, Dautancourt, slaves to discipline and self-abnegation. Behind them, in the shadows, lurked Fouché and Talleyrand . . .

BOOK II

THE GUARD KEEPS WATCH

CHAPTER 1

The Imperial Guard

THE order of the day on 10 May 1804 read as follows:

'The Guard is informed that today the Senate proclaimed Napoleon Bonaparte Emperor of the French and vested the imperial succession in his family.

'Long live the Emperor! . . .

'Today the Guard takes the title of "The Imperial Guard".

'The officers will report to Saint-Cloud tomorrow at 1.30 p.m. to be presented to the Emperor.

'The Guard will form under arms at 4.30 p.m. tomorrow in the Champ de Mars to take the oath of allegiance to the new Emperor that is required by the Senate . . .

Bessières,

General of the Guard in waiting upon the Emperor.'

The veterans, forage-caps in hand, listened in silence. Then the cry '*Vive l'Empereur!*' that was to make Europe tremble for the next ten years burst from their throats.

'You have succeeded in teaching a people whom civil effervescence had rendered impatient of all restraint and inimical to all authority', said Cambacérès the following week, in addressing the Emperor, 'to cherish and respect a power exercised uniquely for its glory and repose'.

The word *imperator* – he who commands the legions and transmits power to the empire – derives from *imperare*, to command or order. Thus, in one sense empire means 'order'. The new emperor of the Republic was the heir of both Caesar and Charlemagne, the founders of Empires. Napoleon adopted as his own emblem the spread eagle of the Roman legions, which was also the emblem of Saint John the Evangelist and of Jupiter.

He needed great dignitaries of court and household to add luster to the principle of authority, a necessity for all those in power who wish to attract the ambitious and dazzle the crowd. However, these posts – though handsomely remunerated – were only sinecures. Those of marshal of the Empire (instituted in May) and colonel general were indispensable to command the conglomerate forces of French, Italian, Batavian, Swiss, and German troops that the Emperor had christened the '*Grande Armée*' without a national designation. This was the army of a new Europe including Italy, Holland, Switzerland, and the German states allied with France, to which Bonaparte had introduced the concept of liberty and the rights of man.

Since March 1804 he had succeeded in bringing order into equality through the new civil code. The kings of Europe trembled on their thrones. Gentz, the Aulic Councillor, wrote the Austrian Emperor: 'If the sovereigns recognize Bonaparte's title, and those of his pretended dynasty, the magic of supreme power will be forever dissolved. Revolution will be sanctioned, if not sanctified, and thereby transmitted, with all its pernicious precedents, to our most remote posterity.' Gentz was a prophet.

By becoming Emperor Napoleon had made the Revolution universal. Nevertheless, by August he was officially recognized by all the kings of Europe except the Tsar (with his satellite Turkey), and the King of England with whom Napoleon was at war. The ambitions of these two sovereigns could not reconcile them to a unification of Europe.

The warlike preparations at Boulogne were progressing. In Paris the Emperor was planning a journey to the Rhine to visit the tomb of Charlemagne, 'his illustrious predecessor'. Before leaving, he decided to unite the civil and military hierarchy of France, admitted to the newly-formed Legion of Honor, overtly in a ceremony of investiture at the church of the Invalides, and award the new insignia.

On 14 July the Imperial Guard paraded before the Emperor in the court of the Tuileries. Then the regiments lined the route to the Invalides, and to the booming of cannon the Empress and princes with their consorts drove in carriages to the Hôtel. Then the Imperial procession set forth, led by chasseurs of the Guard, their standards already embroidered with eagles. Next came the marshals, the Emperor on horseback, the colonel generals of the Guard, and the aides-de-camp. The horse grenadiers brought up the rear.

Received at the door by the Archbishop of Paris, the Emperor occupied a throne erected near the spot where he lies today, surrounded by Invalids and Polytechnicians. At the close of the Mass the Constable of France[1] decorated Napoleon. Then the Emperor decorated each dignitary in turn, including grenadier Coigniet,[2] with the order that has retained its prestige to this day, though its significance has been somewhat vitiated by the ever increasing number of its recipients.

Soldiers of the Guard, magistrates, savants, generals, dignitaries of the church, and artists bent over the dais to receive identical insignia, having first sworn on their honor to 'devote themselves to the service of the Republic, to guard her territory, defend her government and laws . . . and to maintain liberty and equality'.

The Emperor was escorted back to the Tuileries with the same ceremony as before. By now a number of officers and soldiers of the Guard wore crosses of gold or silver.

Brilliant uniforms had already transformed the members of the Consular Guard. Now the admission of its bravest men, alongside the most illustrious civilians, into the Legion of Honor completed the transformation.

We shall hear no more of those who were expelled from the corps like one 'Laurent, chasseur of the 5th Company', who, 'having behaved in a manner unworthy of a

---

[1] Louis Bonaparte.
[2] The published *Cahiers* of Grenadier Coigniet, frequently quoted in this book, give a vivid account of the ceremony. – Ed.

soldier of the Guard, and having taken to drink in a shameful way, will be stripped of his uniform and drummed out of the Corps . . . Guardsmen must realize that their position requires them to set an example and behave in an irreproachable manner . . .'

In July the organization of the Guard was fixed for the following year. The elite legion of gendarmes became officially part of the Guard. A magnificent troop of foot and horse, it was posted on the garden terrace of the Tuileries. Savary, now a commander of the Legion of Honor, was its chief. Quartered in the former residence of the Archbishop of Cambrai, the gendarmes were comfortably housed. Though the men still slept two in a bed, the corporals and trumpeters had beds to themselves.

The strength of the Guard was not otherwise increased. The grenadier and chasseur regiments remained at three battalions, including one of *vélites*, and the cavalry regiments at four squadrons. The Mameluks were attached to the *chasseurs à cheval*. The artillery was a separate corps which included a squadron of horse artillery and four companies of train, plus the park and artificers.

In becoming 'Imperial' the Guard's prestige increased. The colonels of the four regiments now held the rank of major general and received a bonus of 6,000 francs over and above their pay which was 24,000 francs for the colonel generals.

Although the Consulate had ceased to exist, the etiquette of the Monarchy seemed hardly applicable to the new Empire. Who would be capable of reviving it? Who in the Emperor's entourage would know its minutiae of detail? Consecrated as this etiquette was by tradition and royal precedent, was it even appropriate to a man elected by the people?

Napoleon established two categories of attendants to ornament and dignify the state and maintain his personal prestige: symbolic attendants, inspired by royal custom, and functional attendants who, while taking due account of the honor due his office, were organized to encompass the ardent life of a Napoleon. Both groups were aware of his popularity and his genius as well as of his close association with the army and affection for the Guard.

The colonel generals served a week in rotation in waiting upon the Emperor and never left his side from the time he got up until he went to bed. They marched just behind him and were responsible to him alone. (The Guard was under their orders while serving as his guard or escort.) These officers lived near him in the palace and slept in his tent in the field.

The colonel generals administered the oath to Guardsmen of all ranks and presented those newly promoted to the Emperor. At ceremonies they surrounded his carriage, marching two by two at either door. When on foot, they walked just behind him; when mounted, the Master of the Horse occupied this post. The colonel generals were entitled to the same honors as marshals of the Empire, and commanded the troops at great parades. But no one of them commanded the Guard which was never under the command of anyone but the Emperor. The four colonel generals were simply intermediaries.

A letter from Napoleon to his brother Joseph, King of Naples, dated May 1806 says: 'Do not organize your Guard so as to have to name a single commander. Nothing is more dangerous . . .'

Under the new organization Napoleon was in constant contact with his Guard. He knew every incident that occurred and heard all complaints.

'We should be paid in francs but we are paid in *livres*',[3] some grenadiers wrote their chief, addressing him as 'Monseigneur Murat, Marshal of the Empire'.

'The Emperor must not be surprised to find us very well dressed when we appear before him . . . But the moment we return to barracks the clothing issued for the parade goes back to the magazine . . .'

Was this true?

It was. Rapp, sent to investigate, concluded his report: 'There is general discontent and we hope that His Majesty will put a stop to the abuses.'

Consequently, an order was issued on 9 November: 'The Guard will receive new clothes and new buttons' (see tailpiece page 59).

Each nomination to the Guard was submitted to the Emperor. Three drivers and three assistant storekeepers were needed in the artillery park. 'No use to present the list to His Majesty', wrote Berthier. General Songis and Marshal Mortier disregarded his advice. They were right. The Emperor chose six veterans of Italy and Egypt and signed their admission papers himself.

The Guard enjoyed special privileges. Its flags and standards were kept in the Emperor's salon.

'Wherever the troops of the Guard shall find themselves in company with those of the Line, the former shall occupy the place of honor.'

Officers and NCO's of the Guard took precedence over their opposites in the Line when engaged in the same duty.

'When a corps or detachment of the Guard meets a corps or detachment of the Line en route, the latter shall form in line of battle and port arms or present sabers . . . Flags and standards shall be dipped, the drums shall beat *Aux Champs*, and the trumpets sound the March until the troops of the Imperial Guard shall have passed. The colonels or commanders shall exchange salutes.

'The corps of the Imperial Guard shall render the same honors as it receives in such cases, but shall not halt its march.'

When the Emperor crossed a river or put to sea in a boat, the craft was manned by the Imperial Guard.

'A noncommissioned officer of the duty detachment of the horse Guard shall be in attendance at all times in the guardroom adjoining His Majesty's apartments.'

How could the Guard fail to be proud of these privileges?

Here is a list of the honors rendered by the Guard:

'Outside the palace, the Imperial Guard shall present arms and line the route for the Emperor and Empress. It shall port arms and form in line of battle for princes and

---

[3] Old coin minted at Paris at 25 sous, and at Tours at 20 sous. – Ed.

princesses of the Imperial family. The trumpets shall sound the March and the drums beat *Aux Champs*. It shall also port arms for the colonel generals of the Guard, the drums beating and the trumpets sounding.

'When the Emperor is present with the army, guard posts of the Imperial Guard shall turn out under arms for the general in chief; they shall turn out unarmed for other generals, the drums not beating and the trumpets not sounding.

'When the Emperor is not present, the Guard sentries shall render the same honors as the Line to the general in chief and other generals.'

In traveling, the colonel generals accompanying the Emperor on horseback took station at the right and left carriage doors and officers of the Imperial Guard rode just ahead or behind the colonel general, on the same side.

'Only the Imperial Guard shall precede and follow His Majesty's carriage.'

The new regulations were put into effect at the Camp of Boulogne.

At this camp near Moulin-Hubert, stars of the Legion of Honor were awarded to the army on 16 August 1804. The Emperor sat on a throne surrounded by trophies, facing the sea, with the ministers, marshals, and colonel generals of the Guard grouped behind him. In front, the Imperial Guard was drawn up in a line. The army was massed by columns in fan formation with the men to be decorated in front and the cavalry formed in line of battle on the slope above (see Plate 30).

Aux Champs was beaten by 1,300 drums. After the men were decorated the massed bands of Guard and Line paraded the troops to the strains of the *Song of Departure*, led by Méhul, and cries of '*Vive l'Empereur!*' Most of the officers and many soldiers of the Guard were decorated at this grandiose ceremony.

The skies were lit that evening by fireworks, during which the fire bombs shot off by the artillery and star cartridges by the infantry were visible in the camp of Wimereux. The town and ramparts were illuminated.

That night the Emperor ordered an escort of horse grenadiers for a long journey to Belgium and the Rhine.

Napoleon left Saint-Omer on 27 August, arriving in Brussels on 1 September and in Aix-la-Chapelle the following day.

It had been presumed until then that he was to be crowned in the Church of the Invalides by the Cardinal Archbishop of Paris, and that the ceremony would be consummated by a constitutional oath in keeping with the spirit of the Republic.

On 7 September Napoleon heard a Te Deum in the Cathedral of Aix where he was presented relics of Charlemagne. He meditated long before the tomb of the Emperor of the West. Did he seek the same crown? At any rate, he wished the one he wore to be consecrated. Therefore, he wrote from Cologne to the Pope, inviting him to perform the sacred rite of coronation, and sent his aide Caffarelli to Rome with the letter.

The ceremony was ultimately fixed for Sunday, 2 December 1804.

CHAPTER 2

Coronation

THE Pope arrived at Fontainebleau on 26 November. As he entered the château the Guard presented arms. The orders of the day read by the company clerks were chiefly concerned with the problem of 'His Holiness'. Those of the Grand Marshal (Duroc), the Governor of Paris (Lebrun), and the ministers dealt also with the coronation, ceremonies, entertainments, and protocol. Fearing to commit a *faux pas*, these gentlemen were all tangled up in titles, ceremonial, and salutes, and literally besieged with requests. The women needled their husbands; Caroline nearly drove Murat mad, while Elisa and Pauline exasperated Napoleon on the subject of precedence, jewels, and dress.

The Guard had no complaints. As promised, it received brand new uniforms on 9 November. These were unchanged except that eagles and other imperial emblems replaced those of the Consulate. Dandyism was the rage. Anciaume, a *vélite*-chasseur stationed at Mirecourt, asked his family to send him money for two pairs of nankeen breeches, low shoes and stockings for walking out, cotton pantaloons, and breeches 'with pockets', since they were 'cheaper at Mirecourt than Paris'. (It was probably a hoax, as he had just contracted for a pair of silver buckles at 20 francs.)

The infantry officers were resplendent and the cavalry dazzling. The Mameluks were flamboyant in all the colors of the rainbow. The dress of the kettledrummers recalled the splendor of the *Maison du Roy*.

The coronation was a triumph for the Guard which was either present or represented at every ceremony.

On 29 November detachments of grenadiers, chasseurs, and elite gendarmes were posted at the Archbishop's palace, the cathedral of Notre-Dame, and in the adjacent avenues, with orders to let no one pass. So no one passed – neither the architect Fontaine who was in charge of the decorations, nor the workmen themselves. To simplify matters, the ground was covered with ice.

On the morning of the great day there were frightful complications. From 6 a.m. on, when the doors opened, crowds of curious and impatient people – with and without invitations – swept into the Cathedral, engulfing the ninety-two ushers and the workmen hastily putting the finishing touches to the draperies.

No carriages were allowed in the vicinity of Notre-Dame, so the first ladies of the Empire, the pretty with the plain, were obliged to walk in their low-cut gowns and thin slippers all the way from the Palais de Justice, wending their way through tortuous and dirty alleys, shivering in the icy wind. Judged not respectable by the wags of the Cité, they were showered with propositions en route.

PLATE 25

a) Sapper

b) Drum major

FOOT CHASSEURS, GUARD OF THE CONSULS

Note the green plumes and epaulets and the bonnet without plaque

(*From contemporary engravings published chez Jean*)

PLATE 26

PLATE 27

Project for the First Consul's triumphant entry into London
(*From an original sketch by Naudet with engraved montage*)

PLATE 28

PLATE 28

Regiment of horse grenadiers of the Consular Guard
(*After Hoffmann, from an engraving colored by the artist*)

PLATE 29

Tambour de la Garde à pied.

a) Grenadier drummer, Imperial Guard, in *surtout*
(*Contemporary watercolor*)

b) Italian grenadiers
(*After C. Suhr*)

PLATE 30

Napoleon awarding the Legion of Honor at the Camp of Boulogne
(From an original sepia wash by Martinet)

PLATE 31

PLATE 32

PLATE 33

PLATE 33

Napoleon in his coronation dress
(*After Isabey*)

PLATE 34

PLATE 35

PLATE 36

THE IMPERIAL FAMILY
Top row, left to right: Lucien, Letizia ('Madame Mère'), Joseph.
2nd row: Jerome, Hortense Beauharnais, Caroline, Elisa, Pauline, Louis.
3rd row: Josephine, Napoleon, Marie-Louise (Empress, 1810)
(From a lithograph by Becquet)

PLATE 37

Napoleon accepting the surrender of Ulm
(From an original drawing by Martinet)

The order of precedence in the cathedral was enforced from the entrance doors. At nine o'clock the diplomatic corps arrived, escorted by cavalry. Official France, civil and military, took its place according to precedence, appropriately costumed. The tribunes near the throne were reserved for officers of the Imperial Guard. 'This reminds me of the old regime', someone whispered.

Grenadiers and chasseurs rendered the honors at the Tuileries while others lined the square. Several 'old moustaches' had been there before to worship the Goddess of Reason . . .

At eleven o'clock – the Papal procession having arrived an hour earlier – the Emperor's cortege appeared.

First came Murat and his staff, preceded by the kettledrums and trumpets of the carabineers. Then came squadrons of carabineers, cuirassiers, and chasseurs of the Guard 'interspersed with detachments of Mameluks', the heralds of arms, the carriage of the master of ceremonies, those of the great officers of state, ministers, great dignitaries, princesses, and then . . .

The Emperor's coach, drawn by eight horses and driven by César, the coachman of the 'infernal machine incident',[1] with the colonel generals – now also marshals of the Empire – flanking both doors. Inside were the Empress, dressed in white and gold and wearing diamonds; Joseph and Louis, in white also, and the Emperor in purple and gold velvet with a Spanish cloak (see Plate 33).

The carriages of the officers and ladies of the suite were followed by four squadrons of horse grenadiers and horse artillery and a squadron of elite gendarmes.

In these sumptuous surroundings Paris could scarcely recognize either the General or the Consul it had chosen as its sovereign. At the Imperial couple's entrance into the cathedral the band of the Guard broke into a grand triumphal march. Throughout the ceremony the colonel generals never left the Emperor's side. General de Beauharnais bore the coronation ring, a twenty-carat emerald engraved with the arms – not of the new Empire but of the Holy Roman Empire – with the additional device of a dove holding an olive branch: a threefold symbol of divine revelation, Charlemagne, and peace.

Three days later the distribution of eagles took place on the Champ de Mars. The Emperor had written on 27 July: 'The spread eagle as displayed on the seal of the Empire shall be placed, as on the Roman standards, at the head of the staff. The flag shall be placed below it in place of the *labarum*.[2] The standard shall be inscribed: "The Emperor of the French to the ——— regiment". The eagle itself shall be the standard, the flag being replaced as its condition demands' (see Plate 111).

The Emperor considered the regimental emblem to be the staff with its eagle,[3] and the flag to be of secondary importance. From this time on the eagle and staff represented

---

[1] The attempted bombing of Napoleon's carriage on the day of the plebiscite, 24 December 1800. – Ed.
[2] Rectangular metal ornament below the eagle on Roman standards. – *Ibid.*
[3] The eagles presented by the Emperor, surmounting tricolor flags consisting of a white lozenge set in alternate angles of blue and red, were sculptured by Chaudet and cast in bronze by Thomire.

the Emperor who was henceforth symbolically present at the head of every regiment that received one at his hands. Consequently, whereas under the old regime the loss of a flag was a regimental bereavement and disgrace, the loss of an eagle would involve dishonor to the Emperor and the nation. This notion has persisted in the French army.

Between a double row of grenadiers of the Guard, preceded by *chasseurs à cheval* and Mameluks and followed by horse grenadiers and gendarmes, the Emperor rode in state to the École Militaire where a throne had been erected. On the steps stood the colonels appointed to bear the eagles for the army; at the right stood the eagle-bearers of the Guard; opposite were massed the national guard flags of 108 departments.

The Emperor raised his voice:

'Soldiers, here are your flags. These eagles will always be your rallying point. They will be wherever your Emperor deems necessary for the defence of the throne and his people. Do you swear to lay down your lives in their defence, and by your courage to keep them ever on the road to victory? . . .'

'We swear!' the colonels cried in unison, raising their flags on high. The troops presented arms, placing their bearskin bonnets on the point of their bayonets. The bands of the Guard played and the drums beat the *March of the Flags*.

It rained in torrents during the parade. Napoleon, the elect of the people, had referred to them as '*my* people'. Which of the two was sovereign?

Who worried about a possessive pronoun during that glorious month whose every day was marked with fêtes and orations?

On Sunday, 20 January 1805, Napoleon was indeed sovereign of the people. Pressed against the fence surrounding the Tuileries, they watched a dazzling parade of the Imperial and Italian Guards in honor of President Melzi of the Republic of Italy who had come to offer the Emperor the crown of Italy.

On 26 May the Italian Guard, with detachments of *vélite*-chasseurs and horse grenadiers from Paris under Major Bourdon, were drawn up before the Cathedral in Milan where the King-Emperor placed the iron crown of Lombardy over his imperial crown, the one supporting the other.

Piedmont was annexed to the Empire which was now bounded by Boulogne, Hamburg, Genoa, and Tarento. This was the empire of Charlemagne; however, to give full validity to the device on the coronation emerald, there must be peace.

There could be no peace in Europe while England remained outside the common cause. Orders went out from Milan to speed the preparation of the coastal army and flotilla. General Hulin, left in Paris with the rest of the Guard, received the following instructions from Bessières, revealing the Emperor's intentions:

'Form six companies of grenadiers with 75 veterans and 45 *vélites* . . . and six of chasseurs. Leave with the two battalions for Wimereux without revealing your destination . . . All troops must be in prime condition, clothed and armed.'

Reaching Genoa on 30 June, Napoleon left for France and went to his headquarters near Boulogne on 3 September. There he found Hulin's battalions ready to board the pinnaces manned by marines of the Guard who had been assigned the task of transporting the Emperor with his household and staff across the Channel.

In the mornings Ensigns Barberi, de Rigny (a favorite of the Emperor and a *légion-naire* at twenty-two), Gérodias, etc. drilled the marines in marching and marksmanship. In the afternoons, at a signal from the Guard drummers they embarked the horses and heavy equipment. The grenadiers were made to swim and practise landings under various conditions of wind and sea.

The enemy was often in evidence. The marine lieutenants Boniface, Gerdy, Grivel, Kerveguen, and Saizieu had already made names for themselves in the Guard by their exploits. Thanks to good wages paid regularly, the marines' warlike activities were punctuated with sprees ashore in the cabarets of Boulogne where they drank and sang to the tune of *The Baker's Wife:*

> 'From England we'll bring back treasure
> That won't have cost us a sou . . .'

or else:

> 'Before Boulogne,
> Nelson raised hell on the firing line;
> Many poor sailors were heard to groan,
> And drank salt water instead of wine
> Before Boulogne . . .'

They also danced. A sailor cap or printed neckerchief knotted fisherman style identified the improvised 'girl' partner. On Sundays the marines of the Guard organized races across the sand in small canoes on wheels, propelled by enormous sails. If the helmsmen were awkward they capsized to the delight of the spectators. Free-for-all fights and swordplay by candlelight between the marines and grenadiers were not unknown.

What was the *Tondu* waiting for? When would he give them the signal to go? All right, so Admiral Villeneuve would collect the Spanish ships at Cadiz and those at Ferrol, and would sail to Boulogne and make an all-out attack on every craft flying the English ensign. If he could hold out for three days, twenty-four hours, even twelve – then the army of 100,000 might cross the narrows, England would be beaten, and there would be peace . . .

On 7 August Napoleon still believed the operation feasible, for he wrote Bessières:

'Send the grenadiers and chasseurs of my Guard, equipped for war, to Boulogne under Dorsenne and Gros, with General Soulès in command. Also send half the foot gendarmes in battle trim, and the infantry of the Italian Guard – even without uniforms provided they are armed. Rush the horse chasseurs and grenadiers from Genoa . . . Be ready to leave yourself . . .'

But next day he wrote:

'My Cousin: I wrote you yesterday, ordering you to make various dispositions of my Guard and send some to Boulogne. If some of the troops have already left, allow them to proceed; but I now intend that you hold the rest and prepare for any eventuality while awaiting my orders.'

Had the Emperor no confidence in the arrival of Villeneuve?

No. The Admiral had not understood the sacrifice demanded of him.[4] And now – with forces paid by a frightened England – Russia and Austria were arming, and also Prussia. Talleyrand had written from Vienna that the danger lay in the east, not the west.

The chips were down. On 23 August the Emperor wrote his minister:

'... We must wait until winter is past before undertaking the crossing ... I am in a great hurry ... I am striking camp ... The 1st *vendémiaire* (23 September) will find me in Germany with 200,000 men ... I am marching to Vienna ...'

On the 25th he sent his cavalry with the coastal army – newly christened the 'Grand Army' – to the Rhine. On the 28th he ordered the concentration of the Guard at Strasbourg, as follows: Berthier was ordered to send the units from Boulogne with their fifteen guns; Bessières was ordered to leave a guard at Saint-Cloud and send from Paris two battalions of the Italian Guard and all available men, with 'surgeons, field hospitals, caissons and wagons to transport food and baggage, and everything necessary for a campaign ...' Finally, Mortier was ordered to organize the artillery into three batteries of eight guns each, with caissons of artillery and infantry ammunition, a forge, spare gun carriages, etc, and to equip each drummer with a musket and 20 cartridges.

Orders went forth to buy 400 horses, and 100 mules – 'for their greater endurance' – as well as wagons and harness. The clothing magazines were emptied and Larrey made preparations for the field hospitals.

On 19 September the Emperor created 800 cavalry *vélites*, half grenadiers and half chasseurs, from conscripts with an income of 300 francs who could produce a pair of buckskin breeches, gauntlets, and boots. The Guard depot was instructed to furnish the cadres and organize, train, and clothe the new units, and Majors Clément and Clerc were put in command.

On 30 September, 2,700 men and 1,200 horses from Boulogne entered Strasbourg exhausted from marching day and night. Overcome with sleep, the soldiers had often locked arms to keep from falling. Sometimes whole platoons tumbled into a ditch, despite the drummers' efforts to keep them awake by beating the Charge. Finally, at Saverne the sleepers had to be loaded on carts.

The Paris column had already arrived, sent 'by post' in wagons and carriages, 'which was exceptionally hard on the equipment', according to the commissary.

'And on the grenadiers!' exclaimed the victims who had been packed four and five to a buggy, or a dozen to a carriage, and had traveled over 60 miles a day.

On 1 October the Emperor reviewed his Guard, by then refreshed and assembled. 'This reserve corps', he wrote Bessières, 'is really a division of infantry, cavalry, and artillery with autonomous auxiliary services ...' adding: 'My Guard must lack nothing the army has.'

---

[4] Namely, to lure the English fleet from the vicinity of Boulogne and engage it at all costs so as to clear a passage for the flotilla across the Channel. Villeneuve was later beaten by Nelson at Trafalgar, taken to England as a prisoner, and upon his return, committed suicide rather than face Napoleon. – Ed.

The Guard now consisted of brigades of grenadiers, chasseurs, Italian infantry, and horse Guards, a general staff, and a corps[5] of horse artillery. One company[6] of artillery was made up of Italian gunners.

The elite gendarmes were attached to Imperial Headquarters. Except Commander Roquebert's crew, the marines were left in Boulogne with the flotilla under Marshal Brune. The overage men of the other corps had been left to guard the palaces, or at the main depot in Paris.

Several majors sent to the Line as lieutenant colonels had been replaced by Friederichs, ex-soldier of the Monsieur Regiment; Lonchamp, a veteran of Italy and Egypt; and Boyer de Rebeval, a hero of the campaign of 1800. The infantry was reinforced by 470 *vélites*.

The new commandant of the grenadiers was the 'handsome Dorsenne' whom the Emperor had promoted for gallantry on the battlefield but had hesitated to admit to his Guard because he was 'too attractive'. Lt. Colonel Jean-Louis Gros, a southerner weak in spelling and fine manners but a brave and much-scarred soldier, was in command of the chasseurs under General Soulès, now colonel in chief.

Among the majors serving under Lt. Colonel Oulié in the horse grenadiers were Duclaux, a former officer of the guides, and Chamorin, an old infantryman who became a superb cavalryman in Italy and was wounded at Montebello. Lt. Colonel Morland of the chasseurs was a commander of the Legion of Honor. Major Thiry, who began as a gunner, then turned infantryman, and ended up a trooper in the *Hussards d'Egalité*, had joined the regiment.

With General Roussel as chief of staff, Bessières commanded the Guard division that constituted the reserve of the Grand Army of 200,000 French and 30,000 foreign troops. With 4,500 infantry, 1,600 horse, and 770 artillery, marines, and gendarmes the Guard mustered around 6,800 men in the field.[7]

With this small but solid phalanx, to which the Emperor had just granted two extra pairs of shoes per man, the Imperial Guard began the march to glory that continued for the next ten years.

---

[5] The word 'corps' was used in the Guard in its classic sense to denote distinctive units (grenadiers, marines, artillery, engineers etc.) of varying strength, such as our 'corps of cadets' at West Point, and must not be confused with the army corps, usually numbered and commanded by lieutenant generals or marshals, which contained units of infantry, cavalry, and artillery. – Ed.

[6] A 'company' of horse artillery contained six guns with their crews. – *Ibid.*

[7] The Guard at this date numbered all told 11,500 men of whom about 3,000 were at the depots or on duty at the palaces.

CHAPTER 3

The March to Vienna

THE objective was Austerlitz, 1,200 miles away.

The troops left Strasbourg for Rastatt on 30 September at 6 a.m. The Guard, drawn up between the citadel and the bridge over the Rhine, listened to the Emperor's proclamation:

'Soldiers, the war of the Third Coalition has begun . . . We shall not halt until we have secured the independence of Germany . . . Soldiers, your Emperor is in your midst . . . We shall not rest until we have planted our eagles on enemy territory.'

After this the column crossed the Rhine in the presence of the Emperor who was roundly cheered. On the road through the valley it marched in combat formation, ready for any alarm, as follows:

One squadron of chasseurs
Two eight-pounders
The rest of the chasseurs
Two four-pounders
Light infantry brigade (foot chasseurs)
Artillery park
Wagons of the staff and corps
Brigade of Italian grenadiers
The Emperor's wagons
Elite gendarmes
First division of horse grenadiers
Two eight-pounders
The rest of the horse grenadiers.

The grenadiers remained in Strasbourg with their artillery for duty at the 'palace'. They left an hour after the Emperor the following day. The sick were left behind at small depots. The Guard was making its debut in the dual role of bodyguard and army reserve.

The Emperor's guard was generally organized as follows:

When His Majesty occupied a tent or château, his residence was known as the 'palace' and was guarded by a battalion of infantry and a squadron of cavalry. The governor of the Imperial Headquarters, under the Grand Marshal (Duroc), assigned the troops for sentry duty, security, and ceremonies. The Guard furnished the Emperor's escort on the march and guarded his baggage. The strength of the escort depended upon the

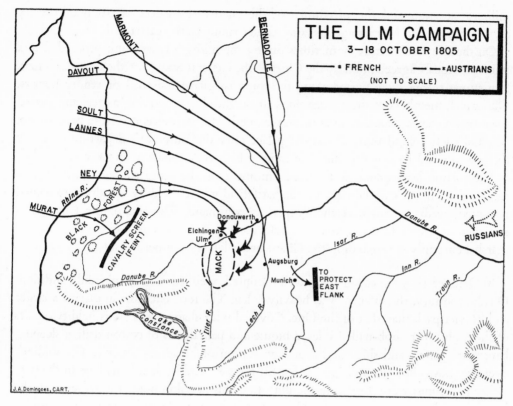

ULM

The Peace of Amiens in March 1802 had ended the ten years' War of the Revolution. But a 'cold war' followed between France and England in which both sides were clearly at fault. Napoleon seriously considered invading England and assembled transports and troops at certain channel ports. Then in 1805, a Third Coalition was formed against France, and Russia and Austria put armies in the field.

Napoleon countered by a 'pirouette' of his forces on the channel coast and led his Grand Army towards the Rhine in its first imperial campaign. In a series of masterly maneuvers, he crossed the Rhine and placed himself on the line of supply of the Austrian Army concentrated at Ulm under Mack. This strategic turning movement was protected by a separate force east of Munich, facing the Russians.

After several days' fighting the entire Austrian Army of 30,000 was captured. Napoleon then turned towards the Russians who retreated beyond Vienna and towards the northeast, pursued by the French Army.

military situation and the proximity of the enemy. However, a troop of cavalry always surrounded his carriage, its commander riding at the carriage door.

On the eve of departure, sometimes during the night, a Guard unit proceeded to a point previously agreed upon by the Chief of the General Staff[1] for the next day's halt. Sometimes troops were posted along the route to guard the road or render honors. On arrival, members of the household, sent on ahead, selected the 'palace' and posted the guard which was already in position when His Majesty descended from his carriage. The units left behind remained at the palace after the Emperor's departure to escort the servants and baggage to the new camp which they joined as quickly as possible.

The escort dismounted at the same moment as the Emperor and immediately surrounded him. It was the same on the battlefield where the duty squadrons remained mounted, ready to move at the Emperor's command. The rest of the Guard was stationed at selected points, or else performed special missions assigned to it. The marshal currently commanding the Guard never left the Emperor's side.

In October 1805 the cavalry was well mounted, well led, and in splendid condition. On the contrary, the infantry was heavily laden. The foot Guardsman carried a larger and heavier pack than that of the Line. Covered with shaggy hide, this held two pairs of shoes plus spare hob-nailed soles, a blouse and pantaloons of cotton drill, a sleeping bag, spare gaiters and shirt, and four days' ration of bread and biscuit. The soldier's overcoat was rolled on top. He carried his mess kit and his hat, in its bag, in the flap. Other provisions were stowed in the bottom of his bearskin bonnet together with the bric-a-brac that has encumbered soldiers of all ages, or were tied onto his person with string in parcels that swung in time as he marched. His plume, in its case, was tied to his sword scabbard of a special design, manufactured at Versailles. The soldiers marched in tail coats or *fracs*, black stocks, and grey gaiters, as did the *Gardes françaises* before them.

The wagon train accompanying the column consisted of 35 baggage wagons, 35 provision carts, five or six forage carts, 20 vehicles carrying medical supplies, and 25 ambulances transporting the field hospital. How could it keep up with the troops?

The first day's march was thirty miles. The great army park of 700 wagons and the division of foot dragoons were already installed at Rastatt, so the Guard camped outside the town 'in the greatest disorder'. Nevertheless, next day, after crossing mountainous terrain on execrable roads, the foot chasseurs rendered honors in full dress to the Grand Duke of Baden who came to visit the Emperor at Ettlingen.

Marching by way of Pforzheim, they reached the palace of the Elector at Ludwigsburg where the Emperor attended the theatre. Up ahead the army marched on without striking a blow. The weather was fine and life was beautiful . . .

Then it began to rain. The troops quickened their pace towards the Danube to turn the flank of the Austrian general Mack whose army was concentrated at Ulm. The French chasseurs and Italian grenadiers were kept on the run day and night – sometimes

[1] Though Napoleon was general in chief, Berthier was designated '*major-général*', actually chief of staff of the army as a whole. – Ed.

both – after the Emperor who traveled by coach, escorted by mounted chasseurs. The foot Guard marched 130 miles in four days to reach the Emperor at Nordlingen. Berthier began to worry.

'Give your brigade some rest at Lauchheim', he wrote General Hulin. 'I shall see that you have bread on arrival (at Nordlingen).'

The grenadiers were privileged to occupy billets but the rest of the Guard, except for the 'palace guard', bivouacked in the rain. The number of worn-out men and horses required the establishment of a small depot; but most of the foot Guard reached Donauwörth on the 8th in time to guard the Emperor as he directed the crossing of the Danube. No one complained. This was their job and they were proud of it.

Apart from the duty squadrons, half the horse chasseurs and grenadiers were galloping after Murat and sabering the Austrians trying to escape from the trap closing on them at Ulm. Victory succeeded victory in south, east, and north: at Donauwörth on the 7th, Wertingen on the 8th, Günzburg on the 9th, and even at Haslach on the 11th, where Dupont, defeated through Murat's error, covered himself with glory.

The foot Guard, in reserve, counted the blows as a spectator as it tramped along in the rain. To cheer it up Bessières issued 5,228 rations of wine. Then it marched behind the Emperor into Augsburg which was illuminated for the occasion.

Here the 1st Cuirassier Division was waiting to join Marmont's corps and form a reserve ready to move 'as circumstances directed into this great theatre of war that varied from moment to moment . . .' It was snowing.

As Marmont's corps was beginning to cross the bridge at Lech the Emperor's horse stumbled and fell on top of him. He might easily have been killed but was not even scratched, and promptly mounted another horse. The army never heard about this from the Guard.

By now a cold rain fell incessantly. The foot Guard had been obliged to leave 550 men behind. Marching to Elchingen, an aide arrived every mile or so to urge haste. Not a word, not a murmur. If the Emperor was calling his Guard, it meant that he needed it to strike a blow.

Actually, it was needed to support the 6th Corps which was attacking the bridge at Elchingen. Formed by brigades in the prairies bordering the Danube, with the chasseurs in front and the Italian Guard in the middle, the Guard occupied the bridge at Leipheim and stood with ordered arms watching the magnificent attack of Marshal Ney.

Then, after a night and day of tramping behind the 5th Corps and Klein's dragoons, who had crossed the Elchingen bridge at a snail's pace, the Guard joined the Emperor on the evening of 15 October at the abbey where the 'palace' was located. In a cold rain and a gale of wind it fought the Line for the occupancy of some half-burned cabins. Bivouacs were formed between Haslach and Thalfingen where the men munched a biscuit after giving up hope of finding a single potato in the ruined villages. The provision train had been pillaged en route.

They greatly envied the troopers with Murat who, together with chasseurs and carabineers of the Line, had thrashed Archduke Ferdinand's cavalry. Colonel

Morland's *chasseurs à cheval*, in mud up to their knees, covered themselves with glory by charging General Mack's own cuirassier regiment.

Vedettes and sentries watched over the Imperial Headquarters and looked up at the Michelsberg towering above Ulm, lit by the campfires of the Austrians whom they would attack on the morrow.

On Wednesday the 16th a bombardment was followed by calm. Perhaps Mack would capitulate . . .

On the 17th a truce envoy arrived in camp. The foot Guard did not stir.

That day Marshal Bessières' orders included the following: 'During sojourns all Guard corps must take the time to put every piece of equipment, arms, and clothing into perfect order, with special attention to their appearance and cleanliness.'

Sojourn indeed! You would think this was a pleasure trip!

The men inspected their uniforms. (The Emperor did not like ragged gaiters nor torn shirts.) They had to groom their bearskin bonnets, to brush and brush the fur and hang them up by their chin straps so that when they wore them again they could be trimmed and puffed out in proper Guard style. Forming single file, each man dressed the hair of the man in front, tied his queue just two inches from the end, stuck the eagle pin into the knot, and spread the powder with a brush.

Nevertheless, Hulin published the following:

'The Commandant has noticed several soldiers wearing black gaiters on the march and reminds them of the regulations expressly ordering them to wear grey . . .'

These were cotton gaiters; those of black cloth must be kept for duty at the palace. This is what it meant to belong to the Guard.

The Italian Guard and the foot chasseurs left the battle area with a squadron of horse grenadiers and the artillery to await the Emperor at Augsburg. The units with Murat were ordered to join them there.

The grenadiers stayed at Elchingen where the foxy ones searched the battlefield, since a horse fetched 100 francs 'on the spot and in silver'; a cannon, 60; a good musket, one franc; a saber, 4 sous; and cannon balls, a sou apiece.

20 October. Before Ulm. The Austrian army filed past the Emperor and laid down its arms. On a knoll near a great bonfire, which burned a hole in his grey coat, Napoleon received the captured flags and handed them to his grenadiers. Sixteen Austrian generals, including Mack himself, were present. 'All empires come to an end', Napoleon told the vanquished general (see Plate 37).

Ah, yes! This was 1805. In just ten years . . .

The campaign had lasted twenty days and the foot Guard had not fired a shot. The main Austrian army had not been involved, but remained intact under the errant Archdukes[2] in the Tyrol and Bohemia and Archduke Charles, engaged against Masséna in Italy; and 25,000 men had been sent to garrison Vienna.

From Augsburg, which was illuminated and where the grenadiers paraded the forty trophies of Ulm destined for the Senate, the Emperor and the Guard pushed on to

[2] John and Ferdinand.

Munich. Napoleon had just learned of the disaster at Trafalgar on the 21st. France was now ringed with maritime powers; but there was still Europe.

The *Grande Armée* now included 180,000 Frenchmen, 22,000 Bavarians, 3,000 Württembergers, and 2,500 Badeners – all commanded by compatriots and fighting under their own flags – in addition to the Poles and Piedmontese serving in French regiments. It was the beginning of a European Army. Its reserve, the Guard, included Italians and Mameluks as well as men from twenty-four departments in Savoy, Switzerland, Holland, the Rhineland, and Piedmont.

Napoleon's present mood was one of enthusiasm. He was gay, familiar with his suite, and generous to his Guard, granting it a thousand pairs of shoes and rations of bread. The capital of Bavaria was 'illuminated with great taste' and gave him a warm welcome. A number of houses were decorated. Horse and foot Guard, reunited at last, resumed the gay life of Paris, accompanying the Emperor to the theatre and to the Cathedral where a Te Deum was sung. They rendered honors to the ministers and deputies of the Elector who came to be presented to His Majesty.

Whoever opposed the Imperial design based on the Roman Empire must be pushed back to his own territory. Prussia watched the proceedings. An eternal tightrope walker, she moved east or west, ready to come to the aid of the victor. The Tsar Alexander had come to Berlin and sworn eternal friendship for the King of Prussia at the tomb of Frederick the Great.

Kutusov was on the Inn with 32,000 tired men and a large number of sick. Learning of the disaster at Ulm, he turned and fell back rapidly towards his reserves en route from Russia. The Emperor unleashed the Grand Army and deployed it in three masses, preceded by an advance guard under Murat, with orders to make contact with Kutusov and destroy him.

It was a fast race over the snow. Behind the center mass followed the 'eternal reserve' protecting the Emperor, marching thirty miles a day, preceded by 400 horse, who marched the night before, and by pickets posted along the route. The men were billeted on the natives who had to feed them as well. As many as eighty were stuffed into one house. The gardens were devastated.

The soldiers crossed the Inn at Mühldorf on a bridge that 'trembled under the weight of a single infantryman', and passed through Braunau where they ate, thanks to the stores there.

The dynamic Major Guyot was ordered back to Munich to command the small units of the Guard left there, and receive the reinforcements from France; also to buy horses 'of whatever breed' for the cavalrymen arriving on foot; procure shoes, food, and forage, and establish magazines. A fine job for a *chasseur à cheval*!

But an urgent one. The troops were melting away. Ten thousand stragglers and pillagers were dishonoring the army and indiscipline was filtering through its ranks. On the breathless marches by night and day over miserable roads in the snow, everyone grumbled from the colonels to the smallest drummer. The infantry jeered at cavaliers and carters trying to pass the columns, and even stopped the wagons of the Chief of Staff's topographical service.

The cavalry of the advance guard arrived first at the halting places and took the best billets. The infantry took the rest, so that the last detachments reporting to Imperial Headquarters found no lodgings available and staged pitched battles against the quartered troops to avoid sleeping in the snow. The men abused their officers. There was nothing to eat. The Russians had destroyed or carried off everything. If the French could only catch up with them and force them to do battle, all their miseries would end . . . But those *Russkis* were some marchers!

5 November. Linz. There was a rumor that the headquarters would remain there several days. The men hoped for some rest and provisions; but the magazines had been pillaged and the population was in revolt. The troops had no one to rely on but themselves.

Marshal Bessières 'bore witness to the whole garrison of his displeasure'. Venomous quarrels had broken out between the different corps over billets. 'Too much discontent over small things without any foundation is being aired before the troops,' he wrote. 'Orders must be accepted with patience and executed with accuracy and zeal and without thought or discussion. Whoever discusses them does not know how to obey . . .'

A basic truth, worthy of meditation by the soldiers of all ages.

The Emperor himself was in a bad humor because the Russians traveled too fast. But still he thought of everything. On 2 November he created two new battalions of *vélites*: one of grenadiers and one of chasseurs. While anticipating battle losses from future clashes with the Russians, he must also raise cadres for a northern army in case of a Prussian offensive in Hanover.

The Guard calmed down, rested, and polished arms and equipment. The Elector of Bavaria was due. And the army? It must be halted while the stragglers caught up. The men must be fed, shod, clothed. Even the Guard was wearing pantaloons of every color of the rainbow – Austrian, Russian, and whatnot. As for the mounts: 'I do not wish horses given shelter in preference to men', the Emperor wrote Marshal Lannes. The horse grenadiers were strangely mounted on what looked like ponies. And the Russians kept ahead of them . . .

'I shall have news in five or six days', the Emperor wrote Josephine.

In less than that . . .

During the night of 8–9 November Kutuzov crossed the Danube at Krems, burned the bridge, and escaped towards his reserves. Murat, ordered to pursue him and keep a sword in his back, let him slip through his fingers; then he galloped off to Vienna and entered the city on the 13th.

'You rush on like a madman!' the Emperor wrote him.

A look at the map shows that at this point the army should have made a grand detour. However, this would have lengthened still further its line of communication and diminished its strength. The Emperor decided instead to join Murat without delay. The night of the 13th found him en route to Schönbrunn. The Guard would follow as best it could.

It is hard to imagine by what supreme effort of will two detachments of foot and horse managed to arrive at Schönbrunn in the middle of a blizzard at the same moment as the Emperor, and watch over him as he slept and worked on the night of 14 November. By the 15th the whole Guard was there.

They learned that Murat had captured the bridge at Vienna by the ruse of pretending an armistice had been signed, and had then allowed himself to be duped in turn by Kutuzov at Hollabrunn. For the second time, the Russians escaped to Olmütz.

The Emperor was furious. 'It is impossible to find terms to express my displeasure. You were commanding only my advance guard. You had no authority to conclude an armistice . . . You have cost me the fruits of a whole campaign. . . .'

After four days of forced marches through storms and snow to Hollabrunn, Znaim, Brünn, and Pohrlitz the foot Guard caught its breath for a moment in the Moravian capital.[3] Meanwhile the mounted troops under Bessières followed the Emperor in all his moves. During a reconnaissance near Wischau on 21 November, four squadrons of the escort vigorously charged some Russian cavalry and threw them back to their outposts. Returning the same evening, the chasseurs dismounted simultaneously with the Emperor five miles from Brünn.

An icy wind was blowing. Standing on a knoll, Napoleon looked south upon an undulating plain bounded on either side by small streams. The eastern horizon was hidden by a long plateau on whose slope they saw the steeple of the village of Pratzen.

'Examine this terrain carefully', he said. 'We shall fight on it.'

[3] Brünn.

CHAPTER 4

Austerlitz

PREPARATIONS were made for a decisive engagement. Kutuzov and the Austrians had joined forces with the Russian reserves and formed a front. Would they await the arrival of Archdukes Charles and John from Carinthia before attacking the French? Napoleon watched their movements closely. Reconnaissances increased and there were skirmishes with the enemy horse and foot.

The Emperor received many visitors at Brünn: a Moravian delegation led by a bishop, his marshals, Austrian plenipotentiaries, a Prussian . . .

Napoleon was taking a terrible chance. Over 1,200 miles from Paris, he had lost a fifth of his army since Boulogne, and had employed half the rest to guard his flanks and rear which were menaced by Prussia. With 60,000 to 70,000 men at his disposal, he did not wish to attack from 100,000 to 200,000 Austro-Russians massed at Olmütz by his ordinary method. The problem was how to exaggerate his misfortune to a degree that would tempt the Allies to try and profit by it.

The offer of an armistice to the envoys Stadion and Gyulay; the surrender of Wischau to the Cossacks; the retirement of the French army, during which its cavalry refused combat; the evacuation of the Pratzen plateau; the defensive earthworks and batteries thrown up feverishly before Brünn – all these were clear indications that Napoleon was seriously embarrassed and was retreating to Vienna. The Allied Emperors were jubilant.

On the arrival of his reinforcements at Olmütz, Kutuzov prepared to maneuver on the French right to cut them off from Vienna and throw them back to Bohemia. Prussia armed and waited. Little by little, as the maneuver unfolded, the Emperor's gaiety became more articulate.

'Those chaps across the way think they have nothing to do but gobble us up,' he observed to a grenadier on sentry go at his door.

'We'll serve 'em the meal the other way 'round,' replied the veteran.

Bessières performed his function in a scrupulous manner and under no circumstances let anything escape him. He was perpetually unhappy. At the Emperor's review on the 27th the Guard was turned out in a pitiful state. The corps commanders were ordered to take their men in hand. Dorsenne prescribed 'blue cloth pantaloons, cut loose, with no buttons down the side' for his grenadiers, forbidding any variations. But he forgot to mention how such pantaloons could be acquired. Pouches, scabbards, and bayonets needed repair; cap plates were attached insecurely; hooks were missing from collars; the haversacks were not worn at a uniform height; the chalk for whitening the cross-belts did not have enough blueing in it. In vain had they run day and night for the past month through mud and snow, rain and hail; a grenadier of the Imperial Guard, 'who ranks as a noncommissioned officer', must do more . . .

At Kritschen, a small village six miles east of Brünn, the Imperial Headquarters was set up in a shanty on 29 November. The 'guardroom' was a tumble-down shack. The Emperor slept in his traveling carriage on a hill by the Olmütz road while waiting for the sappers of the Guard to finish constructing a temporary shelter with benches laid on the bare earth. He was in an excellent humor, distributing tobacco and tweaking the moustaches of the workmen.

Next evening he climbed the plateau of Pratzen and observed: 'I've got them! They won't escape me now . . .' Nobody understood why.

The weather was abominable.

Sunday, 1 December 1805. The eve of the coronation was a year ago today. What would happen tomorrow?

'Let us go see the Guard', the Emperor said to his officers, to whom he had been expounding at dinner his predilection for the tragedies of Corneille.

The night was dark and a mist obscured the first quarter of the moon; but the whole plain of Schlapanitz was dotted with campfires. The grenadiers and chasseurs were warming themselves and eating their evening meal. On the right, in front, at the left, and behind they saw the fires of Murat, Caffarelli, Lannes, and Bernadotte. Far off behind the plateau, a faint glow lit the sky. It came from the Russian camp.

Before the grenadiers' bivouac the men caught sight of the *Tondu* as he suddenly tripped over a log and fell. The officers helped him up, but the men of the Guard hastened to twist handfuls of straw into torches which they lighted and carried before him. Then, one by one, all the bivouacs lit his passage, their cheers reaching to the camp of Caffarelli's division and the horse Guard beyond. 'Watch your pouches!' the officers warned, fearing the explosion of irreplaceable cartridges on the eve of battle.

'It was the eve of the coronation anniversary', Horse Grenadier Leblois wrote his parents. 'We all carried torches of straw and cried *"Vive l'Empereur!"* – and there he was in our midst . . .'

Across the way, the Grand Duke Constantin and the generals were rubbing their hands. At dawn they would attack the French, cut them off from Vienna, destroy them . . .

Monday, 2 December. 6 a.m. A thick fog. The Guard shouldered arms and mounted their horses. 'To the right by flank', they marched towards Turas and took up a position in reserve with ten battalions of Oudinot's elite grenadiers, making 9,000 bearskin bonnets in all. The great baptism was fixed for today.

The Emperor arrived, escorted by mounted chasseurs. The band played an operatic air. 'Have they forgotten the *Song of Departure*?' he asked Bessières. Immediately, Drum Major Gebauer led them in the old song of triumph, accompanied by shouts of *'Vive l'Empereur!'* Thiard, Count de Bissy, a former émigré who was present, diagnosed the demonstration as 'enthusiasm for the chief and devotion to the cause'.

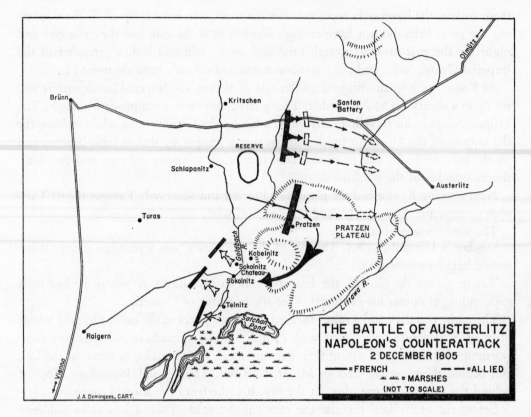

THE BATTLE OF AUSTERLITZ
NAPOLEON'S COUNTERATTACK
2 DECEMBER 1805
══ = FRENCH   ╌╌ = ALLIED
⚓ = MARSHES
(NOT TO SCALE)

J. A. Domingoes, CART.

AUSTERLITZ

With his supply line seriously overextended, Napoleon halted his eastward course at Brünn and took up a defensive position east of that city. The French were convinced that the Allies would attack. Napoleon hoped for a battle, being confident of his superior tactical skill.

The Allies did attack west of Austerlitz, making a wide envelopment of the French south flank and a secondary attack on the north. Napoleon counterattacked, driving back the weak Allied center. The French then struck the main Allied attacking force in its flank and rear. Austerlitz, called the first great battle of modern history, ended in a complete triumph for the French.

The Allied Army was thoroughly disorganized, the Austrians asked for terms, and the Russians marched out of Austria.

PLATE 38

PLATE 39

a) Clerc
(*After miniature: Collection Mme. Soulet*)

b) Clément
(*After Lagrénée, 1808*)

c) Berthier
(*Aquatint by Levachez*)

d) Gros
(*Contemp. engraving*)

e) Morland
(*Contemp. engraving*)

PLATE 40

GENERAL RAPP PRESENTING HIS CAPTIVES TO THE EMPEROR AT AUSTERLITZ
On horseback at right, left to right: Berthier, the Emperor, Duroc, Bessières, Junot, and Roustam
(*From the painting by Gérard in the collection of Hugh Bullock, Esq.*)

PLATE 41

a) Desmichels
(*Engr. Réville*)

b) Dahlmann
(*Engr. Réville*)

c) Grand Duke Constantin as colonel
of the *Chevalier Garde*
(*Colored engraving by Henne*)

d) Kutuzov
(*Engr. Vendramini after Saint-Aubin*)

A proclamation read throughout the army was greeted with roars of approval:

'Soldiers, the Russian army faces you to avenge the Austrians at Ulm. During a march to turn my right they will present their flank to me . . . I shall direct your battalions in person . . . This victory will end the campaign . . .'

True, the French were confident; however, for five days the Russians had been advancing and the *Grande Armée* retreating. The headquarters of the Russian and Austrian Emperors was now at Austerlitz.

Patience!

These slow marches – less than 36 miles in five days – had allowed Napoleon time to bring up 25,000 reinforcements, and estimate correctly the enemy maneuver to turn his right. This enveloping movement was made too late and in insufficient force. Only that morning the enemy had been led to make a perilous flank march – a fatal one.

7 a.m. In the mist the Guard formed behind the knoll on which the Emperor stood, near the Brünn road. On the left was Lannes' corps. Ahead, Oudinot's grenadiers were posted behind some trees bordering the Goldbach. On their right were the cuirassiers, Murat, and the whole cavalry reserve, with Bernadotte's corps behind them. Soult's corps was further to the right, across the stream. A few hundred yards from the frozen waters and marshes of the Littawa a brigade occupied the château and park of Sokolnitz. This zone was covered with ice, but the temperature was rising and a thaw commencing. On the road from Raigern to Sokolnitz 5,500 men of Davout's division were advancing under Friant and Bourcier.

The Russian columns could be seen descending the Pratzen plateau towards the Littawa. On the right a violent fusillade was coming from Sokolnitz, Telnitz, etc . . . On the left the cannon thundered. Bagration and Liechtenstein were attacking Lannes and Santon (a solitary hill which the veterans of Egypt had christened 'the pyramid'). Between these two actions the Emperor had grouped 65,000 men on a front two and a half miles long and a mile deep.

8 a.m. The sun was rising behind Pratzen. The valleys were still filled with mist and smoke from the campfires. At a signal from the Emperor, Lannes advanced. A cavalry contest between Murat, Liechtenstein, and the Russian Guard began in the plain. In the center Soult pressed the main attack towards the village of Pratzen, beyond which the Russians marched off by the flank, following their vanguard which was attacking Davout at Telnitz.

Suddenly a desperate struggle developed. Schiner's brigade of Soult's corps was badly mauled and his 4th Line Battalion thrown into disorder by the cuirassiers of the Russian Guard. Then the cavalry of the Imperial Guard reversed the situation.

According to the Bulletin of 3 December, the Emperor 'ordered Marshal Bessières to the aid of our right flank with his Invincibles'. General Desmichels, at that time a captain of chasseurs serving as orderly to Marshal Bessières, has this to say in a letter of 19 April 1834:

'The glory of this memorable episode belongs entirely to the Marshal who ordered and led those brilliant charges, made under the eyes of Napoleon the Great and the

Emperors of Austria and Russia, which contributed a powerful impetus to the victory.'

General César de Laville, Bessières' aide, confirmed this in a letter dated 1 December of the same year:

'General Desmichel's letter about the charge of the duty squadrons of the Imperial Guard at Austerlitz is confirmed absolutely by what I saw with my own eyes. I was then a major of cavalry serving as aide-de-camp to Marshal Bessières and never left his side – and neither did Major Barbanègre, who was later killed as colonel of the 9th Hussars at Jena, nor Desmichels, an officer of the *chasseurs à cheval* serving as the Marshal's orderly during this campaign.

'I ought to add a particular episode. The Marshal was standing with the other officers mentioned in front of the chasseurs and grenadiers of the Guard. The ground before him rose to a height that cut off our distant view. He was on his way up to investigate, as was his custom, when he noticed some infantry running rapidly down the slope and constantly looking back. Then he said: "Laville, we are going to have a cavalry engagement".

'He ran back to the chasseur squadrons and ordered them up to the heights to charge, supporting them with horse grenadiers which he led in person. The engagement took place. General Rapp behaved with great bravery and, though wounded, delivered the commander and standard of the *Chevalier Gardes*[1] to the Emperor. Meanwhile, Marshal Bessières had succeeded in rallying the 4th Battalion of the Line, and forced the Russians to retreat from this sector.

'The evening after the battle I asked him how he had guessed so opportunely that a cavalry engagement was imminent. He replied: "Because the retreating soldiers kept looking back. When infantry retires before infantry they never turn their heads."

'This feat of military sagacity led to a brilliant result. The honor of its conception is due to the Marshal, and the merit of co-operating in its execution, to General Rapp. It remained profoundly engraved on my memory.'

The memoirs of participants convince one that official bulletins are motivated by politics rather than justice. 'He lies like a bulletin', the men said after Marengo. Later the soldiers said 'Communiqués are nothing but eye-wash.'[2]

The charge of the cavalry of the Guard appears to have been ordered by Bessières and carried out in two phases. The first, led by Colonel Morland with two squadrons of chasseurs and supported by three of horse grenadiers under Marshal Bessières, rescued the 4th Battalion and threw back the cuirassiers of the Russian Guard. Then the French were thrown back in turn by the *Chevalier Gardes* whom Rapp put to flight in disorder with his last three squadrons and the Mameluks.

'I took off at a gallop', wrote Rapp. 'The enemy cavalry was slashing our troopers. A short distance in the rear we could see masses of foot and horse waiting in reserve. Then the enemy let go and turned on me. Four pieces were brought up at a gallop, unlimbered, and set up in battery. I advanced in good order with the brave Colonel Morland on my left and General Dallemagne (Dahlmann) on my right. We charged

---

[1] Elite cuirassier regiment of the Tsar's bodyguard. – Ed.
[2] *Bourrage de crâne* – literally, 'head-stuffing'.

the artillery and captured it. The cavalry stood firm awaiting our attack, then broke under the shock and fled in disorder. A squadron of grenadiers came to my support at the same moment as reserves arrived to support the Russian Guard. The shock was terrific. The infantry did not dare fire since we were all jumbled together, fighting hand-to-hand.

'At last the intrepidity of our troops carried all obstacles. The Russians fled the field and disbanded. The guns, baggage, and Prince Repnin were all in our hands. With my broken saber and covered with blood, I went to give an account of the affair to the Emperor. A victory won by so few troops over the elite of the enemy inspired him with the idea for the picture painted by Gérard' (see Plate 40).

The chasseurs lost Colonel Morland, a captain, eleven NCO's[3] and troopers killed, and 17 officers and 50 men wounded; 153 horses were put out of action. The horse grenadiers had only six officers wounded but they lost 99 horses.

By 1.30 p.m. victory was assured.

The forces of Lannes and Bagration were still fighting; however, at the day's end the Russians were finally beaten by Murat's cavalry. Meanwhile the Emperor, followed by the foot Guard and the artillery, reached the plateau and halted near the chapel of St. Anton.

At this point Soult's corps cut the Russian line in two and pursued the vanguard to Telnitz which was well defended by Davout and the surrounding ponds. The batteries of the Guard joined forces with those of the 4th Corps on the banks of Satschan Pond and shelled the enemy columns still engaged on the dike and in the frozen marshes.

Major Clerc of the horse chasseurs captured a gun on the banks of the Littawa, winning a gold star of the Legion of Honor. The Russian defeat turned into a rout in the chill darkness of an early night.

The Emperor remained at his post, guarded by foot chasseurs. Sergeant Heuillet, who joined the regiment on 17 October, had beaten the charge of the 27th Regiment on the bridge of Lodi at the age of fifteen.

'Among the prisoners', he relates in his memoirs, 'was a Russian artillery major, a young man who spoke very good French. He begged vociferously to be shot, preferring death to capture. The men told him to shut up. "The Emperor will hear you!" The Emperor saw him and ordered him to approach. "Sire", the captive implored, "order them to shoot me. I am unworthy to live for I have lost all my guns!" The Emperor replied: "Calm yourself, young man. It is no dishonor to be defeated by *my* army". And the Russian stopped crying.'

The foot Guard had not been engaged. 'It cried with rage', said the bulletin. Surgeon Maugras of the foot chasseurs was wounded while ministering to the soldiers in the field.

In the snow that started falling again Dahlmann led a reconnaissance with two squadrons of chasseurs on the enemy's right which was in full retreat. The Emperor, followed by his staff, toured the battlefield, gave money to the wounded of the three

---

[3] Although NCO's in the French Army did not include corporals (*brigadiers* in the cavalry) we have lumped them together wherever possible for the sake of brevity. – Ed.

nations and encouraged the surgeons and hospital attendants. Passing a severely wounded Russian officer, Bessières presented him with 600 francs.

In the château of that sly fox von Kaunitz, whose architecture recalled the days of Voltaire and a Francophile Europe, the Emperor announced to the Empire his remarkable victory in these words:

'I have put to flight the army of the Coalition under the personal command of the Emperors of Russia and Germany.' Then he added: 'Soldiers, I am pleased with you'.

In the poor little village of Austerlitz, its thatched roofs covered with snow, the grenadiers found six hundred sheep and distributed them throughout the Guard. This windfall was long remembered in the barracks and bivouacs.

CHAPTER 5

A Packful of Glory

On 4 December the whole Guard marched towards Hungary. The weather was superb. Bessières halted the troops in front of the Emperor on several lines near the mill of Nasedlowitz. The sappers built benches and lit a great fire; then they went to collect straw to cover the ground to the edge of the road. Pickets of chasseurs scanned the horizon.

An hour passed. Then a troop of horse appeared. These were Kienmayer's hussars and Schwarzenberg's lancers, escorting several carriages. In the last one rode the Emperor Francis II.

The drums beat *Aux Champs* and the trumpets sounded the March. Napoleon went to meet the vanquished sovereign, embraced him, and led him to the fire.

Towards four o'clock, when the interview ended, the bands played *Let Us Watch over the Empire* and the Guard cheered the Emperor.

'Gentlemen', he announced, 'the peace is made. We shall return to Paris.'

Not all of them returned. At Brünn, in Fröhlichstrasse Nr. 163, Morland lay dying. Next day he expired and his body was embalmed by Larrey and transported to Paris under escort by his faithful chasseurs. The burial of his viscera took place with great pomp in the Brünn cemetery on 7 December in the presence of his brother, a trooper in his regiment.

Bessières visited the wounded at the hospital and distributed 1,700 francs.

The Emperor stayed at the governor's palace with his household. On the 12th he arrived at Schönbrunn and occupied the room adjoining the Porzellanzimmer whose clock would one day toll the death of his son.

The grenadiers strutted about the palace. The great wood stoves roared. Snow covered the gardens, coifed the marble statues, and adorned the fountains, arbors, and gazebos. From the terrace of the Glorietta they saw a range of mountains to the west. The *vélites* were thinking that behind them – very far behind – lay France.

'You will return', the veterans told them, 'with a packful of glory'. Meanwhile they were in Vienna, sleeping in the palace of the Austrian Emperor. Without the *Tondu* they should never have had that honor!

The lackeys moved about performing their small tasks. The Guard danced with the girls of Leopoldstadt. Due to the Emperor's generosity, the men were rigged out like the Versailles aides. They ate *Wiener Schnitzel* and 'paradise potatoes', washed down with wine far superior to what they could buy in the 'heroes' canteen', or sipped a '*double*' at the Greek café, or spent an evening at the Kasperle-Theater. Of course, there were sergeants' inspections, and more by the captains who tugged away at their gaiter-straps to make sure they were secure. There were also reviews by the Emperor in the court of the château. The men watched for a glance from his eagle eye and 'trembled all over when he spoke to them'.

Napoleon's work was crushing. He received the great of the world, heard concerts of Haydn and Cherubini, and appointed kings of Bavaria and Württemberg and grand dukes of Berg and Baden as if they were corporals. He also granted exceptional rewards to the Guard: a pair of shoes to each foot soldier and a bayonet to each trooper.

On 18 December the vacancies in the cavalry were filled. Dahlmann succeeded Colonel Morland, and Guyot became lieutenant colonel of the chasseurs. Daumesnil and Delaître were promoted to major. Corbineau of the staff was given a company command and Trumpet Major Krettly was brevetted ensign.

The new lieutenant colonel of the horse grenadiers was Lepic. He was a great talker. Once a corporal in the Constitutional Guard of the king, he had received seven saber cuts – one of which cracked his skull – at Pastrengo. Chastel, a veteran of Egypt, was promoted to second-in-command.

In the foot Guard Dorsenne and Gros were made colonels of the grenadiers and chasseurs. These agreeable bits of news did not prevent Bessières, his face 'furrowed like a currant bun', from counting the buttons on the gaiters and ordering the men to wash the cases of their bearskin bonnets.

Only the Guard left for France on 27 December, the day the Treaty of Pressburg was signed. Those who survived in the Line would not see their native land until they passed through it en route to Spain two years later. The bulk of the army was left in Germany which Napoleon wished to control.

Before leaving Vienna Larrey organized a ward for the sick and wounded of the Guard in the hospital of the Dominican Fathers, leaving a sergeant and twenty-two Austrian attendants and Invalids to care for them under the supervision of Viennese doctors. The director promised that the wounded would be well cared for.

Now the troops repeated the long, hard marches of the previous month in the opposite direction; but this time they were received as victors everywhere. In Munich they celebrated the New Year, which would never again be termed the 10th or 11th *nivôse*, since now the Revolutionary calendar was a thing of the past.

On 13 January the Italian Guard stopped in the Bavarian capital to attend the wedding of their Viceroy, Prince Eugène, to the charming Princess Augusta, daughter of the Elector Maximilian Joseph whom Napoleon had just made King of Bavaria.

On 4 February Hulin made a triumphal entry into Nancy at the head of the two foot brigades. The men wore black gaiters, a luxury hitherto denied them. By this time many women were marching at their heels – not all *vivandières*[1] and laundresses.

On this day the Emperor, who had reached Paris on 26 January, signed a decree renaming the Quai du Mail 'Avenue Morland' in memory of the heroic colonel of the

---

[1] Uniformed women sutlers traditional in the French army. – Ed.

chasseurs of the Guard. The whole quarter, including the new bridge,[2] was dedicated to the victory.

At last, on 16 February the Guard entered Paris. It was greeted at the Porte de La Villette by the municipal authorities and cheered by an immense crowd. At the Porte Saint-Denis the soldiers passed under a triumphal arch erected in their honor and marched to the Champs-Elysées. It was raining. Under tents they were served food copiously sprinkled with water from on high, and wine from bottles they uncorked with their sabers.

At this epoch victories were celebrated with fêtes and rejoicing, not as today, with lugubrious memorial services. A grand dinner was given the Guard under the galleries of the Palais-Royal by the City of Paris, and a complimentary performance of *The Passage of the Great Saint-Bernard*, complete with monks and dogs, at the Porte Saint-Martin. Taps did not sound until 2 a.m, according to Coigniet.

In his study the Emperor dreamed of the Roman Empire. He planned to erect a column like Trajan's with bronze melted down from enemy guns, and an arch of triumph like those of Titus and Septimius Severus in the Place de la Carrousel to serve as a gateway to the Tuileries. Another was to be erected at the end of the Champs-Elysées, on top of the hill where many roads met and formed a star.

He also remembered his Guard and awarded each man an extra fifteen days' pay.

The victory of Austerlitz, known in the Guard as the 'Battle of the Three Emperors', ended the war. Now the regiments resumed their peace time role of 'troops de luxe'.

In 1806, a year of triumphs, the Emperor shared his glory with the Guard. Representing the army still in Germany, the Guard participated in the daily fêtes celebrating the victory of Austerlitz in this immortal spring that marked one of the grandest years of the reign.

On 21 and 22 February the clothing magazines were emptied once more for great parades at the Tuileries, and plumes, epaulets, and coats distributed – 'on loan', it must be admitted, since they were returned the following day.

The foot grenadiers turned out in full dress on 2 March at the reception for the Prince of Baden who was engaged to Stephanie de Beauharnais, Napoleon's adopted daughter; and again for the Legislature.

'My armies had not ceased to be victorious when I gave the order to stop fighting', the Emperor announced to the legislators. 'The whole Italian peninsula is now part of the Grand Empire . . . I desire peace with England . . . I shall do nothing to postpone this event . . . I stand ready to conclude it on the basis of the Treaty of Amiens.'

The moment was perhaps propitious. On 28 January Pitt died, after ordering the map of Europe rolled up 'since it would be out of date in ten years'. His successor Fox seemed to favor Napoleon whom he described as 'one of the men best fitted to appreciate greatness'.

On 3 March the Emperor commissioned a series of paintings depicting the principal events of the campaign of 1805, assigning to Gérard the 'capture of the Imperial Russian

[2] Called thereafter the 'Pont d'Austerlitz'. – Ed.

Guards'. This was to show Rapp presenting the flags, cannon, Prince Repnin, and more than 800 captured noblemen of the Russian Guard to the Emperor at Austerlitz. And since Napoleon was precise in all things, he specified that the canvas should be 3·3 meters high and should cost 12,000 francs.

This and thirteen other canvases were destined for the Tuileries after a public exhibition in the salon of the Musée Napoléon in August 1808.

CHAPTER 6

Precarious Peace

THERE was no war in prospect at the dawn of 1806. The federation of western Germany was proceeding rapidly, according to plan. The civil code had been introduced and favorably received. Industrial development was progressing. Therefore the increase in the Guard cadres was designed primarily to raise its prestige and, incidentally, to make it more efficient in case the peace were threatened.

Three engineer officers, including Major Boissonnet, were added to the staff.

Michel, a brilliant veteran of Santo-Domingo married to the niece of Maret, the Minister of Foreign Affairs, was appointed lieutenant colonel of the 2nd Grenadiers. The grenadier corps was magnificent at this epoch with the brave Sénot as drum major, six master drummers wearing gold brandenburgs,[1] and 48 drums – soon increased to 72 – beating the Reveille of the Guard. Among the new majors brought from the Line were Darquier and Dupin.

In the chasseurs, Colonel Curial of the 80th *Légère* was appointed commandant, and Lt. Colonels Rottembourg and Lanabère were brought from the Line as majors.

General Walther, an ex-hussar of Berchényi who had been wounded at Hohenlinden and Austerlitz and wore the grand eagle of the Legion of Honor, was named colonel in chief of the horse grenadiers.

On 11 June the Emperor decided to raise 2,000 additional infantry *vélites* to replace those already commissioned in the Line, or admitted to the Guard as privates and NCO's. One hundred and sixty more were incorporated in the artillery and paid 300 francs a year for their board, etc.

The great innovation in the Guard of 1806 was the creation of a regiment of dragoons (*dragons*) of the Guard. This name was originally given his mounted *arquebusiers* by the Maréchal de Brissac after the dragon guarding the apples of the Hesperides, revered as a symbol of courage by the ancient knights. Twelve troopers and several officers were levied from each dragoon regiment of the Line to form the first two squadrons, and a third was composed of *vélites*. The rest of the cadres came from the cavalry of the Guard.

The intrepid Arrighi de Casanova, twenty-eight-year-old cousin of Napoleon, was appointed colonel in chief. He was a superb soldier, having made his debut in the Liamone Volunteers in 1796. He had served with the Armies of Italy and Egypt, been severely wounded at Acre, and had recently commanded the 1st Dragoons at

[1] Ornamental strips of lace or braid on revers, on the breast of hussar dolmans, and the full dress coats of West Point cadets, etc. (see Plates 6a, 13). – Ed.

Wertingen. His lieutenant colonels were Fiteau, former captain in the 7*bis* Hussars in Egypt, and Colonel Letort of the 14th Dragoons. Among the squadron commanders were Jolivet and Rossignol of the horse grenadiers.

The dragoons were quartered in the Rue de Grenelle-Saint-Germain and mounted on bay or chestnut horses. Their uniform was like that of the horse grenadiers except that it was green and was worn with a brass helmet trimmed with a panther skin band or 'turban', and a black horsehair crest and red plume. On the front of the metal crest was stamped an eagle holding a thunderbolt in its talons (see Plate 42b).

When the regiment was complete the Emperor reviewed it and presented it to the Empress. *Noblesse oblige!* It promptly took the name '*Dragons de l'Impératrice*' or 'Empress' Own Dragoons'.

The artillery park was given an artificer company and 10 storekeepers. Captain Chauveau, whose battery had rendered signal service at Austerlitz, was promoted major, and Lallemand to captain.

Its train battalion was commanded by Captain Leroy, former adjutant of the Egypt wagon train, a twice-wounded *légionnaire*.

Concerned by the breakdown of his auxiliary services during the last campaign, Napoleon granted assistants to the inspector and commissaries, and created six new adjutants to take charge of food, forage, clothing, and hospital supplies. He also decreed: 'So that the officers and soldiers may be familiar with the problem in case of war, 30 bakers will bake bread for the peace time Guard in portable ovens'.

Each infantry battalion and cavalry regiment was assigned two 4-horse covered wagons, 10 ammunition caissons, and 2 baggage wagons, all painted grey with 'a crown on one side and a grenade or hunting horn[2] on the other'. The artillery caissons were drawn by six sleek horses which contrasted favorably with the three or four sorry hacks pulling those of the Line.

The barracks were comfortable, with large, well-ventilated rooms, and the stables trim and sanitary. Little light was provided in the common rooms; however, each man bought 'dozen candles' – 12 to the pound and very thin. Light was a common lack of that period when, except for the Tuileries and a few private residences, one could see little after dark, indoors or out.

The Guard hospital was improved. A heating system was installed in every room and a modern ward opened. Directions for procedure in case of fire were posted everywhere. The medical officers of the different corps practised there, assisted by 16 staff physicians.

The Emperor rewarded individual merit with promotion, the Legion of Honor, or gifts of money. Sometimes he even paid the men's debts.

Bessières bought the château of Grignon and entertained the Emperor there. The Guard was granted lodging allowances, allotments for mounts, and a groom for every two horses. In the infantry the two senior captains and all officers over fifty were mounted.

The colonel generals signed all the contracts. Nothing was too good for the Guard. Cloth for their overcoats cost 29 francs a meter. If their credit ran out the Emperor

[2] Insignia of the grenadiers and chasseurs, respectively. – Ed.

paid the deficit. He ordered troop movements without even informing the Ministry, except in the case of long journeys. If he forgot, what did it matter, since the Minister was answerable to him alone?

Even the Guard's horses were privileged characters. To begin with, they were fed, which could not always be said for the Line's. Their daily ration was $6\frac{1}{2}$ kilos (about 15 lb.) of hay, 5 of straw, and $8\frac{1}{2}$ litres of oats.

The ministers, and the generals and soldiers of the Line, all jeered at those 'asses of the Guard' who 'had it better than the marshals', fuming with rage and bursting with jealousy. Yet they dreamed only of belonging to it.

This year every Line battalion was ordered to send a man to the foot Guard by 1 July. The candidates must be under thirty-five, five-foot-ten for a grenadier and five-foot-eight for a chasseur, with ten years' service, a good conduct record, and a citation for bravery. The elite battalions and cavalry regiments were ordered to send six, and each artillery regiment, 15 gunners five-foot-ten. It soon appeared that these conditions could not be fulfilled, even by lowering the term of service to six years and exempting légionnaires[3] from the measurement rule.

Fontaines, a Line grenadier of six-foot-four, winner of a weapon of honor and cited for saving the life of his 'corpulent commandant' in Egypt, fulfilled the requirements; so did Corporal Menin of the Line whom Berthier described as 'a good and handsome man, worthy of the honor'. However, Corporal Sauvé with eleven years' service and the Legion of Honor seemed a mite tall for a foot chasseur at six-foot-one[4]! All three were approved by the Emperor whose furious 'N', scratched under the arabesques signifying 'Approved', is appended to the list of candidates. Napoleon signed it himself – this is what they were proud of, even those who could not read.

The veterans of the Guard were the finest soldiers of their day. Born under the Monarchy and brought together in the royal army, then dispersed and demoralized, they had been reunited by hunger under the tricolor flag and had found bread and glory serving the Republic against the invader, after losing their faith and memories of home. Now both had been replaced by the *Tondu*. He was the first person who had ever honored them. He knew them, called them by name, offered them tobacco, pulled their ears, and awarded them his cross or a few gold pieces with his likeness. He mentioned them in his bulletins.

These habitués of the revolutionary clubs, these worshippers of the Goddess of Reason, these anarchists had now become privileged characters – even pets. Now they guarded their privileges more jealously than they ever had their claims to equality. Living apart, they prided themselves on merits which they ended by acquiring. They held their heads high, asserted themselves, childishly assumed a superiority which obliged them to obey certain rules, and ended by considering themselves indispensable instruments of the Emperor's grand strategy.

'As the Emperor said to me in Moravia: "Soldier, I am pleased with you".' Charlet quoted this under his portrait of an Old Guardsman, for he knew them well.

[3] Members of the Legion of Honor.

[4] These are English equivalents, since the French foot measured 12·8 English inches – Ed.

The Guard's renown required that its discipline be severe. A grenadier caught sleeping out of barracks got fifteen days' arrest and thirty more 'on bounds'. A second offence was punished by imprisonment. For misconduct a Guardsman was 'drummed out' and expelled from the Corps.

It was forbidden to walk out with women; if absolutely necessary, a soldier might escort one but might not take her arm. Crossing the Palais-Royal was tolerated, but lingering there or frequenting places of ill-repute was not.

The soldiers of the Guard were formal with one another, not addressing their comrades as 'thou', and were called 'Monsieur' by their officers and NCO's. They did not brawl at the canteens nor were they seen drunk on the street. Duels, which had been common though punished severely, were now rare.

Grenadiers were seen dancing at the Pavillion de Flore in white stockings and buckled shoes. Sergeants, cane in hand, frequented various cafés in Nanterre and Surèsnes to drink a bottle of new wine and play a game of piquet or *drogue*. With arms crossed and short pipes between their teeth, chasseurs and grenadiers expounded definite opinions on the most weighty problems. These could never be solved without the Guard. 'The *Tondu* would do well to think of that!'

True, all this did not prevent amorous intrigues with the laundress nor debauches of mammoth proportions. Nor being always impeccable under arms. Nor fighting in the field and getting killed . . .

Napoleon kept this in mind when planning the Guard's organization for 1806. 'In case of war two companies of *vélites* will march with each battalion of the Guard . . .' This meant that the foot Guard was to be rejuvenated by the infusion of young blood, while 420 old chasseurs and grenadiers would be left at the depot in Paris. Each cavalry squadron of 250 sabers was to include 50 *vélites*; each battery of a hundred veteran gunners, 25.

The train battalion now had a thousand horses. Each corps had its own transport wagons, drivers, and horses ready to march, and its own field hospital. The Emperor had learned from experience that service troops and transport could not be suddenly improvised in war time.

There was no talk of war at the moment. On the contrary, the chief topic seemed to be peace. However, since all Europe was talking peace, the peace must be endangered.

Louis Bonaparte was King of Holland. Venice was joined once more to the Kingdom of Italy, and Joseph Bonaparte was King of Naples. In a letter to the Pope Napoleon wrote: 'Your Holiness is sovereign at Rome but I am Emperor . . .' and received the reply: 'The Emperor of Rome does not exist'.

In the east, Marmont was in Dalmatia and Sebastiani in Constantinople, sent there to preserve the integrity of the Ottoman Empire. Russia was in Cattaro and England at Malta. To whom did the Mediterranean belong?

The Austrian Emperor was no longer Emperor of Germany. In Frankfurt the throne of Charles V had been removed from the Diet Hall. Germany was occupied by the Grand Army, and the Confederation of the Rhine had been established. A national movement was being fanned by the speeches of Fichte and sermons of Schleiermacher, and the publisher Palm had been shot at Braunau.

Engineered by Talleyrand, an agreement was about to be reached between the Empire, Russia, and England. In spite of this the English declared a blockade of the coast from the mouth of the Elbe to Brest. And Fox was about to die.

In Prussia, now an ally of Russia, sabers rattled in their scabbards in response to the appeals of Queen Louise, a beautiful Amazon.

At the beginning of September the Emperor's orders went forth in rapid succession:

On the 5th: '. . . Recent events in Europe oblige me to think seriously of the situation of my armies . . . of a conscription of 50,000 men of the class of 1806, and of calling up 30,000 from the reserve . . . The probable point of concentration is Bamberg.'

On the 10th: '. . . Prussia's movements continue to be most extraordinary. She must be taught a lesson . . . On Friday the 12th I plan to send on an advance guard of 1,000 horse from my Guard, and the rest eight days later . . . I shall have 3,000 cavalry in all, 6,000 elite infantry, and 36 pieces of artillery . . .'

On the 11th His Majesty reviewed the Guard minutely on the Plaine des Sablons from eight in the morning until four in the afternoon. Then he wrote Bessières: 'Give me a clear account of . . . who will be ready to leave within four or five days . . .'

On the 12th, to Bessières: 'Procure sufficient harness for 1,200 horses. I need 24 provision caissons, 24 baggage wagons, 6 for tools, and 20 for the field hospital . . .

On the 15th Napoleon wrote the King of Holland: '. . . I imagine that this crisis will soon pass, and that Prussia will not want to be crushed . . .'

On the 17th he wrote Dejean: '. . . If Prussia declares war on me, the move against this power would seem to pivot on Mainz . . .' And on the 18th: 'The foot Guard . . . must be in Mainz not later than the 28th . . .'

Then followed a detailed order for the execution of these movements: the hours of departure and itineraries for the troops, their arms and baggage, and instructions for the prefects, sub-prefects, commanders, etc.

Hulin, Gros, Dorsenne, and the lieutenant colonels harnessed their private vehicles. The commissaries left to prepare the relays, stage stations, and meals. The men stowed their knapsacks and the officers packed their trunks. By early morning of the 20th the last soldiers were on their way.

'We march through some villages on foot and get back into the wagons at the far end', reported the *vélite* Anciaume. In Luxembourg the human cargoes collapsed in the streets and the men fell asleep on the sidewalks.

Next day the horse Guard departed, except for the dragoons who remained in Paris where Arrighi was obliged to engage grooms, since he had more horses than men.

The staff carriages left on the 23rd and Bessières on the 24th, so as to reach Mainz on the 28th.

On that morning, stiff, bruised, and exhausted after traveling 550 kilometers in eight days, the grenadiers, chasseurs, marines, and artisans of the Guard descended from their vehicles in Mainz a few hours before the Emperor, the Empress, and Bessières.

There was no news of the enemy and war had not been declared.

CHAPTER 7

Jena

BEFORE leaving Paris the Emperor ordered the creation of a regiment of fusiliers of the Imperial Guard with cadres from the infantry *vélites* and officers from the chasseurs. Men of five-foot-six recruited from the departmental reserves were eligible for the new regiment which was attached to the chasseurs and wore the same uniform with shakos instead of bearskin bonnets (see Plate 46).

Boyer de Rebeval was named lieutenant colonel, with Lanabère as one of the majors, Maugras as surgeon major, and Lieutenants Rosey, Suisse, Beurmann, Labusquette, and Jullien as captains. Other officers were brought from the Line, including Schramm, a veteran of Egypt who had captured a gun at Wertingen.

At the beginning of October the army was in the Main valley, rushing towards the enemy at such a pace that the horse Guard could not catch up with the Imperial Headquarters. The Emperor was escorted by the 1st Hussars and guarded by the foot Guard whose daily marches were of an appalling length. They paused for breath at Bamberg where the Emperor arrived on 6 October. That day General Walther crossed the Rhine with 1,300 horse Guards and 300 gendarmes who would not make contact with the Emperor until they reached Berlin.

Marshal Lefebvre was given command of the foot Guard, to which General Oudinot's two regiments of foot dragoons had been attached. These elite troops, together with 1,100 grenadiers and voltigeurs of the Line, served to reinforce the infantry of the Guard. The Guard park consisted of 24 guns plus 12 from the Line. But when would the gunners catch up?

When its units could be assembled, the Guard would muster around 8,700 men, including the marines and service troops. Meanwhile, Napoleon was obliged to improvise many units and organize large magazines at Bamberg.

He was obsessed with the problem of bread. This time the Guard carried four days' supply; its wagons were loaded with 10,000 rations, and the Emperor's own caissons with 3,000 rations of biscuit. A commissary was left at Würzburg to load 40,000 more on all available vehicles, and to prepare 20,000 for the horse Guard due at Bamberg the 10th.

The first bulletin outlined the political situation, and reported the entry of Prussian troops into Saxony and the advance of the Grand Army.

Prussia had not profited by taking the initiative. Her forces were dispersed, with only 140,000 men under Reichel, Brunswick, and Hohenlohe defending the route to Thuringia. True, 120,000 Russians were expected, but not for another month or two.

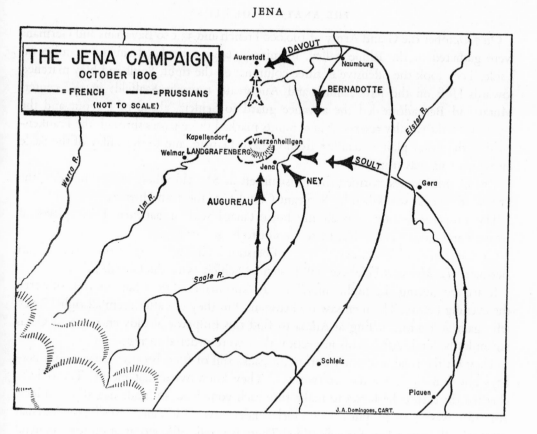

JENA AND AUERSTÄDT

The French remained in Germany and the Prussians sent an ultimatum demanding their withdrawal. Napoleon accepted the challenge and advanced in a brilliant strategic maneuver that separated the Prussian forces.

The Prussians, retaining the inflexible methods of Frederick the Great, had a firm belief in their own military superiority. But they were no match for the Grand Army. The French crossed the mountains in three columns and, in a wide turning movement, confronted one Prussian force at Jena and a second at Auerstädt. In two separate battles fought the same day, 14 October 1806, the Prussians were decisively defeated and retreated in disorder. A relentless pursuit by the French resulted in the capture of most of their army.

Superior tactics had won the battle.

On 7 October the Grand Army of 190,000 French and 33,000 Bavarians and Germans were gathered in the Rhine valley, forming a large articulated square 37 miles on a side. They took the offensive in three columns: on the right, Soult and Ney marched towards Hof; on the left, Lannes and Augureau, towards Saalfeld; in the center, Murat and Bernadotte led the advance guard to Schleiz, ahead of Davout and the Guard with the cavalry reserve. These points marked three passes through the Franken-wald to the Elster plain extending from Gera to Leipzig, and to the valley of the Saale on which Jena was situated.

On the 9th Lannes stormed the Prussian left at Saalfeld where its commander, the Prince of Prussia, was killed by Sergeant Guindey of the 10th Hussars.

The Emperor wrote: 'I await my horse Guard with impatience. Forty pieces of artillery and 3,000 cavalry like these are not to be sneezed at!'

On the 10th the foot chasseurs were at Ebersdorf. That morning an order came from Berthier: '*Le Maréchal* Lefebvre will hasten to Schleiz with the Guard. . .'

It arrived during the night, marching 15 kilometers after a famous trek of forty the evening before. The men saw no Prussians, but they ran after them all right! They left again at 3 a.m., halting at Auma to find the Emperor already en route to Gera, ten miles beyond. After arms inspection they were ordered to rest.

They hit the road again at 1 a.m. with packs full of food because 'they would per-haps not find any for a day or two . . .' They knew what that meant! The officers checked the cartouche-boxes to make sure each contained 50 'undamaged' cartridges. An order was given to 'put the gun locks under cover if it rained'. Really, the Marshal must take the grenadiers for conscripts! There was talk of 'concentration for a general engagement . . .'

The agreeable maneuver of enveloping the enemy had succeeded. By evening on the 12th 'the veil was lifted'. The Prussian army, disoriented by orders and counter-orders, left one corps northwest of Jena and beat a retreat to the northeast. Immediately, the Emperor, whose vanguard was three days' march ahead, lured the Prussians on by pivoting on his own left, under Lannes and Augureau at Jena, with a turning move-ment under Bernadotte and Davout designed to cut the enemy off from its rear-guard and throw it back to the west. The Guard, Soult, the dragoons, and the curassiers were brought up to Jena on the double.

'I am traveling from twenty to twenty-five leagues[1] a day', the Emperor wrote Josephine several hours before his departure for Jena. The Guardsmen could say as much!

13 October, 4 a.m. Escorted by the 1st Hussars, the Emperor passed Jena and climbed the Landgrafenberg occupied by Lannes' corps, halting '600 yards from the Prussian lines'. The grenadiers of the 40th Regiment built him a shelter a little way back and guarded him until Lefebvre arrived and deployed his three brigades along the southern slopes in five lines, 'the first one along the summit'.

Noticing that the general commanding the Line artillery was absent, Napoleon spent part of the night, lantern in hand, supervising the widening of a ravine to allow

---

[1] Roughly 50–63 miles. – Ed.

PLATE 42

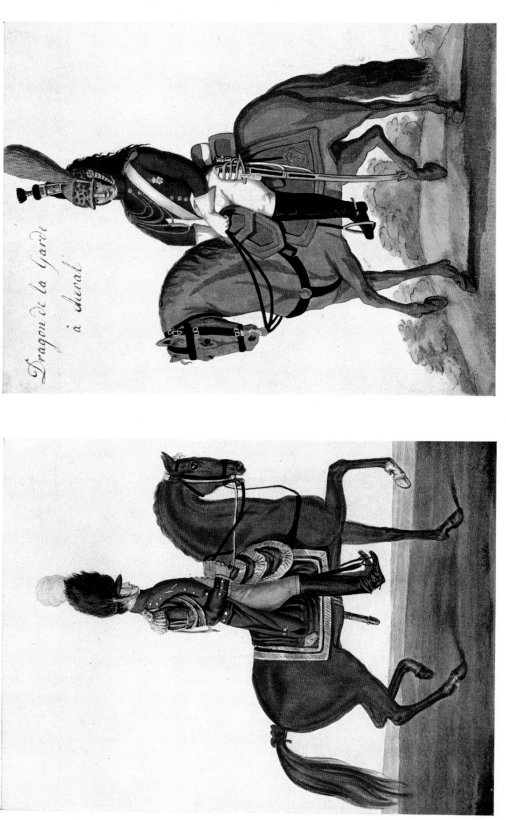

Dragon de la Garde
à cheval

PLATE 43

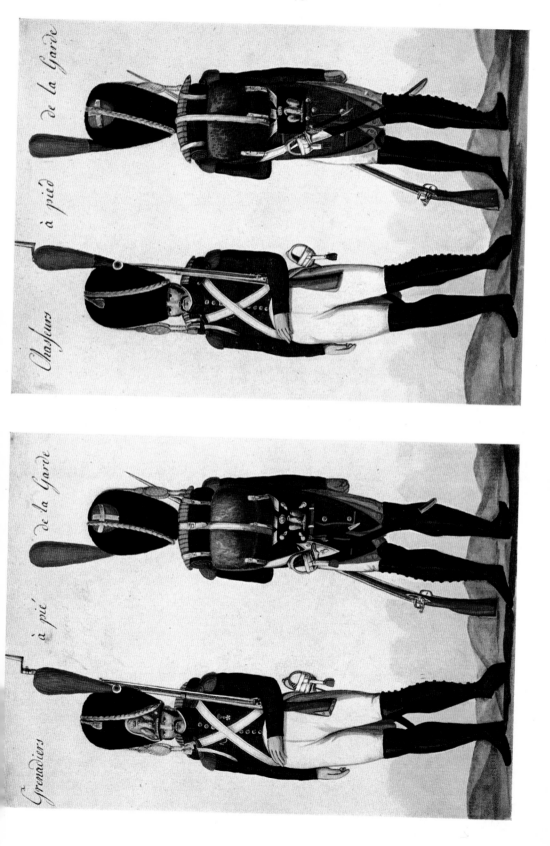

PLATE 44

a) Ney
(*Engr. Tassaert after Trezel*)

b) Dejean
(*Col. lithograph*, chez *Rosselin*)

c) Lefebvre
(*Colored engr. by Freisinger after Mengelberg*)

d) Guindey
(*After miniature: Collection M. Maurice Castellar*)

e) Arrighi de Casanova
(*Contemp. lithograph*)

PLATE 45

Entry of Napoleon into Berlin
(From an original sketch for the painting by Debret)

PLATE 46

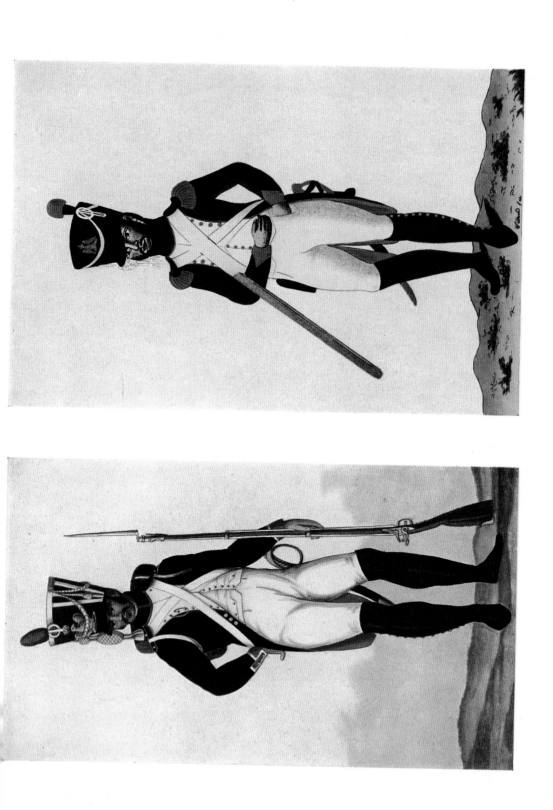

the passage of Lannes' artillery and the Guard's. The exhausted gunners were given food and hot wine by the grenadiers who had been foraging in the abandoned houses and wine cellars of Jena. 'Each had three bottles', reports Coigniet, 'two in his bearskin cap and one in his pocket – and plenty of spirits in his gullet!'

On the 14th came victory.

Lannes captured the Landgrafenberg. Augureau on the left and Soult on the right moved through the fog and stormed Hohenlohe's left which was facing south at Kapellendorf. Surprised, the Prussian general executed a change of front toward Vierzehnheiligen.

A premature attack by Ney between the corps of Lannes and Augureau led Napoleon to order a general offensive. Attacked simultaneously on both flanks and in front, the Prussians were thrown into disorder and fell back upon Weimar. Meanwhile, a few miles to the north, unknown to the Emperor, Davout won a victory at Auerstädt.

The foot Guard remained in reserve, neither stirring nor firing a shot. The horse Guard was still thirty-six hours' march behind. In the evening the Emperor, overcome with fatigue, slept on his maps in the middle of a square of silent grenadiers.

'. . . The foot soldiers of the Imperial Guard watched everybody engaged while they stood idle with unconcealed bitterness. Some were heard to cry: "Forward!" "What is that?" asked the Emperor. "Only a beardless youth would presume to judge in advance what I should do. Let him wait until he has commanded in thirty pitched battles before he dares give me advice!" It was the *vélites* who were impatient to show off their courage . . .'

Thus the Emperor described the scene in the bulletin from Jena where he slept on the 14th. Conquering its ill-humor, the Guard watched over the inn that served as the 'palace' and thirty flags captured from the Prussians.

The pursuit began on the 15th. The Emperor went to Weimar where Murat's cavalry was harassing the fugitive Prussians, but the Guard remained behind at Jena. 'The *Tondu* doesn't give a damn for anybody', it grumbled. 'Look – his horse Guard escorts the wagon train and his foot Guard rounds up the pillagers, while the Line licks the Prussians!'

By way of Naumburg and Merseburg, where it joined up with the cavalry, the Guard accompanied the Emperor in his race towards the Elbe, pressing his troops forward to prevent the debris of the Prussian army from joining forces with the Russians. He preferred to destroy the enemy piecemeal.

CHAPTER 8

Berlin

AT Wittenberg on 23 October the grenadiers learned of the departure of their chief. Hulin had been named commander of the Berlin garrison in recognition of the Emperor's satisfaction 'with his conduct at the battle of Jena'.

Other changes occurred. Oudinot's foot dragoons were detached from the Guard and, equipped with Saxon horses and sabers, converted into cavalry. Major Rottembourg of the chasseurs was made a colonel in the line, and Captains Dupin and Flamand were promoted to major.

On 24 October the foot Guard entered Potsdam at nine in the evening after a march of 35 miles. The horse Guard was so exhausted on arrival that the 1st Hussars continued to escort the Emperor.

The Chief of Staff (Berthier) wrote of the captured flags: 'The Emperor wishes them bound together in bundles and placed on a caisson of the grenadiers . . . to spare the vanquished troops the humiliation of seeing all these trophies[1] . . .' But the 'vanquished' seem to have had other worries, since every one who could find a horse or wagon was flying in disorder towards Stettin, hoping to reach Koenigsberg . . .

Potsdam was a military town. Somber and beautiful in normal times, it was now deserted. The wide streets were empty and the inn *At the Sign of the Prince of Prussia*, bereft of patrons. Having spent half the night polishing its equipment, the Guard forgot its fatigue next day when a great parade took place before the palace of the king.

The soldiers would long remember the luxurious barracks of the Prussian *Garde du Corps* where the chasseurs and grenadiers groomed their horses; the French church; Sans-Souci where the bedroom of Frederick the Great was adorned with a single portrait of Gustavus Adolphus; the tombs of the King's dogs; the 'Isle of Peacocks', a short way from town, favorite resort of the beautiful Queen Louise. Wearing the uniform of a colonel of his own grenadiers, Napoleon meditated for some time at the tomb of Frederick the Great.

At the Charlottenburg, the summer palace of the Prussian king in a forest outside Berlin, the Emperor prepared his entrance into the capital.

October 27 was a day of triumph. About two o'clock, surrounded by his Guard, the Emperor advanced between a double rank of curassiers to the Brandenburger Tor where he was received by General Hulin and the governor, president, and nobles who had come to present the keys of the city to its conqueror. The Mameluks, foot chasseurs,

---

[1] Letter from Marshal Berthier in the collection of Raoul and Jean Brunon, reproduced in *Les Français à Berlin* by Lt. Col. Bernard Druène.

and grenadiers in full dress – their plumes waving in the breeze – passed in succession. Then came the *chasseurs à cheval*.

Finally, amidst the splendid marshals came Napoleon in his simple green uniform 'with his penny cockade, the most poorly-dressed man in the army'. The horse grenadiers brought up the rear as the procession swung down Unter den Linden, packed to the roof tops with Berliners, to the Old Palace. The statue on the bowling green in front was not of the great Frederick but of the Prince of Dessau, creator of the old Prussian infantry.

In the evening the Lustgarten was ablaze with bonfires lighted 'on the usually immaculate lawns' as far as the palace square.

'Each soldier has the bearing of an officer, and each officer that of a corps commander and a hero', wrote a spectator. 'The Guards sang, danced, and feasted far into the night . . . I never witnessed such a spectacle . . .'

In the Duke of Kurland's palace at 7 Unter den Linden Hulin organized the occupation. The men were billeted on the inhabitants and fed at their expense with 'a bottle of wine a day included' which was obligingly changed to beer, since wine was too expensive.

'Everywhere peace and good fellowship reigned', says Coigniet, but the duty was rigorous and the discipline severe. Hulin was not tender with transgressors. He decreed: 'Soldiers must live but must not enrich themselves at the natives' expense.' Several thieves were shot.

The cavalry was housed in the superb royal stables, but the artillery was still en route from Mainz. The officers occupied luxurious dwellings vacated by their owners. They had plenty of leisure to enjoy the theatre, and visit the opera house seating five thousand, the Cathedral with its tombs of the Electors, and the garrison church hung with flags and paintings showing the death of four great warriors: Kleist, Schwerin, Keith, and Winterfeldt. The colossal bronze statue of the 'Great Elector' weighed over 150 tons!

The Freemasons, famous for their 'brilliant concerts and splendid meals', welcomed the initiated to the Royal Lodge of York. The great hostelries *City of Paris*, *Golden Eagle*, and *Russian Sun* on Unter den Linden received in true imperial style all who honored them with their patronage.

The problem of exchange, currencies, and measures was complicated. In Austria they reckoned in *Kreutzer*; in Prussia, in *Groschen* and *Pfennigs*. *Napoléons*[2] were accepted by the natives with enthusiasm, but the soldiers were naturally forbidden to use French money. The quartermasters had difficulty reckoning quantities in pounds and *aunes*,[3] *Faden* of firewood, *Webe* of cloth, *Zimmer* of leather. But in conquered countries the victor is always right.

The forward-looking Larrey had his wagons repaired and painted, and was copied by all the regiments. The painter and master farrier presented bills in *écus* and were

---

[2] 20-franc piece with the effigy of Napoleon. The *écu*, or crown, was worth 3 to 5 francs; the florin, at this period, $2\frac{1}{2}$ francs. – Ed.

[3] An *aune*, or ell, was the equivalent of about 2 yards. – *Ibid.*

paid in florins. The Guard depots rushed out convoys of shoes, shirts, and cloth, but Paris complained of waste.

The Council of State gave notice on 4 November that 'in future the Guard must submit its administration and economy to the statutes in force for the army'. The Emperor, upon reflection, approved this judicious suggestion.

On 7 November the next to last Prussian unit was obliged to surrender; only the last, Lestocq's, escaped. The victory was complete and crushing.

'Soldiers, you have justified my expectations', the Emperor proclaimed at Potsdam on 26 October. '. . . You are worthy defenders of the Crown and of the glory of a great people . . . All provinces of the Prussian monarchy up to the Oder are in your power . . . The Russians boast of marching on us, but they will only find another Austerlitz . . .'

Towards the middle of November the Emperor ordered his army corps on the Oder rushed to the Vistula where Bennigsen had arrived with an army. Grand strategy was luring Napoleon to Warsaw. A reconstituted Poland might serve as a Catholic 'March' of Western Europe against the Russian menace and prevent the Tsar, with England's help, from destroying the Ottoman Empire.

Estimating that England was 'the enemy of the continent', the Emperor countered her blockade of the French and German coasts by a decree 'applying to England the same treatment sanctioned by her maritime laws against other nations', and declared a blockade of the British Isles which he signed in Berlin on 21 November.

On the 24th Napoleon quit Berlin with his Guard to join the army. 'Be assured', he wrote Murat, who entered Warsaw the 28th, 'that I shall not beg a throne (there) for one of my own people.'

He announced to his soldiers that 'new armies raised in the interior of the Empire' were coming to relieve them. These were Dutch and Italian regiments, plus troops of the Confederation of the Rhine, provisional regiments raised by Kellermann in Mainz, Saxons, and new units of the Imperial Guard, bringing Mortier's corps to 30,000 men. Strung out in echelon along the stage routes, these detachments of miserably dressed soldiers were on their way to Prussia where they would be paid, fed, and clothed at the Prussians' expense. Thus Napoleon guarded his communications while reinforcing his army and easing the drain on his treasury.

Back in Paris, Arrighi was in a dither. His dragoons, ordered to march on foot to Berlin where they were to be mounted, had no overcoats. Without them, they would die of cold en route. He wrote the Archchancellor Cambacérès, who looked after the Guard 'by the book', begging him to intervene with the Minister.

Here is the Archchancellor's letter of 14 November 1806:

'Monsieur,

I transmit herewith a letter just received from Colonel Arrighi, commanding the Dragoons of the Imperial Guard. The claim contained in it seems just to me, and I beg Your Excellency to grant it. The 200 dragoons left in a body yesterday. They cannot survive the long journey they must make unless they can be guaranteed against the rigors of the season by the overcoats their Colonel requests. Obliged to travel on foot, these men cannot make use of their capes . . .

'Kindly inform me, Monsieur, what reply I am to make to Colonel Arrighi. I expect to inform His Majesty the Emperor tomorrow of this letter, and tell him that I have sent it on to Your Excellency.

'With renewed expressions of my warm regard and highest respect, I am, etc.

Cambacérès,

Archchancellor of the Empire.'

Dejean reacted at once:

'. . . I hasten to reply to the letter Your Highness did me the honor to write me concerning the request of M. the Colonel Arrighi, colonel of the Dragoons of the Guard, for overcoats for 200 dragoons who left yesterday on foot for the *Grand Armée*.

'Were the dragoons going to campaign on foot, doubtless I should have granted them the overcoats indispensable to such service. I should thus equip any cavalry in a similar situation; however, their situation is quite different. On a journey . . . conditions are not the same as on campaign where bivouacs and night marches make it mandatory to equip foot soldiers with overcoats. On the contrary, this garment, though useful, has never been considered indispensable on a journey, however long . . .'

Dejean's arguments were patently absurd. The Minister did not like the Guard because it was on the periphery of his administration. But Arrighi stuck to his purpose.

The fusiliers were in an equally embarrassing situation. This regiment, raised in December, was quartered at Rueil and Courbevoie. Its instruction was well advanced; yet Boyer was having trouble procuring clothing and funds for his men. If the Emperor knew this . . .

He did – through Arrighi – and he reacted promptly, as follows:

'Monsieur Dejean:

I learn that my Guard is in difficulties in Paris, that they are not paid, and that my regiment of Fusiliers is not clothed. Remove these obstacles promptly, for I shall summon this Guard in a very few days . . .'

On 21 December, 1,549 fusiliers of the Guard – with no overcoats, though they were infantry – left for Mainz, squeezed into wagons. They traveled in a hard frost, making seventy-one stops en route. Their treasurer carried in his strong-box the cash to pay them through 1 February 1807.

Now only the cadres for the mounted *vélites*, plus 500 men unfit for campaigning, remained in the Guard depot.

A new regiment of fusilier-grenadiers had been raised from conscripts of 1807. Lt. Colonel Friederichs of the *vélite* grenadiers was put in command. This regiment, initially called the '2nd Fusiliers', was not sent to the Grand Army until the following April.

CHAPTER 9

Eylau

THE Emperor was due in Warsaw with the Guard on New Year's Day 1807. He was hesitant about re-creating the Kingdom of Poland. In spite of the ovation given him by the Poles, he wrote: 'Only God can arbitrate this vast political problem . . . It would mean blood, more blood, and still more blood . . .'

Unconcerned with the future of Poland, the Guard observed that this miserable country was nothing but mud, more mud, and still more mud . . .

The marines had been sent ahead to ferry Davout's light infantry over the Narew in pursuit of Bennigsen. Beyond Posen, where the women could not have been more friendly had they been French, the horse Guard had only been able to move at a snail's pace. (Its commander Bessières had just been transferred to the command of the 2nd Cavalry Corps.)

As for the infantry, stumbling along rutted trails through a mournful landscape of marshland and dripping pines, crossing rivers on tree trunks, passing through sordid villages whose names they could not even pronounce, both men and beasts faint from hunger, they cursed the Prussians, the war, the Russians, and even the *Tondu*!

Nevertheless, he had not forgotten them. On 2 December at Posen he ordered erected in Paris before the Madeleine a monument in honor of the soldiers of the *Grand Armée*, to be guarded and maintained by the Legion of Honor. Surely, thought the soldiers, this will be a monument to the dead, for we shall all be buried alive in these cursed bogs!

Napoleon announced that day that the Prussian campaign had yielded 280 flags and 700 cannon. Some of the guns would be assigned to the artillery park of the Guard. 'The eagle of France soars over the Vistula . . . The Poles regard us as the reincarnation of Sobieski's Legions', the bulletin concluded.

Well, thought the Guardsmen, this fellow Sobieski – who was unknown on the muster rolls of the Guard – surely lived in one hell of a country where the sun set at two in the afternoon!

They spent Christmas at Lopaczin, a wretched collection of wooden hovels. The Emperor's hat drooped limply over his shoulders and the Guard's bearskin caps, swinging from their belts, were full of water. 'He' was in a foul humor like everyone else. It was here that he gave the men of his Guard the nickname of *Grognards*.[1]

The next day at Golymin they wallowed in water 'up to their bellies', obliged to pull up their hind legs by hand 'like carrots from the garden' in order to move them

[1] 'Grumblers'. – Ed.

forward. They occupied the Bishop's palace whose household slept on the floor. After battling the horse grenadiers with sabers for the possession of a pig, the foot grenadiers finished by eating their gaiter straps.

Finally, at Pultusk on 31 December the Emperor announced: 'I believe the campaign is ended'.

Hollow-eyed, their sunken cheeks covered by an eight days' growth of beard and their cloaks in tatters, the foot grenadiers halted at the gates of Warsaw where they noticed a scowl on the face of Dorsenne. Without mincing words their commander accused them of cowardice in adversity and told them of the Emperor's displeasure. 'He calls you "grumblers"', he said.

At eight in the evening of 1 January the Emperor arrived in the capital, on horseback and almost alone. Having ridden to Warsaw at break-neck speed, he had been obliged to leave his carriage and escort, bogged down in the marshes behind.

Happy New Year!

Down packs!

The soldiers' rest in Warsaw consoled them for their miseries. The city was less tidy than Berlin, but full of palaces. The Emperor occupied the handsome residence of Stanislaus Augustus on the Place de Saxe. Triumphal arches had been erected everywhere. The women were pretty and amiable; it appeared that even the *Tondu* had noticed one who was very pretty indeed.

The army's bread was baked in Prague. The Emperor had confiscated all the wine. The Jews were making a fortune. Thanks to them the Guard ate. There was a succession of fêtes and balls, and a review and parade each day. An embassy reception, too. The Austrian ambassador was especially popular. M. de Talleyrand had long conversations with him, though people hinted that the Emperor was not told every word.

Now Napoleon tried to improve the lot of his unfortunate soldiers and stiffen their morale which had wilted in the Posen sands and Masurian marshes.

The whole army, from the marshals to the least drummer boy, received a bonus for the Polish campaign that doubled their pay, though this fact was not published. The allotments of the foot and horse grenadiers and chasseurs were increased and paid in advance. Soup kettles were distributed and the quota of provision wagons and horses was doubled. The soldiers were paid in person, which was not strictly regulation, and each was issued an extra shirt, a cotton sleeping bag, a pair of boots if mounted, and three pairs of shoes if on foot. Cloth was issued for overcoats and capes. Officers drew a supplementary food allowance of 150 francs.

Equipment, harness, clothing, and arms were shipped from Prussia and France. There was little bread in Warsaw and the bakers, unpaid, refused to work. 'It is only the matter of a *louis*', Napoleon wrote Daru. 'Your storekeepers are nincompoops.'

Larrey replenished his ambulances. A number of them were still en route. The stage stations between Posen and Mainz were veritable ant hills and the Guard depots beehives of activity. The roads of France and Italy were clogged with convoys and troops on their way to join the Grand Army.

85

The Emperor's activity was intense. He wrote the Prince of Peace[2] advising him to keep the English off of the Iberian Peninsula, and to the Shah of Persia offering his friendship. He organized a provisional government for Poland and a Polish army. He requested Decrès, the Minister of Marine, to concentrate vessels at Toulon and 'make a show of fitting them out for Constantinople' to support Sebastiani in his negotiations with the Grand Turk.

On 23 January the Emperor transferred Marshal Lefebvre to the command of the 10th Corps and put him in charge of the siege of Danzig and Kolberg. The Marshal replaced General Victor who had been captured by Schill's men en route to his post. Lefebvre had French, Baden, Polish, and Italian troops under him.

On the 30th, before leaving Warsaw for Willenberg, preceded by the Guard, the Emperor directed Berthier 'to raise a corps of Polish light-horse to be composed of men with sufficient education to guarantee their morality'.

Duroc, assisted by Rapp, who had been wounded at Golymin 'in his bad arm as usual', stayed in Warsaw to direct the organization. The corps was to consist of a staff and, to begin with, four troops of 120 men each. Count Vincent Corvin-Krasinski of Dombrowski's lancer regiment was given command. Kozietulski, commander of the Warsaw Guard of Honor, together with some officers from the new Polish regiments, were appointed later.

Bennigsen had just broken the winter's lull. Based on Koenigsberg, he advanced on Ney's corps which was holding the left wing of the Grand Army. On 27 January Napoleon ordered a countermarch.

With his forces divided into three columns (Davout on the right, Ney on the left, and Murat, Soult, Augureau, and the Guard in the center), Napoleon hurried after the Russian army which he claimed was 'running away without knowing whither'.

This was not strictly true. The Russians had turned round in an effort to escape to Koenigsberg. On 7 February they took up a position before a wretched village called Eylau which the 28th Infantry entered at ten o'clock that night to find the whole Russian army bivouacking a gunshot away in two lines east of the cemetery.

The great engagement would take place on the morrow.

Where was the 'palace'? At Eylau?

No. In the midst of the service battalion which, tonight, was the grenadiers. When the troops had nothing to eat and slept in the snow on the eve of a decisive battle, their chief shared their lot. Behind the little church on the cemetery ridge the grenadiers lit great fires.

The Emperor begged a log and a potato from each squad, and each mess brought him twenty. As he sat on a bale of straw, stick in hand, they saw him share them with his aides-de-camp. By the light of the fires, with soap melted in the embers, the barbers shaved their comrades. Whatever the circumstances, a grenadier of the Guard must present himself shaved on the battlefield.

8 February, 8 a.m. A grey sky, heavy with snow, lowered above the white plain. The Russians saluted the wan daybreak with salvos from all their guns. The Guard was

2 Godoy, Spanish minister in the pay of Napoleon. – Ed.

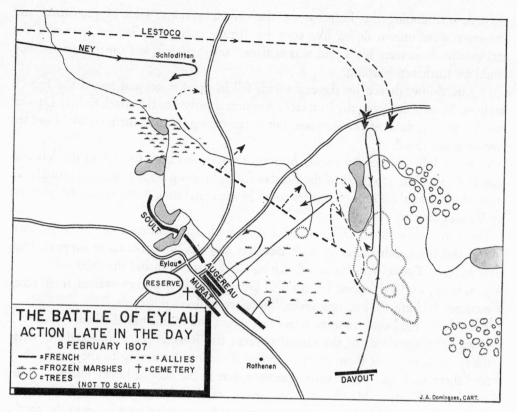

EYLAU

In midwinter the Russians under Bennigsen surprised the French west flank under Ney and drove it back. Then Napoleon marched east in an attempt to encircle the Russians; however, Bennigsen retreated and refused battle. Finally, at Eylau the Russians made a stand and fought back an unco-ordinated French attack. The French Third Corps under Davout arrived late in the day and turned the Russian east flank, but was in turn outflanked by the Prussian Army under Lestocq which came up in a surprise move, evading the holding force under Ney.

The battle was tactically indecisive, with heavy losses on both sides. The Russians retreated from the field but the French were unable to pursue. Both armies retired to winter quarters.

massed, surrounding the Emperor on the cemetery ridge. Files of grenadiers and chasseurs were mown down like corn by Bennigsen's guns. Several horses of the service squadron were hit. Eylau was in flames on their left, and on their right they could see Rothenen burning.

11 a.m. Snow, driven by the east wind, fell in great flakes and lashed the French soldiers. At an order from the Emperor, Augureau moved to the attack to help Davout envelop the left flank of the Russians; but in the raging blizzard the men could not see twenty paces ahead.

11.30. A lull. Blinded by snow, Augureau's divisions bore too far to the left and marched to within 300 paces of the Russian front, bristling with 72 guns. Through the snow and smoke their broken squares could be seen retreating to the cemetery, pursued by Russian cavalry.

The Emperor ordered Dahlmann forward with six squadrons of chasseurs; then Murat and the cavalry reserve, with Bessières and the horse Guard in support. One after another, Grouchy, d'Hautpoul, Klein, Lasalle, and Milhaud marched off.

'Heads up, by God!' Lepic cried to his horse grenadiers as they waited their turn, sometimes ducking the bursting shells, 'those are bullets – not turds.'

Behind the 'big heels' six squadrons of chasseurs and Mameluks charged.

'Twice the squadrons of the Guard overran the Russian mass, knocked out their artillery, then ran over them in the opposite direction. Returning to the attack, they forced them back and broke their resistance, but at the cost of heavy losses . . .' recounted Jean-Baptiste Martin, adjutant major of the *chasseurs à cheval*. He offered his canteen to General Dahlmann who was mortally wounded by a bullet in the thigh. Then he beat off the Russians with his saber and was led back to the French lines by Chasseur Brice who himself was wounded in the shoulder.

Dahlmann died next day at Eylau, Martin took his commander's heart back to his widow in France, and Brice went his way.

The chasseurs lost 21 officers and 224 men in killed and wounded, and more than 200 horses. Captain Guyot of the second squadron and the standard-bearer, a veteran of Egypt, were among the killed; Thiry, Desmichels, and Rabusson were wounded. The Mameluks had covered themselves with glory. Abdallah, already pierced seven times by lances at Golymin, was wounded again; so also was Chahin'.

The horse grenadiers had 143 horses killed. Captain Auzony of the first squadron received a mortal wound. His men wished to carry him off the field, but left him in the snow upon his express command. Three lieutenants were killed, and 13 officers wounded including Lepic. Major Maucomble, General Walther's aide, received six saber cuts and had his horse shot from under him.

The foot Guard, covered with snow, remained glued to the cemetery under fire without flinching. As the ultimate reserve, the Emperor wished to preserve it until a decision was reached. This did not occur until darkness fell when Ney arrived and attacked the Russian flank.

Towards the close of the cavalry fight a Russian column of 4,000 men stormed the cemetery. The Emperor sent Dorsenne against them with a battalion of grenadiers.

Without firing a shot the Grumblers hurled them back with bayonets while the service squadrons attacked their flanks. Major Lonchamp and Captain Rogéry were wounded. Two lieutenants of the grenadiers and chasseurs were killed and three officers wounded. The artillery of the Guard lost few gunners, but left a lieutenant in the snow.

At last calm was restored along the front. The Emperor gave orders to bivouac in position without breaking ranks. He kept watch in the midst of his Guard in a shack a mile from Eylau. They had neither wood to burn nor potatoes to eat. Some Jews came from Warsaw to peddle their wares at the price of jewels – 6 francs for a pony of brandy.

In Eylau and on the battlefield the medics picked up the wounded and cared for them as best they could. Larrey worked forty-eight hours without a respite. A 'Guard hospital' was set up in the village. The surgeons worked with the Russian doctors who were later 'reimbursed for medicines' costing 443.85 francs.

At three a.m. Soult's aide-de-camp came to announce to the Emperor the enemy's retreat. This was an immense relief.

Touring the frightful field of carnage, Napoleon was saluted with cries of '*Vive l'Empereur!*' But he heard others of 'Bread and Peace!' and 'Hurrah for Peace and France!'[3] As if echoing these sentiments, he was heard to exclaim:

'This spectacle was devised to inspire princes with a love of peace and a horror of war.'

Next evening he wrote Josephine: 'My horse Guard covered itself with glory'. And five days later: 'The countryside is covered with dead and wounded. This is not a pretty side of war. You suffer and your soul is oppressed to see so many victims.'

Was he victorious? The enemy had not been destroyed . . . In his adversaries' estimation he had received a setback.

What was he doing in Poland, 1,250 miles from Paris?

He was there because the Russians were on the Danube. His drive to the Vistula was a counterstroke to the Russian push towards Constantinople, which Sebastiani was resisting, as well as to the pressure from England who was now mistress of the Mediterranean.

In their icy bivouac the gunners of the Guard gave little thought to the problems of Europe. Captain Marin dressed his wounds. Major Chauveau, who had been made an officer of the Legion of Honor, wrote his mother: 'The battle was a bloody one – the bloodiest I have seen yet. I am well . . .'

[3] '*Vive la paix et la France!*'

CHAPTER 10

The Household Troop

BACK in September, before going to join the army, Napoleon had sent the following note to Champagny, the Minister of the Interior:

'Enclosed is a project you may handle as you see fit. Pass it on . . . to Marshal Kellermann . . . I do not need troops, but I should like to reopen the military profession to men alienated from their Fatherland by the Revolution who would like to join the army, which is a natural career for Frenchmen . . . I do not know what the scheme will bring forth . . .'

Napoleon was planning to invite the nobility to enlist in an elite troop attached to his household. This was the third time he had made overtures to this group.

At the time of Marengo the Bonaparte Hussars – known in Paris as the 'Canaries' from their yellow jackets – had been recruited among aristocrats and bourgeois who wanted to campaign with the First Consul. Among them were Robert de Choisy, son of a brigadier under Rochambeau; the young Count de Ségur, grandson of Louis XVI's marshal, who commanded a brigade of guards of honor in 1813; Count de la Billarderie, a son – perhaps – of Louis XV's guillotined *maréchal de camp*;[1] Count de Piré, an émigré wounded at Quiberon who ended as a lieutenant general at Waterloo. The corps had been disbanded in 1801.

In 1805 a regiment of guards of honor had been projected to attract the same group, but the war ended before its volunteers had a chance to prove themselves. The future Marshal Boni de Castellane, the Duke de Mortemart, etc., upon expressing a simple desire to serve in the army, had been brevetted second lieutenants in the Line.

The Emperor christened the new corps '*gendarmes d'ordonnance*', the name Charles VII gave the *gens d'armerie* (men-at-arms) of his *ordonnances*, or personal retinue. These became the *Gendarmes des Ordonnances* of Henri IV and eventually, the famous Gendarmes of the *Maison du Roy* under Louis XIV who recruited them from the noblest families of the realm and commanded them in person.

'Every man between eighteen and forty', the project ran, 'possessing sufficient fortune to provide his own horse and equipment and travel at his own expense, will report to Marshal Kellermann at Mainz where he will be admitted to the Corps of *Gendarmes d'ordonnance* of the Emperor. Those entering the cavalry troop must have an income of at least 600 francs, either from their parents or in their own right.'

The Minister of War wrote Kellermann on 2 October: 'General Lacuée will design their uniform of the Emperor's dark green, trimmed with silver, with silver epaulets

---

1 *Maréchal de camp* was the title of a major general under the Monarchy. – Ed.

like those of the old bodyguards'. Kellermann, the future colonel general of the corps, was put in charge of its organization; but he did not understand what was required of him until six weeks later when the Emperor reached Berlin.

The new corps was eventually attached to the *chasseurs à cheval* of the Guard. Marshal Kellermann finally grasped the Emperor's real intentions concerning this corps and addressed the officers and NCO's in his orders in such anachronistic terms as: 'We order Messieurs the Gendarmes . . . to obey in this respect . . .'

At the beginning of December the Marshal received word from Berthier that, when completed, the first two companies 'should join His Majesty, wherever he may be . . .' These were now practically complete.

The nobles rushed through this open door into a corps more consonant with their taste and traditions than the Guard, with whose origins they were all too familiar. Nominations poured in from Caulaincourt, Cambacérès, Senator Chasset, etc. to the troop whose members were pleased to term themselves *gendarmes d'ordonnance de la Maison de l'Empereur*.[2]

The first company of 135 horse was commanded by Mathieu-Paul-Louis de Montmorency, Viscount de Laval, son of the marshal of France under Louis XVI. A *mousquetaire* in 1764 and later captain in the Dauphin Dragoons, in 1769 he took part in the Corsican campaign, then commanded the Auvergne regiment in Martinique where his superiors reported him 'one of the best colonels in the King's service'. In 1788 he was promoted *maréchal de camp*.

MM. Carion de Nisas and de Montullé were appointed lieutenants, and the roster of gendarmes included Vergennes, de Bouloz, etc., etc.

The second company under the Count of Arberg, a scion of one of the most illustrious families of Brussels, numbered 150. Among the lieutenants were MM. de Norvins, ex-officer of the Wittgenstein Regiment and future biographer of Napoleon, Charles de La Bedoyère, and Hippolyte d'Espinchal whose mother was a friend of the Empress. Sergeant de la Platrière had been a captain of infantry under Louis XVI.

A certain mystery shrouded this privileged corps. The Minister of War sent a rush order for eight trumpeters, farrier majors, carbines, pistols, and funds. He specified that the hussar jackets be lined with red and the red waistcoats trimmed with silver lace, 'to make them less somber' (see Plate 47b).

What rank should the new gendarmes hold in the hospital? How did they rank in the army? Were they part of the Guard? Kellermann must get his instructions direct from the Emperor. Dejean was suspicious. Were they entitled to officers' allotments? Certainly not, since they must pay for their own equipment.

'Beg pardon', queried the quartermaster, 'who is to pay for repairs to their kit?' Papers piled up in Paris and Mainz to no avail.

'Nevertheless, the gendarmes should live decently', wrote the inspector. And this was not easy on their pay plus 20 *louis* (400 francs) a year, since their pouch alone cost 5 *louis*; their shabrack 9; their saddle and bridle 6; their two horses 62; and their

---

[2] 'of the Emperor's Household', an analogy to the old *'Maison du Roy'*. The small foot company was judged 'useless' by Kellermann and disbanded in April 1807.

servant's horse 10 – for each gendarme had a groom. Moreover, 'kept on the run day and night', they must eat from time to time. Fortunately, their families came to the rescue.

The first company crossed the Rhine on 4 December; the second, on 3 January 1807. Splendidly equipped and admirably mounted, their mission during their march to join the Emperor was to destroy the bands of Hessian partisans operating around Marburg that were harrying the stage route. The *gendarmes* of Count Arberg were soon supported by the fusiliers of the Guard who joined them at Cassel on 10 January.

'It is a superb regiment', d'Espinchal wrote of the new bodyguard. But the weather was frightful and to reach Berlin the gendarmes were obliged to cross the Harz mountains in three feet of snow. When would they join the Emperor?

They did not even know where he was.

After leaving Mainz, where Josephine had fêted them, and skirmishing with the Hessian partisans along the route, the *gendarmes d'ordonnance* stayed at Magdeburg where one or more enjoyed the favors of the late Prince Louis' mistress.

At length, 'in a beautiful northern frost', with trumpets sounding and cloaks rolled on their saddles, they made their entry into Berlin on 23 January and drew up at the barracks of the Royal Prussian Guard.

'Pass them in review', the Emperor wrote Clarke, the new governor, 'and hold them for further orders. You shall inform me what you think of them . . .'

Clarke thought well of them. However, he warned them that, like the fusiliers, they must receive their baptism of fire before joining their chief.

The *gendarmes d'ordonnance* left Berlin on 7 February to hunt for the partisans of Major Schill and camped that night at Schwedt-on-the-Oder. They reached Stettin on the 11th and joined the Italian general Teulié who was ordered to chase the Prussian guerrillas out of Pomerania.

At Stettin they joined forces with the fusiliers of the Guard, and together they captured Neugarten where Colonel Boyer of the fusiliers and Lieutenant d'Espinchal of the *gendarmes* distinguished themselves.

At Treptow, Greiffenberg, and Degow the second company of *gendarmes* sabered the Prussian infantry and, supported by the first, attacked the cavalry with great vigor. Montmorency had his shako split by a saber and La Bedoyère was pierced by another. Fusiliers and *gendarmes* shared honors in the 63rd Bulletin.

On 8 March the division reached Kolberg, a small fortified town on the Baltic. An attaché of the Emperor arrived at Zernin with decorations of the Legion of Honor for Colonel Boyer and d'Espinchal. Six days later the *gendarmes* received their grand baptism near this spot, losing five or six men killed or missing, with many wounded including de la Platrière, de Bouloz, etc.

In the *Monitor* of 2 April the Emperor expressed his appreciation:

'On the 8th, and particularly the 20th March, the *Gendarmes d'ordonnance*, commanded by M. de Montmorency, defeated both infantry and cavalry sent against them by the enemy. The impetuosity of their charges was admirable and put the enemy to flight . . . Having been put to the test in these skirmishes, (they) will soon be called upon to

participate in more important engagements in a larger theater . . .' Several, includ
ing MM. d'Albuquerque and Carion de Nisas, were cited for particular bravery.

An order from His Majesty on the 22nd directed General Teulié to send the *gendarmes*
to Imperial Headquarters.

'*Gendarmes d'ordonnance*', the General wrote in his order of the day, 'accept my
congratulations and my sincere regrets at being separated from you. You carry with
you the esteem of all the troops I have the honor to command. Your honorable
conduct during this short campaign . . . and the constant proofs you have given of
your brilliant courage . . . are a sure guarantee of the favorable welcome awaiting you
at Imperial Headquarters.'

The Emperor had been at Osterode since 21 February. Meanwhile, the Grand Army
was encamped along the Passarge, ready either to face a Russian attack to raise the siege
of Danzig or retire by the bridges of Marienburg and Marienwerder, when repaired
by Commander Roquebert's marines.

Bennigsen was granting his troops a much-needed rest.

At the castle of Orden, where Napoleon was staying, his labor was enormous. He
must consider both Europe and the Orient, direct Sebastiani and the Viceroy of Italy,
'stir up' Joseph and Louis on their thrones, keep the senators informed, and reassure
Cambacérès. He must support Dejean in Paris, Kellermann in Mainz, Clarke in Berlin,
Poniatowski in Warsaw, feed the army, reorganize it, fill up the gaps, reward the
deserving, and then . . .

An order went to Duroc to hurry the reorganization of the 'Regiment of Polish
Light-Horse of the Imperial Guard', and to send from Warsaw 'in undress coats'
whatever remained of the Guard except for '50 horse and 50 foot'.

He ordered Bessières to send him marines and pontooneers to rebuild the bridges at
Marienwerder and some marine officers to reconnoiter the Danzig shipping.

He ordered Cambacérès to review the Guard depots and send all available men to
Mainz in battle trim – infantry, cavalry, and artillery – and 820 horses in charge of 410
grooms to remount the horse Guard in Berlin.

He ordered Dejean to study the formation of wagon train battalions to replace the
train company, of which he 'did not wish to hear another word'.

He ordered Berthier to issue a daily ration of brandy to the Guard.

He informed Bessières that he would grant 160 eagles of the Legion of Honor to
the Guard and asked for nominations. Then he promoted Lt. Colonels Michel and
Curial of the 2nd Grenadiers and 2nd Chasseurs to colonel. Captain Leroy of the
grenadiers was promoted to major. Fifty NCO's were commissioned in the Line.
Captains Hennequin and Harlet were named majors in the new fusilier regiment.

The Emperor passed a special review of his horse Guards to congratulate and thank
them for their bravery at Eylau. He called his 'comrades' and 'invincibles' by name
and patted them on the back. Guyot was named colonel of the chasseurs; Thiry,
lieutenant colonel; Martin, Corbineau, and Desmichels, majors. Thirty-five NCO's
were commissioned in the corps.

Napoleon ordered *vélites* recruited for the infantry. 'Young men who volunteer', he wrote, 'may enlist in the two fusilier regiments if they are strong and healthy and measure not less than 1·733 meters (5 foot 8). They will have no board to pay and will receive an allotment at the Guard depot in the École Militaire.'

The Guard depots worked day and night. The administrative councils had massive orders from the fighting units. Counting upon local resources, the Emperor had discontinued the allotments to the troops of the Grand Army.

Dejean was not happy. The chasseurs made fun of the administration. They were great moguls and hard to please. These gentlemen turned up their noses at Prussian goods; the shirts were too small, the pistols too long, the carbines too short, the sabers unwieldy... As for the cloth for their capes, they found it exactly what they needed for stable jackets. The horse grenadiers, remounted on Prussian horses, considered them 'worthless', and disdained the Glogau cloth. 'Of course one only dresses well in Paris...'

On 7 March, 45 caissons of furnishings for the Guard left the École Militaire. Everything was packed, tied, and tagged, with detailed invoices in duplicate and papers carrying enough signatures and stamps to make the most punctilious commissary swoon from joy.

Osterode, 23 March. The Emperor wrote: 'I intend to move my headquarters to Finkenstein. My Guard will be encamped at Riesenburg, Rosenberg, Freistadt, and Deutsch-Eylau. Today Marshal Bessières will send his chief of staff to reconnoiter the positions... He will keep the army separate from the Guard... My small staff will go to Finkenstein tomorrow to select billets...'

That same day the *gendarmes d'ordonnance* were detached from Teulié's division and sent to Marienwerder to await the Emperor.

On 1 April His Majesty came to Finkenstein to inspect the works erected in that charming little town on a hill overlooking the right bank of the Vistula. A bridge had been built and stores collected. Commissary stores, hospitals, and bakeries had been opened.

Accompanied by Murat, Bessières, and a squadron of chasseurs, the Emperor reviewed the artillery of the Guard and the *gendarmes d'ordonnance*. He expressed his satisfaction to Monsieur de Montmorency and his troop for the 'bravery they had shown in the various engagements they had fought', and awarded them seven crosses of the Legion. This silenced the gunners who had been inclined to sneer at the silver-laced dandies who 'could not go to war without their valets'.

'One can find neither fatuousness nor pretension in them', wrote General Boulart in his memoirs.

The corps' roster read like a book of heraldry: Marshal of the Empire Kellermann, colonel general; General Viscount de Montmorency-Laval, lieutenant colonel commandant; MM. de Carion de Nisas and de Sourdis, majors; de Montullé, d'Albuquerque etc, adjutant majors ... Even the surgeon major was an 'ex-nobleman' from Brussels!

The house where His Majesty was staying had been built by Count Finkenstein, the tutor of Frederick the Great, and now belonged to Count von Dohna, Marshal of the

Prussian Court. The castle had 'many fine mantels' and was 'handsomer than Bessières', Napoleon wrote Josephine.

Never had the Emperor found himself in a more dramatic situation. 'You made a stupid mistake in not attacking me after the battle of Eylau', he told the Austrian ambassador. 'I was in a fine fix!'

'Ah, if only I had been Archduke Charles!' cried Jomini.

The Emperor inspected the army encamped along the Passarge, directed the siege of Danzig, sent for the marines at Boulogne, encouraged Lefebvre and lent him engineer officers from the Guard staff, exhorted Eugène, counseled Joseph, now King of Naples, berated King Louis of Holland, sent for reinforcements from France and posted them on the Rhine and the Elbe, arbitrated disputes at the Opéra, organized plays in Paris, supervised the University and the teaching of history, and sent Talleyrand in Warsaw instructions for the Polish light-horse.

'I want one squadron with me in two weeks' time', he wrote. 'I have sent an officer of my Guard to Posen for sabers, carbines, and pistols. He will take them to Warsaw at once. By paying the light-horse the same as my Guard, I intend to procure educated men and experienced horsemen, and not peasants who need polishing, which would be a lengthy operation.'

A later decree specified: 'Candidates must be landowners, or sons of landowners, between eighteen and forty, and must furnish their own horse, uniform, equipment, and complete harness of the prescribed model . . .'

The four squadrons were organized like the chasseurs. Count Krasinski, the colonel commandant, had two French majors, Dautancourt of the elite gendarmes and Delaître of the Mameluks. The latter were now commanded by Captain Renno whose conduct at Eylau had been magnificent.

The Emperor was worried about the food situation. But the Guard's interest in life revived with the thaw, the spring, and the provisions found in the secret caches of the peasants.

A camp square was laid out at Finkenstein with the 'palace' in the center, surrounded by barracks like those at Boulogne, in a clearing seven and a half miles in perimeter. There was an 'Austerlitz Street', a 'Jena Street', and a 'Marengo Street' – 'all straight as a die'. The officers' lodgings were very comfortable. All this was accomplished in two weeks.

The Emperor often visited the camp accompanied by beautiful Polish ladies. It was grand to hear the *Diane*[3] beaten by all the drums, and accompanied by all the trumpeters. In the evenings the men sang *In the Regiment I had a Mistress*, and *Chasseur Whom I Adore*.

Clean, combed, and powdered as in Paris, the men on guard duty pocketed several *napoléons* in tips whenever there was a fête at the castle.

The marines of the Guard were on their way. The winter at Boulogne had been a hard one. Stormy seas had prevented the flotilla from putting out, as well as British raids. The camp at La Tour d'Ordre was deserted.

[3] Reveille.

With the coming of spring the men resumed their monotonous duties. Rocked to sleep by the waves, Chief Boatswain Fontaine imagined that the marines of the Guard had been abandoned; that the marshals had won out. 'These marines spoil everything', they said. 'It's foolish to give muskets to these characters who go barefoot, walk with a slouch, wear rags, and reek of tar and tobacco . . .'

Easter came and went. Then on 30 April the marines heard the news that they had been sent for to join the army before Danzig.

On 4 May Lieutenant Grivel was ordered to leave to prepare the way for the battalion. Captain Daugier made preparations for their departure. Forty-five four-horse wagons, plus the officers' carriages, were required to transport 500 men. The distance from Boulogne to Danzig was over a thousand miles. The Emperor had written Cambacérès to 'see that the move was made speedily', so a tour de force was indicated.

The departure was fixed for 5 May. On the 11th, having averaged 75 kilometers a day on roads dredged with deep ruts, they reached Wesel, bruised and exhausted. General Piston, in command of the garrison, reported that despite all his efforts, no further transportation was available. They must march as far as Cassel where they would find wagons.

No one in the battalion complained. The 260-kilometer hike ahead was preferable to the jolting carts which were much worse than tossing ships.

Marching from Boulogne in thirty days flat, the marines reached their destination – but too late. Danzig had fallen to the French the end of May.

CHAPTER 11

Friedland

AFTER a sharp if abortive attack by Bennigsen, Napoleon began maneuvering towards Friedland on 6 June.

That day he moved his headquarters to Saalfeld. The horse Guard was already there and the foot Guard was ordered to follow 'without delay'. Napoleon sent Marie Walewska back to Warsaw and ordered the *gendarmes d'ordonnance* to take over his escort.

The 'grass was green in the Prussian prairies', and the earth trembled under the feet of Napoleon whose horizon extended to Asia. The muddy roads had turned to dust under the feet of the Guard. It marched 100 miles in five days. The Emperor wanted to catch up with Bennigsen, who had begun his retreat to Koenigsberg, before he crossed the Alle.

At Guttstadt the *gendarmes* of his escort imprudently attacked a party of Cossacks, crying '*Vive l'Empereur!*' and would have been decimated had not the chasseurs of the Guard intervened – reluctantly. So, they grumbled, the Emperor now preferred these elegant cavaliers of the nobility who had been serving with the enemy while the plebeians were fighting to clear his path to glory and lead him up the steps to the throne?

Silence!

Two days later at Heilsberg the Russians made a stand. In the action that followed, the brave General Roussel, chief of staff of the Guard, had his head blown off by a shell. Curial was severely wounded marching at the head of the fusilier-chasseurs who covered themselves with glory. Major Vrigny and Captains Schramm, Deshayes, and Labusquette were among the wounded. Chauveau's artillery performed yeoman service during the engagement.

On 13 June the Emperor assigned his 'household troop' the following mission:

'The *Gendarmes d'ordonnance* will make a reconnaissance. If they find no obstacle in their path, they will advance to Legienen, taking care to proceed with caution, and inform themselves of any armed parties on the road from Bartenstein to Eylau, sending me word at Beisleiden. They will then probe Legden where they will keep themselves informed of all enemy movements, sending me a second report . . . They will send me a third at Gross-Kärthen where they will halt and send on to headquarters all persons who shall have left Bartenstein or Schippenbeil this morning to be thoroughly interrogated.'

At seven-thirty that evening, within sight of Bartenstein, a Russian column had been marching along the road to Koenigsberg for the past hour.

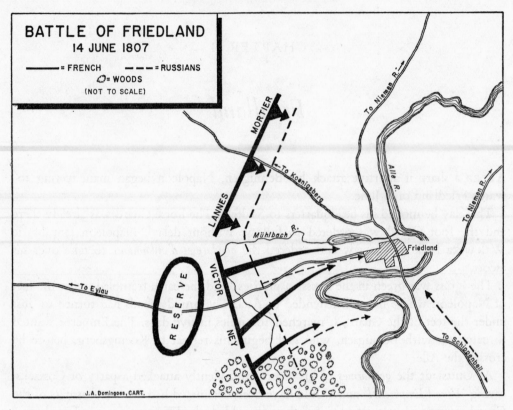

BATTLE OF FRIEDLAND
14 JUNE 1807

———— = FRENCH   — — — = RUSSIANS
◯ = WOODS
(NOT TO SCALE)

J. A. Domingoes, CART.

HEILSBERG–FRIEDLAND

In May 1807 the French broke out of winter quarters and prepared for a mid-June advance against the Russians. However, the Russian army under Bennigsen surprised their advanced forces under Ney and attacked them in force. The French made a countermove, obliging the Russians to retire to prepared positions at Heilsberg.

Napoleon attacked at Heilsberg and sent a turning force to cut the Russians off from their base at Koenigsberg. Both sides suffered heavy losses.

The Russians retreated to Friedland to avoid being outflanked and crossed the river Alle, sending part of their army back across the river to attack Lannes before he could be reinforced. Lannes held out until Napoleon and the main body arrived and launched a well co-ordinated attack, piercing the Russian left and cutting them off from the Alle bridges. The French inflicted heavy losses on the Russians and pursued them to the Niemen where the Tsar joined his army.

The Tsar asked for a truce which resulted in the Peace of Tilsit.

At 11 p.m. at Eylau, near a shack guarded by foot grenadiers, Marshal Bessières was sleeping under a caisson. Brusquely awakened, he sent to the devil – and to the Imperial shack – Lieutenant d'Espinchal of the *gendarmes d'ordonnance*, bearer of dispatches. Norvins, the officer on duty, led him to the Emperor's apartment where His Majesty was stretched, fully dressed, on a cot of planks. Jumping to his feet, Napoleon went to a table where a map dotted with red and black pins was lit by two candles. During the report he stuck new pins into Friedland and Koenigsberg.

'Have you eaten?' asked the Emperor, satisfied.

'Not for twelve hours, Sire.'

'Very good – go to my canteen and help yourself.'

His intentions were good, but nothing remained there but a loaf of bread – one Imperial loaf – which was taken off and devoured by the famished patrol of gendarmes.

Sunday, 14 June 1807. Lannes, whose corps was stretched out before Friedland on the left bank of the Alle, was attacked by the Russians who had occupied the town and were forcing a passage to Koenigsberg. The Marshal impatiently awaited the Emperor's arrival with reinforcements.

10 a.m. Alerted at Eylau, Napoleon galloped to Friedland, preceded, escorted, and followed by the cavalry of the Guard. He halted on a mound and watched the battle raging before him. The artillery of the Guard was set up on his right, supported by the *gendarmes d'ordonnance* and *chasseurs à cheval*. On his left the dragoons formed in line of battle. Behind were the big bearskins of the horse grenadiers and elite gendarmes.

Noon. The foot Guard arrived, marching to battle in parade dress with plumes and gloves. It was the anniversary of Marengo, and Bennigsen, with the four bridges over the Alle his only line of retreat, was in the same fix as Melas had been. Ney, on the right, would take him in flank by attacking Friedland. Lannes would form his corps in a double line in the centre. On the left Mortier, not stirring until ordered, would serve as a pivot. Victor (initially) and the Guard would remain in reserve.

At four o'clock the plan was executed. Ney attacked Friedland furiously. He captured and recaptured it three times. The bridges were finally destroyed. The Russian army was cut in two and finished off by Mortier who went into action on an order delivered by Lieutenant La Bédoyère of the *gendarmes d'ordonnance*.

By ten that evening the Russian debacle was complete. Only the Guard's artillery and fusiliers had been in action; the rest had not fired a shot. Captain Deshayes had received a fresh wound.

'A good day', the Emperor remarked to the grenadiers.

'For you, perhaps . . . The bulletin will say we have put on full dress to stand with folded arms.' grumbled an old-timer.

The cavalry of the Guard joined in the pursuit of the Russians towards the Niemen, during which the dragoons drew their sabers for the first time and one of their captains was wounded.

On 19 June the Emperor and his Guard entered Tilsit where an armistice was signed on the 21st. The campaign had lasted two weeks.

'Here is the boundary between the two Empires', Napoleon said to Prince Lobanov, the Tsar's envoy, pointing on his map to the Vistula. Europe on the west, Russia on the east.

The town of Tilsit was in full fête. The Guard was never out of full dress and each man took out his decorations for an airing. The clothing caissons were emptied of their contents.

On 25 June the marines of the Guard were rewarded for their fatigue and disappointment. The Emperor and the Tsar were to meet on a raft built by the artificers of the Guard artillery and anchored in the middle of the Niemen. Since he would embark upon water, His Majesty's escort was assigned to the marines.

Unfortunately, the river was very low at this moment. Captain Daugier predicted that the Emperor's barge would not be able to move more than fifty yards before running aground, a fact 'that irritated His Majesty . . .' It was therefore on a common scow, manned by sailors of the Guard, that Napoleon put out from the left bank to meet Alexander.

Their two Guards, massed on either bank, cheered them lustily. Then the Tsar and the King of Prussia, having nowhere to dine but at the Emperor's table, found themselves in the midst of the French army in the neutralized city. Arrighi made friends with the Grand Duke Constantine, and the *gendarmes d'ordonnance* found several old comrades of their emigration days in the Russian Guard.

The great attraction was the camp of the Bashkir and Kalmuck prisoners. They had flat faces and large ears, ate their meat raw, and nibbled candles as if they were candy. A sign prudently posted at the entrance read: 'No Admittance – Inmates Rather Wild'.

Grenadiers, chasseurs, dragoons, and gunners busied themselves with preparations for a mammoth feast to be given by the Imperial Guard for that of the Tsar. They erected tents and sheds. By special permission, fifty peasant carts brought in pine trees and provisions from twenty miles around.

On the morning of 30 June the final touches were put to the floral decorations on the lawns and parterres. Sixty pieces of artillery under Lariboisière paraded before the three sovereigns. Passing the King of Prussia, a Guard drum major warned his drummers: 'Don't beat so loud – he's only a king!'

'You are young to have gained so much glory', the Tsar remarked to a colonel of dragoons while reviewing the regiment and admiring his superb helmet, a gift from Princess Pauline.

The collation, served by men with powdered hair in white aprons, began at noon. It continued until evening and ended in an orgy.[1] Simultaneously, the *gendarmes d'ordonnance* entertained the Tsar's *chevalier gardes*, as befitted the household troop of the Emperor of the French, since the horse Guard was already on its way to Koenigsberg to prepare for the Emperor's arrival in the capital of East Prussia.

On 9 July, before leaving for Koenigsberg, Napoleon signed the peace with Alexander and Frederick William III. Prussia lost her territories west of the Elbe, which

---

[1] According to Coignet, the Russians stuck their fingers down their throats after consuming one meal and promptly started on another.

became the Kingdom of Westphalia, and her Polish provinces. These were presented as a grand duchy to the King of Saxony who had just joined the Confederation of the Rhine. In her turn, Russia was evicted from the Mediterranean and halted on the road to Byzantium. Nevertheless, the Tsar undertook to mediate the quarrel between England and the Empire. If he failed, Alexander promised to ally himself with Napoleon.

Was he sincere? Impressed with the defeat the French had inflicted upon his forces at Friedland, he was now 'imbued with the atmosphere of Tilsit'. 'What do you think?' Napoleon asked Daru.

Installed in the old castle that had served as the 'cradle of the Prussian monarchy', Napoleon considered the Empire at its zenith. To give this glorious peace the most magnificent possible setting he decorated Tilsit in the style of an Epinal print,[2] with the Imperial Guard as the spectacular frame. He wished his Guard to be beautiful, gilded, and gay.

Gros, Curial, and Arrighi were promoted generals. The latter, only twenty-nine, was awarded the eagle of a commander of the Legion of Honor, while 146 NCO's of the foot Guard and 100 cavalry *vélites* received commissions in the Line and a bonus of 1,500 francs. Hulin, Soulès, and Dorsenne were given 100,000 francs each; Lepic, Gros, and Curial, 50,000; Friederichs and Major Henry of the gendarmes, as well as Michel, Chastel, Dogureau, Digeon, and Jacquin, were each given 30,000. Three hundred *napoléons* were given each staff officer, 100 to each captain, 50 to each subaltern, and 800,000 francs divided among the NCO's and soldiers who had taken part in the last campaign.

Many officers and men were decorated with the Legion of Honor. The Guard also received foreign decorations such as the orders of St. Henry of Saxony, St. Alexander Nevski and St. Andrew of Russia from the other sovereigns.

In July 1807 the Guard at Tilsit was resplendent. Dorsenne and Curial had emptied the Russian and Prussian stores, turned out the knapsacks, shaken the portmanteaux, inspected the bearskin bonnets, the endless pockets, and opened the parcels that had been trailed through the mud. The accumulated riches, plus the contents of the caissons from France, Berlin, and Warsaw and the confections of the master tailors and bootmakers, gave the Guardsmen an appearance worthy of the Emperor.

Brushed, polished, and resplendent, they marched behind their gold-laced musicians and plumed drummers before the Emperor and the Tsar. They rendered honors to the beautiful Queen of Prussia, of whom Coigniet remarked naïvely that 'he would give his ear to stay as long with her as the Emperor.'

On 12 July Marshal Bessières mounted the *gendarmes d'ordonnance* in Koenigsberg to announce in the name of His Majesty the disbanding of their corps. Its members might remain in the army, however. General de Montmorency was attached to the Emperor's household and made governor of Compiègne, a post formerly held by his father, the Marshal. The officers were transferred at a higher rank to the Line;

[2] Home of the famous 'Imagerie' where popular prints – many showing soldiers – were published during the 19th century. – Ed.

the gendarmes were commissioned subalterns. Those of the fourth and fifth companies, who had fought no campaigns, were assigned to the *vélite* squadrons for one year, after which they were to become officers.

Thirty-six gendarmes refused these favors and asked permission to return to their homes. Out of a total of 378 effectives, the *gendarmes d'ordonnance* yielded 10 generals, 24 colonels, and 300 officers to the army; however, few ever forgave the Guard for their humiliation at Koenigsberg. 'Their families will espouse their griefs', one commentator observed, inferring that after the aristocracy had served loyally, according to its traditions, on the battlefields of the Empire, Napoleon had made a political blunder in yielding to the jealousy of his plebeian Guard.

In his *Military Reflexions* of 1764 M. de Boussanelle wrote: 'True emulation seeks to imitate and surpass the brilliant actions of others, since it knows what they cost and respects them, whereas false emulation thinks only of abasing the rival and destroying him...Wherever there are men there is envy... Who would believe that this honorable profession, which seems to have no object but glory, is ... the one in which ... the success of others arouses the greatest fury, or at least chagrin? ...'

The Guard of 1807 confirmed the testimony of this cavalry general of Louis XV.

Yet the men whose jealousy had destroyed the *gendarmes* were now masters of Europe. The Emperor had often said that to them nothing was impossible, and now the Guard thought it perfectly natural to walk about Koenigsberg, the 'first city of East Prussia', as though they were in their native villages. Were they not at home everywhere? Who was the King of Prussia anyway? Just another chap they had licked! When they planted trees along the highway and spread fresh sand on it, it was not for him, but for the Emperor.

He was a magician. By a promotion, a bit of ribbon, a few *napoléons*, he inspired emulation. With a mark of attention, a casual phrase, he turned his hard-boiled veterans inside out, so that they talked of the incident in the bivouacs and dreamed of it at night. Later they repeated it in the barracks and canteens with embellishments. 'The Emperor said to me "I need you." Well, then?'

The Prussians, the Poles, the conscripts of the Line might bawl: 'Long live peace!' Peace? What did it matter to the men who ate herrings from the Baltic, drank brandy flecked with gold, slept in linen 'as white as snow', smoked Elbing tobacco, used – or failed to use – the cuspidors the *Hausfrauen* provided. Whether in Koenigsberg, Berlin, Vienna, or Paris, they belonged to the Imperial Guard. Nothing counted but that.

The Emperor ordered the evacuation of Prussia. Then he ordered the Guard recruited up to strength. Without delay, the cavalry of the Line was to furnish for the horse Guard 700 men, chosen from those who had distinguished themselves at Austerlitz, Jena, and the battles fought since, regardless of their length of service.

The artillery left for France on 1 July. The rest of the Guard departed in three columns from Koenigsberg on the 14th, 15th, and 16th.

Where were they bound? They did not know; they only knew that they 'tramped the road' in sweltering heat and would march until the *Tondu* ordered them to halt.

CHAPTER 12

Paris

THE artisans, hospital attendants, surgeons, sick, and wounded of the Guard, traveling by water from Koenigsberg and Marienwerder cooped up like merchandise in horse-drawn barges, arrived in Berlin after a terrible voyage.

The marines were in Stralsund with Brune who had been ordered to neutralize 'that archfool, the King of Sweden' since, under pressure from England, he had lately denounced his treaty with Mortier.

The rest of the Guard was in Hanover with Bernadotte who was watching Denmark. The British Admiral Gambier was bound there, intent on destroying her shipping and arsenals, for England was still at war.

Neither infantry nor gunners were amused by their sojourn on the sandy banks of the Leine where they found little to do but visit monuments, walk in the Ellernried woods, and drink quantities of beer.

Orders to return to Paris arrived – but not for the artillery. Soon the infantry and cavalry, 'fêted and fed', were en route, marching by easy stages to the capital. Before entering large cities like Frankfurt, Mainz, Nancy, and Châlons they changed from their marching kits into dress coats to parade under the arches, past the cheering girls.

Full of play, General Soulès of the foot chasseurs ordered the custom officials, so indiscreet as to wish to inspect his wagons, restrained at bayonet point. Neither the officials nor the Emperor appreciated his little joke. Soulès, a senator with a handsome income, was retired in February 1808. Later he revenged himself by participating in the Emperor's downfall, which was not very noble of him, and cast his vote for the death of Marshal Ney, which was worse still.

At Châlons, Letort received an order to send 200 dragoons to Bordeaux immediately. There were great lamentations from the troopers who were hardly given time to change their shirts.

Letort did not know that on 18 October Junot had crossed the Bidassoa, marched across Spain, and was now on his way to Algarve in Portugal . . .

Porte de La Villette. 25 November 1807. Noon.

Under a winter sun an immense crowd waited at both sides of the Claye-Paris road and around the triumphal arch erected near the gate. Under arcades decorated with portraits of celebrities the stands were filled by members of the municipal council and an orchestra conducted by Monsieur Méhul.

'Here they come!' The Imperial Guard was returning to Paris

Marshal Bessières rode at the head of his staff, followed by the eagles of the different corps. He was greeted by the prefect of the Seine who attached a wreath of silver leaves, tied with a blue enameled ribbon, to the eagle of each corps as a gift from the City of Paris.

'The wreaths with which you crown our eagles', declared Bessières, 'give further proof of your affection for the Emperor, and render a glittering homage to the *Grande Armée*.' Then music burst forth. The choirs of M. Méhul chanted the *Song of Return* that he had composed for the occasion.

With drums beating and trumpets blaring, the Guard marched between rows of enthusiastic Parisians. The horses were groomed, the men shaven. Though the plumes had molted and the coats were threadbare, at least a third of the shabby revers bore the Legion of Honor. Under the fur bonnets, grown bald in patches, the sunburned faces registered indifference to the applause. For these men were the Guard.

At the Porte Sainte-Marie and on the boulevards the ovation increased. To the rhythm of drums beating the *March of the Camp of Boulogne* and bands playing *What Better than to be Home with your Family?* the corps filed past in order.

Behind their sky blue trumpeters marched those privileged characters the 'invincibles'. '*Chasseurs whom we adore . . .*' hummed the girls.

The troopers were wearing undress coats with aiguillettes. The crowd missed their gaudy dolmans and pelisses, and the march-past 'at the trot'. At their head, surrounded by chasseurs wearing the Legion of Honor, was a wagon bearing Dahlmann in his coffin, followed by his faithful lieutenant colonel, Guyot.

Numerous holes left in the ranks of the *chasseurs à cheval* had not been filled. Some newcomers who had not yet acquired uniforms of the corps were easily spotted.

Renno and his Mameluks clattered by, then the fusiliers, still without overcoats. A worse dressed corps could not be imagined. The public made fun of their sleeves which were too short and coats which were too tight. Could they have grown?

Boyer, their colonel, was convinced of it. Nevertheless, his juvenile regiment was covered with glory and the Emperor would soon grant it a privileged place in his Guard. Among the officers of the fusilier-chasseurs were some veritable monuments: one major, a captain, the eagle-bearer, and Lieutenant Colomban had all been charter members of the foot chasseurs.

The chasseurs' drummers rumbled by, preceded by sappers in leather aprons. Among the virtuoso drummers was Estienne, a *légionnaire* known as 'the drummer of Arcole', who rolled out thunderclaps with his silver-mounted sticks of honor. Behind Soulès and Gros marched the chasseurs with their 'battle-wise air'. All their officers and many chasseurs were *légionnaires*.

The foot grenadiers passed, led by the 'handsome Dorsenne', with Michel at his elbow. These old-timers were the foundation stone upon which 'he' had built the Guard. Captain Lemarois and Lieutenant Mirabel had served in the same regiment in the Consular Guard.

Young Arrighi, dapper on his chestnut horse and tightly cinched into his green uniform with its white plastron, pranced by at the head of the dragoons, leading the one surviving squadron christened by the Empress. Lt. Colonel Letort rode just behind him. He was a daredevil of Lasalle's ilk; if his skin was as full of holes as a colander it was for the Emperor's sake, for France, and for the uniform he wore.

Walther, chamberlain to His Majesty, marched by at the head of his horse grenadiers whose 'beehives' had lost their plumes. Lt. Colonel Lepic, the vice-commander, had recovered from his wounds and resumed his post beside Chastel. These giants, severe and calm, were greeted with wild applause. Among them rode Clément and Duclaux.

A squadron of 'immortals' from the depot of the elite gendarmes closed the parade.

The day advanced. It rained as the regiments formed in line of battle in the courts of the Carrousel and the Tuileries. The Emperor was not there to review them, congratulate them, and welcome them as only he could. He had left for Italy to inspect his kingdom, study the Mediterranean situation, supervise the implementation of the Treaty of Tilsit, present awards to the Army of Italy, and recruit its men for his Guard.

The troops rendered honors to the eagles to be deposited in the Emperor's cabinet. Then they marched up the Champs-Elysées where the municipality gave a feast in their honor. Tents lined the sidewalks on both sides of the road from the Place de la Concorde to the Étoile. At the circle was a tent for the staff.

A fine reception, to be sure, but exhausting for the Guardsmen. The journey back to the Tuileries for their packs and muskets, the return to their barracks in Courbevoie, Panthémont, and the École Militaire which they had not seen for a year – and which the recruits had never seen – ended *'in grisaille'*[1] the grandeur of this day which finally expired in the flicker of a damp rocket.

We can imagine the homecoming of these tired, overwrought men, searching by the dim light of a few smoking lamps through endless corridors for their own rooms; the bawling of the sergeants, the jostling, the packs and parcels collapsing in heaps on the floor, the mumbled replies to the corporals' roll calls, and the final tumbling of two men into a bed three and a half feet wide – not to mention the cavalrymen who could not go to bed until they had looked after their horses. And we understand why the Emperor had scheduled the banquet for the following day.

The fête lasted for a month. Military festivities are rarely agreeable for the participants. To them, they are simply a multiplication of miseries: furious polishing by the light of flickering candles with encouragements laid on thick by the NCO's; extra inspections by the adjutant majors for days in a row with the specter of the guardhouse ever present; then finally, a nocturnal departure.

This celebration involved more pleasures than usual. The Paris theatres gave free performances for the Guard. The Vaudeville presented a piece entitled *They Arrive*, written for the occasion. For more serious fare, the Emperor's own troupe presented *Gaston et Bayard*, a tragedy claimed by the critics to 'offer a true and noble portrait of soldierly virtue and knightly zest which no audience has ever been better fitted to appreciate'.

[1] Literally 'in grey tones', as opposed to color; a technical term in painting. – Ed.

The Imperial Academy of Music put the orchestra pit, parterre, and all its best boxes at the Guard's disposal for the current hit. This was *The Triumph of Trajan* which was greeted with enthusiasm, since Trajan was none other than Napoleon. The *Monitor* reported brightly that the Guard – 'the elite corps that has visited so many climes . . . recognized Rome, and its emotion was impossible to describe . . .' Actually, the Guard's emotion was due less to recognizing Rome, which it had never laid eyes on, than to the charms of Mademoiselle Maillard and the evolutions of Franconi's six white horses hitched to the hero's chariot.

On the 28th the Senate gave a function in its palace for the officers of the Guard. This was a mammoth *kermesse* in the gardens which had been transformed into several ballrooms for dancing and waltzing. Immense buffets tempted the guests who were received with flourishes of trumpets and drums and the music of bands stationed on the grand staircase.

At the arrival of Bessières, followed by the officers of the Guard in full dress, Lacépède welcomed them with the rhetoric in fashion at that moment: '*Monsieur le Maréchal*, invincible Imperial Guard, the Senate goes forth to greet you . . .'

At the banquet that followed, the toasts were accompanied by ritual speeches, poems, and songs addressed to the 'gracious sons of victory', 'brilliant elite of heroes', etc. etc. *ad nauseam* . . .

In the gardens Franconi gave an exhibition of trick riding and Forioso walked a tightrope – like a grenadier on the road to Jena. Balloons 'filled with fire' ascended and bouquets of rockets swished through the night sky.

On 3 December a dinner of 600 was given by Bessières to the ministers, marshals, prefects, and mayors, followed on the 19th by a fête in the old Military School 'to celebrate the triumph of the Grand Army and thank the City of Paris for its welcome to the Imperial Guard'.

In the middle of the illuminated Champ de Mars a shell was erected framing a colossal statue of the Emperor who was unfortunately absent. However, the Empress arrived at eight o'clock. The officers of the Guard did the honors. For half an hour the grenadiers and chasseurs executed a 'fire by files' with star cartridges on the Champ de Mars with a most beautiful effect. The guests were entertained by a ballet, followed by supper and dancing until dawn. The quadrilles were led with drill manual precision by officers more familiar with the evolutions of the parade ground than the ballroom.

Outside, the Champ de Mars was aglow with fireworks – the indispensable complement to all official rejoicing along with *Te Deums* and salvos of artillery. The display was presented by gunners of the Line. The artillery of the Guard – still en route to Paris with the marines – could never be consoled.

The Japanese lanterns were finally extinguished by the December wind, but the eagle remained at the zenith. Drunk with glory, the Guard went into winter quarters. It was the keystone of the arch supporting the Imperial edifice; the order founded by the living god who held dominion over the world and who had assigned it, as a rule, the cult of honor. Napoleon had founded this lay religion on French pride, and raised it to sublime heights of virtue and sacrifice. It imbued the soldiers of the Guard with the self-confidence, self-respect, and fidelity that the old aristocracy had acquired by education and tradition.

'It is a virile religion, without symbols or images, without dogmas or ceremonies, whose laws are nowhere inscribed', wrote de Vigny in his *Servitude et Grandeur Militaires.*

Now, through its cadres, the Guard must infuse this cult of honor into the whole army, and beyond, into the Imperial institutions through which the Emperor hoped to establish true equality among the peoples of France and Europe.

Over the Imperial Guard in the twilight of 1807 hovered the figure of Napoleon the Great whom the Guardsmen saluted with the cry that summed up all their hopes:

'Vive l'Empereur!'

BOOK III

THE GUARD SUFFERS

THE WAR IN SPAIN AND THE PENINSULA CAMPAIGN[1]

Napoleon was obsessed by his 'continental system' by which he hoped to bar England from the ports of Europe, thereby forcing her to make peace. Supported initially by Russia and Austria, he took steps to control first Italy and Sicily, then Portugal and Spain.

Napoleon decided to occupy Portugal and cede it to Spain in exchange for territory north of the Ebro. To this end he sent Junot with an army to Portugal, via Spain.

At that time Spain was nominally ruled by Charles IV but actually by Godoy, the Foreign Minister. Charles was opposed by his son Ferdinand. When the people rose against the monarchy both appealed to Napoleon who countered by abducting both and placing his brother Joseph on the throne.

Despite their inadequate army, poorly equipped and trained, the Spaniards revolted. The first French troops sent to Spain to support Joseph were far superior to the Spanish, but the country, cut up by rivers and mountains, was difficult, lacking in provisions, and infested with guerrillas. Notwithstanding French victories the Spaniards did not submit. Both sides resorted in desperation to extreme cruelty. After a week Joseph was obliged to quit Madrid which led Napoleon to move a large part of the Grand Army from Germany to Spain.

Napoleon underestimated the difficulties in Spain. When England sent an expedition to Portugal, Napoleon underestimated the quality of the English troops. In the Peninsula Campaign the French battalion columns were beaten for the first time by Wellington's battle line, deployed two deep so that its volley fire could reach the front and flanks of the French. Meanwhile, Wellington kept reserves in the rear to counterattack when necessary.

Eventually Napoleon went to Spain where his Grand Army reached a peak of a quarter million men. Less than 150,000 Spanish opposed him, plus the English under Moore who moved from Portugal to Spain.

The Spanish war was a popular insurrection, supported by patriotic enthusiasm, good fighting units, and a strong Ally whose fleet controlled the sea. Napoleon conducted a fine classic campaign and overran the country, but when he left Spain for Austria he had not actually reduced any part of the Peninsula to subjection.

---

[1] See pull-out map at end of book.

PLATE 47

PLATE 48

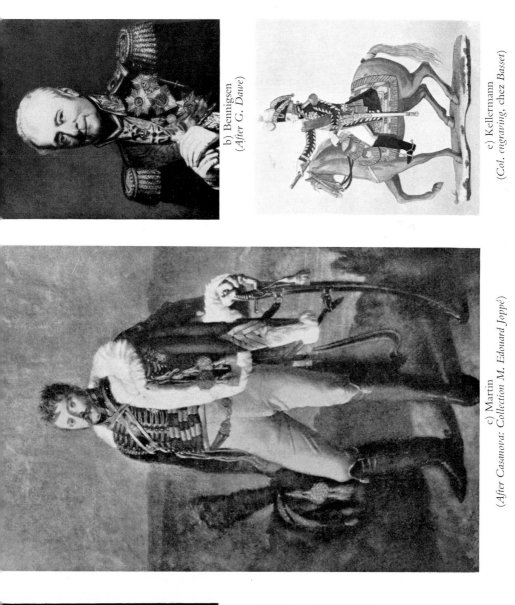

b) Bennigsen
(After G. Dawe)

e) Kellermann
(Col. engraving, chez Basset)

c) Martin
(After Casanova: Collection M. Edouard Joppé)

a) Marie Walewska
(Engr. after Lefèvre: Musée Marmottan)

d) La Bedoyère
(Contemp. engraving)

PLATE 49

'They grumbled ... and kept on following him'
(From a lithograph by Raffet)

PLATE 50

PLATE 51

a) Fête given for the Russian Guard by the grenadiers of the Imperial Guard at Tilsit
(*From a contemporary colored print published* chez *Chereau*)

b) Kalmucks and Bashkirs
(*From an original drawing by Horace Vernet*)

PLATE 52

The Imperial Guard parading before the three sovereigns at Tilsit
(From an engraving by Couché after Swebach)

PLATE 53

PLATE 54

a) Daru
(*Col. engraving by Meyer*)

b) Walther
(*Engr. Réville*)

c) Guyot
(*Contemp. engraving*)

d) Letort
(*Contemp. engraving*)

PLATE 55

a) Krasinski
(*Contemp. lithograph*)

b) Lefebvre–Desnoëttes
(*Engr. Forestier*)

c) Delaitre
(*Contemp. lithograph*)

d) Lariboisière
(*Col. engraving by Meyer*)

PLATE 56

Gunner of the Guard foot artillery
(*From an original watercolor study by Edouard Detaille*)

PLATE 57

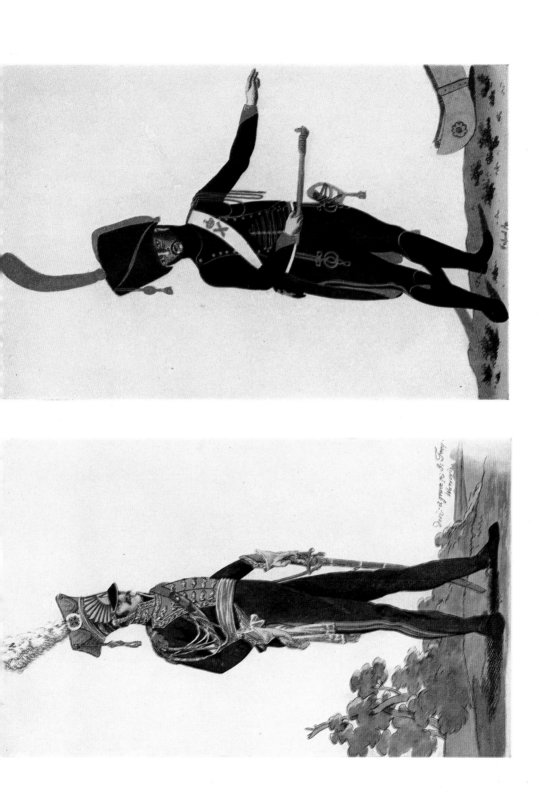

CHAPTER 1

South by Stealth

AT the beginning of 1808 the artillery of the Guard left Hanover and arrived at its new garrison at La Fère on 14 January. More cunning than the chasseurs, the gunners had managed to smuggle in large quantities of British goods hidden in their kits.

This corps was beloved by the master and enjoyed a reputation it hardly deserved. It was teeming with officers. General Lariboisière, the commander in chief, wore the grand eagle of the Legion and was a remarkably fine officer. The vice-commander, Major General Couin, was a vigorous trooper and as brave as his own sword. Colonel Dogureau was young, proud, and peremptory; Colonel Digeon, commanding the park, was intelligent, amiable, and the most capable of the lot. Major Chauveau was difficult, and the 'handsome Greiner', though susceptible and conceited, an excellent officer. Boulart was newly arrived from the Line.

In charge of 450 NCO's and men and 36 guns were 50 officers, besides 16 in the train and three or four in charge of the artificers and park. This plethora of officers had engendered a certain laxness among men whose devotion to the Emperor consisted of simple adoration mixed with jealousy.

The corps' long sojourn in Hanover had not improved Lariboisière's opinion of it. An old comrade of Lieutenant Bonaparte in the La Fère regiment, he warned Napoleon that a reorganization was imperative.

The tour at La Fère began badly. The inhabitants rented the officers lodgings at exhorbitant prices on the pretext that Guardsmen could pay. Numerous incidents were handled without tact or courtesy. Officers and gunners complained of their 'exile', for which General Couin and Colonel Dogureau persuaded some of their colleagues that Lariboisière was responsible.

While downing the daily 'bracer' issued to keep them alert in the service of the Emperor, these gentlemen grumbled and blamed the *Tondu*. Why had they been cooling their heels in Germany while the cavalry and infantry were amusing themselves in Paris at the public expense? Was not the Guard supposed to guard the Emperor? Well, then, since he was in Paris, what were they doing at La Fère?

The Emperor issued orders without explanation, even to the artillery of his Guard.

On arrival at La Fère, Boulart's *vélite* squadron was warned to be ready to depart immediately. Where was it going? The officers emptied the magazines and purchased horses, dispatching 600 with 1,400 sets of harness to Tours.

Some train soldiers were appointed sergeants and some conscripts, corporals – in the Guard! The people in Paris must be out of their minds. A second train battalion, raised the previous year, was detached to serve in the wagon train of Dupont's corps. Was the whole Guard to be emptied into the Line?

'There is talk of a coastal observation corps being raised to watch the English', Boulart wrote. Actually, this corps was already on its way to Tours with orders to bypass Paris.

The marine battalion returned the same day as the artillery. Tired of piloting those infernal barges and convoying wounded and venereal cases down the Vistula and the Frisches Haff, 650 officers and men had quit Stralsund with joy on 25 November and had marched 750 miles to the École Militaire.

They arrived destitute, lacking shoes, uniforms, equipment, and funds. A dispute between the Ministries of War and Marine left them suspended in mid-air. After exchanging notes, reports, and memoranda, the commissaries and inspectors decreed that the marines should draw navy pay from the War Ministry, supplemented by the treasury of the Guard, with the result that not a sou was forthcoming. Their quarter-master did not know which saint to propitiate.

Daru quibbled endlessly, though Captain Daugier needed money to pay the arrears in wages and clothe his men. He had also to fill vacancies caused by age and war. Ordered to march, Daugier emptied the depot and departed at the beginning of February with four crews under Vattier, Baste, Roquebert, and Kerveguen. Others joined them later at Bayonne.

Colonel Arrighi of the dragoons was also in difficulty. The December decree ordering the dragoons increased to four veteran squadrons and one of *vélites* had not been implemented. Rushed out on campaign before they were fully organized, and shorn of the 200 already sent to Bayonne, the regiment would have been in a sorry plight had not its energetic young commander been determined to make it a crack corps of up-to-date cavalry.

He forthwith abolished queues, powder, breeches, stockings, buckled shoes, and long-tailed coats. Marshal Bessières, a stickler for tradition, was scandalized. However, Arrighi had permission from his cousin the Emperor to do as he pleased.

One morning he dressed two NCO's and took them to Saint-Cloud. The Emperor examined them, turned them round and round, pinched their ears, and approved their uniform. This consisted of a short-tailed green cutaway coat with an aiguillette on the right shoulder (to distinguish them from the chasseurs), white buckskin breeches, high boots with spurs, gauntlets, and a brass helmet with a leopard skin band, or turban, eagle-stamped crest, and red plume. They were given light muskets, elegant capes, and small square portmanteaux in place of the large round ones used formerly. For full dress, white plastrons and waistcoats were worn (see Plates 42b, 88).

Bessières was furious. He regarded them as fops and berated their colonel. 'When His Majesty has prescribed a uniform', he wrote, 'no one has the right to alter it in any respect. It is my recollection that he specified red plumes. Inform me by what authority you now order white ones . . .'

More weighty affairs occupied Arrighi by the end of the month: incorporating troopers from 30 Line regiments, reassigning promoted officers such as Captain

Pucheu and Lieutenant de Montarby, procuring vast orders from the master artisans, and obtaining funds.

Money was the universal preoccupation of the corps commanders. The Guard must be impeccable and ever ready, and its enemies were jealous. At the end of December General Walther demanded 250,000 francs to pay his horse grenadiers on 1 January, since his funds had been spent to clothe 300 dragoons for Poland and buy horses for the *vélites*. His men's pay was five months in arrears.

The situation of the *chasseurs à cheval* was no better. They had drawn no pay since Tilsit. Their new chief, General Lefebvre-Desnoëttes, had just left Westphalia[1] so that he might continue to serve the Emperor whom he had previously served as aide-de-camp and master of the horse. His wife was a cousin of Napoleon.

Desnoëttes combed the stables of the horse merchants of Caen and Paris and demanded 150,000 francs to settle the 'shocking arrears in pay'.

Lariboisière also demanded the money due his artillery to meet current bills. 'Pay the forage bill', the Minister told him, 'and wait for funds before paying the rest.' But no funds were forthcoming.

Napoleon knew the situation, but his mind was on economy. He abolished the baking, heating, and forage allotments, and cut the hospital allowance for troops on campaign. Henceforth, portable ovens and pine kneading troughs would be issued to provide the men in the field with bread. For the rest, they must live off the country. But what country, no one knew.

All was calm at Rueil in January 1808. The chasseurs and fusiliers felt themselves at the ends of the earth in the old barracks of the Gardes Suisses where they were reorganizing the troops at Panthémont with conscripts and veterans. It was monotonous with Malmaison empty, though a guard was still mounted in the park. They were forbidden to go to Paris, which left only the canteen for amusement. To hear them talk you wondered what the *Tondu* would do without his foot chasseurs. He might send them some news . . . He was neglecting his Grumblers, preferring to hunt at Fontainebleau. Well, that was his affair; but he would think of them soon enough when the time came to shoulder packs again . . .

25 January. Afternoon. An order arrived from the Emperor. The barracks were alerted. Two battalions of chasseurs were ordered to leave under Colonel Friederichs in battle trim, with wagons loaded and ammunition issued, before dawn next day. They had just fifteen hours in which to form companies, pass inspection, and draw equipment. It was impossible to say goodbye to friends. Where were they going? No one knew.

What did the Grumblers say? They cried '*Vive l'Empereur!*'

Like the chasseurs, units of the horse Guard were alerted. Daumesnil rounded up 200 chasseurs and Renno, 90 Mameluks. These were joined by Major Jolivet with 200 dragoons, a squadron of elite gendarmes, and Colonel Krasinski with 350 Polish light-horse fresh from Warsaw.

[1] Now become an independent kingdom under the Treaty of Tilsit. – Ed.

The Poles upped sabers and cried *'Vive l'Empereur!'* These were no mercenaries, but fine young men who had volunteered to join in the liberation of peoples. Dressed in slate blue *kurtkas* (double-breasted lancer jackets) with crimson plastrons and crimson *czapkas*[2] with the cypher 'N' emblazoned on their sunburst plaques, they wore white epaulets and an aiguillette on the right shoulder. The latter were silver for officers.

The troop's organization had been fraught with difficulties. In October the first squadron had arrived at the sumptuous stables of the Prince de Condé in Chantilly. Lt. Colonel Delaître had to wait for the second which had been held up in Warsaw for lack of funds. In vain had Marshal Davout, the governor, given dinners and proposed toasts. He had even lent them 600,000 francs. Finally, the squadron left for France.

A third detachment appeared in January. Passing through Châlons it ran afoul of the chief of police who reported: 'Each trooper is a law unto himself and races through the streets at full gallop. Drunkenness is rife and discipline nonexistent.'

Marshal Kellermann gave the Poles a warm welcome. He had known them of old and spoke their language, being a veteran of their war of independence from Russia. He recognized the silver Maltese cross – adopted as their national emblem forty years before – attached to their tricolor cockades.

Davout wrote the Emperor: 'Colonel Krasinski has risen above serious opposition, even from his own family, to go to Paris to join his troop. He is leaving Lt. Colonel Dautancourt behind to bring on the rest of the regiment.'

In Paris the Polish troopers and officers were warmly welcomed by the Guard and entertained at banquets at the Emperor's expense. The regiment was proud that its members all came from Old Poland rather than 'South Prussia'. Because of their hasty departure for Spain the handsome parade dress of a white *kurtka* with crimson overalls could not be made in Paris as planned. (Though worn by a few officers and the musicians, this uniform seems never to have been worn by the troop as a whole, see Plates 57a, 114.)

General Lefebvre-Desnoëttes was in command of the 1,000 horse Guards ordered south, with Lepic in charge of the first detachment and Dériot as chief of staff. Lepic alone knew the troops were heading for Bordeaux to join Boulart's squadron of horse artillery.

Something must be up. Since the Emperor's wagons, horses, cooks, and valets were preparing to leave Paris in charge of his equerry M. de Canisy, Napoleon's departure seemed imminent.

The Peninsula affair was the sequel to events that had dragged on since 19 July 1807. On that day Napoleon wrote Talleyrand: 'Take all possible precautions to ensure that Portugal closes her ports to the English, failing which I shall declare war on her and confiscate all British goods . . .' On 2 August Dejean had been ordered to organize the Observation Corps of the Gironde. Junot took command of this corps and crossed the Bidassoa on 18 October.

[2] Square-topped Polish headdress resembling the academic 'mortarboard', except that the earlier version had a tall connecting piece between cap and top. – Ed.

The Spanish government was aiding the French; however, Napoleon was suspicious of the court which was ruled by intrigue. On 11 October Charles IV and the Prince of the Asturias had both written letters to Napoleon. The former denounced his son, while the latter asked the Emperor's protection and the hand of a French princess in marriage. Since then Napoleon had pondered over the Spanish succession.

He knew that Godoy, who was in the pay of the French, was old, perfidious, and detested by the Spanish people and that both King and Prince were mortally afraid of him. If a revolution broke out in this proud, stubborn, and fanatic country, England would surely take advantage of it to intervene. Perhaps the Emperor should anticipate her. 'I must have peace in my rear', he told Metternich.

A moment when the rest of Europe was either conquered or submissive seemed propitious. But he must proceed cautiously, without alerting Spain or the rest of Europe or compromising his coming interview with the Tsar.

'If anyone mentions this affair to you', he wrote Caulaincourt, 'say that the anarchy prevailing at the Spanish court obliges me to intervene . . . that the people have been clamoring for my presence . . . and that I shall go to Spain; but that this must not prevent our interview . . .'

Meanwhile the Emperor remained in Paris, hunted, showed himself at the theatre with Josephine, and watched St. Petersburg and Madrid in turn. Most of the Guard remained with him.

In March, 1808, with a view towards establishing an imperial nobility, he inaugurated a *Livre d'Or* inscribed with the names of the most distinguished men in France.

Beginning where the Legion of Honor left off, Napoleon established a sort of 'general staff' composed of descendants of illustrious men, as well as his illustrious contemporaries, to be united in a new nobility. He believed the government should not break all links with the past or exclude any group, but should regard the generations as mutually interdependent; that under all regimes service rendered the nation should be rewarded by 'sovereign and citizens'; and that 'a patrimony of honor and glory should be as much revered as any other'.

The Guard was specially favored in the new investiture. Savary became Duke of Rovigo, and while waiting to be Duke of Istria, Bessières drew an income of 100,000 francs from Milan. Dorsenne, Lefebvre-Desnoëttes, Walther, and Lariboisière were made counts; and Guyot, Delaître, and Gros (despite his egregious gaffs) barons.

Though it caused gossip in the salons of the Faubourg Saint-Germain, where the ladies snickered behind their fans at Marshal Lefebvre's wife being the Duchess of Danzig, Napoleon's system derived from the honors conferred during the great days of the Monarchy rather than the last two hundred years; just as the Imperial Guard of 1808 was more nearly analogous to the guards of Philip Augustus and Saint Louis than to the *Maison du Roy*.

The master psychologist had already revived the title of *chevalier* (knight) in the Legion of Honor and had created a number in the Guard. For the Guard was the 'high school' of the Empire, the nursery in which were reared the officers and NCO's Napoleon sorely needed. The Grand Army could absorb every youth trained in the schools

For the Peninsula Napoleon had to raise two new corps under Moncey and Dupont and two divisions under Merle and Duhèsme, totaling 110,000 men of whom two-thirds were foreigners. The rest were provisional regiments of conscripts, neither uniformed nor paid, whose equipment was stamped: 'Rejected by the *Grand Armée*'. The Guard had to furnish cadres to instruct these units and build their morale.

Since he might have to leave for the frontier in a hurry, the Emperor ordered detachments of the Guard posted in echelon along the route to guard him, provide his escort, and form a small reserve for the young troops operating in the Peninsula. The first units had already left secretly under Lepic 'without knowing where they were bound'.

They reached Bordeaux on 23 February where Lepic reported the arrival of 1,180 foot chasseurs, 1,046 horse, and 174 gunners – in all, 2,400 men with 6 guns and 71 new vehicles.

The Emperor's deputy, Murat, came galloping into Bordeaux at top speed. In passing he tossed Lepic an order 'to get under way at once for Bayonne, arriving by 3 March . . .' Canisy would follow with the Emperor's baggage . . .

CHAPTER 2

Madrid

'BAYONNE is a pleasant little town in the Spanish style. Its pretty approaches are bathed by the waters of the Adour', wrote the Duchess of Abrantes (Junot's wife).

This was true. However, two hundred years ago when the Adour's course was diverted from the town, Bayonne had lost its importance and become a mere fortress enclosed by walls and bastions overlooking the green-carpeted glacis. Except for Saint-Esprit, the suburbs and monasteries had vanished. Both old and new castles were still standing, but few fine houses remained in the dark, winding streets. The largest was the old Governor's Palace on the Place D'Armes which the Grand Duke of Berg[1] occupied on his way to Spain.

The city was now alive with officers and many soldiers were encamped on the glacis. Those from Spain wore shabby uniforms, while those from the north were better dressed. The curious crowded round the horses, caissons, and baggage trains. The arsenal and magazines were teeming with activity. The roll of drums created an air of excitement. Saint-Étienne was crowded, and the road to the Bidassoa jammed with troops.

M. Detchegaray, the mayor, had the Government House prepared to receive the Emperor who was expected momentarily. His Majesty's approach was heralded by the arrival of the first detachment of the Imperial Guard on 3 March. The city was in the midst of the Mardi Gras carnival.

The town major forwarded to General Lepic an order to continue his journey to Vitoria and Burgos, leaving a squadron of Poles at Bayonne to await the second Guard detachment. This consisted of four fusilier battalions arriving from Fontainebleau, Cherbourg, Compiègne, and Rouen 'with new uniforms and four pairs of shoes per man'. At Poitiers, Colonel Boyer of the 2nd Chasseurs had received them and divided them into a regiment each of fusilier-grenadiers and fusilier-chasseurs under Lt. Colonels Lanabère and Harlet. Together with 600 horse Guards escorting the bakers, forage wagons, caissons, and field hospital from Paris, the fusiliers were due in Bayonne on 20 March.

Lepic's chasseurs were very tired and the marines were exhausted. The sailors had been marching continuously for two years – even faster than the grenadiers. For this reason Lepic allowed them to rest and follow the column at a day's march.

The road was secure and the reports encouraging. Rumor had it that the natives were welcoming the French as liberators, and the people of Viscaya building triumphal arches . . .

[1] Murat.

Where, for God's sake? Ten miles from the Bidassoa the troops marched through a mountainous country inhabited by sheep, wild bulls, and people, ragged and proud, who regarded them with indifference or hostility. They ate *fritada*, a kind of omelette, and had to 'play a whole pantomime to buy wine that stank of goatskin', wrote Lepic. They passed through Vitoria on 10 March. On the 14th they arrived at Burgos where they were reviewed by Murat.

The Grand Duke of Berg was going to Madrid next day, escorted by 300 Polish light-horse, the Mameluks, and three companies of dragoons, chasseurs, and horse grenadiers. General Lepic remained at Burgos with the rest of the Guard, with orders to have biscuits manufactured for the army, maintain cavalry posts along the Emperor's route, and welcome the fusiliers.

Events developed rapidly. On 17 March a revolution broke out at Aranjuez to which the Spanish court had repaired. The populace invaded the palace crying 'Death to Godoy!' – not because he was the Queen's lover but because they suspected him of plotting to remove the King and deliver Spain to the 'Franchutes'.

Charles IV abdicated on the 19th and Ferdinand VII was proclaimed king. On the 21st Charles protested to Napoleon against his abdication which he claimed had been forced upon him.

On the 23rd, dressed in green velvet with a white-plumed hat and red leather boots, Murat made his entrance into Madrid, escorted by the cavalry of the Guard and followed by the Line. On the same day at Bayonne the fourth squadron of Polish light-horse escorted Marshal Bessières across the town and on to Burgos where he took command of the Imperial Guard and Northern Spain.

On the 26th at Saint-Cloud Napoleon announced his departure on 3 April. He sent the following orders to Bessières:

'Send all my Guard at Burgos to the capital. Also send the rest of the Guard – infantry, cavalry, and artillery – as soon as possible to Madrid where I shall join them without delay. You must realize how important it will be for me to have all the artillery of my Guard, as well as the infantry and cavalry, in the capital. The Grand Duke of Berg has already taken between 300 and 400 men with him; the rest must follow as soon as possible.'

'Divide them up into several columns. The best marchers should be able to do 25–30 miles a day. From Burgos you can reach Madrid in nine days. The second part of my Guard, composed of the fusiliers and about 500 horse, will wait at Burgos where it should arrive on 2 or 3 April. The men will be tired and will need rest. Take steps to secure some means of transport for my baggage and suite from Burgos to Madrid. If the road . . . is very bad I should not be afraid to travel on horseback . . .'

These imprecise orders, and the movements of the Guard by weak detachments ordered six weeks in advance, were not characteristic of the Emperor. They indicated hesitation. What did he wish to do in Spain?

Madrid was a large city whose dreary streets, paved with black cobblestones, were very dirty. Ordure was piled up to the front stoops of the houses. The chasseurs and

Mameluks were billeted in a monastery near Murat's palace and declared themselves 'living in luxury, with plenty of wine . . .' The Poles joined the dragoons and horse grenadiers at the King's palace. The elite gendarmes were quartered separately, and the infantry and artillery were at the Pardo, a palace as far from Madrid as Saint-Cloud from Paris, where the Emperor was to stay. The marines guarded Murat's palace.

Here was yet another capital. After Milan, Vienna, Berlin, Warsaw, the Guard now slept in Madrid from which 'the Americas were governed'. The Sons of Glory had heard *'Vive l'Empereur!'* in all languages. However, they felt ill at ease in a country where every cobbler called himself a 'noble', though he be only a 'gutter hidalgo', loquacious, proud, and intemperate; and where the black-haired girls with thick lashes crossed themselves before and after making love, spitting out insults and curses the while.

The Grumblers were right. Since the revolt organized by the Count de Montijo at Aranjuez the Spanish affair had become a trial of strength. Godoy's arrest, the abdication, the acclamation of Ferdinand VII, the cries of 'Long Live France and Spain!' and 'Long Live Napoleon!' (who was credited with having inspired the coup d'état), the fiery caresses bestowed on the *chasseurs à cheval*, the reception of the Spanish *Carabineros* to the officers of the Guard were followed by dagger play and cries of 'Death to the French!'

In the city the number of beggars, vagabonds, and sorcerers increased. One had to keep an eye on the Lavapies quarter and Maravillas whence came the female warriors, the ruffians and revolutionists.

On 7 April the Emperor's ambassador Savary persuaded Ferdinand, the king proclaimed but not recognized by the French, to visit Napoleon 'just a few miles away . . .' Ferdinand's entourage was in favor of this act of courtesy, but the people were anxious – and not without reason.

The road from France to Spain was dotted with posts and planted with patrols. At Somosierra on Palm Sunday eve the Madrid lackeys escorting Ferdinand on horse and muleback met up with Krasinski's light-horse and hurled insults at them. The procession halted at Burgos, expecting to find the Emperor there, but found only Bessières with a picket of the Guard. Lepic observed that 'the people's affection for their young king approached fanaticism', and that in Spain royalty was a 'cult it would be dangerous to meddle with . . .'

On leaving a bullfight the chasseurs noticed that the women, who were 'cruel and had a passion for massacres', threw them glances full of hatred, and that the peasants were buying daggers and gunpowder.

At this moment the foot grenadiers arrived in Bayonne.

'My little rabbits', their commander Colonel Michel announced, 'the Emperor arrives this evening and you must not be standoffish. You must prepare to give him a good welcome.'

Wherupon the 'little rabbits' of five-foot-eleven began to brush their bearskins, roll their overcoats, polish their scabbards, whiten their breeches and cross-belts, shine their belt plates, buttons, and muskets . . . Then the 'accomplished barbers' braided their queues and powdered them with flour, and the dandies waxed their moustaches. In full dress, with drums beating, a battalion of grenadiers crossed the wooden bridge and marched to Saint-Esprit where the mayor and notables, escorted by the Guard of Honor of Bayonne, awaited the Emperor. A large crowd filled the road. The cavalry went out to meet him and reported him still a long way off. Night fell.

Nine o'clock. Here at last came the procession. Although it was Maundy Thursday, the bells of the cathedral pealed, guns thundered from the citadel, and the streets and windows were lighted. Stopping in front of the mayor, who bid him welcome, the Emperor inspected the guards of honor in their red coats. He did not like that color – it reminded him of the English.

At a brisk trot, followed by Berthier and Duroc, he crossed the Mayou bridge, glanced at the battalions of the foot Guard drawn up in the Place de la Liberté, and went to Government House.

Don Carlos had arrived two days before.

His brother Ferdinand was en route to Vitoria where he did not find the Emperor, but found instead a reassuring letter. If his father's abdication were 'an honest move', the Emperor wrote, 'if it was not forced by the Aranjuez revolt, I shall make no difficulty and shall recognize Your Royal Highness as King of Spain. Therefore, I desire to talk with Your Highness to this purpose . . .'

Ferdinand decided to proceed. But, shouting 'Viva el Rey!' the crowd barred the way to his coach and cut the traces. The elite gendarmes dispersed the mob which Ferdinand himself tried to appease. Neither French nor Spaniards knew that the Emperor had written Bessières: 'If Ferdinand retreats to Burgos, you are to arrest him'.

On 21 April the royal coaches passed the frontier. It was an abduction; even a double abduction, for the old King and Queen arrived at Bayonne with their suite on the 30th. The Spaniards would make the Emperor pay for this . . .

In Madrid in the dens of the Cebadería, Calle de San Antonio, and the sordid alleys swarming with chisperos,[2] she-asses, and prostitutes, the crapulous love-making turned to murder. Moncey's soldiers were nailed to doors under obscene placards reading: 'That p—s-pot calling himself Napoleon . . .' etc, etc. In the pulpits, the monks preached a Holy War.

Soldiers were forbidden to leave their quarters alone. Officers had to go fully armed to the theatre. Chasseurs, fusiliers, marines, dragoons, and Poles, brightly polished each day to parade 'under the most beautiful eyes in the world', grit their teeth, kept silent, and awaited orders from the Emperor. This was what it meant to belong to the Guard.

A letter written on 2 May by Charles IV to his son set the stage for disaster.

'Now Spain can be saved only by the Emperor. I have taken refuge in his camp. The Emperor has shown me letters written by you declaring your hatred for France. In wresting my crown from me you have forfeited your own. You have despoiled it of that which made it sacred to others . . .'

[2] Ruffians.

So neither Charles nor Ferdinand would return to Spain, and Napoleon was now the ruler.

Only the night before, Murat had written the Emperor from his palace in Madrid: '. . . I trust that at the moment at which I have the honor to address Your Majesty the Spanish business is finished . . .'

Was he blind? The marines and light-horse who guarded him were not. The revolution took place under their windows.

Sunday, 1 May was market day in Madrid. The parade was beautiful. Many *madrileños* visited the Emperor's tents which Canisy had erected in the gardens of the Pardo. However, what Napoleon and Murat termed the 'canaille of Madrid', and the many peasants come to town, swarmed about the Puerta del Sol and greeted a party of dragoons with catcalls.

In the evening the patrols noticed that the squares and church porches were filled to overflowing with men and women engaged in noisy discussions. They overheard such phrases as: 'Treason!' . . . 'Death to the French!' . . . 'They have kidnaped the King . . .' 'The Infante Don Francisco, who was to leave town tomorrow with his sister, will not leave . . .'

Next morning the sun rose over the royal palace. The ex-Queen of Etruria's carriage left without difficulty, but the Infante's was suddenly surrounded and its horses unhitched by the grooms, assisted by an enraged mob. Major La Grange of Murat's staff, who had come on horseback to pay his respects to the departing Queen, was unhorsed and beaten. He was eventually rescued by a patrol of the Guard. Colonel Friederichs marched to the palace at the head of the fusilier battalion and the Polish light-horse. In a few moments they charged the mob, sweeping it back into the Plaza Mayor.

'Hide your cockades, gentlemen', a passing priest advised two marine officers, 'or you will be massacred'.

By this time Murat had ordered the drummers to beat the General Alarm, and had alerted the Mameluks at Carabanchel in the southeastern quarter, leaving the marines to guard his palace. He galloped to the Portillo de San Vicente, where the Guard was concentrated, and ordered it to march in concentric circles on the Plaza Mayor and the Puerta del Sol. The fusiliers, led by the cavalry of the Guard, filed through the Calle de la Platería.

The Mameluks and cuirassiers were met in the Calle de Toledo by a hail of rocks and bullets fired from the windows above. Below, the mob was thrown back and sabered without mercy. The chasseurs and several patrols of Mameluks under Daumesnil and Renno were ordered by Murat's aide-de-camp to the Retiro to join Grouchy, which meant crossing the city from west to east. Near the crowded Puerta del Sol they slashed right and left with their sabers to open a passage.

The popular fury was loosed upon the Mameluks. These 'pagan sons of dogs' were assailed by women who jumped onto the cruppers of their horses and bit them until the blood flowed, knocking them to the ground. Heads rolled under the scimitars. In the Calle de Alcalá Daumesnil was pinned under the second horse shot from under him that day. Wounded in the knee, he was rescued by Lieutenant Chahin' who himself had been hit and blinded by his own blood. Before a house in the Carrera de San Jeronimo two Mameluks fell to the pavement, shot from the window above. Furious, their comrades entered the house, killed all the occupants – both men and women – and threw their heads into the street. 'An even hundred . . .' Murat wrote the Emperor.

Towards two in the afternoon the canaille was finally subdued; but then the reprisals began. Tied in pairs to the stirrups of the Mameluks and chasseurs, the condemned were dragged to the Pardo, the Retiro, and the Convent del Jesús where firing-parties awaited them. Meanwhile, the Spanish garrison, faithful to its orders, had not stirred.

Between two thunderstorms which rent the calm of the fine night one heard stray shots, fired at Frenchmen lost in the alleys of the southwest quarter.

What were the consequences? At first, bloodshed – how much, we do not know. We know only that 31 Frenchmen were dead and 114 wounded; among the latter were Daumesnil and 20 chasseurs, all the officers of the Mameluks, and Commander Kerveguen of the marines. Then – war.

The Emperor was preparing for it.

CHAPTER 3

The Marines at Baylén

THE events in the Peninsula were bound to have repercussions in Europe. Consequently, on 12 April 1808 Napoleon signed a decree increasing the artillery of the Guard to a staff, four horse batteries, six new companies of foot, a pontoon company, a park of 60 guns, and two train battalions.

Lariboisière proposed as commander of the foot artillery 'a lieutenant colonel of the Line who can organize the new companies and instruct them so as to make them capable of appreciating the honor of belonging to His Majesty's Guard . . .' This man was Lt. Colonel Drouot of the 3rd Foot Artillery. Boulart of the *vélite* regiment was appointed major and several captains and lieutenants were transferred from the horse batteries, among them Lallemand and the Polytechnician Le Français.

In Lariboisière's opinion every man in the corps, whatever his job, should be an artilleryman – even the drummers and the mathematics professor (who in this case happened to be a veteran of seven campaigns). What the General really proposed was a purge.

On 14 August he recommended that fourteen officers of the horse batteries whom he considered undesirable be transferred to the line, and gave his reasons. The Emperor accepted his recommendation; but the plebeians of the corps like Couin and Dogureau protested that Lariboisière was a '*grand seigneur* of the old regime', and therefore prejudiced. It was an artillery war.

On 4 September the Emperor assigned the task of arbitration to the new war minister. Next day Clarke proposed a solution.

He wrote that General Lariboisière had suggested dropping the officers because they had not served in the artillery before entering the Guard. It seemed quite proper to the Minister that the corps should be officered only by men trained in gunnery . . . 'however, His Majesty might conciliate all parties concerned if, instead of sending these officers of the artillery to the Line, he approved their transfer to other corps of the foot or horse Guard'.

Clarke presented two decrees for the Emperor's signature: the first nominating the fourteen officers to the infantry and cavalry of the Guard; the second annulling the decree of 27 August.

The Imperial decision read as follows:

'Saint-Cloud, 6 September.

'To the Minister of War:

'I am undecided about the two decrees you presented to me concerning the artillery officers of my Guard. The decree already signed by me concerns those serving there today . . . I cannot conceive how one can say that these officers have not served in the artillery. I do not know whether they graduated from any school, but all of them have served on battlefields for the past 14 years – which should certainly be worth as much as the study of polygons! For the rest, if there are some among them who should be dropped from the Guard I must have a separate report on each. The decrees I sign in confidence should never involve exclusion from my Guard unless I have individual reports . . .'

The Emperor alone commanded the Guard. No one had the right, nor the power, to touch this prerogative. Whoever belonged to the Guard was under his authority and protection. His gratitude to those who gave him loyalty and devotion conferred grandeur upon the word 'service' which the vain and the mediocre consider demeaning.

But Napoleon's bounty and indulgence towards the soldiers of his Guard did not exclude firmness, severity, or justice. The Guard had no judge but the Emperor. On 31 December Quartermaster Robert, who was a liar, was arrested by order of the Emperor. General Couin and Lt. Colonels Dogureau and Digeon, who had failed to administer their commands in a wholesome manner, were turned out of the Guard. They would have honorable careers in the Line, but would not be readmitted to the order of popular knighthood whose grand master was Napoleon.

'Palace troops are terrifying', the Emperor wrote at Saint Helena, 'and become more dangerous as the sovereign becomes more autocratic. My Imperial Guard would have been a fatal instrument in any hands but mine.'

On 17 April the Emperor moved into the Château of Marrac at Bayonne. The grenadiers slept in tents outside and the duty squadron of the Polish light-horse kept watch, their horses always saddled.

Learning of the insurrection in Madrid, the Emperor took advantage of it to force the abdication of both Ferdinand VII and Charles IV, sending the first to Valençay and the second to Compiègne. He had issued the following order to Bessières:

'Avoid deploying troops in garrisons and small detachments. Hold the capitals by concentrating your forces . . . If the countryside revolts, send out mobile columns to teach it a lesson.' And to Murat: 'Do not spare the canaille of Madrid if it rises.'

'Since he loved us so much, and since we would have given our lives for him', wrote Lieutenant Grivel of the marines in his memoirs, 'why could not the Emperor have listened to our ideas on his Spanish campaign? He could thus have appreciated the effect his policies were having on the hearts of his soldiers . . . However far we came from predicting the misfortunes that were soon to befall us, we were revolted by the injustice of it all.'

Orders went forth to prepare for demonstrations, win over public opinion, and begin at once to regenerate the government so as to win support from the more enlightened citizens.

Meanwhile, Bessières was ordered to fortify Burgos, and Murat to put several buildings in Madrid into a posture of defence and recall all Swiss troops serving outside the capital.[1] This last was of the utmost importance. The Emperor concluded: 'Soldiers – especially those of my Guard – must be forbidden to walk about the towns.'

He was right. For, led by the clergy, all Spain was on fire within two weeks. Minor rebellions broke out in Arragon and Catalonia, and Lefebvre-Desnoëttes was sent to Toledo and Saragossa with a few squadrons of the Guard and 5,000 infantry. There was a large uprising in Galicia and a terrible one in Andalusia. Bessières was ordered to suppress the first, and Dupont to put down the second.

Meanwhile, Joseph Bonaparte had been proclaimed King of Spain and was en route from Bayonne to Madrid on 9 July. But he could enter his capital only behind an army sounding the trumpets of conquest.

The trumpets of Lasalle and the drums of the fusiliers of the Guard sounded on 14 July at Medina-del-Rio-Seco where Bessières with 16,000 men – including 2,200 from the Guard with six guns – destroyed a force of 21,000 under La Cuesta and Blake on the parched banks of the Sequillo. Informed of this at Burgos on the 15th, Joseph resumed his journey and entered his deserted capital, escorted by Guard veterans, on the 20th.

Murat, ill and full of spite for not being made King of Spain himself, had quit the city on 12 June. General Savary was sent by the Emperor to command the garrison and arrived on the 14th, bringing instructions to abandon the system of mobile columns and guard all the important points. However, the task begun must be finished; all Spain must be brought under subjection.

Dupont had left on 4 May for Andalusia and Cadiz with Barbou's division, Fresia's cavalry, and the marines of the Guard and had not been heard from since. The latter were ordered to reinforce the crews of Admiral Rosily which had taken refuge in Cadiz after Trafalgar.

The marines left Toledo under Captain Daugier on 24 May and crossed La Mancha singing. Daugier was a witty man and his officers well educated. Their gaiety on the march must be credited to Don Quixote; for there were Maritorne and Dulcinea, the peasants and windmills, the brigands' dens and oak forests, unchanged.

There were also the 'jagged silhouettes of the Sierra Morena' and the black rocks of Dispeña Perros, the gateway to Andalusia, so named by the Vandals. Granary, cellar, garden, and stable of Spain, the loss of this country had been eternally regretted by the Moors who had occupied it for eight hundred years.

The marines formed the rear-guard of the army with Privé's dragoons. 'The air here is more pungent with balsam', wrote Grivel, 'and the aspect more smiling.'

The Emperor had predicted correctly that this 'would be a military promenade'. The journey ended on 5 June at Andújar on the green waters of the Guadalquivir. Though perfumed by pink laurels, the town was very hot.

Bad news arrived from every quarter. There had been a general uprising in Andalusia and Estremadura. The road to Portugal was cut and the French left flank was menaced by the Army of Granada. Ahead, the Army of Andalusia was marching from Seville to Cordoba. The bridge at Alcolea was strongly defended by the enemy.

[1] Some Swiss troops in Spanish service had joined the French. – Ed.

On the 7th this bridge was captured by Dupont. The marines, supported by dragoons, halted an enemy column that appeared in their rear. 'Though few in number, and though it was the first time the sailors had ever formed a line of battle', Daugier wrote Marshal Mortier, 'these brave men displayed the greatest ardor'.

While Dupont was advancing on Cordoba the marines stayed behind to repair the bridge and its defences and guard the passage of the troops, field hospital, wagon train, and baggage which were continually harassed by enemy sharpshooters. Then they proceeded to Cordoba which was given over to pillage. They stayed in a monastery outside the walls.

A wave of terror ran through the army. Not a single courier sent by Dupont to Madrid to ask for help had got through. Many Frenchmen had been massacred. After the column left Andújar the natives had emptied the hospital, and sick, wounded, orderlies, and doctors were tortured to death, buried alive, sawn in two between boards, hung, or mutilated. Finally, they learned that, overwhelmed by the Cadiz artillery, Admiral Rosily had been obliged to surrender.

General Castaños was marching from Seville to Cordoba with 27,000 men. Dupont ordered a retreat. He halted at Andújar on 18 June.

Torrid heat, clogged wells, and the stench of burnt corpses in houses still burning made the town unbearable. An immense convoy of wagons loaded with gold and treasure pillaged in the city of Cordoba was there, but nothing to eat. The marines harvested grain, built ovens, baked bread, and maintained order. Their patrols roamed the streets and detachments guarded the unloading of several requisitions of food.

The marines were unhappy. Accustomed to warfare beyond the Rhine, where they had met the enemy only in combat, they were exasperated to find him in their midst. They had nothing but scorn for these loquacious, miserable, arrogant people, and counted men and women traitors whose hatred was ferocious and who boasted of their determination to drive the French out of Spain, regardless of reprisals.

'You are now masters of the land under your feet', they hissed, 'but by God, we will drive you off it!'

That evening at the inn, where the officers were having supper, Ensign Barberi dressed up in an old cape and, with a shabby *montera* of black velvet on his head, proceeded to lampoon the *alcalde*:[2] 'Alas, *señor*, we have no bread – we have only clear water and the wind that blows ...'

Then they danced and made merry.

Vedel's division had left Toledo on 16 June to join Dupont whom he had not heard from since. The march was a nightmare through scenes of horror that upset the conscripts. At 5 a.m. on the 27th Vedel's advance guard made contact with Commander Baste in the village of Santa Elena.

Baste was a good sailor and an energetic infantry commander. He had marched out from Jaén where he had been requisitioning food. Things were terrible in Andalusia, he reported. The officer he sent ahead had been killed by the Spaniards who were scattered through the mountains. Baste had had to fight a bloody engagement to gain

[2] mayor.

PLATE 58

Soldats
de la marine
de la garde

PLATE 59

Entry of King Joseph into Madrid
(From an original wash drawing by J. L. Rugendas)

PLATE 60

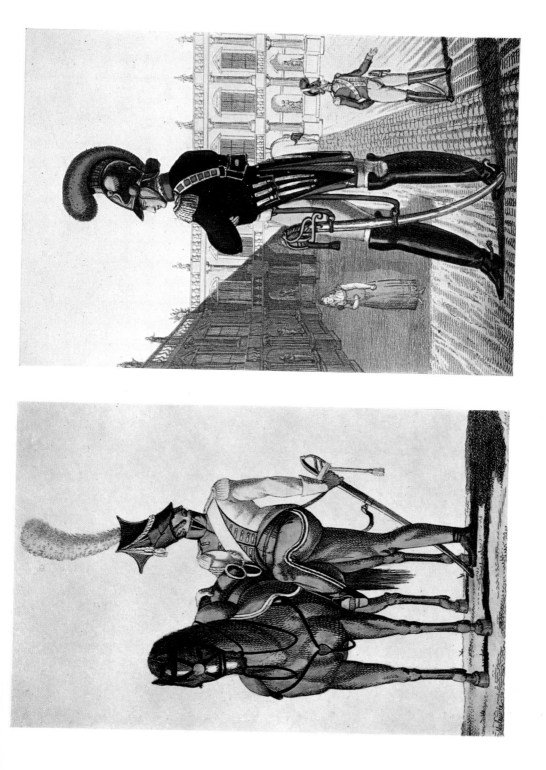

PLATE 61

a) Grivel
(*After contemp. portrait*)

b) Dupont
(*Engr. Forestier*)

c) Royal Family of Spain
(*Colored aquatint by Donas*)

d) Murat as Grand Duke of Berg
(*Col. engraving*, chez *Basset*)

e) Drouot
(*Engr. Charon after Aubry*)

PLATE 62

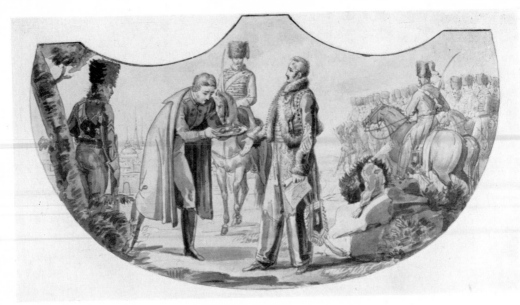

a) Lasalle at Stettin
(*From an original drawing attributed to H. Vernet*)

b) Subjugation of Estremadura by the French
(*From an original drawing by Naudet*)

entrance to the town whose narrow streets were steep and winding. Soldiers who entered the houses never came out. His own men had killed women and children. Finally, he had succeeded in taking out 15,000 rations, and his men took a lot more. 'Ah, there's a good commander!' they said. 'After three of his speeches we gave the houses back voluntarily . . .'

It was a bad war, and the Emperor in his Château of Marrac did not realize it. He wrote optimistically to Joseph on 14 July: 'With 20,000 men Dupont will sweep all before him . . . With 25,000 he will have more than sufficient forces to accomplish great things . . .'

But he had barely 15,000. . .

Napoleon continued: 'If Dupont should suffer a reverse, it would be of little consequence . . .' We shall see about that.

At Andújar Dupont found himself in a vulnerable position which could easily be turned from the roads to Mengibar and Baylén. He was finally joined by Vedel whom he left at Baylén to watch the road to Jaén. Later several battalions of Gobert's division appeared. These he detached to guard his communications. Then he strung out his units in echelon and waited.

The Spaniards did not. Castaños, commanding an army of 34,000 in Andalusia, decided to immobilize Dupont at Andújar while the Swiss Colonel Reding and the French émigré Coupigny marched from the south with 18,000 men to join forces at Baylén and take him in the rear.

Dupont believed himself lucky to have an old soldier and brave general like Vedel, to whom he had attached Captain Baste, holding the ford of the Guadalquivir at Baylén. But Vedel was no longer there. He had left to seek a nonexistent enemy reported at Santa Elena, leaving the Jaén road defended by only two battalions.

At 9 a.m. on 18 July, 35,000 Spaniards reached Baylén from the south and straddled the road to Andújar, taking up positions in the woods and hills west of the town on the plateau descending to the pass of La Cruz Blanca and the bridge over the Rumblar.

Hearing this news, Dupont decided that he and his 9,000 men would have to run the gauntlet through this force to escape from Castaños who was separated from the French only by the stone bridge at Andújar.

At ten that night Daugier's marines and the sappers collected all the matériel and prepared to leave quietly at midnight. The battalion was ordered to guard the rear of Dupont's little force which had set out at six that evening. There was not a breath of air; the night was sultry and depressing. The men marched in silence. The long train of wagons, heavily loaded with loot, kicked up clouds of dust.

At nine the next morning Lieutenant Grivel's crew, the last of the marines, reached the Rumblar bridge with orders to defend it to the death. A battle was raging ahead. Daugier's battalion was rushed forward to attack the redoubt north of the road but was unable to penetrate it. With great bravery the marines returned twice to the attack but were repulsed each time.

If only Vedel would come! He had left La Carolina at 4 a.m. but it took him twelve hours to march 28 kilometers.

Towards evening Dupont placed himself at the head of the marines of the Guard who were ployed in column along the road. Sword in hand and followed by his staff, he ordered the drummers to beat the Charge and advanced. What remained of his division moved forward under a withering fire. Dupont was wounded, the marines' attack repulsed, and some of the Swiss, refusing to fight against their compatriots, deserted to the enemy. (The Emperor had foreseen this when he ordered Murat to recall all Swiss troops to the capital.)

Under a broiling sun 3,000 men, worn out after marching all night and fighting for ten hours, were left with the colors. But they still held out. The marines even advanced, but were pushed back into the olive groves with heavy losses. Daugier lost a third of his men. Ten officers were wounded, among them Grivel who had been trying to defend the Rumblar bridge against the whole Spanish division that had surrounded it since four that afternoon. 'We were in a mouse-trap', he said.

Barbou returned from the front and announced: 'We have arrived at the Caudine Forks'.[3] Then Grivel realized that Dupont was going to surrender.

On 22 July the convention of Andújar was signed. Under its terms Dupont, the army, and the marines of the Guard were all prisoners of war; as was Vedel who was surrendered with the rest without having taken part in the action.

Only one regiment refused to surrender. This was the 116th Line Infantry which succeeded in rejoining the French army under cover of a rear-guard led by Second Lieutenant Bugeaud, the young aristocrat who had written his sister for sympathy from the *vélite* school at Fontainebleau. The convention stipulated that the French were entitled to the honors of war and guaranteed repatriation to Rochefort.

The evening before, Napoleon left Bayonne for Paris full of confidence as to the outcome of affairs in Spain. He was more concerned about affairs at home, since Austria was arming and Talleyrand had turned traitor.

News of the capitulation at Baylén reached him at Bordeaux on 1 August. His first reaction was: 'The battle of Medina-del-Rio-Seco crushed the army of Galicia; the battle of Andalusia has removed 15,000 men from my army. Doubtless the two events do not cancel out; however, they balance to some extent . . .'

Napoleon had congratulated Dupont upon taking Cordoba and had anticipated his subsequent defeat. The result of his surrender was aggravated by the fact that the Spaniards reneged on their signed convention and failed to release their captives.

The Emperor's temper was aggravated to the same degree. His cries of rage hid his remorse for having isolated 15,000 men, including a unit of his Guard, in an exasperated Spain, and his suffering at this military rebuff to the *Grande Armée*. The moral effect of the capitulation at Baylén was considerable.

After Joseph fled from Madrid Napoleon had nothing left in Spain but Barcelona, where Duhèsme was beseiged, and a small area around Bilbao, Burgos, and Tudela.

[3] In 321 B.C. a Roman army was trapped in that pass and forced to surrender and 'pass under the yoke' by the Samnites. – Ed.

Portugal was eluding his grasp. An English army under Wellington had debarked at the mouth of the Mondego on 1 August. This lightning stroke rocked the foundations of the European Confederation, raised the hopes of his enemies, and frightened Joseph and his general staff out of their wits. Only the Emperor remained calm.

The Grand Army was disbanded. The Army of the Rhine of 90,000 men under Davout held the territory between the Rhine and the Elbe. The Army of Spain, composed of six army corps and a reserve of 200,000 men, was sent to the Pyrenees under the Emperor's command.

CHAPTER 4

The Poles at Somosierra

Now Napoleon had to prepare a maneuver with armies grouped in echelon on interior lines, and the whole of Europe as his theater of operations. Since the Guard must be prepared to follow him, he ordered all its matériel and administration based on Paris from where it could be sent either to Spain or Germany.

The remainder of the Guard in Paris prepared to leave for Spain on 20 September. This included 2,400 horse (chasseurs, dragoons and grenadiers) and 3,200 veteran infantry, with two companies each of horse and foot artillery and 36 guns.

The Emperor introduced a new principle, already tested in the Line, into the Guard. He increased the number of regiments by dividing one regiment of 800 men into two of 400. This had the twofold advantage of stiffening inexperienced troops with a higher proportion of officers and NCO's, and facilitating sudden expansion, since it was easier to procure conscripts than cadres. But the new system was costly.

General Walther, commanding the Guard in Paris, was ordered to bring it up to strength with levies from the Line, including the 36 regiments in Italy, Naples, and Dalmatia, and 20 in Germany with Davout.

Walther was given only forty days to do the job. Infantry was hard to procure. For example, how long would it take the 79th Regiment in Dalmatia to find ten soldiers five-foot-nine with four years' service and deliver them to Paris? The 29th in Rome had only four, and asked if five-foot-eight would do for a grenadier. The Minister advised the Emperor to refuse – the day he was encamped before Somosierra.

Even the cavalry was having trouble filling its ranks. Some Walloon Guards Daumesnil had recruited for the Mameluks were expelled by the Emperor who was 'astonished that this good man should be possessed of such an idea'.

In the last three months of 1808, 3,125 conscripts were assigned to the Guard, of whom 3,122 showed up at the Paris depots. Only 116 were subsequently lost through desertion, retirement, or death.

The uniform problem was becoming serious. 'The color blue is the best ... Besides, it is known as our color throughout Europe', the Emperor wrote Dejean on 11 July. But because of the blockade, there was no more indigo. Now that the grenadiers' coats were dyed 'with plants grown in the Empire' (principally woad), their color was quite unpredictable.

In Burgos Lefebvre-Desnoëttes requested red plumes for the colpacks[1] of his chasseurs who would keep the old red and green ones for their felt hats (see Plate 113).

---

[1] Cylindrical fur headdresses worn by the chasseurs (see Plate 65). – Ed.

Was such foppery necessary when the artillery was still lacking some indispensable fittings required to hold its gun carriages together on the execrable Spanish roads?

Walther was given until 1 October to double the number of foot and horse Guard regiments, as well as procure 36 guns with teams and transport for 48,000 rations.

Everyone worked like beavers; however, their task was like Penelope's[2] since every day men were being transferred to the Line as officers and NCO's, requiring new clothing to be drawn and training begun for the replacements.

Napoleon reviewed the Guard minutely on 11 September. Finally, on the 27th he went to Erfurt to meet Alexander. The Tsar would not commit himself to oppose Austria and Napoleon had to be content with a mere promise of future assistance.

On 2 October he ordered Clarke to dispatch General Walther to the Pyrenees with half the infantry of the Guard and 24 guns. Half the cavalry was to be at Bayonne on the 30th. Lefebvre-Desnoëttes was left in Paris with the rest, ready to leave.

This seemed only prudent; for though the Tsar would probably renew the alliance eventually, nothing had yet been signed. Time pressed, and it was a long way to Spain where Joseph was piling one stupidity on top of another. The rest of the Guard was to follow after 12 October, the date on which Napoleon was to renew his convention with Alexander. Meanwhile, he 'shut his eyes to avoid seeing the future'.

Still master of his movements, if uneasy in his mind, Napoleon rode back to Paris from the meeting at Erfurt. Surely this war would spread to the east since both Russia and England were fanning the flames. The Emperor had granted the Tsar a few concessions so as to keep his hands free for the next few months – or even weeks.

A new Grand Army was commencing operations beyond the Pyrenees under Victor, Moncey, Lefebvre, Gouvion-Saint-Cyr, and Ney. The Emperor's orders proliferated. He warned his ministers he would need a powerful reserve for the new army and for Germany.

On 28 October he created the 'conscripts of the Guard'. Recently, 5,360 conscripts from the classes of 1806–9 had been assigned to the fusiliers and the first 500 had already left for Bayonne. The rest were now at Rueil and Courbevoie where they did nothing but draw – rather slowly – their coats, shakos, and the buttons of the Guard.

Now, around 5,000 more conscripts were divided between the chasseurs and grenadiers of the Old Guard in Paris at the rate of 300 to a company of 100 veterans. The latter functioned as their NCO's and the company officers directed their training. Paid the same as the 'Paris infantry', at least half would be ready before the middle of December. In the chasseur barracks at Panthémont and the École Militaire, and those of the grenadiers at Versailles, the veterans had to train the conscripts in six weeks, in addition to guarding the palaces. The conscripts were carefully rated and the best assigned to the fusiliers.[3]

On 30 October Napoleon left Rambouillet. Four days later he entered Bayonne, 530 miles away. The weather was miserable; nevertheless, except for the artillery which

[2] Odysseus' wife who wove a tapestry each day during his twenty-year absence and unraveled it each night to avoid committing herself to her suitors. – Ed.

[3] The rest were known as 'conscript-grenadiers' and 'conscript-chasseurs', later becoming *tirailleurs* and *voltigeurs*. – *Ibid.*

had left La Fère on 10 October, the Imperial Guard was already in Bayonne, quartered in shacks around the Château of Marrac.

Where was the army? What were Victor, Ney, and Bessières doing? No one knew anything but it was rumored that things were going badly. Actually, the troops were scattered and the corps confused. Lefebvre was making blunders; Joseph was frightened and understood none of the strategy. As for his chief of staff Jourdan, 'his ineptitude defied all comprehension'.

Fortunately, the main Spanish forces were isolated. Blake was shut up in the Durango valley with 35,000 men and Castaños and Palafox were on the Ebro, near Tudela, with 60,000. These might be divided and beaten from Burgos. Thirty thousand English under Sir John Moore were still in Portugal, near Almeida.

Beware, fanatic Capuchins, furious women, rebel hidalgos, and jealous marshals! 'The Emperor is taking command of his armies in person.'

At 6 a.m. on 4 November the Emperor and his Guard entered Spain, escorted by Lefebvre-Desnoëttes' chasseurs and guarded by horse grenadiers posted along the route. The Guard carried provisions for four days and planned to 'advance as far as possible'. They marched thirty miles to Tolosa which was lighted as bright as day. The weather was cold and the road was swept by an icy wind; but the men sang because all was strange and picturesque.

Lasalle's division galloped ahead, policing the countryside with a heavy hand. The soldiers found the villages deserted, ravaged, and burned. Spain was a mixture of squalor and grandeur, drenched in poverty.

On the evening of 5 November, having ridden 87 miles in thirty-six hours, the chasseurs led the Emperor into Vitoria as the bells pealed. The fusiliers of Lepic and Friederichs were at their posts. Daumesnil's chasseurs and Jolivet's dragoons shivered at the communication posts along the route. King Joseph was in Vitoria with his household and bodyguard, also Canisy with the Emperor's baggage.

The Emperor ordered his headquarters set up apart from Joseph's, to the latter's chagrin. Lepic's foot chasseurs took over the Emperor's guard. They felt lost and abandoned in this miserable country where the men waged war with knives, the women bewitched then murdered you, and the priests were miserable scoundrels.

The Guard, now commanded by General Walther, had to use the utmost vigilance in protecting the Emperor and his headquarters as well as themselves. Several dragoons lured to a drinking bout were massacred. General Lasalle apprehended the culprits, one of them a woman, and hanged them. Arrighi's men guarded the scaffold. Spaniards were forbidden to cut down the corpses on pain of being strung up in their stead.

To compensate for these horrors the resourceful men 'liberated' some chests containing precious objects which turned out to be silver trumpets consigned to the Royal Guard of Spain. They were appropriated by the dragoons. Not until after Wagram did Napoleon present them to his brother Joseph.

His right flank covered by Lefebvre and Victor and his left by Moncey, the Emperor, with 50,000 troops of Soult's division, defeated Belveder's small corps on the road to Burgos.

The horse Guard found plenty of entertainment after the battle. At Gamonal there was a luncheon party with excellent wine, followed by a hunt with oxen for game. In the evening the officers gambled away their pay. Arrighi lost 100 *napoléons* – a large sum even for a colonel of the Guard.

After a lively fight and a brilliant charge by Bessières and the horse Guard, the army entered Burgos on the 11th amid scenes of pillage defying description. The streets were lined with corpses. Carrying lighted tapers, thousands of famished soldiers of the Grand Army sacked the deserted houses, starting fires, and threatened the inhabitants who had taken refuge in the Cathedral. Pickets of the Guard were sent to protect the latter with orders to shoot anyone who approached. The Cartuja and other monasteries were ravaged and converted into stables. Tombs were opened and soldiers walked over bones and bits of shrouds. Accursed country! Accursed war!

A squadron of horse grenadiers tethered their horses in the garden of a monastery and fell into a trap. Lured by an urchin to 'come in and quench his thirst', one trooper did not return. A grenadier who went in search of him also disappeared. Some men of their troop returning from a foraging detail conducted an investigation, sabers in hand. They found the child, followed him, and discovered their two comrades with their heads cut off. They arrested eight monks and threw them all out of the window.

Meanwhile, the foot artillery from La Fère arrived in Burgos with some of its gun carriages hitched to cows. Lt. General Count de Law de Lauriston, commander of the Legion of Honor and aide-de-camp to the Emperor, had relieved Lariboisière as chief of the Guard artillery.

The Emperor assigned six guns to each infantry corps, twelve to the cavalry, and set up a reserve of six twelve-pounders from the park of the 1st Corps.

Feeding the army was a problem in this barren land. The artisans had not yet been grouped into a single work battalion, but were divided as before into five companies under an adjutant in charge of bread and wine, assisted by a lieutenant in charge of forage and a second in charge of livestock. All three belonged to the Old Guard and wore the Legion of Honor.

The transport chief Lapierre commanded a train company of 48 drivers; however, each Guard regiment had its own wagonettes, caissons, and carts drawn by mules and donkeys, since horse-drawn vehicles were unwieldy on the bad Spanish roads.

A company of 25 men and an officer manned the ambulances carrying the field hospital and medical personnel of the Guard.

The Guard in Spain mustered around 10,000 men, though most of its units were under strength, a situation prevailing throughout the army in general. Used to thinking on a grand scale, the Emperor's optimistic orders inspired confidence in the men who had to execute them, even when he asked the impossible.

Soon the Guard began to curse the war in Spain. It was high time the *Tondu* put a stop to it. The soldiers could not stomach misery without end or compensation. Forty-three fusilier-grenadiers had deserted during the retreat from Madrid. The youngsters were gloomy and no longer sang. They came to dread the smoky huts in

133

the villages where men and beasts were huddled together and where the fleas in their pallets were simply indestructible. They had been better off in Germany where the hog was king. There the women did not look at them with fire in their eyes – quite the contrary! What were they doing in this ruined land where, marching thirty miles a day, one ate only what he could carry?

'Shut up, little monkeys! That's the affair of the *Tondu* who knows more than we do and depends on us.'

An order was issued to 'shoot any man caught looting'. And another: 'The colonel and grenadiers of my Guard will be responsible for my large coach. An officer and three sentries will be posted each day to guard it. The coach contains the state papers which must never fall into enemy hands. The colonel shall set fire to it and burn its contents before permitting anything whatever to be removed . . .'

To whom could the Emperor confide his secrets if not to the Guard? 'You have not followed my private life closely enough to realize how well I am guarded, even in France, by my most trusted and experienced soldiers', he wrote the King of Naples in 1806.

The Polish light-horse had been sent away to be trained in maneuvers and discipline by General Durosnel, the Emperor's aide-de-camp and governor of the Corps of Pages. 'He took us under his wing', one of his pupils wrote. Then Lasalle, who – were he not a holy terror – would have commanded the cavalry of the Guard, had been assigned the task of pulling the regiment together and had succeeded brilliantly.

'It was in General Lasalle's school that we learned outpost duty', wrote one of the officers. 'We have kept a precious memory of this general in whom all the lovable and imposing qualities of a born marshal were combined . . . He should have replaced the Grand Duke of Berg (Murat) to whom he was vastly superior . . .'

In honor of the Poles, this extraordinary man composed a terrible verse to the tune of their regimental march which he immortalized by singing it as he led them into battle:

'The French were once in Poland,
Now the Poles have come to Spain;
Europe will see them both command
Her peoples without shame;
What nation is so strong
As to resist for long?
For Poles and Frenchmen, in one breath,
Could put all men on earth to death!'

Now fully trained and in daily contact with the horse grenadiers and chasseurs of the Guard, the Poles had acquired a polish and discipline that made their regiment outstanding. They were soon to prove themselves.

Due to a misunderstanding between Ney and Moncey, the Emperor failed to envelop Castaños. Palafox had shut himself up in Saragossa. Joseph must be brought back to his capital at all costs. Therefore, Napoleon decided to march on Madrid by way of Aranda and Somosierra where the road crossed the Guadarrama mountains.

On 29 November he marched with Victor's corps, the Guard, and the cavalry reserve to Boceguillas, a village north of the mountains.

When Friederichs' and Lanabère's fusiliers of Savary's advance guard were thrown back by armed peasants, Kozietulski's light-horse squadron was relieved in the Emperor's escort by horse grenadiers and chasseurs and sent forward on outpost duty. Then Savary was brought to the rear by Berthier who explained that 'His Majesty does not propose to expose the soldiers of his Guard in advance of the army'.

The rest of the light-horse joined the bivouac around the Emperor.

30 November. Dawn. A thick fog enveloped the army. The Emperor arrived, followed by the third Polish squadron, now restored to his escort. The cavalry of the advance guard was formed in line of battle in a meadow bordering a stone bridge across the Duratón. Colonel Piré, their commander, reported that the Spaniards were badly frightened. He could hear them talking. (In the fog one could see nothing.)

Sent on reconnaissance, Lejeune confirmed the report. A detachment of Poles sent to the right flank returned with a prisoner and brought him to the Emperor who was sitting on a stool before the fire. The man was terrified of reprisal. (All along the route from Burgos the French had run across corpses with their noses and ears cut off.) Finally, a swig of brandy loosened the prisoner's tongue and he gave a clear report.

The road ahead was good. Marked with stone pillars, it wound for three kilometers between rocky cliffs up to the *puerta*, or pass, 1,500 meters above. At the mouth of the gorge was a house and, farther on, a small village inhabited by shepherds. Since the 18th, 9,000 infantry of Benito San Juan's army had been entrenching themselves on the heights. A battery of four guns was posted at each bend in the road.

A light-horseman standing by the fire lit his pipe in the Emperor's presence.

'You might at least thank His Majesty for the privilege,' his lieutenant scolded.

'What good would that do here?' replied the trooper. Then, pointing to the top of the mountain, he added: 'I'll thank him up there.'

The soldiers of the 96th Regiment passed by on the road. To the right and left the 24th and 9th Light Infantry were already engaged on the heights. These belonged to Ruffin's division of Victor's corps, the vanguard of the army.

9 a.m. The battle was joined. The men could not see thirty feet ahead. They must wait for their flanks to advance. The fusillade increased and Spanish cannon balls began falling at the Emperor's feet.

11.30 a.m. The sun pierced through the fog, revealing the rock-bound and barren landscape. Piré's cavalry advanced and then retreated.

'It's impossible!' Piré exclaimed.

The Emperor cracked his riding-whip. 'Impossible? I do not know the meaning of the word!' he rasped. Then, turning to the escort: 'Take that position for me – at a gallop.'

The order struck the third Polish squadron as a challenge. A provocative, extravagant, impossible order – but nevertheless an order from the Emperor.

'Trot!' Immediately, Kozietulski raised his saber and led his 150 horsemen forward in columns of four. Under a withering fire, he knocked out three batteries in succession while Lieutenant Niegolewski took the fourth with the last troop, then fell, his body pierced by eleven wounds. The Spanish gunners and foot soldiers, slashed, pierced, pounded under foot, fled in wild disorder towards the pass and Somosierra, Buitrago – even Madrid.

Eighty-three horsemen were left on the road. All seven officers were either killed or wounded. The aide-de-camp Philippe de Ségur, who had galloped off with them for a lark, was severely wounded. The sergeant major of the first troop captured a flag.

The charge had lasted just seven minutes. The rest of the light-horse took off at a headlong pace with the cavalry of the Guard and rode like a whirlwind into Buitrago that evening by moonlight.

Leaning over the bleeding Niegolewski, as he lay beside the guns he had captured, the Emperor took off his own cross of the Legion of Honor and pinned it on the wounded man.

'Would that many a youth might live to see such a day!' this heroic scion of the Polish knights wrote forty-seven years later.

At Buitrago on 1 December the Emperor ordered the *Demi-ban* sounded by the trumpeters of Colonel Krasinski's regiment to which, drawn up in line of battle, he awarded sixteen stars of the Legion of Honor, divided equally between officers and men. Then he took off his hat and cried: 'You are worthy to belong to my Old Guard. Honor to the bravest of the brave!'

The foot grenadiers drained a bumper in their honor, and the 13th Bulletin reported: 'Guns, flags, muskets, soldiers – all were taken, destroyed, or captured; the Regiment has covered itself with glory and shown itself worthy to belong to the Imperial Guard.'

Inspired by such praise, the Poles marched down the road to Madrid in a thick fog. Finding the outskirts strongly defended, they wiped out a battery and overran the infantry guarding the Los Pozos gate. Then they returned to Chamartin dragging a gun captured by the brave Wilczek and saluted the Emperor with raised sabers crying: 'Long life to Caesar!' (This was the anniversary of Austerlitz and the coronation.)

The dragoons, drawn up in line of battle, cried: '*Vive l'Empereur!*' Far off they heard the tocsin rung from the 133 *campanarios* of Madrid which was bathed in a golden morning light. Would the capital dare resist? Crying 'Here comes the Anti-Christ with Joseph, the phantom King of Spain!' the prisoners released from the jails had sworn on the Gospel to assassinate all Frenchmen. Napoleon hoped to appease them, but the magic of the tocsin bells impressed his staff, quartered in the shrubbery around the Duke of Ossuno's palace where the Emperor was lodged.

The Guard posted sentries in the woods while the infantry bivouacked, without food or water, in the park as far as the Aranda road. Some foragers returned leading a convoy of donkeys loaded with wine. 'We had to shave in wine', reported Coigniet.

Except for the Poles sent with the fusiliers to Guadalajara and Santa Cruz where the remnants of the army of the interior were caught and defeated, all the cavalry was installed in the stables of the palace. The dragoons were quartered near Fuencarral. The provision carts as well as the cellars and casks had been emptied. On the veterinarian's advice Arrighi bathed his horses in rivers of wine. The night was cold and sharp; it was hard to find wood.

Sent in town with a summons to surrender, Bessières received an emphatic 'No' from the Junta. This was echoed by the populace, crying 'Long Live Fernando VII and damn the tyrant Emperor!' and 'Death to Bessières!'

The Guard was drawn up in two lines, supporting Lapisse's and Ruffin's divisions, in the northern suburbs and the Retiro. The chasseurs and grenadiers were posted near San Bernardino, and the horse grenadiers 1,000 meters behind, near a pine wood. Nearby, the Emperor's tents were guarded by the duty battalion and a squadron of Poles, in liaison with the dragoons who were deployed a mile from the Retiro. A full moon lit the artillery emplacements. The Guard batteries were trained on the northwest positions and were ordered to open fire if the second summons were rejected next day.

On 3 December at 9 a.m. the guns barked, opening breeches for the infantry who entered the city and shot everyone in sight. The Retiro was captured. Daumesnil, at the head of a few chasseurs, advanced to the Puerta del Sol. He returned to the Emperor's tent in time to hear Napoleon 'give Lauriston rats' for being such an ass as to punch a hole with his artillery in the barracks of the Royal Bodyguard.

That night the capitulation was signed in the Emperor's tent in the presence of King Joseph, and the army entered Madrid next day. Though a few fine mantillas, disdaining politics, appeared on the balconies, the atmosphere was gloomy and depressing. Where were the triumphal entries into Vienna, Berlin, Warsaw? The Guard did not participate but remained at Chamartin with the Emperor. Only the artillery was quartered in town, in the monastery of San Jeronimo which had been sacked and devastated.

The general exasperation, the laxness of the commanders, and the misery everywhere provoked a disciplinary crisis. A fusilier of the Guard who had stolen some mattresses was executed in the presence of fifty men from each corps. Such severity did not improve relations between the *madrileños* and the French.

A pall of sadness descended upon these men who, however resigned to their fate, were nevertheless fearful of the future. The squadron escorting the Emperor to the palace moved through deserted streets. No one saluted the procession. French vanity was humbled before Castilian pride. At the Chamartin parades Chassé's Dutchmen and the Baden and Nassau troops were disdained alike by this rigid, haughty people, driven to fanatacism by priests who hid muskets in the confessionals.

Would the Emperor's review on the 19th lure a few beautiful ladies?

Presented by General Walther, the Guard was drawn up in two lines with the chasseurs, grenadiers, dragoons, Poles, gendarmes, and Berg lancers on the right; then the foot chasseurs, grenadiers, and fusiliers. The artillery, with its guns and caissons, was ranged in front in battle formation. Its new lieutenant colonel, D'Aboville, was on horseback behind Lauriston; Boulart commanded the foot gunners, and Marin the horse artillery. The third rank contained the transport wagons and pack animals. Here were the donkeys of the Guard that the Line had christened 'mules', since the Guard always rated a rank higher.

The parade was in full dress, with overcoats rolled on the packs, capes buckled to the saddles, and ammunition complete. Of a total roster of 11,242, there were 428 officers and 9,008 men reporting under arms.

The review was splendid. One hundred and ten captured flags were parceled out among the regiments until de Ségur should be well enough to take them back to the Legislature (where half of them repose today). The inspection was detailed: 60 cartridges, four days' rations of bread, and two pairs of shoes were counted in each pack.

A dispatch rider brought the Emperor a note from Marshal Soult.

On the night of 14 December the British cavalry, with 5,000 infantry of Moore's army and a crowd of delirious peasants, had overrun Soult's posts at Rueda and Tordesillas. Valladolid was in upheaval and Franceschi's cavalry had been forced to evacuate it.

The review ended abruptly.

CHAPTER 5

Benavente

THE English at Valladolid? Moore must be mad! If this were true he could be cut off, encircled, destroyed . . . 'It is manna from Heaven that the British have at last sent their army to the continent . . .'

The French would maneuver to cut the English communications with Salamanca, then fight them. Soult would lure them on as far as possible; then the Emperor, with Ney, the Guard, and the cavalry reserve, would attack their flank. Meanwhile, Joseph would hold Madrid with the troops of Victor and Lefebvre.

Ney was ordered to advance to the Guadarramas, followed by Lefebvre-Desnoëttes and the cavalry of the Guard. The foot Guard was to march with the Emperor. The departure was scheduled for 21 and 22 December. The weather was fine, the skies clear.

But not for long . . .

The moment the troops reached the Escorial snow began falling and the wind blew at gale force. The higher they climbed into the mountains the harder the ground froze underfoot. Ney's troops got over the pass with the greatest difficulty. Lefebvre-Desnoëttes followed, but the weather became so bad that it was impossible to advance. The squadrons lost their way and a whole troop of dragoons disappeared into a gorge. Worse, in the gusts of wind and sand that penetrated to their very bones they were hurled back upon the infantry who were climbing on foot, and upon the artillery, throwing it into a welter of confusion.

Night fell. Up ahead Krasinski judged the ascent of the Guadarramas impossible. Behind the Poles Lefebvre-Desnoëttes was hardly more optimistic. But the troopers murmured: 'The Emperor is ahead . . . He will make a fine face when he learns that his Guard has not followed him, while the Line got through.'

'Each man leading his horse by the bridle', the squadrons followed one another up the nine kilometers to the pass. Half the dragoons were left on the road, tormented by a frost of minus 12 degrees.[1] At dawn, numb, famished, their crests rimed with frost, the two squadrons reached Espinar. The 'big heels' behind them suffered less, since by then the storm had moderated.

Four kilometers beyond, the Emperor worked in the chapel of San Rafael, surrounded and guarded by Lapisse's division of Victor's 1st Corps whose men bivouacked in the snow. It was the Emperor himself whom they had cursed and insulted while crossing the pass the night before. 'Oh, shoot the bastard!' a soldier was heard to mutter in the depths of his misery, but his suggestion had not been followed. Nevertheless,

[1] 10.4° Fahrenheit.

His Majesty had marched over the pass in the midst of his soldiers, his hat pulled down over his eyes, his boots full of snow, leaning first on the arm of Duroc, then Savary.

Yet he thought of everything. Darricau's infantry found wine and brandy waiting on their arrival at the bivouac. Thanks to this, at reveille next morning the men of Lapisse's division cried '*Vive l'Empereur!*' on learning that they had still twenty-five miles to go. What was the point? To catch and beat the English.

The foot Guard saw the point. It arrived the evening of the 23rd at Villacastin where the Emperor was already established. Leaving Madrid at dawn on the 22nd, it had traveled 82 kilometers in two days. Though the passage of the Guadarramas was easier, it reminded the old-timers of the passage of the St. Bernard eight years before.

A magazine was set up in the village. The Guard was able to replenish its stores of wine and brandy. The surgeons established a field hospital in the pass, and the gendarmes cleared the road of stragglers and organized communication posts for the couriers.

Now it rained. It even hailed, which drove the horses mad and made their muzzles bleed. A sharp thaw transformed the valley of the Douro into a sea of mud.

It was the 24th December. The Poles were a hardy lot. This country reminded the Guard of Poland, yet the Poles claimed they had never seen anything like it before. Just two years ago today the French were pulling out of Warsaw.

That night at the Christmas feast the crusts of bread stowed in the soldiers' packs were reduced to pulp and their canteens were empty. Yet the *Tondu* kept on going. Fortunately, they were approaching the sea.

The English were, too. Learning that the Emperor was on his heels, Sir John Moore had turned around and was retiring rapidly towards Corunna 'with its ships and resources'. He had given the slip to Soult who reported him first 'here – then there'. On the night of the 23rd he was at Sahagún, less than 100 kilometers from the Douro.

Colbert and Lefebvre-Desnoëttes had just reached that river. Though they could not cut off the English from Salamanca they hoped to cut their communications with Astorga. It was a question of speed.

The pack took a breathing-spell on Christmas Day. The horse and foot Guard surrounded the palace which was set up at Tordesillas on the Douro. The church bells summoned the faithful and the churches were filled.

It was the feast of peace and joy – also a reminder of man's duty towards God. Nevertheless, at 5.30 p.m. the horse and foot Guard got under way behind Ney for Medina-del-Rio-Seco. It rained in torrents. The grenadiers and chasseurs, rigged out in motley blankets, were munching their black bread. Up ahead two Englishmen were taken prisoner.

Faster . . .

'We could end this war at a single stroke . . .' Surely the heads under all those bear-skin bonnets understood that Soult was luring the English off to the east, and that the *Tondu* was about to take them in the rear. Here they were at Medina where the victory was won last year on 14 July. The Guard had been there. Bessières guided the Emperor over the battlefield, escorted by the Polish light-horse who were half-submerged in water on the north and west roads.

Where was the enemy? Durosnel, commanding the west wing, reported that Colonel Krasinski had found the bridge over the Esla at Benavente occupied by British infantry. A little way upstream his men had attacked a convoy escorted by the 10th English Hussars. Lefebvre-Desnoëttes was promptly ordered to Benevente with his chasseurs and the rest of the light-horse. 'Do not jeopardize my Guard', the Emperor added.

Then he marched north alone, accompanied by the duty squadrons, impatient for a meeting with his eternal enemies. The men riding after him through the mud were out of breath as he galloped furiously ahead of his advance-guard so that Ney's scouts took the chasseurs of the escort for English hussars.

Faster!

The infantry, too, was out of breath. The Guard followed, harassed, in water up to its knees – and sometimes to its waist – but the men drew a triple ration of wine.

Faster!! The *Tondu* was ahead. They must stop the English tonight, the 28th, on the Esla. But they were too late. Moore's army had already crossed the river.

Faster!!!

They must catch up with them, stop them, fight them. This, at any rate, was the opinion of Lefebvre-Desnoëttes who arrived at Castrogonzalo on the Esla the night of the 28th. Durosnel's Poles were already there. Both chasseurs and Poles were brought up short by a deep torrent, 100 meters wide, roaring between steep escarpments on either bank. Beyond were the English guns, a battalion of foot, and several troops of horse, already in position. The bridge above the town had been cut. The French saw bivouac fires at the outskirts of Benavente. They decided to cross by the ford at dawn.

Actually, they had to swim across. Led by Desnoëttes, three squadrons of chasseurs and a small detachment of Mameluks and light-horse, 550 troopers in all, plunged into the water a mile upstream from the bridge under the eyes of La Houssaye's dragoons who were encamped at Castrogonzalo. They crossed the river, re-formed into squadrons, and marched towards Benavente at a steady pace.

The alert was given by the English hussars watching the river who now fell back. Lord Paget took his time preparing his response. Lefebvre-Desnoëttes beat off an attack by 350 light dragoons from Benavente; however, outflanked at 300 yards by the 10th Hussars, followed by the 7th and led by Lord Paget, he took off and retreated at full gallop towards the river.

One hundred and sixty-five men were killed, wounded, or captured. The standard-bearer and a lieutenant of the Mameluks were killed. Lieutenants Schmidt and Sève were captured and five officers, including Captain Cayre, wounded.

Galloping back with the last of his men on his wounded horse, Lefebvre-Desnoëttes was caught near the Esla by a German dragoon named Bergmann who gave up his prize to Hussar Grisdale. This trooper relieved the General of his sword and sabretache which are still exhibited in the Royal United Service Museum in London.

'Console his wife', Napoleon wrote Josephine on 31 December. Lefebvre was the one to be consoled, for he had not a sou in his pockets, having lost all his money at cards.

While Colbert pressed on towards Astorga, where he was killed by a ball in the forehead, the cavalry of the Guard threw a human dam across the river to protect the artillery as it forded the stream. Several troopers were swept away by the current and drowned. The infantry reached the right bank by means of ladders placed across the gorge and rejoined the Emperor at Benavente.

The English had set fire to the Duke's palace and the magazines, pillaged the town, and fled in disorder, leaving behind them some cavalrymen too drunk to move, and some women – several of them pretty and well dressed – who were put up at auction indiscriminately with the burros, and sometimes sold for less.

'I should never have believed that an English army could fall apart so quickly', Moore wrote Lord Castlereagh on 13 January 1809. 'Its conduct during the last marches has been infamous beyond description.'

'We never saw anything like it', the old Grumblers agreed.

'We will string up the French with the guts of the English', the Spaniards concluded.

On New Year's Day, having marched 61 kilometers along the road to Astorga, Napoleon was met by a courier from Paris bringing bad tidings. Cambacérès had uncovered a plot hatched by Fouché, Talleyrand, and Murat, and there were further threats from Austria. In a somber mood he entered the town, surrounded by strong and ancient walls.

After floundering in mud for ten days over 225 miles, the foot grenadiers and chasseurs paraded on the Plaza Mayor. Then, by order of the Emperor, they returned to Benavente. 'Who knows', they were thinking, 'with Lefebvre-Desnoëttes holding Lord Paget in check and Moore stopped and probably crushed, perhaps the English are fed up with the struggle and the conquest of Portugal . . .'

But Napoleon understood only too well that he could not stop the English. On 6 January he entered Valladolid. There he ordered Soult to pursue Moore, and gave orders to retire all Guard depots in Madrid, as well as the *chasseurs à cheval* and the Poles, to Vitoria.

On the 15th he wrote Bessières: 'My Guard will remain here under your orders', meaning that he was leaving Spain without the Guard.

The Guard grumbled. 'To wear out your legs running after him and follow him through all his caprices is one thing. It's your job, and one you can be proud of. But to be left behind in this land of brigands – that's too much!'

Dark clouds were gathering on Napoleon's horizon. Was the Peninsula under a curse? The surrenders at Baylén and Cintra, his personal failure at Benavente, the incapacity of Joseph would make it seem so . . . And beyond the mountains there were the menace of Austria, the evasions of Russia and the Pope. And now the treason of Murat, his brother-in-law whom he had made a king, of his sister Caroline, of Talleyrand, that 'thieving, cowardly, faithless prince', and of Fouché, a common police inspector.

Was the Guard mixed up in it?

PLATE 63

a) Kozietulski
(*After portrait: Collection Princess Lubomirska*)

b) Niegolewski
(*After contemporary portrait*)

c) Suchet
(*Lith. Delpech*)

d) Philippe de Ségur
(*Engr. Forestier*)

PLATE 64

The Poles at Somosierra
(From a colored aquatint by Debucourt after Horace Vernet)

PLATE 65

PLATE 66

The French Army crossing the Guadarrama Mountains
(*From a lithograph by Gelée after Taunay*)

PLATE 67

a) Retreat of the English from Corunna
(From an original drawing by Naudet)

b) English gunners evacuating their guns
(From an original drawing by Benjamin West)

PLATE 68

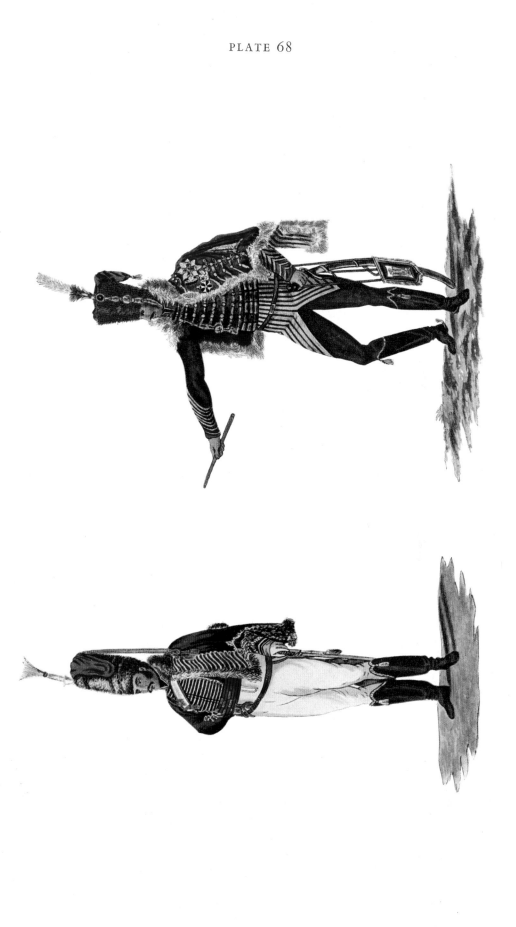

The storm broke at Valladolid during a review before the palace of the kings of Spain. Passing down the ranks of the foot grenadiers Napoleon suddenly seized one by the collar, disarmed him, threatened him, and pushed him back in ranks.

'What is the meaning of all this talk I hear?' he thundered to the motionless troop. 'So you want to return to your trollops in Paris? Ah, but you are not there – you are here where you shall see plenty of others! . . .'

With an abrupt nod to the drum major, he signaled the drummers to close the *Ban*.[2]

The corps commanders[3] were ordered back to Paris immediately.

'The Guard is not part of the army', Napoleon wrote on 15 January to the Chief of Staff (Berthier). 'Only when the Emperor sends for his baggage and his Guard can it be announced in the orders that the Emperor has turned over the command.'

The same day, he wrote Bessières: 'Take care of my Guard . . . I intend to move the depots to Bayonne.' And to Joseph: 'I want my Guard to remain at rest so as to be in condition to move to another front in case of need.'

Finally, he sent word to Prince Eugène, the sovereigns of the Confederation, Jerome, Marmont, and the ambassadors: 'I am on my way back . . . My Guard and part of my army are retiring for the time being . . . If Austria persists in her folly, I shall invade her with 400,000 Frenchmen . . . The business in Spain is finished; the Spanish armies are destroyed, and the English thrown into the sea . . .'

On 17 January, while galloping towards Burgos on the road to Paris, he learned that on Soult's arrival at Corunna he had seen the English board their vessels. But first, they had lined all their cavalry horses up on the beach and shot them through the head.

On the previous day, Sir John Moore had been killed.

---

[2] The *Ban* and *Demi-ban* were the rolls or calls for 'attention' before announcements, proclamations, etc. 'Closing the *Ban*' gave notice that the announcement was terminated. – Ed.

[3] That is, commanders of Guard 'corps' such as the grenadiers, *chasseurs à cheval*, artillery, etc.; not to be confused with the Line corps (corps d'armée) commanded by marshals, etc. which were equivalent to the modern army corps. – *Ibid*.

The French use of the word corps for distinctive military organizations, though classic (as in 'corps of cadets' at West Point) is very loose, and has little to do with numerical strength. Thus, the 'corps' of grenadiers contained one regiment in 1802 (see p. 24) and 4 in 1815, not counting the 10–12 Young Guard regiments 'attached' to it in the interval; and the 'corps' of artillery, more than 100 companies in 1813, whereas the 'corps' of engineers never mustered more than a few companies of sappers.–*Ibid*.

CHAPTER 6

The Young Guard

THE year 1809 marked a turning point in Europe and the Empire as well as in the army and the Guard.

Arriving in Paris on 23 January, Napoleon counted the breaches in his continental defences: in Portugal, Spain, Sicily, Rome, the Tyrol, and Turkey, not to mention 'a thousand dissidents in Prussia'. The duplicity of Russia and the treason at home had been confirmed, and an attack by Austria was imminent.

He believed that the Peninsula could be subdued within a few months. While the results so far were disappointing, nevertheless Joseph was in Madrid with 200,000 veteran European soldiers, 10,000 horse, and 500 guns under commanders like Soult, Victor, Ney, Mortier, etc. This was an imposing force which should be able to adapt itself to the exigencies of warfare in a rough and primitive country defended by fierce and elusive inhabitants.

Since the Emperor had left Joseph his supreme reserve – the Guard – he evidently planned to return to the Peninsula after he had settled affairs in Austria, the Empire, and the European Confederation. For this task he had only the Army of the Rhine under Davout, stationed in Franconia and Saxony, and the Hanseatic command of Bernadotte; about 100,000 men in all. These provided reconnaissance as well as a temporary deterrent to the ponderous Austrian army which was hardly an 'army of maneuver'.

These forces would ultimately be reorganized into an Army of Germany; but first there was the problem of the reserve – namely, the Guard. The Emperor might recall it from Spain, but at what cost? From Valladolid to Vienna was a journey of 1,750 miles, involving an enormous effort from men and matériel and considerable expense. Such a march could only be accomplished by small units traveling at varying rates of speed. True, Dejean was a virtuoso of wagon transport; but even he could not be expected to deliver the whole Guard at the right spot at the right moment.

With war threatening on several fronts, requiring the Emperor to move rapidly from one to the other, the Guard could neither follow nor escort him. Therefore, it must resume its role of reserve, its chief military function.

Napoleon had to think of economy. On 13 January at Valladolid he had decided that his aides-de-camp and those of the marshals, the colonel generals of the Guard, officers of the Crown, and generals commanding Guard corps should be removed from the Guard and attached to the general staff of the army whose perquisites were more modest. It was a bitter pill for these men to swallow; however, their old privileges had been abused.

As to the rank and file, the grenadiers and chasseurs were 'extremely expensive'. 'Being so precious, one fears to expose them', the Emperor wrote. He planned to keep the 1st Regiments only, disbanding the 2nd. Soldiers with ten years' service in the Line would continue to be admitted to the 1st Regiments with the rank of NCO.

The fusiliers would also be retained, though they were 'in an awkward spot between Guard and Line, costing twice as much as a Line corps'.

Some junior regiments were now formed from selected conscripts of the Guard and trained by Old Guard cadres. 'In war', the Emperor wrote, 'I profit more from the fusiliers and conscripts than from the grenadiers and chasseurs. If the word "conscript" has an unpleasant connotation', he added, 'we might call (the new regiments) "tirailleurs".'[1]

To distinguish them from the Old Guard these regiments were given the corporate title of 'Young Guard', to which they clung tenaciously. Attached to the grenadiers and chasseurs and administered by them, the Young Guard proved itself a magnificent weapon forged by the Old. It ended by equaling the latter's performance and sharing its glory, so that posterity made no distinction between them but lumped them together under the proud title 'Imperial Guard'.

When first proposed in 1803 Bessières, reflecting the Guard's opinion, had shown reluctance to mixing conscripts with veterans. (Plebeians who belong to an elite organization invariably become snobs.) So the vélites, who did not officially belong to the Guard, were created instead.

These had proved valuable. The Emperor had increased their number, commissioning some in the Line and admitting others to the Guard. Many fusiliers were recruited from their ranks. Drilled by the men of Arcole and the Pyramids and commanded by officers like Friederichs, Henniquin, and Chéry of the grenadiers, and Boyer, Labusquette, and Beurmann of the chasseurs, these agile youngsters had behaved gallantly at Eylau and Friedland. Reinforced by selected conscripts from the reserve, the fusiliers had whipped the canaille of Madrid and charged at Medina and Guadalajara.

In consequence, the Emperor had increased their pay and allotments and given them the title 'fusilier-grenadiers' and 'fusilier-chasseurs' as a New Year's gift. Though they did not belong to that august body the Old Guard, they were now the 'old soldiers of the Young Guard', uniformed like their elders except for the bearskin bonnet, wearing swords – and (in the fusilier-grenadiers) even queues (see Plate 46).

The new tirailleur-grenadiers and tirailleur-chasseurs were created at Valladolid on 16 January 1809. Composed of 3,200 of the 'strongest and best-educated' conscripts of the Guard, these regiments were assigned excellent cadres consisting of officers and NCO's of the disbanded 2nd Grenadiers and 2nd Chasseurs and graduates of Saint-Cyr. The cadres retained their Old Guard status and pay.

'At the end of two years' service, tirailleurs may be admitted to the fusiliers; and after four more, into the Old Guard; but only by virtue of an Imperial decree.'

Thus the hierarchy within the Guard was preserved.

[1] Literally, skirmishers or sharpshooters. – Ed.

Only four depot companies were left in Paris to guard the palaces and receive the conscripts. The fusilier depot was filled by 1,100 conscripts of the classes of 1808–9. Now 4,000 more arrived for the new *tirailleur* regiments, followed shortly by 10,000 from the class of 1810.

Transient barracks were opened in the Rue Verte and at La Pepinière whose fleas were direct descendants of those that had tormented the king's soldiers. General Dériot, vice-governor of the Palaces, was named commandant of the Guard depots which had to clothe, administer, feed, and instruct the lads soon seen drilling on the Champs-Elysées, Champ de Mars, and Plaine des Sablons.

From the old barracks of the *Gardes du Corps* at Versailles the nineteen-year-old conscript Etienne Rimmel wrote his parents, telling how he spent his time. He had musket drill from 7.30 a.m. to 10 a.m., roll call at noon, then more drill from two to four. Soup was served at ten and four. 'It is good', he reported, 'and you can always find a piece of beef in it.'

Each recruit was issued a shako trimmed with a white cord, eagle plate, leather cockade, and pompon, plus a coat, sleeved waistcoat, breeches, overcoat, forage-cap, and two shirts and pairs of stockings, shoes, and gaiters; a black stock, bedroll, haversack, cartridge pouch and belt, musket bandolier, and – though no saber[2] – the buttons of the Guard. The whole outfit cost 154·26 francs. Morale was high, 'We live like lords', wrote a conscript of this period.

Naturally there were some deserters and conscientious objectors; however, of the 26,875 conscripts handled that year by the Guard depots, only 117 failed to appear, including 44 from departments in Belgium and Switzerland.

On 8 February the two *tirailleur* regiments received their officers and cadres. Colonel Lonchamp, who joined the Guard in 1804, was appointed lieutenant colonel of the 1st *Tirailleur*-Grenadiers, and Poret de Morvan a major. The captains were old grenadiers of the pre-Consular Guards like Faucon, or else battle-scarred newcomers such as Léglise and Cicéron.

Colonel Rosey, a hero of Acre, was named lieutenant colonel of the 1st *Tirailleur*-Chasseurs. Major Cambronne came from the Line with three citations and the Legion of Honor. Several captains, including Malet, had served in the Guard of the Consuls.

Forty-eight virtuoso drummers beat the *Grenadière* and *Carabinière*.[3] The regiments were uniformed and their officers proceeded with the training (see Plate 76a).

And well they must, for the Emperor was beginning to concentrate forces between Strasbourg and Ulm. Meanwhile, he organized the Army of Italy and made plans to bring his old foot Guard back from Spain.

Reassured by the capture of Saragossa on 19 February, two days later Napoleon ordered Bessières to leave a few units of infantry and cavalry in Spain and send the rest of the Guard – including the artillery, field hospital, and train – to Paris. The generals and corps commanders were to leave by post the moment their orders arrived.

[2] Actually the *tirailleurs* were probably issued sabers. – Ed.
[3] The respective drum rolls of the corps of grenadiers and chasseurs. – *Ibid.*

Napoleon had finally yielded to temptation, requiring a supreme effort from his old soldiers. He could not be separated from the Guard.

At a review on Sunday, 19 March the conscripts of the Guard made a good impression on the Emperor who was pleased with their alert air; so between the 29th and 31st he ordered four new regiments raised at Paris to be known as 'conscript-grenadiers' and 'conscript-chasseurs'. These were paid the same as the Line and wore the same uniform, except that they wore short-tailed coats, and the shako cords and buttons of the Guard.

The staff officers and captains from the Guard retained their status and pay, and the subalterns were either *vélites* or Saint-Cyrians. Most of the NCO's – 'veterans of Friedland, at least' – came from the fusiliers. Stripped of 450 men for this purpose, the fusiliers were replenished by a levy from each department of four conscripts who were 'intelligent, literate, robust, and of suitable height'. The depot of the conscripts of the Guard received 6,000 men from the classes of 1808–9.

The memoirs of the Guard conscripts reveal their keen desire to prove worthy of the veterans and share in their glory. The Emperor could count on the devotion of these eager young regiments, led by seasoned veterans whose medals and scars commanded their respect, for they were animated by the same ardent faith. They were of the Guard, the Guard of an Emperor they loved, to whom nothing was impossible.

CHAPTER 7

The Long Road Back

'WAR seems almost inevitable', the Emperor wrote Joseph on 28 March 1809.

Clarke's ministry was in a continual turmoil. The Chief of Staff (Berthier) was busy concentrating the various corps of the Army of Germany, which 'must be accomplished by the 30th . . .' so as to present a front to the Austrians who were 'already in motion', according to Davout.

The office of Dejean was an inferno. On 24 March he was ordered to send to Strasbourg, via Paris, the infantry of the Guard strung out from Bayonne to Poitiers, also the artillery staff, surgeons, and hospital personnel. Relays and relay stations provisioned with food must be arranged, and a rate of seventy-five miles a day maintained. The cavalry and artillery were ordered to 'travel as fast as possible without foundering their horses . . .'

Would they arrive in time? An order went to General Walther, commander of the Paris Guard, to send officers ahead to expedite the move, and to send Arrighi with 300 men from each cavalry depot and 12 guns to Strasbourg. Walther himself was due in Strasbourg on 6 April with the led horses and the Emperor's baggage, and the Chief of Staff two days earlier.

Decrès was directed to make up a crew of 140 marines of the Guard under Captain Baste to replace the battalion captured at Baylén. Commanders Kerveguen and Roquebert were transferred to the Line. What had become of their comrades imprisoned through Spanish treachery?

After the surrender at Baylén the captive marines were marched to Rota, a small port north of Cadiz, escorted by Spanish troops. On the march they were abused, threatened, and even bitten by mobs of furious men and women. Guarded in their new barracks by the local militia, they were at last sheltered from the mob. Their energetic officers, Grivel, Gérodias, Gerdy, etc, joined in their defence.

Ensign Barberi, a six-foot Corsican, was surprised at his toilet by the *alcalde* on a tour of inspection. Thinking his comrades were being abused, he rushed from his room, stripped to the waist, his face covered with lather, and leaped over the bannister on top of the *alcalde* as the latter reached the landing below. He seized the astonished Spaniard by the throat in an iron grip, shouting '*Sangre de Dios, señor!* . . .'[1] Grivel and his companions intervened just in time to avert disaster.

---

1 'By God's blood, sir!'

Such incidents provided some merriment, for the young officers could not spend all their time lamenting their fate. To be sure, they reviewed their navigation, read the books the doctor brought them, studied Spanish, and wrote their memoirs. But they also sang *Mère Gaudichon*, laughed, danced, got their keepers drunk, and even went on an occasional bender and engaged in amorous adventures, despite the dangers involved.

Lieutenant Boniface, whose curly mane was carrot-red, made a conquest of a neighboring charmer who saw him lean bareheaded out of the window. But since this provocative creature happened to be the lawful wife of a local official, his comrades urged Boniface not to appear in the street without his hat.

Life in the barracks was quite bearable for the sailors as well. Many worked in the town, went fishing, and received favors from their *queridas*, thanks to whom there are said to be descendants of the marines of the Guard around Cadiz today.

These pleasures ceased on 21 February 1809. Since the French were marching south, the Junta at Seville ordered the captives transferred to prison ships in the harbor. Then the escapes began. With the help of smugglers, Vattier gave his jailers the slip and took refuge in Morocco from where he made his way home in February 1810. Grivel, who was ill, was sent to the hospital.

These were the lucky ones; for on 3 April the rest of the officers and 180 marines were deported with 5,000 Frenchmen to the island of Cabrera, off Majorca, a hell from which only a few managed to escape.

The artillery of the Guard would serve sixty guns at the height of the coming campaign. D'Aboville, Henrion, Greiner, and Boulart arrived at La Fère from Spain on the 28th. Boulart had only ten days in which to organize two new batteries and start them on the road for Strasbourg on 8 and 10 April.

On the 7th, 150 'well-mounted Poles' left Paris with the veteran grenadiers and chasseurs who could be spared from the depots, and two *tirailleur* regiments only 80 days old. Leaving in small mixed detachments on successive days, the Guard had never before departed on campaign in such disorder.

Time pressed, however. Berthier, given temporary command of the Army of Germany by the Emperor, hurried to Stuttgart on the 10th. Napoleon kept in constant touch with him, having only a limited confidence in his ability. Through the courier service, dispatches took less than a day and a half to go from Donauwörth to Strasbourg, a distance of 175 miles, and only two days from Strasbourg to Paris, 300 miles. But in clear weather news could travel this distance in six minutes over Chappe's new telegraph.

On 11 April at Courbevoie, Generals Dorsenne and Michel solemnly inaugurated the 1st Conscript-Grenadiers and -Chasseurs. Colonel Darquier, lieutenant colonel of the 1st Conscript-Grenadiers, was present with his majors, including Carré, a former Guard of the Directory. Among the captains were old lieutenants of the Guard, including Mirabel. Half the lieutenants were from the *vélites* and half from Saint-Cyr. The subalterns were all present but half the privates were not.

Colonel Vrigny, ex-major of the fusiliers, was lieutenant colonel of the 1st Conscript-Chasseurs. The men were well dressed in short blue coats, black shakos with white cords, and wore sabers and pouches. About 600 were still lacking.

The second conscript regiments were still in the process of formation. Colonels Robert and Mouton-Duvernet from the Line had been appointed but had not yet arrived. Majors Rogéry and Maillard of the Old Guard awaited them.

'Inform me', the Emperor wrote Lacuée,[2] 'whether two regiments of conscripts cost more or less than a Line regiment of three battalions, and the difference in cost . . .' He went on to say that with two regiments of the Old Guard and two of fusiliers, plus four regiments each of *tirailleurs* and conscripts, he 'would have 20,000 men which makes a fine army corps'.

On the evening of 12 April a courier arrived from Berthier. The Emperor announced: 'They have crossed the Inn. It is war . . .'

He left with Josephine on the 13th. Napoleon entered Strasbourg before sunrise on the 15th to find a frantic appeal from Berthier in Stuttgart. At midday he crossed the bridge at Kehl.

Where was the Guard?

Poitiers, 4 April. Morning. A file of 3- and 4-horse carts surrounded by gendarmes was drawn up on the side of the road to Châtellerault. In them were the 1st Fusiliers, leading the Infantry of the Guard back from Spain. All was in good order. The bayonets and musket locks had been demounted and carefully wrapped. Each wagon contained twelve men. They paid 5 francs per horse (300 for a dead one.) at the relay stations where they found a fresh relay hitched and ready to go. At the 'refreshment billets' the men stopped to eat at tables prepared in advance. They were allowed three quarters of an hour for a meal. No other stops were permitted. They traveled between 50 and 60 miles in twenty-four hours and were due in Paris the 9th. They would be there.

Many officers traveled by carriage. Some had more than one. Officers' carriages were sent through posthaste, since the Guard did not travel as the Line but led the life of great lords, riding in imposing equipages and scattering money along the route. What did it matter? Their future was assured. The Emperor protected the Guard. Nothing was too good for it since it was his.

On 9 April the fusiliers, cramped and bruised from the journey, descended from their vehicles at Paris and Versailles. They reassembled their muskets and changed their shirts as thousands of idlers looked on; then, to drums beating the *Carabinière*, the fusilier-chasseurs entered Paris.

At Versailles the fusilier-grenadiers buckled on their packs and made the rest of the journey on foot. This pleased the soldiers who preferred marching to riding in wagons. Day after tomorrow they would be off again in those miserable vehicles, as the Emperor was calling for them.

The old grenadiers and chasseurs arrived the 12th, followed by the horse grenadiers, chasseurs, and gendarmes strung out behind them on the road. The artillery reached

[2] Military representative in the Council of State. – Ed.

Bordeaux on 10 April. The last of the rear-guard under Lt. Colonel Chastel of the horse grenadiers quit Spain on 24 March and reached Paris on 30 April.

The infantry had only 24 hours at Courbevoie, Rueil, or Versailles before leaving cheerfully for Strasbourg and, eventually, Germany where the air was pure, the beer foamy, and the girls amiable. Meanwhile, the Emperor was burning up the roads and winning victories, escorted by Württemberg and Bavarian cavalry.

General Walther left Paris on 3 April after dispatching several columns to Strasbourg under General Roguet. These included about 300 Polish light-horse, two large battalions of Old Guard infantry, the two *tirailleur* regiments, a small detachment of artillery, and Daumesnil's chasseurs who had escorted the Emperor from Spain until their horses gave out. More chasseurs, remounted at the depot, brought up the rear with the field hospital, bakery, etc. The soldiers were forbidden to give news of the army in their letters home.

The convoy marched in the greatest disorder. Walther left with the last detachment and rode past the columns in his carriage, speeding up the stragglers and exhorting the commanders to hurry. Entering Strasbourg on 15 April with Roguet, he estimated that the Emperor might expect 4,200 infantry and 2,000 horse in addition to the artillery and service troops. But – the Emperor had left that noon to join Berthier at Stuttgart without leaving any orders.

Walther took it upon himself to send the leading units after him by wagon, not knowing that at Pforzheim Napoleon had received from the King of Württemberg in Ludwigsburg an hysterical letter which decided him to go there instead.

Returning to Stuttgart on the 17th, the Emperor heard that there were wagonloads of harassed infantry of the Guard in the suburbs of Cannstadt; but he was in a terrific hurry. Escorted by Württemberg cavalry, he hurried on to Donauwörth to repair the blunders made by Berthier (see Plate 70).

On the 18th Walther sent off the rest, reinforced by the first convoy of chasseurs and fusiliers from Spain who had reached Strasbourg only the night before. The General figured that the order he had received that day from Donauwörth 'to send all the available Guard there' was being carried out to the letter.

However, by the 19th Napoleon was already far away. That night he slept at Neustadt, 80 kilometers beyond Donauwörth. On the 20th he won the battle of Abensberg; on the 21st, the battle of Landshut; and on the 22nd, the battle of Eckmühl, escorted the while by the 1st *Chasseurs à cheval* of the Line.

It would be difficult to keep up with him at such a pace, even if one knew where he was; but since one did not know . . . The Guard was not even present when he was wounded at Ratisbon on the 23rd; however, it was on its way.

On that day the first battalion of chasseurs and the fusilier-chasseurs slept at Augsburg, 75 miles away, about a day's march by wagon. But since all was chaos, their wagons were halted outside of Augsburg 'because of the proximity of the enemy!'

The rest of the Guard traveled by the stage route. During the halts the officers ate at the tables of their hosts while the men were issued bread from the commissary, with soup, a pound of meat, vegetables, and either wine or beer provided by the inhabitants. All would have been well had the stage route not been 25 miles south of the Emperor's itinerary.

April 26 was a memorable day. Leaving his 'palace' in the convent of Prüll, near Ratisbon, Napoleon decided, after visiting the wounded from Eckmühl, to return to Landshut for the night. There he found the first battalion of chasseurs and 1,200 fusilier-chasseurs.

Where were the *tirailleurs*?

The day before, he had received Lacuée's estimate showing that the Young Guard brigades cost him nearly half a million francs less than a Line regiment. This decided him to raise a second pair of *tirailleur* regiments from the 3,000 conscripts left at the Paris depot.

The 1st Regiments, in excellent condition, were at Augsburg with the second chasseur battalion, the grenadiers, light-horse, and cavalry of the Old Guard. The field hospital and service troops were only a day's march behind.

'Let them double their marches – this bungling must stop!' The Emperor wanted his Guard with him.

On 1 May he brigaded the two *tirailleur* regiments together under Roguet, and the fusilier regiments under Gros. Together they formed Curial's division under General Mouton.

Dorsenne was put in command of the Old Guard with 24 guns, of which only eight had arrived as yet. Boulart's two foot batteries, en route from La Fère, were due in Strasbourg that day.

'I want action, action!' the Emperor wrote. 'In a month we shall be in Vienna.'

They would be there before that . . .

CHAPTER 8

Essling

AFTER defeating General Hiller at Ebersberg on 3 May, the Army of Germany began its march to Vienna. On the march against Archduke Charles in Bohemia, its left flank was covered by the corps of Masséna, Davout, and Bernadotte, echeloned along the Danube; its right flank, by Lefebvre in the Tyrol.

The Emperor took his Guard in hand again, for it had been too long dispersed. On 7 May he ordered Walther to 'take the division of *tirailleurs* and fusiliers and the Polish light-horse to Amstetten and camp along the river Ips' (now Ybbs).

Next day new orders came to 'send all the foot and horse Guard to Neumarkt and Ips'. The *tirailleurs* and fusiliers marched to Neumarkt with eight guns and 300 light-horse; the Old Guard, with the dragoons and horse grenadiers under Arrighi, to Ips; meanwhile, 300 chasseurs and 90 Poles joined the Emperor at St. Pölten.

The Army of Germany was concentrated on the right bank of the Danube and the main Austrian army on the left bank. Step by step the Guard reached the head of the French army.

On the 10th Lannes received orders to march to Vienna. Several hours later the Emperor was at Schönbrunn, guarded by twenty-five faithful grenadiers who had volunteered to march fifty extra miles to present arms upon his arrival. For the second time the double-headed eagle was replaced in the Austrian capital by the eagle of France.

Curial's 5,000 men were quartered in Hetzendorf, south of the Palace park. The chasseurs were at Meidling, the grenadiers at Schönbrunn with Arrighi's 1,500 horse, and 3,160 horse Guards en route from Spain were approaching Vienna.

The dragoons of the Guard had made the 2800-kilometer journey from Valladolid in sixty-three days without losing a man or a horse. On 22 May, as they marched past the high bluff on the Danube crowned by the magnificent Abbey of Melk, Fiteau, Letort, and their troopers heard in the distance a dull, continuous roar – the guns of Essling.

This battle was a feat of sheer determination. The operations of the past six weeks had led the main Austrian army under Archduke Charles and the French army under Napoleon into parallel positions across the Danube. Neither could maneuver any longer to east or west without endangering its communications. One or the other must be destroyed.

The shock of collision came a short distance downstream from Vienna on 21 May. Since the bridges had been destroyed the Emperor crossed the river on pontoons.

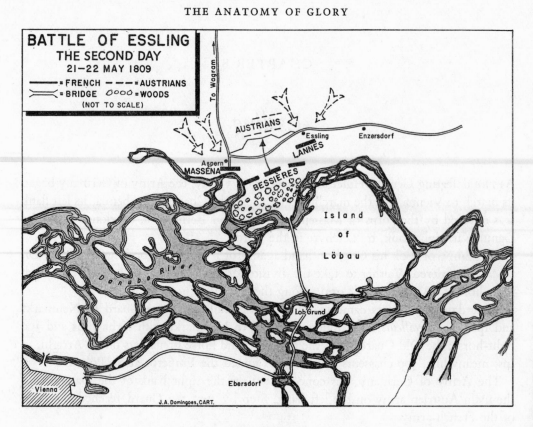

ESSLING

Without waiting for his major reinforcements to come up Napoleon decided to force a crossing of the Danube at Lobau Island, southeast of Vienna, in the face of the main Austrian army. The first French units crossed and occupied the villages of Essling and Aspern to protect the bridge-head, but failed to fortify them against a certain Austrian attack.

The French bridge across the river was completed on 20 May. The Austrians did not attack in force until the afternoon of the 21st. The conduct of the French troops was irreproachable. On the first day some 20,000–30,000 French opposed 80,000–100,000 Austrians; on the second, the French were reinforced, but still inferior. In bloody fighting exceptional losses cost each army over 20,000 men. Each side claimed victory, the Austrians clearly with more justification since Napoleon's tactics had been faulty. Napoleon retired his forces to the Island of Lobau and prepared for another crossing.

By 19 May the French army had reached Ebersdorf on the right bank where the river meanders around several islands to a width of about two and a half miles from bank to bank. The largest island, being in a branch called the Lobau, the French christened the 'Island of Lobau'. Here Masséna and Lasalle crossed on two pontoon bridges to establish a foothold on the 19th, and were followed across next day by the Emperor with part of the Guard and the cavalry reserve.

'Cross over with your troop', the Emperor ordered a lieutenant of the Polish light-horse. When the officer hesitated, he added: 'I know for a fact that the Tartars swam the Danube in Sobieski's time'.

Less than a mile away rose the steeples of Aspern, Essling, and Enzersdorf whose bells rang out this Whitsunday morning. The fields beyond, covered with haystacks, extended towards the wooded slopes of the Bisamberg which hid the horizon.

From the Island of Lobau the troops marched across a shaky bridge to the left bank of the Danube where Masséna occupied Essling and Aspern and the cavalry reserve deployed between the two. Curial's division re-formed at the bridgehead, near the Emperor who occupied a sandy beach beside a small wood.

The rest of the Guard was supposed to follow. However, the enemy sent rock-laden ships against the bridges and the strong current carried them away.

Archduke Charles chose this moment to attack the French force of 16,000 foot and 6,800 horse, supported by 90 guns, with his army of 100,000 men with 200 guns, in an effort to throw them back into the Danube.

The battle raged furiously from the start. The Austrian fire was concentrated upon the cramped French position where Masséna's heroic men were put to a severe test. The enemy advanced to within 200 yards of the bridgehead while Bessières, Lasalle, and General d'Espagne's cuirassiers attempted through massive, repeated, and costly charges to draw the fire of the overwhelming Austrian artillery.

Night fell. The Austrians did not press the attack. They would have had they but known that, under cover of night, the sappers and pontooneers were repairing the bridges by which Lannes, Oudinot, the artillery, and the Guard infantry crossed – slowly and by the grace of God – to reinforce Masséna.

Reaching the left bank safely, the reinforcements found Boulart forming an artillery park with the batteries of Bizard and Le Français in front of Dorsenne's division, near the tile works.

At 3 a.m. the Emperor mounted his horse and inspected the front which ran parallel to the enemy's, 400 yards away. He was frantically cheered by the soldiers.

The day about to break was a critical one. The French would be fighting in the proportion of two to one in a witches' cauldron with the widest river in Europe at their back. Although Davout and the cavalry divisions were still on the right bank, Napoleon prepared to attack the enemy with 48,000 infantry, 7,000 horse, and 144 guns the moment their artillery opened fire.

A desperate struggle commenced during which Marshal Lannes was mortally wounded. Masséna held the village of Aspern with admirable tenacity while the

Austrian grenadiers wrested Essling from Boudet's division. Then the Emperor's aides, Generals Mouton and Rapp, recaptured it with troops from Curial's division.

'Forward in columns! Keep your heads down and don't bother about the number of enemies', the Emperor ordered. The Guard batteries supported the attack, firing at top speed. Captain Bizard had his arm shot off. Some of the gun crews were reduced to two men. Durosnel, Drouot, Curial, and Gros were all wounded, as was Mouton who was created Count of Lobau after the battle.

The *tirailleurs* drove the enemy out of Gross-Aspern. Then Captain Cicéron was sent to the cemetery where he was overwhelmed by a superior force and obliged to retreat. Wounded, and with the rear-guard of his company surrounded, he had to surrender.

In its baptism of fire the Young Guard lost a quarter of its effectives. Lt. Colonels Lanabère and Lonchamp as well as Rousseau, Secrétan, Labusquette, and Cicéron were all wounded more or less severely. Yesterday's conscripts had proved worthy of the veterans who stood motionless in reserve with ordered arms under heavy bombardment by enemy artillery. 'The shells blew off our bearskin bonnets', reported Coigniet.

The Guard had always to be a model of courage and sang-froid since victory sometimes depended upon the forces not engaged. At the height of the battle, the Emperor admonished the frantic Berthier: 'Before yielding victory to the enemy, wait until he wrests it from you.'

At one point, when Napoleon had unduly exposed himself, the veteran grenadiers cried: 'Lay down your arms unless the Emperor falls back!'

Posterity has produced a miserable few who would tarnish the glory of this man and his soldiers. But with their imperturbable good sense the French people persist in admiring the 'old of the Old', and even envy them for having had someone to love.

At their bivouac on the Island of Lobau, infantry, cavalry, wagons, prisoners, stray horses, hospital units swarmed about in the dark in a space twenty kilometers square, jumbled together in a wood crisscrossed with ditches filled with water. The Line was forbidden to go near the Guard.

In a hunting pavilion the wounded screamed under the scalpel of Larrey. Shots rang out in the bushes and an imperial stag and some stray horses fell and disappeared into the regimental kettles, for the men were famished. Daru had ordered bread, biscuit, meat, a little wine, and lots of brandy brought by water from Vienna. These treasures were hard to find in the general disorder.

Fortunately, Archduke Charles did not stir.

Across the small branch of the river between the island and the left bank some oarsmen struggled against the current. The Emperor, Berthier, and Savary landed 600 yards from the enemy. Masséna joined them, and the four sat together under a tree.

It was the consensus of opinion that they should leave behind what they could not carry – artillery, horses, wagons – and cross to the right bank.

'But that is equivalent to advising a retreat to Strasbourg!' the Emperor exclaimed. 'If I retire across the Danube I give up Vienna; for the enemy will cross on my heels and drive me before him – perhaps all the way to Strasbourg . . .'

The left bank must be held. Masséna would stay. Berthier wrote him: 'You must hold the head of the first bridge . . . The Emperor will cross to the opposite bank to arrange for reinforcements, and especially provisions.'

Napoleon reached the right bank in a skiff and slept for two hours at Ebersdorf, guarded by the Portuguese Legion (see Plate 102a). He had left the Guard to cross next day after the wide bridge had been repaired.

The Austrians were exultant. 'Napoleon is among the dead . . . Our army has crossed the Danube . . . Bonaparte killed two of his generals in a moment of rage . . . His prestige is destroyed . . .'

Europe was agitated. Spain trembled; prices fell on the Paris *bourse*; the Chouans[1] took up arms again. The Kings looked towards England. Fouché reflected, his finger between his teeth . . .

'They have made an engagement to meet at my tomb, but they do not dare go there together', Napoleon told Savary.

Of all the European rulers Napoleon was the calmest. At his 'Imperial Camp at Vienna' he annexed Rome and the states of the Romagna. He needed a month at least to prepare his great battle against Archduke Charles.

'But what if he should attack you in the meanwhile?' the worriers inquired.

---

[1] Bourbon sympathizers among the peasants of Brittany, etc. who conducted effective guerrilla operations against the Republic until 1803, and sporadic ones against the Empire until their leader was executed by Fouché in 1807. – Ed.

CHAPTER 9

Wagram

THE French army needed boats, wood, tools, artisans, sailors, ditch diggers; also provisions for the men on the Island of Lobau, transport for the wounded, a 500-bed hospital in Vienna with food, wine, and money for the sick, and decorations for the men who had distinguished themselves.

Meanwhile, it had to watch the enemy and prepare his destruction. The Army of Italy under Prince Eugène and Macdonald, the victor of Laybach, were gradually approaching Vienna. These would take care of Archduke John; then the Emperor would concentrate all his forces against Archduke Charles.

In a royal lodge at Ebersdorf, where the Old Guard and escort were quartered, the *Tondu* 'attended to business' which meant putting the island into a state of defence, constructing batteries on the left bank, and safeguarding his communications which improved from day to day.

He devoted much time to visiting the wounded in the Guard hospital that Larrey had set up in the village. Preceded by a secretary who called their names, and followed by soldiers carrying baskets of *ecus*[1] from his privy purse, he questioned each man in turn, consoled him, talked of his future, of glory, gave him 60 francs, listened to his troubles and his hopes, and awarded him a cross and a pension. The officers received from 150 to 1,500 francs.

Tears flowed. Many men never spent these silver pieces stamped with the Imperial profile, but kept them to gaze at until they died.

The Young Guard spent the rest of the month at Himberg. The cavalry was strung out as far as Hetzendorf where the horse grenadiers were encamped. The dragoons were quartered in a suburb of Vienna, and the chasseurs near Schönbrunn. They were all in need of rest, horses, breeches, and boots. They accepted Austrian mounts with reluctance, but spurned their clothes. The Guard could be dressed only in Paris.

The Emperor's wrath burst forth. This time it would be dressed in Vienna, because it was 'better to wear Austrian breeches than no breeches at all.'

In spite of his promises at Tilsit and Erfurt, Alexander did not lift a finger to help the Emperor who now stood alone, excommunicate and without allies. He needed all his energy to persevere in his designs. Orders went forth to secure his line of communications which was threatened by a revolt in Germany. His paternal advice led to the defeat by Prince Eugène of Archduke John at Raab. The Archduke was then kept immobile by Macdonald, and later by Marmont.

[1] Three-franc pieces. – Ed.

PLATE 69

Napoleon in his undress uniform of the *chasseurs à cheval* of the Guard
(From an aquatint by F. Arnold after Dähling)

PLATE 70

Württemberg and English Household Cavalrymen
(*From an original watercolor by Rowlandson*)

PLATE 71

a) Archduke Charles
(*Engr. Velyn after Noireterre*)

b) d'Aboville
(*Engr. Chrétien: Collection Vicomte d'Aboville*)

c) Mouton, Count of Lobau
(*Contemp. engraving*)

d) Masséna
(*Lith. Delpech*)

PLATE 72

Death of Marshal Lannes at Essling
(From a colored engraving by J. J. Wolff after Carle Vernet)

PLATE 73

PLATE 74

Prince Eugène, Viceroy of Italy
(*From an original drawing by Antonio Calliano*)

PLATE 75

THE FRENCH ARMY AT VIENNA, 1809. Compare the same artist's impression of the French army in 1800, Plate 7

(*From a colored aquatint by Rahl after Wilhelm Kobell*)

Napoleon assembled his forces at Vienna facing Archduke Charles whose destruction he was preparing in minute detail.

On the Emperor's return to Schönbrunn the Guard occupied its former billets and resumed its watch. The artillery from Spain had arrived at last and was quartered in the suburb of Wieden. For the first time the foot batteries were united in one place. Each morning they were seen exercising on the glacis.

On 7 June the whole Guard was reviewed by the Emperor. It was high time. Most of the Guardsmen had not seen him for six months and had traveled 1,750 miles to have him pinch their ears. The conscripts who had fought at Essling were quite cocky. The Emperor granted a pair of shoes to each man from Spain, and decided to send for the new Guard conscript regiments in France.

Three new companies of foot artillery with 24 guns were being formed in Strasbourg for the fusiliers, *tirailleurs*, and conscripts of the Guard.

'I now have a dozen twelve-pounders', Napoleon wrote the Minister of War, 'and shall have eighteen.' He called them 'his cherished daughters'.

The Emperor ordered an extra conscription of 40,000 men to replenish the depots, including 6,200 for the Guard. Cadres from the *tirailleurs* were sent off to Paris, followed by Lieutenant Colonels Flamand and Deshayes of the 2nd *Tirailleur*-Grenadiers and 2nd *Tirailleur*-Chasseurs together with 17 captured flags. Major Vézu, wounded at Essling, was assigned to the *tirailleur*-grenadiers, and Captains Pompéjac and Secrétan promoted majors in the *tirailleur*-chasseurs.

Davout, Eugène, Marmont, Macdonald, Vandamme and his Württembergers, Wrede's Bavarians, Nansouty's and Lasalle's horse were all concentrating their forces around Vienna. The Island of Lobau – now rechristened 'Île Napoléon' – had become a veritable fortress, bristling with batteries and depots of food and munitions.

Lt. Colonel Drouot was seized with the desire to organize a band for the foot artillery. He found a bandmaster, hired him for 180 francs a month, and dressed him in a coat 'with two gold stripes'. He negotiated for instruments in Vienna, and sent in a requisition for a bass drummer so he could 'use the drum he had ordered'.

Imagine his delight at receiving three 'distinguished artists' including Maestro Klein, a virtuoso of virtuosi. (Possibly Mr Beethoven's presence in Vienna at the time and the Augarten concerts had provided the inspiration.)

A great lover of walking, the robust and vigorous Larrey was no longer seen promenading on the ramparts. Instead he was busy organizing a Guard hospital on the Rennweg with 16 wards, 2 pharmacies, and 4 kitchens. He engaged 58 Austrian attendants and several surgeons for the staff.

After the battle of Essling the medics buried 243 Guardsmen and picked up 943 wounded, half of whom had already been returned to their corps. About a hundred died of their wounds but the survivors had excellent care. Each morning the steward distributed rolls (Vienna rolls of course!) costing ·05 francs apiece, eggs at ·10 to ·15 francs, rice, meat, and French brandy at 3·50 francs a bottle. Larrey was preparing to evacuate the sick and wounded to Paris. He must make room, for the great battle was imminent.

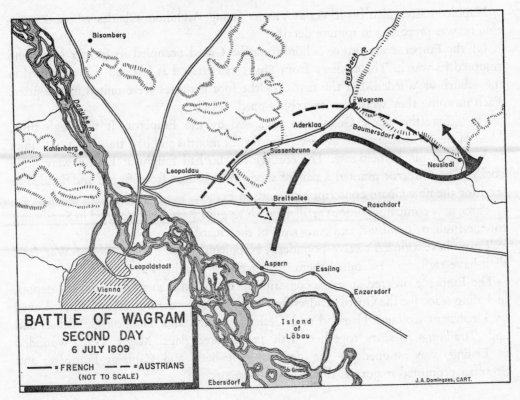

BATTLE OF WAGRAM
SECOND DAY
6 JULY 1809
—— = FRENCH - - - = AUSTRIANS
(NOT TO SCALE)

J.A.Domingoes, CART.

WAGRAM

Napoleon concentrated all his available forces for the next crossing from Lobau and made careful preparations, constructing several bridges and accumulating ammunition and supplies. On the night of 4–5 July he crossed the river with his main force, prepared for battle.

The first French attack was repulsed. Early on the second day, while the Austrians were making progress towards enveloping the French left, the French attacked the Austrian left. To resolve the situation, Napoleon made a mass attack on the Austrian center. The French were successful and Wagram ranked as one of Napoleon's greatest victories, though the Austrians succeeded in withdrawing in good order from the field. On 12 and 14 July the Austrians fought again at Znaim, then proposed a truce. On 18 July the campaign ended in an armistice.

Île Napoléon. 1 July. Morning. Since 4 a.m. the grenadiers of the duty battalion and chasseurs of the escort had been doing their chores around the Emperor's tents. These were pitched to the west of the island near Lob Grund, a wooded beach bristling with entrenchments that protected the bridges, now solidly constructed, leading to the right bank at Ebersdorf.

Though they were the 'old of the Old' whom nothing could surprise, the Grumblers had never seen anything like this. In six weeks the Emperor had 'abolished the Danube' and transformed the miserable island, on which the army had once floundered about for two days, into a town 'with streets lighted like those of a city' and canals lined with workshops, forges, food stores, and ammunition depots. It was surrounded by trenches, with a double line before the old bridgehead, garrisoned by Masséna's 4th Corps and policed by 'immortals'[2] who had never seen Austrians at such close range before.

Deceived by the redoubts and batteries facing Aspern, Essling, and Enzersdorf, Archduke Charles massed his armies between the three villages. He established outposts so near the French lines that on one of his tours the Emperor found himself within 150 feet of one. 'Retire, Sire', the Austrian officer called out. 'You have no business to be here!'

'Admirable words', Las Cases comments in his *Memorial*, '. . . words that reflect everlasting credit upon the army that uttered them . . .'

The Emperor would not cross the Danube where the Archduke expected him to, but downstream, south of a small islet the men had christened 'Alexander' after Berthier. Napoleon planned to send the army across during the night of 4 July and the following day, after Captain Baste of the marines, commanding the 'fleet', had cleared a path for Oudinot's troops, and the sappers had thrown bridges across.

4 July. 9 p.m. A violent storm broke, sending torrents of rain down upon the troops massed on the Island of Lobau. Thunder from heaven joined that of the guns deployed the whole length of the island as they shelled Enzersdorf which was soon in flames.

'Nasty weather,' the Emperor observed to a grenadier at the door of his tent.

'Better than none at all', rejoined the old soldier.

Baste pushed off with his flotilla and let his boats drift downstream to cover Oudinot's grenadiers and voltigeurs as they crossed the river. At 2 a.m. Masséna's corps crossed on rafts and bridges, followed at 9 by the foot Guard and the cavalry. The artillery did not join them on the left bank, where the rest of the army was concentrated, until four in the afternoon.

The weather cleared, revealing a superb view. In the distance the Poles saw the Kahlenberg, its summit still haunted by the ghost of Sobieski who had delivered Vienna from the Turks in 1683. Executing a left wheel into position at 7 p.m., the French found themselves in three lines, facing the Austrians who had retired to the Russbach with their right flank at the Bisamberg, center at Wagram, and left at Neusiedl.

The Emperor had his tents pitched half a mile northeast of Raschdorf. He ordered an immediate attack, fearing the Austrians would escape during the night.

[2] Elite gendarmes.

The Archduke had no such desire, for he was hoping his brother Archduke John, who should be just ahead of his left wing, would arrive and outflank the French.

Bernadotte, Eugène, Oudinot, and Davout halted on a front extending from Breitenlee beyond Neusiedl. Their troops were tired, parched with thirst, and in disorder. Some showed signs of panic; however, the divisions 're-formed around the Guard, that immovable reserve in time of danger'.

So far only the Guard's artillery had been in action and had suffered casualties. Major Greiner had had his arm shot off.

The evening was warm and muggy. The smoke of battle, hanging motionless on the air, enveloped the field. Tonight's bivouac would be short. The men had no fuel and the wet straw burned poorly. However, the prudent Guardsmen carried many treasures in their packs – in their caissons, too – and fed their horses grass they had brought with them.

The Emperor slept in the lee of twelve grenadier drums stacked in groups of three. The staff worked under the stars. It was certain by now that the great engagement would take place next day.

At dawn the skirmishers of both armies were engaged and cannon thundered along the whole front. From their assembly point at Raschdorf the Guard could see the whole battlefield except the parts obscured by smoke. Breaking ranks to get a better view, the soldiers followed the movements of the army from the sound of musketry.

Marshal Davout was advancing on the right. In front a battle was raging near Baumersdorf. Sounds of gunfire came from the rear and left flank.

The Emperor and Archduke Charles had taken the offensive simultaneously, and each was maneuvering on his own right flank.

With the evident intention of supporting Davout, towards eight o'clock the Emperor ordered the Guard to shoulder arms. He then mounted the cavalry reserve to lead them to the right flank. A moment later Bernadotte's Saxons on the left, near Aderklaa, were seized with panic, sweeping Masséna's troops before them in a rout. The Austrian right promptly advanced ten kilometers and occupied Essling and Aspern, threatening Enzersdorf, the bridges, and the line of retreat.

The Guard and cavalry reserve were brought back to their point of departure. From a mound half a mile from Aderklaa, at the angle of the Austrian line, the Emperor watched the battle 'in a rain of round shot'. Then he mounted Euphrates, his snow-white Persian horse, and traversed the battle line from end to end. His mere presence halted the fugitives. Retracing his steps, he carried them forward again under heavy fire.

11 a.m. Having returned the combatants to their positions and brought back his reserve intact, the Emperor reversed his original dispositions at the height of the battle. He now decided to penetrate the center of the enemy line which had become overextended. Although his own left flank was wavering dangerously, using his reserves to shore it up might diminish his chances of destroying the enemy.

With great care and sang-froid the Emperor took his time mounting the new maneuver. He ordered Masséna to Essling by a flank march, a feat only this commander could have executed, sending Lasalle's and Saint-Sulpice's cavalry in support. Then he sent Eugène to Aderklaa. He ordered Macdonald to form his two divisions in columns of attack facing Süssenbrunn, supported by the Bavarians, the cavalry reserve, and the Guard, while Lauriston opened a path for them with the 72 guns of the Guard and 40 from the Army of Italy.

D'Aboville and the horse batteries advanced at a gallop, followed by Boulart and Pommereul. Then Drouot came up with a battery of twelve-pounders which his gunners unlimbered under fire and set up in front of the infantry, within easy range of the enemy.

Deployed along a mile of front, this formidable artillery silenced the enemy guns and stopped all movement between Breitenlee and Süssenbrunn; however, its losses were lamentable. D'Aboville's right arm was shot off; Martin was mortally hit; Boulart and Drouot were wounded. In all, 28 officers were put out of action. When several gun crews were reduced to one or two men the Emperor called for volunteers from his old grenadiers and chasseurs.

He called for 20 from each company and 50 stepped out of ranks. They crossed the Raschdorf plateau at breakneck speed, passing Macdonald's column in a narrow valley on their left. Under a hail of balls they advanced to the point where Major Henrion was waiting to receive them and send them forward.

The Emperor came to see how they were getting on. This is a sample of what he saw:

'Depold, Jean-Claude, chasseur of the first battalion, being posted at No. 6 gun of a battery of twelve-pounders, most of whose gunners had been killed, took the place of the right-hand gunner. Through his industry and courage he contributed largely to the defence of this important position in the face of sharp attacks by the enemy.'

'The detachment of chasseurs and grenadiers sent to the foot batteries of the Guard artillery behaved with the greatest gallantry', Drouot added to his report – and he should know.

Led by Reille, the Emperor's aide, the Young Guard advanced to support Macdonald on the right of the grand battery. Farther to the right, before the mound occupied by the staff, the Poles and chasseurs advanced, their cloaks slung over one shoulder, ready to charge. Bessières and Nansouty's divisions supported the left flank.

Formed in columns of attack behind the hill, the last reserve of dragoons, horse grenadiers, and infantry of the Old Guard stood motionless under the enemy fire. All was ready. Then, from Baumersdorf to Aspern the whole front line advanced.

Macdonald reached Süssenbrunn, supported on the right by the light cavalry of the Guard under Guyot. At this moment Bessières was needed to charge Liechtensteins' cavalry – but the Marshal had just been hit. This was a double calamity, for neither Nansouty nor Walther dared charge without orders, and no orders arrived.

Bessières was borne unconscious from the field on a litter. His men thought he was dead and some were sobbing. All swore to avenge him.

'That was a fine shot, Bessières', the Emperor told him later. 'It made my Guard cry . . . but it also cost me 20,000 prisoners which you would have taken for me . . .'

Time passed. In front the light-horse, led by Delaître, crushed Schwarzenberg's uhlans. Meanwhile, the *chasseurs à cheval* upset the dragoons of Rysz and together they overran three battalions of infantry.

'The 1st Regiment was thrown back once', Guyot wrote Daumesnil, 'because the infantry was formed in squares and killed ten of our men and as many horses. But I gave a lecture to the 2nd Regiment that convinced them we were the stronger. Of the enemy's three guns, we captured one ... That, my dear friend, was about the end of our day ...'

By six, Masséna had reached Leopoldau; but Lasalle was dead, shot down during a charge. The artillery of the Guard had fired all its ammunition. 'Hurry up!' Boisselier shouted to his gunners as he stood there exhausted, his coat on the ground. 'The sooner done the sooner ended.'

The battle was won. The enemy was in retreat but was not destroyed. Archduke Charles retired slowly into Hungary, unpursued. The skirmishers of his brother John appeared in Drouot's rear. They were too late.

Halfway between Raschdorf and Wagram the Emperor, worn out, retired to his tent. The Old Guard stood watch. Initiated into the mysteries of the military art, they understood the situation perfectly.

CHAPTER 10

Schönbrunn

SINCE 13 July the Emperor had been at Schönbrunn drafting the peace treaty and reorganizing the army. After the battle of Znaim, where the Guard remained in reserve behind Marmont's corps, it returned to its camp and billets around the château.

The Emperor visited the wounded of his Guard and rewarded them with citations and medals. Sixty silver stars were granted to the artillery whose losses at Wagram totaled 28 officers and 357 men in killed and wounded. Captain Martin of the foot artillery died of his wounds. At his funeral Boulart, the new colonel commandant, delivered the eulogy of this veteran officer 'of sterling merits'. Then, at the end of the ceremony, he received into the corps a young graduate of the École de Metz named Hubert Lyautey whose nephew became a famous marshal of France.[1]

The Old Guard was in need of reinforcement. The two foot regiments were replenished with 456 selected NCO's from the Line; the cavalry, with 410 from the curassiers, light cavalry, and dragoons.

The 1st Conscript-Chasseurs and 1st Conscript-Grenadiers arrived in Vienna the day after Wagram, having journeyed by forced marches from the Tyrol where they fought Andreas Hofer's insurrectionists. The units, 3,000 strong, were well dressed, well led, and provided with vehicles. The Emperor reviewed them immediately.

The Young Guard was now formed into a division of two brigades under Curial. The first contained three regiments of conscript-, *tirailleur-*, and fusilier-chasseurs under General Gros; the second, the three corresponding grenadier regiments under Roguet. They were quartered at Enzersdorf.

The enterprising men soon learned that balls picked up on the fields of Wagram and Essling and brought to the park would fetch 5 sous each. It was estimated that there were 100,000 of them. (This represented quite an inflation since 1805 when those on the battlefield of Ulm had fetched but a sou apiece.)

On the stage route there was considerable activity in both directions. The 2nd Conscript-Grenadiers and -Chasseurs were training at Augsburg and Friedberg under Lt. Colonels Robert and Mouton-Duvernet. 'I wouldn't have believed a soldier could be in such good shape', wrote a recruit of the 2nd Conscript-Chasseurs. 'I used to be skinny, but now I look as fat as a commissary! . . .'

The soldiers' morale was high. At morning and evening drill the awkward youths were drilled separately in special squads. The instructors were forbidden to lay a hand

---

[1] Hero of the conquest, then administrator, of Morocco, whose tomb was honored as a shrine at Rabat until 1961 when his body was returned to France. – Ed.

on the men, to address them by the familiar 'thou', or to 'suggest that they stand treat for drinks'. Here at last was a case where sergeants had to treat privates in bars. But the privates had to salute their NCO's 'with hand to shako'.

It was forbidden to leave quarters without permission. Infractions were punished with eight days' arrest and fifteen extra drills 'with the third class awkward squad'. Punishments were especially severe for NCO's. According to Mouton-Duvernet, the latter were 'veterans from whom one had a right to expect the zeal and exactitude that warranted their appointment by His Majesty'. (In the Young Guard, as in the Old, the nominations for NCO were submitted to the Emperor for approval.)

The master drummers of the fusiliers taught their drum corps to beat the Assembly, To Arms, To the Colors, Mess Call, Dismissal, Quickstep, Retreat, and Charge as well as the *Aux Champs, Ban, Diane, Rigodon*,[2] and the Roll for the Emperor in 'proper Guard style'.

On 15 August the Emperor's birthday was celebrated throughout the Empire. After the parade the soldiers had a gala dinner with 'beer, brandy, bread, and roast meat'. The officers, 'in ball dress if possible', attended a banquet and ball at the house of the governor, General Moulin, a former enemy of Bonaparte and Sieyès in the Directory, whose political opinions had changed.

At the review the sergeants and corporals of the Young Guard wore the epaulets of the Guard for the first time. The chasseurs wore overalls and short gaiters, and the grenadiers long gaiters of nankeen.

Drouot proudly presented his band, but was vexed by his gunners' dress. His regiment had been awarded sixty stars of the Legion of Honor but so far, no uniforms. Transferred from the Line, the men still wore their old regimentals with shakos. The first arrivals managed to draw 'a few grenadiers' epaulets, white waistcoats, blue fatigue jackets, and foot grenadiers' sabers'. However, something must be done about their caps. Drouot was chagrined to present them in shakos, since his gunners belonged officially to the Old Guard and should wear bearskin bonnets like the rest.

The Emperor passed along the ranks, congratulated the bravest soldiers, and decorated Captain Cicéron, whose conduct was brilliant at Essling, with the gold star of the Legion. 'Monsieur Cicéron', wrote Dorsenne, 'is the son of the director of the Imperial Polytechnic School. Colonel Krasinski and the Count de Pac received gold eagles for exceptional bravery and Dessaix, the trumpet major of the Polish light-horse, a silver eagle.'

The grenadiers marched past at their ordinary step, and then at a quickstep of 100 paces a minute.[3] However, the chasseurs distinguished themselves by marching 120.

Finally, a great marksmanship competition took place in the regiments. The conscripts fired three rounds at 100, 200, and 300 yards. The first prize was a pair of shoes and new overalls; the second, overalls and gaiters; the third, gaiters.

One festivity followed another at Schönbrunn where a *Te Deum* was sung, followed by banquets, receptions, and awards. The Emperor presented marshal's batons to

[2] The Salute, Announcement, Reveille, and the call announcing a 'bull's-eye', also used as reveille.
[3] Route marches were made at the rate of 85 to 90 paces a minute.

Macdonald, Oudinot, and Marmont and signed numerous patents of nobility. All colonel generals of the Guard were now dukes. Mortier became Duke of Treviso in 1808, and Bessières Duke of Istria in May 1809. Soult had been made Duke of Dalmatia in 1808 but was annoyed not to be Duke of Austerlitz. Some marshals, and Davout who was Duke of Auerstädt, were given the titles of their greatest feats of arms. At this birthday celebration the Emperor created Davout Prince of Eckmühl as well, naming Berthier Prince of Wagram and Masséna Prince of Essling.

The colonels commanding Guard corps received bonuses of 6,000 francs, and all amputees were compensated. General de Saint-Sulpice, the Empress' master of the horse and a brilliant cuirassier commander, was named colonel of the dragoons of the Guard, replacing Arrighi, now Duke of Padua, who inherited the cuirassiers of General d'Espagne, killed at Essling. One man was missing at the ceremony. 'Monsieur le Maréchal', as Bessières was known in the Guard, had been sent to Paris to rest and recuperate from the wound that had made his Grumblers cry at Wagram.

In his hospital on the Rennweg, Larrey was exhausted. He put away the scalpels and saws he had used to amputate the legs of Daumesnil and Corbineau of the horse chasseurs and Captain Ponsard of the foot, and the arms of d'Aboville, Greiner, etc. Larrey made his report, heaping praise upon his colleagues.

Of 1,200 wounded, 600 had been returned in a few days to their corps where the medical staff looked after them; 254, including 38 amputees, were evacuated to France; 145 died of their wounds (from tetanus, gangrene, fever, etc.); 80 amputees 'completely recovered'; 150 seriously wounded were retired as 'unfit for duty' and pensioned with a certificate engraved on paper for privates and on parchment for NCO's.[4]

At Schönbrunn the Emperor drew up plans for a new order to be called the 'Order of the Three Golden Fleeces'. This was to be an imperial order, outranking the Legion of Honor instituted under the Consulate. Its badge, an eagle holding a golden fleece in its beak and in its talons the ancient fleeces of the King of Spain and Emperor of Germany, was designed by the Emperor himself.[5] Among the Guard officers nominated to the new order were Dériot, Krasinski, Letort, and Marthod, Captain Baste of the marines, and the field officers Albert and Rabusson.

Finally, Napoleon signed the list of awards for Wagram. Berthezène, Boyer, Colbert, Decouz, Friederichs, and Lepic all became commanders of the Legion of Honor. Kozietulski – the 'only officer intact after the charge at Somosierra' – was made an officer, and Captain Fredro, Lieutenant Zelouka, etc. of the Polish light-horse were awarded silver stars. Many troopers became chevaliers.

Montholon quotes the Emperor as follows:

'The French have two equally strong passions which seem mutually contradictory, but which nevertheless spring from the same sentiment: a love of equality and a love of distinction. A government cannot satisfy both at once except by exercising the most strict justice. The laws and actions of government must be equal for all; honors and

---

[4] If one consults the medical records of the Crimean, Civil, and Spanish-American Wars, one will find this recovery record unsurpassed in the annals of military medicine before World War I. – Ed.

[5] This project was shelved when the Emperor married an Austrian Archduchess.

rewards must be bestowed only on those most worthy of them in the eyes of all. Merit is pardonable, but never intrigue. The Legion of Honor has served as a vast lever for virtue, talent, and courage. Misused, it could have been a plague. We should alienate the entire army if the court or clique spirit were ever allowed to dominate either its awards or its administration.'

The fête ended in the evening with fireworks prepared by officers of the Guard. The Emperor watched them from a terrace at Schönbrunn, then left with Berthier to view the illuminations in Vienna. Above the waltzes and laughter, cries of 'Vive l'Empereur!' rent the night. It was a magical evening. But not for all . . .

On his bed of pain in the Esterhazy palace Daumesnil listened to the shouting and singing of the crowd and watched the fireworks. In the next bed his comrade-in-arms Marie-Louis-Hercule-Hubert Corbineau was bleeding to death from a sudden hemorrhage. Daumesnil shouted for the attendants who were outside watching the fireworks.

In a burst of energy he got out of bed, holding onto the clasps that held the edges of his wound together. Hopping on one leg and pushing a chair before him, he reached the staircase and started to descend. Then, overcome by pain, he fainted in the arms of a servant who was attracted by his cries and carried him back to bed. On regaining consciousness he looked over and saw Corbineau still alive. 'But you don't realize', Daumesnil explained, 'that I too wanted to go see the illuminations!'

These were now extinguished. Parades, visits, theater parties in the court theater at Schönbrunn, and shopping expeditions in town occupied the spare time of the officers of the Guard. The Trinkhallen in the Prater, the *Kaffee mit Schlag*,[6] the brandied plums enchanted the soldiers who also like to '*coquettiren*', dance the polka and mazurka, and frequent the small theatres. But the veterans noticed that the Viennese *Gemütlichkeit*[7] was not what it had been in 1805.

During a parade the Emperor just missed being assassinated by a student named Stabs who 'admired and hated' him. This expressed pretty much the prevailing Viennese sentiment towards Napoleon and his soldiers.

On 14 October a peace was signed at Schönbrunn. With Russia banished from Europe, and Prussia muzzled, Austria was now disarmed. There was no longer any Europe, for Europe was now the Empire.

The guns of every town saluted the peace that the Emperor had sought but that England did not want. On the day of the signing the Guard received orders to return to France by easy stages.

'If all goes well in Austria send them to Strasbourg', the Emperor wrote Berthier the day after his arrival at Fontainebleau. (This letter, dated 27 October 1809, is still at Schönbrunn.)

The ceremonial battery at the Tuileries fired 101 guns and the Imperial standard was raised over the palace.

Europe was silent.

[6] Coffee served with whipped cream.
[7] Sympathetic friendliness.

BOOK IV

THE GUARD IN SPLENDOR

CHAPTER 1

Imperial Bridegroom

THE Emperor was obsessed with the idea of 'finishing the devilish business in Spain' where, removed from supervision, his brother and the marshals were playing sovereign and courtiers and permitting the guerrillas and a few English to beat the best soldiers in his army.

After the battle of Talavera in June Kellermann – now Count of Valmy – wrote Berthier; 'This is no ordinary war. One could not end it unless he possessed the head and arms of Hercules . . .'

Napoleon thought otherwise. Having fought several successful battles there within a few weeks, he hoped by going to Spain to finish the war at one stroke.

'Call a meeting of my Guard to settle its finances and prepare it for a campaign in Spain', he wrote the Duke of Feltre (Clarke) on 23 November. 'I propose to march . . . with 4 regiments each of conscripts and *tirailleurs*, 2 of fusiliers and Old Guard, 5,000 cavalry, and 60 guns – about 25,000 troops in all, including the surgeons and service troops. They must be ready to leave on 15 January.' Then he appointed Berthier chief of staff of the Army of Spain.

The council of generals inspected the depots and went over the clothing accounts. Then they visited the magazines and appealed to everyone's patriotism and devotion to the Emperor with the result that the Young Guard returning from Strasbourg was decently clothed in time to take part on 3 December in the fêtes celebrating the fifth anniversary of the coronation.

These were magnificent – the finest since the coronation itself. One hundred and twenty grenadiers and gendarmes and a battalion of fusiliers were on duty at Notre-Dame. General Dériot commanded the guard of honor. Sixty chasseurs were posted at the Legislature. Two battalions of Guard conscripts lined the route to the Tuileries while the elite gendarmes policed the grounds. The palace guard was doubled.

The rest of the foot Guard was stationed on the Quai Bonaparte, lining the route to the Place de la Concorde where the cavalry was massed between the bridge and the Garde-Meuble. The white Imperial standard, edged with red and blue and blazoned with a gold crowned eagle holding a thunderbolt, floated over the palaces.

In the evening the Guard gave a dinner to the regiments of the Duke of Abrantes (Junot). The 'black sheep' remained on duty at the barracks, but the men 'confined to quarters or under arrest' (except the 'deserters and thieves') were freed.

A great parade took place the following day in the Place de la Carrousel. The soup was made the night before and served at eight in the morning.

171

Four thousand guests, including the Kings of Württemberg, Saxony, Holland, Bavaria, Westphalia, and Naples[1] with their courts, attended the evening reception in the Hôtel de Ville. After many speeches 'a unique event in the history of Europe occurred when a majority of its rulers sat down together at a banquet as members of a powerful confederation'. This was followed by an elegant ball and supper and a display of fireworks for the Parisians. In the course of the evening the Emperor and Empress visited the barracks, which were illuminated, and distributed gifts of money.

During the hunting parties that followed at Fontainebleau the fusiliers guarded the Emperor, receiving a month's extra pay.

There was general rejoicing over Bessières' victory in Holland where, with the help of the national guards from the northern departments, he had driven the English from Walcheren Island.

Rumors were rife concerning the Emperor's impending divorce. Since Josephine had produced no heir to the throne, the problem of the succession had become crucial. Whatever the Emperor's personal feelings, he decided to divorce her and remarry for reasons of state. The divorce proved to be a lengthy affair. The final decree was pronounced on 15 December. On that day he reviewed the Young Guard in the Empress' presence. 'You showed courage', he wrote her that evening.

Two weeks later, when the Emperor appeared alone at the parade, the Grumblers thought of Josephine whom they had liked to see on the balcony watching them march. Years after, amid the miseries of 1812, one of them exclaimed: 'He hadn't ought to have left the old one . . . She brought him luck, and us too.'

The coronation fêtes had barely ended before Napoleon advanced the date of the Guard's departure for Spain. It was to march in three divisions. The 1st and 2nd under Generals Roguet and Dumoustier were each composed of two regiments of conscripts and two of *tirailleurs*, with two route[2] regiments of horse Guards, a division of artillery, a company of gendarmes, and a detachment of service troops. The 3rd Division, composed of fusiliers, grenadiers, and chasseurs, was to follow. The orders concluded:

'All the cavalry, with 60 guns, 4,000 tools loaded on wagons with teams, and 6 pontoon bridges with pontooneers and marines shall present themselves to the Emperor, ready to leave on 1 January . . . The lancers of the Grand Duke of Berg will be attached to the Guard . . . The Duke of Istria (Bessières) will proceed to the Peninsula . . . In a short while I shall be in Spain . . .'

He ordered Roguet to divide his force into three columns and leave for Bordeaux on 19 December, and Dumoustier to take his division to Tours and wait there for orders.

In Chartres on 16 December Roguet inspected his division.

On the 19th the cavalry and first brigade of conscript- and *tirailleur*-chasseurs departed with four guns and several caissons under Mouton-Duvernet, followed next day by the second under Lt. Colonel Robert. The roads were bad all the way to Tours. It rained and the marches were long for the conscripts; nevertheless they sang.

[1] Murat, who was also Grand Duke of Berg. – Ed.
[2] Made up of mixed detachments. – *Ibid.*

At Tours they crossed the Loire by a beautiful bridge with elliptical arches. There were pretty promenades on the ramparts but all the trees had been cut down. Food was dear and the subalterns had difficulty making ends meet. Beyond the Loire each soldier received a bonus from the Emperor of ·20 francs a day plus campaign rations.

In Poitiers the countryside was fertile and the weather improved. In Angoulême the soldiers saw women in wide-brimmed white hats, enormous 16th-century ruffs, and short skirts. On the 30th Roguet reached Bordeaux where General Boivin found billets for the troops and markets where provisions might be had. He arranged for the lame men, who were numerous, to stay in Saint Raphael's Hospital.

With reinforcements acquired along the route, six thousand men and 1,150 horses turned up for the review on 14 January 1810. The men were drilled twice a day; however, target practice had to be curtailed for lack of cartridges.

On the 25th the first brigade left for Bayonne with the cavalry and elite gendarmes, followed next day by the second. The road was so crowded with men and vehicles marching to and from Spain, with prisoners (the Spanish ragged and the English arrogant) and wounded that Roguet had to enlist the commissary's aide to find food and lodging for his men.

By 4 February the whole division was at Bayonne with orders to proceed to Spain immediately. The infantry had marched 500 miles since leaving Paris and the men had worn out three pairs of shoes. Those coming from Augsburg had gone through six pairs. However, the Chief of Staff's orders must be obeyed.

As barrels of shoes were **being** emptied Roguet was briefed on the military situation:

At the end of 1809 Marshal Jourdan had been relieved in command of the theater by Soult. Joseph now had 78,000 men including Victor's 1st Corps, Sebastiani's 4th, Mortier's 5th, and Dessolle's division. Concentrated in La Mancha, this army was preparing to invade the south. Suchet's 3rd Corps and Augureau's 7th were occupying Arragon and Catalonia. An army under Masséna with units commanded by Ney, Junot, Montbrun, and d'Erlon was poised to enter Portugal. A northern army under the Duke of Istria (Bessières) was being formed around Burgos as a reserve to guard the rear of the Imperial armies and protect the stage routes.

The French were opposed by Blake and O'Donnell, guarding Valencia; Arizaga, guarding the Sierra Morena; the Duke of Albuquerque and Graham's English division operating in Estremadura; and the divisions of the Marquès de la Romaña and Hill operating around Ciudad Rodrigo. The guerrilla bands of Mina were in Navarre and Viscaya, and Wellington was organizing an Anglo-Portuguese army of 60,000 in Beira.

The French morale was low. The half-organized units had been hastily dispatched to Spain where they found the King uneasy and the marshals tired and jealous of each other. The guerrilla bands were formidable and inaccessible, the English solidly entrenched, and the population hostile and cruel.

Lt. Colonel Delaître left Bayonne on 4 February with a route regiment of light cavalry of the Guard, followed on successive days by two infantry brigades, and a second regiment of dragoons and grenadiers under Lt. Colonel Marthod.

On the 16th Roguet reached Logroño where his men camped on the outskirts of the town. Since they were raw recruits, half of whom had never fired a shot in anger, he had no impression of commanding the Imperial Guard. Their discipline left much to be desired. Many reported sick. Yet it devolved upon them to uphold the reputation won by the Guard in 1808.

'It is useless to shout at a soldier', Roguet wrote in his orders. 'An officer inspires confidence by keeping calm.'

The rations had improved, with two pounds daily of 'almost white bread', four ounces of soup bread, a bottle of wine, half a pound of meat, and four ounces of dried vegetable or two of rice. The forage ration was 13 pounds of hay plus a bushel of oats or barley and 20 pounds of straw.

A modus vivendi was reached between the *alcaldes*, colonels, and commissaries; but the soldiers were confined to camp. After some *tirailleurs* were assassinated no detail of less than eight or ten was permitted to leave a village. Grenadiers and chasseurs had to sleep with a full pack and a musket with 'flint inserted' at the head of their beds. Any sentry post commander failing in vigilance was obliged to mount guard as a private, without stripes or saber.

Roguet's division was put under the command of General Dorsenne, governor of Burgos, Soria, and Aranda, who in turn was responsible to Marshal Bessières.

'Our foothold is precarious', wrote Roguet. 'Life is difficult and dangerous, and the condition of the roads and communications beyond belief. The influence of the monks and priests, the indolence of the men, their arrogant pride . . . are all anachronistic. The form – as well as the spirit – of the government is opposed to any progress. On the contrary, it seems deliberately to keep the nation in a splendid, somber, and sterile isolation, despite its contacts with other civilizations, despite Cervantes and Murillo . . .' He concluded: 'Only Napoleon's genius could put it back on the right track.'

Saint-Cloud, 30 March 1810. 5 p.m. The Emperor and Archduchess Marie-Louise of Austria arrived from Compiègne, escorted by the cavalry of the Guard. The foot grenadiers lined their route from the bridge and the horse artillery fired 101 guns. Their marriage was scheduled for the following day.

What marriage? In the dormitories at the École Militaire the men did not understand what had happened. Prince Berthier had gone to Vienna on 11 March and 'married' the daughter of the *Kaiserlik* Emperor 'by proxy'. By simple logic, since the Marshal had married her first he 'must have been the first to sleep with her'. Sergeant Coigniet, a simple soul, told Captain Belcourt 'he would like to have been in his shoes'. Well, then, so the *Tondu* was *cocu*![3]

When his bride arrived at Compiègne on the 27th, Napoleon went to the Chancellery while the new Empress stayed at the Château. However, he seemed happy enough – even in love. The cuirassiers of the escort related that at Courcelles, the last relay station, the Emperor was waiting for the procession. In a hurry to see his bride, he jumped into her coach 'like a cuirassier' – tearing her dress in the process.

[3] A cuckold.

174

On Sunday he would marry her himself. The day before, 25 NCO's went to the Archbishop's Palace to fetch the imperial crown – which proved that the Emperor's marriage was more than just a grenadier's night out.

To the booming of guns the civil ceremony took place in the presence only of the Imperial family, household, and Guard whose bands played during dinner that evening at Saint-Cloud and afterwards in the salons. The Emperor himself chose the program. The fountains, gardens, and *orangerie* were illuminated. The weather was bad, with wind and rain, just as on the night of the coup d'état ten years before, the grenadiers recalled.

But Monday, 2 April, was a day of radiant sunshine. The Emperor was due in Paris at noon; however, Conscript-Chasseur Rimmel, quartered in the 'rue Mouftard', tells us he got up at 5 a.m. in order to be under arms at 5.30, and remained so until 6 p.m.!

Noon. The guns had been firing for the past half-hour. The Polish light-horse arrived with Guyot's chasseurs and Mameluks, then the dragoons led by Saint-Sulpice, and the thirty-six carriages of the great officers of state and Imperial family, followed by the Empress' coach drawn by eight horses, but it was empty. Covered with diamonds, she was seated beside the Emperor in the coronation coach, surrounded by the colonel generals. Thirty Guard NCO's followed the coach ahead of the gendarmes and princes' carriages, and Walther's horse grenadiers brought up the rear.

The foot Guard rendered honors in the Grand Court and lined the route along the avenue to the bridge. The bands played *What Better than to Be Home with Your Family?* Passing through the Bois and the Champs-Elysées, the procession joined the grenadiers and chasseurs in the Place de la Concorde.

In the great gallery of the Louvre the officers seated the important guests. NCO's in bearskin bonnets with sabers, stockings, and buckled shoes were presented to the ladies by Dorsenne as 'their knights who would bring them refreshments'. After the party each received a bottle of the Emperor's own wine. They 'had never drunk such good wine before'.

The Mass and marriage ceremony were performed by Cardinal Fesch, the Grand Almoner. Afterwards the Guard paraded as Their Majesties watched from the balcony, and 'cheered them with inexpressible enthusiasm'. A double guard was left at the palace and the bands were posted in the salons and gardens.

'The Empress is beautiful but she looks very young and fragile', Rimmel observed.

At the gates of a somber and silent Malamaison, where Josephine wept alone, the *tirailleurs* waited to be relieved . . .

The Paris revelers gorged at buffets, drained fountains of wine, and applauded the fireworks. But to the sensitive Parisians something was lacking. They had not been allowed to see their Emperor, to worship him, to rejoice with him, to follow his coach to Notre-Dame, nor even to cut their last candle in two to light their dormer windows. They had been cheated out of a glance from the man whom they had elected emperor six years before because he believed in justice, equality, and glory.

Why had he not presented his young wife to them? With one smile she would have conquered this crowd who desired nothing more than that. An Austrian? Never mind, she carried in the folds of her imperial robe the third peace treaty of the reign – peace with Austria whom they had fought for centuries. The final peace . . .

The people of Paris and France were right. Neither poems nor songs nor celebrations nor gifts of money could replace the presence of the man they loved. He had not discovered this. Would he ever, now that he was also Emperor of Rome, of Europe?

On 17 February the Senate decreed: 'The Imperial city of Rome is the second capital of the Empire. The Emperor's eldest son will . . . bear the title "King of Rome" . . . The Imperial couple will be crowned in St. Peter's . . . on the tenth anniversary of the coronation at Notre-Dame . . .'

The Emperor's eldest son? So that was why they needed a new empress!

'Let us watch over the Empire.' The band of the Guard regiment on duty played this every morning in the court of the Carrousel.

This watchword was relayed throughout France to her natural frontiers. Beyond, through the mortar of the imperial edifice, it was transmitted to schools where the French administrative system was being taught, and applied to the dependent peoples.

His brothers' failure to grasp his Imperial designs had obliged Napoleon to found a dynasty. Kings by the grace of Napoleon, they had pretended to be kings by the grace of God and pursued their own designs. No, the family system had had its day.

The European Confederation had its own institutions and legal code and its own army which, though its basic component was French, combined units from the Rhineland, Baden, Württemberg, Bavaria, Hesse, Saxony, Prussia, Nassau, Holland, Portugal, Spain, Italy, Croatia, Greece, and Poland. This federal army of between 600,000 and 700,000 men was arrayed against England, the enemy of a united Europe. It needed a large, solidly-framed reserve capable of rallying to the Imperial standard units as disparate as those of the *Grande Armée*.

The Imperial Guard, without losing its special character, was to become the reserve of the European Army.

CHAPTER 2

The Gilded Phalanx

RETURNING to Paris after his victory in Holland, Bessières advised the Emperor to keep with the colors the national guards of the northern departments, since the Marshal had formed a high opinion of them during the campaign.

'I cannot hold them against their will', replied the Emperor. 'They must send me a written request . . . or else give tacit consent to serve.'

Napoleon thought it would be good policy to admit a regiment of national guards to the Young Guard and signed a decree to this effect on 1 January 1810. He directed the Duke of Istria (Bessières) to submit a list of officers and NCO's, and General Soulès to organize the regiment.

The inauguration took place on the Esplanade at Lille on 1 April. The regiment was commanded by Colonel Couloumy, an old soldier of the Bourbonnais Regiment and officer of the Guard of the Legislature. Without private means, Couloumy could not compete with his colleagues in the Guard, so the Emperor granted him Old Guard pay and allowances.

Meanwhile, two Italian units were attached to the Imperial Guard. These were the *Vélites* of Florence and Turin, raised as bodyguards for the Emperor's sister Elisa, Grand Duchess of Tuscany, and his brother-in-law Prince Borghese, governor of the Transalpine departments.

The Florentine *vélites* numbered 600 men under Major Dufour, a former officer of the Guides of Bonaparte and captain in the foot chasseurs, wounded at Marengo. The officers and NCO's came from the chasseurs, and the men from the Tuscan departments, being youths of eighteen and over, five-foot-ten, who could 'pay 200 francs for their board'. The battalion was uniformed in Florence in blue coats faced and lined with scarlet, white waistcoats and breeches, white epaulets with red centers, and shakos with scarlet plumes.

The guard duty with 'Her Imperial Highness the Grand Duchess' was not very arduous. Nevertheless, Major Dufour found his troop expensive and sent a request for additional funds, which was returned with 'Refused' scrawled above an imperial 'N'.

The *Vélites* of Turin mustered 475 men under Major Cicéron who was already well known in the Guard. The officers and NCO's came chiefly from the grenadiers. The inauguration took place in the Riding School on 28 May, the *vélites* wearing blue coats lined with scarlet, white waistcoats and breeches, shakos with white cords and scarlet pompons, and scarlet sword-knots.

Prince Borghese was very proud of the battalion and spent much time training its cadres. He wanted it to be magnificent and to be dressed in Paris, hoping vainly that the ministry would foot the bill. He paid his twelve drummers 64 francs instead of the usual 50, and requested a band, a flag, and additional funds for office expenses.

The Emperor refused him the band and the office expenses. As for the flag, the Minister wrote: 'We could hardly propose to His Majesty that an eagle be awarded to the *Vélites* of Turin . . . Only the regiments of the Old Guard have eagles . . .'

In the spring of 1810 the Emperor endeavored to dazzle his young empress. 'When a young and beautiful wife fell to my lot was I not to show my pleasure?' he wrote. Journeys and fêtes succeeded one another. The court was brilliant and the Old Guard was kept busy with ceremonies.

At Compiègne where the Emperor went stag-hunting, and at Saint-Cloud where there were daily receptions, the guard duty was arduous. But who complained? The grenadiers and chasseurs were served soup, boiled meat, chicken, salad, and good wine. The sergeants ate separately and the officers dined with those of the Imperial household.

Each corps of infantry and cavalry took turns performing the guard and ceremonial duties. The Paris guard was relieved every three months. The foot grenadiers were quartered in the Bonaparte barracks on the Quai d'Orsay, and the chasseurs at Panthémont. The sappers and band of each corps, being required to conduct the guard to and from the Palace daily, lived in permanent barracks.

A cavalry patrol was held ready at the Tuileries to escort the Emperor in his goings and comings. The palace guard was under the grand marshal of the Palace who posted one officer at the Pavillion de Flore, another in the guardroom, an officer and eight gendarmes at the bridge leading to the Tuileries, an officer and twelve men at the Louvre, and five men at the Guard hospital.

On Sundays when His Majesty went to Mass in the chapel, where the Empress and the Household awaited him, the colonel of the regiment on duty followed him with the Grand Almoner (Cardinal Fesch). The colonel generals and their aides walked at the end of the long procession which moved from the throne room up the grand staircase – lined with a double row of grenadiers and chasseurs – across the guardroom to the chapel. The drums beat 'To the Emperor' at the entrance and a grenadier or chasseur stood motionless with ordered arms at either side of the altar.

The guardroom was furnished – as today – with a leather armchair, rush-bottomed chair, table, and wardrobe for the officer. The eternal lead inkwell filled with black mud stood on a massive table and the room was heated to the point of suffocation by a wood stove. The straw mattresses and bedrolls of the men were ranged along the wainscot; their muskets were in a rack, their bread on a shelf above. A bait can held the *marrons*[1] for the visiting officer. At night a single candle in an iron sconce shed a sepulchral light. A pair of snuffers was supposed to rejuvenate the candle when it threatened to expire. The men slept, ate, yawned, and played *drogue* while awaiting the corporal's summons. But outside the sentry kept his eyes open, for he was guarding the Emperor.

[1] Circular copper pieces inscribed with the hour at which the officer would make his rounds. These were placed in a can and drawn by the officer with his eyes closed. – Ed.

In the winter of 1810 Napoleon received a list of grievances from Daru. During the Austrian campaign no infantry corps except the fusiliers had sent a statement of its accounts to Paris. The company clerks refused to submit their barrack lists for verification, or pay for damages. The canteen proprietors paid no fees. Daru called the Emperor's attention to the enormous clothing bills – over a million and a half francs to dress and equip the conscripts in 1809, not counting the shoes provided by the Emperor. Many bills were unpaid and the merchants complained.

During the past four years the Guard's uniforms had cost 20 million francs, and the cost kept rising. In the Line, coats and waistcoats had to last three years, overcoats four, hats five, and heavy equipment twenty; but no term was specified in the Guard. The resulting waste appalled the honest Daru.

The Emperor read his report without lifting an eyebrow. The Guard must shine. Its uniforms must be resplendent. The made-over clothes worn in the Line would not achieve this result.

However, Napoleon decided to reinforce the administration and finance departments and raise the pay and allowances of the inspectors and commissaries.

A 1st class commissary drew 6,000 francs plus 1,200 for his house, 1,800 for heat, 2,555 for four horses, and 3,000 for office expenses. The paymaster, who administered the pay of 35,000 men, drew an aggregate of 12,000 francs with 4,000 more for office expenses.

The councils of administration were directed to 'make a thorough inventory of the contents of the magazines' before ordering new clothing.

On 18 February the Emperor created the 'artisan battalion[2] of the Guard', placing it under the Chief Commissary.[3] Its five companies, commanded by Captain Gubert, were in charge of food, forage, livestock, medical service, and transport. The battalion numbered 33 officers and 163 men from the Old Guard and its captain drew the pay of a captain in the horse Guard.

The Emperor's sudden interest in the Guard's economy inspired Inspector Félix to question a forage allotment for ten horses to Kirgener, the new general of engineers. His Majesty must be mistaken – the engineers were not mounted. Baron Félix refused to honor the requisition, pending an appeal to the Minister of War.

The answer was not long in coming. 'What is he meddling in this for?' the Emperor wrote the Duke of Feltre. 'Let Baron Félix confine himself to carrying out my orders.'

The Guard of 1810 was at the apogee of its glory, reflecting the glory of the Empire. The regiment of horse grenadiers had been completely refurbished. Its horses, $14\frac{1}{2}$ to 15 hands high and between four and five years old, were black with full manes and tails, bought in Caen for 680 francs apiece. Their daily ration was 10 pounds of hay, 15 of straw, and $\frac{2}{3}$ bushel of oats or $1\frac{1}{3}$ of bran.

The troopers were quartered at the Napoleon barracks in the École Militaire where they slept in solid oak beds six-feet-eight by four feet with a shelf at the head. NCO's

---

[2] *Bataillon d'Ouvriers d'administration.*

[3] *Commissaire ordonnateur*, the comptroller of the Guard. This post was held by Dufour. – Ed.

and trumpeters had single beds three and a half feet wide. The bedding consisted of two mattresses – the lower one of straw – a bolster, blanket, and two sheets. The stores contained five sheets per man.

The horse grenadiers' large wardrobe was made by Bosquet, the master tailor, a celebrated artist in his craft. Their bonnets were made by Maillard of the Rue Saint-Honoré, their doeskin breeches by Garel of the Rue d'Échelle, and their boots by Fabritzius. A new dress coat costing 60·41 francs was issued to each trooper this year. The trumpeter's hat was of the same quality as a general's (see Plate 5).

Baron Félix reproached their quartermaster for spending all the regiment's funds on horses etc. before paying the forage bill. What could he do? Did Baron Félix, who never set foot out of Paris, have any idea what escort duty with the Emperor entailed? The cavalry of the Guard had to answer for his safety to the army, the nation, and Europe.

In the *chasseurs à cheval* the uniform and harness were even more expensive. This corps, billeted in the École Militaire and 'at Prince Eugène's', had lost 159 horses on campaign. The dealers were asked to provide 300 bay or chestnut horses the same height as those of the grenadiers. Paulmier furnished the chasseurs' mattresses which were covered with checked ticking and 'filled with 30–36 pounds of carefully carded ewe's wool'. The straw mattresses were covered in grey muslin and the white blankets were of the quality specified for the Old Guard.

The kit of a *chasseur à cheval* called for five different qualities of green cloth, two of scarlet cloth, and five kinds of wool lace, not counting the guimp, braid, cord, and twist of gold bullion, wool, or gold and wool mixed. The furrier Koenig charged 30 francs for their colpacks[4] and furnished the marmot's fur to trim the NCO's' pelisses. The lining of the officer's pelisse 'of short grey fur' cost 50 francs, and the collars and edging of 'throat of Canadian fox' cost from 100 to 120. Their 'shabracks of panther skin, lined with striped drill and bound with gold braid', cost from 300 to 350 francs.

The chasseurs needed new coats, waistcoats, overalls, and boots. Wagner furnished them 1,295 pairs of boots, and 469 pelisses and dolmans, 918 undress coats and waistcoats, and 950 pairs of Hungarian breeches were ordered from the master tailor Hartmann and the breechesmaker Garel (see Plate 10).

'Why not make economies by ordering in quantity?' the administration inquired.

'The diversity of uniforms in which our corps goes to war is an obstacle to our negotiations . . .' the council replied. 'The uniform changes prescribed by His Majesty make a considerable difference in the kind of goods the corps requires . . . It is impossible to estimate in advance the consumption of each article . . .'

General Lefebvre-Desnoëttes did not sign the report since he was a prisoner of the English. Nor did Corbineau or Daumesnil who had been retired for wounds. The former was now receiver-general of the Seine-Inférieure and the latter, governor of the Fort of Vincennes which was garrisoned by the Guard.

The Polish-light horse, quartered at Chantilly, had become lancers to satisfy the demand of their chief Count Krasinski. Their training in the new weapon began

---

[4] Cylindrical fur headdress whose cloth crown, known as the 'bag', hung over the side. – Ed.

in earnest when Major Fredro returned from leave in Poland bringing back manuals and exhibiting amazing skill in handling the lance.

Colonel Dautancourt studied the changes to be made in the uniform (such as moving the aiguillette to the left shoulder), harness, and schooling of the horses. These were five or six years old, between $14\frac{1}{4}$ and $14\frac{1}{2}$ hands high, 'in uniform groups of chestnut, bay, black, and dark grey'.

Dautancourt proposed permitting only the front rank of a squadron to carry lances for fear that in charging those in the second rank might injure the horses and men in front. Furthermore, a light-horseman armed with a lance, carbine, bayonet, saber, and two pistols would hardly continue to be a light-horseman! But Dautancourt was voted down. All troopers of the regiment were armed with lances of straight-grained oak, nine feet four inches long, with an iron point and a fitting for the crimson-over-white pennant.

Experience proved Dautancourt correct. In 1813 the 'light-horse-lancers' of the Guard carried 66 lances to a company of 125 men, the troopers of the second rank and NCO's being armed with carbines and pistols.

The most expensive cavalrymen were the Duke of Rovigo's[5] 'immortals' who were quartered in the Célestin barracks and commanded by Colonel Baron Henry, the Emperor's confidant for 'delicate missions'.

The purveyors to the elite gendarmes were proud of the confidence reposed in them. These included Madame Colleau the linen-draper, Master Malicot the 'trimmer', Blouet the cabinetmaker, who furnished their drums, and the celebrated breechesmaker and glover Mottet of the Palais-Royal. The master artisans did not all make fortunes. Fert, ex-bootmaker of the elite gendarmes, failed and ended up at Saint-Pélagie,[6] a humiliating retreat for a master of his craft.

As usual, the artillery engaged the Emperor's special attention. Besides La Fère, there were units stationed at Vincennes and at the Vaugirard barracks in Paris. The six Old Guard companies were commanded by Majors Boulart and Marin; the three conscript companies, by Major Henrion. General d'Aboville had been retired for wounds and appointed commandant of the Artillery School.

Lt. Colonel Drouot had finally obtained for his gunners a bearskin bonnet with a visor, chin strap, and cord. In the evenings his officers wore a hat, coat, casimir breeches, silk stockings, buckled shoes, and a 'court' sword. In the day they wore sabers and 'fur bonnets trimmed with gold cords and cockades with the Imperial arms', and their saddlecloths were edged with gold. The 'sergeant drummer', as well as the drum major and his band, wore swallow-tailed coats with sleeved waistcoats, blue Hungarian breeches with a trefoil worked in gold bullion and wool, felt hats, and top boots. The gunners wore blue overcoats and the sergeants grey. Their cockades were embroidered with the cypher 'N' (see Plate 56).

The horse artillery was magnificent. The NCO's' blue coats were lined with scarlet and trimmed with gold lace; the trumpeters' were sky blue lined with crimson and

[5] Savary.
[6] Prison in Paris. – Ed.

laced with gold. The NCO's of the train wore grey coats laced with silver. The coats of the sergeant artificers were trimmed with lace nearly two inches wide, but no grenades. The fur colpack added great chic to the horse gunners' appearance. The trumpeter's was of white fur, costing 90 francs. The artillery of the Line never forgave them this headdress (See Plate 16).

During the spring fêtes Drouot, Marin, and Boulart were all made barons.

In March 1810, 38 marines of the Guard captured at Baylén arrived in France. On 8 March two officers and 58 more marines made contact with the 1st Corps operating around Cadiz. Some had escaped to Tangier and gone fishing in the waters of the Sultan of Morocco while waiting for a chance to return to Spain.

To honor the marines, who had suffered much, the Emperor made Captain Baste a count and ordered 140 marines to accompany him on a tour of Belgium and Holland by land and sea.[7]

The following September he revived the marine battalion of the Guard at a strength of 1,100 with 32 officers. Captain Baste, its commander, was assigned the delicate task of clothing the battalion, which inspired some involuntary humor when the commissary proposed that, since the cost of 'navy blue' cloth had risen so high, they be dressed in 'sky blue'.

The quarrels between the Ministries of War and Marine over the officers' pay did not cease until after Waterloo. Napoleon was often accused of neglecting his marines, but he knew how to touch their hearts. Here is a letter from one:

'Pierre Requin[8] (a good name for a sailor) very respectfully informs you that he entered the service in year VI and took part in the campaigns of Egypt and America in year X, and all subsequent campaigns until the present.

'Sire, he is the one who had the honor to carry you on his back on board the barge of the frigate that took you back to France. You had the goodness to promise him at that time that you would remember him. I dare beseech Your Majesty to think favorably, if he considers me worthy, of honoring me with the Legion of Honor. The severe wounds he has suffered and the unbounded devotion he has given Your Majesty make him hope that you will deign to look with favor upon his request.'

This is how Pierre Requin, marine 2nd class of the Guard, became a *légionnaire* . . .

[7] The Emperor's barge used on this visit is in the Musée de la Marine in Paris.
[8] *Requin* means 'shark'. – Ed.

CHAPTER 3

The Fêtes of 1810

JUNE 1810. The season was at its height in Paris. The fêtes in honor of the Imperial couple were numerous; however, the etiquette was more rigid than formerly and good humor and cordiality suffered in consequence.

On the 10th there was a fête at the Hôtel de Ville, and on the 12th a gala at the Opera where *Perseus and Andromache* was sung. On the 14th a fête was given at the Princess Borghese's château in Neuilly consisting of a dinner and theatrical performance. In the park, which was illuminated, there was a reconstruction of the aviary at Schönbrunn and music by the grenadiers' band. Those who knew Vienna recognized the 'Glorietta' in which trumpets sounded *The Victory is Ours*, as well as the Palace – complete with Austrian grenadiers – and the 'Temple of Love'.

On the 21st a fête was given by the Minister of War with a play staged by Feydau and a military spectacle.

The officers of the Guard had hardly any sleep, and the soldiers none at all. They were busy preparing for the great fête to be given on Sunday the 24th in honor of the Emperor and Empress. The Champ de Mars was transformed into an amusement park, and a ballroom constructed in a court of the Military School with 24 rows of *banquettes* mounted in tiers for the ladies. Behind these, for the men, was a promenade of planks supported by columns and lighted by candelabra. The ballroom itself, of frame construction, was decorated with painted canvas scenery and artificial flowers.

On the evening of 22 June there was a dress rehearsal at which the soldiers of the Guard occupied the stands. Invitations were issued and a number of ladies were present. The Empress' uncle the Grand Duke of Würzburg, who never missed anything, was there with Madame Mère[1] and the Empress' two sisters. Sixty dancers from the Opéra, with Madame Gardel and M. Vestris as the principals, rehearsed the ballet to be presented. Nothing could be more graceful, the spectators agreed.

Sunday, 24 June. The military celebration of the age commenced before sunrise. The fête of the Guard began traditionally with the beating of the *Grenadière* and *Carabinière* at 3 a.m. The officers living off post left their houses at dawn with their gala uniforms under their arms and deposited them in rooms rented for the night in Paris hotels. Returning to their posts, they prepared their commands for departure. The men's appearance had been fussed over by the barbers and NCO's since the evening before.

[1] Napoleon's mother.

The troops left at midday, in stifling heat. From 4 p.m. on the corps marched in succession to the Champ de Mars where men and horses, dripping with sweat and covered with dust, were drawn up in the broiling sun. Those whose quarters were just across the street or in the neighborhood were lucky.

Five o'clock. The crowd surged along the embankment between the Champ de Mars and the Seine. Since two o'clock a stream of carriages stretching to the Invalides had been discharging guests in the Court of Honor. The parade lasted until midnight.

6 p.m. Their Majesties arrived in a procession of six glass coaches. The Emperor's was drawn by eight horses and surrounded by mounted grooms, a double row of *chasseurs à cheval*, and a double file of grenadiers. The artillery of the Guard fired 60 guns. A short dinner was served; then the Emperor and Empress repaired to a balcony to watch the spectacle which included horse races, chariot races by Franconi's troupe, tightrope dances, and finally, an ascent in a balloon by Mme. Blanchard.

For a while the balloon remained suspended in mid-air at the level of the balcony on which Their Majesties were seated. Then, at a signal from a cannon, it rose and disappeared in the direction of Sèvres.

Night fell. With a linstock presented by General Lariboisière the Emperor lighted a firework in the form of a dragon. This was attached by a long fuse to a scaffolding overlooking the Champ de Mars on which a magnificent set piece had been prepared by the artificers of the Guard. Then, by the light of flaming torches, a battalion of grenadiers formed a square before the Emperor and fired by files, using star cartridges of every color.

'Never', wrote Coigniet, 'has such a bouquet of flowers been seen. The Guard was crowned with stars.'

About ten o'clock, amid loud applause by the crowd and the assembled guests, Their Majesties entered the ballroom, overheated by 3,000 lighted candles and 15,000 people. The stands were filled to bursting and were fragile.

'For the love of God, get down!' It was Lt. Colonel Harlet, swearing at an acrobatic civilian who had climbed up on one of the slim columns supporting the elevated promenade. Under his weight the whole framework might have collapsed and caught fire. Not a soul would have escaped from a furnace from which there was but a single exit. Heedless of the danger, the Duke of Istria and the officers of the Guard did the honors.

It was a gigantic fête, a magnificent one, costing two millions. 'There is no better way to spend the money presented to the officers and soldiers of the Guard by His Majesty the Emperor on the occasion of his marriage than by paying the expenses of the fete', Bessières wrote, by way of an order. (Several 'big hats' are said to have greeted this pronouncement with a wry face.)

The season was over. One could breathe again.

'The art of giving fêtes has not kept pace with the art of multiplying the occasions for giving them', Victor de Broglie wrote Marshal Marmont.

The last one of the season took place at the Austrian Embassy on 1 July and ended in tragedy. The ballroom erected in the garden caught fire. The Russian Ambassador was injured and the Princess Schwarzenberg, the Ambassador's sister-in-law, was burned to death.

After escorting the Empress back to the Tuileries, the Emperor returned to the Rue Mont-Blanc, wearing his grey overcoat, and directed the rescue proceedings until 3 a.m. Profoundly impressed, he concluded that the fire protection of the Imperial palaces was inadequate.

Several days after Marshal Lannes' funeral at the Invalides at which, to the strains of Beethoven's *Funeral March for a Hero*, a procession of eight grenadier NCO's of the Guard bore the urn with his ashes, the Emperor wrote from Rambouillet:

'There shall be raised before 1 January 1811 a company of sapper-firemen[2] of the Imperial Guard under the Commandant of Engineers. This company will be assigned to serve pumps at the Imperial palaces of Paris, Saint-Cloud, Versailles, Meudon, Rambouillet, Compiègne, Fontainebleau, etc . . .'

Commanded by a captain and two lieutenants, the company was to have 121 NCO's and sappers, a four-horse caisson, and 8 pumps drawn by two horses and maintained by 6 specialists.

'The sappers will receive instruction in the theory and practice of pumps and the rescue measures to be taken at fires . . . The captain, one lieutenant, and two sections of four pumps each will always be on duty at the palace where the Emperor is in residence. In wartime the company . . . will be attached to Imperial Headquarters.

'The uniform of the sappers of the Guard shall be like that of the Line except that the former shall wear brass helmets' (see Plate 76b).

Napoleon was satisfied with the medical service of the Guard. Chief Physician Suë and Chief Surgeon Larrey had made the hospital of the Gros-Caillou into a model establishment. For two francs a day the superintendent Montessuy had to feed the sick, according to the doctors' prescription, on 'white bread, Malaga and Burgundy wines', and such delicacies as 'good fat chickens, fish, and baked potatoes' as well as to provide 'heat and light in the wards' and maintain the linen and the 'furnishings and utensils'. Though the number of employees was fixed by the commissary, the superintendent had to select, pay, and feed them. He must also provide the deceased with a coffin and shroud for 7·50 francs.

In 1810 the hospital had 24 wards lit with 'reflector lamps and fixtures of white metal' and 'furnished with benches and a fountain'. The storeroom was well stocked with sheets and blankets, as well as hair mattresses and bolsters of wool and down.

Chief Pharmacist Sureau and five assistants worked in the vast laboratory. The bathroom contained eight copper tubs. Next year there would be twenty more, fed with hot water from a large cauldron. The pantry was equipped with 500 pewter teapots for making herb tea.[3] A flourishing garden was tended by the convalescents.

Originally planned for 450 patients when the Guard numbered 7,500, the Gros-Caillou was altogether too small now that the turnover of wounded and sick averaged

[2] *Sapeurs-pompiers.*
[3] *Tisane*, made of camomile, mint, etc. – Ed.

from 1,300 to 1,400 a month. Infirmaries had to be established in the barracks. In the conscript regiments the serious cases were sent to the Val-de-Grâce. Temporary hospitals were established at the Hôtel-Dieu, Saint-Louis, and Saint-Antoine.

Larrey headed a large medical staff. Each Old Guard regiment had three medical officers; each of the Young Guard, two. The artillery had five. Larrey chose them with great care before submitting their names to the Emperor. Each regiment in Spain had four field hospitals and a train detachment to take care of the stores.

The Emperor took a deep interest in the medical service of his Guard and the care of its wounded and sick. He formed a permanent board to examine those eligible for retirement and the candidates for the Young Guard.

The new national guard regiment of the Guard was about to depart for Spain. Reduced to two battalions on 29 May, it was reviewed by General Curial who reported the men 'of good height, quite well trained, and apparently animated by a desire to do well'. However, the number of desertions was deplorable. Quartered at Lille, these soldiers from the north were too near their families.

'Several have returned', the General wrote, 'but most of them will never return'. He found the company officers 'zealous, intelligent, and well mannered'. The gaps were filled with 197 conscripts of 1811. Fifteen surplus lieutenants were sent to the Line.

On 27 June Curial wrote the Minister of War:

'Monseigneur,[4]

Since the uniforms of the National Guards of the Guard have not been prescribed as yet, their manufacture is being held up. It is even more important to settle this question than to stop dressing this corps in clothing that does not belong to it, but which is nonetheless charged to its account.

I have proposed as its uniform a short coat with vertical pockets, white revers and tail facings piped with red, and red collars and cuffs; white waistcoats and pantaloons, black half-gaiters, shakos with yellow eagle plates, and yellow eagle buttons. I beg Your Excellency to bring my request once more to the Emperor's attention.'

From Saint-Cloud the Emperor wrote on the margin of this letter: 'Returned to the Minister of War to decide as he wishes'. Clarke replied to Curial on 5 July: 'The regiment of National Guards of the Guard will be ready to campaign the end of August 1810 . . . The uniform shall be that prescribed by General Curial . . .'

The officers and NCO's of the two nonexistent battalions were en route to join General Suchet in Spain. The regiment was leaving shortly to reinforce the 1st Young Guard Division on the Ebro.

Since Napoleon suspected the English might land at Quiberon, he had held up Dumoustier's division at Angers. With four regiments of conscripts and *tirailleurs*, eight guns, and the Polish light-horse, this unit now went to join Roguet's division in the Guard corps commanded by General Dorsenne.

Dorsenne took his orders direct from Berthier. His corps was the reserve of the armies of Spain. In case of disaster, it had to guard Masséna's retreat from Portugal,

[4] Clarke, the Minister of War, was now Duke of Feltre. – Ed.

the King's from Madrid, Suchet's from Catalonia, Augureau's from Arragon, and Soult's from Andalusia.

The horse Guard in Spain was reorganized and put under General Lepic. This included the lancers of Berg and a light cavalry regiment under Delaître containing two squadrons of Polish light-horse, a squadron of chasseurs under Major Martin, a company of *vélites*, and one of Mameluks. The regiment of heavy cavalry under Lt. Colonel Marthod contained two squadrons of dragoons and a squadron of horse grenadiers under Baron Rémy. Rémy had entered the Guard in 1807 and had received eleven citations and six wounds.

'Reinforce the cavalry in Spain with *vélites*, who have had little war experience', the Emperor wrote Bessières, 'and replace the *vélites* with conscripts. The veterans must be conserved since they are harder to replace . . .'

Colonel Marin commanded the Guard artillery in Spain which consisted of two companies of horse artillery, three of foot, two train companies, and a large number of mules.

'Dorsenne is in absolute command of the province of Burgos', the Emperor wrote. 'He is to keep the troops in motion in order to hold the bandits in check, and to organize seven or eight mobile columns with the Polish light-horse and the younger men. He must keep my old soldiers together so as not to lose any man by surprise . . . General Dorsenne holds a personal command . . . From one moment to the next he is apt to receive a direct order from me . . .'

When was the Emperor coming to Spain?

During May he changed his way of life. His home, his relatives, the Empress' friends, and Prince Metternich absorbed his attention. At forty-one he was jealous of his young wife who was only nineteen. He became suspicious, worked less, gave fewer orders, and those he gave were less clear.

Napoleon, the captain, sovereign, and administrator, endowed with almost universal genius, was also a man . . .

CHAPTER 4

Days of Anxiety

THE Spanish wound was festering. The bad news irritated the Emperor who sent on the dispatches to Bacler d'Albe[1] to be digested. They were returned with assurances that Spain was in the process of 'regeneration', and that the people's hate would 'wear itself out'.

The soldiers of the Young Guard in Burgos had not noticed it. Their expeditions against the partisans were increased. The troops were tired but war-wise. Subjected to the strict discipline of the Guard, they had absorbed its spirit despite the horrors around them.

Colette, a soldier of the 2nd Conscript-Chasseurs 'operating against the partisans', wrote in June 1810 that he was 'marvelously well'. But when he and his comrade Renier had three sous they were 'afraid of suddenly dropping dead', so they 'drank them up the same day'. He complained of 'not getting bread' and being miserable. 'In this wretched country if you wear a shirt ten days you are covered with vermin . . . We can't rest . . . We must spend two weeks at a time in the mountains . . . The partisans blockaded us four days without bread so we ate the captain's horse. Then we charged them with bayonets and made an opening. When we leave a town the partisans enter it and come out to attack us every night. It takes 100 men to form a post that can stop them . . . Where we are, they are all around us . . .'

In his memoirs and reports Roguet tells of the capture of a treasure of 20,000 francs under escort from Burgos to Lerma, and the breathless chase by Deshayes and 400 *tirailleurs* in pursuit of the bandits.

The French lacked everything – cartridges, flints, money; yet they had to organize expeditions with infantry, cavalry, and artillery to procure wine!

At the end of May Dorsenne ordered a general offensive against the bands proliferating in Navarre. Kirmann with some chasseurs, lancers, and Mameluks annihilated 200 partisans at Lavio and captured their arms depot. His only casualty was a wounded Mameluk.

Captain Baste heard there were insurgents at Almazán and led a punitive expedition against them in June. Leaving Soria with several companies of conscripts and marines, he reached the outskirts of the town at dawn on the 10th and surrounded 2,000 partisans who had taken refuge there, taking 500 prisoners.

Dorsenne himself, directing a large scale operation with the conscript-grenadiers and horse grenadiers, drove the enemy temporarily out of Navarre, capturing Logroño,

[1] Chief of the Emperor's topographical bureau. – Ed.

Santo Domingo, Aro, Pancorbo, Miranda, etc. But all towns had to be garrisoned with from 50 to 500 men, making it difficult to organize the taxgathering expeditions ordered by the Emperor.

The troops were out of breath keeping up with Mouton-Duvernet and his conscripts; with Major Secrétan, Marthod, and Robert in their pursuit of Longa, alias Papel, whose dragoons threw down the gauntlet to them in true picaresque style; with hunting the bands of the fanatic monk Merino. Not content with massacring their prisoners, killing cattle, and raiding the vineyards, the *guerrilleros* killed the *alcaldes* who turned over tax money to the French. Some of the chiefs wore French uniforms stripped from corpses, and even decorated their horses' manes with the Legion of Honor. But most of them wore felt hats and leather breeches, the espadrilles on their bare feet thrust into wooden stirrups, and reserved their stock of regimentals to disguise their men in ambush.

Goya saw all this – the massacres, murders, and atrocities. He saw generals sawed in two and soldiers boiled in oil, buried alive to their shoulders, hung by the feet, or mutilated . . . Such horrors spurred the French to frightful reprisals during which they killed old men, women, and children, and burned villages.

On the Island of Cabrera sixty marines of the Guard, sent out with 5,000 French prisoners after the capitulation of Baylén, were dreaming of escape. They lived in a log cabin roofed with sacking under the walls of the castle where Lieutenant Gerdy and several officers were sweltering in the July heat.

Their diet consisted of bad bread and beans, when the sailing barks from Palma brought them; fish, when they caught any; and, for those who were not afraid to die, lizards. All the water had to be brought from Majorca. There had once been a spring on the island but 5,000 thirsty men had drunk it dry. Since many were transferred each day to the cemetery, the living shielded their bodies from the sun with the garments of the dead.

One night the marines were reminiscing as usual about their campaigns, their junketings in Germany and Paris, the Emperor . . . They, too, would celebrate the birthday of their Saint Napoleon. So that nothing should be lacking, each man decided to save five beans a day from his ration.

15 August. Since dawn the marines had been scrubbing the cabin floor. The men were freshly shaved. They congratulated one another, shook hands, and hung up garlands of greens prepared the night before. In the center of a worm-eaten table a stewpot held the daily ration plus 150 beans horded for the occasion.

The men ate with gusto, recalling past reviews, fireworks, illuminations, and free shows. They sang, danced, and drank – precious mouthfuls of water from a tin cup or a bit of broken pottery – to the health of the *Tondu*.

'Through sheer force of illusion we got quite drunk', one of the celebrants wrote afterwards, 'and our hearts were wafted back to France, to the Emperor.'

Next year, after a dramatic escape, most of them celebrated the feast of Saint Napoleon in Paris.

In spite of his determination Napoleon did not go to Spain. Two great problems detained him: Holland and Russia.

Louis had renounced the throne of Holland, and relations with Russia were becoming strained despite protestations of friendship on both sides. Following his brother's abdication on 1 July, Napoleon incorporated the kingdom of Holland into the Empire on the 9th.

In September he admitted several Dutch regiments to the Guard. When Louis' *Garde du Corps* was dissolved its NCO's and men had been appointed *vélites*. The first two companies were assigned to the Dutch grenadiers; the last two, to the Old Guard grenadiers and chasseurs.

The Dutch grenadiers became the 2nd Grenadiers of the Imperial Guard, while the hussars of the Royal Guard became the 2nd Light-Horse-Lancers of the Guard. (Its German members were given the choice of joining the Berg lancers or the Dutch cavalry.) King Louis' light artillery and train were incorporated into the Guard artillery. The native-born members of the Veterans Company remained in Amsterdam for guard duty at the palace.

The Dutch guardsmen's uniforms lost their brandenburgs, and their buttons were replaced by those of the Imperial Guard.

A detachment of 2,100 infantry, 740 cavalry, and 160 gunners arrived at Versailles the end of August. The Emperor reviewed the grenadiers who were much admired by the people of Versailles. Their commander Colonel Tindal was a Scot who had served as captain of the Grand Pensioner's bodyguard in 1805. Tindal was a tall man with a stentorian voice. The Emperor was favorably impressed with him.

On 6 September the Old Guard gave the newcomers a reception at Versailles that ended in an orgy of catastrophic proportions. Women were chased and attacked, men were beaten, and shops were rifled. Drunken soldiers 'committed outrages' despite efforts to stop them by the police commissioner whose feeble national guard units were no match for the grenadiers of the Old Guard. Finally, towards midnight, order was restored. Next day the corps commanders called on the mayor to express their regrets and promised that the guilty parties would be punished.

On 21 September His Excellency Marshal Bessières and Baron Dominique-Xavier Félix, Inspector of the Imperial Guard, officially inaugurated the 2nd Grenadiers at Versailles. In addition to 46 officers and 1,188 NCO's and men the regiment numbered 16 sappers, 40 fifers and drummers, and 153 *vélites* plus supernumeraries and aliens working for subsistence alone.

Nearly all the Dutch *Gardes du Corps* were officers' sons. The father of one Chassé made a name for himself at Waterloo. Among the officers, Lt. Colonel de Contamine was attached to the foot chasseurs and Lt. Colonel Roque to the grenadiers.

The 2nd Light-Horse-Lancers was inaugurated by Bessières and Félix the same day, with Colonel du Bois de La Ferrière in command, assisted by Lt. Colonel Van Hasselt, Majors Coti, van Ticken, and de Watteville. Its four squadrons mustered around 800 men. A fifth was formed later under Colonel van Merlen of the 1st Dutch Hussars which King Louis had incorporated into his Guard shortly before the abdication.

PLATE 76

a) Tirailleur-grenadier

b) Officer, sappers of the Guard

(After Martinet)

PLATE 77

Funeral procession of Marshal Lannes
(*From a contemporary colored print published chez Chereau*)

PLATE 78

Vûe de la
prise de la lanterne

de Paris

jardin de St Cloud.

PLATE 79

b) Drummer, *Vélites of Turin*
(*From an original drawing by S. Puyo*)

a) *Tirailleur cooking in bivouac*
(*From an original drawing by Ernest Crofts*)

The new lancer regiment was garrisoned at Versailles. Major General Baron Colbert, the colonel in chief, was a brilliant cavalryman and veteran of Austerlitz, Eylau, Heilsberg, Friedland, and Wagram. He was concerned about the uniform, believing that the 2nd Lancers should be dressed like the 1st, although the *czapka* and *kurtka* were essentially Polish garments.

Whole essays were written on the subject. Lieutenant Georges Fallot, a Belgian known as 'the bear' from his hairy chest, Herculean strength, and commanding presence, was chosen to model the proposed uniform for the Emperor. He made a favorable impression and the uniform, consisting of scarlet *czapka*, *kurtka*, and overalls faced with Imperial blue and trimmed with yellow lace, was adopted. The trumpeter's *czapka* was white. The plumes were white, black and white, or red tipped with white, and the aiguillette and embroidered trefoil worn on the left shoulder were yellow (see Plate 91).

The marching uniform was a blue *kurtka* and overalls for the lancers, and a swallow-tailed coat worn under a blue cloak with a cape and collar for the officers. The trumpeter, like all those of the cavalry of the Guard, wore sky blue.

As the year 1810 drew to a close dark clouds gathered on the eastern horizon before those in the west had dispersed. Under the terms of the Trianon Decrees, signed in August, the blockade was lifted. However, the Trianon Tariffs, promulgated simultaneously, laid a prohibitive duty on foreign goods. The columns of the *Monitor* were filled with accounts of British goods being seized and burned at Strasbourg, Cherbourg, Cleves, Coblenz, Bayonne, Leghorn, and Koenigsberg.

The Tsar refused to have anything to do with these sanctions. Alexander was a hypocritical ally and never offered to help Napoleon – whom he professed to 'love like a brother' – force England to make peace; therefore Napoleon had to treat directly with the English.

Their response was negative – even more emphatic than that Masséna had received at Torres Vedras.[2] After the sinister picture of the Spanish situation painted by Foy, Masséna's emissary, Napoleon considered marrying Ferdinand VII to a Bonaparte princess and restoring him to the throne.

These problems arose during the hunting parties at Fontainebleau, in which the grenadiers participated as beaters and bearers; the fêtes, reviews, and evenings at the opera in honor of the Emperor's marriage, and the state baptism of his adopted children. Nevertheless, the atmosphere at Court was one of anticipation, for the Empress was awaiting a 'blessed event'.

On 13 December Napoleon annexed the Hanseatic cities and the Duchy of Oldenburg. He could no longer trust anyone but himself to defend the Empire against the Tsar and the 'man up North' – the unreliable Bernadotte.

[2] Strong line of fortifications established by Wellington before Lisbon where, after a blockade by the French under Masséna, the English refused to surrender and forced Masséna to retire from Portugal. – Ed.

The last days of the old year were traditionally dedicated to the Guard. The Emperor remembered those in Spain who were in daily combat against the guerrillas. This warfare was difficult, costly, and hard on the nerves as well as on discipline and morale. Weighed down with misery and a 63-pound pack, the soldiers in Spain were ill-nourished, and the officers unpaid.

'In this country', said Henri IV, 'large armies are always starved, and small ones always beaten . . .' Why had the Emperor not listened to him?

Opposed by small groups of partisans who joined forces, scattered, then joined forces again, the French had neither time to prepare for their attacks nor the means to resist them. The commanders were obliged to disperse their units and dissipate their efforts. Roguet's and Dumoustier's officers were on the road twenty-four days of every thirty. Bessières, cold and formal, ordered a reign of terror, seizing hostages and arresting magistrates and priests. Dorsenne, haughty and hard, used the same tactics.

The fear – often imaginary – inspired by the rapidity of the partisans' movements and the fluidity of their numbers imposed constant changes in the plan of operations so that a coherent master plan was impossible. Generals were left to their own resources. The number of French units increased as their strength diminished. This dissipation of forces seriously affected the discipline of the troops.

Did Napoleon in Paris really understand the situation?

'We have been running around the mountains for almost two months', wrote Corporal Franconin of the 1st *Tirailleur*-Grenadiers from Logroño in December. 'We set out in the morning and sleep in whatever village we land in at the end of a fruitless search. We have seen the partisans several times. Two of our mobile columns . . . came across one of the largest bands on a hillside two musket shots from Belorado. We gave them a good beating . . . killing more than 800. I did not know what to think of these rascals until I had tested their valor at first hand. It isn't much . . .'

At Vitoria the fusilier-grenadiers were similarly engaged. The Emperor awarded them, as well as the *tirailleurs* and conscripts, a bonus of 120,000 francs.

On 30 December Napoleon signed a decree making changes in the Guard. The *tirailleur*-chasseurs and conscript-chasseurs were to be known henceforth as 'voltigeurs of the Guard', and the regiments numbered from 1 to 4. The corresponding regiments attached to the grenadiers were called '*tirailleurs*' and numbered likewise (see Plate 82).

Each of the new regiments was to form an elite company of 200 men called 'corporal-voltigeurs' and 'corporal-*tirailleurs*'. Meanwhile, a company of 'sergeant-fusiliers', recruited from the most intelligent and promising fusiliers, was incorporated in that corps.

General Dorsenne was directed to select the men and organize the new units which were to be sent to a 'school of the guard' at Fontainebleau.

The Emperor wrote Bessières on 3 August: 'I intend that the Young Guard subalterns and NCO's shall rank with those in the Line;[3] its NCO's shall be drawn from the fusiliers, and those of the fusiliers from the Old Guard. In the Line I shall use *tirailleurs* as

[3] Unlike those of the Old Guard and fusiliers who held superior rank. – Ed.

corporals, and fusiliers as sergeants. Therefore, the best conscripts should go to the *tirailleurs* and fusiliers . . . The most distinguished and intelligent fusiliers with four years' service or citations for gallantry will be admitted to the Old Guard . . . Thus half or a third of the fusiliers will be recruited from the *tirailleurs* and conscripts,[4] and half or a third of the Old Guard from the fusiliers. This will serve to replenish my Old Guard.

'My Guard should contain cadres for a reserve of 100 battalions. These will require 3,000 sergeants and 6,000 corporals. There are 2,300 fusiliers, and 12,000 conscripts and *tirailleurs* at present. By holding on to the choice men we can eventually train 3,000 sergeants in the fusiliers and 6,000 corporals in the Young Guard. I can easily draw 600 lieutenants from the Old Guard and 600 from the schools. The 600 captains can be furnished by the Line and my Old Guard. A reserve of 100 battalions represents 80,000 men . . .'

'I shall have war with Russia for reasons beyond human control', he told Metternich, 'because they derive from the nature of things . . .'

---

[4] Soldiers with two years' service in the Young Guard were eligible for the fusiliers. – Ed.

CHAPTER 5

The 'Baby Guard'

THE year 1811 marked the zenith of the Empire. It was ushered in by a comet, thanks to which people said the wine was especially good. It flowed agreeably down the throats of the grenadiers and chasseurs in the canteens of the École Militaire while the 'Surèsnes *première*' was quaffed in the bars of Rueil between guard changing at Malmaison.

Believing in their destiny, which the Emperor seemed to rule in his own fashion, the French worked in peace. The echoes of the war in Spain reached their ears but faintly. They could be easy in their minds since the Emperor watched over them. Drunk with glory, happier than they had been in years, the people placed their destiny in his hands, being careful to keep him happy and admire all his works, which is one of the symptoms of being in love.

Even God was on Napoleon's side. On 20 March, 101 guns announced the arrival of the son he wanted, the King of Rome. Paris hoped the Palace of Chaillot would be another Versailles.

The Grumblers rendering honors to the delegations that waited upon the Emperor had tears in their eyes, as if the *Tondu* had become a sort of heavenly father. But now a shadow crossed the soldiers' minds. The greater their chief became the more remote he seemed to his Old Guard. Though he remembered them with bonuses, decorations, and bottles of wine, these did not replace his physical presence.

The Grumblers did not pose as heroes; they did their job and set an example to the conscripts, but they were the Old Guard. They had known the Emperor since the days when they tramped the roads of Europe together, dealing blows to the *Kaiserliks* and Cossacks. They did not know as much as he who knew everything; but surely he must distrust the Golden Greek in Moscow . . .

The Old Guard was right. The Emperor did distrust him. But Europe was peaceful at the moment. Every nation of the Empire had its own institutions, political and social. Their community of interests had wiped out frontiers. Interior markets were beginning to develop. Fairs were inaugurated at Frankfurt and Leipzig, and industries in the Ruhr and the Saar.

The Emperor was ubiquitous. He traveled through Belgium, Germany, Holland, and Italy. Strasbourg and Antwerp owed him their new prosperity. Imperial highways were being built to Mainz, Leipzig, Warsaw, Wesel, Hanover, Berlin, and through Dalmatia towards Constantinople.

He ordered the Roman monuments restored. Perosini was drawing plans for an imperial palace on the Capitoline hill. Meanwhile, the Quirinal served as his palace.

Never had Napoleon's intellectual and moral vigor been greater nor his clarity of mind more dazzling. 'I want to finish a job that has just begun', he told Fouché and Caulaincourt. 'We need a European code, a European court of appeals, a universal currency, a uniform system of weights and measures, a code of laws. I must forge the peoples of Europe into one people.'

A Mediterranean brought up in the tradition of the Roman Empire that lasted for centuries, he realized that the partition of Europe had resulted in 250 years of war out of the past 300. His project for confederation was based on the Roman Republic and the democratic Roman Empire which had brought 300 years of peace to Europe by placing in equilibrium two principles often opposed: those of order and liberty.

The peoples of Europe understood only later the Declaration of the Rights of Man and the Napoleonic Code. But after the peace of 1802 their rulers, starting with the King of England, were quick to see the danger to their thrones inherent in the wars that followed.

At Tilsit Napoleon had thought Alexander understood England's insular attitude towards the continent. Since 1808 he had not been so sure; however, he still believed in his own star. By 1811 he began to suspect that, like England, Russia had no place in a unified Europe and was basically hostile to its federation. No matter how grave affairs became in Spain Napoleon considered them of secondary importance. The principal danger lay in the east. The Russians talked peace; but their troop movements in Moldavia led him to suspect that they had designs on the Grand Duchy of Warsaw.

Alexander had annexed Finland, Moldavia, and Walachia. All the Turkish forts on the Danube were in his hands except Choumia which barred the road to Constantinople. Czartoryski was planning an insurrection in Poland in the spring to spark an invasion of the European Empire. With his right flank resting on Sweden, where Bernadotte had just turned against the French, Alexander counted on help from Austria, Prussia, and the British Navy to which he opened his ports on New Year's Day 1811.

The lesson of Rome and the barbarian invasions haunted Napoleon's imagination; for the Russian push threatened to travel the 'Visigoth route' that Hauterive had been studying under the Emperor's direction.

Could this fatal war be avoided? Napoleon would propose peace to England. Lauriston, the new ambassador to Moscow, would try to reason with Alexander.

While simulating friendship, the Tsar was already a whole year and a whole army ahead of the Emperor; but he did not know it yet. 'I shall not make war', he wrote his minister Champagny on 5 April, 'unless Russia wants more than the left bank of the Danube, or tears up the treaty of Tilsit and makes friends with England.' But what if Russia attacked him?

Alexander preferred a 'cold war', leading the enemy to the point of desperation.

The Emperor said to the Russian Ambassador: 'I have no stomach for a war in the north, but if the crisis is not past by November I shall raise 120,000 more troops. I shall continue thus for two or three years, and if I find it more exhausting than war, I shall go to war . . .'

Simple prudence led the Emperor to increase his vigilance. Early in 1811 he instituted a system of covering forces at key points. The 1st Observation Corps of the Elbe under Davout was stationed at Hamburg; the 2nd at Munster and Osnabrück, under Oudinot. The Observation Corps of the Coast under Ney had its right flank resting on Danzig, and the Observation Corps of Italy under the Viceroy covered Verona and the Trentino. Three cavalry corps were held in reserve.

Under the protection of these corps the Emperor formed a European army to face any eventuality from Russia. Its supreme reserve, the Imperial Guard, had to be increased, concentrated, and officered.

What were its needs? The Emperor cut himself off from the world of receptions, fêtes, parades, and travels and dictated answers to this question, based on figures. He added up his battalions, batteries, men, and horses. The totals were sometimes erroneous and always optimistic; however, they represented goals to strive for.

Wherever the Emperor should find himself the Guard must be ready to move with all its equipment. The move must be made gradually, without compromising the homogeneity of the units or attracting undue attention, and without recalling Dorsenne's small corps from Spain. He must increase the strength of the Young Guard and the artillery, fill up the cavalry, and centralize the services of supply. Finally, he must provide experienced officer cadres to each corps and create a reservoir of generals and commanders who could take the field on short notice.

In 1811 there were 532 Guardsmen who had served under the 'Little Corporal' in Italy and Egypt; however, recruiting for the Old Guard men with ten years' service, or its equivalent in wounds and citations, was becoming increasingly difficult. Nevertheless, the Emperor refused to trifle with the rule. He approved the transfer of twenty-five Dutch grenadiers to the Line for bad conduct, but refused Clarke permission to lower the service requirement by two years for Dutchmen entering the regiment.

Magnificently turned out by Colonel Tindal, the 2nd Grenadiers was inaugurated early in 1811. The regiment did not belong to the Old Guard; nevertheless, its Major Duuring was among the last Guardsmen to remain with Napoleon at Waterloo.

The uniform resembled that of the 1st Grenadiers; however, the coats were white faced with crimson, since large stocks of white cloth were on hand in Holland and economy was in order. The officers' coats were faced with crimson velvet. Their bearskin bonnets bore scarlet plumes 40 centimeters[1] high, but no eagle plates. The regiment eventually had a band dressed in sky blue coats faced with jonquil yellow and trimmed with silver lace brandenburgs and shoulder knots. They wore hats 'bordered with wide gold lace and feathers, and trimmed with a plume and cockade' (see Plate 84a).

The corps was granted an eagle on 30 June.

Saint-Denis, 21 March. The city had a festal air. The 'baby regiment', dressed in white and led by a band and drum corps, paraded before Admiral Decrès, Minister of

[1] About 15 inches.

Marine, and a crowd of spectators. The youngest drummer was twelve and the oldest sixteen. They were tired after eighteen route marches from Amersfoort in Holland. The lame boys rode in the baggage carts with the packs that had proved too heavy to carry.

At the Hague these orphans of men killed in the service of their country, attached by Louis Bonaparte to his Royal Guard, had been known as *vélites*. After his abdication they had come to France to join the navy.

They reached Saint-Denis the day after the King of Rome's birth. This was celebrated by a big dinner for which the barrack master furnished 540 pints of wine and 165 kilos of beef.

On Sunday, 24 March the 1,063 Dutch *vélites* were the chief attraction at the Emperor's review in the Place du Carrousel in honor of his son's birth. Struck by their aplomb, agility, and the precision of their drill, Napoleon said to Admiral Decrès: 'You can't have this regiment', and ordered Berthier to attach it to the Guard.

So now the Baby Guard was added to the Young and Old Guards.

'Soldiers of my Old Guard', the Emperor said, 'here are your children. Their fathers were killed in battle. You shall replace them. By imitating you, they will be brave. By listening to your counsel, they will become the first soldiers in the world . . .'

'And you, my children', he continued, 'in attaching you to my Guard I assign you a duty that is hard to perform. But I count on you and hope that one day people will say: "These boys are worthy of their fathers" . . .'

The review ended, the regiment of *pupilles* (minors) of the Guard marched off behind their miniature sappers and drummers to an air from *La Favorita* at the head of the other corps, according to the tradition of the Guard.

Following the advice of the Duc de La Rochefoucauld-Liancourt, Napoleon decided to open their ranks to the foundlings and orphans of the Empire who were four-foot-eleven and healthy. (Moustaches were not obligatory!) Thus many unfortunate legacies of public charity were rescued from rags and vagrancy. Made presentable, educated, and trained, they became good soldiers and good Frenchmen.

Recruits under sixteen poured into Versailles and were quartered near their seniors. Colonel Tindal of the 2nd Grenadiers took them in hand. By 30 August the corps had eight battalions of 800 each, plus a depot battalion. In all, the 8,000 boys from France, Italy, Brabant, Holland, and Germany comprised one-sixth of the Guard.

Officers and NCO's were needed to handle these youngsters. The Emperor appointed captains from the Dutch grenadiers and other Guard regiments to command their battalions. French NCO's conducted classes which were less academic, but also less onerous, than those taught by professional tutors.

Among the *pupilles* were several 'disobedient and delinquent' characters whom the Minister of War wished to turn over to the navy.

'The navy is not a sink', the Emperor wrote abruptly on the margin of Bessière's request to transfer to that corps Pupille Guillaume 'who had induced two of his comrades to desert . . .'

CHAPTER 6

The School of the Guard

THE marines were reorganized in a 'crew' of 1,136 officers and men under Captain Baste, assisted by Commander Vattier. Vattier had recently returned to France after escaping to Tangiers in a smuggler's bark from the prison ship *La Fortuna* and making his way to the coast of Spain.

The companies were widely scattered. Two were serving in Portugal where they fought courageously in the rear-guard at Fuentes de Oñoro; two were at Brest and Antwerp, and two were serving on vessels at Toulon. The last company, commanded by Lieutenant Grivel, was at the siege of Cadiz under Marshal Victor.

The rest of the marines were still at Cabrera where many died of thirst. A hundred, including Lieutenants Boniface and Gérodias, managed to escape by seizing the bread bark and sailing it to the mainland near Barcelona. There the two officers were re-captured and interned in Majorca. The English moved them to Fort Portchester in Portsmouth harbor from which they escaped in the spring, crossed the channel, and turned up at the Mont-Blanc barracks in Paris.

In July 1811 Captain Count Baste was made a rear admiral and given command of the fleet at Boulogne.

Bessières left Spain in August and returned to Paris to reorganize the cavalry of the Guard. After his departure General Dorsenne became governor of the northern provinces. Important changes were taking place in the Peninsula. The new governor gave his troops plenty of action, increasing the number of expeditions into León and Galicia.

At the end of August the whole Guard marched against Abadia and the Army of Galicia. Attacked and pursued to Astorga, the Spanish rear-guard was slashed to pieces by Major Martin's chasseurs and light-horse.

Meanwhile, Roguet's division reached the foothills of the Asturias. In September it was sent to Zamora to collect taxes and gather crucial provisions for Marshal Marmont's forces encamped before Ciudad Rodrigo. Roguet's troops crossed country stripped of every resource. For three days all they had to eat were a few potatoes. A few NCO's – and unit commanders – closed their eyes while houses were pillaged. 'Old Man Roguet' did not trifle with discipline which he termed 'the soul of armies'. On their return three courts-martial were convened. Two of the malefactors were shot and a corporal and sergeant, 'who for the honor of the flag should have preferred death to disorder', were stripped of their chevrons in front of the troops. Roguet added: 'I shall remember the commanders who permitted this relaxation of discipline'.

That was what it meant to belong to the Guard.

It was impossible to keep track of the Guard detachments sent all over the provinces. Their operations were sometimes made in conjunction with Marmont and Suchet. Napoleon said of Suchet: 'If I had two generals like him this war would be over . . .'

Five or six bands were operating around Vitoria. The partisans rode into town one day and raided the markets. Five hundred fusiliers and some horse grenadiers with 'rations for 12 days' were sent in pursuit, returning empty-handed and famished at the end of two weeks. This was ruinous on men and horses, also on shoes and overcoats. These Dorsenne asked to have replaced even though they had not lasted the prescribed term.

In each engagement, and even in camp, the Guard sustained losses which mounted during the year to twice the number of men in the two route battalions sent from Paris. The officers were beside themselves worrying about food with bread at two francs a pound and wine unprocurable unless begged from the peasants. They had to post sentries and guards day and night since guerrillas sprang up on every hand.

Nevertheless, the officers enjoyed the evening *tertulias* given by the few Spanish families who invited the French, and the balls at General Caffarelli's, a former Guard officer who was affable and popular. Elegant ladies were not lacking. One saw them on Sunday at the military Masses which everyone attended in full dress. Some attractive adventuresses came from Bayonne and Toulouse – and even Bordeaux. The elite gendarmes, who rated the best lodgings, cut a fine figure with them at the everlasting card parties.

Valladolid. 10 September. A strange convoy was traveling to Bayonne. It contained more than a hundred vehicles, with 40 coaches and carriages and 60 wagons taking to Paris the Danish Ambassador, a Portuguese general, ten French generals, clerks, commissaries, surgeons, wounded, fifty females – including Countess Dorsenne and her maid – a seven-year-old boy, a nurse, and a baby a year old. The escort was composed of 2,000 soldiers of Guard and Line.

Naturally this impressive procession was attacked, but the partisans were speedily repulsed to the great relief of the passengers.

The Line troops of the convoy were veterans of Friedland and the Peninsula. The Guardsmen were the 'handsomest fusiliers with the longest service' whom Dorsenne was sending to the 2nd Grenadiers and 2nd Chasseurs, disbanded two years ago, that the Emperor had decided to revive. (At this news Captain Deblais of the fusiliers began to sing his name 'de Blais'.)

By now, the Young Guard had been magnetized by the Emperor and had proved its worth. Napoleon planned to increase the number of voltigeur and *tirailleur* regiments and to pay and clothe each corps alike. As the first regiments had finished their training their Old Guard officers were transferred to the 2nd Grenadiers and 2nd Chasseurs and the Dutch regiment, newly rechristened the '3rd Grenadiers'.

To maintain its esprit de corps, the Emperor preserved the hierarchy of the regiments within the Guard wherever possible.

The 1st Voltigeurs and 1st *Tirailleurs* were reorganized in Spain with officers, NCO's, and *vélites* of the Guard. Baron Longchamp commanded the 1st *Tirailleurs*, assisted by Major Poret de Morvan, etc.; and Baron Mallet, the 1st Voltigeurs. Meanwhile, Baron Rosey commanded the 2nd Chasseurs, with Captains Rignon and Maillard as majors; and Baron Harlet the 2nd Grenadiers, assisted by Majors Albert and Lavigne. The cadres were completed from the Line; the ranks, from 500 men with five years' service plus 1,000 from the instruction battalions at Fontainebleau.

In April 100 Young Guardsmen from Spain, reputedly chosen for the King of Rome's bodyguard, were sent to Fontainebleau to join the nucleus of the 'instruction battalions' of the Guard, a valuable military school attached to the Old Guard. Established to furnish cadres for the Line, these battalions were composed of 'the best and most experienced fusiliers, voltigeurs, and *tirailleurs*', as well as Guard conscripts.

They were received at Fontainebleau by Drouot and divided into 'sergeant-fusiliers', 'corporal-voltigeurs,' and 'corporal-*tirailleurs*'. Administered by their parent corps, they were students at the school commanded by Colonel Christiani of the grenadiers, assisted by Majors Sicard, Laurède, Desalons, and Castanié, and Old Guard officers and NCO's. The subalterns were from Saint-Cyr.

The faculty included an engineer officer, commissary, fencing master, and masters of arithmetic and writing. Each pupil was given an infantry manual, grammar, arithmetic textbook, pencils, pens, penknife, and lead inkwell. He also had the use of artillery and engineer matériel.

The schedule was tight. The pupils got up at 3.30 a.m., had infantry drill from 4 a.m. to 7 or 8, artillery drill until 10, and soup at 11, followed by a course in administration for the best scribes. A rest period from 1 to 1.30 p.m. was followed by classes in writing, grammar, and arithmetic until 4, and dinner at 4.30. From 5 to 6.30 came more theory, with instruction in garrison and campaign duty and fortification.

'You have to know your lessons by heart, although you are not given a moment to study them', Corporal-Voltigeur Rimmel complained. 'A musket has 54 parts and each has a different name – and even parts of parts. A cannon is still more complicated. Yet we earn the pay of a Line corporal, 8 sous a day, of which 4 go to the mess, 2 to the underwear fund, and 2 into our pocket, which is not enough to buy pens and paper. It's a second Saint-Cyr . . . One would think they were trying to make engineer officers of us.'

General Curial inspected the battalion and reported: 'The school is designed to produce excellent NCO's within a short time. The officers and men are willing and assiduous; however, the voltigeurs and *tirailleurs* are better educated and learn more easily than the fusiliers . . .' (Possibly because they were younger.)

Curial observed that the levies from the Old Guard this year had seriously reduced its strength. For example: after furnishing half the cadres for the sergeant-fusiliers, and all those for the corporal-voltigeurs, the chasseurs had only 14 officers, 13 NCO's, and one drummer left.

The Duke of Treviso (Mortier) was recalled from Spain to command the Young Guard. On 2 July he announced that the Fontainebleau School had furnished 946 men with the required five or ten years' service to the 2nd and 1st Grenadiers and Chasseurs. By June the school had 3,400 students.

The Emperor proceeded to organize subaltern cadres for the 120,000 troops he proposed to raise against the Russians. These were the most precious, but also the most difficult, men to find. Then he raised new regiments for the Young Guard.

In May the 5th Voltigeurs and 5th *Tirailleurs* were raised in Paris with men from the Guard depots, conscripts of 1811, and cadres from the Line; and in August a sixth pair were raised in Brussels with conscripts from the reserve and cadres from the Line, Fontainebleau, and the *vélites*.

The senior officers were chosen with great care from the Old Guard. Major Hennequin, 'who laughed when he burnt himself', became lieutenant colonel of the 5th *Tirailleurs*, with the stern Léglise as one of his majors. Major Carré was given command of the 6th, with Golzio of the grenadiers as a battalion commander.

In the voltigeurs, Major Sicard of the chasseurs was appointed commandant of the 5th, and Major Rousseau of the fusiliers, of the 6th.

At first the new units were all dressed like their 1st Regiments,[1] but later their shako plates were stamped with regimental numbers and their pompons dyed different colors.

On a fine summer's morning a column of 1,500 youths wearing blouses, bourgeois frock coats, or peasant smocks poured into the barrack yard at Rueil. They marched more or less in step behind 16 drummers. They had been selected from the Guard depot on the basis of parentage, education, appearance, and locality. They came from Brittany, Gascony, Paris, Lorraine, Flanders, Italy, and Germany.

This ethnic brew was stirred for the sake of discipline; then the adjutant majors drew them up in three ranks and divided them into eight companies forming the two battalions of the 5th *Tirailleurs*. Twelve privileged characters were appointed sappers who would carry axes and wear aprons and bearskin bonnets. Guessing which of the youths would grow beards – and black ones, for red or blond beards were out – was something of a problem.[2]

Their dress was left to the NCO's who presented them to their captains an hour later transformed into dandies in their blue, white, and red uniforms. They were issued muskets so heavy that, in their first attempt to 'port arms', the barrels trembled dangerously. Nevertheless, these fine youngsters were full of ardor and gaiety and were proud to wear buttons with the crowned eagle (see cut on page 59).

---

[1] As a company clerk in the 5th Voltigeurs, Rimmel described his uniform as a short coat with pointed lapels, a yellow collar, red cuffs and lining, and a white waistcoat and trousers. On leaving for Russia in 1812 the NCO's were ordered by their colonel to wear 'grey overalls with buttons down the side, boots, and blue waistcoats'. For these garments he spent his last 55 francs (see Plate 82b).

[2] Sappers of French infantry and cavalry regiments traditionally wore beards. – Ed.

The Young Guard already considered itself an elite corps. Thanks to the spirit of emulation fostered in its men, it eventually proved worthy of this still imaginary distinction.

Though the Emperor always championed equality of human rights, he knew how to create esprit de corps in his Guard by granting titles and distinctive dress to its men and addressing them in simple phrases that stirred their hearts.

In September a regiment of 'flankers'[3] was attached to the chasseurs. This was recruited from 'sons or nephews of the headquarters, foot, or horse rangers of the Crown Forests, or those of the public domain, who have reached 18 years of age and measure 5 feet, 6½ inches'. After serving five years, flankers might succeed to their fathers' posts.

To recall their forester origin, their uniforms were green, faced with yellow. However, the Old Guard officers clung to their blue and white coats, which clashed with the green ones, so that the flankers were usually conspicuous at Guard parades. Only men in desk jobs were eligible since the Line could not be bled further. (The colonels were complaining that the Guard levies had left them nothing but conscripts.) Pompéjac of the voltigeurs was appointed commandant of the flankers. The captains came from the Line and the lieutenants from the Guard (see Plate 84b).

The Emperor now used the term 'Middle Guard' for the fusiliers and instruction battalions, to distinguish them from the Young Guard composed of voltigeurs, *tirailleurs*, national guards, and the 3rd Dutch Grenadiers. As the difficulty of bringing the regiments up to strength increased the Emperor adopted the following rules:

The Young Guard was to be replenished with selected conscripts; and their cadres, with Line officers, *vélites*, fusilier NCO's, and occasionally Saint-Cyrians. As far as possible their senior officers would be chosen from the Old Guard.

The fusiliers were to be replenished with voltigeurs and *tirailleurs* with two years' service and some education, and selected conscripts. Their cadres would come from the Line, the instruction battalion, or the Old Guard.

NCO's and soldiers of the Line with ten years' service and good conduct records, and fusiliers with more than six years' service replenished the Old Guard whose officers were drawn from the same sources. Old soldiers were sent to the gendarmerie, Veteran's Companies, Imperial household, or the Invalides.

The reshuffling of men within the Guard – and back and forth between Guard and Line – involved much traveling about Europe, with sudden arrivals and departures and the adventures common to all soldiers whom nothing can surprise or disconcert.

But, compared to the soldiers' life, that of the councils of administration was a hell. Clothing and housing the troops became more and more difficult, since the merchants complained of their unpaid bills and declined to accept further orders. For example, against a budget of two million francs to clothe their 2nd Regiment and the voltigeurs, the chasseurs had contracted for 448,000 francs' worth of goods but had received only 145,000 in cash.

[3] *Flanqueurs*.

The new 2nd Grenadiers complained that at a December review in the Carrousel the Emperor's attention seemed fixed on a regiment of Croats rather than on them. 'We marched right under his nose so he could inspect us at his ease', wrote Captain Deblais who now commuted from Rueil by cabriolet at 12 francs a ride.

The regiment was even handsomer than the 1st, the generals admitted. The men were 'younger, with better figures', but their esprit de corps was 'not of the highest'. They went poaching around Courbevoie and stole grapes from the vineyards of Argenteuil. General Michel of the 1st Grenadiers sent the offenders to prison. Life in Spain had corrupted them.

Summoned to guard the Empress Josephine at Malmaison and the Princess Pauline at Neuilly, the men were taken in hand by their commanders who inspected their cap cords, saber hilts, cuffs, and sword knots, and the leading of the musket flints. A few stiff punishments brought them into line.

'The Marshal wishes to know when the 2nd Grenadiers will be ready for guard duty with Their Imperial and Royal Majesties . . .' The grenadiers were acutely sensitive to this criterion, for there was even a hierarchy within the Old Guard.

The 1st Regiments drew extra pay and allowances and were better housed. They also ranked higher in the Line. 'I wish it clearly understood that this privilege does not apply to the 2nd Chasseurs and 2nd Grenadiers, nor to the fusiliers, voltigeurs, *tirailleurs*, nor the 2nd Light-horse-Lancers', the Emperor wrote Bessières, adding: 'Keep this decision for your guidance alone'.

The Emperor created six adjutant generals of the Guard to command the Young Guard brigades with the rank of major general. For the grenadiers he appointed Barons Boyeldieu, a veteran of Egypt and major of grenadiers in 1806; Rottembourg, former major of the chasseurs, wounded at Wagram; and Berthezène, a sergeant at Toulon who had been wounded at Eckmühl and Wagram. For the chasseurs he named Lanabère, Mouton-Duvernet, and Boyer de Rebeval.

CHAPTER 7

Cavaliers and Guns

THE cavalry of the Guard was increased. The regiments were expanded to five squadrons and grouped in divisions of 3,000 light and 3,000 heavy cavalry. The hussars, chasseurs, and Polish lancers of the Line replenished the light division, and the carabiniers, curassiers, and dragoons the heavy division. The horse grenadiers were granted eight kettledrummers, dressed in light blue laced with gold and armed with short infantry sabers or *briquets* (see Plate 87).

Vélites were brought in to fill up the ranks of the 2nd Lancers which belonged to the 'Middle Guard'. Those who had served less than a year were not entitled to wear the headdress or aiguillette of the Guard, or guard the Emperor.

Count Lefebvre-Desnoëttes, still on parole in England, was living in Cheltenham. He went out a great deal in London society while his Countess pined alone in Paris. A great-niece of Madame Mère and thus a first cousin of the Emperor, he took a special interest in her. 'General Lefebvre-Desnoëttes, Colonel of the *Chasseurs à cheval* of our Guard', he ordered on 5 November 1810, 'shall be paid his salary and allowances from the time he became a prisoner of war, and shall continue to receive them as though present with his corps'.

Lieutenants Sève and Schmidt had returned to their corps after a perilous escape. The troopers left behind were in revolt against their harsh treatment. They smuggled out a letter that found its way to the Emperor's desk.

'I beg you', he wrote the Minister of Marine in April 1811, 'to have this brought to the attention of the Transport Office . . . with a demand that these men be treated more humanely. If this is not remedied the same number of Englishmen will be thrown into dungeons. The conduct of the English towards these brave men shows definite laxity and is doubtless unknown to the Prince of Wales, since it is unthinkable that he would tolerate treatment so vile as to be unknown in civilized nations . . .'

Some months later the Emperor saw ten English prisoners jump into a boat to help some soldiers lay a pontoon bridge. He wrote Clarke: 'Give orders for those men to be given new clothes, 5 *napoléons* each, and a travel order to Morlaix where they will be turned over to the Transport Office, while making known the reason . . .'

During Lefebvre-Desnoëttes' absence Baron Guyot commanded the chasseurs, seconded by Lt. Colonel Lion, a battle-scarred Belgian, wounded at Marengo and Essling, whom his comrades considered a bit of a boaster because of his name.

Nevertheless, the Emperor missed Desnoëttes who was brave, intelligent, and devoted. Berthier's aide-de-camp Lejeune, captured in Spain in April, had just returned to France. By chance, the British had forgotten to make him sign a parole. Naturally he did not call attention to the fact and an agent of Savary arranged for his passage from Folkestone.

'Did you see Lefebvre-Desnoëttes?' the Emperor asked when he presented himself on arrival.

'No, Sire, but I have been in correspondence with him. He is extremely anxious to return to Your Majesty, but he is beginning to lose hope of ever being exchanged. He would already have done what I did were he not afraid of incurring Your Majesty's displeasure, since he is on parole.'

'Oh, let him come! I shall be very glad to see him.'

'Does Your Majesty authorize me to deliver that message in his name?'

'Yes, yes – and don't lose any time.'

At the end of the year the Countess Lefebvre-Desnoëttes left with her son for England 'to bring her errant husband back to the straight and narrow path'. On a fine spring evening of 1812 Desnoëttes, disguised as a 'Russian count', together with his wife in men's clothes and his son, left Cheltenham for London by post-chaise, accompanied by his aide and a servant. From there they went to Dover, Calais, and Paris where the General resumed his place at the head of the chasseurs of the Guard.

In this case the parole – a verbal but nonetheless formal agreement – had been patently violated. However, the Emperor needed such commanders badly and they were hard to find. For example:

'Communicate my displeasure to the colonel of the 9th Curassiers', he wrote the Minister on 18 July 1811. 'He has sent the Guard a bad character who has spent three months in jail. Order him to place the responsible parties under twenty-four hour arrest and publish the fact in his orders. To send bad characters to my Guard is to fail me in an essential respect.' Then he added: 'The inspectors will select the men for the Guard hereafter'.

Baron Colbert was whipping the 2nd Light-horse-Lancers into shape to escort Their Majesties to Holland in the autumn. Some men tried on the new shakos, and the trumpeters their colpacks, then resumed the Polish *czapkas*. They had far overspent their clothing allotment of 584 francs. An idemnity of 1,000–1,200 francs per man was asked from the state to 'repay the regimental fund for three uniform changes' by which they had docked their pay of 40 francs a month for the next three years!

The 2nd Lancers were inexperienced in escorting the Emperor, and he began to miss his chasseurs. He wrote Bessières from Amsterdam: 'Recall from Spain 50 chasseurs accustomed to duty in my escort'. A few days later he added: '. . . also the horse grenadiers and chasseurs, General Lepic, and all the cavalry of the Guard . . .'

Whether because it was his old branch or because it was indispensable, the artillery was the principal object of the Emperor's concern. 'In battle', he wrote, 'the Guard furnishes artillery to the whole field.'

In February he had ordered the foot gunners and dismounted train soldiers brought from Spain. Then he directed Lariboisière to increase the Guard artillery to 72 guns with 60 caissons and a double ammunition supply. Leaving three conscript companies with 24 guns in Spain, Napoleon ordered five Line batteries with 40 guns prepared to serve as auxiliaries to the Guard in case of war. This brought the Guard park to 136 pieces.

On 8 February Napoleon wrote: 'I do not wish to spend the money now, but I want everything in readiness so my plans may be implemented within a month after I give the signal . . .'

Lariboisière was appointed Inspector General of Artillery, and General Count Sorbier ordered to prepare the Guard artillery to take the field in force in case of a Russian attack. The general staff under Sorbier included General Baron d'Aboville, the surgeon major with two assistants, a professor of mathematics, a quartermaster, and officers in charge of provisions, forage, and the park.

The four horse batteries[1] of the Old Guard were under Baron Desvaux de Saint-Maurice, former aide-de-camp of Marmont promoted general at Wagram, assisted by Lt. Colonels Marin and Chauveau. The six foot batteries were commanded by Colonel Drouot, assisted by Lt. Colonels Boulart, Lallemand, and Pommereul. Majors Cottin and Henrion, veterans of Santo-Domingo, commanded the four Young Guard companies, and Captain Leclerc the pontooneers. The two train battalions under Leroy were recruited up to strength.

On the eve of 1812 the Guard contained 30 regiments. The administrative and medical staffs were increased. On 24 August the Emperor decided to combine the companies of artisans and transport troops into two autonomous units under the Chief Commissary. The work battalion,[2] containing the companies in charge of the bakery, meat, forage, and field hospital, was increased and made sufficiently flexible to answer calls for masons and locksmiths. The pay of these troops had not changed since 1809 and was most inadequate. Attached in small details to different corps, they had difficulty in feeding themselves.

Captain Gubert commanded the new battalion whose soldiers wore short steel-blue jackets piped and lined with scarlet, with waistcoats and pantaloons to match, and beige overcoats. Their shakos were trimmed with orange braid and cords, the eagle plate of the Young Guard, and red bean-shaped pompons. In 1813 they wore plumes. The NCO's wore tail coats with overcoats, and their shakos were trimmed with gold – or gold and wool – lace and cords. They were armed with musketoons, bayonets, and *briquets*.

The transport service was centralized in a 'wagon train battalion'[3] created in August out of the fifth company of the work battalion. All corps vehicles were abolished,

---

[1] Though the modern term 'battery' is sometimes used in this book to distinguish an artillery unit from a company of infantry or squadron of cavalry, the artillery of the Imperial Guard was actually divided into 'companies' of foot and horse, and 'battalions' of foot and 'squadrons' of horse artillery. – Ed.

[2] *Bataillon d'Ouvriers d'administration.*

[3] *Bataillon du Train des Équipages.*

PLATE 80

a) Lepic
(*Engr. Forestier*)

b) Tindal
(*Contemp. lithograph: Collection M. Dronkers*)

c) Dorsenne
(*Contemp. colored engraving*)

d) Mouton Duvernet
(*Engr. Forestier*)

e) Clarke
(*Contemp. engraving*)

PLATE 81

A Spanish guerilla chief in his camp

(From a contemporary colored engraving 'after a drawing in the possession of the Marquis of Buckingham')

PLATE 82

PLATE 83

a) Recruits for the Guard

b) Chasseur on the march

(*From lithographs by Charlet*)

PLATE 84

PLATE 85

PLATE 86

PLATE 87

PLATE 88

Drummer, Empress' dragoons, 1810
(*From an original watercolor by Lucien Rousselot*)

because of widespread abuses, and the wagons, horses, harness, and drivers' clothing turned over to the new battalion.

On 1 October the Inspector and Chief Commissary Dufour inaugurated the unit, the latter assuming overall command. The battalion lacked men and horses, and the corps caissons and wagons were still in the shop being repaired and repainted. New four-wheeled, four-horse wagons painted olive green with the crowned eagle and inscription 'Garde Impériale. Bataillon des Équipages, Compagnie no.—', were on order.

The first company had charge of transporting the baggage and papers of the different corps and the cavalry forges; the second, the field hospitals; the third, the provision wagons. The battalion mustered 17 officers, 800 men, 268 vehicles, and 1,200 horses.

The uniform was like that of the work battalion except that the collars, cuffs and facings were brown, piped with scarlet. Shakos with white metal eagle plates, chin scales, and white cords were worn, shoulder belts and pouches with the cypher 'N' and crown, shoes and gaiters for the men on foot, and leather breeches, gloves, and boots with 'Prussian spurs' for the mounted men.

The artisans and train troopers were no fashion plates. Their uniform cloth was not the same as the grenadiers', despite the Emperor's decree that cloth would be of the same quality throughout the Guard. The historians do not pay much attention to them, but devote their pages to the grenadiers. However, without these loyal and long-suffering men the Guard could not have been fed nor its wounded cared for or evacuated to safety.

Because it was their duty the train troops, dispersed in small detachments under sub-alterns and NCO's, drove their rawboned nags over the rutted roads of Germany and Russia to bring their heavy wagons to the right place at the right time. For they, too, belonged to the Imperial Guard.

What can one say of a man like Lapierre, adjutant of the work battalion, who was sixty-five, who had enlisted in the Mestre-de-Camp Cavalry five days after the *Tondu* was born and had dragged his carcass over every battlefield in Europe? It is to the ever-lasting honor of the French army to have produced such men who knew their trade thoroughly, and whose modesty and devotion could be summed up in the word 'service'.

Though the Emperor was enlarging his Guard, the budget for the previous year was already two millions in arrears. The bureau of accounting sent the ministry the following report:

'Since His Majesty has attached so many new regiments to the grenadiers and chasseurs, a single quartermaster now has to keep the accounts of ten to twelve regiments; a single procurement officer is burdened with the details of clothing 18,000 men; a single council has to administer a number of corps whose organization, pay, and allotments are vastly different. This results in much confusion . . . The funds for various fiscal years are all mixed up . . . For example, the Guard is still owed 1,200,000 francs for 1808. The purveyors are unpaid . . . Such chaos is harmful to the public treasury . . . The accounting system of the infantry of the Guard has become a labyrinth in which no inspector can find the thread . . .'

On 9 June the whole Guard attended the baptism of the King of Rome at Notre-Dame. The long procession was escorted by cavalry whose trumpets sounded the glory and enthusiasm evoked by the occasion. Stationed along Their Majesties' route, the foot Guard lined the pavement and rendered honors. Paris was illuminated.

So was Rome. The Capitolio and Forum; the Temples of Concord, Antoninus and Peace; the arches of Septimius Severus, Titus, and Constantine, and the Coliseum were all lighted for the occasion. The Royal Guard of Italy paraded in Milan.

On 23 June mammoth banquets were given by the Emperor's order to the regiments stationed around Paris and Versailles. These were organized by Duroc in the Bois de Boulogne and the park of Saint-Cloud. The troops at Fontainebleau and Chantilly were entertained locally. The anticipated cost was thirty sous a man plus a bottle of wine, but the Emperor provided three francs apiece from his privy purse to regale the Guard. The Grumblers and conscripts never forgot this.

Having granted a month's extra pay to the soldiers of the Guard on duty at the King of Rome's baptism, the Emperor wrote on the margin of a complaint from the inspector: 'Did they not line the route?'

This was but a minor incident. The Emperor knew the faults of his Guard, but he also knew its mind and soul for which he was responsible; and he knew that at a signal from him it would march to its death.

CHAPTER 8

The Music of the Guard

EXCEPT for Paisiello's, the Emperor did not care for music; but he understood the power it had over his soldiers.

We owe to Louis XIV our military bands, bugle calls, the long roll for the General Alarm, and the military airs commissioned from the great masters of the *Grand Siècle*. Lully composed the calls for Order Arms and Retreat, the marches of the *Régiment du Roy* and the fusiliers, also the celebrated *March of the Musketeers* still played under the Empire. The court musician Philidor composed the first collection of drum rolls and trumpet calls.

Louis XV borrowed the clarinet, which originated in Nürnberg, from the bands of Frederick the Great, also the Hanoverian cornet and the *Marche des Dragons de Notre-Seigneur*[1] used by Meyerbeer in his opera *L'Étoile du Nord*.

'Make them all march in step', the Maréchal de Saxe wrote in his *Rêveries* when discussing infantry. 'That is the whole secret of marching and performing rapid evolutions without fatigue, and that was the military step of the Roman legions.' Ever since, bands have played, trumpets sounded, and drums beat at military Masses, parades, route marches, and ceremonies.

In his youth Napoleon had heard the bands of the *Gardes françaises* and the national guard that gave birth to the Conservatoire and the School of Declaiming and Singing, both founded in his day. He had sung the *Marseillaise* which Sarrette's musicians played in the streets, learned from the Parisians the *Song of Departure*, and heard the first notes of the trombone, and the serpent invented by a priest in Auxerre. He had been struck by a remark of the Abbé Raynal: 'If Frederick II owed some of his victories to the speed of his marches, surely he owed others to his military bands'.

In 1802 Bonaparte abolished cavalry bands – not because he believed with Saint-Germain that 'military music that gives no signal is fit only to make ladies dance' – but because they deprived him of 3,000 fighting cavalrymen. Later he revived them.

During the Empire the drummers, trumpeters, and musicians were pampered. They wore elaborate uniforms and received high pay. These artists increased the corps' prestige, rendered honors, and led the troops on the march and into battle. By prescribed signals, drummers and trumpeters transmitted commands to the troops at drill and in battle and ordered their lives in barracks and camp. In the Guard these indispensable functions were performed by virtuosi.

[1] March of Our Lord's Dragoons.

In 1811 the Emperor established a school for 120 student drummers of the Guard so that its tradition might be maintained and the calls remain uniform in all units. David Bühl was appointed musical director of the school which was soon opened to fifers and trumpeters as well. At first he worked without compensation beyond the five francs a day paid a musician of the Old Guard.

Bühl was well known to the Emperor to whom the musician had dedicated 28 trumpet calls, some of which survive today. These included a fire alarm which the Emperor fancied. Bühl had played the trumpet since the age of ten. He once sounded the calls before a commission of generals presided over by Louis Bonaparte. Hearing him sound the Charge, General d'Hautpoul exclaimed: 'I feel as if I were there!'

Twenty-four students for each regiment of grenadiers, chasseurs, and fusiliers, and 48 for each regiment of voltigeurs and *tirailleurs* were enrolled in the new school which opened on 5 April. Candidates were recruited from the children of Veterans and Invalids and from the *pupilles*.

Painters and historians have recorded the uniform of the drum majors who led the Guard columns. These wore coats trimmed on all seams with gold lace, gold brandenburgs and epaulets, gold-trimmed white Hungarian breeches and black Hungarian boots, and hats with red and white plumes and a tall white panache. The drum major wore gauntlets. His left hand rested upon the gilded hilt of an officer's sword, carried on a red velvet baldric edged with gold and embroidered with gold laurel leaves and grenades. In his right hand he held the heavy baton with its silver pommel, chain, and tip (see Plate 85).

Though less ornate, the undress coats worn on the march with plain black boots to the knee were laced with gold and worn with gold epaulets. The undress hats carried the plume of the corps when the troops wore plumes (see Plate 89).

The drummers' dress was the uniform of the corps with extra lace, brandenburgs, and epaulets of mixed gold and red silk. Their brass drums had sky blue rims and were decorated with the corps insignia. With brass-bound ebony sticks they beat the March, Charge, Quickstep, triple *Rat-tat-tat*, quintuple *Rat-tat-tat-tat-tat*, and the Roll dating from the 17th century. Sometimes accompanied by fifers, whose ancestors had played at Marignan,[2] they beat the *Diane*, *Rigodon*, General Alarm, and Assembly, the calls To Arms, To the Colors, Mess, Dismiss, Retreat, Charge, the *Ban*, and *Aux Champs* (the old call to the field that evolved into a salute to the general).

There were distinctive beats for the ordinary step, and the quickstep they beat at the head and flanks of a column. The famous syncopation erroneously called the 'Lame Duck' was borrowed from the Prussians whose drummers beat this singular rhythm when their officers were late for assembly.

The band of the 1st Grenadiers was the best in the Guard. The regiment was proud of it, and so was the Emperor. This band usually performed at the fêtes, dinners, and balls at the Tuileries under Sergeant Major Michel Gebauer, the first oboist, who drew the pay of a subaltern. For special occasions its 48 musicians were supplemented by professionals paid by the corps and engaged from Feydau, the Opera, or the

[2] Famous victory of Francis I over the Swiss and Milanese in 1515. – Ed.

Conservatory where the best artists were to be had. The band contained clarinets, flutes, oboes, bassoons, horns, trumpets, trombones, a serpent, base and snare drums, cymbals, and a Chinese bells, or 'jingling Johnny'.

The musicians' dress uniform cost a fortune. It consisted of a grenadier coat with crimson revers, collar, cuffs, cuff flaps, and lining until 1810, and scarlet thereafter. All seams were laced with gold. They wore top boots, and their hats were bound with gold lace, bordered with red and white plumes, and topped with a tall white panache. Except for the percussion group, each musician owned his instrument which he maintained at his own expense. Though paid only 2·22 francs he received a substantial gratuity from the Emperor for each concert (see Plate 86a).

Every day at nine in summer and noon in winter the band of the corps on duty accompanied the guard mounting at the palace occupied by the Emperor, and played a serenade during the changing of the guard. The varied repertory included the vaudeville and dance tunes that had been the chief source of military music since the days of the Monarchy.

It would have been useless to invite a Tyrtaeus[3] to compose poetry to inspire the Grumblers. They preferred *I Like Onions Fried in Oil* or *The Victory Is Ours*, set to vaudeville tunes or hunting songs. A popular song familiar to all, *Dans la rue Chiffonnière*, provided the air for the pertinent lyric 'We will pierce their flank' sung at Marengo.

To soldier songs like *Malbrouck* – whose air was borrowed from the Saracens by the soldiers of Saint Louis – and *Auprès de ma Blonde, Il Pleut, Bergère*, etc. they added the Emperor's favorites: the *Song of Departure, What Better than to Be Home with Your Family?* and *Let Us Watch over the Empire*. They also played the *March of the Consular Guard*, the *March of the Pupilles* (improvised by Cherubini in the salon of Queen Hortense), the Solemn Marches of Ferdinand Paer played at the Emperor's marriage to Marie-Louise, and the Quicksteps in 6/8 time by Gebauer whose *March of the Grenadiers* was played at Waterloo.

'Here comes the band, the war is over . . .' This unjust sally sometimes greeted the brave musicians who had often to restore courage to wavering troops under fire. Nevertheless, the Guard marched behind them into the capitals of Europe and on into history.

The trumpeter was the idol of the cavalry. The trumpet first appeared as a celestial instrument in the *Book of Numbers* and the *Apocalypse*, and its long career extends clear to the Last Judgment, via the reign of the antichrist (to whom it announced catastrophe), the siege of Jericho, the Pass of Roncevalles, the medieval battles, tournaments, and cavalcades, and the victories of the Empire.

To be sure, a cavalier who had the honor to wear a sky blue uniform laced with gold, and attach to his trumpet – often of silver – a banner so richly embroidered that it was sometimes called a 'standard', was not – as in the *Gospel according to St. John* – necessarily an angel, though we are tempted to add: 'He ought to be'. But perhaps it is to his celestial origin that he owes the incontestable prestige he has always enjoyed among his comrades in the troop, the duty NCO, and the opposite sex.

[3] Athenian poet who inspired the Spartan soldiers with his songs in the 7th century B.C. – Ed.

In the Guard the trumpeter rated a bed to himself and his pay was 10 francs instead of 4·50. It would require another volume to describe his various uniforms. The trumpeter of the horse grenadiers wore a sky blue coat faced with crimson and laced with gold with gold brandenburgs, and a white bearskin bonnet with a gold cord and a white plume tipped with light blue. His cloak was sky blue and his crimson housings and holsters were trimmed with gold lace.

The uniform of his colleague in the chasseurs was positively theatrical, consisting of a sky blue dolman trimmed with scarlet and gold, a scarlet pelisse trimmed with sky blue and gold and edged with white fur, and a white fur busby with a scarlet bag. The saddlecloth, crimson at this period, was sky blue in 1812.

The dragoon trumpeter wore a white coat with a blue plastron laced with gold, and a helmet with a black[3] horsehair crest (see Plate 112).

The lancers' trumpeter wore a white *kurtka* whose crimson plastron was laced with silver; and in the Polish regiment, a crimson and white *czapka*. The same, trimmed in scarlet and gold, was worn by the trumpeter of the 2nd Regiment who also wore a white *czapka* (the trumpet major a white colpack) in full dress (see Plate 114).

The trumpeter of the horse artillery wore a rose pelisse trimmed with sky blue and gold, and a white colpack with a sky blue and white plume. The uniforms of the trumpet majors were trimmed with extra lace and their pay was high (see Plate 16).

The Emperor liked being escorted by these dazzling cavaliers. Whenever he heard a trumpet sound a false note he remembered that the trumpets of Hercule had helped him win the battle of Arcole. Since his day Bühl had recruited 600 musicians for the Guard, arranged all its calls and marches, and composed for it the famous fanfares 'The Standards', 'To the Emperor', and 28 calls, many of which are still used.

Long surpassed by the German and Russian military bands, nevertheless the Guard had an excellent corps of trumpeters, many of whom were of foreign origin. Krettly, the son of a professor at the Conservatoire, was trumpeter of the Guides of Egypt, then trumpet major of the chasseurs. He possessed both a sword and a trumpet of honor and was now a commissioned officer of his corps.

Besides the trumpets, the *fanfares* of the Guard included horns, drums, and kettledrums. In the Line, only the carabineers and a few cuirassier regiments were privileged to have kettledrums, for which Louis XIV had had a special weakness. Dressed in Turkish costumes under the Monarchy, kettledrummers of the Imperial Guard also wore Polish or Hungarian dress and rode richly caparisoned horses. It required supple wrists, a good ear, and perfect balance to manage on horseback a pair of drums surrounded by dazzling aprons of the regimental color (see Plates 32, 87, 88).

All the drums, bands, and trumpets of the Guard were massed in honor of the supreme fête of the Empire – the birth of its heir.

'With one accord your people salute the new star risen on the horizon of France whose first rays have dissipated the last shadows of the future.' These words were pronounced in the name of the Senate by its president on 21 March.

In 1811 the Guard was the staunchest supporter of the regime and defender of its destiny.

[3] Both Martinet and Hoffmann, the principal contemporary sources, show black horsetail plumes. – Ed.

'My Cousin', the Emperor wrote the Duke of Istria (Bessières) on 20 September, 'go and see the King of Rome often and talk with Madame de Montesquiou. Take all precautions necessary for his safety. Inform Madame de Montesquiou that in case of emergency she is to call on you and keep you informed . . .'

To whom, if not the Guard, could the Emperor entrust the safety of the King of Rome?

The Guard's splendid days ended on 16 September 1811. On this day the Emperor wrote Bessières:

'My Cousin, you will prepare the Guard to leave on campaign.'

BOOK V

THE GUARD IN ACTION

CHAPTER 1

The 'Majestic Migration'

In 1812 the Grand Army of Europe consisted of eleven infantry and four cavalry corps totaling 550,000 men with 1,300 guns. These included 270,000 French in 15 divisions, 40,000 garrison troops, and 15,000 foreign mercenaries serving in Swiss, Spanish, Illyrian, and Croatian regiments and the Portuguese Legion. All these wore the French cockade.

The 170,000 troops of the European Confederation were divided between Polish, Bavarian, Saxon, and Westphalian army corps; Italian, Neapolitan, Württemberg, and Danish divisions; and brigades from Baden, Berg, Hesse, and Mecklenburg. Finally, an Austrian corps and several Prussian divisions contained 60,000 'allies'.

This was a considerable force, well led, trained, and organized. Its grand reserve was the Imperial Guard of 50,000 men, including Dutch, Polish, and Mameluk units. In March the Emperor added the Legion of the Grand Duchy of Warsaw, composed of four Polish regiments under General Claparède; and later, battalions from Berg, Neuchâtel, and Hesse, and Swiss and Prussian batteries, bringing the Guard's total strength to 60,000.

Russia, never having disarmed, was still a threat. Though the Tsar declared he would not be the first to draw his sword, he kept Czartoryski in Poland to organize an uprising as a prelude to an invasion of the European Empire. Napoleon believed that Russia must be pushed back into Asia, and the Kingdom of Poland restored. However, mobilization was not war.

The 'majestic migration' – in the words of Louis Madelin – advanced eastward in silence, if not in secret. Would it give Alexander pause? Could the spirit of Tilsit be revived on the banks of the Niemen? Napoleon's first step was crucial, since it was final. He could not turn back.

Flattered by kings who masked their deceit by contemptible toadying; surrounded by secretive diplomats, rancorous malcontents, frightened ministers, and the weary marshals who were either unco-operative or downright prophets of doom, Napoleon, the sovereign, statesman, and commander in chief, stood alone on the horns of a dilemma stretching from the Guadalquivir to the Niemen.

What did the soldiers think?

'I had plenty of trouble last year', wrote Tirailleur Mignolet of the 1st Regiment from Spain. 'If I never have another year like it I shan't complain . . . We are surrounded by 40,000 brigands whom we must fight every day – and the situation gets no better, but worse. Their bands grow bigger every year, for we burn their towns and villages . . .'

Tirailleur Delvau of the 6th Regiment wrote his father, an innkeeper on the Meuse: 'The Emperor must go to Russia to make war on that little emperor. Oh, we'll soon have him in the soup! When there's no one left but us there, there'll still be plenty. O Father, this is some army! Our old soldiers say they never saw anything like it. And it's true, because they are bringing up food and large forces, but we don't know for sure if we are going to Russia. Some say it might be India and some say Egypt. You don't know which to believe. It's all the same to me. It would suit me all right to go to the ends of the earth . . .'

Alas, Tirailleur Delvau did not realize that his wish would be granted! Nevertheless, this conscript of 1812 had the true spirit of the Guard. If their officers were dreaming of promotion and the pay that was accruing, the soldiers were filled with boundless confidence in their chief whom they loved with unflagging devotion. They would go wherever he wished.

The battle-wise old-timers showed the young enthusiasts how to dodge cannon balls. 'The Russians?' asked the veterans of Austerlitz and Friedland. 'We beat them . . . we smashed them!' 'The Tsar?' 'Just a chap the Emperor outsmarted at Tilsit.' 'Egypt?' 'We've been there. Now we're going to Russia where the Cossacks eat candles. Or to India where there's diamonds and treasure and dancing girls . . .' Nothing could match the cockiness and gaiety of these Gauls marching to glory behind their god.

Shoulder packs!

No, not yet . . . Paris was preparing for the Carnival which the Emperor wanted to be brilliant and gay. Nevertheless, at Rueil, Courbevoie, Brussels, and Burgos the Guard was not playing. On 10 February – the eve of Mardi-Gras – a column left quietly for Brussels. It included the 6th Voltigeurs and 6th *Tirailleurs*; the 2nd Light-horse; a company of gunners with eight pieces; caissons, commissaries, surgeons, and ambulances, under Adjutant General Lanusse. General Colbert left Paris simultaneously 'without saying goodbye to anyone'.

The 3rd Guard Division, made up of the Old Guard infantry under General Curial, had been ready to leave since the beginning of the month. Each regiment formed a company of overage men to guard the Empress and the King of Rome during the Emperor's absence.

The 1st Grenadiers and 1st Chasseurs took their eagles with them on campaign. New flags, 33 inches square (22 in the cavalry) excluding the gold fringe, with equal vertical bands of blue, white, and red, embroidered inscriptions and gold emblems, had been ordered.[1] Tricolor *cravates*, or streamers, hung halfway down the staff. The eagle was carried on a gold-trimmed leather belt by the 'eagle-bearer', and flanked by the 'eagle guard'.

Like those of the Line, the tricolor, blue, white, red, and yellow battalion guidons borne by the Old Guard, fusiliers, *tirailleurs*, voltigeurs, and flankers had no symbolic significance. Each cavalry regiment carried but a single standard. Only the horse grenadiers and chasseurs carried theirs on campaign.

[1] These were not delivered to the Guard until the spring of 1813. – Ed.

Taking their guidons only, the 3rd Grenadiers left Versailles at dawn on 20 February with their artillery, caissons, etc. Four squadrons of the 1st Polish Lancers left Chantilly the same day. A fifth would be formed at Posen. Where were they bound?

Colonel Krasinski was ordered to Compiègne where he found 150 *chasseurs à cheval* and 50 elite gendarmes waiting with a packet of sealed envelopes. Each day he was to open the one for that date only, which would give him his itinerary. He was ordered to depart before daybreak. 'No one may know where he is going', the Emperor repeated several times. Step by step, Krasinski's regiment reached Mainz.

At almost the same moment the horse grenadiers left Paris in new fur bonnets and cords made by the Emperor's hatter Poupard, together with the chasseurs under Guyot and Exelmans. Three or four hundred of each corps were left to come in April with two horse batteries from Spain. Lefebvre-Desnoëttes resumed command of his chasseurs on 6 May.

The dragoons' movements were complicated. The battle squadrons left their quarters on 3 March under General Letort and crossed the Rhine the 28th. They were joined in Hanover by Captain Pictet's detachment, which had left in January, and 400 troopers from Spain under Marthod. The last company left Paris under Captain Chamorin on 8 May.

To spare the horses, the marching discipline was strict in the cavalry. The squadrons set out at a walk which they continued for the first hour. After a ten-minute halt they cinched up their mounts, redistributed their pack equipment, and walked for another mile. Finally they started trotting at intervals of 100 paces, continuing at this gait for two hours. The riders dismounted on steep grades, both ascending and descending. The gaits were regulated at 100 meters a minute for the walk, 220 for the trot, and 300 for the gallop. The quartermaster rode ahead to arrange the bivouacs, rejoining the troop to assign the officers' billets on the march.

By order of the Duke of Istria (Bessières) the 2nd Grenadiers and 2nd Chasseurs were ready on 1 March to leave at a moment's notice. But of course! They had been told that every day for a month. Every evening pickets were detailed for the van and rear-guards, and the wagons loaded. All was ready . . .

It was just as well, for at 4 a.m. on 2 March they were alerted for departure. The chasseurs left at 6 a.m. and next day the grenadiers, followed by Pompéjac's flankers. They reached Metz in twelve stages.

Baron Gros (who, being from the Aude, called himself 'Grosse') was in command and everyone was delighted. Though not a 'Grumbler' – that name being reserved for the rank and file – he was certainly a character. Loudmouthed, rather plump, pictur-esque, and uneducated, he declared that he 'slept in the arms of the goldsmith'[2] – thinking Morpheus was some pimp at the Palais-Royale. He bullied his *'bélites'*, as he called them, whose education he envied and whose pranks he feared. He had difficulty paying the debts of his coquettish and extravagant wife who profited handsomely from his long campaigns. The Emperor put up with his gaffs at the Tuileries because of his loyalty and his magnificent bravery in the field.

[2] *'L'orfèvre'* for *Morphée*.

The 5th Voltigeurs and 5th *Tirailleurs* under Berthèzene, and the 4th regiments still in Spain, formed the 1st Guard Division under General Delaborde who had been a general longer than Napoleon and had known the *Tondu* in his Toulon days. Berthezène, son of a simple workman, was 'worthy of any position he might occupy, and merited the esteem and affection in which he was universally held', according to the inscription carved on the façade of his château at Vendargues.

General Roguet was recalled from Spain in the midst of a campaign, as were Boyeldieu's fusiliers who were chasing bandits in Aranda. General Dorsenne was much embarrassed to be stripped of his forces at that moment and did not relay the order until 23 February.

Indeed the troops had neither shoes, shirts, nor money to buy the barest necessities. Carrying seventy-pound packs, the fusiliers, voltigeurs, and *tirailleurs* marched to Bayonne where an officer from the general staff was waiting with carriages to take them to Paris. The fusiliers left on 15 March, and the rest next day. The 4th Voltigeurs and 4th *Tirailleurs* were already on their way to join Delaborde, marching 468 miles in twenty-three days – a famous marathon.

Reaching Paris on 6 April, Roguet gave his men a twelve days' breathing-spell. They needed it after two years of hard campaigning, ending in a bone-crushing ride. The General had to round up his orders, weed out the unfit, and fill up his ranks from the depot. Thanks to careful selection, his recruits were excellent, physically and morally sound, well dressed and educated. His was the 2nd Guard Division composed of Boyeldieu's 1st Voltigeurs and 1st *Tirailleurs* and a brigade of fusiliers and flankers under Lanabère. But the latter had left Rueil on 20 February! Each brigade left a company cadre for 300 conscripts at the depot. With these, new regiments would be formed and sent on at the end of the month. Roguet's division left for Metz on 18 April.

In the midst of these rapid troop movements, for which orders were issued by men with no means of communication but goose quills and horses, you might think the general staff of the Guard had enough to do without having to verify whether so-and-so of such-and-such a regiment fulfilled the Emperor's requirements for becoming a grenadier. Well, you are mistaken. Each candidate was subjected to a regular inquest.

The mayor of the commune of Ohey wrote the sub-prefect: 'You ask about the morals of one Paul-Joseph Poulard of the 4th Cuirassiers, and about his family, since he is a candidate for the Horse Grenadiers of the Imperial Guard. Before he left town I kept my eye on this individual and I cannot praise his conduct too highly. It was exemplary. His parents, too, were good people and are both deceased.'

Not everyone who wished to could enter the Old Guard. The Emperor saw to that.

On 21 February the Emperor reviewed the *pupilles* in the Place du Carrousel. There were nine battalions, 8,000 strong. This was no parade, but a minute inspection. He found their state satisfactory, but the uniforms varied. Napoleon had originally planned to dress the regiment in green; but the stocks of white cloth in Holland were so large that the minors wore white with green or crimson facings. When their commander Bardin, a man 'of great merit and learning' who was very strict about dress, protested the Emperor replied: 'It is a question of economy'. So the *pupilles* continued to wear white uniforms with Young Guard shakos. They carried short dragoon muskets (see Plate 116a).

The Emperor had his 'children' carefully examined by the top Dutch and French doctors who found 400 – nearly all Dutch or Belgian – in poor condition and sent them to orphanages. Bardin declared that though this regiment was the largest in the Guard it had the lowest pay and allotments. A *pupille* drew 45 sous, and his captain 150–300 francs. The cadres were far from complete. The elite battalions, composed of seventeen- and eighteen-year-olds, lacked both captains and NCO's.

The Emperor was enchanted with the blonde, clear-eyed youngsters. After the review he sent for seventy-five officers and NCO's from the instruction battalion at Fontainebleau, and nine company clerks from the *lycées*. The Paris Guard furnished the rest. Some 'veterans of eighteen' were made corporals, and even sergeants. They were much stricter than their elders.

All nations, creeds, and classes were represented in the regiment. The Dutch, who had been longest in the army, tried to dominate the rest; the Italians bullied the dull Germans; the French jeered at those who did not understand their language. Justice and brotherhood were restored only by confinements to barracks. The greatest punishment was to be sent to the awkward squad, known as the 'future company' by its members.

Soon only the depot was left at Versailles. The other *pupille* battalions were garrisoned at Rouen, Le Havre, Fécamp, Dieppe, Dunkirk, Caen, and Grandville. This further complicated the administrative problems of Bardin, the lowest paid lieutenant colonel in the Guard, who drew the pay of a Line colonel.

Monsieur Courtois, the Guard's new chief of personnel, soon discovered the Emperor's weakness. 'Nothing is to be denied our Guard', Napoleon wrote on the schedule of food and clothing allowances. Courtois established once and for all the distinction between Old, Middle, and Young Guards in the following extract:

RANK AND FILE

a) OLD GUARD.

1st Chasseurs, and NCO's of the 2nd; 1st Grenadiers, and NCO's of the 2nd; Veteran's Companies; NCO's of fusiliers; horse grenadiers; *chasseurs à cheval*; dragoons; 1st Light-Horse-Lancers; Mameluks; elite gendarmes; foot and horse artillery; storekeepers of the park; pontooneers; sappers; marines; NCO's of the artillery attached to the Young Guard.

b) MIDDLE GUARD.

3rd Grenadiers; 2nd Light-horse-Lancers; corporals and soldiers of 2nd Chasseurs and 2nd Grenadiers; fusiliers; artillery train; *Vélites* of Turin and Florence; work battalion (artisans); Veteran's Company of Amsterdam

c) YOUNG GUARD.

Voltigeurs and *tirailleurs*; flankers; national guards; *pupilles*; wagon train battalion; corporals and gunners of artillery attached to the Young Guard.

OFFICERS

OLD GUARD:

All officers of: 1st–3rd Grenadiers; 1st and 2nd Chasseurs; fusiliers; horse grenadiers and chasseurs; dragoons; light-horse-lancers; Mameluks; artillery (including Young Guard detachments); pontooneers; sappers; artillery train; marines; lieutenant colonels, majors, and captains of voltigeurs, *tirailleurs*, flankers, and national guards.

The Guard's departure was carried out discreetly so as to attract the least possible attention. The regiments were scattered in small mixed columns commanded by subalterns. They left town by night and followed different routes to their first destination which was Mainz and the Rhine valley.

The senior commanders remained in Paris to supervise the organization of the reserves, the departure of the troops, and to receive orders from Bessières. By their presence at court and in society they hoped to divert the public's attention.

The Emperor ordered numerous moves by post which were tiring and costly but quick. Fortunately, horses were plentiful. The troop movements caused great confusion, as the divisions were scattered and had difficulty collecting their components.

At La Fère the Guard artillery had been preparing a grand departure since the first of the year. On 12 January the Emperor created a company of 'Veteran-Cannoneers'[3] for garrison duty, composed of five-year Guard veterans unfit for campaign. They were paid 20 sous a day and wore the uniform of the Old Guard with hats.

During January General Sorbier came to La Fère several times to inspect the vehicles of Colonel Pellegrin, the batteries of Drouot and Desvaux, and to direct maneuvers and target practice. Distinguished, dry, and severe, Sorbier enjoyed an incontestable prestige which was increased by his penchant for parties and receptions.

The manners of General Baron Desvaux de Saint-Maurice were quite as fine. He was both amiable and kind as well, with a gay and charming wife who entertained everyone with such grace that La Fère society – heretofore rather stiff – burst into tears at the departure of the troops.

They left between 1 and 4 March in four columns that reached Metz between the 10th and 13th. Lt. Colonel Boulart was attached to the Old Guard and Major Henrion to the Young. Six foot, four horse, and ten train companies from the Line, and companies of pontooneers and artisans had been attached to the Guard. No one was left to console the ladies at La Fère but the pontoon artificers and numerous cripples sent by the Medical Board, to the great annoyance of Colonel Pommereul who was left in command.

Delaborde's division set out from Brussels on 2 March. It was raining and the officers wore their *surtouts* and thin blue *redingotes*[4] (double-breasted topcoats) over which some also wore hip-length capes. The men had plenty of overcoats.

---

[3] *Canonniers-Vétérans.*
[4] Napoleon wears a *redingote* in Plate 115b. – Ed.

On the Louvain road the columns marched to Liège and Aix where the troops took sulphur baths and visited Charlemagne's tomb in the Cathedral of Notre-Dame. By easy stages they reached the Elbe at Madgeburg in a carefree mood.

General Delaborde traveled by carriage. Only forty-eight, his bent back and protruding paunch made him look much older. He was suffering from rheumatism and could not mount his horse. This valiant warrior, usually gay and benevolent, harangued his men in a few sonorous words interspersed with picturesque military slang. When he was again able to ride at the head of his division, who adored him, he became suddenly rejuvenated and electrified his men.

At last the marines departed. One company left from Paris under Boniface, and another from Toulon under Bouvier-Destouches. Fresh from Portchester prison, the extraordinary Lieutenant Gérodias was appointed adjutant major in command of the detachment.

Among the marines was one Ducor, a former quartermaster in Rosily's squadron who had escaped from Cabrera in 1811. He obtained leave to go to Paris to see his mother whom he had not seen since before the Consulate. Presented to Lieutenant Boniface, Ducor swapped reminiscences with his old companion in misery. Suddenly the Lieutenant asked: 'How would you like to join my company?'

'To serve in the marines of the Guard under the giant Boniface', Ducor wrote in his memoirs, 'had been my ambition for so long that you can imagine what my answer was . . .' So, after plowing through every ocean, starving in Cadiz, and thirsting at Cabrera, Ducor wound up freezing in Russia, proud to be a marine of the Guard, who ranked with a petty officer.

The 'immortals' were also on their way to Mainz. One detachment had followed Krasinski's lancers. At Antwerp another joined forces with the battalion of marine artificers attached to the Guard whose commander claimed they could 'make anything from a pendulum to a 100-ton ship'. The rest of the gendarmes remained in Paris.

On roads furrowed with the tracks of the army, heavily-laden horsemen and foot soldiers followed the indispensable wagons and the less indispensable officers' carriages. In the Guard the least subaltern had a servant. Numerous 'officials' followed the detachments on horseback, or in carriages laden with everything from food to beds and chairs. One lieutenant general had six servants and was followed by his *calèche*, two baggage wagons, and twelve horses. He kept open house, entertaining every officer who returned from a mission. As for the paladin Count Corvin-Krasinski, no boots were too soft for him nor handkerchiefs too fine. He left on campaign with his cooks and valets, his furniture, and his 'household'. The lieutenant colonel of the dragoons took along 40 saddle horses, 4 mules, and 18 horses for his carriages. The equipages of other officers were commensurate.

But the Emperor and the Chief of Staff set the pace for luxury. A transport battalion was organized for His Majesty's vehicles alone. One company was assigned to Duroc for the Emperor and his household, a second for Berthier and his retinue, and four more for the headquarters troops, casual personnel, prisoners, etc, carrying a month's provisions for 6,000 men.

The Emperor's transport required 500 horses and mules, 50 carriages, 130 saddle horses, and a mobile dispensary. The 'light service', consisting of 60 magnificent mules led by 30 liveried grooms, followed him everywhere. Each groom, mounted on one mule carrying a portmanteau, led a second carrying two leather trunks on a pack saddle. These contained provisions and a silver service blazoned with the Imperial arms.

An 'elite squadron' of a captain and 93 men was attached to Supreme Headquarters to furnish the necessary escorts. 'The Guard has become too important a corps to provide this service', the Emperor wrote; but it still guarded the Imperial camps, consisting of eight tents covering roughly fourteen acres. The Emperor's tent, transported in a single wagon, had a 'first drawing room', 'second drawing room', study, and bedchamber. The other seven were reserved for the Emperor's personal staff and aides, orderlies, secretaries, etc. The Chief of Staff's own camp was pitched about 300 yards behind the Emperor's.

On the march the elite company, two infantry battalions, the sappers of the Guard, and a picket of elite gendarmes escorted the Emperor's vehicles. In camp a canteen was held ready to follow the duty squadron, and a kettle kept on the fire to provide soup for the Emperor and his household at a moment's notice. (This was a new regulation.)

The camp and the Emperor's person were guarded by a battalion of chasseurs or grenadiers, with muskets always loaded, who performed ceremonial and police duties. The officers attached to the 'palace guard' ate with the Emperor's aides. A squadron and picket of horse Guards under the command of the colonel general in attendance were ordered daily for the escort. The horses of the duty squadron were kept saddled, and were bridled an hour before sunrise and unbridled an hour after sunset, the troopers remaining in the saddle all day with loaded weapons. The picket horses were kept saddled, bridled, and mounted twenty-four hours a day. The officer spent the night in the 'first drawing room' of the Emperor's tent. In the presence of the enemy the picket never left the Emperor's side. A special escort and officer were in charge of the Emperor's carriage, and the coach containing his papers which they were not permitted to leave under any pretext whatever.

Before the Emperor left for the army 1,900 foot and horse Guards were held in Paris to provide these services, joining their corps later. Afterwards only the company of convalescents, under a subaltern of the foot grenadiers and two lieutenants of chasseurs, were left to guard the Empress and the King of Rome.

Who would guard the capital?

'My renown', replied Napoleon.

CHAPTER 2

Poland

WHILE the 1st Guard Division marched to the Elbe other units marked time at Mainz. They reached the Rhine around Easter which fell this year on 29 March. Krasinski's detachment was at Würzburg, a beautiful town in Franconia. It was time to bring order to the confused mass that had left France so hastily; to re-form the regiments under their own commanders, and consolidate them under a unified command for their eastward push to the Elbe to join General Delaborde.

General Walther had arrived by post at Würzburg where he occupied the superb Episcopal Palace. From there he dispatched his columns to Dresden between 1 and 6 April. The three cavalry regiments of Walther's division were put under Saint-Sulpice. General Sorbier arrived in Würzburg on the 8th to direct the artillery's movements and assemble the units scattered throughout the vicinity.

On the 10th the Chief Commissary arrived with Baron Larrey, now Surgeon General of the *Grande Armée*, and the four field hospitals of the Guard. If the great practitioner's art was considerable, his administrative talent was even greater. Speaking in a commanding voice with an imposing assurance, he could teach Fourcroy chemistry and Monge mathematics. 'An honest man withal – in fact the greatest man I have known', the Emperor said of him later.

The Old Guard left Würzburg between 1 and 4 April under Baron de Rebeval. After resting two days in Dresden, Krasinski went on to Glogau with his lancers. The Emperor ordered small depots established at Würzburg and Magdeburg, and enjoined Bessières to send off the rest of the vehicles and baggage which seemed reluctant to leave Paris.

After their departure nothing was left in Paris but the first battalions of the grenadiers and chasseurs, scheduled to leave for Mainz by post with the Emperor on 9 May, and 240 foot and 300 horse at the depots. This minimum was needed to post a guard of 28 men at the Tuileries, 20 at the Elysée, and provide escorts and patrols in Paris.

On 14 May Berthier wrote Roguet that the army would assemble on the banks of the Pregel at the beginning of June, adding that the Emperor 'would be happy to see the General's division there'. A desire of the Emperor's was virtually an order.

Marching through Thuringia, lovely at this season, the 2nd Division reached Leipzig whose fine gardens and urbane inhabitants recalled to the soldiers those of Frankfurt. After a short stay they pushed on, arriving on 12 June at Marienwerder where they found their artillery, field hospitals, and artisans. Roguet's soldiers had covered a distance of 465 miles by wagon and over 700 on foot. But life was beautiful, for they were back in good old Germany where the beer was foamy and the *Fräuleins* friendly. They were billeted on the inhabitants who fed them cheerfully.

A few philosophers speculated in their diaries upon the eternal stupidity of man who could not be as peaceful as nature in May; however, the soldiers' life went on with its servitude and discipline and its monotonous orders of the day. 'Hunting is forbidden. Men convicted of pillage will be shot.'

In Spain the troops had got out of the habit of being inspected. Now they were made to roll their overcoats on their packs, wash their queue ribbons, whiten all belts the same shade, polish their arms, and answer three roll calls a day. These were the orders issued in the Guard. But it was natural for a soldier to obey. Only at night, in listening to the charming tune of Retreat played by Young Guard fifers, did he forget his misery. Then he went to bed and dreamed of glory and the Emperor.

Meanwhile, to the south on the roads of Saxony the Old Guard was marching to Dresden which it entered on 23 April by a magnificent tree-lined avenue. With trumpets sounding the three cavalry regiments made a fine entrance, to the cheers of court and army. Then the old chasseurs and grenadiers gathered at Steinbach, west of the city, at eight in the morning in full dress with their plumes and cap cords, and paraded under arms behind Marshal Lefebvre who had taken command of the Old Guard on the 10th. The Royal Guard of Saxony rendered honors.

But the Saxons did not seem to care for artillery parades. The Guard artillery had taken advantage of its stay at Grumbach to give its caissons, horses, and gunners a good bath. The men trimmed their bonnets in the fields and donned their somewhat crumpled plumes to make a fine entrance into Dresden. But on their arrival at the city gates their hopes were dashed, for they were sent outside the walls to a gate adjoining the district where they were to be quartered.

The officers of the Guard were lodged and fed by the burghers at the King's express command. This ruler's devotion to the Emperor was complete and sincere. The soldiers were ordered to appear only in full dress, to keep on good terms with the Saxon troops, and to 'salute all officers, whether French, Saxon, or foreign . . .' They were forbidden to smoke their pipes on the street. Retreat sounded at 8 p.m. Cases of drunkenness or objectionable conduct were punished by 'fifteen days in prison on bread and water'.

Walther's regiments remained in the capital a week. The royal castle, with its 350-foot tower and Hall of the Giants where the Elector Augustus II had given sumptuous entertainments, was the pride of the Royal family. The Grosser Garten of Prince Max was open to the officers of the Guard. On Sundays they heard Mass in the Chapel-Royal where the singing was superb. They visited the library with its treasures, the Japanese Palace, the romantic Heilige Hallen in the Plauen valley, and Neustadt, the town across the large Elbe bridge.

Lefebvre's division, as well as Walther's horse Guards, reached Glogau between 4 and 6 May and camped in and around the town. Forage had become scarce and the cavalry had to make shift while waiting for the hay to ripen.

General Curial arrived with his 3rd Division on the 15th and installed his staff at the Countess von Dohna's castle. The grenadiers were commanded by General Baron Michel, and the chasseurs by Boyer de Rebeval. Claparède's division, known officially as the 'Polish Division attached to the Guard', arrived in Glogau the 10th. Dautancourt's light-horse were due the end of the month with General Konopka who had joined them in Luxembourg.

By now the countryside, stripped bare by the 4th Corps on its march from Italy, had nothing more to offer so campaign stores had to be issued. Hay and oats for the horses were also issued and, when necessary, were carried on the march on the troopers' valises.

Ranged in five camps around Glogau, the Guard put its equipment and boots in repair and replaced its worn-out horses. 'If His Majesty the Emperor and King visits the camp, the men will turn out under arms and will line the route in full dress with their officers at their head. They will be sure to warn their commanders immediately of His Majesty's approach. *Messieurs* the Commanders, when given warning, will assemble their troops as promptly as possible in the main square, taking care to summon them to a single location.'

This order was issued by the Duke of Danzig (Lefebvre) on 18 May. His Excellency desired to add an officer from each Old Guard regiment to his staff. Those chosen were much honored; but the honor cost them two saddle horses and their commands, as well as their independence. Besides, the Marshal talked drivel and amused himself by telling them over and over the story of his life, beginning with his enlistment in the *Gardes françaises* and including every detail of his love affair with the Duchess – an Alsatian peasant lass – which had not been regularized for some time.

The Emperor arrived at last. Followed next day by his foreign minister, the Duke of Bassano (Maret), he had quit Saint-Cloud on 9 May. He had left the Tsar's ambassador, Prince Kurakin, in Paris without means of obtaining his passports, should he ask for them. Thus the ambassador would have to remain at his post, the semblance of peace would be maintained, and an abrupt severing of diplomatic relations avoided.

Napoleon went to Dresden where Frederick Augustus had been unable to sleep for fear of missing his arrival. It was a triumphal march all the way. 'The Germans, whether from pride or a natural love of the marvelous, regarded Napoleon as a supernatural being', Ségur reported. They lined his route. The princes thronged to town to hear his words and greet the Empress and courtiers. Nobles and plebeians threw themselves in his path, spending whole nights beneath his palace window in Mainz, Würzburg, Bayreuth, Plauen – not only to admire his grandeur but also so they might tell their grandchildren that they had seen Napoleon.

At Freiberg, 20 miles from Dresden, the King and Queen of Saxony came to meet the Imperial guests. On 16 May, to the pealing of bells and booming of cannon, they led them by torchlight to the apartments of Elector Augustus II, King of Poland. It was the eve of Pentecost. The Emperor of Austria and all the kings – except the King of Prussia who was on his way – were in Dresden.

Escorted by the splendid Saxon *Garde du Corps* in yellow coats faced with blue and white-plumed helmets with black chenille crests, Napoleon wore his simple uniform and felt hat. In this costume he greeted the Allied rulers, resplendent in full dress with cocked hats. He outlined his plans and gave them his orders.

At 8 p.m. on 30 May the Emperor entered Posen, where his Grumblers awaited him, amid a storm of hurrahs. Poland welcomed him with triumphal arches. Soldiers, burghers, officials, and ladies all came to pay homage to their 'liberator'. They even named a principal street after him.

Napoleon took leave of the Empress and went alone to join his army. The Guard resumed his escort, marching ahead of his coach and guarding the crossroads. They marched with the army to Thorn. The officers of the Guard organized relays to guard the Emperor's passage at all hours of day and night. The Poles were cordial, but food was scarce and the billets were terrible. Swarming with servants, the 'castles' were wooden dwellings, larger than their neighbors but no cleaner. The mean little villages, wallowing in mud and crowded with unfortunate Jews, had nothing to offer in the way of provisions or forage. Usually the stables offered better bedding than their wretched hovels. In such surroundings the army's discipline relaxed. Some marauders were shot.

For Poland the Guard received an extra bonus double that of the Line. Each regiment was trailed by a small herd of cattle, and wagons loaded with bread, flour, and vinegar; but the convoys were often delayed by the bad roads and arrived at dawn, just as the troops were leaving.

A large Guard depot was established at Thorn where on 5 June the Emperor reviewed the 3rd Guard Division on the glacis. Napoleon walked between the ranks on foot, talking to officers and men in the paternal manner that endeared him to all. 'He seemed truly in the midst of his family', Captain Fantin des Odoards of the 2nd Grenadiers wrote of this occasion, adding: 'Foster parents are sometimes better than real ones'.

'Where are you from?' the Emperor asked him.

'From Embrun, Sire.'

'In the Low Alps?'

'No, Sire, the High Alps.'

'What, contradicting the Emperor?' scolded Lt. Colonel Harlet after the interview. This was not done. However, Napoleon was in a good humor and ignored it. He promoted fourteen NCO's in the 3rd Grenadiers to subalterns, congratulated Boulart's gunners on their fine uniforms, and remarked on the splendid condition of their horses. Unfortunately for the latter, the Emperor ordered the artillery to leave immediately, before it had time to procure hay or oats. The teams ate green rye in consequence and died.

The army marched to Danzig where the Emperor reviewed the troops and appointed Major Darriule of the 25th Regiment, a hero of Saragossa, to the 1st Grenadiers. Then they passed through Heilsberg and Friedland of bloody memory, almost five years to the day since they had beaten the Russians there. How could they stop Napoleon now? Surely they would recoil from a whole Europe in arms!

Yet some warned that the French were wasting precious time; that the Russian summer was short. If a war was to be fought they had better get on with it.

Silence! The Emperor was with them and that sufficed.

Delaborde's division paraded at Koenigsberg. Then at Gumbinnen, in blistering heat, it crossed the Pregel River of accursed memory.

On the evening of 21 June the Emperor's tents were pitched at Wilkowiczki, surrounded at last by the whole Guard, behind the center of a formidable army.

Only yesterday the Guardsmen had been dirty and unshaven. Laden like donkeys on their march from Salamanca, short pipes between their teeth, their bonnets in bags swinging from their belts, their forage-caps pulled down over their eyes, they had been lashed by rain or stifled by heat and dust. The horsemen had been kept down to the pace of their famished mounts. Often walking beside them to spare their chafed and bleeding backs, the troopers dragged their heavy sabers along, hampered at every step by their mud-caked overalls. The gunners had suffered tortures trying to pull their caissons and gun carriages out of ruts baked hard by the sun, or out of axle-deep mud. Everyone had grumbled and cursed Russia, the army, and even the *Tondu*. 'One day he'll be left to shift for himself, and he'll see!'

But 'he' never would see anything. However, he had the forethought to dictate and sign the following order the night before he crossed the frontier:

'Gumbinnen, 20 June.

'The Guard will take on the march six days' bread rations which the soldiers will carry on their persons. This ration must contain 12 ounces of bread, 5 of flour, and one of rice per day . . . Tomorrow rations for six more days will be issued to the Guard. Each battalion will assign pickets and wagons to carry them. The bakers will remain at Gumbinnen today and tomorrow the 21st to bake bread . . .

'It is urged that the soldiers save their rations and eat them sparingly. The officers will inspect them each morning to see that each man eats no more than the ration for that day and saves the rest for the required number of days.

Napoleon.'

Next day the whole Guard cheered the Emperor. The Old Guard in white gaiters and the Young in black, shaved, polished, spic and span, presented themselves to him in a forest of scarlet plumes, their horses 'polished to the hoofs', to hear the following proclamation:

'Soldiers! The second Polish War has begun . . . Russia . . . has violated her oaths . . . She has left us the choice between dishonor and war . . . The second Polish War will be as glorious for French arms as the first . . . The peace will put an end to the arrogant influence that Russia has exerted for the past fifty years over European affairs . . .'

One and all, the Guard believed that now it was going to finish the Russians' education. However, since it was marching through Poland, well then, 'Long Live Poland and Long Live the Emperor!' It would go anywhere he wanted – to Moscow, Persia,

India – 'since the genius who ran the show at Essling and Wagram is still in charge', Sergeant Franconin of the 2nd Grenadiers wrote his father.

Songs of glory, dreams of carousing and booty, and a bad bivouac eighteen miles behind the Niemen ended this unforgettable day.

Was it really war? It was. The Tsar had refused to receive Ambassador Lauriston at his headquarters in Vilna. He had refused to parley unless the Emperor evacuated Prussia. But the European Army was on the Niemen.

All was proceeding according to Alexander's plan. 'I will not be the aggressor', he had said to Narbonne.

'And I do not want war', Napoleon had replied.

The cold war, waged deliberately since 1810, was suddenly heated up as the exasperated Emperor passed to the attack.

22 June, 5 p.m. Escorted by a squadron of Polish light-horse and followed by Duroc, Caulincourt, Bessières, Berthier, and Haxo, the Emperor passed down the lines of his infantry, massed in a beautiful pine forest on the banks of the Niemen, and inspected the impatient cavalry which Murat held with difficulty behind the frontier. Then he stopped for supper at the presbytery of Strawden.

'For whom are you praying, Father?' he inquired. 'For me or the Russians?'

'For Your Majesty', replied the old priest.

Meanwhile the cavaliers of the Guard pawed the left bank of the Niemen and observed in dim outline the right bank opposite. No enemy was in sight.

The Emperor changed into the cloak and forage-cap of a lancer of his escort and rode through the last village, Nangardyski, at one in the morning. A pallid light veiled the landscape. In this latitude during the summer solstice it is hard to distinguish between sunset and dawn. Suddenly his horse Gonzalon shied at a hare and the Emperor rolled on the ground. A bad omen.

'The Russians are retreating to their own country', a Jew reported.

'The Tsar will refuse battle and will draw out the war', Caulincourt prophesied.

'Go with God', an old peasant called after his guest, an officer of the Guard.

The pontooneers and marines completed the bridges, and Boissonnet's sappers built a cabin for the Emperor on an eminence a short way behind them. For the first time on this campaign, his tents were raised nearby and guarded by grenadiers.

CHAPTER 3

Smolensk[1]

AT midnight on 24 June 1812 the Army of Europe began to cross the Niemen. In 1807 this had been the end of their line; now it was the beginning. All the 'old moustaches' were bursting with enthusiasm, for no sound of war was heard to mar the fanfares and cheers. The Russians were retreating without firing a shot.

On the 25th, as fine a day as they had seen at the Tuileries, the Imperial Guard cheered the Emperor and crossed the bridges. 'We'll celebrate the 15th of August in St. Petersburg this year', they said.

On the road to Vilna neither quicksand nor rain nor oppressive heat could dampen the soldiers' ardor. As the bridges were destroyed before the town, Kozietulski's light-horse (the heroes of Somosierra) jumped into the water to reconnoiter the left bank. Then they entered the city. The Lithuanians welcomed them cordially, for Old Poland dreamed of independence.

At Vilna the Emperor attended a ball at the house of the Count de Pac, now an aide-de-camp to His Majesty. The officers of the Guard danced with the society ladies who were wearing the French colors. Mlle. Sophie de Tyzenhaus shied away from His Majesty's compliments, having eyes only for the Count de Narbonne.

All the Guard was at Vilna. The 1st Regiments of the foot Guard were lodged near the 'palace' and excused from chores since they were on duty with the Emperor. The rest were quartered in the suburbs and bivouacs. General Durosnel, the governor, could issue no provisions, for on leaving, the Russians had destroyed all the stores. Five thousand horses had died of colic due to improper food. Horses were taken from the artillery of the Line to replenish the Guard's.

The Guard was given two weeks' extra pay but ordered to save bread. Some pillage occurred. Some inhabitants complained. Marshal Lefebvre reacted vehemently. The marauders were returned to the Line, and the pillagers shot.

Why was Roguet's division dragging its feet and why was the artillery late? Why did they tarry in Vilna?

Napoleon went about a great deal and visited the countryside and the advance posts. He found the enemy elusive. Barclay de Tolly was retiring rapidly to Drissa, and Bagration to Minsk. A general envelopment was now impossible; but the French might succeed in surrounding Bagration ... Davout's corps was sent to Minsk with Colbert's light-horse; and Murat's cavalry, with a squadron of 1st Lancers, to harass Barclay.

[1] For campaign map, see first pull-out map at end of volume.

A large depot was established to handle the Guard's stores. The bakers made bread and biscuit day and night. 'I shall have no peace until the Guard and the Imperial Headquarters have twenty days' rations in hand', the Emperor said.

8 July. At Vilna the Emperor reviewed the Guard, except for Claparède's division which had left to support Davout. The Italian Guard had arrived with the Viceroy. The troops were in superb condition. Each man had twelve days' rations, half of which he carried with him. The cavalry and artillery had new horses; however, the Russian beasts were smaller. Three Young Guard battalions were due in two days from Koenigsberg.

Between the 'old ones' nearing an age at which campaigning becomes painful and the novices of the Young Guard, Roguet's division was the best in the army. The fusiliers were vigorous men between twenty-five and thirty, well trained and educated, disciplined, and led by excellent officers. They had finished two years of hard campaigning in Spain. On the march from Burgos to Vilna they had left only sixty-three men behind. The Emperor congratulated and rewarded them. Then he marched at their head across the city. 'Take good care of them', he said to General Roguet.

And with good reason; for under the best possible conditions the Guard at Vilna mustered barely 16,000 infantry and 4,000 horse. The Emperor foresaw his needs and ordered the Minister to fill up the 2nd Voltigeurs and 2nd *Tirailleurs* from Spain with men from the national guard cohorts and send them to Berlin. The *vélites* and guards of honor of Florence and Turin were due there momentarily.

The Emperor received the members of the Polish Diet, wearing cockades of blue and crimson. After Mass, which they had attended in force, the beautiful Polish ladies flirted with the officers and men, waltzing with them as they had with the Russians a few days before. Could one trust these people?

The Emperor took advantage of the Poles' good will to create a third regiment of light-horse in the Guard. It was recruited from members of Polish landowning families who could ride and provide their own equipment. It was uniformed like the 1st, with yellow buttons and lace instead of white. General Konopka was appointed colonel in chief and put in charge of organizing it (see Plates 100, 101).

The time had come for the French to tear themselves away from Vilna. On 12 July Delaborde's division with eight guns and Lefebvre-Desnoëttes' chasseurs left with four Bavarian cavalry regiments, the sappers, marines, and part of the Emperor's baggage for Gloubokoye, 150 miles away. Under the command of Mortier, they were ordered to prepare a passage across the Dvina River.

Up ahead, the maneuver against Barclay was worked out in detail. The plan was to outflank the Russians at Dünaburg and Drissa and attack them on the march by a wide turning movement to the left, pivoting on Murat at Drissa. The French would then cross the Dvina between Drissa and Vitebsk.

The Old Guard left Vilna full of gratitude towards the Lithuanians, but lost it by nightfall. At Sventziany, where it bivouacked, all the inhabitants had vanished, leaving nothing behind. To make matters worse, at dawn the grass was covered with frost. Nevertheless the soldiers must follow the Emperor who reached Gloubokoye on 18 July.

Never was a greater reward conferred upon a finer soldier. Originally a *garde française*, then a colonel at Fleurus, Friant had been a major general in Egypt, a lieutenant general under Davout at Auerstädt, and been wounded at Wagram. He wore the grand eagle of the Legion of Honor.

The enemy could not go on retreating indefinitely without trying to halt the invader. The Emperor expected a Russian attack – perhaps because he hoped for one – and made his preparations. Redoubts were built before Vitebsk and batteries installed. Meanwhile, there were rumors of peace; for what was the use of going on?

Napoleon paid no attention to them. Impatient to come to grips with the enemy, he organized a fast expeditionary corps with four army corps and the Guard. With this he would attempt to cross the Dnieper under cover of the forest between his forces and the Russians in Smolensk, and fall upon their rear.

The Guard, in reserve, left Vitebsk on 11 August. Downstream from Smolensk they crossed the Dnieper, the boundary of Old Poland, and re-formed west of Krasny. At last they heard the roar of cannon. Barclay de Tolly must be making a stand . . . But no – he had escaped to Smolensk, after repulsing no less than forty charges by Murat.

Each night the soldiers believed themselves on the eve of an engagement only to find next morning that the enemy had vanished. And the Russians left nothing behind them – not even water. They had cut all the ropes in the wells.

On the good post road from Grodno to Moscow, planted with four rows of birches by Catherine the Great, the Guard marched all day on the 14th. The next night they marched through a burning village, passing near the barrier the Jews were not allowed to cross, and smelled the buckwheat in the fields of Old Russia. They halted at last around the Emperor's tents, pitched in a wood near the post house of Boyarinkovo.

It was 15 August, the Emperor's birthday. The Guard artillery fired salvos with powder captured the day before. The Emperor received the congratulations of the marshals, generals, and officers of the Guard, and distributed rewards and gifts – 500 francs to each major, and 333 to each captain of the Old Guard. Some would not cash their vouchers until 1817.

He appointed Generals Durosnel and Mouton special aides to transmit the Emperor's orders to infantry and cavalry for the movement of troops on the battlefield. This function they performed on the 17th before Smolensk.

After a forced march the Guard was posted at dawn that day on a bluff overlooking Smolensk which bristled with steeples. The Russians, drunk and yelling like men possessed, were defending it desperately against the troops of Ney, Davout, and Poniatowski. The enormous city, corseted with ramparts, was aflame. Under a terrific cannonade Lefebvre's ten battalions maneuvered, sometimes stepping out of ranks to admire Murat who stood alone amidst the projectiles aimed at Boulart's batteries from the front and sides. What was he doing there, taking a walk?

The Russians defended the suburbs until nightfall. Then they retired, after setting fire to the ancient city by order of Barclay de Tolly. As the Emperor reconnoitered his positions his escort of Polish lancers was obliged to chase off several parties of Cossacks.

'In the midst of the horrible spectacle', Boulart reported, 'the enemy sharpshooters posted on the ramparts were silhouetted against the flames like so many devils in hell.'

Delaborde's division fought its way into the suburbs with difficulty. Voltigeurs and *tirailleurs*, parched by the heat, devoured green apples they found in the orchards. Amid toppling houses, screaming women, and wounded roasting in the flames they penetrated to the center of the burning city which lay under an immense pall of flame-colored smoke. The Russian grenadiers, easily distinguished by their low-crowned shakos with a triple grenade on the front, fought from house to house.

At last, near the burned bridge, the Young Guard joined Claparède's Polish legionaries who were firing on the retreating enemy. There they saw Davout, Prince of Eckmühl and Marshal of the Empire, musket in hand, shooting a Russian who was trying to escape in a boat.

Half a mile from Smolensk the ten Old Guard battalions bivouacked in a square around the Emperor's tents. Their 'august chief', safer here than in the citadel, was convinced that the Smolensk maneuver, too, had failed. Would they go on to Moscow?

'It would be better to go there in two campaigns', said the Emperor, 'but . . .'

CHAPTER 4

Borodino

THE army had already lost 150,000 men in killed, wounded, and stragglers, including those left at the depots and on the line of communications.[1] Desertion was rife in some of the foreign corps.

Already the guns of the vanguard could be heard thundering near Valutina. Before a portrait of the King of Rome sent him by Madame de Montesquiou, the Emperor resolved to deliver to an expectant Europe a victory like Friedland under the walls of Moscow.

After inspecting Sorbier's artillery, the Emperor left his 'palace' at Smolensk at midnight on 24 August. He left Delaborde to garrison the ruined city with his 4,000 men and 8 guns. This was bad news for the Young Guardsmen; however, three route battalions of the Guard were summoned from Vitebsk to relieve Delaborde. Meanwhile, he had a quantity of bread baked, reassured the inhabitants, and formed the stragglers into battalions.

The march behind the Emperor continued through broken and devastated country. The troops suffered from heat by day and froze in the bivouacs at night. On the 28th they marched over twenty-three miles to Viazma, once a lovely town but now ruined and deserted. Though there was not exactly a famine there, food was both scarce and expensive. Then it rained.

'If this rain continues', the Emperor announced on 30 August, 'we shall retire tomorrow to Smolensk.' Their fate hung in the balance.

But the sun shone on the 31st and they marched fifteen miles further along the road to Moscow. Next day the Emperor sent for the route regiments that Delaborde had left at Smolensk with General Lanusse.

Napoleon's luck might change. Now that Barclay had been relieved by Kutuzov, the Russians had altered their tactics.

On 5 September Murat reported that the enemy would make a stand 85 miles from Moscow on the Borodino plateau, situated on the right bank of the Kaluga river, a tributary of the Moskva. Redoubts straddling the Moscow road indicated that the Russians intended to defend the city.

That day the Emperor's army debouched into the plain. The Shevardino redoubt in front of the river was captured by the 61st Regiment, supported by the batteries of the Guard. The gunners lost a captain, a lieutenant, and 20 men wounded.

[1] These figures are somewhat misleading since the author does not specify the number of troops stationed at the depots and guard posts on the exceedingly long route between Paris and Moscow. The French losses from dysentery and starvation had actually been far higher than from combat. – Ed.

The Emperor had his tents pitched in the middle of a copse near the Moscow road. After sunset the Guard took station around him, with Bessières' cavalry in a hollow on the left, the fusiliers in front, the Old Guard behind, and the artillery on the right. A foot battery covered the front and Marin's two horse batteries protected the cavalry. The whole force numbered 6,500 Old Guard, 4,500 Middle Guard, and 4,900 horse, with 109 guns.

Next day the old chasseurs and grenadiers occupied the Shevardino redoubt. The army rested and the Guard spruced up. The gunners replenished their ammunition and the infantry polished their weapons and brushed their dress coats. Beyond, along the river, several culverts and three breastworks were built. The right-hand works adjoining the woods was armed with two dozen twelve-pounders from the artillery reserve. These were trained on the enemy redoubts.

That evening the Old Guard bivouacked in a square around the Imperial tents. It was a miserable night, cold and damp, in rude contrast to the suffocating heat of the past few days. The herds furnished meat to a few soldiers, but the foraging parties went far afield without finding any for the rest and many ate horsemeat for the first time.

Tomorrow's battle would be decisive. No one doubted the French would win it. The Emperor worked through the night.

7 September, 2 a.m. From right to left in the bivouacs the *Diane, Grenadière, Carabinière*, and Reveille of the Guard were beaten, regiment by regiment, by the drummers as the trumpets sounded. The Polish light-horse, turned out as at the Tuileries, mounted their chargers, followed by the rest of the cavalry. The service squadrons escorted the Emperor to his position 450 yards east of the Shevardino redoubt.

Already in contact with the enemy, the corps of Ney, Davout, and Prince Eugène were massed for a frontal attack on Semyonovskoye and Borodino. On the right, Poniatowski's Poles prepared to make their way through the woods and envelop the Russian left flank. In a reserve position on two lines the foot Guard, in column by battalions sixty paces apart, surrounded the Imperial Headquarters. They could see the Russians alternately praying and drinking, and hear them singing.

In the French camps cries of '*Vive l'Empereur!*' rang out after the order of the day was read: '. . . The victory depends on you.'

5 a.m. Though suffering from a cold and a bad headache, the Emperor mounted his horse and rode down the lines. The weather was misty; the wind 'was blowing towards the enemy' and clouds of dust obscured the horizon. Then the sun came out.

'The sun of Austerlitz', murmured the Guard.

At six o'clock three shots from one of the batteries near the Emperor unleashed a fierce cannonade. One hundred and eighty guns, including sixty of the Guard, promptly went into action in front of the Shevardino. 'At the first command, General Sorbier will prepare to detach all the Guard howitzers and mass them against one redoubt or the other', the Emperor ordered.

The battle was joined. Soon the long shots from the Russian guns, fired slowly at a high elevation, began to fall on Roguet's Middle Guard. Sorbier's batteries deluged the Semyonovskoye redoubts with projectiles as Davout and Ney attacked. In front of the

PLATE 89

Drum major of the Guard on the march
(*From a lithograph by Charlet*)

PLATE 90

a) Delaborde
(Contemp. lithograph)

b) Desvaux de Saint-Maurice
(After Victor Huen from contemp. portrait)

c) Sorbier
(Engr. Bovinet after Vauthier)

d) Claparède
(Engr. Couché)

e) Barclay de Tolly
(After G. Dawe)

PLATE 91

PLATE 92

a) Friant
(*Engr. Forestier*)

b) Durosnel
(*Engr. Bovinet after Vauthier*)

c) Ney
(*Col. engraving by Charon after Aubry*)

d) Mortier
(*Lith. Delpech*)

PLATE 93

b) Old chasseur in Russia
(From an original watercolor by Charlet)

a) Italian vélite and guard of honor evacuating wounded at Smolensk
(From an original drawing by Albrecht Adam)

PLATE 94

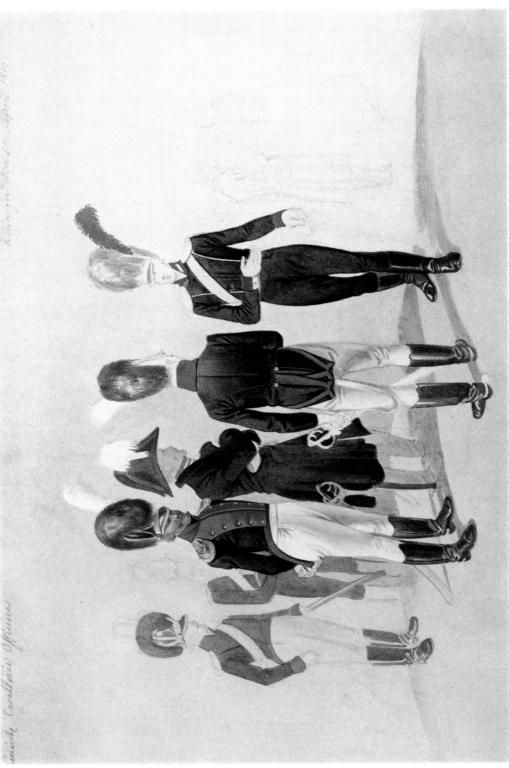

redoubts the fighting was furious. The Emperor took Junot from reserve and sent him to Semyonovskoye, supported by the heavy artillery of the Guard.

Ney advanced with difficulty and heavy losses. He was soon subjected to a massive counterattack by Bagration and called for reinforcements. The Emperor hesitated, ordered Claparède forward, then upon reflection, stopped him and sent Friant's division instead. At the same time he ordered Lanabère to advance with one of Roguet's brigades to support the Viceroy[2] who was hard pressed at the center.

Lanabère replaced General Morand who had been wounded during the attack on the large redoubt. As he rushed over the parapet at the head of the 9th, 16th, and 30th Regiments, Auguste Caulaincourt, replacing Montbrun who had just been killed, charged the mouth of the redoubt with his cuirassiers. The position was carried, but both generals were mortally wounded (see Plate 95).

Lanabère died at Mozhaisk on 16 September. Promoted major after Marengo, he had been admitted to the chasseurs of the Guard on the eve of Jena, had been wounded at Essling, and had commanded the 1st Fusiliers in Spain. He was adjutant general of Roguet's division with the rank of major general. After the battle the Emperor had planned to give him a division. His attack in conjunction with the cuirassiers made possible the capture of the enemy's first line of defense.

The Old Guard was optimistic. The *Tondu* drank a toddy. Then he mounted his horse and, preceded by lancers and escorted and followed by chasseurs, rode along the front. Just after he had sent his Poles to counterattack the Russian cavalry on the left, an officer of the Guard artillery came from Sorbier to warn him that Kutuzov was mounting an attack on Semyonovskoye.

'Let him come and tell me himself', was the Emperor's rejoinder.

It was too late. Sorbier could not leave at that critical moment. He was in the process of moving all 24 twelve-pounders from the right-hand works, bordering the woods, to the center to shell the Russian columns. Soon crushed by the fire of a hundred guns, the remnants of the Russian infantry fell back under cover of their cavalry.

Twice the soldiers of the Guard heard the command: 'Forward in the name of the Emperor! Advance, Guard!' once from Lefebvre and once again from Lobau's[3] aide. Both times they advanced only a short distance before the order came to halt. Now Murat with his 'Coquerico panache' – as Marshal Lannes called it – came to ask for their support to force a decision. The answer was 'No'. As at Wagram, the Guard was held as a last reserve to avert disaster. Besides, the French had won the day, for the enemy was now retiring.

The army planned to spend the night at Mozhaisk whither the King of Naples (Murat) rode at top speed with the Emperor's baggage and part of the horse Guard. Though the French had been victorious, Murat was halted en route by Platov and his Cossacks.

In the middle of squares formed by the 1st Grenadiers and 1st Chasseurs, the Emperor's tents were pitched near the Shevardino redoubt, as on the eve of the battle. Patrols of chasseurs and dragoons roamed the grisly field, covered with dying and dead. From

[2] Eugène Beauharnais.
[3] General Mouton, Count of Lobau.

all directions during the night they heard cries of: 'To arms! Here come the Cossacks!' Fortunately, the intruders were only stray horses.

It had been a terrible battle, with Davout wounded and 14 lieutenant generals, 34 major generals, 7 adjutants, 32 officers of the general staff, 86 aides-de-camp, and 37 regimental commanders killed or wounded. Friant, Boyer, de Turenne, and Krasinski were all wounded, and 18 officers of the Guard artillery were either wounded or killed. The French, Poles, Württemburgers, Saxons, Bavarians, and Neapolitans had all suffered. The European Army lost 28,000 men; the Russians, 50,000.[4]

The enemy was retreating, but slowly. Before Mozhaisk Murat had to send Friant's division – which had been badly mauled – to attack the enemy's rear-guard.

'General', the King of Naples said to Claparède, who was standing beside him, 'march on the enemy's flank and attack it boldly.'

Without making any reply, General Claparède turned to his second in command: 'You heard the King's order, Colonel.' and he kept his countenance before Murat who was 'stupefied by such effrontery'.

Mozhaisk was captured. The Grumblers nicknamed it 'the cabbage city', since each squad harvested a prodigious quantity in the surrounding fields.

[4] Prussian reports estimate the Grand Army's casualties at 32,000 and the Russian at 42,000. – Ed.

CHAPTER 5

Moscow

JUST as the Egyptians cried 'Thebes!' on first beholding the city of a hundred gates, and the crusaders cried 'Jerusalem!', the Guard peered into the distance at the golden cupolas of the metropolis and cried 'Moscow!' There was pride, hope, and relief in the cry, and their faces were joyful. For this proved that nothing was impossible to their '*sacré Tondu*' who had brought nearly a half-million men from Paris to the capital of the grand dukes of Muscovy.

On the evening of 14 September 1812 Napoleon and His Guard entered the deserted suburbs and stopped before the Smolensk gate where they waited for the authorities to arrive. The general sent to fetch them returned to report that there was no longer any authority in Moscow. The city was deserted. Sebastiani had occupied the Kremlin, and the Vladimir Gate through which Kutuzov's army had fled.

A caterer's house near the Smolensk Gate was converted into the 'palace'. The Old Guard bivouacked in the garden and the Young in the suburbs. Claparède had gone ahead with Murat. Provisions were scarce. 'The rascals are in hiding, but we'll find them – we'll bring them to their knees . . .' But they would not.

Leaving Delaborde's division outside the walls, the Emperor mounted his horse Emir at seven next morning and made his entry at the head of the Old Guard. The bands played *The Victory Is Ours* and the trumpets sounded, raising no echo in the streets lined on either side with boarded-up houses.

As they reached the Kremlin, the fortress surrounding the palaces of the tsars in the center of the city, no one rendered honors. The cavalry and artillery poured into the great square where the foot batteries formed a park. Guns were posted at each corner of the square while companies of grenadiers and chasseurs guarded the gates.

The troops must eat but were forbidden to loot. Foraging parties sent under lieutenants to comb the neighborhood for food found all doors barricaded against them. Some French residents brought whatever they had, even offering them hospitality.

The day ended hideously when near midnight a rocket exploded over the city. Immediately, from post to post, the sentries were crying 'Fire!' A terrible clamor arose as the flames devoured the Solenka, the rich Chinese bazaar near the Foundlings' Gate. The whole horizon lined with palaces burst into flame . . . As the last word of their fiery oration to the invader the Russians were burning their capital, their Holy City . . .

The Guard flew to arms. Fanned by a strong wind, sparks rained down on the artillery barracks while firebrands of pitch fell on the roofs of the Arsenal, and the kitchen and stables of the Kremlin.

Armed with brooms and pails of water, grenadiers and chasseurs climbed on the roofs and wet down the iron sheathing. The Emperor came through a flaming arch to watch. This was no place for him! Distressed at his danger, the gunners of the Guard pressed so close that Lariboisière had to beg them to move back. But by that time, however dangerous it was to stay it was difficult to leave.

Not until 5.30 p.m. on the 16th did the Emperor, astride his horse Tauris, leave the Kremlin by the river postern. He reached the Mozhaisk road, followed at a distance by his Grumblers in single file who ran as fast as their legs would carry them through the flames, half-asphyxiated by smoke. After waiting for the stragglers to catch up they went in search of their chief.

They found him at Petrovskoi, a bizarre castle in the Asiatic style about three miles from town. The service squadrons were already there. The Old Guard in their burnt cloaks and grilled bonnets, their moustaches singed red, bivouacked in the park. Turning night into day, the vast funeral pyre behind them was a flaming symbol of heroism and barbarity.

On the 18th the Emperor made his way back through the rubble to the Kremlin, followed by the foot Guard. Where was Kutuzov?

Bypassing the capital, one Russian corps had taken up a position on the Smolensk road to guard Kutuzov's rear. On the 22nd General Lanusse marched out with some Guard units and ran head-on into Dorokhoff's troops. The Cossacks captured both men and matériel before the French could return to Moscow.

On the 23rd Saint-Sulpice was sent to Bezovka, halfway to Mozhaisk, with the dragoons of the Guard, two horse batteries, and an infantry regiment to guard the line of communications. Two days later a patrol of 200 dragoons fell into an ambush set by 4,000 Cossacks near the estate of Prince Galitzin. Lt. Colonel Marthod was mortally wounded in the action and died on 4 October. A major was killed and Major Hoffmayer, Captain Ligier, and three officers wounded. More than 80 dragoons were killed, wounded, or captured. This was a grevious loss.

Saint-Sulpice's squadrons found their communications so precarious that on the 26th Lefebvre-Desnoëttes was sent to a post halfway between Bezovka and the capital, taking a horse battery with him to support his chasseurs. These were eventually relieved by the cavalry of the Italian Guard.

Farther south Bessières and 1,400 of Colbert's light horse camped near Voronovo on the Kaluga road to wait for General Konopka's 3rd Lancers.

The 2nd Lancers, officered by stocky Dutchmen and supple Parisians and looking spectacular in their red uniforms, had by now proved themselves in combat. The 1st Lancers, bold, capricious, impulsive, and garrulous, were already famous. Ardent in temperament, the Poles cut capers in the field and drove their attacks home; but in camp they led the life of great lords. Their cooks roasted whole pigs and sides of beef on spits in the open, and their *cantinières* made coffee at all hours of day and night, serving it with sugar to all ranks. Sitting in armchairs upholstered in gold brocade or on bare planks, depending upon the locale, they smoked their long pipes and sat up half the night damning the Muscovites, serenaded the while with the latest Paris songs by General Colbert's aides who had remarkably fine voices.

The Young Guard was quartered in the rubble around the palace of Count Rostoptchin, governor of Moscow, where Count Delaborde and his staff were quartered. The voltigeurs and *tirailleurs* made themselves comfortable and ate off gold-rimmed porcelain. Their staff took in some French refugees who provided gaiety at the excellent dinners organized by the aides and Lieutenant Bourgoing, the interpreter, and caused the young men's hearts to flutter.

These were Mesdames André and Anthony of the French Theatre which was directed in Moscow by the witty Madame Bursay. When their theatre was burned, leaving the actors quite destitute, M. de Beausset, prefect of the palace, undertook to lodge them, dress them from the rich stores in the Kremlin, and organize performances. Michel Kovatchevitch reported that at a performance of Marivaux's *Game of Love and Chance* 'the orchestra was filled with soldiers of the Old Guard, in full dress and wearing the Legion of Honor, who greeted each significant line with cries of "*Vive l'Empereur!*" . . . while their comrades mounted guard outside'.

Some Guard officers lodged in the priests' houses near the Cathedral in the Kremlin used altar cloths for sheets and vestments for blankets. The cellars were stocked with six months' provisions of rum, coffee, sugar, chocolate, tea, meat, salt fish, and jam. The mulled wine and punch they concocted were much appreciated by the grenadiers who drank them from silver goblets.

Nevertheless, great precautions were eventually taken to guard the Kremlin and stop the pillage. Marshal Mortier, the governor, and General Durosnel, the garrison commander, detailed a regiment of the Old Guard under Generals Gros, Michel, or Tindal, to stand watch day and night. Posts of 100 men guarded the five gates in use. In addition, two companies of marines, and two of Prussian gunners with 8 guns were on picket duty. Ten patrols of horse grenadiers guarded the inside of the Kremlin, to which no Russian was admitted, and the ramparts were ringed with sentries. Outside in the city sentries were posted day and night and patrols of horse and foot toured each district.

Still there was looting. Mortier reported that some soldiers of the Guard sacked the flour stores and beat the guards in the vaults of the Foundlings' Hospital. Some Line soldiers were sold stolen goods at high prices. Major Labiffe of the horse chasseurs was robbed of his valise while guarding the Emperor, and sacks of coins were put up up for auction.

Lefebvre came down on the offenders with a heavy hand, turning them over to the provost marshal who arrested the officers and put the Grumblers in confinement. 'A soldier of the Guard who cannot appreciate the honor of serving in the Corps does not deserve to belong to it', he wrote in the orders.

Had the Guard lost its discipline? No; but its soldiers, especially the young ones, had been hungry ever since Smolensk. 'A soldier is like a sack – he can't stand up when he is empty.' In one of Delaborde's brigades 99 Young Guardsmen died of starvation between Smolensk and Moscow. The soldier of that day lived chiefly on bread. This

243

commodity existed only in the depots and stores which were rarely accessible during rapid troop movements.

On reaching Moscow the Guard's first concern was to guard the Emperor; its second, to eat and find forage for the horses. Despite the fire there were large stores in the capital. These were distributed as efficiently as circumstances permitted by Consul-General Lesseps, the governor of the province; nevertheless, excesses were committed, though some authors have charged the French Army with crimes committed by the Russians themselves.

'While we still had hopes of extinguishing the fire', General Berthezène wrote in his reminiscences, 'the most strict orders on the subject of looting were issued and rigorously executed. I saw guards prevent a soldier from taking a yard of cloth from a shop already in flames. But when the fire went out of control the surveillance was relaxed, and for two or three days we saw appalling disorder, with French and Russian soldiers, peasants, and serfs all engaged in indiscriminate looting. It was almost impossible to prevent this. However, these disorders ended as quickly as they had begun.'

The Emperor, Mortier, Durosnel, Lesseps, and the local commanders organized the city. They distributed money to the afflicted and opened hospitals, asylums, and stores of food and supplies for the Guard and Line stationed outside. Larrey reports that enough food to feed the army for six months, as well as reserves of cloth, fur, leather for boots and shoes, and immense quantities of wood and iron, were stored in the cellars of Kitai-Gorod.[1] There were even 40,000 muskets and 200 tons of gunpowder.

The soldiers had as much wine as they wanted and the surplus was put in depots. Brandy was so plentiful that thirty rations per man were issued to the troops on their departure. There were quantities of flour, vegetables, and oats; but these commodities were inadequately distributed so that some corps had plenty while others were in want. It must be remembered that the Emperor and his Guard stayed only thirty-three days in Moscow, and the problems were immense.

As for the spirit of the Guard, it had not changed. Would the army winter in Moscow? Would it go to Saint Petersburg? Or to the Ukraine where it was pleasant? Nobody worried. Napoleon was there. It was for him, their living god, that the Guard marched and suffered, and thanks to him that it lived 'on a different scale from everyone else'. For a long time each Guardsman had submerged his individuality in that of the corps, seeking no glory for himself but only for the Guard.

Naturally they were no angels. They felt the pangs of hunger. Stiff with cold and fatigue, they froze in the bivouacs so he might sleep and work in his tent. They swaggered, but they would have eaten their gaiter straps rather than admit any weakness. As for the Muscovites' gold, that belonged to the Treasury. Nevertheless, some of them sold sacks of copper *kopeks* above the official rate because their pay was overdue, though they knew in their hearts that money soiled one's fingers. They ordered fur-trimmed pelisses and finery and planned to wear three or four shirts at once when winter came. But they would keep the new blue overcoats and bearskin bonnets made in Moscow to impress the Cossacks – and Kutuzov.

[1] 'Chinese City', the commercial center of Moscow up to the Revolution of 1917. – Ed.

The Emperor knew all this. He knew his Guard. The aristocratic Dorsenne had wanted to fill up the Guard with 'sons of good families' to bolster His Majesty's prestige in the Empire and Europe. He had discussed the matter with Roguet. But Napoleon never dreamed of changing his method of recruiting the Guard.

'The officers of my Guard', he said later, 'had little education, but they fitted into my scheme. They were all old soldiers, sons of laborers and artisans, who depended entirely upon me. Paris society had no hold on them. I had more influence over them and was surer of them than if they had come from a higher class.'

He saw them daily at the noon parades on the Kremlin square. The troops wore full dress, as in Paris. The light-horse regiments were absent, prancing behind Murat on the Podolsk and Kaluga roads, fighting Cossacks.

Foraging parties were sent out every other day. These important expeditions were commanded by a general and joined in turn by units of the Emperor's entourage and each corps of infantry, cavalry, and artillery under the direction of the Duke of Treviso (Mortier). The enemy was becoming bolder and Napoleon was worried. He still had hopes that his presence in Moscow would lead Alexander to sue for peace. But if the Tsar wanted peace, why had he burned his capital?

The Emperor stuffed all the advance depots with men and attached Charrière's brigade of 4,000 dismounted cavalry to Delaborde's division. He ordered the 120,000 conscripts of 1813 sent forward on 10 November; route regiments of horse and foot Guards formed in Paris and sent by post with 100 gunners to Magdeburg, and the 2nd Voltigeurs and 2nd *Tirailleurs* from Spain sent to Berlin. These orders reached Paris in two weeks, thanks to the relay posts organized between Paris and Erfurt, and teams of four couriers posted every 75 miles in Poland and every 12 in Russia.

'What are the Polish nobles doing?' the Emperor inquired. His 1st Lancers were dwindling and he appealed to Warsaw for recruits. Five hundred of the 1,200 horses bought by General Konopka to mount his 3rd Lancers were diverted to the senior regiment. The Guard and the Emperor's household ordered rough horseshoes for ice, with which only the lancers were so far equipped.

On 8 October a corps of Tartar cavalry was organized under Lt. Colonel Mustapha Mursa Achmatowicz of the Polish cavalry, an influential Lithuanian Tartar. 'These people are burning with the desire to serve their country which has granted them the privileges of nobility for the past 500 years', General Sokolnicki wrote Napoleon.

Achmatowicz's 1st Tartar squadron of the Guard wore colpacks with yellow turbans, green jackets, crimson boleros trimmed with blue or gold braid, crimson sashes, and wide green trousers.[2] They carried sabers and lances with green and white pennants.

By the Emperor's order, no troops were sent to Moscow after 14 October.

The reviews of the Guard on 7 and 8 October gave Napoleon pause for reflection. The troops were in good condition. The infantry had regained its strength and was well clothed and shod. The Old Guard's cavalry horses were healthy, though those of the artillery were mediocre. The guns were plentiful, the wagons well stocked, and there was a plethora of munitions, but – the men had dwindled.

[2] In 1813–14 they wore white turbans, red jackets, blue trousers, and boleros of blue, green, or yellow. – Ed.

The Emperor examined the muster rolls. The 'situation of the troops composing the army corps of H. E. the Duke of Treviso as of October 1812' was as follows:

1ST DIVISION – GENERAL COUNT DELABORDE. The first voltigeur brigade (4th–6th Regiments) reported 1 officer and 838 men in hospital; 1 officer and 792 men in depots between Danzig and Smolensk; 814 'remaining in the rear without authorization'. (These included sick, lame, and wounded men as well as deserters.) In short, General Lanusse's three regiments mustered only 90 officers and 1,561 voltigeurs; General Berthezènes', 89 officers and 1,583 *tirailleurs*. Adding 309 gunners, pontooneers, and artisans, Delaborde had 3,632 men left of the 5,797 who had crossed the Niemen.

2ND DIVISION – GENERAL ROGUET. This division was somewhat better off since the fusiliers were more solid. Boyeldieu was the only brigade commander present, for Rottembourg had not yet arrived to replace General Lanabère. (He left Paris the end of October with two route regiments of the Guard and did not reach Stettin until 10 December.) The 1st Voltigeurs and 1st *Tirailleurs* reported 2 officers and 1,251 men in the depots, hospitals, and rear, and 67 officers and 1,382 men present under arms. The four fusilier battalions reported 66 officers and 2,501 men. The artillery mustered 245 officers and gunners. The division totaled 143 officers and 4,118 men, or 10 officers and 2,030 men less than at Marienwerder in June.

Pompéjac's flankers (23 officers and 1,172 men) were at Vitebsk and Vilna, in good condition but short of cartridges. Claparède's Polish division, which had arrived from Spain with 101 officers and 5,546 men in April, had only 87 officers and 1,683 men left.

In short, Mortier could muster but 373 officers and 8,199 men with 49 guns, (counting the 6th Voltigeurs on loan to the Old Guard cavalry, some reserve gunners, and Portuguese chasseurs) to keep order in Moscow and defend it if necessary.

Only Curial's Old of the Old gave a reassuring report. The 3rd Division commanded by Lefebvre had hardly varied since July. Here are the returns:

REGIMENT	10 JULY	10 OCTOBER
1st Chasseurs (General Gros)	33 officers—1,359 men	42 officers—1,504 men
2nd „ (Col. Rosey)	41 „ 1,210 „	40 „ 1,324 „
1st Grenadiers (Col. Laurède)	32 „ 1,278 „	39 „ 1,346 „
2nd „ (Col. Harlet)	34 „ 1,030 „	35 „ 1,117 „
3rd „ (General Tindal)	38 „ 1,074 „	39 „ 714 „
Totals	178 officers 5,951 men	195 officers 6,005 men

The units remaining in Paris with the Emperor had rejoined their corps along the route; however, 308 Dutch grenadiers had 'gone astray' in the rear.

From this time on, due to its solidity, resistance, and devotion, the Old Guard infantry was permanently attached to the Emperor, guarding him on the march and in camp. Moreover, it had plenty of artillery.

Major Pion des Loches commanded the two foot batteries of the chasseurs and Lt. Colonel Boulart, those attached to the grenadiers. Each detachment had 16 guns. Their 104 caissons carried 6,700 projectiles and 200,000 infantry cartridges.

So far the infantry had lost few men in battle. The artillery had lost heavily at Smolensk and Borodino; but not a single gun or caisson had been left on the field. Sorbier had kept his reserve and park intact by replenishing them along the route.

The horse artillery reserve under General Desvaux mustered 337 officers and gunners in two divisions commanded by Lt. Colonel Marin and Major de Lemud. Colonel Drouot commanded five reserve foot companies with 530 officers and gunners. The park had 300 vehicles. Depots had been established at Kovno and Vilna. Three companies from Spain had just arrived under Major Henrion. In all, the artillery of the Guard mustered 176 guns.

The cavalry of the Guard was in a satisfactory state. Engaged less often than the Line and better cared for, only the lancers and dragoons at the advance posts had suffered losses. Reinforcements, including a mixed detachment under Captain Chamorin of the dragoons, had arrived from France. The old troopers were in good condition, with full squadrons, and were dressed in handsome new colpacks, bonnets, furs, and pelisses.

On 18 October the Moscow cavalry mustered 4,009 horse as against 4,500 on 24 June. The remount horses were not too good; however, the Emperor was justly proud of his horse Guard, half of which had come all the way from Burgos.

Commanded by General Kirgener, a brother-in-law of Lannes, the engineers numbered 155 officers and men in one sapper company and one of Berg pontooneers and miners. Its 5 wagons carried 700 tools. Fifty sappers had been detached. There were no stragglers.

Thus, at the beginning of October the Imperial Guard numbered 17,000 infantry, 4,000 cavalry, and 176 guns. The Grand Army at Moscow mustered less than 100,000 men. The Emperor had reason to believe that Kutuzov's army was becoming more aggressive. Lauriston was unable to conclude an armistice. Under these circumstances it was impossible to winter in Moscow.

The foraging parties of the Guard now found nothing in the fields but apples as big as their thumb. Forage was harder to procure each day. With Cossacks descending upon them in clouds, no road was safe. No unit of less than 3,000 could hope to defend itself. And winter was coming on . . .

CHAPTER 6

The Retreat

ON 13 October the Old Guard was ordered to be ready to leave Moscow at a moment's notice with two weeks' rations. Mortier was ordered to hold the city; and Murat, reinforced by Claparède's division, the town of Voronovo on the Kaluga road against Kutuzov.

18 October. 3 p.m. The Emperor reviewed the 3rd Corps and General Charrière's dismounted cavalry. The generals of the Guard were present and Berthier was deep in conversation with His Majesty. Roguet, a caustic Gascon who knew the world, said to Berthezène: 'They are laughing – the news must be bad.'

It was. The day before, near Tarutino on the Kaluga road, Murat had allowed himself to be surprised by Kutuzov and the whole Borodino army. The French had lost much of their cavalry and 36 guns. General Lefebvre-Desnoëttes and a lieutenant of chasseurs had been wounded. Claparède's division had saved the day by recapturing the Tchernishna gorge and the town of Vinkovo. Murat's whole corps had just missed being captured. Were Kutuzov now marching to Moscow on both the old and new Kaluga roads, the situation in the capital would be serious indeed.

Everyone alert! The Emperor ordered the army to march to Kaluga at once.

'The Duke of Istria (Bessières) and my horse Guard will spend tonight ten miles from Moscow on the Kaluga road. I shall leave tonight for Desna. The small staff, the Duke of Danzig (Lefebvre) and the Imperial Headquarters will leave at once by the Kaluga gate. The Guard will bivouac in a square around the Emperor's quarters. General Roguet will leave tomorrow, escorting the treasury and the major-domo's staff.

'The Duke of Treviso (Mortier) will remain in the Kremlin with Delaborde's division and its artillery, Charrière's brigade, 500 horse, two companies of sappers, and one of artillery.'

Then he continued, to Mortier: 'Even if the whole enemy army attacks you, you should be able to hold out there for many days. You have 200,000 pounds of powder, two million cartridges, and 300 full caissons. An artillery major will blow up the Kremlin when so ordered. I cannot call your attention too strongly to the fact that we still have wounded here. Put them into the vehicles of the Young Guard and all others you can find. The Romans conferred civil crowns on those who saved the lives of the citizens. The Marshal Duke of Treviso will deserve one if he saves those of the soldiers...'

On the 19th the army began to march slowly in the following order: Eugène, Ney, the Emperor and the Old Guard, Davout, then Roguet's division reinforced by 1,200 dismounted cavalrymen. Next came 400 troopers of the 2nd Lancers who remained under arms from 8 a.m. until 10 p.m. on the day of departure and then bivouacked in a wind so strong that it upset the soup kettles.

The convoy was a valuable one. The 'treasury' contained minted money as well as gold and silver ingots, trophies – including Turkish and other flags taken from the Kremlin – and the famous cross from the Ivan Tower. Morand's division marched behind Roguet, and Colbert's brigade guarded the rear.

The troops could not travel very fast since both men and horses were heavily laden, and the road was choked with wagons filled to bursting with men, women, and children fleeing from Moscow.

Jerzmanowski's lancers appeared long before the end of the convoy which was lagging behind. 'Hurry up', said the Emperor. 'In twenty days we must be in winter quarters!'

At last the soldiers were leaving this unhappy country. They were heading south-west towards Kaluga and, eventually, the rich and smiling Ukraine where the Emperor was expected. It was a good day on the whole.

But not for everyone. The newest regiment of lancers would never join Colbert's brigade. General Konopka and the first two squadrons had been surprised at Slonim on the road to Minsk by a large body of Cossacks. 'They defended themselves valiantly and lost sixteen officers and many men before they were finally beaten. All who escaped with their lives were made prisoner.' Nothing was left of the regiment but a small depot at Grodno.

On the 20th, from the poor little castle of Troitskaya where the Old Guard watched over the Emperor, orders went off to Mortier to leave Moscow the 23rd and join Napoleon on the Kaluga road.

On the morning of the 24th the army heard gunfire ahead. Already harassed by Russian cavalry, it pushed on towards Kutuzov who was barring the road to Malo Yaroslavetz. Prince Eugène's corps was promptly engaged by a large force deployed on a plateau across the steep, wooded ravine of the Luzha River.

The Guard took up a position about a mile to the rear and watched 'anxiously', Boulart reported, as the battle took place. The chasseurs, grenadiers, and *vélites* of the Italian Guard fought 'with the utmost self-sacrifice'. The other corps had great difficulty entering the line because the ravine was so narrow. The horse batteries of the Guard went into action and Lt. Colonel Marin and a captain of the train were wounded.

The dreadful day ended at last and the Russians retired to Kaluga. The Emperor rode over the battlefield and through the burning city. Then he returned to Gorodnia and spent the night, surrounded by the Guard, in a weaver's cabin near the bridge over the Luzha. The first battalion of the 2nd Grenadiers was on duty. Great precautions were taken for the Emperor's safety, for the Cossacks were all around them. Sorbier mounted guns behind and west of the cabin and everyone slept with one eye open.

The Emperor was up before dawn on the 25th. 'I am always beating Russians', he told Caulaincourt, 'but it has yet to settle anything. I must make sure that the enemy is really retreating. My horse!'

Bessières, Berthier, and Caulaincourt reminded him that it was still dark and that they were not sure where the outposts were; but the Emperor was already on his way. Durosnel, Lauriston, Rapp, and the picket of chasseurs overtook him at a gallop. Half a mile from headquarters they heard loud cries and the sound of hoofs galloping through the artillery bivouacs; but they could not see more than twenty-five paces ahead.

'Halt, Sire, here come the Cossacks!' cried Rapp.

'Take the chasseurs and go ahead.'

The Emperor and his generals drew their swords. A dozen chasseurs dashed forth to join the picket, and together they attacked the Cossacks. Soon reinforced by the four service squadrons, Kirmann's Mameluks, and Colbert's brigade, they continued their pursuit until daybreak when they lost contact.

They could now see the whole plain, alive with Cossacks. The troopers of the Guard freed the gunners who had been taken prisoner and brought back the captured guns. A number of cavalrymen including Kirmann, Captain Schmidt, and two officers of the chasseurs, four dragoon lieutenants, and Major Kozietulski of the lancers were wounded. One of Berthier's aides who had killed a Russian and appropriated his lance, was run through by a horse grenadier who took him for a Cossack because of his long green coat and fur cap.

The Emperor had just missed being captured in the midst of his Guard. It was often said that his Grumblers fought well but guarded poorly. Actually, the Cossacks had spent the night just 300 paces from a battalion of grenadiers!

The Emperor's safety posed a difficult problem to his escorts. He would mount his horse without warning at any hour of day or night. Though the picket horses stood always ready, the service squadrons bridled their horses only when the Emperor ordered his own. Consequently, he usually set off with no more than three or four companions, and the rest caught up at a gallop.

That morning the service squadrons had not been relieved for three days and the men and horses were tired. Yet that night they were attacked again.

The Emperor did not finish his reconnaissance until 5 p.m. when he determined that Kutuzov was preparing another battle on the Kaluga road. In his hut at Gorodnia, where he was seated at a table studying his maps, Berthier, Murat, and Bessières stood silent for over an hour, their hats under their arms. The army's shortest route, leading through country that – though not rich – was at least not devastated, was now barred. They must return by the route over which they had come through a virtual desert.

Orders were issued: 'The Army will turn around'. Kutuzov would, too.

On the road to Borovsk the Grumblers complained. To begin with, the Emperor was not there. Claparède's division was guarding him. Then why this countermarch? Were they going back to Moscow? Why not go after the Russians? It began to rain. The horses fell down, and the wagons got stuck and had to be abandoned. No use to talk or think. The *Tondu* had his reasons.

Vereya, 27 October. Mortier arrived with the Young Guard and the dismounted cavalry. He had left Moscow at 6 p.m. on the 22nd but, because of his numerous vehicles, had not crossed the Moskva until midnight. At 11 p.m., under the protection of Berthezène's brigade which left last, General Noury had lighted the fuses and blown up the Kremlin.

'Why should it be I, rather than someone else?' Mortier asked bitterly, regretting the awesome destruction. He was known for his sweet nature and was 'endowed with every civic virtue'. He brought with him General Wintzingerode, a Württemberger in the Russian service, and Prince Narishkin, both captured in civilian clothes trying to enter Moscow with their cavalry. Wintzingerode sang the praises of the Marshal and of Lt. Colonel Sicard of the 5th Voltigeurs whose prisoner he had been; but the Emperor was inclined to be less cordial.

Delaborde's staff was full of Polish officers and Prussian artillerymen. A painter, and the actors André and Anthony with their charming wives, followed them in a carriage. Life was beautiful. At night food was plentiful in the bivouacs where the men burned whole pine trees. The civilians made fun of the soldiers' fur coats and the dissimilarity of their 'uniforms'.

Stretched out along the Mozhaisk road, where next day Mortier was due to join Claparède and the Old Guard, was a file of wounded whom the Duke of Treviso had sent out of Moscow to prevent their being maltreated by the Russians. The first cold arrived with a frost of −4°[1] and the nights were hard. The column crossed the battlefield of Borodino – a gruesome sight.

The order came to burn all useless baggage and load several wounded on each wagon, including the Emperors'. Dressed in a Polish costume consisting of a green pelisse and a cap of marten fur, Napoleon had so far traveled in his closed carriage.

The army reached Viazma. The cavalry of the Guard and Lefebvre's infantry were five miles ahead. The Young Guard halted beyond the town where there were provision depots to replenish the stores and forage of every corps. They must wait for the army to catch up.

Having discovered their route, Kutuzov kept harassing the army's left flank with Platov's Cossacks, and attacking the rear-guard under Marshal Ney (see Plate 97b).

'It's like marching in Egypt', the old-timers said. The Emperor's carriages were in the middle of the column. In front were the artillery and baggage trains, preceded and followed by infantry and cavalry, and flanked on both sides by battalions in single file surrounding several cannon. In this formation the troops could respond immediately to an attack.

From now on the Emperor, marching either on foot or horseback in the midst of the 'old of the Old', was always escorted by the Guard. He knew that Platov had promised his daughter to 'bring Napoleon back alive'.

4 November. It snowed and froze. The vanguard trampled the road into a skating rink. The horses fell down and the men fell repeatedly. They soon learned to fall without resistance, like a cat. On the hills the resourceful men simply slid to the bottom 'at the

[1] Centigrade, equal to 25·8° Fahrenheit.

crouch' – as Masséna described it when chasing the Austrians across the Alps. Others hung onto the wheels of the wagons, braking them to spare the horses. Crossing bridges the columns became separated. Boulart's gunners had to double their teams and leave some of their caissons behind. Some of their men, too.

6 November. Bad news. In Paris on 11 October General Malet had announced that the Emperor had died in Russia, and had imprisoned Savary, the former commander of the 'immortals'. Then he attempted to seize power and overthrow General Hulin. It had taken some time to bring him under control.

This was an incredible coup, carried out under the noses of the Empress, Cambacérès, and the depots of the Guard. Everyone had completely lost his head. Grivel's marines, who had arrived from Spain several days before the coup d'état, were alerted and occupied the Senate. The Empire had escaped falling by a hair's breadth.

Eventually rigorous measures had been taken. Drums beat, troops were mobilized, and everyone pretended that the authorities had never lost control and that Malet's abortive enterprise was no more than an act of folly; but they laughed in their sleeve at the predicament of the Minister of Police. By his order General Dériot had increased the guards at the Ministry, Senate, Cambacérès' house, the Abbey, the Tuileries, and the Place Vendôme.

On 7 November, in the Castle of Pnevo near Slobpneva, where the Emperor was guarded by the fusilier-grenadiers, General Roguet said to him: 'Everything depends on your life, Sire . . .'

Napoleon replied: 'Are you forgetting my son? Do you discount our institutions, and France itself which is immortal? Have we accomplished so much believing that it would all be in vain? The Empire was no chimera of mine but the filling of a pressing need, a compromise between past and future. It was inevitable. What, if not the Empire, ended the anarchy and laid a new foundation on the ruins? Though blind at the moment, all men, the peoples, the kings – whether allies or enemies – have a vested interest in the Empire. Believe me, the masses understand it by instinct better than the intelligentsia. We must be patient. "Sufficient unto the day is the evil thereof." If our task became even harder, still no man – even I – could stop the movement led by France and the Empire, and something stronger than either of them – time itself. The generation that comes after us will want to go even faster.

'And now – to answer the question you did not dare ask – no individual, apart from his mission, was ever indispensable. France is great, her influence in Europe is assured. It was no vain ambition that brought you here, and I have most pressing interests elsewhere. This campaign will lose me time and, to some extent, momentum. The 600,000 men I brought to Russia provide only part of the prestige I need. Many things cannot be accomplished by force. Do not confuse the conqueror with the builder, or a man's duty to vanquish the stubborn and prejudiced and defend himself with a love of adventure. It was Louis XIV's weakness and discontent, his weariness of everything at the close of a long reign – not his death – that produced Louis XV, and ultimately the Revolution . . .

'On the day that Caesar fell did the sun stop giving light to the world?'

Roguet, to whom we owe this extraordinary profession of faith from the Emperor, added: 'All that fickle fortune brought him later has not succeeded in diminishing the impression the words of this genius made on me. Doubtless he alone saw the end . . .'

For the actors in this drama the worst was just beginning.

'We think of nothing but how to get warm', General Desvaux wrote his wife, 'and sleep four hours a night . . . We get up at 2 a.m. to be ready to leave at four. We halt at six in the evening and spend the time until ten eating and trying to get warm . . .'

'It's a villainous country. There's nothing here to put your teeth in', the soldiers complained.

The snow fell in whirling masses so that one could not tell whether it came from the sky or the earth. It took two hours to kindle a fire with the green wood. The *cantinières* sold coffee at 5 francs a cup. The men kneaded dough in the snow and made cakes which they cooked on sticks held between their toes. Anyone who went off alone to find food was lost.

'Show a little more courage, damn you!' said the men. 'The retreat is well covered.'

Oudinot, Gouvion-Saint-Cyr, and Victor were guarding the main route; Macdonald was on the left, at Riga; the Saxons and Austrians were guarding the right flank in Poland. Reinforcements were on their way.

The Guard was only twenty-five miles from Smolensk, a well-stocked city at the frontier of Old Poland. General Baraguay-d'Hilliers, the governor of the province, and General Charpentier, the garrison commander, would surely furnish men and beasts with food and fuel, lodge them, and let them recover. This hope kept them alive.

Sent from the rear to Smolensk on 4 September, the 8th Corps of the Duke of Belluno (Victor) was still garrisoned there on the 27th. Then, by the Emperor's order, it had left to guard the army's line of communication to the Berezina. There it was exposed to a double menace: on the one hand from Tchitchagov, whom Reynier and Schwarzenberg had failed to halt in his march north to Minsk, and on the other by Wittgenstein who was marching south after chasing Gouvion-Saint-Cyr from Polotsk.

As he was setting out for Kaluga the Emperor had ordered Baraguay-d'Hilliers to proceed with his division from Smolensk to Yelnia on the Kaluga road. Meanwhile the battle of Malo Yaroslavetz had changed the army's itinerary. Ordered back to Smolensk on 4 November, Baraguay was attacked on the 9th at Baltutino by one of Kutuzov's corps. Caught in a salient at Liakhovo, his vanguard under General Augureau was overpowered by a superior force and obliged to surrender. The Emperor was furious.

Napoleon arrived at Smolensk at the same moment as the remainder of Baraguay's division. His principal unit had not been engaged. This was a route regiment of the Guard commanded by Major Pailhès of the 4th *Tirailleurs* who had been promoted at Austerlitz and served as Dorsenne's aide in Spain. The regiment numbered 1,374 foot and 249 horse from every Guard corps and was a welcome reinforcement. This unit, plus Colonel Pellegrin's artillery, brought the Guard's effectives to 14,000, including Claparède's division.

Berthezène's brigade was ordered to cover Smolensk on the south where hordes of enterprising Cossacks were operating. Quartered in the suburbs of Roslavl, they pushed their outposts to the junction of the roads to Roslavl and Yelnia. The thermometer descended to $-18°$ ($-0·8°$F.) and the sentries froze to death. Several units of Delaborde's division were quartered in Krasny.

Lefebvre's chasseurs and grenadiers and the artillery were camped along the Dnieper between the old and new towns. Climbing the icy bluffs above the river with difficulty, they bivouacked on the promenade below the citadel where bread, biscuit, meat and hay were distributed. The men lighted fires against the terrible cold. Soldiers coming from the rear reported that Vitebsk and its stores had been captured by the enemy.

While on a looting expedition several chasseurs took shelter in some houses where they proceeded to thaw out by drinking grain alcohol. A general more concerned with his comfort than his duty dislodged them.

'The dog! The filthy bastard!' cried the men, and they began to rail against all officers, including their own, not realizing that the latter had been evicted before them. That night thirty chasseurs froze to death as a result of their eviction.

At evening roll call on 13 November the Old Guard reported 183 officers and 5,777 men present, and the cavalry, 2,000 horse; another 2,000 dismounted troopers were occupying the villages between the Dnieper and the Orsha road.

The three army corps in the rear followed one another at a day's march, constantly harassed by Cossacks who never let them out of their sight. It was hard to get news of them, since the cavalry had dwindled. So far 30,000 horses had died of cold or starvation. The Emperor still risked a few officers on courier service, escorted by Polish lancers whose mounts were roughshod; but these liaisons were dangerous and often fruitless.

'I am very tired', General Walther wrote his wife from Smolensk. 'At fifty-two you do not make such journeys painlessly . . .'

Under the circumstances it was useless to think of wintering in Smolensk. The troops must push on to the west. If they waited for the corps of Eugène, Davout, and Ney to catch up, Kutuzov's army would outstrip them on a parallel route and attack their van. On the contrary, if left to themselves these isolated corps were in danger of annihilation.

In Smolensk the storekeepers and bakers worked day and night. Nevertheless, the company officers paid for bread in gold, and the Emperor's servants sold his Burgundy for a *napoléon* the bottle.

PLATE 95

PLATE 95

Death of General Caulincourt before the
Grand Redoubt at Borodino
(*Detail of an original watercolor by Franz von Habermann*)

PLATE 96

The Russian Army at Borodino
(From an original watercolor by Denis Dighton)

PLATE 97

a) Napoleon and his suite
(*From an original watercolor by Dietrich Monten*)

b) Platov and his Cossacks in 1812
(*From a colored aquatint by G. Schadow*)

PLATE 98

Italien.

Offizier
in Marschanzug

Reiter,
Marschanzug mit Mantel.
Offiziere in Lageranzügen
(Surtout u. Überrock)
Ehrengarden

Reiter
Lageranzug mit Mantel. Paradeanzug. Lageranzug.

Das Italienische Heer unter Vicekönig Eugen.

1812.

PLATE 99

The burning of Moscow

(From a colored engraving published by Artaria, Vienna)

PLATE 100

Officers, 3rd Polish Lancers, parade dress, and
1st Polish Lancers, stable dress
(*From an original watercolor by Victor Huen*)

PLATE 101

General Konopka, colonel of the 3rd Polish Lancers
(*From an original watercolor by William Heath*, 1812)

PLATE 102

b) Russian artillery officer
(From a drawing by Bachelin after Gottfried Schadow)

a) Grenadier captain, Irish Legion; Lithuanian Tartar of the Guard; grenadier, Italian Legion;
chasseur, Portuguese Legion
(From a watercolor sketch by A. de Moltzheim after H. Vernet)

PLATE 103

a) Colbert
(*After portrait: Collection Marquis de Colbert*)

b) Michel
(*Col. lithograph after Hess*)

c) Morand
(*Contemp. engraving*)

d) Berthezène
(*Contemp. lithograph: Bibliothèque Nationale*)

PLATE 104

Grenadier sentry before the Emperor's tent
(*From an original watercolor by Eugène Lami*)

CHAPTER 7

Krasny

ON 14 November the foot and horse Guard were bogged down in six feet of snow around a shanty in Korytnia where the Emperor was quartered. To the south Kutuzov's campfires were visible. Some shots rang out . . .

Alert! The Cossacks!

It was a false alarm. The sudden attacks of these savages had made the men jittery. It was only a party of train soldiers returning to camp with thatch filched from the roofs of neighboring cottages. The men ate their last biscuit, restoring life to their swollen gums. It took twenty horses now to pull a forge.

At Reveille next morning some horses procured in Smolensk were found dead. The farriers spent the following night removing the shoes from the rest and wrapping their hoofs in rags and bits of church vestments – and even ball gowns – against the ice.

'This distresses you', General Sorbier said to Major Pion des Loches who was heart-broken at having to abandon his guns. 'As for me, I don't give a damn! The sooner you lose them, the better for the gunners who are killing themselves trying to save them . . .' But what if the gunners of the Guard preferred to die?

Ten miles beyond, buried in a deep valley, was Krasny. The road to it led through a hilly region crisscrossed by tributaries of the Dnieper. The last one, known as the Losmina, flowed through a steep gorge which could be crossed only by a bridge at right angles to the road.

Junot's 900 Westphalians, burdened with noncombatant stragglers, led the way. Men and horses followed, numb with cold, stumbling over one another in the silent white landscape. If the enemy barred the road, only the Guard could open a passage for them.

At this very moment Miloradovitch, supported by artillery, was formed in line of battle before Krasny. It took General Exelmans of the horse grenadiers to galvanize the indifferent French army. A fearless soldier and superb horseman, he organized the column, putting each man – general, infantryman, and gunner – into position, and led it towards the enemy. This so impressed the Russians that they were content with shelling the road and harrying the flanks of the column with their cavalry.

Supported first by Claparède, then by the Emperor and the Old Guard, Exelmans crossed the gorge and entered Krasny, chasing out Ozharovski's cavalry. The remnants of the Guard band played *What Better than to Be Home with Your Family?*

'You would do better to play *Let Us Watch over the Empire!*' the Emperor observed.

255

The gorge soon became congested. The Guard's artillery was hoisted by manpower up the plateau overlooking the vast expanse of snow they had just crossed. It had taken them twenty-two hours to march twelve miles. All General Desvaux's gunners were now afoot, but thanks to the surviving horses they had not lost a gun since leaving Moscow. As for the Young Guard artillery, its teams were still healthy due to the foresight of Colonel Villeneuve who had loaded his caissons in Moscow with plenty of oats.

The fires of the Russian bivouacs burned to the south and southwest across the Losmina, but the enemy did not attack.

'The Emperor Napoleon is at Krasny which is full of soldiers in fur bonnets', a peasant reported to Kutuzov.

'You wish me to take a risk now when in a few days victory is certain?' Kutuzov asked his generals who were pressing him for action. He had 90,000 men to Napoleon's 50,000. The enemy was held in check only by the prestige of the Guard.

Surrounded by the 2nd Chasseurs, the Emperor appealed to the Guard: 'I count on you, as you can count on me, to perform great feats . . .' he told the officers and NCO's. Then he ordered his tents and wagons burned in their presence, commanding the officers to do likewise.

On 15 November at 9 p.m. Roguet was ordered to attack Ozharovski's bivouacs, containing large forces of every branch, two miles south of Krasny on a five-mile front. He formed his four fusilier battalions in three columns directed towards Buyanovo on the right, Malievo in the center, and Chirkova on the left. They advanced noiselessly, their watches synchronized for a simultaneous attack. Roguet marched with the center column.

At midnight, in cold that had put the Russians into a coma, the fusiliers fell upon them with bayonets in their camps, throwing them into disorder and inflicting heavy losses. The fusiliers lost 300 men, with two officers killed and Major Vionnet and 5 officers wounded.

After this Kutuzov was more circumspect. He halted his enveloping movement and ordered Tormasov's corps, sent to cut the road from Krasny to Liady, to suspend operations. But this did not prevent the Cossacks from plundering the treasure wagons stuck in the Losmina gorge. They had to be burned on the 16th.

'I have played Emperor long enough', Napoleon announced. 'It is time I played general.'

He was faced with the dilemma of running the gauntlet to safety with the Guard, or waiting at Krasny for Prince Eugène whose guns could now be heard, and for Davout and Ney behind him. He chose the latter course.

General Durosnel was sent back towards Smolensk with a battalion of foot chasseurs under General Boyer, and two squadrons of the 1st Lancers with two guns under Chlapowski, to open a passage for the Viceroy.

Durosnel marched to the left of the main road towards Katova, driving clouds of Cossacks before him. A little later he saw a line of enemy cavalry on his right. He ignored it and sent some Polish lancers to warn Prince Eugène of his approach. Coming within sight of the Russian lines he opened fire and was promptly charged by a large body of cavalry, supported by horse artillery. His men, firing in squares, stopped every charge; but when reinforcements arrived for the enemy Durosnel ordered a retreat. Slowly, in good order, the old troopers returned to their lines just as the anxious Emperor sent Latour-Maubourg to order them to retire.

This action permitted the Viceroy to come up during the night. Napoleon was happy to have saved both his stepson's corps and his own chasseurs. He invited Eugène and Durosnel to supper.

Now, if possible, he must rescue Davout and Ney.

Near the Smolensk road on 17 November Napoleon climbed a hill on Murat's arm, wearing his green pelisse and carrying a stick. He scanned the horizon. To the east lay a snowfield under an inky sky. On the right were Cossacks, then the strong columns of Strogonov, Galitzin, and Miloradovitch – at least 80,000 men with 100 guns – marching to Krasny. Skirting the town to the south, he saw them turn west towards Liady and Orsha. If he would clear a path for Davout and Ney and keep open his line of retreat, these Russian columns must be stopped.

Stopped with what? With the Guard, which meant 14,000 famished men, a few squadrons, 400 horse under Latour-Maubourg, and the few guns that still had teams to move them.

The Russians loomed over the horizon in front, on the right, and behind them.

Posting Mortier with 5,000 Young Guard east and southeast of Krasny along the Losmina gorge, the Emperor said: 'I leave you here with confidence. You will be attacked by the van of the Russian army. I ask you to hold out for a whole day. Its advance must be held back as long as possible. I shall be grateful for every hour you gain.'

'Sire', Mortier replied, 'I shall hold the enemy back throughout the day.'

Except for a battalion of chasseurs supporting Mortier's left flank, stationed near the icebound road to Smolensk, the Old Guard remained with the Emperor.

Roguet and his fusiliers were posted in front and on the left, facing Katova. Claparède, escorting the remains of the baggage train and treasure, was posted west of Krasny to cover Eugène's retreat to Liady. Tindal, with a battalion of the 3rd Grenadiers, the wounded, and the dismounted cavalry, barricaded the town and prepared to defend it. Having given Drouot their last horses, the foot gunners burned most of their caissons and threw their ammunition into a small lake near the Orsha road.

The Duke of Treviso (Mortier) made his dispositions on the bluffs above the Losmina. Drawn up in front and along the bank occupied by the Old Guard, he placed Prince Emil of Hesse's brigade of 600 men on the left, the 1st *Tirailleurs* and 1st Voltigeurs in the center, and a battalion of 3rd Grenadiers on the right at Voskreseniye. By placing his troops in two lines instead of three he was able to extend his front by a third. 'And very thin it is', a Grumbler observed, 'like a bone thrown the Muscovites to chew on . . .'

The rest of Delaborde's division, with a squadron of 'Red lancers' and a Portuguese squadron under the Marquis of Loulé, occupied the second line.

Early in the action the Russians opened fire on the Hessians and shelled them furiously with 30 guns. Soon 100 were in action along the whole front. Poor Drouot 'could only make noble efforts, alas!' in retaliation. One of Captain Evain's caissons blew up, burning him seriously.

'Let's go, boys!' cried Old Man Delaborde. 'Run across the battlefield and lift your noses the moment you smell powder.' His fine lads answered with lusty cheers. Reaching the left flank, where the Hessians were in mortal combat, the General said: 'I congratulate Your Highness on the courage of his soldiers and thank him for holding firm at this important position.'

'You can see, General, that I am losing many men.'

'Our French troops are being punished as severely as their allies. We have never played favorites on the battlefield.'

'My remark was not a complaint, General', replied Prince Emil. 'My soldiers will continue to do their duty.'

On the right, Voskreseniye was taken and retaken several times. Captain Arnaud of the 1st Voltigeurs, 'sent forward with his company to block a Russian column which threatened to outflank the town, withstood many charges' before being wounded and brought to the rear by his men. A veteran of Egypt, cited for bravery at Eylau and Ratisbon, Arnaud was later wounded at Lützen, and again at Pau in 1814.

4 p.m. The light was fading, which was a blessing. Ahead and on the left, Davout's guns and the musketry of Roguet's troops at grips with Miloradovitch were audible. To the south, east, and west the whole horizon was ablaze. Claparède reported that Bennigsen had cut the road to Liady. Now only one road remained open – the road north to the Dnieper.

But alas, it was open no longer! An enemy horse battery had appeared on the left and opened fire on the Old Guard and the Emperor.

'A battalion of my chasseurs shall go capture it', Napoleon said calmly. He was haunted by the thought of Mortier under furious attack, and a bombardment to which Delaborde's guns, maneuvered by hand, could make only a feeble response. Could the Marshal hold out a quarter of an hour longer?

The Duke of Treviso, on horseback in the thick of the fire, would hold out until night.

At last the 1st *Tirailleurs* fell back to Krasny 'at an ordinary pace', by the Marshal's express command, repeated by Delaborde. On their right the 1st Voltigeurs fought on furiously. At one moment there were shouts and cries of '*Vive l'Empereur!*' mixed with Russian 'Hurrahs!' then there was silence.

The Novgorod Dragoons took possession of the field. The 1st Voltigeurs had vanished, and with them the 3rd Grenadiers who were promptly replaced by Russian guns shelling the rest of Delaborde's division which was deployed in support of 120 survivors of Boyeldieu's brigade.

Meanwhile, on the left, the Old Guard had been fighting gloriously to save the fusiliers and clear a path for Davout who was driving a Cossack horde before him. Fortunately, Kutuzov, fearing Miloradovitch would be trapped between Davout and the Emperor, had ordered him to retire to the south.

At 7 p.m. Davout crossed the gorge and bypassed Krasny on the north, pursued by Russian cavalry.

With death in his soul the Emperor was obliged to leave the field before he had rescued Ney. He ordered Mortier and Davout to make every effort to save him. Then he left with the Old Guard to try and break through to Liady.

Roguet's fusiliers and flankers relieved the Old Guard. Shelled by Russian artillery, these brave fellows tried to hold back the enemy in order to clear the Smolensk road for the passage of the 3rd Corps. The flankers charged the Russian hordes and were repulsed, but the fusiliers succeeded in stopping them.

Under cover of night the Russian cuirassiers attacked the plateau and charged the lot, engaging them in mortal combat. The French guns had to be brought off the field by manpower. Finally, Mortier ordered Roguet's division to retire from the field of carnage – but slowly, as if on maneuvers, dragging their wounded along under the bursting shells.

Krasny was on fire, revealing a Dante's inferno. The Russian troopers, yelling like banshees, were sabering everyone they met. The battalion of 3rd Grenadiers made several charges in the crowded streets, being the last to retire behind the Young Guard and Roguet's division.

General Tindal's companies were reduced to 20 men apiece. Roguet's division lost 760 men, including 6 officers of the 1st *Tirailleurs* and 14 of the 3rd Voltigeurs. Lt. Colonel Mallet and Major Pion des Loches were wounded, and several officers of the Old Guard killed. In the single battalion of the 3rd Grenadiers, 13 officers including the battalion commander were put out of action. Delaborde's division lost 31 officers in killed and wounded. The artillery had 6 officers killed, and an officer of the wagon train was missing.

The Old Guard had covered itself with glory. The Russian infantry had never dared attack it.

The Emperor and his staff made slow progress towards Liady. The foot and horse Guard and the artillery advanced with difficulty on a precipitous road covered with ice. The town was at the bottom of a steep hill. The gunners unhitched the horses and let the guns and caissons coast down, braking them as best they could by means of ropes. Naturally the matériel landed at the bottom in poor condition.

The cavalry dismounted and horses and riders slid down the hill together, several riders being crushed by their mounts. Next came the infantry, descending rapidly 'at the crouch', followed by the staff, and the Emperor who preferred to descend in the same fashion rather than trust himself to the arm of an aide.

'I have lost thirteen horses since 13 November, which doesn't help', Count Delaborde wrote his wife. 'But may God spare us from losing a great man! He is well, notwithstanding his immense labors . . .'

Simultaneously the Duke of Danzig (Lefebvre) wrote Senator Clément de Ris: 'Our hero is well, as ever. We love him in spite of (the conspirators) and shall defend him with our last breath . . .'

The whole Guard – Young and Old – felt the same way. 'We're "cooked,"' said a horse grenadier wearing a bald fur bonnet and a single boot, 'but "*Vive l'Empereur!*" all the same.'

Forty-five miles west of Krasny the road crossed the Dnieper at Orsha, a squalid village inhabited by destitute Jews. A thaw had set in and the streets were a sea of black mud a foot deep in which the dazed and hungry soldiers broke ranks and floundered grotesquely.

At noon next day Mortier, Claparède, Delaborde, Roguet, Lefebvre, and the Guard joined the Emperor near the bridge and together they contemplated the disaster.[1] Yesterday they 'had been lucky to save him from capture during a Cossack attack'; but today the outposts had been surprised and the Emperor was alarmed.

He assembled the Old Guard at his headquarters in Princess Lubomirska's château and said:

'You are witnessing the disintegration of the army. By fatal delusion, most of your brothers-in-arms have given up the fight. If you follow their tragic example all is lost. The fate of the army rests with you. I know you will justify my confidence in you. Your officers must not only maintain strict discipline, but you yourselves must keep a rigorous watch over each other and punish those who try to leave the ranks. I count on you. Swear that you will not abandon your Emperor!'

'We swear!' cried the Grumblers. Near Dubrovna the Count of Lobau (Mouton) called for a similar oath from the Young Guard which it took with enthusiasm.

'Let's have a tune to warm us up', the Emperor said to the band as they continued their march. 'Let's have the *Song of Departure . . .*'

---

[1] After Krasny a large number of soldiers in the Grand Army threw down their arms and refused to fight any more. – Ed.

CHAPTER 8

Crossing the Berezina

20 NOVEMBER was their darkest day. Ney had not put in an appearance. Ahead at the Berezina the armies of Wittgenstein and Tchitchagov were lying in wait with 175 infantry battalions, 150 squadrons of cavalry, and horse artillery. If Kutuzov attacked their rear and left flank they would be destroyed.

That evening the Guard bivouacked in melting snow; but there was bread and meat, since Orsha harbored a depot under a 'very efficient' commissary. The elite gendarmes, mounted and magnificent, had arrived on the 17th. The artillery of the Guard was quartered in the courtyard of a large building on the edge of the village. Against heavy odds, several detachments had come from France with officers, gunners, and matériel. These included Lieutenant Lyautey and a pontoon section. Of what use was such a contraption now? Apparently the Emperor thought the game was up, for he burned his papers and the eagles and had Sorbier consign the 60 pontoon boats to the flames. A week later twenty could have saved nearly all of them . . .

The horse Guard and the Emperor's household were still mounted since their horses had been cared for, watered, and reasonably well fed. Each evening the half-frozen troopers and grooms went in search of water. They broke the ice and hauled water to camp in pails, then went to look for forage.

Berthier worked late at the 'palace', a shack of vertical planks, while the exhausted Emperor dozed on a map of Russia spread before him on a table. No officer or servant was there; only the grenadier sentry before the door.

Ney finally arrived. By sheer force of energy the 'red-faced fellow' had saved the elite of his 3rd Corps – 3,000 heroic men including Colonel Pelet and General Ricard. As Mortier and the Young Guard went to meet him, Oudinot's aide burst into the room where the Emperor was dozing. With a start Napoleon jumped up in the midst of a nightmare, crying: 'How shall we cross? How shall we cross?'

The situation was as follows: the Duke of Reggio's (Oudinot's) corps of 10,000 fresh troops was at Bobr, 37 miles beyond. Twenty-five miles further north at Tchereya, 12,000 men under the Duke of Belluno (Victor) were in contact with Wittgenstein. Tchitchagov was believed to be near Minsk, marching to Borisov. Meanwhile, the Cossacks were everywhere and growing bolder by the hour.

Orders were issued to rest the following day at Orsha. Such a decision required great courage when minutes were worth hours. However, at the risk of losing all, the troops still able to fight must be given a breathing spell.

The Emperor and the Guard spent the night seven miles beyond at Barany.

'Burn half the wagons and carriages', the Emperor wrote Claparède, 'and give Sorbier 120 horses to salvage what he can of the Guard's artillery . . .' Only thus might he hope to beat Tchitchagov to the Berezina and face Wittgenstein only. And if not? Duroc and Daru dreamed of sending the Emperor across in a balloon!

Oudinot was sent ahead to Borisov and Minsk to form the vanguard while Victor took command of the rear.

The Berezina, the right-hand tributary of the Dnieper, flowed roughly north and south. At Borisov, a village of 350 wooden houses on the left bank, it had two forks spanned by a narrow bridge. Here on the 22nd Oudinot had met and defeated Tchitchagov who burned the bridge in his retreat to the right bank.

Seven and a half miles downstream on the left bank was a collection of hovels called Studianka. There the river, cluttered with ice floes, was a single stream 100–120 feet wide meandering through a wide, marshy valley. Westward from the right bank, which dominated the left, extended a pine forest punctuated with flimsy shacks forming the hamlets of Kostulitzy, Brili, Zanivki, and Stakhov. The road from Borisov to Vilna ran through these villages. Though a thaw had set in the ground was still covered with snow.

Corbineau's brigade arrived in this theatre. On the 25th Napoleon examined the terrain with a strong escort of around 3,500 Old Guard infantry, 1,400 mounted horse Guards, 1,500 dismounted cavalry under Dautancourt, and an ephemeral troop of cavalry officers under Murat and Grouchy known as the 'sacred squadron'.

Oudinot was put in charge of the crossing. His artillery chief Colonel Chauveau, former major of the Guard horse artillery, demolished some houses in Veselovo to procure wood for a bridge which he built with 'indefatigable zeal' at daybreak on the 26th. With a wagonload of nails salvaged from the boats burned at Orsha, General Eblé and the Guard pontooneers, marines, and gunners built trestles and rafts. They were encouraged by the Emperor in person as the Cossacks looked on from the right bank.

A battery of 40 guns was installed on the left bank while the infantry of the Guard, 5,000 strong, calmly prepared to protect the crossing of Oudinot's infantry as they forded the stream on the cruppers of Corbineau's horses, or were ferried across in rafts.

This operation was successful. The grenadiers saw the black forms of the vanguard in the snow on the opposite bank, around the huts at Brili and at the edge of the forest.

Behind the Guard on the left bank were Eugène, Ney, Poniatowski, the Westphalians, and Davout – in all, 10,000 men. Then came the stragglers, and finally Victor with 11,000 men of the rear-guard, posted east of Studianka to hold Wittgenstein's 24,000 and Kutuzov's 30,000 Russians at bay while the others crossed.

Early on the 27th the troops began to cross on two trestle bridges which the sappers, pontooneers, gunners, and marines of the Guard virtually held up with their arms among the ice floes. First came the Emperor with the Old Guard and the wagons of the household. With the Duke of Danzig (Lefebvre) in the lead, they marched between a double row of Grumblers to Zanivki where a pair of sheds measuring six by seven feet were designated as the 'palace'.

Delaborde's voltigeurs and *tirailleurs* crossed next, followed by Roguet's fusiliers, the cavalry, Claparède and his wagons, and the artillery, crossing slowly. The vehicles advanced with caution, a wagon at a time, so as not to shake the bridge whose deck looked as though it were built of matchwood.

The commanders of each unit crossed last. Larrey made several return trips, spending the whole day of the 28th on the left bank looking for his wagons and ambulances and forcing them into the line. At the mere mention of his name the ranks opened and people rushed to his aid. 'I owe my life to the soldiers', he recalled. 'In the end I was seized by strong hands and literally pushed across the bridge.'

At nightfall on the 28th the last Guard wagon crossed the vehicular bridge on the left. Luckily it was colder and the ice held in the marshes; otherwise not a vehicle would have been saved.

At Zanivki, a trio of rickety shacks rechristened 'Miserovo' by the Guard, the Old Guard watched in silence as the regiments crossed, their passage constantly threatened by a howling mob of stragglers whom the commanders held back with difficulty. 'Why such feverish anxiety?' the soldiers thought. Did they think safety lay at the far end of this ridiculous structure only a few yards long?

Ordered to cover the Vilna road, which the corps traveled in succession after their difficult crossing, Mortier posted his 1,500 Young Guard on either side of the road in the snow-covered forest, facing Borisov. On a ridge in front, a battery of the Guard's twelve-pounders returned the fire of the Russian guns on the heights beyond.

Ney came to relieve Oudinot who had just been wounded for the thirtieth time in his career. Mortier, Delaborde, Roguet, Claparède, Berthezène, Tindal, Doumerc, the Prince of Hesse, the Marquis of Loulé and their aides stood round him within range of the bombardment. Fortunately the Russians were firing too high.

Their combined units drove Tchitchagov's 30,000 infantry and 12,000 horse from the Brodnia defile, between them and Borisov, while on the left, towards the river, Berthezène's *tirailleurs* delivered a flank attack.

While leading his 5th *Tirailleurs*, Colonel Hennequin's horse was suddenly decapitated. Officers and soldiers rushed to his aid as he went down in the snow with the bloody carcass; but he was already on his feet. 'I am at my post, *messieurs*', he said. 'Let others remain at theirs.' Hennequin, of whom it was said that he 'would laugh only if he were burning', was very rude, but also rather pathetic. As his servant was saddling another horse a piece of bread fell out of one his holsters. 'If one of you needs this more than I', he said to the soldiers, 'you are welcome to it.'

Ahead and on the right, Doumerc's 400 cuirassiers debouched like a waterfall into a clearing and took 1,000 prisoners. Among the cuirassiers was Colonel Ordener, a twenty-five-year-old who had served under his father in the horse grenadiers in 1805. While charging at Austerlitz alongside his father the latter said to him: 'Go ahead and salute the enemy – that's your privilege when you meet him for the first time – but a really brave man does not repeat this courtesy.' Stung to the quick, the youth proceeded to be wounded three times in the action and lose his horse.[1] He was ultimately saved from death by his uncle Captain Walther, the regimental standard-bearer.

That evening the Emperor stood at the bridgehead surrounded by the Old Guard and watched the crossing of the army. He himself placed a Guard battery to cover the retreat of Victor's corps which was putting up an heroic defense against Wittgenstein.

Victor's 9th Corps crossed the following night, under fire from the Russian guns which shook the bridges that Eblé's pontooneers and the marines of Bouvier-Destouches, etc. struggled to support until the last troops had crossed. Then they burned them. Most of the 10,000 stragglers left behind were taken prisoner.

'It has been said that the bridges presented a hideous spectacle', Berthezène wrote in his reminiscences, 'due to the crowding and confusion . . . In reality, the crossing of the Berezina in the face of the enemy was a very large military undertaking that reflects further glory on the army and its chief.'

Naturally there were heavy losses. On 29 November the Old Guard mustered barely 2,000 men, and the Young Guard 800. Hunger and cold had taken a heavier toll than the enemy. Claparède and numerous officers of the Young Guard, fusiliers, and horse Guard were wounded. The 2nd Lancers lost heavily. Lt. Colonel van Hasselt and two officers were mortally wounded, and Majors Verdière and de Watteville and an officer missing. Two officers of the foot artillery, a captain of the horse artillery, and four officers of the artillery and wagon trains were wounded or missing.

'If we succeed in crossing the Berezina', the Emperor had told Daru and Duroc, 'I shall be master of the situation; for the two fresh corps (Oudinot's and Victor's) and my Guard will suffice to beat the Russians.'

At dawn on the 29th the Guard began its march to Vilna over a corduroy road of pine logs laid across the marshes. From now on they would be marching towards the promised land of Vilna with its stores, and Poland. Had the Russians been in their shoes, the soldiers said, and they in the Russians', not a man would have escaped.

Lefebvre asked Roguet during the march for some more men to 'guard his *Tondu, the Corporal*'. All the remaining fusiliers volunteered. The Emperor had never known such devotion as now. Though the army had been virtually destroyed, the flag had never been dishonored. If any eagles were captured it was because there had been no one left to defend them.

The thermometer descended to —26° (—14·8°F.) and men died of cold before the fires in the Lithuanian forest. Far and wide through the night they heard drums beating the 'Refrain of the Regiments', followed by the call To Arms. Men isolated and exposed to attack by enemy cavalry pricked up their ears, took courage, and marched towards the 'cadenced rhythm' that brought them comfort and recalled them to their duty.

People have confused the servants and noncombatants marching with sacks of flour on their backs and sticks in their hands, an ever-growing band of pillagers swelled by stragglers and deserters, with the army in being. Most of these 30,000 good-fornothings were left behind at the Berezina, for they were the least deserving and were left to go last.

[1] 'Saluting' was a euphemism for 'ducking' in French soldier slang. – Ed.

It is repugnant to regular soldiers to leave the ranks. They would rather die under the eagle than live with the stragglers. Leading their shrunken but orderly units, the commanders were often invited to share grilled horse or a bowl of gruel in the bivouacs.

'All honor to the French', Caulaincourt wrote. 'Honor to the nation that bred such men! And shame on the cowards who would tarnish the glory they earned – a glory even more precious than the laurels coveted by their descendants, and that of the Europeans who were never able to beat them . . .'

The Guard lived up to its reputation by covering the retreat of the army to the bitter end, establishing outposts around the villages where they halted, and sleeping in the huts. At the cry 'To arms!' the whole Guard assembled at the rendezvous. 'It is remarkable the way they assemble so promptly without warning from the drummers', wrote an officer of the foot chasseurs.

'This corps set an admirable example with its vigor and its martial air', wrote Caulincourt. 'The "old moustaches" brightened up the moment the Emperor appeared . . . Each day the duty battalion was dressed with amazing care . . .'

One day an officer of the *chasseurs à cheval* whose regiment had been wiped out set off for the rear, followed by a trooper leading his horse.

'Where do you think you're going?' the Emperor asked him.

'To join Marshal Ney', he replied, referring to the commander of the rear-guard. 'I heard my old chief had no one to carry messages – that his aides were all wounded or had lost their horses.

'Good for you! You, at least, have not lost your courage.' the Emperor exclaimed.

Neither had the Guard artillery who on 4 December, the feast of their patron Saint Barbara, drained a cask of wine that Drouot had been saving for the occasion.

The following morning at the Lithuanian village of Smorgoni, before the 'palace' (an *izba*[2] on the village square) the duty battalion was already in its bivouac when the four escort squadrons drew up and the Emperor descended from his carriage.

'I am going to give you some fur-lined boots and a bearskin pelisse', he said to Captain Count Wonsowicz of the Polish lancers. 'You will leave at once with Caulaincourt for Vilna. Tell no one of your mission . . .'

At 7.30 p.m. Mortier left the 'palace' with Bessières, Ney, Duroc, and Murat, deep in conversation. Such phrases as 'Rally the army at Vilna . . . Take up winter quarters on the Niemen and beyond . . . Hold on to Kovno . . .' were overheard.

The Duke of Treviso (Mortier) said to General Delaborde: 'A most unexpected event is about to occur, but in my opinion a necessary one. Let us resign ourselves and not be discouraged.'

By lamplight the generals read the following order: 'The Emperor will leave at ten tonight . . . accompanied by 200 Guardsmen. From the relay station beyond Smorgoni to Oshmiany he will be escorted by a route regiment which will spend tonight ten miles from here. One hundred and fifty Guard horses still fit for duty will be sent to a point $2\frac{1}{2}$ miles this side of Oshmiany. The staff of the route regiment and a squadron

[2] Cottage.

of lancers of the Guard will form relays between Smorgoni and Oshmiany. The King of Naples will take command of the army.'

Delaborde and Roguet agreed with the Marshal that the Emperor's course was proper. 'As Emperor in Paris he will be ten times as valuable as marching with an army in disorder. His job here is finished.'

Napoleon's anxieties, such as the Malet affair, Schwarzenberg's failure to co-operate,[3] etc., were chiefly political. In times of victory he had played the roles of ruler and commander in chief successfully; could he continue to play them in defeat? 'In the present state of chaos', he said, 'I can impose my will on Europe only from the Tuileries . . .'

8 p.m. The thermometer in Larrey's buttonhole registered −30° (−22°F.) Thirty chasseurs, hand-picked by Lefebvre-Desnoëttes, were already in the saddle, wearing their dark green capes, their colpacks rimed with frost and their moustaches caked with ice. The duty battalion was under arms. As four scouts detached from the picket rode up, one of their horses fell and the rider rolled on the ground. Alas, he was not the last!

Captain Wonsowicz entered a sleigh drawn by six horses and flanked by the grooms Fagald and Amodru. Behind was the Emperor, accompanied by Caulaincourt, in his sleeping carriage with Roustam on the box, followed by the escort. Duroc and Lobau (Mouton) followed in a second carriage, and Lefebvre-Desnoëttes, the secretary Baron Fain, and the valets in a third.

The drummer beat a funereal '*Aux Champs!*' and the Emperor was gone . . .

Oshmiany, Midnight. In an inhuman frost of −30° the escort could not keep its footing. There were only fifteen chasseurs left, all at the end of their tether. However, Colonel Stokowski, Major Fredro, and 100 Polish lancers of the Guard, newly arrived from the Koenigsberg depot, were already in the saddle.

Seslavin's Cossacks had raided the village and the garrison had been called to arms. Arriving an hour before the Emperor, Captain Wonsowicz had ordered the Poles to relieve the chasseurs.

'You will surround the carriages while the relays are being changed', the Emperor ordered. 'We shall depart immediately.' Then, handing the officer a brace of pistols, he added: 'I count on you. In case of certain danger I want you to kill me rather than let me be captured.'

'Will Your Majesty permit me to translate what he has just said into Polish?'

'Yes, tell them what I said.'

'We shall all be hacked to pieces rather than permit anyone to approach you!' the lancers cried.

Alas, after eight miles there were only 50 troopers left; and at the relay station of Rovnopol but 36. The Guard had gone the limit of its endurance. Neapolitan horsemen escorted the procession next day. After that the Emperor's three carriages were on their own on the icy road, at the mercy of a handful of Cossacks. But Napoleon's star was still in the ascendant.

[3] Commanding the 'allied' Austrian corps, Schwarzenberg eventually signed an armistice with the Russians. − Ed.

At Château-Thierry he changed into grenadier uniform and transferred to a cumbersome post-chaise with enormous wheels and traces in which he flew on at breakneck speed.

On 18 December he passed under the Arc de Triomphe. The clock on the Tuileries struck a quarter to midnight as the grenadier sentry halted the carriage at the gate of the Carrousel.

'No one may pass.' (The countersign would not open this gate to any but court carriages.)

Amodru burst out: 'But it's the Emperor!'

'You're joking! Only yesterday I read in the *Monitor* that he was in Smolensk.'

The officer of the guard came up to investigate. Suddenly he bowed, surprised and moved.

CHAPTER 9

The Remnants

THAT night the Imperial Guard was at Insterburg in East Prussia, fifty miles from Koenigsberg. Except for the Emperor's remaining carriages, escorted by dragoons, the men had had nothing to guard since Smorgoni. Their reason for living had disappeared at the depth of their misery. From now on for whom would they fight and suffer? What was the use of going on?

Because they were the Guard. The *Tondu* had told them: 'I leave you to go and get 300,000 soldiers, since for the first time one campaign did not finish the war . . .'

They froze on the march, their vitals gnawed with hunger. On 3 December the Emperor had said: 'Only my Old Guard has kept together, but hunger is beating it, too.'

Lieutenant Charles Faré of the foot grenadiers, Curial's aide, had not lost confidence. He wrote his mother that his eyes were burned and that he had lost everything, but his courage and gaiety had not left him. 'Whatever they say, life is a blessing', he wrote, 'and we have learned through resignation and hope – if not how to be happy – at least how to eat horse meat with relish.'

How many of the Guard were in Koenigsberg on Christmas Day, 1812?

Mortier's corps mustered 278 officers and 795 men including the Hessians and the Neuchâtel battalion. Adjutant Major Gérodias counted 4 or 5 officers and 35–40 marines of the Guard. Bessières commanded 800 more or less frozen cavalry. General Colbert still had 19 officers, 200 Dutch light horse, and 150 Poles. Curial and Michel between them mustered 159 officers and 1,312 Grumblers, as follows:

REGIMENT	OFFICERS	MEN
1st Chasseurs	28	435
2nd „	30	257
1st Grenadiers	38	369
2nd „	39	234
3rd „	24	17

The artillery still had 200 gunners, 130 train soldiers, 9 guns, and 5 caissons.

The Duke of Danzig wrote the Chief of Staff on 21 December that 500 of the above were 'more or less in fighting condition', but that all the rest were 'frozen and gangrenous'; that he had 'sent off that day 200 of the sickest in a sleigh to Danzig where they could have their frozen fingers and toes amputated as soon as possible'.

The old Marshal had finally lost his spirit. In the crowded town of Oshmiany near Vilna, with his white beard and his baton in his hand, he had been magnificent in his courage and energy, crying 'To arms!' to his Grumblers and leading them to the ramparts to repel the Cossacks. But then his son was killed.

Beaten down, plunged into a sort of torpor, he emerged thereafter only to harangue his soldiers: 'Look at this Old Guard that was once the terror of Europe . . . See what a condition it is in!. . . You think you will see France again. . . Not one of you ever will!'

The first time, a chasseur muttered between his teeth: 'Shut up, you old fool! If we must die, we will die.' After that they let him talk. Finally he went to ask Murat for permission to return to France.

The elite corps had been destroyed and its survivors were in a sorry state. Bessières was 'ill from the cold', drained of every physical and intellectual resource. Rapp's face was frozen. After crossing the Berezina Durosnel, dazed and delirious, had ridden to Vilna in a small sleigh drawn by his gendarmes. Their major, Janin, was severely wounded. Their adjutant major died the day after Christmas at Koenigsberg, and their standard-bearer on New Year's Day.

General Saint-Sulpice was worn out and asked to be retired. Walther requested a leave he would never get. Lariboisière died of exhaustion on 21 December, and the famous Eblé of the Berezina followed him to the grave on the 31st.

General Delaborde, ill and exhausted by the retreat, had nothing left but his 'indomitable courage'. He had made some stages of the journey on horseback and some in his heavy traveling coach until his horses gave out. At Smorgoni he had bought a sleigh in which his aide-de-camp Burgoing found him each evening at the bivouac or relay station. His division was reduced to 155 officers and 323 men, including 71 officers and 272 men of the Hessian battalion who had saved their artillery. The 6th Voltigeurs had only 12 officers and 8 men 'present under arms'.

At forty-two, Old Man Roguet was a tough soldier and a natural leader. Neither the rigors of climate nor the misfortunes of war had shaken his confidence in the 'rising again of the good star'. Wearing regulation uniform with a white stock and rags for boots, he had marched on foot at the head of his orderly division, eating gruel and drinking melted snow, sleeping in camp, happy when he had a fire.

His servants all froze to death, and his horses followed him, finding forage for themselves. A few survivors had arrived in East Prussia covered with long hair, like wool. His aides, Albert and others, less war-wise than he, had had their faces, hands, or feet frozen. Roguet himself never even had a cold in the head, though he had stood watch in the bivouacs, and each dawn had forced his benumbed men to their feet. He picked up the bodies of the unfortunate men who had died of hunger and saw that food was prepared each evening for the sick.

He had lost everything he possessed and hadn't a sou. A *cantinière* gave him 1,000 francs and Prince Eugène gave him a pelisse. Two hundred and eighty-eight fusiliers, in good order and disciplined, remained with him, led by 57 officers including Suisse Vionnet, and Vrigny (who died of exhaustion at Elbing in January 1813). A major wounded at Krasny had died on 8 December.

Each evening Roguet had posted sentries around the bivouacs. When the troops stayed in a village he organized a 'small parade' at guard mount. He claimed nothing for the losses he had suffered because the disaster was even more terrible 'for France, the army, and the Empire'.

Such were the Guard officers who had come, full of illusions, from nothing. They were trained by strict chiefs, dedicated to the highest traditions, who led them through the severest trials which constitute the best school for a soldier.

As for the Old Guard, though some companies had only 15 men left, 'no man had quit the ranks unless sick, frozen, or killed'. Not one had been demoralized or had deserted. At each loss the rest had closed ranks. It was the Grumblers who had thrown back the Cossacks at Vilna. In the Ponary hills they were forced to abandon the 'treasury'[1] and leave the *napoléons* scattered in the snow. Finally, on the march to Kovno, they had been the only force able to protect the crossing of the Niemen. The marshals and the 800 horse had marched with them.

In Prussia they could breathe freely and eat once more. Some died there, like the eagle-bearer of the foot chasseurs. Berthier called for a report which was hard to procure. General Exelmans was wounded; three lieutenants of the horse grenadiers and one of the chasseurs had been mortally wounded at Kovno and Vilna. Two majors, including de Watteville, and three officers of the 2nd Light-Horse were killed, wounded, or missing, and nine officers of the artillery had been left at Ponary and Kovno. The wagon train had been completely wiped out.

'Many lacked the energy and moral courage that extricate men from the worst difficulties', General Sorbier wrote Captain Evain's brother. 'Your brother, though wounded, withstood a cold of −25° which strewed the roads of Russia with our fingers and toes.'

With Generals Sorbier, Desvaux, and Marin, and with de Lemud, Mancel, Lallemand, Boulart, Pion, a dozen horse artillery officers, and 136 foot gunners, cadres were organized. 'But we also need men who have not been through the ordeal of this campaign', Berthier wrote.

On 10 December General Rottembourg, adjutant general of the Guard, had arrived at Stettin from Spain with two route battalions of the Guard from the 2nd Voltigeurs and 2nd *Tirailleurs* numbering 37 officers and 1,318 men under Lt. Colonels Deshayes and Flamand. These units were brand new and had a band.

Murat had 45,000 men, not counting the Austrians. These were more than he needed to face the Russians who reached the Vistula utterly exhausted. The Poles were being reorganized at Warsaw. If the Prussians and Austrians remained faithful, the King of Naples (Murat) would have two armies totaling 85,000 men. But perseverance, self-sacrifice, and strength of character were required to handle them. Had Murat these qualities? The Army and Guard did not think so. They were right.

On 1 January the Prussians defected and Schwarzenberg prepared to recross the Vistula. Murat thought all was lost. But the administration remained serene.

At Elbing on 8 Januray 1813 the lieutenant generals of the Guard received an astonishing communication from the Secretary of State complaining that since 5 January,

[1] This contained 6,000,000 francs and all the loot from the Kremlin. – Ed.

PLATE 105

PLATE 106

a) Platov
(*Engr. Godby after Orlowski*)

b) Oudinot
(*Engr. Forestier*)

c) Miloradovitch
(*After contemp. miniature*)

d) Lauriston
(*Col. engraving by Meyer*)

e) Victor
(*Lith. Delpech*)

PLATE 107

The Guard at the Berezina
(From an original drawing by Peter Hess)

PLATE 108

PLATE 109

Crossing the Berezina: the second day
(From a colored lithograph by Victor Adam)

PLATE 110

Scenes of the retreat from Russia: 2 December (below) and 1 January (above)
(*From original watercolors in the field sketchbook of Faber du Faur*)

'disbursements had been made for almost twice as many men as the Guard's present effectives . . .' Such a document, when men and horses were dying of hunger, left the commanders quite stunned. The 'overpayment' to the survivors of this terrible campaign seemed to dominate the government's thinking, when in fact it was faced with a crucial situation.

For lack of any plan since Vilna the army was in great disorder. Murat decided to move it beyond the Oder and set up headquarters at Posen, making that city a rallying point for the Guard.

The Duke of Treviso (Mortier) formed a detachment with the Young Guard, and 300 horse assembled at Koenigsberg from the route regiments of the Old Guard and light-horse. With this unit he left Elbing on 13 January. The column was harried by Cossacks en route. On 20 January near Kamin the infantry repulsed a sharp attack.

At last the Guardsmen reached Posen where they found the cavalry depots formed at Bromberg on 14 January by the Duke of Istria (Bessières), 100 men of the 3rd Lancers, the horses of the two Lithuanian regiments, the Italian Guard, General Roguet, and the Old Guard. These were later joined by the *Vélites* and Guards of Honor of Turin and Florence who arrived from Warsaw with 832 infantry and 130 horse in good condition. Finally, the two fresh Young Guard battalions arrived from Stettin and also the Hessians.

On 16 January a new order was published in one sentence: 'His Majesty the King of Naples being ill, His Imperial Highness the Viceroy has taken provisional command of the army in the Emperor's absence.

The Prince of Neuchâtel, Chief of Staff,
(signed) Alexander'

So Murat had deserted!

Having received the Emperor's instructions, Prince Eugène began the large task of reorganizing the army on 24 January. He formed an Observation Corps of the Elbe with seven divisions, including a Guard Division under Roguet who kept a company cadre for each 100 men and sent the surplus cadres to Mainz.

At noon on 26 January the Viceroy reviewed the Guard in the great square at Posen. It needed a complete overhaul. Its spirit and discipline must be restored. The pay and correspondence with the depots must be resumed and the fantastic dress abolished.

Daily parades 'in the best uniforms available' were ordered at noon on the theater square. From now on the sentinels would strictly observe the passwords and the officers make their rounds. Men would march in an orderly manner to draw their rations. 'All soldiers who forget the rules concerning looting . . . will be arrested and turned over to the War Council to be shot.'

A Guard hospital was opened in the seminary. The men must be on the alert. Every day a detail of 200 men with 2 guns was posted at the outskirts of Posen, ready for action in case of need.

General Roguet took his men in hand again and organized his little division. He sent 725 officers and NCO's of the Old and Young Guard to Mainz with Lt. Colonel Flamand, keeping Lt. Colonel Deshayes with him. The Emperor ordered Friant,

Curial, Saint-Sulpice, Walther, and the marshals to Paris where Mortier arrived on 1 February.

The day the sick and lame left for Frankfurt the Guard division prepared to leave Posen and retire to the Elbe. It was composed as follows:

1ST DIVISION – GENERAL ROGUET

Young Guard	—2nd Voltigeurs	916
	2nd *Tirailleurs*	884
	Hessian battalions	208
Middle Guard	—Fusilier-chasseurs	126
	Fusilier-grenadiers	118
	Vélites of Florence	342
	„ „ Turin	461
Old Guard	—Chasseurs	415
	Grenadiers	408
	Royal Guard of Italy	279
	Total	4,157

CAVALRY OF THE GUARD – LT. COLONEL LION

1st Lancers	125
2nd „	31
Chasseurs	260
Dragoons	120
Grenadiers	127
Guards of Honor (Turin)	73
„ „ „ (Florence)	85
Total	821 men
	(773 horses)

265 gunners and train soldiers with 9 guns and 26 sappers should be added to the total. By now the Emperor had already kept the promise he made at Smorgoni: 'I am leaving you to go and get 300,000 soldiers'.

BOOK VI

THE GUARD TAKES CHARGE

CHAPTER 1

Improvisation

ON his return to the Tuileries Napoleon set to work rebuilding the armed forces of the Empire.

He planned to raise a new Grand Army over and above the survivors of the Russian campaign now in Germany with the Viceroy. He had some illusions on the subject, for he did not yet realize that the peoples of Europe – who only understood later what he had done for them – were about to rise against him.

The Guard as such no longer existed. But there were still the Paris depots; the Veterans and four battalions of *pupilles* in Versailles, and four more in coastal garrisons; four instruction battalions at Fontainebleau; the artillery at La Fère; the units in Germany under Roguet and Lion; depots of artillery and cavalry and reserves of matériel at Mainz and elsewhere. In Spain there were the 3rd Voltigeurs and 3rd *Tirailleurs*, and elements of the 1st; the national guard regiment, some cavalry, and ten guns. The Guard tradition lived on in the generals and cadres. Whether this would be sufficiently strong to inspire a whole new phalanx was the Emperor's principal anxiety.

His next concern was resources, for he needed men, horses, clothing, and equipment. About 8,000 conscripts of the class of 1813, called up last September and barely trained and equipped, were in the Guard depots. After 9 February the levy of 100,000 conscripts of 1809–12 would furnish 10,000 men to the Young Guard, and 20,000 of the Class of 1814 would report by 1 April. Several thousand from the national guard cohorts would provide men with some training and experience for the army at the beginning of February; and on 3 April a special levy of 80,000 from the same source would yield 24,000 men for the Young Guard.

On 5 January an extra remount of 3,000 horses was ordered for the Guard to supplement 1,500 furnished by the war ministry. Six hundred were assigned to each cavalry regiment and 300 to the gendarmes and horse artillery. (The black horses were reserved for the grenadiers and gendarmes!) The rest were drawn from a large army purchase of 24 December 1812.

The Emperor ordered the infantry wagons replaced by pack animals and drastically reduced the number of mounts allowed generals and other officers. There were still wagons, caissons, and gun carriages in France and Germany.

On 6 January the Emperor asked the Minister to draft a decree creating a 'bodyguard of six squadrons . . . to guard the persons of the Emperor and the King of Rome'. The Malet plot had disturbed Napoleon. He was now bereft of his Old Guard whose survivors had lost their morale, according to Bessières. Meanwhile, the Grand Marshal of the Palace Duroc was put in charge of reorganizing the Imperial Guard. The Duke of Treviso (Mortier) commanded the infantry and General Walther the cavalry.

Duroc, Duke of Friuli, that imperturbable gunner 'with lively secret passions', knew the Guard well. A faithful friend of the Emperor's since the Italian campaigns, he not only administered the Emperor's household, being omniscient and omnipresent, but had been entrusted with many special missions by Napoleon. Duroc set to work at once and nothing more was heard of the new bodyguard for the time being.

First, since the men must eat, the commissaries bought 26,000 quintals[1] of wheat to feed the Guard. Where would they live? How many men would the Guard barracks accommodate? General Dériot was asked to furnish this information.

His report listed available quarters in and around Paris[2] for 18,000 men and 7,000 horses. The Emperor judged these altogether inadequate, for he had large projects in mind for the Guard.

During the current political upheaval in Germany Prussia's defection might not be the only one. The duplicity of the Austrian cabinet, the poor quality of some European contingents in the last campaign, and the youth and weakness of the new army he must raise in haste led the Emperor to enlarge his Guard whose morale and performance had been maintained throughout the retreat from Moscow.

The Guard could no longer be considered merely the reserve of a European army of dwindling strength and vacillating loyalty, for after Smolensk – and especially Krasny – the Guard had become its chief component. Had it been larger the disaster might have been averted. Consequently, in the crucial campaign about to begin, it must be large and solidly framed to support the green troops of the army and bring them victory; or, in case of defeat, to guard their retreat.

Between the beginning of January and the end of February the Emperor ordered a number of regiments raised at the depots of France and Mainz; and units at way stations like Fulda, Gotha, etc. which could be brought up in a hurry in case of need.

This program demanded enormous labor and dispatch from the men responsible for its execution. For the hundredth time the Emperor insisted that he would accept no ifs, buts, or becauses. Why should he? With commanders like Friant, Michel, Curial, Bessières, Walther, Lefebvre-Desnoëttes, Colbert, Sorbier, and Drouot miracles could be performed. And the Guard was still the Guard.

Were its members skeptical? Ask Colonel Griois, who had commanded Latour-Maubourg's horse batteries in Russia, what he thought of his appointment as lieutenant colonel of the Old Guard foot artillery on 24 January. 'Many ambitious men have aspired to this post', he wrote in his memoirs.

'It is better to be a private in the Guard than a sergeant in the Line', wrote Cajot, a conscript in the Guard artillery.

[1] 1,300 tons. – Ed.
[2] In Paris, Courbevoie, Rueil, Sèvres, Vincennes, Saint-Denis, Versailles, Chantilly, Beauvais, Fontainebleau, Melun, Rambouillet, Compiègne, and La Fère.

On 19 March the Emperor wrote: 'An officer or NCO may not be admitted into the Old Guard until he has served twelve years and fought in several campaigns; a soldier must have served ten years and fought in several campaigns; but eight years' service is sufficient to enter the 2nd Chasseurs and 2nd Grenadiers. If nominations contrary to this rule are made they shall be presented for confirmation to the Emperor before taking effect.'

Whatever his needs, Napoleon recruited the old regiments with great care. He often demanded the impossible and imagined work in progress that had not even begun. He took no account of time, and seemed ignorant of the fact that it took a courier six days to travel from Paris to Posen. However, while his imagination worked overtime, he was not naïf. Exceptional circumstances demand extraordinary activity as well as optimism and the will to succeed.

He held reviews at the Trianon and in Paris, made appointments, awarded stars of the Legion of Honor to Dériot, Lepic, Digeon, Kirgener and others, distributed 20,000 francs to Pac, Dumoustier, Mouton-Duvernet, etc, and aroused confidence in his officers and enthusiasm in his men by speeches ending: 'I count on you'.

And with reason. When he promoted Captain Deblais, who had commanded a grenadier battalion in Russia and was now serving with Roguet, a major in the 1st *Tirailleurs* the latter wrote: 'I shall do my utmost to please my superiors and be just and humane to my subordinates. I shall try to earn the esteem and friendship of the former and win the affection, respect, and obedience of the latter.' This was the magnificent program of the Old Guard veterans.

On the evening of 2 March, after visiting the terrace of Chaillot where he planned to build a palace for the King of Rome, the Emperor received the generals and officers of the Guard at the Tuileries. They came (some on crutches, others with their arms in slings) to celebrate the Mardi Gras, for it was up to these men to reassure the populace and revive the courage of those who mourned loved ones; to show by their smiling faces and confident air that the Russian campaign had been only an episode in a war they would ultimately win because they could not help winning. This was still the Guard.

France's morale was intact. The losses and the Malet plot did not dampen the spirits of the Carnival nor dim the colors of the flower market in the Quai de l'Horloge. The country was sure its sovereign would triumph over disaster and win final victory. Filled with patriotic enthusiasm, the cities of the Empire, the departments, the Senate, the Council of State, and even the bishops contributed money, bought horses, and raised cavalry troops. The manufacturers donated cloth; the princes of the Confederation of the Rhine, 2,000 horses.

The rebuilding of the Guard proceeded in two phases. Up to the middle of February, the Emperor raised what he needed most, for time was pressing: new companies, battalions, squadrons of every branch that could be combined into regiments and, eventually, divisions. He must work fast but not hurriedly. In his decrees one can trace his plan to utilize the resources of the depots to complete the first phase, and then proceed to the second.

The Emperor drew the indispensable cadres needed for the first phase from the armies of Germany, Spain, and Italy. He ordered the Viceroy to reserve a company staff for every 100 men, a battalion or squadron staff for every 500, and to send him the remaining cadres with all possible speed. 'Send as many for the Young Guard as you can . . . with those of the 3rd Grenadiers to Paris; and to Mainz, the elite gendarmes, horse grenadiers, dragoons, chasseurs, dismounted train soldiers, and their cadres. They will find the Duke of Istria (Bessières) there with horses, uniforms, and equipment.'

He repeated these orders to Berthier. 'Send the artillery depot at Mainz to La Fère with cadres, gunners, and train soldiers.'

On 6 January he created two auxiliary or '*bis*' battalions of grenadiers and chasseurs with men from the depots, and ordered the 250 seasoned battalions of the Army of Spain to send him 3,000 veterans, half with eight years' service and half with four. Five battalions serving aboard ships would furnish six veterans per company, and the rest of the army yield 2,000. These detachments, ordered to 'proceed by triple marches to their destination', were combined to form the infantry of the Old Guard.

Simultaneously, two auxiliary fusilier battalions were formed at Panthémont from the depots and, on the 10th and 17th, the 3rd–6th *bis* Voltigeurs and *Tirailleurs*.[3]

'This is a fine regiment', wrote Voltigeur Ghys of the new 6th *bis* Regiment, stationed at the École Militaire. 'I am content with my lot. We have good beds but we never see a fire. We have to buy wood out of our pocket money as we are not issued any.'

The flankers' depot was moved hurriedly to the Saint-Denis barracks, 'before the Minister could get his hands on it', and a new battalion formed.

Caffarelli, commanding the Northern Army in Spain, was ordered to send by post the 3rd *Tirailleurs* and 3rd Voltigeurs and the cadres of the national guard regiment (whose men were turned over to the 1st Voltigeurs and 1st *Tirailleurs* in Germany).

On 17 January the Emperor ordered all *pupilles* seventeen and over at Ostende and Boulogne sent to Lille to be incorporated into the Young Guard. Armed with dragoon muskets, they were ready to march on 15 February.

The reorganization of the cavalry was more difficult. Apart from the Italian guards of honor, a few lancers of Berg, and 100 dragoons of the Italian Guard serving with Prince Eugène, there were only about 500 troopers of each branch serving under Lieutenant Colonel Lion.

All available cadres were sent by post to Paris or to depots at Gotha and Fulda. General Walther took 1,000 dismounted officers and men to Fulda where he was ordered to form four squadrons with horses donated by the Rhine princes, and clothing, harness, and arms sent from France and Mainz.

For political reasons the troops furnished by the towns and departments near Paris were assigned to the grenadiers, chasseurs, dragoons, and 2nd Light-Horse-Lancers, forming 'Young Guard squadrons' whose members were designated 'second troopers' and drew Line pay. Their initial allotments were modest and they wore no aiguillette.

[3] These were in being barely a month. – Ed.

General Lefebvre Desnoëttes was told to sort out the newcomers and hold on to the men of 'good physique and conduct', exchanging the rest for good specimens in the Line.

'I have ordered the thirty regiments in Spain to furnish 20 men each', the Emperor wrote Duroc on 6 January, 'and have called up another 200 for the *gendarmes d'élite.* I believe the Mameluks can be recruited from their children at Melun and Marseilles. As for horses, we are still short a thousand. You must see the Minister . . . and choose the best from the departmental requisition.'

On 2 January the Emperor reorganized the Guard artillery whose strength would be a vital factor in the coming battles. He ordered two horse and four foot batteries formed in the Old Guard, serving 44 guns, with a double ammunition provision. For these, 1,500 horses and harnesses must be purchased, and gunners furnished by the horse artillery depots, marine artillery, and Army of Spain. Meanwhile, five train companies were formed from the Grand Army, and the 7th Train Battalion attached to the Guard.

This was a beginning.

On 24 January the Emperor ordered a number of new batteries formed for the Young Guard. The first four were manned by gunners from the cohorts of the national guard. The Old Guard foot companies were eventually increased to six. Pontooneers were recruited from the Line depots. The 800 conscripts assigned to the train and gunners from the cohorts were designated '2nd gunners' and received the pay of the Line.

'They have put all the farmers in Paris into the train of artillery', wrote Conscript Cajot on 20 January. 'We are much better off than the *tirailleurs.* We have only two horses to groom, we are better dressed and better paid, we draw 6 sous a day and 15 on the march, and we belong to the Old Guard. They take us for gunners!'

The company of sappers was raised from marine artificers and depots of the sappers and miners battalions. By 8 March the Emperor would have 120 '2nd sappers' from the conscripts of 1809–1812, paid as the Line and wearing shakos.

On 26 January the wagon train battalion was reorganized in Paris and filled up with conscripts. The artisan companies were reorganized at Vincennes under Captain Gubert.

'We harrived [sic] 10 April at Mainz', wrote Guermont of the second artisan company of the Guard to his parents. 'The next day they issued us carbines and drilled us. The Emperor arrived today (the 16th). I won't be sorry to leave for Frankfurt, for there you eat in the peasants' houses. We left Monday the 12th of this month at 8 to excort [sic] the flour boats, and came back yesterday . . .'

Alas, the good Guermont would never again see his native village, for he disappeared in the debacle of August 1813.

Nicolas Decresson, a soldier in the wagon train of the Guard, could not read or write; however, he kept his family informed through an obliging comrade. Reaching Courbevoie on 13 March, he was sent to the train depot at Vincennes where he promised 'always to do his duty like a good soldier', and announced with joy that white bread cost only 6 sous a pound, meat 10 sous, and wine 6 sous a bottle.

Organizing these units required a vast amount of effort. The generals and most of the lieutenant colonels were old-timers, used to throwing themselves wholeheartedly into their work. Their willingness and zeal were exemplary; but they often lacked the means to accomplish their ends.

'Several thousand men must be clothed immediately and provided with 3,000 horses', wrote a quartermaster, 'but we cannot make the necessary purchases. We have only 1,250,000 francs which will not even buy the horses!'

To reorganize the work and transport troops of the Guard alone cost two and a half million francs – most of which went to buy matériel. The Emperor began to finance the army out of his own pocket to relieve the war budget. Up to 15 April 1813 he advanced it seven million francs.

CHAPTER 2

The New Guard

STUDYING the old invoices, one finds the furnishings delivered at the beginning of 1813 – the beige cloth for the men's overcoats, the 'fur bonnets for the sappers of the Young Guard', the trumpet banners, etc. – ordered with the same attention to detail as before. The administrative councils seemed to attach the same importance to the frills as to the necessities, regardless of time or money.

It was the same throughout the Guard. What would happen if the cavalry had no aiguillettes and the grenadiers no bonnet cords? The Emperor's prestige, as well as the corps', depended on these items. This vanity, which is a component of discipline, indicated that the Guard had not lost its traditional spirit at the beginning of 1813. The morale that the Duke of Istria (Bessières) had found low after Smorgoni had risen, thanks to General Roguet and the Emperor.

Despite the difficulties involved in providing beds, light, medical care, clothing, and instruction for masses of conscripts, the life of the Guard went on. It performed the same duties as before, guarding the Tuileries, the Louvre, and the Elysée-Napoléon. The sentries at the barracks and quarters, the Guard hospital, and Vincennes were furnished by the Young Guard who also manned the posts at Meudon, the two Trianons, Malmaison, and the residences of Madame Mère in the Rue Saint-Dominique, Queen Hortense in the Rue Lafitte, and Princess Borghese in the Rue de la Chaise.

But time pressed. The Fatherland was in danger. The Russians were in Germany. Warsaw had fallen. Would Austria remain loyal? Would the covering forces organized by the Viceroy on the Oder, and later on the Elbe, be sufficient to contain the enemy while the Grand Army was reorganized and the Guard reborn?

'It (the Guard) is being reorganized in great strength', the Emperor wrote the Viceroy on 22 January. 'I need officers and cadres to receive the recruits arriving from all directions. I already have a division of 10,000 men . . .'

Was this an illusion or was it a miracle?

It was a miracle.

On 15 February at La Fère General Drouot inspected its artillery, consisting of four foot companies with 32 guns, a double ammunition supply, and 18 caissons.

On the same day the Emperor reviewed the Young Guard division, commanded by General Barrois who had been in Spain since 1808. The first brigade, containing two battalions of fusiliers and the 2nd Voltigeurs and 2nd *Tirailleurs*, was commanded by General Rottembourg; the second, composed of the 6th Voltigeurs and 6th *Tirailleurs* and two battalions of *pupilles*, by General Tindal, the new adjutant general. The division was assigned a company of sappers, Grivel's marines, a commissary with two assistants, a wagon train company with 6 field hospitals, bakers to prepare 24,000 bread rations a day, and a squad of masons to build ovens.

Naturally this 1st Young Guard Division was not impeccable; however, it mustered 12,000 men with sound cadres. It left for Mainz on 15 February to be organized and trained.

General Barrois took with him five squadrons of assorted horse Guards under Lt. Colonel Leclerc. Each trooper led an extra horse, 'harnessed and equipped', for the dismounted troopers at Fulda. Two horse batteries with 12 guns from La Fère joined the division in Germany.

The Emperor was satisfied that his formula was working. That night he signed a decree organizing the infantry of the Guard for 1813 as follows:

GRENADIERS: 1st and 2nd Grenadiers; Company of Veterans; fusilier-grenadiers; 1st–7th *Tirailleur*-Grenadiers; instruction battalion at Fontainebleau (four companies of 200 men each).

CHASSEURS: 1st and 2nd Chasseurs; fusilier-chasseurs; 1st–7th Voltigeurs; flankers; four battalions of *pupilles*.

There was a depot for the grenadiers, one for the fusiliers, and two for the *tirailleur*-grenadiers under Lt. Colonel Robert; and the same for the chasseurs. Each depot company numbered 300 men with double cadres.

Roguet's grenadier and chasseur battalions were filled up with reinforcements from France. These were designated the 'first battalions of the 1st Regiments' and granted eagles by the Emperor. The second battalions were formed in Paris.

The 2nd Grenadiers and 2nd Chasseurs were formed at Fulda and assigned to the Middle Guard. Only their officers and NCO's belonged to the Old Guard. Veterans of the Russian campaign, including fusiliers with three years' service, were assigned to the first battalions of these regiments; veterans from the Line, to the second battalions. Since the Guard always marched in reverse order, the first battalion of the 1st Grenadiers represented the ultimate reserve. The 3rd Grenadiers was disbanded and its men turned into the 2nd.

The *bis* battalions raised in January were abolished, those of the fusiliers becoming the first battalions of the fusilier regiments. The two combat battalions of *pupilles* became the 7th *Tirailleurs* under Lt. Colonel Pailhès who had managed to escape from Krasny; the national guard regiment became the 7th Voltigeurs under Couloumy.

The flanker-chasseurs, raised from the second flanker battalion and conscripts from the forestry service, was commanded by Lt. Colonel Pompéjac. A regiment of flanker-grenadiers, which wore the same uniform, was raised on 25 March.

The men returning from Spain thought they were going to Russia. 'I would like to go to Russia', wrote a corporal of the 3rd Voltigeurs, 'because that would be my last campaign.'

'We leave on 24 March to dance with the Russians', wrote another.

'I should like to have some butter on my bread', wrote Tirailleur Colette the day after he reached Versailles, 'but I must eat it dry . . . We have no coffee, but the wine makes up for it.'

A number of majors of the Guard, including Jouan, Schramm, Castanié, Darriule, Vionnet, and Trappier, were given command of the Young Guard regiments. Colonel Poret de Morvan commanded the 3rd *Tirailleurs* and Colonels Rousseau and Flamand the two fusilier regiments. Meanwhile, Deshayes, Roguet's only surviving lieutenant colonel, took command of the 2nd Chasseurs and Baron Christiani, of the 2nd Grenadiers.

Despite the wars, promotions were slow in the Old Guard. A sergeant major of the 1st Chasseurs who had served since 1792 was only now commissioned. Twenty corporals promoted to sergeant had entered the service before 1793.

The Dukes of Friuli and Treviso (Duroc and Mortier) were in charge of training the new Guard. Mortier arrived in Frankfurt on 14 February and took charge of the recruits, prescribing each detail of their drill and maneuvering them by battalions and regiments.

'The corps commanders shall drill the battalions in rapid deployment into double columns under cover of platoon fire', the Emperor ordered, 'as well as in forming squares, columns, and lines of battle. The men must be drilled in one hundred yard charges, the first ranks with bayonets lowered and drums beating.'

With the men from Spain and the two conscriptions, the Emperor found himself with a surplus of 6,000 with which he raised the 8th Voltigeurs and 8th *Tirailleurs* under Lt. Colonels Secrétan and Lepaige-Dorsenne. Before long the levies from the cohorts and the Classes of 1809–12 enabled him to increase the voltigeur regiments from eight to thirteen; and, after forming the 9th *Tirailleurs* under Lt. Colonel Bardin from *pupilles* at Versailles, to organize the 10th–13th *Tirailleurs*.

The new regiments, under Old Guard commanders like Martenot, Vézu, Laurède, Suisse, etc, were formed very rapidly. For example, the flanker-grenadiers were created by decree of 25 March, their cadres were appointed on 8 April, and part of their clothing and equipment was delivered on the 19th.

The reorganization of the cavalry was more difficult and took more time. Each regiment was expanded to a brigade containing one Old and one Young Guard regiment.

Lefebvre-Desnoëttes complained that he had no funds to buy horses for his chasseurs who were gradually increased to 2,411 officers and men, including the five Young Guard squadrons. General Baron Guyot was vice-commander, assisted by Colonels Meuziau and Lion and a number of old-timers like Major Cayre and Captain Barbanègre. The squadron of Mameluks under Kirmann was reinforced with Frenchmen. Though its troopers wore oriental dress, half of them spoke with a Parisian accent and were designated '2nd Mameluks'.

The 2nd Light-horse-Lancers numbered the same as the chasseurs and also included five Young Guard squadrons, recruited in part from the municipal horse guard of Paris. General Colbert remained colonel in chief, assisted by Du Bois as commandant and several of the old majors such as van Ticken, Coti, Verdière, etc. The troopers drew 1,300 *czapkas* at 35 francs, silk lance pennants, and 2,500 pairs of Mameluk boots. The prefect of the Seine was informed that corporations wishing to sponsor the regiment must contribute 466.40 francs to clothe and equip a lancer, and 200 francs to caparison his horse.

The 1st Lancers was reorganized at Friedberg by Dautancourt at a strength of 1,500, with horses contributed by the Rhine princes plus 600 purchased in Hanover. Its personnel included veterans of Russia, 500 picked men of Dombrowski's division, the remnants of the 3rd Lancers, and the company of Lithuanian Tartars under Sultan Ulan who had succeeded Achmatowicz when the latter was killed at Vilna.

Dautancourt commanded the 'Old Guard companies' assigned exclusively to the Emperor's escort. The other nine squadrons of Krasinski's regiment were attached to Lefebvre-Desnoëttes. Among the officers were Prince Radziwill and Majors Jerzmanowski, Chlapowski, and Kozietulski.

A sixth Young Guard squadron of 300 horse was attached to both horse grenadiers and dragoons. Half the troopers were rated '2nd' grenadiers and dragoons, wore no aiguillette, and drew Line pay with a bonus for serving in Paris.

Count d'Ornano, a cousin of the Emperor, succeeded General Saint-Sulpice as commander in chief of the dragoons of the Guard. (After the Russian campaign the latter had been named governor of Fontainebleau.) Though only twenty-nine, d'Ornano had performed distinguished service in Santo-Domingo during the Consulate, had fought at Austerlitz, and in Portugal and Spain. Promoted general after Fuentes de Oñoro, he had charged at Borodino and Malo Yaroslavetz and had been left for dead at Krasny.

The redoubtable General Letort and Colonel Pinteville from the Line were co-commandants, assisted by Majors Pucheu, Clément de Ris, Pictet, and Captains Ligier, Chamorin, Despierres, de Montarby, etc. One squadron was still in Spain.

Count Walther, though not yet fully recovered from the Russian campaign, still commanded the horse grenadiers, assisted by Generals Castex and Levêque (now Count de la Ferrière) as the commandants. Castex, who had been colonel of the 20th Chasseurs under Lasalle, had been promoted general at Wagram and been wounded at the Berezina. Laferrière-Levêque had served under Marshal Brune and had been a gunner, infantryman, and hussar in turn before receiving four wounds in Spain and being promoted general in 1811. All the majors and company officers and many NCO's wore the Legion of Honor.

The elite gendarmes were filled up with 200 national gendarmes. General Durosnel had recovered his wits and resumed command of the corps, assisted by Lt. Colonel Henry and Major Jacquin, etc. A third of the 640 newly recruited '2nd gendarmes' were required to speak German.

On 29 March General Dulauloy was named commander in chief of the Guard artillery. He arrived full of ambition and zeal and poked his nose into everything, creating such confusion that the quartermasters were beside themselves.

Artillery was needed for each of the 34 infantry regiments of the Guard. The Old Guard had six horse and six foot companies, and the Young Guard 14 of each. A foot company was assigned to each infantry brigade. The four reserve batteries had 32 twelve-pounders or long range howitzers, bringing the Guard total to 196 guns.

General Desvaux, seconded by the faithful Marin, commanded the horse artillery with Majors de Lemud and Boisselier and many old-timers like Captain Mancel and Lieutenant Lyautey on the roster. Lieutenant Colonel Griois, a very learned man, commanded the Old Guard foot artillery, with Major Couin as a division[1] commander and Pion des Loches in charge of the depot. The 'New Guard' – as the rest were called – was under Lt. Colonel Henrion. Lt. Colonel Lignim commanded the train which was increased to two regiments, though the second was not completed until August.

The wagon train had to be increased, though both time and means were lacking. The Emperor called for ten train companies with wagons built in Paris and horses bought in Mainz; meanwhile, he ordered the depot drivers to Frankfurt with eighty-eight caissons for which there were no horses.

Though the Young Guard received the pay and allotments of the Line, the clothing and equipment were supposed to be of the same quality for both Old and Young Guards. On the march the soldiers' pay was increased to permit them to buy bread and meat.

With the complications involved in raising so many regiments, one might expect some administrative laxity. But though the infantry wore out enormous quantities of shoes, and the shoemakers were not paid and were threatened with bankruptcy, the commissaries refused to grant them an increase of 50 centimes a pair.

The provision caissons were often empty but the paper chests were full. The bookkeeping equipment carried on the march included innumerable forms, returns, and ledgers. In comparison, the medical equipment was comparatively simple. Larrey's ambulance kits contained the following:

72 rolled bandages	72 kgs.
Sheets	22 kgs.
Towels	12 kgs.
Gauze	12 kgs.
30 surgical splints	
12 stretchers	
6 pallets	
1 roll of tape	
1,000 pins	
50 needles	
2 skeins of thread	
60 grams of beeswax	
250 grams of string	
80 grams of sponges	

The medicine chests contained:

250 grams Goulard's Extract (subacetate of lead)

[1] A division of foot artillery served 8 guns. – Ed.

100 grams cerate of lead
600 grams spirits of camphor
50 grams camphor
125 grams laudanum
180 grams Hoffmann's Liquor (compound spirits of ether)
90 grams ammonia
125 grams sticking-plaster
500 individual plasters
15 packages emetic
2 liters brandy.

Many medical students among the conscripts were admitted to the Guard, ranking as sergeant majors and wearing blue uniforms with Medical Corps buttons. Their service began with a tour of duty at the hospital of the Gros-Caillou where they were sorely needed, for in April 1813 the number of hospital days in the Guard totaled 12,940.

In that month the Emperor advanced the Grand Marshal three million francs from his privy purse 'for the Guard', hoping 'for reimbursement when the war paid off'.

He eventually decided to raise four regiments of guards of honor, 10,000 strong, from among the nobles and bourgeois who could afford to pay substitutes to serve in their stead. As an added inducement he offered the candidates, who must provide their own uniforms and equipment, a subaltern's commission after twelve months' service. In a final paragraph he added: 'At the close of this campaign, when we proceed to form a bodyguard, part of (it) shall be chosen from the guards of honor who shall have most often distinguished themselves' (see Plate 117a).

Lt. Generals Counts de Pully, Lepic, de Ségur, and Saint-Sulpice were named colonels in chief of the new regiments on 8 April. However, they were unable to organize them until June.

PLATE III

PLATE 112

Trumpeters in parade dress, Empress' Dragoons
(*From an original watercolor by Lucien Rousselot*)
NOTE: The horsetail plumes were actually black.

PLATE 113

NCO, trumpeter, and *chasseur à cheval* of the Guard in walking-out dress
(*From an original watercolor by Lucien Rousselot*)

PLATE 114

Trumpet major and trumpeters in parade dress, 1st Polish Lancers of the Guard
(*From an original watercolor by Lucien Rousselot*)

CHAPTER 3

Lützen

THE Grand Marshal (Duroc) made preparations for the Emperor's departure. His Majesty decided to set an example by reducing the size of his retinue. This time he planned to take no pages with him and to make do with two beds, two tents, and one dinner a day consisting of 'soup, boiled and roast meat, vegetables, and no dessert'.

He first chose Fulda and Gotha as concentration points for the Guard; but on 5 March he decided to concentrate it at Frankfurt instead. The convention of Kalisch, signed on 28 February, had completed the break between France and Prussia and confirmed the latter's alliance with Russia. After the evacuation of Berlin, camps had to be maintained in Hesse, Thuringia, and Franconia for the armies being formed. The Army of the Elbe comprised five corps, Roguet's Guard division, and three cavalry corps; the Army of the Main, three corps and the rest of the Guard.

The whole Guard was assembled at Frankfurt. By 15 March Mortier's command included Leclerc's cavalry and the artillery from La Fère, all the depots at Fulda and Gotha, the cadres of the 1st Voltigeurs and 1st *Tirailleurs* from Paris, the conscripts sent to various regiments, the 1st and 2nd Lancers, and 268 vehicles of the wagon train with capacity for six days' rations.

The Emperor planned to take command of the army in April with headquarters at Frankfurt. During March and April his orders proliferated. The staff, administration, surgeons, etc, were sent to Frankfurt on 5 April. The Duke of Istria (Bessières) went to Gotha the 12th to take command of the horse Guard composed of Lion's 500 horse, Colbert's cavalry, and the cavalry, raised in Frankfurt by General Walther, attached to Lefebvre-Desnoëttes.

On 11 March the Emperor outlined to the Viceroy, Prince Eugène, a grandiose plan of operations against Berlin, Stettin, and Danzig. He originally intended to take the offensive in May and ordered a concentration of the Army of the Main. However, the Allies' march on Wittenberg and Dresden decided him to lure their commander in chief Wittgenstein towards the upper Saale as far as Bayreuth to cut him off from Prussia. Then Napoleon proposed to march on Dresden, his first objective.

On 9 April the Army of the Main was marching to Coburg, Meiningen, and Eisenach, ready to execute this maneuver. But on the 11th the Emperor learned that Wittgenstein had crossed the Elbe at Dessau with 40,000 Russians and Prussians, evidently intending to join forces with Blücher and his 40,000 Prussians behind the Mulde. A Russian corps of 30,000 was marching on Dresden, and the intelligence at Bayreuth reported that an Austrian corps was being formed against an imminent break with France.

The Emperor took command of the army on 12 April. By then Wittgenstein and Blücher had marched into Saxony with 80,000 men. Napoleon must try to reach their right flank and throw them back into Bohemia, cutting them off from the Elbe. Consequently, the Army of the Elbe of 58,000 men was concentrated on the lower Saale, and the Army of the Main of 100,000 deployed as follows: Ney's 3rd Corps was at Meiningen-Gotha; Bertrand's 4th Corps, at Coburg; Marmont's 6th Corps, at Eisenach. Behind Marmont was the Guard.

On 10 April the 1st Guard Division under Dumoustier contained three brigades totaling 9,400 men, as follows:

1ST BRIGADE (General Berthezène): 2 battalions each of grenadiers and chasseurs; 2 battalions of fusiliers: 2,200 men.

2ND BRIGADE (General Lanusse): 1st and 6th Voltigeurs (Colonels Jamin and Castanié): first battalion of the 2nd Voltigeurs; 2nd *Tirailleurs* (Colonel Flamand): 3,500 men.

3RD BRIGADE (General Tindal): 1st, 6th, and 7th *Tirailleurs* (Colonels Christiani, Trappier, and Coucourt): 3,700 men.

The artillery under General Desvaux contained five foot companies (including two of Young Guard), two horse companies, 800 train soldiers, and 52 guns. Two small companies of sappers and marines, an artisan company, and a wagon train battalion with 524 men, 800 horses, and 174 vehicles, completed the division.

The Duke of Istria (Bessières) was marching to Gotha with the lancers of Berg, 3,080 horse Guards[1] under Krasinski, Colbert, Desnoëttes, Ornano, and Walther, and 50 elite gendarmes.

Berthier left Paris on 13 April. Two days later, on Holy Thursday, the Emperor left Saint-Cloud at 4 a.m., arriving in Mainz at 8 p.m. on the 16th. There he found General Curial busy organizing Delaborde's 3rd Guard Division whose first brigade – containing the 4th, 5th, and 8th Voltigeurs – was assigned to General Gros. The 9th–12th Regiments, when ready, would be assigned to the other brigades.

Meanwhile, General Barrois' 2nd Guard Division of around 8,500 men was nearly complete. It was organized as follows:

1ST BRIGADE (General Decouz): two battalions each of grenadiers and chasseurs; flanker-chasseurs: 2,400 men.

2ND BRIGADE (General Mouton): two battalions of fusiliers; 3rd Voltigeurs: 3,300 men.

3RD BRIGADE (General Boyeldieu): 7th Voltigeurs; 3rd *Tirailleurs*: 2,800 men (his third regiment, the flanker-grenadiers, was due to leave Paris the 26th).

Barrois' artillery included two Old and two Young Guard foot batteries, a horse battery, 400 train soldiers, and 38 guns. A detachment of 220 marines and sappers, 4 wagon train companies, and a company of artisans were ready to go.

On the 22nd the Emperor reviewed this division and sent its completed units to join Dumoustier at Eisenach. By the 24th, when he left for Erfurt, Roguet's division had been detached to the Army of the Elbe under the Viceroy.

[1] These included 530 1st and 700 2nd Lancers, 750 chasseurs, and 550 each of horse grenadiers and dragoons.

The 4th Guard Division was being formed in Paris by Generals Friant, Michel, and Boyer de Rebeval with the 4th, 5th, 8th, and 10th–12th *Tirailleurs*. General Caffarelli was recalled from Spain to command the Guard units in Paris, including the infantry and cavalry depots.

The Emperor reviewed the Guard corps at Erfurt and ordered his armies to rendezvous west of the Saale. He had decided to attack the Russo-Prussian corps whose position had been revealed by spies.

The Guard arrived at Naumburg the morning of 29 April and bivouacked around the Cathedral. Sapper Winckel of the 2nd Grenadiers hauled down the Prussian flag from the steeple and raised the French colors. Around 4 p.m. the Emperor arrived on his dappled horse, escorted by chasseurs and Mameluks. He stopped at the grenadiers' bivouac and said to Captain Ranchon:

'They say the Prussians and Russians have started quarreling already . . . Well, in a few days we shall oblige them to make up!'

They heard gunfire ahead. It was Ney, fighting the '*Moscoss*', as the grenadiers called them.

That evening Grenadier Philippe Ballut of Ranchon's company consoled a seventeen-year-old who was brought in with a shoulder wound. 'I could only find a small shell splinter', he wrote in his diary. 'I took it out with the point of my knife and a little salt water, and in three days there was nothing to be seen.'

Next day an engagement was fought at Weissenfels between Souham's division of Ney's Corps and a brigade of enemy cavalry. 'These lads are heroes!' the Prince of the Moskva (Ney) exclaimed as he watched the conscripts. The troops crossed the Saale and bivouacked in fan formation east of the town, their outposts in contact with the Russian cavalry.

On 1 May the commander of the Guard, Marshal Bessières, took breakfast with his aide de Baudus at Weissenfels on the pretty salmon river known as the Saale. The weather was clear and springlike. Mirza the Mameluk was holding their horses and the Polish lancers of the escort were forming up.

The Marshal was depressed. He had no appetite. When his officers insisted, he said; 'All right, if a ball comes my way this morning I'd rather it did not find me empty.'

The Emperor had spent the night at Weissenfels in the house of a rich bourgeois named Ulrich. Drenched in a sudden shower, he had to wear borrowed garments while his valet dried his uniform. General Berthezène's Old Guard and the cavalry watched over him. As usual, the men off duty were lodged with the natives. While making coffee, Ninon, the weaver's daughter, told how she had put some over-importunate Cossacks to flight with a roasting spit.

The enemy did not budge from their positions on the Mulde and Elster between Leipzig and Pegau. They seemed to be undergoing a command crisis. The vanguards of the two French armies concentrated on the left bank crossed the Saale. Macdonald's 11th Corps and Latour-Maubourg's 1st Cavalry Corps of the Army of the Elbe

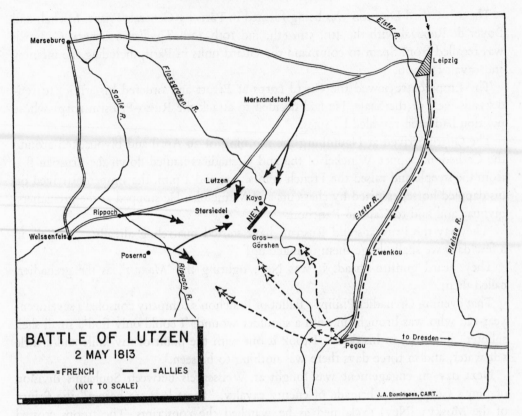

BATTLE OF LUTZEN
2 MAY 1813

―――― = FRENCH ― ― ― = ALLIES

(NOT TO SCALE)

J. A. Domingoes, CART.

LÜTZEN

With incredible speed Napoleon assembled a new army on the Elbe to supplement the decimated Grand Army retreating from Russia. Strong in artillery, this new force consisted largely of half-trained conscripts, and was deficient in cavalry. Once more the French faced the combined armies of Prussia and Russia.

Lacking cavalry for reconnaissance, Napoleon advanced to develop the situation. As he moved towards Leipzig the Allies concentrated southwest of the city and struck the French in the flank, surprising the flank guard under Ney who was occupying three small villages south of Lützen. The Allies attacked in successive waves, none being strong enough to break the French. The main French forces, echeloned in movement towards Leipzig, were able to concentrate rapidly and join the battle under the control of Napoleon.

At the critical moment 16 Young Guard battalions in column attacked the Allied center and carried the field. The Allied retreat degenerated into a rout which was inadequately pursued by the French, due to their lack of cavalry.

It was a brilliant but indecisive French victory. The Allies withdrew to the vicinity of Bautzen.

crossed the river at Merseburg, and marched towards Markrandstädt, while the Army of the Main drew closer to Weissenfels.

Dumoustier's Young Guard division marched with the cavalry of the Guard in support of Ney's 3rd Corps. Behind them was part of General Decouz's brigade, consisting of two Old Guard battalions and one of flanker-chasseurs. The rest of the brigade was at Erfurt with orders to proceed at once to Naumburg, thirty miles from Weissenfels.

Though his cavalry was scarce and inferior, the Emperor had 150,000 men. Therefore he pursued his plan of massing his armies between Leipzig and Lützen to take the enemy in flank and crush him against the mountains of Bohemia.

Wittgenstein tardily ordered 65,000 infantry and 28,000 crack cavalry sent to join him on the Elster and its tributary the Flossgraben. Though his flanks were covered at Weissenfels and Leipzig, he expected Napoleon's main force to attack near Naumburg.

1 May, 11 a.m. The 3rd Corps left for Lützen under cover of Kellermann's cavalry and soon made contact on the banks of the Rippach with Lanskoi's horse who fell back rapidly upon their infantry and a few guns installed on the heights of the right bank. Beyond, a broad plain extended towards Lützen whose round tower and belfry were visible over the tiled roofs of the village.

12.15 p.m. The Emperor arrived with his staff and halted in the village of Rippach overlooking the ravine, where he dismounted at the post house and took up a position under a linden tree. Bessières, having left his horse Guard west of the village, accompanied him. The Marshal's face was grave. Baudus said to a comrade: 'The Marshal burned his wife's letters this morning. If we fight today he will be killed.'

Up ahead a lively fusillade was in progress. Ney reported that Souham's division was making slow progress across the ravine towards Gross-Görschen.

12.45 p.m. The Emperor ordered Bessières to cross the ravine with his cavalry, push back the Cossacks and Lanskoi's horse, and knock out the enemy batteries. The Duke of Istria promptly went into action along a sunken road opposite the inn. He galloped towards the firing line to reconnoiter the terrain beyond the ravine. When within range of the Russian guns his orderly, Sergeant Jordan of the Polish lancers, had his head blown off by a shell.

'What are you doing here all alone?' Ney asked Bessières. 'If you had your cavalry with you, you could do some good work here.'

'I'm just going to send for it', the Marshal replied. Retracing his steps past the body of the NCO, he ordered it buried immediately so that in case the position were recaptured the enemy would not 'think the Guard had been engaged'. He put his spyglass back in his pocket, and then . . .

12.55 p.m. A cannon ball hit the wall enclosing a neighboring field, ricocheted, and struck the Marshal, hurling his mutilated body under his horse's hoofs. Monsieur de Saint-Charles dragged it clear of some charging enemy cavalry, then placed it in the ravine. 'He is dead', he told Marshal Ney who rode up for news.

'Such is our fate', observed the Prince of the Moskva.

The mortal remains of the Duke of Istria, commander of the Imperial Guard, were removed to a weaver's house in the village and covered with a blanket from one of the beds.

'Few losses could affect the Emperor more deeply. The Army and all France will share his grief', read the bulletin of the *Grande Armée*.

That night the Emperor conferred with Ney, Marmont, and Duroc in the inn at Poserna (where the innkeeper scratched the names of his illustrious guests on a window-pane with a diamond). Marshal Soult was eventually named to succeed Bessières.

The Emperor spent the night at Lützen, famous for its castle, and also because Gustavus Adolphus had been killed there in 1632. Guarded by the elite of his army, Napoleon slept in the house where Frederick the Great had stayed on the eve of the battle of Rosbach.

That day Napoleon had summoned Roguet's division from Merseburg to join Dumoustier. Roguet had exchanged some of his Young Guard battalions for Dumoustier's old ones who now went on duty with the Emperor. While the horse Guard bivouacked behind the town the Grumblers watched over the palace. The Young Guard lit fires near the monument to Gustavus Adolphus on the Leipzig road. Sentries were posted to guard the trees around the monument. An advance post exchanged shots with the enemy. Everyone was on the alert, for danger threatened from both Leipzig and Zwenkau.

'Don't tell anyone I told you', a Lützener said to Berthezène, 'but the Russians have left Leipzig. They must be beyond Pegau by now. The Emperor ought to know this.'

It was late and the Emperor was asleep. Neither the Grand Marshal nor the colonel general on duty (Berthezène) nor Berthier dared wake him. Had Bessières been there, *he* would have dared.

Sent with an infantry division to feel out the enemy, Drouot was content to observe the bridges over the Elster and returned without showing the least anxiety. Consequently at 2 a.m., leaving Berthezène at Lützen, the Emperor departed with the Guard for Leipzig where he planned to attack the main enemy force and conduct his enveloping maneuver.

11.30 a.m. The Emperor's equerry brought General Berthezène an order scribbled in pencil. He was to leave but one company to guard his vehicles and march his brigade to Leipzig.

11.45 a.m. Arriving at Markrandstädt, Napoleon reviewed Macdonald's corps.

From the top of the Lützen steeple Berthezène spied the enemy army – 'which seemed immense' – loom over the horizon until the whole horizon was obscured. Its right flank was marching towards Ney at Gross-Görschen and Kaya, and its left towards Weissenfels. There was no longer any question of leaving Lützen.

At noon Blücher's guns opened fire, taking the 3rd Corps completely by surprise. The Emperor heard them. He promptly sent off Dumoustier's division to Lützen and issued the terse command to Berthezène: '*La Garde au feu!*'[2] Then, followed by the cavalry of the Guard, he took off at a gallop for the battlefield.

2.30 p.m. The cannonade was at its height. Ney had lost every village including Kaya, the largest and strongest. Then the Emperor arrived.

'The young troops were throwing away their arms which strewed the ground over which we galloped', wrote Major Chlapowski of the lancers. 'Half an hour later we halted between the road and the village of Kaya, and deployed on a line facing the village in a field where the remnants of Ney's green troops were still in flight. The Emperor ordered us to bar their passage between our squadrons . . .'

Napoleon's arrival had an electric effect, filling both veterans and recruits with enthusiasm and reassuring their commanders. No wounded soldier passed without crying '*Vive l'Empereur!*' Seeing the bonnets of the Old Guard, followed by the Young, the conscripts of the 3rd Corps shouted '*La Garde! La Garde!*' General Lanusse and Dumoustier's first brigade took Kaya with a charge, overwhelming the Russian and Prussian guards defending the village.

At 6 p.m. Macdonald's 11th Corps entered the line on the right of the enemy. Bertrand's corps was operating on their left. The Emperor ordered Drouot to reinforce the batteries of the two corps between Starsiedel and Kaya with the eighty guns of the Guard.

Dulauloy, Drouot, and Desvaux set off at a gallop, unlimbered their guns on the ridge above Starsiedel, and ordered them readied with matches lit.

Formed in four squares with guns at the corners, the Old Guard was posted behind the artillery, near the Emperor, flanked on right and left by the Young Guard brigades and supported by 3,000 horse under Walther, Lefebvre-Desnoëttes, d'Ornano, and Colbert.

'You will defend these batteries', the Emperor told the veterans, 'and if the enemy attacks you shall give a good account of yourselves.'

At that moment a volley of round shot mowed down two files of grenadiers.

'Was anyone killed?' he asked.

'Yes, Sire, two men – and a third had his thigh shattered.'

'Take care of him. We shall give him a good pension.'

The enemy fire increased appallingly.

'What, does the Guard duck?' the Emperor asked the 2nd Chasseurs.

A moment later a bomb fell in front of the first division. No one stirred. Thirty muskets were smashed but not a man was hit. General Curial came up at a gallop, fuming. Captain Heuillet's company had been badly mauled. Why hadn't the chasseurs taken cover?

The Emperor's orders!

Meanwhile, the guns of the Guard continued to fire blank cartridges until the Russians launched their attack. The rattle of drums beating the Charge was heard, and the enemy came within range. Dulauloy gave the order to rake them with grapeshot and their ranks were 'swept clean'.

[2] 'Send the Guard into action!'

Deploying the Young Guard in columns, Marshal Mortier led a counterattack with 10,000 men. In the fierce struggle in Kaya Mortier fell under his wounded horse, and Dumoustier was wounded. The enemy flanks were pressed in until their center collapsed and they fell back to the Elster bridges and the road to Dresden.

The engagement was a bloody one and cost the Young Guard 1,069 casualties, the Old Guard 55, and the cavalry 54. Both majors of the 1st Voltigeurs as well as Lt. Colonels Coucourt of the 7th *Tirailleurs* and Schramm of the 2nd Voltigeurs were wounded. But it was a great victory.

In his bulletin of 2 May the Emperor compared it to Austerlitz, Jena, and Friedland. He had constantly given of himself, entering the thick of the fight on foot and arousing enthusiasm in the ardent youngsters and old veterans alike.

'The Young Guard has fulfilled our expectations', he reported.

The Old Guard had not fired a shot.

CHAPTER 4

Bautzen

BARROIS' 2nd Guard Division was still five days behind, and Decouz's column was en route to Erfurt with the reserve batteries. Ahead, the Guard followed the ponderous movements of the Army of Germany through country infested with spies. When the barns where their horses were stabled caught fire no one could extinguish the blaze.

On 3 May the grenadiers found Pegau deserted. All its houses had been plundered by Cossacks. The church was a heap of smoking ruins. The day before, Blücher had had a Te Deum sung there to hide his defeat, then ordered the church burned. When the priest at Bohlen refused to ring the bells he was hanged.

On 5 May the Russians and Prussians turned to face their pursuers at Kolditz, but their fierce resistance could not halt the Emperor's brats, backed up by their elders. The enemy was soon flying in disorder in the rain, leaving behind their guns and wagons.

After Smolensk, the Berezina, and Vilna, the Guard had a score to settle with Miloradovitch's Russians who now had the misfortune to guard the rear. It was settled with cold steel. Terrified and screaming, the Russians fled barefoot and in rags, taking along their double-headed eagle colors in black cases. Pursued day and night, they were slaughtered without mercy.

The road through the Elbe valley from Wilsdruff to Dresden is lovely in May when the hillsides are bright with flowering trees. But on the morning of 8 May the Saxon capital lay under a pall of smoke, for the Russians had set fire to the bridges on leaving. As the last Russian officer mounted his horse before the Town Hall he heard French trumpets sound the Advance. The natives hastily took down the garlands they had hung to welcome the Allied armies.

At 3 p.m. the Emperor of the French was greeted at the city gates by the regency committee and the municipality as the bells pealed to appease the conqueror's wrath. The escort overheard the Emperor say:

'Gentlemen, are we friends or enemies? I must speak frankly since I know how many insults you have heaped upon France. I wish to forgive you . . . You may thank your King for this, for he is your savior.'

The enemy was still in Altstadt, just across the river. The aide Caraman galloped to the river bank with a horse battery and sewed destruction among the Russians. Then the Grumblers posted a guard of honor at the 'palace', where Durosnel was installed as governor, while the Emperor went to reconnoiter the river, following its course to Priessnitz.

The pontooneers and marines of the Guard spent the night building rafts to cross, but at dawn next day the enemy shelled them with fifty guns. The Emperor went to the shipyard and ordered Drouot to set up 24 twelve-pounders of the Guard on the left of the Priessnitz bridge, and 16 light pieces on the right. Towards noon the coast was clear. The bridge was repaired during the day and night to permit the passage of the Viceroy's troops, sent on the 11th in pursuit of the enemy on the road to Lusatia and Silesia. The Young Guard, quartered in the suburbs, had given up its bivouacs to Oudinot's corps. The Old Guard was billeted on the inhabitants.

12 May, 10 a.m. The whole Guard was under arms on the Pirna road, to the left of the Grosser Garten. Cannon roared and bells pealed. Escorted by General Flahaut and 500 horse Guards, the King of Saxony returned from Prague and entered his capital where he was greeted, embraced, congratulated, and charmed by the Emperor. The pair rode to the palace at the head of the Guard. The same populace that had thrown flowers before the Tsar and the Prussian king eight hours before now cheered the rival sovereigns.

The King brought disturbing news of Austria. The buzzing of the 'Vienna beehive' was audible even in Dresden. There was talk of a peace, with Metternich as arbiter.

Before joining his vanguard at Bautzen the Emperor disbanded the Army of the Elbe and sent the Viceroy to Italy to raise an army in case of war with Austria.

Barrois' division arrived in Dresden on 15 May. It now numbered 5,000, including two *tirailleur* brigades under Rottembourg and Berthezène. Dumoustier's Young Guard division contained a fusilier brigade under Mouton-Duvernet, two voltigeur regiments under Tindal, and three under Lanusse, totalling 8,000 men. Roguet's Old Guard numbered 4,000, with two regiments of grenadiers and chasseurs and two battalions of Italian *vélites*.

The Guard cavalry was divided between a light cavalry division under Lefebvre-Desnoëttes containing 500 Berg lancers and 2,400 light-horse, and a heavy division under d'Ornano composed of 1,500 chasseurs, 1,200 dragoons, 1,200 grenadiers, and 500 elite gendarmes. Counting the gunners, the horse Guard mustered 7,800 men and 18 guns.

On 18 May the three infantry and two cavalry divisions and the artillery left with the Emperor for Bautzen. The Grumblers' packs were loaded with white bread, sausages, and brandy. The women and children cried when they left. The enemy awaited them across the Spree in the mountains of Lusatia.

On the morning of 20 May the Young Guard was camped facing Bautzen on a slope descending to the river. At 9 a.m. the cannon thundered and a fusillade crackled along an eight-mile front whose center was marked by the crenellated walls of the town. Four army corps, forming the front line, crossed the river – which was very low – by fords and pontoons. The Guard followed, leaving Bautzen on its left, and surrounded the Emperor on a hillock. The Old Guard formed a square around him while the Young massed in close order by divisions on his right, with the cavalry on the left. They could see the enemy far off on the opposite heights.

A sudden downpour drenched the field. The firing ceased and was resumed only after the sun came out. The fighting promptly became brisk on the front, consisting of a chain of heavily-wooded hillocks punctuated with redoubts which the enemy defended one by one with great tenacity. Ranged in parallel divisions,[1] the Young Guard attacked several and carried the hill of Klein-Bautzen with gusto. During the attack General Lanusse was kicked by a horse and put out of action.

By evening the Allies' front line had been captured. The Emperor returned to Bautzen and occupied the bishop's palace. In quarters and bivouacs, with plenty of food, the Guard slept on mattresses, watched over the Emperor, and gathered strength for the morrow's battle which would be a crucial one, since the peace everyone wanted depended on it. But these Russians were stubborn – much more so than the Prussians!

At four next morning the trumpets of the duty squadron sounded Boots and Saddles. The Emperor did not leave until seven, though the cannonade had begun an hour before. Napoleon's maneuver had already been mounted by orders issued during the night. The corps on the right were to pin down the enemy while Marshal Ney forced a decision in an advance towards Wurschen, capturing the formidable chain of redoubts en route.

9 a.m. The Emperor took up a position on high ground about two miles from Bautzen. Under fire from the Prussian artillery, the Old Guard formed a square and the 1st Chasseurs suffered some casualties. On the slopes above, the horse Guard formed up within sight of the enemy. The artillery of the reserve was in motion in the rear.

As the advance began, Marshal Mortier led his two divisions up to the line of the artillery which threw up a heavy barrage in an effort to demolish the Prussian redoubts between Besankwitz and Kreckwitz. Simultaneously, Marmont and Bertrand, on the right and left, launched a frontal attack which was both ineffective and costly.

The artillery needed reinforcement. Successive aides sent to the Emperor received no reply but 'Hein?' (meaning to the initiated: 'You don't know what you are talking about!') The *Tondu* must have been sure of victory since he wrapped himself in his cloak and went to sleep under the Prussian shells, ordering Duroc not to wake him for two hours.

This was simply incredible. The Grand Marshal, watch in hand, fended off a procession of couriers. The horizon ahead was ablaze. Whole files of Rottembourg's brigade were mown down. The wounded were tended in the center of the squares and some, as well as the surgeons bound helplessly to their bloody task, were killed. The twelve-pounders on the right were heavily bombarded. On the left Dumoustier's battalions were forced to evacuate a redoubt they had just captured.

It was three o'clock, perhaps four. The Emperor awoke, heard the report of Berthier's aide, and announced: 'The battle is won'. Surely he must be out of his mind!

But no. Victory was now in sight. Ney was nearing his objective.

Orders went forth: 'Barrois' division will capture the heights opposite its position'. The 1st Regiment in close columns by division, followed at 50 paces by the 2nd in squares, approached the salient of the first redoubt. Twenty-four guns supported

[1] A 'division' consisted of 2 platoons, or 300 men. – Ed.

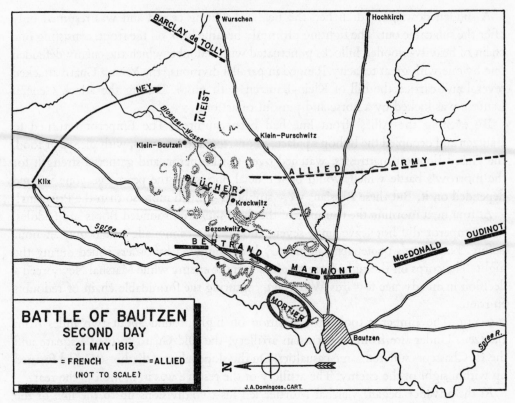

BAUTZEN

The Allies moved into a strong defensive position near Bautzen. Napoleon planned to move with his main force against the Allied front while Ney, marching from the northwest, enveloped their right flank and attacked it from the rear.

On 20 May the French Army attacked and drove in the Allied covering forces to the main line of defense. Next day Napoleon planned a holding attack while Ney moved around the enemy rear; however, Ney's movement was delayed through faulty communications, giving the enemy time to fall back in good order in his path. Napoleon then made a frontal attack and forced the Allies to retire. Both sides suffered heavy losses.

The battle was indecisive because of the delay in co-ordination and, again, inadequate pursuit.

the movement from right to left; the light batteries, placed by Berthezène, enfiladed the defenders. The heights were carried by a charge. The enemy left behind both guns and wounded in their flight.

The sun was sinking behind the horizon when Ney reached the outskirts of Wurschen. The whole Guard, Young and Old, supported by artillery, swept over the enemy and made its way to the inn at Klein-Purschwitz which the Tsar and Blücher had just evacuated.

The Emperor arrived and had his tents pitched near the inn. The whole foot and horse Guard was there. The chasseurs and grenadiers found the debris left by the Russian general staff most uncomfortable. Their meager supper consisted of cakes made of flour captured from the '*Moscoss*' and baked over the campfires. Their bands played *The Victory Is Ours*. Though indecisive, it had been a glorious one for the French.

French and Russians mingled on the road to Görlitz until Miloradovitch rounded up his soldiers to allow the tide of vanquished troops to flow freely towards Reichenbach.

Next morning, the 23rd, the Emperor was in the saddle at daybreak. He rode off with General Walther's cavalry to join the vanguard. The foot Guard followed, leaving the Italian *vélites* at Bautzen.

The enemy was holding the bluffs above the Neisse in front of Reichenbach. The troops of Reynier's corps were making no progress. Clouds of Russian dragoons, lancers, and Cossacks appeared on their right. Annoyed because the horse grenadiers were late, the Emperor stormed:

'But these people have risen from the dead! The cavalry of the Guard will go thrash them.'

Lefebvre-Desnoëttes was soon on his way with two regiments. The troopers knew the Russians of old – how they fired their carbines a few times and fled. The Polish squadrons opened into battle formation and moved off at a walk. The troopers had been warned to prepare their weapons and dress their lines at the command '*Au galop!*'; and at '*Marche!*' to take off at a run, not couching their lances until they could thrust them down the throats of the Russians.

Walther sent the Mameluks and chasseurs in support, then Latour-Maubourg's horse, whereupon the Russian gunners harnessed their pieces and fled. The cavalry lost 264 officers and men. Reynier's infantry entered Reichenbach but soon beat a retreat. The heights above Görlitz were swarming with sharpshooters.

The Emperor, with his suite and escort, forced an entrance into Markersdorf after it was outflanked by Ney's troops. The long narrow road through the village cut obliquely across a deep valley, then turned sharp left up a gentle slope. A group of horsemen pressed through it and ascended the slope in a solid mass. At the top the Emperor was watching the progress of the infantry.

Deep in conversation, Caulincourt, Soult, Mortier, Duroc, and Kirgener reached the hilltop where the Emperor was standing in a grove of trees. The moment they arrived, an officer rode up to the Grand Marshal and Kirgener who stopped to listen to his report. A mile away there was a flash; then a Russian ball hit a tree near the Emperor, bounced off it, cut Kirgener in two, and struck Duroc a mortal blow.

That morning the Duke had confided his papers and watch to his servant, saying: 'Here Coursot, old fellow, keep these for me in case I break my neck'.[2]

This was an irreparable loss for the Emperor. Beside the bed on which Duroc lay dying in a little house in Markersdorf, with Larrey standing by helpless, Napoleon listened to his last words:

'I have devoted my whole life to your service. My only regret is that it might still have been of use to you . . .' With his last breath he added: 'I am leaving a daughter . . . Your Majesty will be a father to her . . .' (see Plate 115).

At 7 p.m. on 23 May Duroc died at the age of forty-one. His body was taken to Görlitz and embalmed. Next day it was removed to Mainz under escort by Soult's aide and a Young Guard battalion, and placed temporarily in the Cathedral.

The Emperor spent the night weeping in his tent in the middle of a field, surrounded by his Old Guard. 'Poor man,' the Grumblers murmured as he passed, 'he has lost one of his children.'

He sent Drouot away when he came for orders and signed only two papers. The first admitted Duroc's aides to the Legion of Honor and appointed his secretary an assistant commissary in the Guard. The second repeated an order already issued to disperse his suite on the battlefield, for doubtless the large group of horsemen surrounding the Emperor at Markersdorf had drawn Russian fire and caused the death of the Grand Marshal.

Two days later the Emperor and the Guard resumed their march to Silesia behind the army. At Dresden reinforcements arrived for the Guard, including 125 Mameluks under Kirmann, 700 mixed cavalry, a horse battery under Lt. Colonel Griois; 4,200 men in all. Durosnel sent provisions to the army and the Guard under convoy of these detachments.

The roads were far from safe. The Young Guard escorting Duroc's body narrowly missed capture by Cossacks. All the hospitals were full. The Guard's contained 500 sick and wounded. Major Roque of the 3rd Voltigeurs died of wounds received at Wurschen. Tindal was down with putrid fever and Lanusse was suffering from wounds, so Colonels Jouan and Couloumy took temporary command of their brigades.

The casualties had been heavy and the commanders' morale was low. Bessières, Duroc, and Kirgener had all been sacrificed to fruitless victories.

'What a war!' grumbled the brass.[3] We shall all meet the same fate . . .'

'The turn of the wheel of fortune had ravaged these souls of iron', was Baron Fain's[4] melancholy observation as he listened to them talk.

---

[2] He kept them, and his descendants guarded them reverently. Jean Coursot had served under Duroc in the Oudinot Grenadiers at Austerlitz. Becoming butler to Madame Mère on the fall of the Empire, he went to Saint Helena as Napoleon's valet in September 1819.

[3] *Grosses epaulettes.*

[4] The Emperor's secretary. – Ed.

CHAPTER 5

The Armistice

GIVING in to pressure from Caulaincourt and Berthier, the Emperor agreed to an armistice which was signed at Pleiswitz on 4 June. During a fifty-six-day truce a congress was to draw up terms for the peace that everyone wanted. But what if the Allies did not?

The Emperor feared the consequences of his weakness. Was it wise to halt a victorious march on the eve of driving the Russians out of Silesia? It appeared that Austria was ready to join the Coalition, as though Metternich were deliberately trying to bring his country's worst enemy back into Europe. England did not want the continent united. Napoleon feared the influence of her diplomacy during the cessation of hostilities.

In urging an armistice, had his marshals considered that in one month he had led his improvised army victoriously all the way to the Oder? That a dozen Young Guard regiments were at Glogau? What did the grenadiers think?

To them the armistice meant fifty-six days without fighting, living comfortably the while in Silesia and Saxony where the country was rich and the girls pretty. For the rest, the *Tondu* knew what he was about.

Times had changed. The old ideals of austerity, duty, self-respect – in short, the spirit of the Old Guard – had been diluted by the influx of conscripts. The veterans of Russia had not lost the habits of plunder, waste, and destruction acquired in that cold and miserable land. The veterans of Spain had been corrupted by an atrocious war which had bred in them, besides hardihood and courage, a fatalistic attitude towards theft and vengeance and a lack of compassion for the misery they brought to others. If their campfire caused a general conflagration they shrugged it off with a '*C'est la guerre!*' Small wonder that this famous phrase was thrown back at the French by their enemies in 1870, 1914, and 1939!

The officers, spoiled by their master's indulgence, now considered it their due and were even more exacting than before. Luxury had become indispensable to them. Their carriages were stuffed, their servants numerous, and their meals lavish, with soup, boiled meat, vegetables, chicken, lamb, beef, fruit, and wine at 12 francs a bottle. Beer was for grenadiers! They held aloof from the men, lived in castles, and hunted and fished with the proprietors. Discipline suffered accordingly.

Tradition demanded that the Guard be brilliant, and the Emperor insisted that its units be full. No one might report sick. Ailing or not, every man must be present in ranks. 'March or die' was the formula – and it did not appeal to the French soldier.

Nevertheless, the old phalanx survived because its bravery in the field and its zeal and devotion to the Emperor remained intact – if not among the generals and marshals, at least from the colonels down. These men worried to see him depressed, but they still believed in his genius.

The Young Guard conscripts, chosen for their vigor and good conduct, showed great courage in the field and were completely devoted to the Emperor. After the bloody combats in May they had cried *'Vive l'Empereur!'* with increasing enthusiasm. But even courage could not banish hunger. Accustomed to regular rations from the commissary (while the Line lived off the country and starved) the Young Guard went hungry on forced marches and soon lost its ardor.

Nevertheless, no one was allowed to lag behind. Special NCO detachments knew how to make the lame walk and showed mercy in inverse proportion to the favors done them. Soon the youngsters fought from fear rather than for glory. In Paris 320 were arrested for desertion and sent to prison.

'It might be embarrassing to bring so many Guardsmen before the War Council', the Minister wrote, proposing to courtmartial 'twenty who had deserted under flagrant circumstances', and turn the rest over to disciplinary battalions. The Emperor concurred.

Some deserters wandered far afield. 'I left my regiment on bad advice', wrote one. 'I was in Italy, Turkey, Croatia, and Hungary before finding a village where I could ply my tanner's trade. Here in Austria banknotes have become worthless. I earn enough to eat, but clothes come high . . .'

Later arrested and imprisoned in Toulon, the soldier wrote sadly: 'If they send me to the colonies, as I expect, it will be my own fault. I shall never see you again . . .'

While the Old Guard followed the Emperor to Dresden, the Young Guard stayed at Polkwitz, near Glogau, with Mortier whose fidelity and gaiety remained intact. This was a regular picnic, as its inhabitants were famous for their naïveté. Orders came to build a cantonment like the one at Finkenstein. The barracks were soon completed by the sappers and marines. The men scoured the countryside for wood, furniture, sand for the walks, and pines, flowers, and turf for the grounds. A pyramid crowned with an eagle was erected at the entrance and a bust of the Emperor adorned the officers' mess. The Silesians came to admire the new wooden city and drank toasts to peace. Every evening a troop of itinerant actors performed in a shed.

Life was beautiful but busy. There were drills twice a day for the recruits and frequent clothing inspections. The uniforms, shoes, and arms were in a sorry state. Some colonels bought white pantaloons and gaiters for their men so their regiments would shine on parade; but those with more foresight ordered loose trousers 'of grey cloth, slit sailor-fashion at the bottom'.

The two Young Guard divisions rolled dice for the privilege of occupying the new camp, and the losers were billeted at Beuthen. The Duke of Treviso, with headquarters at Glogau, visited them often, reviewing and maneuvering the troops.

In Dresden the Emperor occupied the Villa Marcolini at Friedrichstadt, a large summer estate with a beautiful garden reminiscent of the Élysée Palace in Paris. The

PLATE 115

DEATH OF MARSHAL DUROC
a) French version
(*Imagerie d'Epinal*)

b) German version
(*Imagerie of Friedrich Campe, Nürnberg*)

PLATE 116

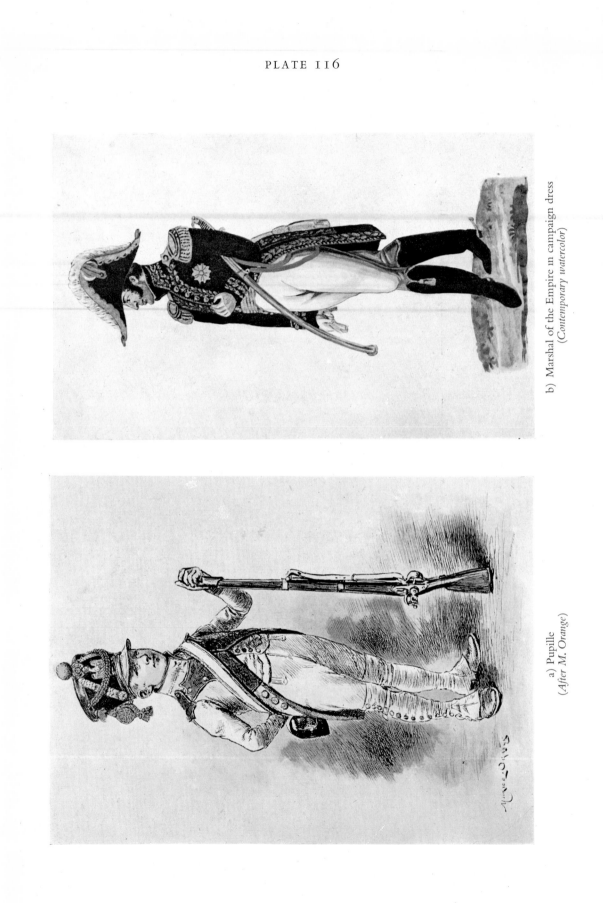

b) Marshal of the Empire in campaign dress
(*Contemporary watercolor*)

a) Pupille
(*After M. Orange*)

PLATE 117

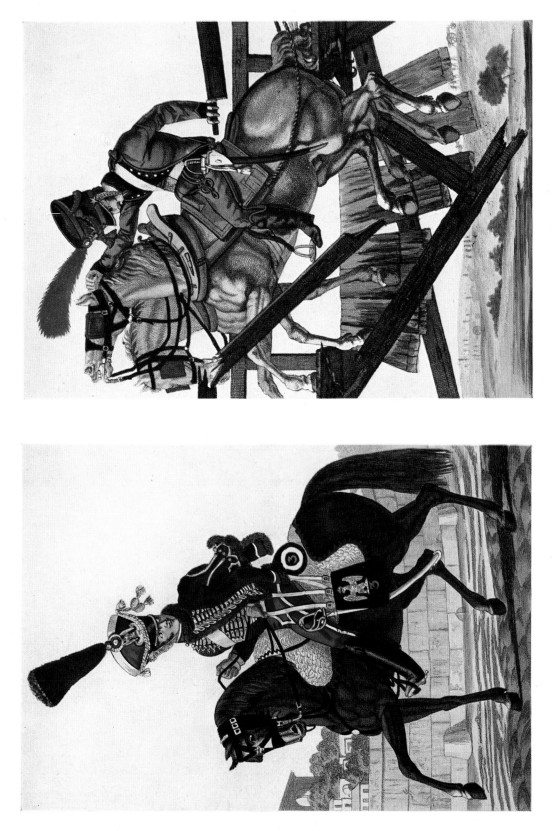

PLATE 118

a) d'Ornano
(*After portrait: Collection Légion d'Honneur*)

b) Duroc
(*Engr. Couché*)

c) Dautancourt
(*Contemp. lithograph*)

d) King Friedrich August of Saxony
(*Col. engraving by Sprinck after Hilscher*)

PLATE 119

A HERO FOR EACH VICTORY

Outer row, left to right: Desaix (top), Lannes, Rapp, Jourdan, Kellermann, Victor, Oudinot, Masséna, Lefebvre, Macdonald, Poniatowski, Foy, Augureau, Kléber, Lasalle

Inner row: Murat (top), Mortier, Berthier, Davout, Eugène, Suchet, Moncey, Soult

(From a contemporary colored engraving by Charon)

PLATE 120

Osterweise meadow in the bend of the Elbe made an ideal parade ground. The Old Guard posted four sentries at the 'palace' gate, two of them mounted. Every day there was a dress parade on the *allée* in front that the grenadiers nicknamed the 'Champ de Mars'.

Soldiers and diplomats abounded in Dresden. The military tailors and bootmakers of Paris took quarters there; the hotels were full and clients were turned away from the inns and eating houses. The Emperor's actors performed in the small theatre in the Marcolini and the Guard wore full dress every day.

Pompéjac's flanker-chasseurs were quartered in Neustadt. Small Guard depots were established in the barracks where General Gros' 4th and 5th Voltigeurs were quartered.

The Young Guard conscripts were issued $1\frac{1}{2}$ pounds[1] of bread a day, with meat at 10 a.m. and *ratatouie* (a kind of stew) at 4 p.m.

Both banks of the Elbe were being fortified. In case hostilities were resumed, Dresden – which, with the fortress of Koenigstein, guarded the gateway to Bohemia – would be the pivot of the Elbe line running through the garrison towns of Torgau, Wittenberg, Magdeburg, and Hamburg. The Emperor wished at all costs to hold this string of the bow formed by Prussia, Russia, and Austria, as well as to secure his line of communications with the Rhine through Merseburg, Erfurt, and Würzburg.

These towns were garrisoned by the Line and detachments of horse Guards. Several squadrons were also quartered around Glogau; but the main forces of Walther, Lefebvre-Desnoëttes, and Ornano were on the right bank of the Elbe at Neustadt, Pulsnitz, and Koenigsbrück. Meanwhile, General Castex was sent with a route battalion of the Old Guard and 900 horse to deal with the partisans interrupting communications between Bautzen and Görlitz.

The artillery reserve remained with the Old Guard in Dresden. Several batteries under Griois, supported by Italian *vélites* and two squadrons of chasseurs and Polish lancers, were stationed near Waldau on the Queis in miserable quarters devastated by successive waves of Russians and Marmont's troops. Nevertheless, Griois reported that he had led a gay life at the hunts and parties given by Marmont at the beautiful castle he was occupying, and had also had leisure for reading.

On the contrary, the Emperor worked eighteen hours a day, making reconnaissances and inspections on horseback and by carriage and wearing out his escorts. He decided to admit some of King Joseph's regiments into the Guard, including two battalions each of grenadiers, voltigeurs, and fusiliers, and the Castile and *Royal Étranger* Regiments. These troops were no longer needed in the Peninsula where the French defeat at Vitoria had left the road to France open to Wellington.

On the morning of 1 July Marshal Soult, Bessières' successor in command of the Guard, received the following order from the Emperor:

'You will leave before ten this evening. You will travel incognito, taking the name of an aide. You will arrive in Paris the 4th and stay with the Minister of War. You will then go to the Archchancellor's, spending only 12 hours in Paris before proceeding to take command of my armies in Spain.'

[1] 500 grams, whereas the English pound was only 453·5. – Ed.

The Duchess of Dalmatia[2] had been in Dresden for the past two weeks. 'I forbid you to return to Spain', she told her husband.

Nevertheless the Marshal sold his horses and carriages and sent his household on leave. At 10 p.m. he entered his carriage. The Duchess left three days later. She did not see him again for a year. General Mouton, Count of Lobau, relieved the Duke temporarily in command of the Guard.

The Congress of Prague was getting nowhere. Though the armistice was extended to 15 August there seemed little chance of peace. 'It is likely', the Emperor wrote on 17 July, 'that the next campaign will begin between 15 and 20 August'.

Meanwhile, there was much to be done. General Boyeldieu and the flanker brigade were sent to put Koenigstein into a state of defence. A camp had to be established at Lilienstein and a pontoon bridge built. A list of Guard NCO's to be promoted subalterns in the Line – which needed them badly – had to be prepared, of Old Guard privates to serve as Young Guard NCO's, and 2,400 veterans of Italy and Spain chosen to replace them.

'But', Mouton objected, 'we have no uniforms.'

'Too bad', replied the Emperor, 'but they cannot be held up for uniforms. Have them made here.'

There was a shoe shortage. The Young Guard needed woolen pantaloons, since cotton would do only for overalls. The following order was issued:

'Coats will be worn under the overcoats. On fine days generals may order the latter rolled over the packs; but in foul or cold weather, or on night marches, soldiers must wear both coats and overcoats.'

Thanks to the gold reserve in the basement of the Pavillion Marsan, the soldiers' pay was forthcoming for once.

The foot Guard was now 35,000 strong. The Old Guard division commanded by General Friant included the 1st and 2nd Grenadiers under Michel and the 1st and 2nd Chasseurs under Curial, plus two battalions of Italian *vélites*. The four Young Guard divisions commanded by Dumoustier, Barrois, Delaborde, and Roguet each contained five regiments alternating between voltigeurs and *tirailleurs*. In addition, the 1st Division contained two regiments of fusiliers and the 2nd, two of flankers.

Mouton-Duvernet, Berthezène, Decouz, and Lanusse were promoted lieutenant generals. Among the new brigade commanders were Couloumy and Pelet, the hero of Krasny.

General Haxo was named commander of the engineers of the Guard. Lion was made a general and Nansouty was given command of the horse Guard which was organized as follows:

The 1st Division under Count d'Ornano contained the Berg lancers, Colbert's 2nd Light-Horse, and Pinteville's Young Guard dragoons. The 2nd under Lefebvre-Desnoëttes contained Krasinski's Young Guard squadrons of Polish lancers and

2 Soult was Duke of Dalmatia. – Ed.

Castex's of chasseurs and grenadiers. The 3rd under General Walther contained the Old Guard squadrons of Lion, Letort, and Laferrière.

The cavalry of the Guard was now 8,000 strong, though some Young Guard squadrons lacked not only epaulets and cap cords but cloaks, sabers, and lances. Its new commander Nansouty was brave, intelligent, and a good horseman; but an unfortunate tendency towards sarcasm and rudeness impaired his leadership in the field.

The artillery now had 200 guns with enough ammunition 'for four Wagrams'.

Since the Emperor's birthday fell on the day the armistice was due to expire it was celebrated on 10 August. The day began with salvos of artillery and the pealing of bells in the morning and a parade at Friedrichstadt of 18,000 men. The Duke of Treviso organized a shooting contest, with cash prizes ranging from 3 francs for the best marksman of each company to 20 francs for the best in the Guard.

On a shady square a banquet was served to the marshals, generals, and officers of the Guard. Mortier proposed the toast to the Emperor which was greeted with thunderous applause. The dinner given by the Grumblers to the Saxon Guard was less convivial, and the hosts found it 'impossible to fraternize' with their guests. At the time for the toasts before dessert the Saxons withdrew under a variety of pretexts.

During the past three weeks the gunners of the Guard had been preparing fireworks which they set off on the Elbe under the 'palace' windows. Boats filled with soldiers launching bombs, star-shells, 'waterfalls', etc. shuttled back and forth across the river. A beautifully illuminated arch, decorated with allegorical figures and portraits of the Emperor and the King of Saxony, was erected on the Elbe bridge. It was a wonderful evening, though it ended on a melancholy note.

This year the birthday bonus would be used to buy shoes for the soldiers, for again the winds of war were blowing.

CHAPTER 6

Dresden

THE Allied armies were divided, with Bernadotte in the north on the Havel, Blücher in the center along the Katzbach in Silesia, and Schwarzenberg in the south at Prague. To cover his adversaries the Emperor posted Oudinot with three corps east of Wittenberg; four corps echeloned along the Bohemian border from Zittau to Dresden; and four corps in Silesia. The Emperor and the Guard remained in Dresden.

Though the French army was superior in numbers its morale was low. To raise its spirits Napoleon sent Oudinot to take Berlin. With the rest, he would maneuver as circumstances demanded and fight Blücher and Schwarzenberg in turn.

The enemy broke the truce on 11 August when Blücher took the offensive. Leaving Gouvion-Saint-Cyr's 14th Corps in Dresden, the Emperor departed on the 15th for Silesia with the Old Guard. By the 18th all the Guard was with him at Görlitz.

News came from Bohemia that Lefebvre-Desnoëttes had climbed the Riesengebirge range and occupied the Gobel pass. His patrols sent towards Prague reported that the Allied sovereigns, together with the traitorous French General Moreau and Prince Schwarzenberg, were marching on Dresden with 80,000 men in several columns.

Since Schwarzenberg was a ponderous commander and neither the Austrians nor the Russians moved fast as a rule, the Emperor believed he had time to finish off Blücher before meeting Schwarzenberg.

Leading his army at the head of the Guard, he marched east. His marches and countermarches, in continual rain and heat over execrable roads, were long and tiring. The army bivouacked in the mud with little to eat.

Whether it was the bearskin bonnets or the Emperor's presence that made him shy, on the 22nd Blücher turned round, refused battle, and retired behind the Katzbach.

Leaving Macdonald on the river, the Emperor turned to face the Army of Bohemia. On the night of the 22nd the Guard was sent to Görlitz in pouring rain. The Emperor recalled the corps of Vandamme and Victor, guarding the passes to Bohemia, and marched to Dresden with most of his army.

It was high time. At the Bautzen bivouac on the 24th alarming news came from Gouvion-Saint-Cyr. The Allied armies had already reached the Dresden plain. Although the 15,000 men of the 14th Corps were doing their duty magnificently, their only hope lay in the Emperor's arrival. The weather went from bad to worse, with thunderstorms, tornadoes, cloudbursts, and hail in succession. Several men were injured by hailstones. If Dresden could hold out until the 28th, the rest of the army would cross the Elbe at Pirna and fall upon Schwarzenberg's flank.

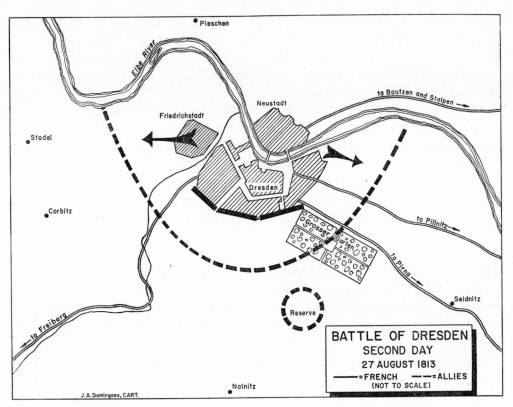

DRESDEN

The Leipzig Campaign, halted by the armistice after Bautzen, was resumed late in August. The Allies were heavily reinforced meanwhile and faced the French in a large semicircle, thus giving Napoleon the advantage of interior lines. The Allies' strategy was to attack Napoleon's marshals, but retreat before the Emperor himself.

As Napoleon moved against Blücher, who fell back, Schwarzenberg took the opportunity to move against the small French forces in Dresden. Leaving a force to contain Blücher, Napoleon moved to reinforce Dresden, sending Vandamme's corps to attack the Allied rear.

At Dresden on 27 August Napoleon attacked the Allied Armies who were separated by a deep defile. The Allied left wing was destroyed and the entire force soundly beaten. However, the enemy's prompt retirement and Napoleon's failure to pursue them in force enabled them to surround and practically annihilate Vandamme's corps on 30 August.

Murat, Haxo, Gourgaud, a dozen officers of the general staff, and troops of lancers galloped through the night to Koenigsberg, Lilienstein, Pirna, and Dresden with orders for the execution of this maneuver. The army was set in motion. Then the orders were countermanded. Dresden could not hold out until the 28th. The enemy was now fighting in the last line of redoubts.

At daybreak on the 26th, despite the 125 miles they had marched in the past four days, the Guard set off at top speed, followed by the army. Exhausted men were left on the road, cheering the Emperor. No one complained. Gunfire was heard. Faster . . .

At the junction of the roads to Bautzen, Stolpen, and Pillnitz the whole battlefield came in sight. The enemy was at the gates of Dresden. Nansouty and the Emperor galloped to Neustadt. Friant's division scrambled down the slopes. The Young Guard ran. Though parched with thirst, they sang *The Victory Is Ours*, and '*Ah! Ah! Nous allons avoir affaire à Papa-Beau-Père.*'[1]

'*Papa-Beau-Père's*' troops had just captured the center redoubt . . .

But the French must have time to catch their breath. They halted at the end of the Neustadt bridge. The men sank to the ground and laid their heads on their packs. The natives brought brandy which they downed in gulps. In the gardens around the Link Baths Roguet's *tirailleurs* 'preened themselves for battle'. The barbers shaved the clumsy men.

Following the artillery, the Young Guard regiments poured into the city across the three bridges and a ferry run by the marines of the Guard, under a hail of shot and shell which fell indiscriminately on roof tops and civilians. Every street leading to the main gates was clogged.

The Old Guard was posted in reserve in the No. 4 Redoubt where the Emperor joined it, after making reconnaissances and calling upon the King who was frightfully upset. Delaborde's and Roguet's divisions were posted at the Ziegel gate; those of Dumoustier and Barrois at the Pirna gate.

Time was pressing. The enemy, supported by abundant artillery sheltered in the Grosser Garten, was storming both positions. The last remnants of the 14th Corps had retired. Furious combats, taking a toll of soldiers and civilians, were in progress before the last line of fortifications. Already the Prussian and Russian soldiers were shouting 'On to Paris!' They were about to force the gates . . .

These now opened before Dumoustier, Tindal, Cambronne, and Jouan with their voltigeurs who charged, supported by fire from the ramparts above. But the Russian gunners stuck to their guns and Dumoustier, Tindal, and Jouan fell, severely wounded.

Dumoustier was charging the enemy at the Pirna gate when suddenly, as the French emerged from the city, the drums of the 3rd *Tirailleurs* stopped beating. Who gave the order to halt? No one. A burst of grapeshot had simply mown down all the drummers.

In column formation, Barrois' division rushed the enemy before the Pirna gate and captured the Russian position. Major Masson and his battalion of the 1st *Tirailleurs* charged six Prussian battalions at bayonet point, taking several hundred prisoners.

[1] 'Oh, we're going to have a fight with Papa-in-Law' – referring to the Emperor Francis I of Austria, Napoleon's father-in-law. – Ed.

Barrois' division occupied the Grosser Garten from where it filtered through to the mills between the Elbe and the Russian right. General Gros' 4th and 5th Voltigeurs captured the trenches at Freiberg.

At 9 p.m. the firing ceased. The troops bivouacked on the spot in the rain, without fires. Two hundred paces off, the Russians followed suit. Since both sides were exhausted a surprise attack seemed unlikely.

Alert! The Austrians, 'drunk with saltpeter and brandy', fell upon Dumoustier's division and a fight took place in the dark. Despite his shattered leg, their commander had remained with his men. Cambronne's 3rd Voltigeurs captured a whole battalion with its flag.

Towards midnight the Emperor, dripping wet, visited the Young Guard bivouacs, complimented the troops, and then returned to Dresden to work.

At dawn the wounded Delaborde and Dumoustier were relieved by Decouz and Curial. Lt. Colonel Vionnet, though wounded also, was given command of Barrois' first brigade.

It was raining so hard the men could not load their muskets. Word was passed to man the batteries and draw sabers. Murat attacked the enemy left, based on Stadel and Corbitz, with his cavalry supported by the horse Guard, as the center corps advanced. On the left the battle was resumed while the Guard artillery gave effective support to the advancing troops. As each Young Guard brigade was accompanied by several batteries, the Duke of Treviso made good progress towards Seidnitz against the Russians retreating towards Bohemia.

The Old Guard remained with the duty squadrons and d'Ornano's division beside the No. 4 Redoubt where the Emperor had established his command post.

On the 28th Mortier occupied Pirna.

The Guard had suffered heavy losses. Nearly all its generals, including Roguet, Dumoustier, Delaborde, Boyeldieu, Boyer de Rebeval, Castex, and Tindal, were wounded. Many unit commanders were put out of action. Lt. Colonel Deshayes of the 2nd Chasseurs and one of his majors were killed. Jouan, Mallet, Secrétan, Hennequin, Pompéjac, and Vionnet were all wounded. More than 100 officers and 2,000 men were casualties.

At the review on 30 August the Emperor took off his hat to the young regiments.

'There go the brave 1st *Tirailleurs*' he said to Major Masson, in temporary command since Darriule fell ill two weeks before. 'Order one hundred out of ranks so that I may award them the cross of the Legion.'

For his fine conduct Masson was named colonel of the 3rd *Tirailleurs*. Commander Grivel was also promoted and eighteen marines were awarded the Legion of Honor.

The Guard had fulfilled the Emperor's highest expectations and justified his confidence. All its regiments had displayed endurance, courage, and devotion during a hard campaign and three pitched battles, ranking its men in the young army as shock troops capable of striking a decisive blow. Their victories, won by a physical feat rarely performed by any corps, had filled them with enthusiasm. Though no longer able to maintain them in the old style, the Emperor still cared for them and praised their qualities, remembering in the midst of his anxieties to award them his share of the glory and inspiring them with the joy of serving.

The cadres of the Old Guard had instilled into these fine lads – sensitive to 'panache' like all good Frenchmen – the desire to appear splendid on the battlefield, to clean their muddy boots and polish their equipment and keep their plumes fresh for the day of battle. The spirit of the Young Guard derived from the Old whose spirit derived from the Emperor; but it was freer and more spontaneous.

By 28 August the conscripts of 1813 were already veterans. The Emperor could pitch his tents within their squares and be guarded, revered, and cheered. Though less stylish than the 'old of the Old', they would nevertheless be able to replace the Grumblers when the last one was gone. Thus the Young Guard was in fact the offspring of the Old.

The Imperial Guard – the largest and soundest corps in the army – filled a crying need at the beginning of September 1813. The battle of Dresden was a triumph of energy and genius on the part of the Emperor, and of courage and endurance on the part of his troops; however, the victory was hardly won before it was compromised.

On 23 August Oudinot had been halted at Grossbeeren on the road to Berlin, and was retreating to Wittenberg. Macdonald had been defeated by Blücher on the Katzbach on the 26th. Finally, Vandamme ventured into the mountains of Bohemia and was captured at Kulm on the 30th.

The Emperor met these strokes of fate with courage and countered them with energy. Ordering Ney to relieve Oudinot and resume the march on Berlin, Napoleon made rapid excursions between Koenigsbrück, where Blücher had gone into hiding again, and Dresden, still threatened by Schwarzenberg. Then, returning to Lusatia, he dealt 'Old *Vorwärts*'[2] a staggering blow which was countered by a French defeat at Dennewitz on 6 September and a retreat to the Elbe.

The Guard never left Napoleon's side during his lightning journeys, inspections, and attacks, doubling their day's marches to guard him by night.

'Keep the Young Guard divisions as fresh as possible', he wrote Mortier on 6 September. 'Keep good order on the march to avoid tiring the troops any more than necessary.'

The officers were worried by these rapid maneuvers, brusque orders, and sudden changes of plan. They sensed that the Emperor was anxious – even hesitant. Meanwhile, his enemies dodged his blows in order to pursue their own ends, and managed to avoid being lured into his traps. Before the Hochkirch presbytery the Guard watched him sitting on a bale of straw, silhouetted against some burning shacks. He was silent, lost in meditation, oblivious of the soldiers who were burning crosses from the cemetery to warm themselves.

The vise was closing on Napoleon. His line of communications was threatened. Macdonald, beaten at Bischofswerda on 23 September, had relinquished Bautzen. A new Russian army under Bennigsen was marching from Bohemia to join Schwarzenberg. It was rumored that Bernadotte had crossed the Elbe.

2 'Old Forward' – the Prussian soldiers' nickname for Blücher. – Ed.

The Guard, strung out along the left bank of the Elbe, was recalled from Dresden while the Young Guard continued to hold Pirna.

The Emperor now decided to enlarge the Guard. Since, left to themselves, his generals were invariably beaten, he assumed that their lassitude and their anxiety to end the war and return to Paris was leading them to obey orders half-heartedly, if at all. Their forces were lacking in vigor and discipline; but the Guard was large and strong. Under the Emperor's sole command it was now the principal component of the army.

It was Lefebvre-Desnoëtte's Poles who, aided by Berg Lancers and infantry, freed the line of communications and whipped the Cossacks infiltrating their positions.

Returning to Dresden, the Emperor reinforced the Guard. Marshal Oudinot, whose corps was disbanded, was given command of the 1st and 3rd Divisions; Marshal Mortier, of the 2nd and 4th. Generals Couloumy and Lacoste were made adjutants general.

Each Old Guard battalion was increased to 800. The 1st Regiments were filled up with soldiers from the 2nd who had served more than six years and won citations. The 2nd Regiments were replenished by 30 choice men from each Young Guard regiment. The *vélite* battalions were also increased to 800 with Young Guardsmen who spoke Italian.

The Old Guard was expanded to two divisions. The 1st under Friant contained the chasseurs and grenadiers; the 2nd under Curial, the fusiliers, *vélites*, a battalion of the Saxon Guard furnished by the King, and a Polish battalion furnished by Poniatowski. The Saxons wore their own uniform and the Poles, Polish uniforms with Saxon shakos. The Neuchâtel battalion escorted the small headquarters staff and a Hessian battalion the large staff.

Cambronne was given command of the 2nd Chasseurs, and Christiani of the 2nd Grenadiers. Rousseau and Léglise commanded the fusiliers. On 1 October the Old Guard numbered 299 officers and 10,443 men including a Westphalian battalion attached to the 2nd Division.

The Young Guard was organized as follows:

The 1st Division was commanded by General Pacthod who had served with Bonaparte at Toulon, where he received seven wounds, and had campaigned in Italy, Poland, Illyria, and Spain. His three brigades, under Lacoste, Rottembourg, and Gros, contained the 1st–4th and 11th Voltigeurs and the 11th *Tirailleurs*. Barrois' 2nd Division contained the 1st–6th *Tirailleurs* under Poret de Morvan and Couloumy; Decouz's 3rd Division, the 5th–10th Voltigeurs under Boyer de Rebeval and Pelet; Roguet's 4th Division, Pompéjac's and Desalons' flankers, and the 7th–10th *Tirailleurs* under Flamand. In all, the young Guard numbered 711 officers and 20,283 men.

The artillery under General Dulauloy consisted of Desvaux's horse and Griois' foot artillery, Colonel Henrion's Young Guard batteries, and two regiments of train, totaling 134 officers and 7,056 men, with 202 guns including those of the reserve.

The three cavalry divisions remained unchanged; however, one squadron from each regiment of guards of honor was attached to the 3rd Division. The cavalry under Nansouty mustered 483 officers and 7,735 men.

Though sappers and marines were scarce, artisans were plentiful, with companies of bakers, butchers, and medical attendants totalling 543 officers and men. The twelve wagon train companies mustered 1,510 officers and men with 527 vehicles.

On 1 October the Guard present under arms numbered 1,684 officers and 47,269 men. In addition, 441 officers and 14,135 men were in depots at Paris, Mainz, and Frankfurt, and the 12th and 13th Voltigeurs and *Tirailleurs* were en route. Numerically the Guard now comprised a third of the army, though its moral factor was far greater.

CHAPTER 7

The Battle of Nations

AT the beginning of October the Allied armies, whose soul was the Tsar, joined forces from the mountains of Bohemia to Magdeburg to rendezvous on the Leipzig plain.

An English prophecy of ten years before ran something like this: 'The rulers of Russia and France will measure their strength at the approximate center of the world. They will fight for territory that they will immediately abandon, leaving one of them master of the field and dictator of the world.'

The Allied generals advanced cautiously and at a slow pace, fearful of an unexpected blow from the terrible warrior who made a practice of profiting from other men's mistakes.

Now Blücher made one. Crossing the Elbe to join Bernadotte, he neglected to hold the bridges in his rear, leaving the road to Berlin wide open.

The Emperor, escorted by elite gendarmes, left Dresden the morning of 7 October. He sent part of the Old Guard ahead to Wurschen and took the rest to Talwitz where he reviewed them on the 9th in the pouring rain. Next day he went to Düben. Meanwhile, Reynier and Bertrand reached the right bank of the Elbe and Berlin trembled.

The whole Guard was assembled around the little moated castle at Düben where the Emperor meditated and poured over his maps. Oudinot and Mortier bivouacked in front at the windmill, and the cavalry guarded the camp from a distance. Curial was escorting the Saxon King. Friant surrounded the 'palace' with 10,000 men.

No one saw the Emperor. The troopers of the picket and service squadrons smoked their pipes; the marshals came and went; the 'red-faced fellow' (Ney) stormed and Berthier bit his nails. Alerts came thick and fast, with orders to prepare to leave; yet nobody stirred except to march to Leipzig and return.

Was the King of Naples (Murat) falling under Alexander's spell? He was certainly retreating very fast before Schwarzenberg! From Munich or Bamberg the Prince of Neuchâtel (Berthier) received a note from his father-in-law[1] announcing the defection of Bavaria. The air was thick with treason.

The French prepared to accept the great battle the Allies were offering on the Leipzig plain. On 13 October Drouot was ordered to send the Guard to Leipzig in the following order: Mortier in the van, then Oudinot, the artillery reserve, and Walther's division, followed by d'Ornano who, with Latour-Maubourg, was directed to 'protect

---

[1] Prince William of Bavaria.

313

the right flank and scout'. Curial and Lefebvre-Desnoëttes were detached to escort the King of Saxony.

Friant left at 4 a.m. on the 14th. The Emperor arrived in his carriage before Leipzig at noon. He had had difficulty finding horses to pull the Guard artillery. It was raining, the road was bad, and the troops made slow progress; but the cheering was endless.

The Emperor halted at Reudnitz, a pretty village a mile from Leipzig. The escort lit a great fire in the field and brought an armchair and a table which was soon covered with maps. The picket kept back the curious while the Emperor got settled. He sat down, stood up, rubbed his hands together, walked up and down with his hands behind his back, kicked the logs into the fire with his toe, took a pinch of snuff, pulled out his watch, wound it . . . He was evidently nervous. From time to time firing was heard to the south. The King of Saxony passed by and had an interview with the Emperor. Then he dismissed Curial's escort and entered the city.

At Kohlgarten, a suburb with a fine park studded with villas, the quartermaster of the palace installed the Emperor on the first floor of the residence of a Leipzig banker named Wester, marking with chalk the rooms in that and the neighboring houses assigned to the suite, high officers, and aides. The first battalion of the 1st Chasseurs posted sentries at every avenue of approach.

The Guard arrived at 4 p.m. The Emperor mounted his horse and went out to meet it. The drums beat, the bands played, and soon bivouacs were formed, rations issued, and fires lighted in Kohlgarten and the surrounding fields, near the junction of the Taucha and Dresden roads. The artillery did not arrive until midnight.

The firing in the distance ceased and wounded began to arrive. Beyond Liebert-wolkwitz a battle had been fought between the King of Naples and Schwarzenberg's Austro-Russians. The outskirts and boulevards of Leipzig were overflowing with troops who had arrived during the day, evening, and night. The enemy was approaching from the north, south, and east.

The 15th was spent in reconnaissance, preparations, and even amusement. From the Meusdorf hills the Emperor and the King of Naples studied the terrain. On the right lay Kleeberg and the wooded marshes of the Pleisse; in front, Liebertwolkwitz and the University Woods; far to the left was the forest of Kirchbach with Holzhausen in the foreground. Murat's troops had fought near Wachau and were tired.

The officers and soldiers went into town and visited the people on whom they had been billeted either last year or in 1807, reviving old memories and renewing old romances. 'A battle is coming', said the townsfolk. 'And we will surely win it', replied the soldiers. They drank wine. The shops were open and heavily patronized. The Italian cafés of Buzzi and Mainoni were full of customers.

At the 'palace' the Emperor dictated his orders. All night carts rumbled by and oaths and cries of 'Make way!' rose above the tumult. The horizon ahead was aglow with campfires and the air was rent by the crackle of musketry.

16 October. The grenadiers relieved the chasseurs at daybreak. The artillery of the Guard was harnessed. By 7 a.m. the misty plain was covered with marching troops.

On the Lausick road a long, dense column was advancing slowly. The Guard was on the march to its positions. In the van marched Oudinot's and Mortier's divisions, followed by the artillery and cavalry. The Old Guard brought up the rear. It halted in a hollow near Probstheida where the infantry deployed in massed battalions at either side of the road and ordered arms.

A great roar of '*Vive l'Empereur!*' rippled across the field as the Emperor arrived in a carriage with Berthier. Napoleon mounted his horse and rode with the service squadron to Meusdorf where he occupied a tobacco mill. Mortier's divisions were massed behind Lauriston at Liebertwolkwitz, flanked on the left by Macdonald, and on the right by the cavalry reserve, Victor, and finally Poniatowski who was supporting Curial's division near Kleeberg.

At 9 a.m. the battle was opened from the Pleisse to the University Woods by three shots fired by enemy gunners. Then followed such a fearful cannonade 'as was never heard before', by all accounts. It was heavily concentrated between Liebertwolkwitz and the river. The columns of Kleist, Wittgenstein, and Klenau advanced and made good progress.

Towards 10 a.m. sixty guns of the Guard and Drouot's reserve went into action before Wachau, pouring an effective crossfire into the enemy infantry and artillery. On Lauriston's left the Young Guard forced its way into Liebertwolkwitz. From there the troops made a brilliant sortie and attacked the Austrians in the University Woods. Firing their muskets effectively and fighting from tree to tree, one of Roguet's brigades succeeded in occupying the park.

Through the mist and smoke Mortier spied enemy cavalry preparing to charge. He formed 3,000 *tirailleurs* of the 7th and 8th Regiments in squares and posted the 9th on their flank.

'Don't make a sound, and don't fire until ordered,' he warned the impatient lads, his shrill voice ringing out above the din. Marguet's and Flamand's *tirailleurs* stopped the cavalry dead at fifty paces. Then the enemy horsemen were counterattacked by Murat, supported by Desvaux's artillery. Alas, Murat's cuirassiers proved too weak and were driven back.

Full of confidence and enthusiasm, the Young Guard impatiently awaited the order to pursue their foe. However, they could not see through the smoke the fierce combat raging on the right in which Wachau was taken and lost several times. They did not know that the Austrians had crossed the Pleisse, nor that Poniatowski and Curial had established a crossfire in a desperate attempt to keep the bridges at Dölitz and Connewitz from falling into enemy hands and causing the whole French line to collapse. They did not know that Macdonald had retired his left flank before Blücher's army of 70,000 men; nor that 25,000 soldiers of Ney and Marmont had been badly mauled and were in retreat towards Pfaffendorf and the Halle gate; nor that the enemy had advanced to within a few hundred yards of the road to France when Bertrand retrieved the situation by recapturing from Gyulay the Elster bridges and the village of Lindenau.

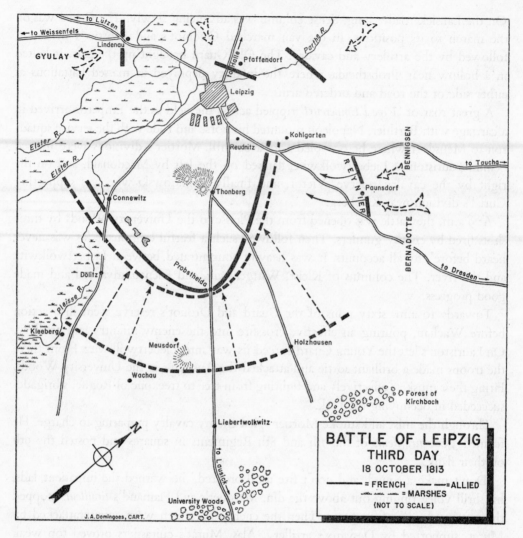

to Lützen
to Weissenfels
Lindenau
GYULAY
to Halle
Pfaffendorf
Parthe R.
Leipzig
Elster R.
Elster R.
Kohlgarten
Reudnitz
REYNIER
BENNIGSEN
to Taucha
Thonberg
Paunsdorf
BERNADOTTE
Connewitz
to Dresden
Dölitz
Probstheida
Pleisse R.
Kleeberg
Holzhausen
Meusdorf
Wachau
Forest of
Kirchbach
Liebertwolkwitz
N
to Lausick
University Woods

BATTLE OF LEIPZIG
THIRD DAY
18 OCTOBER 1813
━━ = FRENCH ╍╍ =ALLIED
⩗ = MARSHES
(NOT TO SCALE)

J. A. Domingoes, CART.

LEIPZIG

After Napoleon's victory at Dresden the Allies won a series of minor battles against the marshals operating separately, gradually surrounding Napoleon. Since the Allies were obviously planning to concentrate around Leipzig and cut his supply line, Napoleon moved his main force to that city and prepared for battle.

The Allies moved in from north, south, and east. On the first day of the battle they were in force only in the south. Napoleon attacked the southern force while holding off the others, but failed to reach a decision. He realized that next day he would be outnumbered 2 to 1. On the third day the Allies made a frontal attack. Though the French lines were not pierced Napoleon was forced to withdraw. On the 19th the French corps retired through the city and across the Elster, losing about 20,000 men in the crossing. The Allies pursued slowly. The French defeated the Bavarians, who tried to cut off their retreat, and retired across the Rhine in a pitiful state reminiscent of the Russian campaign.

Actually, despite local successes, a ring of fire was closing around the French. Even if Napoleon managed to retreat to Weissenfels, he would be obliged to resume the battle on the 18th to give himself room to breathe.

At 9 p.m. the firing ceased. In their bivouacs behind Liebertwolkwitz the soldiers of the Young Guard saw the Emperor arrive on horseback, preceded by two chasseurs with torches. He ordered Mortier's divisions to keep fires going to deceive the enemy and march by stealth to Leipzig, relieving Bertrand's corps at Lindenau and the Elster bridges. The latter would leave immediately for Lützen and Weissenfels to occupy the crossing over the Saale. On this confidential mission depended the safety of the whole army, since a retreat was now inevitable.

Curial and his Poles were left in the valley of the Pleisse. Lieutenant Pleine-Selve, whose platoon had captured General Merveldt as he directed the Austrian attack, was brevetted major and appointed aide to Dumoustier. (Though he had never held the rank of captain, the promotion stood since the Emperor was infallible.)

The capture of General Merveldt might have important consequences. That evening the General was sent back to his own lines with a peace proposal from the Emperor to his father-in-law.

In a hollow behind Meusdorf the Emperor's tents were pitched in the middle of a square of Grumblers who had not left his side despite casualties from the enemy artillery. Tonight they were formed in six lines, the alternate platoons standing under arms while the rest sat on their packs with their muskets between their knees. The guard was changed every hour.

The artillery bivouacked in front and the cavalry in the rear. In the various corps the units were equalized and the stragglers rounded up. Friederichs, the old commandant of the fusiliers, had been mortally wounded; so, too, had Couloumy who died on 29 October. The 1st Grenadiers and 1st Chasseurs had lost 7 officers, and the fusilier-grenadiers 12, including both majors and Lieutenant Sénot who were wounded. The Young Guard had lost 120 officers. The artillery had had 14 officers killed and 31 wounded; the cavalry, 5 killed and 23 wounded.

All the villages in the plain were burning. The steeple in Probstheida had just collapsed.

On Sunday in Leipzig the bells pealed and a Young Guard band played during the mounting of the Saxon and Polish guard before the palace of the Saxon King. A regiment of voltigeurs marched by. The elite gendarmes escorted some prisoners across town. These sights were of little interest to the citizens who were busy guarding their houses against pillagers and trading with the soldiers. A pitiful procession of wounded was wandering about looking for the field hospitals. More than 2,500 were stuffed into the old granary where many died for lack of care.

On the morning of the 18th the sentries on the front line peered into a cold mist. They kindled fires with the muskets of the dead while waiting for the enemy attack. During the night the Emperor had given orders to evacuate the wagons and close up the lines around the city. He had left his bivouac at 3 a.m. and moved his tents to the Thonberg (where the 'Napoleonstein' may be seen today) behind Probstheida.

At dawn he went to Lindenau to inspect the Elster crossing, in charge of Mortier. Around 7 a.m. cannon thundered along the whole front. In a few moments Napoleon was back on the Thonberg. The Old Guard was under arms. Part of its artillery had already crossed the Elster.

Nothing was visible ahead through the mist and smoke. Under a hail of grapeshot the two armies attacked one another ferociously. Oudinot's Young Guard divisions were sandwiched in between Victor on the left and Poniatowski on the right. The Polish prince, created a marshal only two nights ago, and Victor had made a pact not to abandon their positions. Now they were being seriously threatened by the Austrian reserves.

Around the Thonberg the Emperor divided his Old Guard into four strong columns with a battery assigned to each. The artillery reserve was at hand, also the cavalry. Napoleon set off at a gallop towards Connewitz, ordering three of Griois' foot batteries and the Old Guard horse artillery to follow. These were installed so close to the front that the gunners had to defend themselves with muskets. The *Vélites* of Florence had to be brought up to support them, for at that moment Schwarzenberg was making a determined attempt to cross the river at Connewitz to cut off the French line of retreat.

He did not succeed; nor did Wittgenstein at Probstheida, a centre of resistance where Curial's division covered itself with glory. Nor did Blücher at Reudnitz, though reinforced by Benningsen and the renegade Bernadotte, whose arrival provoked the French army to fury, and in spite of the Saxons and the Württemberg cavalry who suddenly turned against their comrades-in-arms.

When Reynier sent an officer to report the latter episode to the Emperor he was greeted with the words: 'Silence! Not another word of this infamy!'

Nansouty's Old Guard squadrons, followed by a detachment of Grumblers, galloped behind the Emperor to Reudnitz. When the colpacks, helmets, and bearskin bonnets of the troops that had made all Germany tremble loomed out of the smoke an awe-struck cry arose: '*Die alte Kaisergarde!*'[2]

Not far from where Ney stood hatless, wounded, his coat in shreds, crying with rage and slashing with his saber at the band of brigands besetting him, the Emperor remained calm. He launched Ornano's and Walther's squadrons across flaming Kohlgarten to the open breach. The shock of forces let loose was tremendous. The ensuing struggle was fought to the death, desperately and without mercy, amid the deafening din of artillery, falling masonry, cries of rage against the traitor[3] whose marshal's baton was bought with French blood, and shouts of '*Vive l'Empereur!*'

The sun went down at 5.19.

The Marshals commanding the right flank had kept their vow. In the center the Guard and Lauriston still held Probstheida; on the left Macdonald still held a salient

[2] 'The Old Imperial Guard!'

[3] Bernadotte, one of Napoleon's marshals, had quit the French army in 1810 on being offered the succession to the throne of Sweden and later joined the Coalition against Napoleon. – Ed.

PLATE 121

Poniatowski
(*From a contemporary colored engraving*)

PLATE 122

a) Arrival of Tsar Alexander I in Germany, 1813
(*From an original watercolor by J. M. Hess*)

b) Russian artillery, 1813
(*From an original drawing by Johann Adam Klein*)

PLATE 123

PLATE 124

a) Bertrand
(*Contemp. engraving*)

b) Nansouty
(*Contemp. lithograph; Bibliothèque Nationale*)

c) Wittgenstein
(*After contemp. portrait*)

d) Bernadotte
(*Engr. after Kinson*)

PLATE 125

Allied sovereigns giving thanks on the battlefield of Leipzig
(From an original gouache by an anonymous 'eye-witness')

to the Parthe; Marmont, Ney, and the Guard were still fighting in Kohlgarten. Bivouac fires were lighted on the spot. It was raining.

In the market place of Leipzig, before the house of the old King Frederick, Dressler's Saxon battalion was standing guard with ordered arms. To belong to the Imperial Guard was a guaranty of fidelity. On the boulevard leading to the horse market, the grenadiers of the duty battalion stacked arms in front of the *Prussian Arms Inn*. The Emperor was expected and a squad of lusty fellows was clearing the 'palace' by throwing excess furniture out of the window. With the debris they kindled a bonfire below.

At midnight the Guard batteries bivouacked on the glacis. Nansouty's cavalry crossed the bridges and joined Mortier at Lindenau. Only last Friday General Boulart of the artillery had been gloating over his stores of matériel. Now, on Tuesday, they were practically exhausted.[4] Passing down the main road that continued for over two miles, crossing thirty temporary bridges and encumbered with troops of every branch, Boulart remembered Krasny and the Berezina.

He collected his attenuated convoy and, regardless of whom he jostled in the process, crossed the bridges[5] over the Elster.

[4] The French had fired 220,000 rounds of ammunition in two days. – Ed.
[5] The 'bridges' over the Elster, which was broad and meandering, were mostly subsidiary structures leading to one high bridge at Lindenau which was the French army's principal avenue of retreat from Leipzic. – *Ibid*.

CHAPTER 8

The Retreat

BEFORE daybreak on the 19th a retreat was ordered under cover of the rear-guards.

'The Emperor has put you in charge of guarding all bridges from Leipzig to Lindenau', Berthier wrote Oudinot at 3 a.m. 'Cross the river at daybreak and follow the boulevards leading to the suburbs. Prepare to blow up all the bridges. Post a guard at each one . . . and form reserves to protect the column and its flanks from interference by the enemy . . .'

Mortier's two divisions had already been alerted. 'Proceed to Lützen with one of your divisions and the Old and Young Guard cavalry', the Emperor ordered the Duke of Treviso. 'Have the baggage train and park follow, flanked by cavalry columns. Leave Barrois' division at Lindenau to guard the positions between it and the road to Halle, until relieved.' These precautions were important, for Langeron's Russians had infiltrated the islands between the Elster and the Pleisse, threatening the French retreat.

Vionnet's brigade went ahead with two guns to clear a passage to the left of the road. The army poured out of Leipzig and Lindenau, fighting as it went. Vionnet, fearing his troops might be stranded, had Major Guillemin of the 2nd *Tirailleurs* build him a bridge across the Elster 'in a secluded spot, out of sight of the road'. Thanks to this bridge, when relieved by Fournier's brigade he led his unit to safety.

Meanwhile, Darriule's *tirailleurs* pushed back the Russian infantry from Rosenthal.

At 6 p.m. the Emperor went to say goodbye to the King of Saxony and release Major Dressler of the Saxon Guard from his allegiance to France. Returning to Lindenau, Napoleon made sure that the Elster bridges were mined. 'Blow them up when the last platoon has crossed', he ordered. Then he went to sleep, oblivious of the bursting shells and flying bullets.

At 9.30 a.m. he awoke with a start as the high bridge blew up prematurely, leaving Macdonald, Reynier, Lauriston, and Poniatowski stranded on the right bank. A corporal of engineers had lost his head![1] Now the unfortunate soldiers of the 5th, 7th, and 11th Corps lost theirs, and the scenes of the Berezina were re-enacted. Something must be done. It was a job for the Old Guard.

The grenadiers and chasseurs were drawn up in line of battle with orders to let no one pass while their officers questioned each soldier, collected those of the vanguard into units, and passed them through under a commander.

Finally, at dawn on the 20th the Old Guard and the artillery reached Lützen. That afternoon they marched to Weissenfels where the gunners dispersed a Cossack attack.

[1] His colonel being absent, when he saw Langeron's troops approaching he lit the fuse. – Ed.

During the retreat Maximilian Joseph, King of Bavaria by the grace of Napoleon, tried to bar the passage of the French from the front while the Allies pursued their rear. The *Tondu* would hand out no more crowns! The Bavarian defection posed a serious problem, since a strong vanguard was needed to fight its way through one enemy, and a strong rear-guard to hold off the other.

The Duke of Treviso (Mortier) commanded the vanguard, consisting of Roguet's and Barrois' Young Guard divisions and d'Ornano's cavalry division. By the Emperor's order Lefebvre-Desnoëttes' light cavalry, with reinforcements from the Line, galloped ahead to 'scour the plain before Weimar'.

Mortier left Weissenfels by night on the 20th for Freyburg to support Bertrand who had led the army out of Leipzig. The Emperor followed with Friant's Old Guard infantry and Walther's cavalry.

Meanwhile, at 3 a.m. on the 21st, the Duke of Reggio (Oudinot) left Lindenau with his two divisions under Pacthod and Decouz to cover the army's retreat. When within sight of Lützen, pursued by enemy cavalry, he received the order to take command of the rear-guard.

Towards 2 p.m. that afternoon Oudinot arrived at Weissenfels, destroyed the bridges behind him, and slept in the house the Emperor had vacated nine hours before. The Duke of Reggio was ill. As he was consulting his maps someone brought him a sword the Emperor had left behind. Decouz reported that the enemy was approaching, and almost immediately shells began to fall.

Oudinot was followed by the Guard artillery which was escorted no longer by the Guard, but by a division of Augureau's corps. Thanks to Boulart's efforts in Leipzig, Dulauloy had 174 guns, 181 caissons carrying 16,500 projectiles, and 38 loaded with 60,800 infantry cartridges.

The rear-guard reached Eckartsberga the next afternoon around five after a difficult march over a steep and narrow road. A dispatch from the Emperor warned: 'Keep an eye on your left and watch out for troops coming from Kösen'. All day they had heard Bertrand's guns thundering from that direction.

Word came that in Leipzig Lauriston had been captured, and Macdonald had swum the Elster. Poniatowski had drowned trying to follow him. There were humble heroes as well. A Young Guardsman captured on the 18th had escaped and made his way into the besieged city of Dresden to warn Gouvion-Saint-Cyr of the disaster at Leipzig.

Lefebvre-Desnoëttes reached Weimar with 2,000 men on 22 October and sneaked into town unnoticed under cover of a heavy fog. He was promptly attacked from all sides by Platov's Cossacks and forced to retire in disorder. The Austrian and Russian cavalry sent in pursuit fell upon Krasinski's Poles who retired in good order to Erfurt where the Emperor arrived next day.

Napoleon's communications with France were now virtually cut. The Bavarian General von Wrede was reported to be concentrating his forces to march on Gelnhausen, a strategic defile on the stage route between Gotha and Mainz, on the 27th.

This left Napoleon exactly four days in which to beat the Bavarians to Gelnhausen, 180 kilometers away, and collect a sufficient force to face the enemy at Hanau on the river Kinzig, a tributary of the Main. It could be done, but with what?

The army was scattered and in a pitiful state. The whole Young Guard was now engaged in the rear where the corps of Mortier and the ailing Oudinot took turns, since the rear-guard had to march all night and fight all day in a ravaged country under incessant rain. Oudinot spent the 23rd and 24th at the tail end of the column to encourage the stragglers. Many were dying of exhaustion.

At Gotha the Emperor dined with the Marshal who was shaking with fever and ate nothing. He had typhus.

The Guard was now the Emperor's only dependable force; but the Young Guard had fought hard and was greatly diminished. At Eisenach the six Guard divisions turned to face the enemy and threw them back. Mortier and Oudinot fought a lively action against Yorck's vanguard until 8 p.m. while Pelet and his voltigeurs guarded the passage of the army. The 2nd and 4th Divisions held the advanced posts through the night; meanwhile, Decouz's division was sent to relieve the Old Guard which had marched all night, then fought all day to capture and hold the village where the Imperial Headquarters was established.

Then the march was resumed. Strung out for 75 miles and harassed in front, in the rear, and on both flanks by Cossacks – who finished off the lame and the typhus victims unable to keep up – the French army fled towards the Rhine. Escorted by Poles, the Emperor marched in the middle with the Old Guard, ready to aid the vanguard in case of resistance ahead, or the Young Guard relentlessly pursued by Schwarzenberg and Blücher in the rear. At the slightest delay this handful of 30,000 men could be caught between two fires and annihilated (see Plate 129b).

The retreat was reminiscent of Russia. Though the cold was less intense, the weather was far from warm. Men were dying of hunger and lack of care.

On the 27th at Hünefeld the duty battalion with a few guns was obliged to chase the enemy from the Imperial headquarters. That day, as a year ago, the soldiers reached the end of their tether. Had the *Tondu* not been with them they would have lain down in the ditches to die. But on that very morning anxiety and exhaustion led Schwarzenberg and Blücher to give up the chase. Now the Bavarians alone remained between the French and the Rhine.

On 29 October, in the castle of Essemburg near Hanau, the Emperor prepared to force the Bavarian blockade with his old Guard, numbering 8,000 foot, 4,000 horse, and 1,100 gunners with 80 guns. There was little sleep that night at Imperial Head-quarters. Lefebvre-Desnoëttes was sent to scout like a subaltern. He reported the roads cut, all the bridges destroyed, and that the enemy was everywhere – in the Lamboy forest, the Kinzig valley, and on both sides of the river. The road to France was blocked and defended in force.

At eight next morning the Old Guard squadrons, drawn up behind Langenselbold, detached six hundred horse to General Laferrière-Levêque of the horse grenadiers.

Then, preceded by Poles, chasseurs, and dragoons and followed by Lefebvre-Desnoëttes, the Emperor set off for Hanau.

Ahead the battle was already joined, with Macdonald and Lamotte engaged. The latter held the edge of the Lamboy forest. The Emperor would have liked to bring up in support the army corps in the rear; but he complained that his orders were no longer obeyed.

Towards 3 p.m., with the grenadiers formed in square behind him, Napoleon flung out his arm and said: 'The chasseurs will charge'.

Curial promptly formed the 2nd Regiment in line of battle and launched it onto the road and into the woods beyond. Though its commander Cambronne fell wounded with a dozen of his officers, the chasseurs pushed the Bavarians back to the Kinzig valley where they retired behind a formidable artillery.

'One is proud to wear the uniform when he sees soldiers like these', wrote General Griois who witnessed the charge.

Drouot led a reconnaissance and, with the Emperor's approval, posted 50 guns in line at the edge of the forest. With these he put the enemy artillery out of action by oblique fire. When the Old Guard batteries were charged by Bavarian cavalry Laferrière led Saint-Germain's division and the horse Guard to their rescue. Captain Sachon charged the enemy with 100 dragoons at the exit of the forest, upsetting three squares, and won a major's epaulet. Colonel Dautancourt and his Polish lancers sabered the Bavarian light-horse so effectively that Nansouty announced that the Colonel 'might consider himself promoted to major general'. The promotion was confirmed on 28 November (see Plate 130).

By 5 p.m. the Kinzig valley was cleared of the enemy. The cavalry suffered heavy losses. Assistant Adjutant Major Guindey of the horse grenadiers, who had dispatched Prince Louis of Prussia at Saalfeld, was killed. Lt. Colonel Radziwill of the Polish lancers and several chasseur officers were mortally wounded. In the dragoons Letort lost two majors and eight officers. Captain Abdalla of the Mameluks and a chasseur major were wounded.

Friant's grenadiers held Neuhof and the bridge at Lamboy, and the road to Frankfurt was clear.

In the dead of the following night Mortier's last brigade marched by stealth into the forest where the battle had been fought. General Marguet, in command, suddenly heard the challenge: 'Who goes there?'

'France!'

One of Mortier's aides stepped out of the bushes to warn him that Hanau had been recaptured by the enemy, and that the troops must bypass the town by a certain detour which would eventually bring them back to the Frankfurt road. 'I knew this detour of old', Mortier wrote later. 'I had used it ever since my first campaigns in Germany with Moreau's army.'

In the Emperor's hour of need neither the Rhine princes nor Murat had lifted a finger to help their friend and sovereign, while many less favored by fortune remained loyal.

An old officer marching from Leipzig with Grivel's marines overheard a young lieutenant complain that he had been forgotten in Spain.

'What is an oversight', the veteran observed, 'when one is sure of the friendship and esteem of his comrades, and feels himself a link in the chain that binds the army together? Do you suppose the "big hats" can do this alone?

'The influence over a soldier of a subaltern who can take what comes without complaining or being discouraged is as powerful as that of the highest ranking officer covered with orders and sashes. This is the modest devotion that bears the daily burdens and sets an example of military virtue to the whole nation. Surely, this role is grand enough to console a man for anything – even injustice.'

De Vigny[2] must have met this old warrior somewhere.

On 1 November at 7 a.m. the Old Guard was drawn up with Oudinot's divisions on the esplanade at Frankfurt and the Emperor was cheered lustily. This was the last 'Vive l'Empereur!' ever heard across the Rhine.

Two days later the Guard, except for Mortier's and Ornano's divisions which remained at Kastel until the 5th, marched into Mainz. The formidable bridgehead, once so green and smiling, was now desolate. Its trees, houses, and inns had all been destroyed; nevertheless, it was the Promised Land to an army that had marched 250 miles through enemy territory, trailed by a long procession of ghosts wasted with dysentery.

As the exhausted soldiers sighted its steeples they cried: 'France!'

---

[2] A reference to Alfred de Vigny's famous classic *Servitude et Grandeur Militaires*. – Ed.

CHAPTER 9

Invasion Threatens

'THE army returned from across the Rhine very tired and much diminished. My regiment was full three months ago, but it has not 300 men left . . . People think the Emperor will at last make peace, else the enemy might march into France. Everyone longs for a rest . . . The Emperor is at Mainz. May he make peace! . . .'

Thus wrote Major Deblais of the 1st *Tirailleurs* to his girl on 6 November 1813. The opinion expressed was general.

More intuitive than the politicians and marshals, the Emperor knew very well that his enemies would not grant him an honorable peace. Alexander preferred to dictate terms from Paris; Metternich and Prussia coveted Germany, and England coveted Belgium and Holland. The Allies were bent on the downfall of Napoleon and his 'insolent nation'. The Emperor knew all this, and prepared to resist invasion. What did the French think?

The old nobility and the rich bourgeoisie, whose business was in the doldrums, had turned against Napoleon. But the people, who had shed so much blood for his glory, still believed in him.[1] Despite his defeat, his prestige as an invincible commander persisted. The people believed he, too, wanted peace, and that if he did not conclude it immediately it was because he was sure of ultimate victory. In the army the marshals demanded peace so as to enjoy the honors and wealth he had showered upon them, while the rank and file and the Guard cried '*Vive l'Empereur!*'

Obviously this was no longer the Guard of 1805 – nor yet of 1809. It was too big and too mixed; but it was still an elite corps with strength and soul and a single chief: the Emperor. Since it was French it continued to grumble, but its tune had changed. At Jena, Friedland, and Wagram the Guard had 'cried with rage' to be left idle while others fought, and the *Tondu* had laughingly replied: 'Your turn will come!' Now their turn *had* come and they complained that the Line left most of the fighting to them. It was the Old Guard that had tramped over the bellies of the Bavarians at Hanau, and the Young that had protected the retreat without flinching.

Napoleon entrusted the country's defence to three men: in the north to Macdonald who was dynamic and honest, but unlucky; in the center to Marmont who was not entirely loyal; and in the south to Victor, a good soldier without other talents.

Mortier's and Curial's divisions were stationed west of the Rhine. The Old Guard remained at Mainz with the Emperor and restored order in the city and environs which

---

[1] This statement seems rather too general in the light of subsequent events. – Ed.

were swarming with stragglers and deserters. Within three days they picked up 26,000 men, sending 8,000 to hospitals and the rest back to their regiments.

On leaving Mainz on 7 November the Emperor left his marshals around 130,000 men from the army, depots, and military districts. He sent the Guard to cantonments on the Saar. It needed rest and reinforcements if it were to continue to play the role assigned to it in the last campaign.

At the end of November the Guard was stationed around Trier, at the centre of the strategic chessboard. The Duke of Treviso (Mortier) was lodged in the Episcopal Palace where his wife and daughters joined him. The Old Guard of 7,000 foot, the artillery reserve, and the horse batteries were quartered in the surrounding country. The 4,000 voltigeurs of Pacthod and Decouz were in Luxembourg with their artillery. The 3,500 *tirailleurs* of Barrois and Roguet were stationed on the roads to Coblenz and Mainz.

Ornano's 800 horse were at Sarreguemines, Lefebvre-Desnoëttes' 600 at Zweibrücken and Walther's 2,500 at Ober Moschel. General Dulauloy still had 2,000 gunners and 166 guns.

At Trier General Roguet took the Old Guard's discipline in hand. Officers of dismounted units were denied horses. On Sunday, 5 December, a *Te Deum* was sung in the Cathedral to commemorate the coronation. The service, attended by all the officers with General Friant and the Duke of Treviso, was followed by a dress parade.

The troops were paid up to 15 November. Glad to be out of Mainz, where typhus victims were dying in the streets and bread cost 5 francs a pound, the chasseurs and grenadiers renewed their zest for life and brought gaiety to the villages. Quartered by companies, they smoked, drank beer, hunted, fished, danced, and courted the Rhine maidens. 'We don't know any German', they said, 'but one does not have to talk to a pretty girl!'

The Emperor ordered the Guard reorganized as follows:

OLD GUARD: 1st Division (General Friant): 4 battalions of grenadiers and 4 of chasseurs: 9,600 men; 2nd Division (General Curial): 4 battalions of fusiliers, 4 of flankers, 2 of Italian *vélites*: 8,000 men.

YOUNG GUARD (Marshal Mortier): 1st Division (General Meunier): 1st–4th Voltigeurs; 2nd Division (General Decouz): 5th–8th Voltigeurs; 3rd Division (General Boyer de Rebeval): 9th–12th Voltigeurs; 4th Division (General Barrois): 1st–4th *Tirailleurs*; 5th Division (General Rottembourg): 5th–8th *Tirailleurs*; 6th Division (General Roguet): 9th–12th *Tirailleurs*. Total – 57,600 men.

The 13th Voltigeurs and *Tirailleurs* were not assigned to a division. Each division was assigned 2 foot batteries which, with 4 reserve batteries and 6 companies of horse artillery, would provide the Guard with 196 guns.

An engineer company was attached to the Old Guard and three to the Young. Each division was assigned a wagon train company and a field hospital.

The depots of Paris and Metz were filled with voltigeurs and *tirailleurs* from former levies. More were due from the Classes of 1804–14. The Emperor planned to add a third battalion, raised from the 20,000 conscripts of 1815, to each Young Guard regiment; and to each Old Guard regiment, one raised from the Line.

To gain time Curial was ordered to send from Metz, and Michel from Paris, the conscripts already clothed, equipped, and armed in units of 1,200 which the Duke of Treviso would form into regiments in Luxembourg and Trier.

On his way to Metz to recuperate from his wounds General Walther died suddenly at Kusel. Perhaps it was merciful that the old Berchény hussar and hero of Hohenlinden and Eylau was spared the ultimate catastrophe. The Emperor wrote his wife: 'I share your grief deeply. In your husband I have lost one of my bravest and most trusted generals. I am asking my Grand Marshal (Bertrand) to go and see you and arrange what is best for you and your daughters . . .'

Walther's death obliged the Emperor to reorganize the cavalry into a light division of Young Guard chasseurs and 1st and 2nd Lancers under Lefebvre-Desnoëttes; and a heavy division under Guyot of Old Guard chasseurs, dragoons, and grenadiers.

On 3 December the Emperor created three regiments of *éclaireurs* (scouts) of 1,000 men each. The 1st Regiment, attached to the horse grenadiers, was to be dressed like the guards of honor and recruited from them; the 2nd, attached to the dragoons, uniformed like the chasseurs of the Line and recruited from 1,000 'Imperial postillions'; the 3rd, attached to the 1st Light-horse-Lancers, raised at Givet with men from the Polish depots at Sedan, and dressed like the Polish lancers of the Line. The officers and NCO's of the 1st Regiment ranked as Old Guard. The rest ranked with the 2nd Lancers (see Plate 134).

The 1st Scouts were christened 'scout-grenadiers' and the 2nd 'scout-dragoons'. Half the regiments would be ready on 1 January and the rest on the 30th, by which date – God willing – all 48 squadrons of the Guard would be mounted.

Would the enemy, who was both strong and fanatical, give Napoleon time to reorganize the guard and the army? He hoped so, for he believed that the Allied sovereigns would go into winter quarters until spring.

13 November. The cry 'Long Live the Prince of Orange!' rang out in the Hague, Amsterdam, and the Ruhr. Proclamations summoned the inhabitants to arms and exhorted them to help Generals Bülow and Wintzingerode. Belgium was in a ferment over the new conscription and requisitions. In Cologne people shouted 'Long live the Cossacks!'

All plans for reorganizing the Guard were upset in consequence. The Emperor knew that Macdonald's troops were unreliable and that their commander was a pessimist.[2] Therefore, he decided to meet the emergency with the means at hand despite the disorder inherent in large improvisations.

He ordered General Roguet to put together at Metz a division composed of the skeleton 12th and 13th Voltigeurs and *Tirailleurs*, 2 battalions of *pupilles,* 150 elite gendarmes, and 200 light cavalry from the Paris depots, and take it to Brussels with a Young Guard battery as soon as possible. On 30 November the 9th–11th *Tirailleurs*

---

[2] Macdonald commanded the left, or northern, wing of the French defense forces. – Ed.

were sent to reinforce him. Cadres of marines were sent to be filled from the Antwerp squadron. Sappers, artisans, surgeons, and vehicles were added to this 'Guard Reserve'. Finally, Lefebvre-Desnoëttes left for Brussels with his cavalry.

The Emperor wrote Daru on 4 December: 'All signs point to a serious war in Holland'.

The Duke of Reggio (Oudinot), barely recovered from typhus, was ordered to Brussels to command the 3rd-6th Young Guard Divisions.

So far the Guard was reorganized on paper only. Most units were still being formed. The 3rd Division, stripped to its cadres and shorn of the 12th Voltigeurs, was at Metz being filled up with conscripts. The 4th and 5th were being formed in Luxembourg. The 6th, being assembled by Roguet, had neither brigade commanders nor chief of staff. The 12th and 13th *Tirailleurs* had no lieutenants; the 10th, no NCO's. Miserable horses pulled the artillery whose caissons were half empty and whose guns were served by ignoramuses and German train soldiers. With these troops Campen had to be policed and brigades sent to Antwerp and Louvain.

'Send me some grenadiers I can use as corporals and sergeants', Roguet wrote Drouot on 21 December.

The 4th Young Guard Division was sent to Brussels by post, arriving after a five days' journey through the Ardennes, packed ten to a cart with their arms and baggage. The wagons had no seats – only straw provided 'at the expense of the owner'.

The 5th Young Guard Division marched by stages to Rheims, leaving on 10 December. From there it was ordered to Amiens to pick up reinforcements from Paris and conscripts from the Somme. This division got no further than Rheims. The cadres of the 9th and 10th Voltigeurs left for Lille on 8 December to pick up 5,200 conscripts from the northern departments and the Pas-de-Calais.

The Emperor issued the following order on 5 December:

'Today the depot commanders of the grenadiers and chasseurs will send officers to Lille and Antwerp by post to establish clothing factories for the conscripts of the Guard, taking with them the necessary funds. The clothing will be completed by 10 January 1814 when there will be 5,000 conscripts at Lille and 3,000 at Amiens.'

Was this an order or a fancy? It was an order which, for the most part, was executed.

Major Deblais of the 1st *Tirailleurs* had been very happy on the Moselle 'lodging with an old lady and giving a ball for the belles of Cochein' when orders came to leave for Luxembourg. Several days later he reached Brussels 'by cart through the Ardennes – a frightful place'. 'Some enemy partisans', he wrote, 'had got as far as Louvain. The country was filled with consternation, but the presence of our four regiments has restored order. They have sent us eight or nine hundred recruits by post, all dressed and equipped. We are busy training them from morning till night.'

Deblais, an 'old of the Old' who had barely escaped from Russia with his life, was neither surprised nor alarmed by the confusion around him. 'I am well off in Brussels', he wrote, 'with good lodgings and good food.' He found it perfectly natural to live at the Princess de Ligne's and 'dine with her from time to time'. He showed no surprise at being ordered to turn over to other units the recruits he had trained, and send the cadres of his 1st *Tirailleurs* to Amiens on 4 January to be filled up with conscripts.

After four days' leave in Paris Deblais joined his new regiment in Amiens. The first battalion was ordered to leave on 17 January for Champagne.

Thus, Barrois' division lost the 1st *Tirailleurs* and was left in Brussels with the 2nd–4th under Vionnet, Masson, and Carré, with a total of 2,519 officers and men plus artillery and train.

The Duke of Albuera (Suchet) was appointed colonel general of the Guard to replace Bessières. General Pelet was named adjutant general. General Petit of the Army of Catalonia was given command of the 1st Grenadiers, and Mallet of the 2nd Chasseurs. Darriule, Henrion, Rousseau, and van Merlen were made generals, and Rottembourg and Boyer given a third star. Lt. Colonel Testot-Ferry, former major in the dragoons of the Guard, was made commandant of the scout-grenadiers, and Hoffmayer of the scout-chasseurs.

The Guard's organization, clothing, and training were rushed in the face of every imaginable difficulty. At La Fère, d'Aboville complained that his most experienced gunners had had a maximum of three months' service, and not a single NCO was ready to campaign. His officers were former quartermasters and supply officers. (Yet of fourteen lieutenants sent to the Young Guard as a whole, 12 were *legionnaires*, and all had fought in from 15 to 20 campaigns.)

Roguet's division was assigned Major Generals Flamand, a veteran of the *Gardes françaises*, and Aymard. These were men on whom Roguet could depend; but he had neither surgeons, commissaries, nor artisans. He conducted the training himself, for he had no cadres. The powder he burned to train the conscripts had left his artillery very vulnerable.

On 28 November the wagon train still lacked 31 officers, 1,428 men, 2,180 horses, 337 caissons, 72 ambulances, and 30 forges; the artisans' battalion, 10 officers and 320 men. The Emperor ordered these units filled and assigned 260 vehicles being built by marines in Antwerp, and others building in Metz and Vincennes.

A thousand uniforms of Sedan cloth and sets of equipment were required for the 1st and 2nd Lancers, and 900 for the scouts. Krasinski reported that the saddler Lapeyre was unable to furnish the scouts with belts, pouches, carbine slings, portmanteaux, or sabre-taches, and that his rival Meunier, 'knowing the fix we are in, has made things very difficult'.

Did he know that the purveyors were in just as much of a fix? That the *chasseurs à cheval* had owed their draper 221,712 francs since 1812, and owed him half a million in all? And that he was owed 426,707 francs by the 2nd Lancers and 91,783 by the horse grenadiers? The Guard owed him more than a million francs. He could 'no longer meet his obligations', and his ruin involved factories in Elboeuf and Berry and was 'plunging the workers into poverty'.

The expense of organizing the Guard in 1813 amounted to some 18½ million francs, and the State still owed the regimental councils 15,587,888 francs. But the soldiers had to be clothed – whether in cloth from Sedan, Charleville, or Timbuktu!

On 1 January the scouts had neither cloaks nor breeches. The 1st Scouts' uniforms were green, trimmed with silver. They were issued undress coats, 'trimmed' pantaloons, grey capes, and stable jackets. Only the NCO's and trumpeters received the prescribed hussar dolmans and pelisses.

Kozietulski, commanding the 3rd Scouts, was organizing the regiment at Givet without farriers or trumpeters, without pay, and sometimes without bread. Colonel Hoffmayer was obliged to appeal to the departments to uniform his 2nd Scouts, and to the Berg lancers for their mounts.

In Metz General Curial was having great difficulty organizing units and sending them out under orders that changed twice a week. He had about 7,000 men all told, including 32 Line depots, stragglers in hiding, and units coming and going from Mainz. Marshal Kellermann suggested the Guard depots be moved from Metz to Lille since the Emperor was sending the corps to Belgium. Depots could be established at Thionville for the cavalry and Saarlouis for the artillery.

Temporary hospitals at the Young Guard garrisons of Thionville, Gorzé, and Bitche were full of typhus patients. Fortunately, Larrey was in attendance with doctors and pharmacists.

The Ministry replied no longer to inquiries. Its bureaus were tired, confused, and swamped with work.

Since the enemy was not waiting for the French to complete their preparations, the Emperor had to turn his attention to the points in the greatest danger.

At the end of November Schwarzenberg's corps began to menace Switzerland and the Rhine bridgehead of Bâle. By 15 December there was no doubt that Alsace would be invaded by the Army of Bohemia, numbering 220,000 Austrian, Württemberg, Bavarian, Russian, and Prussian troops. Victor had less than 12,000. He had done nothing to put the garrisons into a state of defense or arouse the population whose patriotism was proverbial.

Up north the lines of the Ysel and the Lek were already breached. Neuss fell on 2 December. Utrecht and Breda were occupied. The civil authorities lost their heads and ordered mass evacuations, to the delight of the Dutch and Flemings.

Sixty elite gendarmes were routed by von Colomb's hussars and Cossacks on 15 December, and the Walloons were terrified . . .

BOOK VII

THE GUARD AT BAY

THE CAMPAIGN OF FRANCE[1]

In December 1813 several Allied armies crossed the Rhine and, still fearing Napoleon despite his inferior strength, began a slow invasion of France. Napoleon was reluctant to withdraw his garrisons from Italy and Spain for the defense of France. Refusing to face the reality of his position, he made exhorbitant demands in the peace negotiations which the Allies could not accept, even though torn by conflicting interests.

While the Allies halted and fell back temporarily they felt no disposition to treat with the Emperor on his terms. Napoleon's maneuvers showed his old brilliance; however, victories such as Brienne only encouraged concentration of the Allied forces. Repeated defeats of separate French armies made it obvious that the weakened Grand Army could not finally prevail, while Pyrrhic victories of Napoleon and the Guard such as Craonne cost the French irreparable losses.

Finally, at Arcis-sur-Aube Napoleon's reconnaissance failed. He found himself with about 20,000 men practically surrounded by an Allied force of 80,000. His line of retreat was a single bridge across the Aube. A French defeat was unavoidable; however, due to the Allies' failure to attack promptly, the bulk of the French forces escaped.

At last the Allies concentrated their armies and moved on Paris which capitulated. Napoleon abdicated on 11 April 1814.

[1] See map on endpaper on back cover.

CHAPTER 1

Alarm and Confusion

OF what did the Imperial Guard consist in December 1813, besides the troops in Belgium?

The only Old Guard division capable of effective resistance was the 1st at Trier under the command of General Friant, which mustered 150 officers and 5,600 men. The 2nd Division was being formed in Luxembourg under General Michel. Besides artillery, it numbered 155 officers and 1,600 fusiliers, flankers, and Italian *vélites*.

The Young Guard assigned to Oudinot was very weak. General Meunier's 1st Division numbered 117 officers and 4,700 men in two brigades under Generals Lacoste and Rousseau. Its batteries had few gunners. The third battalions formed the depot at Metz. General Decouz's 2nd Division at Thionville could put only 100 officers and 1,250 voltigeurs into the line with two skeleton batteries; its sole brigade commander was General Pelet.

At first the threat to Bâle seemed to worry the Emperor less than that to Holland and Belgium. 'I beg you to inform me the shortest route from Trier to Brussels', he wrote Mortier on 14 December.

Three days later, without waiting for a reply, he ordered the Marshal to leave for Namur with the 1st Division and the cavalry of the Old Guard, plus the artillery, marines, sappers, and service troops.

On the day after Christmas the vanguard entered Namur by the Pont de Jambes. The inhabitants ignored a driving snow to crowd the sidewalks from the bridge to the Place d'Armes. They never forgot the astounding apparition.

'There was Marshal Mortier, sword in hand, his roan charger almost hidden by the voluminous skirts of his greatcoat', wrote Monsieur Delhaize. 'His eyes were large and keen under arched eyebrows and he had a straight nose, thin lips, and a firm chin. His greying hair receded from the temples. All his features radiated vigor as well as tact and kindness. Behind him rode the illustrious soldiers' (see Plate 92d).

Before the Town Hall the Duke of Treviso paraded the grenadiers who looked forward to 'a good night and hospitality' in the natives' houses or the citadel.

'Russian and Dutch Cossacks', it seems, were infesting the frontier. 'And', the Emperor added, 'I believe there are some local Cossacks as well . . .'

'The cavalry of the Old Guard must be at them without delay', he wrote on the 20th. 'Tomorrow it will cross the Sambre . . .'

Meanwhile, Boyer de Rebeval was forming another division at Lille which, with Roguet's division near Antwerp and Barrois' at Brussels, would give the Emperor four

THE ANATOMY OF GLORY

Guard divisions with 6,000 horse and 70 guns between the Escaut, the Meuse, and Lille.

'Recommend that General Maison[1] command the Guard generals as firmly as those of the Line . . .' the Emperor wrote the Minister of War.

While the Duke of Treviso (Mortier) and the prefect of Sambre-et-Meuse were making plans to recapture Breda, the Marshal received an order from the Emperor in Paris:

'My Cousin:

The enemy is pouring into Bâle and marching on Belfort where his vanguard is due the (December) 24th. It is vital that my foot and horse Guard and my artillery reserve get under way for Rheims . . . I need not tell you that the object of this move is to start you along the road to Bâle before it is full of Cossacks . . . The news of your arrival will spread and calm the people's minds . . .'

The invasion had begun. Violating the neutrality of Switzerland, Schwarzenberg had crossed the Rhine on 20 December. The Old Guard must be everywhere at once. Lacking battalions, the 'Kaisergarde' had only its prestige with which to oppose the enemy.

The Emperor knew this. That day (20 December) he ordered a new division formed in Paris with two battalions each of fusiliers and flankers, the third battalions of ten *tirailleur* and voltigeur regiments, and 6,000 conscripts. On 26 December he created the 14th and 15th Regiments of *tirailleurs* and voltigeurs out of the Royal Guard of Spain, since Soult had now retired to Bayonne.

The situation at the front deteriorated rapidly. Morand's 4th Corps was blockaded in Mainz. Before a vigilant foe preparing to cross the Rhine at several points, Marmont retired to Neustadt, near Landau, with the 6th Corps of 10,000 men, Doumerc's cavalry corps of 3,000, and 36 guns.

In Alsace, Victor retreated across the Vosges with 10,000 troops of the 2nd Corps and 5,000 horse without pausing to defend the passes. He was berated by an aroused populace willing to fight and scorned by his own troops who wished to stop the enemy.

In the north Macdonald, commanding the 5th and 11th Corps with two cavalry corps under Exelmans and Arrighi and 88 guns, was threatened with being cut off from France entirely.

Farther north, General Molitor with 4,000 men was retreating before 50,000 Russians and Prussians under Bülow and Wintzingerode. General Maison's Line corps existed chiefly on paper. His only ready force was Roguet's and Barrois' Young Guard. Roguet's division contained 6,574 officers and men with 10 guns, and its morale was good. Barrois' division in Brussels mustered 3,177 on 1 January, plus artillery, but desertion was rife among its conscripts.

Though the Emperor urged him to take the offensive, General Maison was having difficulty defending Antwerp with a garrison consisting chiefly of half a dozen Young Guard depots, and 300 Young Guard cavalry.[2]

---

[1] Commander of the 1st Corps at Antwerp. – Ed.

[2] Actually, though continually prodded by the Emperor, General Maison never succeeded in mounting an offensive with his Northern Army, but confined himself to a few 'offensive reconnaissances' in which

PLATE 126

PLATE 127

Napoleon's bivouac in Thuringia
(From an original watercolor by James Augustus Atkinson)

PLATE 128

THE DUEL

John Bull referees the match between Blücher and Napoleon
(*From an original watercolor by Gottfried Schadow*)

PLATE 129

a) Combat between Cossack and Mameluk
(*From an original watercolor by William Heath*)

b) Cossacks attacking the French stragglers
(*From a contemporary colored lithograph by Vernet*)

PLATE 130

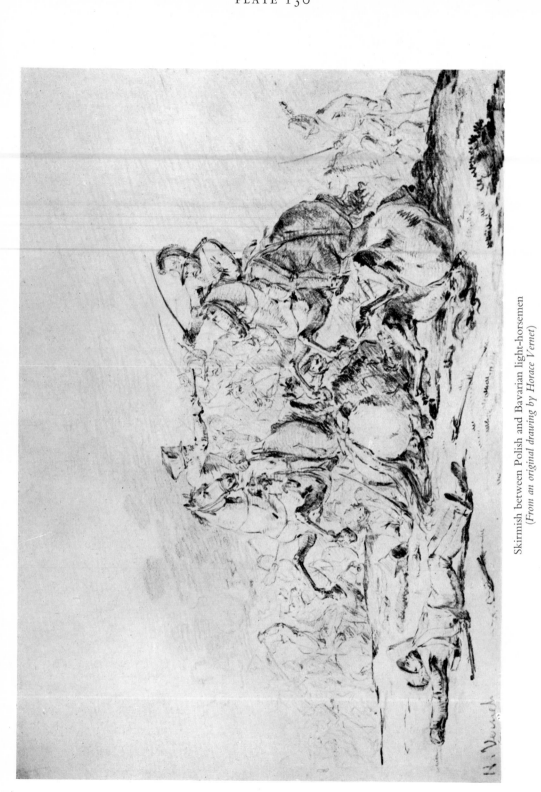

Skirmish between Polish and Bavarian light-horsemen
(From an original drawing by Horace Vernet)

Roguet took up a position at Hoogstraten, 30 kilometers from Antwerp, to guard the roads from Holland. Meanwhile, Lefebvre-Desnoëttes was recalled to Paris with the Polish light-horse, and Castex took command of the cavalry.

On 1 January 1814 a proclamation was issued at Hartwell, signed by the Count of Provence[3] as 'King of France', promising to hold posts in his government 'for those who earned them'.

In Paris, during a reception to the Legislature, the Emperor accused the deputies of treachery when their spokesman openly took him to task. 'Is this the moment for recrimination', Napoleon asked, 'when 200,000 Cossacks are crossing our frontiers? You shall have peace within three months or I shall die in the attempt!'

The situation of both France and the Emperor was precarious. The sovereign should stay in Paris to face the liberals and royalists leagued against him; but then, who would lead the army that disintegrated the moment his back was turned?

While preparing that night to 'don his boots of 1793', he dictated orders to Berthier to speed Mortier to Langres. His vanguard must be there the 10th, and his whole force by the 12th. An army of the right was to be concentrated at Colmar under Marmont, and a Young Guard corps of 18,000 men and 40 guns at Épinal under Curial. The 1st and 2nd Divisions of the Young Guard and the 2nd of the Old were to be filled up from the third battalions at Metz, and an army of 80,000 assembled at Langres under Mortier.

As soon as possible Barrois' division would be sent on from Brussels and Boyer's from Lille. Napoleon instructed the Chief of Staff to rush these orders to Marshal Kellermann at Metz. The weather was clear and the telegraph worked overtime. On 2 January Curial received orders to send Meunier's division from Saarlouis to Épinal, and to alert those still being formed by Decouz at Thionville and Michel in Luxembourg.

Meanwhile, on 1 January, while the Emperor was dictating his orders, Blücher crossed the Rhine at Caub, Baccharach, and Mannheim with the Army of Silesia numbering 80,000 men.

Marmont retreated to Saarbrücken. Victor abandoned Strasbourg. Lacking a supreme commander, the marshals operated individually, without liaison, and offered no resistance.

Since the enemy was proceeding with caution Kellermann still hoped to defend the Vosges. Old General Jean-Laurent Lacoste, the local commander, was a good man but

the Guard divisions participated creditably and suffered some casualties. For the most part, his units remained scattered. Roguet's division was locked up in Antwerp where it was virtually besieged by strong British and Prussian forces under Graham and Bülow, and later by Saxons under the Prince of Saxe-Weimar. Thus the Emperor was deprived of one of his ablest Guard commanders as well as two of his Young Guard divisions during the crucial campaign of France. Though these troops contributed for a time towards the containment of the enemy on the northern front, one can only conclude that the special talents of the Guard – particularly its amazing mobility – were wasted whenever it was separated from the Emperor. – Ed.

[3] The future Louis XVIII. – Ibid.

was terribly depressed by having lost his chief of staff, his nephew, and his aide from typhus in one day. He and the peg-legged General Cassagne had only miscellaneous militia, old cavaliers on donkeys, retired officers, and foresters with which to defend his territory.

Kellermann's only regulars were General Meunier's 1st Young Guard Division, with Generals Rousseau and Clément Lacoste commanding its brigades. The cadres were excellent, though the conscripts had never fired a shot in anger and were poorly dressed and equipped; but they were well armed and their artillery was complete.

Meunier's division left Saarlouis the night of 2 January. By this time the enemy was pouring into the upper Moselle valley, defended by old cavalrymen and young conscripts under the extraordinary General Duvigneau.

In Pont-à-Mousson vehicles were requisitioned to pick up Rousseau's brigade on the 3rd and take it the next day to Nancy where the inhabitants were busy making cartridges. But by the time the voltigeurs reached Nancy the enemy cavalry under Scherbatov was thirty miles from Épinal, and General Cassagne was obliged to order that town evacuated.

General Rousseau hastily issued ammunition to his voltigeurs. He rushed Major Devaux's battalion to guard the Moselle crossing, and a second to Dombasle. Meanwhile, on the 5th, Lacoste's brigade arrived in Nancy where it had a magnificent reception, and the people's courage revived. The troops completed their equipment, ate and drank heartily, and showed excellent morale.

At first the news that the Guard was between Nancy and Épinal 'in three bivouacs' acted as a deterrent to Scherbatov. General Rousseau was able to put Flavigny into a posture of defense and mine the bridge over the Moselle. Then on 7 January old Lacoste, the district commander, made an heroic decision. He ordered Rousseau's brigade of voltigeurs to leave a single company at Flavigny, and march with Duvigneau on Épinal.

The two generals reached the outskirts next day. The voltigeurs fired point-blank into a bivouac of 1,500 Cossacks who decamped in a hurry to Arches, pursued by Duvigneau's cuirassiers without cuirasses, hussars without boots, and gendarmes without hats. 'I have nothing but praise for our youngsters', Rousseau reported. 'They fought well.'

The people of Épinal welcomed their liberators with enthusiasm. The peasants at the outposts, armed with ancient blunderbusses, reported that the Russians and Württembergers had halted in the Moselle valley, and that their troops were frightened and bewildered. Had Kellermann only permitted Meunier's second brigade and his artillery to accompany Rousseau, the latter might have captured the pass of Arches as well.

Meanwhile Ney, ordered to lead the Guard divisions of Michel, Decouz, and Meunier to Épinal and defend the Vosges, did nothing; nor did Victor make a single move.

Rousseau and his voltigeurs held Épinal with a few soldiers of the 139th Regiment and Duvigneau's motley cavalry until the 11th when they were attacked in force and dislodged. Pursued by 4,000 infantry and 2,000 Cossacks, they made an heroic and costly retreat over abominable roads. The brave Devaux and a captain of the voltigeurs were killed, and Rousseau and seven officers severely wounded. One battalion of the 1st Voltigeurs lost half its effectives defending the rear.

Dragging their single gun, the little column finally reached Nancy where they were congratulated by General Meunier and Marshal Ney. The survivors of the infantry and cavalry who had fought alongside them so magnificently were admitted to the 1st Voltigeurs.

Meanwhile, bad news poured into Metz from Kaiserslautern and the Saar. When they learned of Marmont's retreat, Kellermann and Curial decided to move the Guard depots to Rheims, Châlons, and Paris.

Michel reported from Luxembourg that Yorck[4] had entered Trier with 50,000 men. Having only 3,300, Michel retreated. Then Marmont evacuated Saarbrücken.

Michel's division reached Metz on 10 January with around 4,000 men plus artillery. When the governor of Metz requested that some reconnaissances be made, Michel and Decouz – who was still at Thionville – replied that the Emperor had ordered them to Langres and Chalons respectively. Michel left Metz next day, but Decouz did not quit Thionville until the 16th.

Marmont's retreat was very strange. He waylaid Decouz on the road to Metz and dispatched him to Saint-Mihiel to make contact with Victor.

Though the enemy was still scattered and largely inactive, Meunier's division was ordered to evacuate Nancy. The inhabitants were exasperated and heaped insults on the troops in the Place Stanislas.

The weather and roads were bad, and food and order nonexistent on these weird maneuvers. Of the three divisions originally assigned to Ney, only Meunier's was actually under the senior marshal's command. Yet he left it and went off to Ligny with his staff, whereupon Victor took command of it at Toul on the 16th.

Caught in the lamentable tide of retreat sweeping through Ligny, Bar-le-Duc, and Saint-Dizier, Meunier reached Vitry on the 25th where Decouz's division joined him next day.

Fortunately, the enemy's advance was slow. Blücher had only the corps of Yorck and Sacken with him, and both were tired.

[4] The Prussian general Count Yorck von Wartenburg. – Ed.

CHAPTER 2

Bar-sur-Aube

MORTIER alone obeyed the Emperor's orders and hastened to Rheims. Arriving in Rethel on 2 January, he sent Laferrière-Levêque ahead with the cavalry while the infantry and artillery traveled by forced marches. At Rheims Major Lafitte was detached and sent posthaste with 200 chasseurs to Langres where he arrived on the 9th.

He was in the nick of time, for Langres had just missed being captured by enemy hussars. The partisan chief Thurn, patrolling ahead of Gyulay's corps of the Army of Bohemia, had sent an officer up to the ramparts with a flag of truce. Fortunately, the garrison commander was suspicious and posted in ambush outside the walls a patrol who fired at the enemy when they attempted to enter the city behind their emissary. As the latter was being blindfolded by the sentries, a volley from the ramparts put them to flight.

Next day General Chouard arrived with the dragoons, followed by Laferrière who sent scouts south and east to Gray and Vesoul. The Generals reported to Mortier that the people of Langres were uneasy and the royalists numerous; whereupon the Marshal sent 300 foot chasseurs by post to support the cavalry.

On the 12th Mortier entered the city at the head of the Old Guard. His bearing and prestige helped to appease the inhabitants and drive the royalists underground. But the foul weather, with rain on top of frost, delayed Griois' artillery, and the infantry could not keep its footing on the steep streets.

Meanwhile, the enemy was approaching. Lafitte's chasseurs reported a large force on the plateau ten miles from town. A native of Châtenay was sent by the mayor to report that 300 Austrians had arrived in his village that morning.

That night, in a heavy snowstorm, 300 Old Guard chasseurs and grenadiers under Baron Albert advanced noiselessly towards Châtenay with fixed bayonets. With the visibility less than six feet, they made slow progress. After marching three hours they were still a mile away when they heard the challenge '*Wer da?*'[1]

A patrol of Austrian light-horse vanished into the night without waiting for a reply. Since they would doubtless give the alarm, Albert ordered his men forward on the double. They reached Châtenay to find the Austrians formed in line of battle. Twenty-five chasseurs entered the village from the south and twenty-five grenadiers from the north, while fifty bypassed it to cut off the enemy's line of retreat.

At the command 'Forward!' the Austrians were cut to pieces. Half the light-horsemen were killed and a major and 20 men captured. At dawn the French returned to

[1] 'Who goes there?'

Langres, trailed by enemy cavalry who were dispersed by a squadron of Guard chasseurs.

Another skirmish was won at Longeau on the 13th by Major Pictet with 200 dragoons and 400 grenadiers. But despite these successes Mortier believed he had Gyulay's whole corps before him. A large body of cavalry was approaching rapidly from the west and a light corps of Hungarians and Bavarians was threatening his line of retreat. The Guard was short of cartridges. The volunteers also lacked ammunition. (Led by former officers, some of the latter rendered valuable service to Mortier.)

The *chasseurs à cheval* reported that the enemy was approaching in force from Chalindrey and Culmont. Evidently impressed at the sight of 200 *Kaisergarde* bonnets supporting the cavalry, they halted. But behind Gyulay's 3rd Corps was a 1st and a 2nd . . .

Mortier was worried. Though by now a convoy of powder had arrived from Auxonne and been converted by the inhabitants into 60,000 cartridges, he was having difficulty feeding his men and horses. An effective resistance would require the 80,000 men he had been promised, or even 40,000 . . . But they never materialized.

On the 13th the Fays-Billot woods were swarming with Austrians, Cossacks, and Bavarians. Fearing he would be cut off from Chaumont, Mortier sent the horse grenadiers to cover his retreat. Then, to encourage the inhabitants, he solemnly decorated the lieutenant who had saved the city on the 9th.

The 2nd Old Guard Division, whose imminent arrival Berthier had announced, did not put in an appearance. The Chief of Staff was issuing astounding bulletins; for example: 'On 16 January the Duke of Belluno (Victor) and the Prince of the Moskva (Ney) are occupying Toul and Nancy. I have ordered them to defend both cities and halt the enemy.' Mortier knew better. The 2nd Old Guard Division had been at Toul on the 14th, from where Michel reported he would march to Bar-sur-Aube on the 17th – if he survived!

At Vesoul on the morning of the 16th Schwarzenberg ordered an attack on Langres on the 18th with three army corps and a cuirassier division, supported by his guards and reserves.

At noon that day the *Grenadière* and *Carabinière* were beaten. The Old Guard assembled before the Hôtel de Ville. Cartridges were issued and a spectacular departure, timed to reach the Corlée plateau that night, took place. Fifty lame Grumblers were left in Langres with the escort of the Auxonne convoy and the city guard. Mortier made an address 'on the highest plane' to the mayor and populace.

Midnight. In the Corlée bivouacs fires were lighted along a $2\frac{1}{2}$-mile front, facing those of 30,000 Austrians. Then silently Mortier marched his troops to Chaumont.

A courier from Langres reported that the royalists had sent up rockets during the night and the enemy had taken possession of the city.

The 'old of the Old' were exhausted. They had marched all the way from Namur without a day's rest. The dragoons and chasseurs had not slept since Rethel, and their horses were foundered. Still, they had to guard both banks of the Marne at Chaumont against the Württemberg cavalry patrolling in the neighbourhood. Some infantry and cavalry from the depots had been added to the seventy customs officials defending the town, and Michel's division was en route. Mortier hoped these reinforcements would give his Grumblers a chance to rest.

Alert! Marching from Montigny and Langres, the vanguard of 45 enemy squadrons, supported by horse artillery, attacked Chaumont. Mortier's 6,000 tired men held them at bay and finally pushed them back on the 18th. However, the Marshal's situation was precarious. He knew that Victor was at Saint-Dizier, and that the 2nd Old Guard Division was en route to Brienne. Therefore, next day he left Chaumont at 7 a.m. under cover of the dragoons and foot grenadiers, slept at Colombey-les-deux-Églises,[2] and arrived at Bar-sur-Aube on the 20th.

There he found Michel's division with its artillery, also the 113th Regiment of Paris reserves. Guarded by these fresh troops and several squadrons posted along the Chaumont road, the weary Grumblers slept. Meanwhile, a thaw transformed the roads into rivers, aiding the defense.

Schwarzenberg did not seem to be in any hurry to do battle with the Duke of Treviso. Replenished with food and ammunition, Mortier's small corps rested for four days, keeping watch on all roads leading to Bar. The Emperor had sent word that he was ordering a concentration of his forces at Châlons; but since the Marshal was too far away he decided to hold the line of the Aube as long as possible and maintain contact with the reinforcements in Troyes.

The Army of Bohemia had resumed its march. Six thousand Cossacks of Platov, reported at Doulevant and Soulaines, threatened to cut off the Old Guard from Brienne. Chasseurs of the Guard reported the vanguard of the Austrian 3rd Corps at La Ferté-sur-Aube, while the outpost at Colombey announced that the Prince of Württemberg and his corps were 12 miles west of Chaumont on the road to Bar.

Mortier promptly sent General Dufour and a division of Paris reserves to Brienne to cover Troyes. Then he himself with his 13,000 men prepared to do battle on the 24th before Bar-sur-Aube.

Straddling the old Vendeuvre road the small Guard corps, covered by the 113th Regiment with six guns at Dolancourt, occupied the heights overlooking the right bank of the Aube. Letort was at Colombey with 4 battalions, 4 squadrons, and 6 guns; one battalion and the horse chasseurs were at Bayel.

Maneuvering their twelve-pounders with difficulty through the snow, Griois' artillery bombarded the enemy attacking from east and south. The battle was a lively one. Supported by reinforcements, Mortier sent the Florence *vélites* to Fontaine where they covered themselves with glory but lost their commander.

The Marshal spent the night at Bar. During the night, without arousing the enemy's suspicion, his troops disappeared in the fog and fell back to Vendeuvre, ready to resume the battle at noon next day.

Michel's division was massed by battalions in the snow before Vendeuvre, with the cavalry ahead on the right and left. The 1st Grenadiers and the artillery reserve were

[2] The residence of General de Gaulle before he became President of the Republic. – Ed.

behind the village. The 113th Regiment guarded the road to Bar-sur-Seine. But the enemy never appeared.

Guarding the rear, Captain Heuillet, the old drummer of Lodi, and his company of chasseurs lay in ambush on the outskirts of Bar-sur-Aube. As the Austrians emerged at daybreak the chasseurs opened fire point-blank and pushed them back in disorder at bayonet point.

Heuillet's chasseurs arrived at Vendeuvre with 20 prisoners including an officer. Several enemy squadrons appeared and turned tail at the first cannon shot. Meanwhile, the Prince of Württemberg and the partisan chief Thurn marked time while Platov's Cossacks made slow progress towards Sens and Fontainebleau.

Mortier had carried out the Emperor's plan. By his character and talent for maneuver, combined with the valor of his old phalanx, he had managed to delay the invasion of Champagne by more than two weeks.

That afternoon Captain Lamezan arrived at Vendeuvre with orders from the Emperor. Napoleon planned to attack the enemy next day at Saint-Dizier. The Guard was ordered to march to Vitry.

Since the Grand-Orient forest was impassable at the moment, the troops were obliged to start their march that very night via Troyes, crossing the Aube at Ramerupt. As the grenadiers were stealing out of their bivouacs Lamezan outlined the situation to Mortier.

The Emperor was too far away from his marshals to hold them in line. He knew nothing of their movements nor even of their whereabouts. The Chief of Staff had left Paris the 19th to organize the defense of the Meuse and arrange for levies and food; but even Berthier was no longer able to bring order out of the chaos prevailing in the army, the towns, and the countryside. Now the enemy had crossed the Meuse.

Before leaving Paris the Emperor had to mobilize the national guard, review the regiments leaving for the army, and reinforce the Guard with which he still hoped to save the country – if it could be saved.

When Nancy fell he presumed that Blücher and Schwarzenberg were preparing to march on Paris. Only by combining under his command the forces remaining with the marshals, and the Guard units returning from the front, with those in Paris and the national guard would he be able to halt them.

On the 17th he sent Lefebvre-Desnoëttes to Chalons with 1,650 mixed horse Guards under Dautancourt, and Rottembourg's Young Guard division. On the 19th Dériot sent 570 additional troopers with 300 spare horses. Dulauloy was ordered to send three batteries to Châlons to reinforce those of Meunier, Decouz, and Rottembourg. With Mortier's seven, these would bring the Guard park to 128 guns. Clarke was instructed to send 1,000 veteran troopers from Spain by post to fill up the Old Guard squadrons, and 1,000 from the depots for the Young Guard.

On 21 January the Emperor ordered the 14th–19th Voltigeurs and *Tirailleurs* formed from volunteers arriving at the depots at the rate of 400 a day.[3] The men

---

[3] These were known later as 'Marie-Louises'. – Ed.

were carefully chosen, and their officers appointed from the Old Guard, the Royal Guards of Naples and Spain, and the instruction battalions. Among the commanders were old-timers such as Lavigne, Prelier, etc.

Many old soldiers came to the depots begging to serve again. Two NCO's assigned to the 9th *Tirailleurs* had each lost an arm. Captain Magnan of the 66th Regiment, who had won laurels in Spain, was assigned to the Young Guard. He ended up a marshal of France.

On 24 January, Napoleon's last day in Paris, he gave the command of a provisional Young Guard division to General Charpentier with Generals Bauduin and Lelièvre de La Grange – the Emperor's old equerry and hero of Hanau – as brigade commanders. D'Ornano was named commander of the Guard in Paris, with Caffarelli as vice. General Dériot, commanding the depots, was ordered to hold in Paris 10,000 men, with 900 gendarmes (including 100 elite) under Colonel Janin, for any emergency.

Four Young Guard battalions were left to guard the outside of the Tuileries while the Grumblers guarded the inside. In addition, d'Ornano had twenty-two battalion cadres with which to form new units. He was ordered to organize 2,250 scouts as soon as possible, together with 400 horse grenadiers and dragoons and 600 *chasseurs à cheval* and 2nd Lancers, to 'bring the horse Guard in Paris to 3,200'. General d'Aboville was directed to form two artillery companies and reinforce the company of Veteran-Cannoneers. The two batteries from Spain were to remain in Paris.

That day the Emperor wrote Joseph: 'I have put d'Ornano in general command. In case of alarm he will take his cavalry to the Palace, sending between 1,500 and 3,000 horse with 22 guns to the outskirts, depending upon the situation'. Under Ornano's command Napoleon intended to form a reserve of 40,000 men which might either reinforce the army or defend the capital in case of need.

Before leaving, the Emperor reviewed the units being formed with men from the surrounding depots. He ordered 50 drummers from the *pupilles* to fill vacancies in the *tirailleurs* and voltigeurs, and the conscripts of the 6th Corps sent to Curial 'who would make better use of them than Marmont'. General Colbert presented a detachment of 3,500 Guard infantry and cavalry he was taking that day to Nogent-sur-Seine.

After the parade the Emperor, wearing the uniform of commander in chief of the national guard, received at the Tuileries the officers of the Paris garrison, presented by their vice-commander Marshal Moncey. To them he entrusted all he held most dear – the Empress and the King of Rome.

It was his last night in Paris. He appointed his brother Joseph Lieutenant General of the Realm in command of the army and national guard, authorizing him to wear the uniform of the grenadiers of the Guard.

Taking leave of the Empress and the King of Rome, whom he tenderly embraced, Napoleon departed for Châlons at dawn on 25 January.

He never saw them again . . .

CHAPTER 3

Brienne

THE Emperor's arrival at the front was eagerly awaited. Marshal Kellermann and General Belliard worried because the concentrations he had ordered at Vitry had not been carried out. Macdonald was at Mézières, Marmont near Bar-le-Duc, Victor at Saint-Dizier, and Mortier at Troyes. Only Meunier's division, with 3,830 voltigeurs plus artillery under Rousseau and Lacoste, and Decouz's with 2,800, were at the rendezvous with Ney.

Caraman, the Emperor's aide, arrived ahead of his master with orders to send to Vitry Lefebvre-Desnoëtte's division, Rottembourg's *tirailleurs*, and 150 guns from Châlons including 60 of the Guard. Had any one considered the problem of feeding so many troops in so small an area?

Lefebvre-Desnoëttes arrived at the rendezvous with his 2,400 horse and his artillery. These he promptly organized in two brigades under Dautancourt and Krasinski. (The latter's lancers had marched all the way from Belgium.) Rottembourg's division of 3,500 *tirailleurs* plus 313 voltigeurs and flankers and two batteries got under way at Châlons the moment their orders arrived.

On the evening of 25 January the Emperor drew up before the Prefecture at Châlons. Where was Berthier? 'At Vitry, Sire', replied the general sent ahead by the Chief of Staff to meet him. 'The situation is worse than we thought . . . The Duke of Belluno (Victor) has been pushed out of Saint-Dizier . . . The Duke of Treviso (Mortier) cannot be here before the 30th . . .'

Bacler d'Albe stuck pins in a map as information arrived concerning the enemy's whereabouts.

Late that night the Emperor dictated his orders to Berthier. Over-extended in breadth and depth, the enemy was maneuvering in an absurd manner. Learning that Schwarzenberg was spread out along a front running from Neufchâteau through Chaumont to Châtillon-sur-Seine, and that the French were concentrating at Châlons, Blücher had decided to march to Arcis via Brienne. There he would take command of the Army of Bohemia and lead it to Paris.

'I intend to attack (Blücher) tomorrow the 27th', Napoleon's orders read. 'The troops will form on either side of the road to Saint-Dizier, with Victor nearest Vitry and Marmont a mile beyond. Ney, with Meunier, and Decouz, supported by Lefebvre-Desnoëttes and Rottembourg under Oudinot, will be posted a mile beyond Marmont. You must spread the news of the offensive, send back the baggage, and issue bread and wine. If there is no wine but bottled champagne, use that. It had better be drunk by us than the enemy . . .'

Mortier was ordered to leave Troyes only if it were no longer threatened. Colbert's contingent of 870 lancers and scouts from Paris was ordered to guard the bridges at Nogent.

The atmosphere had changed. Questioned as to what reinforcements he had brought with him, the Emperor replied: 'None. We shall try our luck with what we have. Perhaps it will be good. Fifty thousand men and I are worth 150,000.'

Marmont muttered: 'Am I dreaming?'

Next morning the Emperor left for Vitry, escorted by Polish lancers.

Meanwhile, Mortier had received reinforcements. A brigade of 3,000 Paris reserves under La Hamelinaye was at Troyes, and another under Dufour at Lesmont. Bordessoule's cavalry was at Arcis, and Colbert's was en route there. The temperature was below freezing.

On the evening of 27 January the Emperor wrote Mortier and Colbert:

'We have beaten the enemy at Saint-Dizier . . . The Mameluks charged Tettenborn's Cossacks as usual. We are on the enemy's line of operations. Our vanguard is en route to Wassy. The whole Young Guard under Ney and Oudinot will sleep at Montier-en-Der. I shall attack Blücher's rear at Brienne. Leave the Paris troops at Troyes and march with Colbert towards the French right. Vitry is the pivot of operations . . .'

Unfortunately, the courier carrying this dispatch was captured, so Blücher was warned of Napoleon's plans. Mortier was, too, by another courier. He replied that he was ready for anything, but that Troyes would fall if he left it. La Hamelinaye's corps was too weak to defend it and was still waiting for its ammunition and the rest of its arms, due the 29th.

On that date, after a night of thaw and rain, battle was joined at the edge of the woods east of Brienne. Blücher's corps, recalled from the front, were concentrated, facing the French, on the right bank of the Aube.

After their exhausting march through the forest of Der Napoleon's little army had been cheered, warmed, and fed by the inhabitants of Saint-Dizier who took courage because the Guard was there. Peasants and foresters had hitched themselves to the mired gun carriages and taken their weapons out of hiding.

The voltigeurs of Meunier and Decouz, who had been discouraged by constantly retreating without a fight, now laughed, sang, and cheered the Emperor. They brought up the rear of the column, marching on roads already plowed up by the baggage train, Victor's divisions, Grouchy's and Lefebvre's cavalry, and the artillery. The latter began shelling Pahlen's horse and Scherbatov's infantry. Emerging from the thickets at Maizières, Rottembourg deployed his *tirailleurs* in support of the gunners.

Towards 3.30 p.m. Victor's and the Guard's artillery blazed a trail for the infantry. The light was fading under a lowering sky. On Victor's right, Vice-Admiral Baste's voltigeurs, followed by the 7th and 8th under Decouz, advanced from Maizières to Brienne. The streets of the town climbed steeply through gardens and shrubbery to the brightly-lighted castle where Blücher and his staff were dining and drinking the owner's champagne.

'*Heraus! Rasch!!*'[1]

Four hundred soldiers of the 2nd Corps, led by General Châtaux, disrupted the feast and chased out the officers who fled in the dark to the terraces and park.

Blücher himself had a narrow escape. But soon he launched an assault on the slope with his whole infantry in an effort to recapture the castle. In the dark streets below Ney let loose his voltigeurs in the rear of the Russian battalions of Sacken and Olsuviev which were soon caught between two fires.

A frightful slaughter ensued in the darkness, lighted intermittently by burning buildings. The units became hopelessly mixed. Decouz received a mortal wound. After having two horses killed under him, Baste dropped dead in the arms of Lieutenant Saint-Amant while crying '*En avant!*'[2] Lt. Colonels de Contamine and Castanié of the 1st and 6th Voltigeurs were severely wounded. In all, the three Young Guard divisions lost 30 officers and 1,000 men.

By midnight the Prussians were in full retreat. Fires were lighted in the plain between Brienne and the woods and the Guard bivouacked around Maizières. Having narrowly escaped capture in a Cossack raid, during which Lefebvre-Desnoëttes was wounded, the Emperor arrived with Father Henriot, the village priest who had taught the young Bonaparte at the College of Brienne. Astride one of Roustam's horses, the old priest had not left the Emperor's side all day. Now he dismounted to welcome his old pupil to his rectory.

There had been fighting in the college where the Emperor had passed his youth. He heard the wounded groaning in the chapel where he made his first communion.

As the *tirailleurs* and Krasinski's light-horse guarded the 'palace' Napoleon wondered what the morrow would bring forth. Blücher was beaten but not destroyed. Thinking of his absent Old Guard, he wrote Clarke:

'Had I had old troops I could have done better . . . However, considering the circumstances and the troops I had, we should be pleased with the result . . .'

Next morning, the prisoners brought in by the cavalry patrols reported that Blücher's headquarters was located near the camps of the Army of Bohemia; however, there was no indication that the enemy was preparing to attack.

The Emperor went to the castle of Brienne, preceded by the light-horse-lancers, the duty battalion, and General Bertrand. The soldiers had to bury Russian and Prussian corpses and clean up the library which was strewn with serpents, stuffed birds, and human monsters removed from bottles whose alcohol had been consumed by the visitors. Only one room, reserved for the Emperor, had any windowpanes left.

'Ah, the swine!' Napoleon exclaimed as he entered. He shook hands with the porter, an old acquaintance, deploring the ruin of this town that had been the cradle of his glory, to which he was to leave 100,000 francs in his will.

[1] 'Get out! Hurry!!'
[2] Forward!

Oudinot with Rottembourg's division, and Ney with the voltigeurs of Meunier and the dying Decouz, were camped nearby. Curial had been nominated to replace Decouz. Would Blücher attack today?

No, he was joining forces with Schwarzenberg. In that case, should Napoleon retreat? Probably, but in his own good time.

First he must impress the enemy, conceal his weakness, inspire confidence in his green troops, and encourage the populace to rise and defend their homes. He did not yet know that Mortier, in an effort to obey him, had arrived at Arcis-sur-Aube with the Old Guard.

Bordessoule reported to the Marshal that the Prussians had evacuated the valley of the Aube from which Mortier concluded that the Emperor had had a good day. The Marshal sent a detachment of cavalry to the Lesmont bridge to make liaison with the Emperor.

Next day Napoleon sent word to Mortier to return to Troyes which was being threatened by Schwarzenberg. He himself considered retreating – either via Lesmont to Troyes and the Old Guard, or towards the Marne and Macdonald. However, the longer he held Brienne the more apt the Allies were to fold their wings and concentrate their forces for battle in order to keep open their line of retreat. Napoleon even tried to bring this about.

First he sent trusted couriers to make sure that Mortier was at Troyes. Then he sent for everything he could lay his hands on: Colbert's horse, the marines from Vitry, and the two voltigeur battalions from Châlons. He sent Gérard to Dienville, Victor to La Rothière, Marmont to Soulaines, and kept Ney, Oudinot, and the three Young Guard divisions with him at Brienne. He waited . . .

The clock on the college tower struck midnight on 30 January. Outside tramped the voltigeurs, and the duty squadrons surrounded the castle. It was freezing and the moon, nearly full, shone brightly. The French army was in contact with the Prussians; but Blücher did not attack.

Next morning General Defrance's guards of honor and Bordessoule's cavalry were ordered to retire to Piney, and the Emperor prepared to retreat to Troyes.

Meanwhile, Mortier was waiting anxiously in Troyes. His cavalry patrols reported that there were large enemy concentrations between Brienne and Bar-sur-Aube, and that an enemy force of 6,000 had arrived at Vaudes. On the 31st he ordered a reconnaissance in force against Vendeuvre with Old Guard infantry, artillery, and chasseurs. By nightfall he knew that the Seine valley was occupied in force and that Pahlen's Cossacks were galloping towards the Yonne. The next day at 1 p.m. he heard the Emperor's guns at Brienne.

At 9 a.m. on 1 February the Emperor arrived at La Rothière after a quiet night. Nothing was stirring in the enemy camp. The news from Mortier had convinced him that it was useless to remain longer at Brienne. The Young Guard began its retreat from Brienne-la-Vieille. Ney set out for Lesmont. Marching was difficult in the northwest gale blowing. Then it began to snow.

Noon. Alert! Word came from Grouchy and Victor that the enemy was marching in three columns on Brienne from Trannes, Eclance, and Soulaines.

Napoleon decided to accept battle. Ney marched his three divisions back to the Beugné farm, a mile southeast of Brienne; between La Rothière and Petit-Mesnil, Nansouty deployed the horse Guard under Guyot and Colbert on two lines behind its horse artillery; Grouchy posted his corps on their left, and Victor occupied the two villages. Gérard held Dienville and the Aube bridge on the right flank, and Marmont the road to Soulaines on the left. Along a 7½ mile front 40,000 French awaited an attack by 90,000 Austro-Russians.

About 1 p.m. the battle began around La Rothière, held by Duhèsme and already deluged with shot by Nikitin's artillery. As far as one could judge through the blinding snow the Russian guns seemed to be firing at a high elevation. Nansouty seized this advantage to send Guyot's light squadrons to saber the gunners. Then, as Russian horse chasseurs prepared to counterattack, the French fell back behind their own artillery.

Soon afterwards, while cannon thundered from Petit-Mesnil, the light-horse of Krasinski and Colbert easily repulsed an attack by Lanskoi's two hussar divisions, but then were overwhelmed by Vassilitchikov's squadrons and four regiments of Sacken's dragoons. Hard-pressed, the French troopers galloped towards their reserves, posted west of La Rothière under Letort. Piré, watching the action from Petit-Mesnil, saw in a flash their danger. Drawing up his chasseurs in line of battle, he launched them on the Russians' flank and checked the enemy horsemen – but not before the latter had seized twenty-four guns of the Guard horse artillery.

In a howling blizzard the battle raged along the whole front. At Dienville, Gyulay could not broach Dufour's infantry which held fast until night. Duhèsme held the church square and the north end of La Rothière under a withering fire from sixty-two guns. But the French left flank began to crack.

The Emperor ordered Guyot's cavalry, supported by the voltigeurs of Meunier, Rousseau, and Lacoste with one battery, into action towards Chaumesnil on the road to Soulaines, from which Marmont had been dislodged by Wrede's Bavarians and the Württembergers. A desperate struggle took place in the snow-covered woods and marshes, quickly churned into a mire by men and horses. When the voltigeurs were charged by Bavarian cavalry, in the dark and mist the Württemberg chasseurs took the latter for Frenchmen and fell upon them savagely. In the midst of the melée Marmont and the Guard began retiring slowly towards Brienne, leaving Wrede's corps in too much confusion to pursue.

North of La Rothière, which Duhèsme was finally obliged to abandon, the Emperor judged the battle lost; still, he had to keep fighting to cover the retreat of his left flank. Barely 200 yards to the south Blücher and Gneisenau tried unsuccessfully to bring up their reserves. Napoleon launched a counterattack on La Rothière with Colbert's cavalry division and Rottembourg's Young Guard under Nansouty and Oudinot, while Drouot's artillery deployed in the rear.

Night fell. Rottembourg formed Marguet's brigade in three columns. Colbert's squadrons cleared a path for them by pushing back Olsuviev's infantry in disorder as

THE ANATOMY OF GLORY

the latter debouched from the village. While the Young Guard's four guns pinned down the enemy in the first houses, Marguet's conscripts ran to the church and opened fire point-blank at the Russians. Then, seized with sudden fear, they broke ranks and huddled together in groups so that Olsuviev's officers thought they were going to surrender. Then the Russian infantry followed their example. It was a strange situation, lasting several minutes, after which both sides regained their composure and closed ranks. The Russians were soon put to flight by canister shot from the small French battery. As Colbert's troopers pursued them through the village at a brisk trot, they failed to notice that Sacken, taken by surprise, was crouched in hiding between his horse and a house.

At the end of the day Marguet's *tirailleurs* began to weaken. Oudinot personally led Rottembourg's first brigade to their support. It was now 8 p.m. At the Emperor's command, Rottembourg's division evacuated the village under cover of the Guard artillery, directed by Drouot in person. La Rothière was in flames. The retreat through the snow was orderly. Though the Emperor still had in reserve Curial's voltigeurs, who had not been engaged, Blücher had employed his whole force.

By 2 a.m. the following morning the Guard was strung out along the road to Lesmont. Arriving at Piney on the road to Troyes, they found Curial's soldiers under the market arcades, burning chairs from the church to dry their clothes. The troops were famished.

The harassed army bivouacked in mud on either side of the village. The bridge at Lesmont had been destroyed after Milhaud's last dragoon had crossed. Not a Cossack was in sight. They heard guns at Rosnay where, on his way to Arcis, Marmont fought off an attack by Wrede.

'What can the Emperor do about this invasion?' asked the Grumblers.

'His pride is bringing us all to ruin!' the marshals complained.

'Where do we go from here?' cried the conscripts.

Behind the windows of the 'palace' in the house of the notary Collin, the Emperor dictated to Berthier: 'Tomorrow I shall be in Troyes . . .'

CHAPTER 4

Montmirail

THE Emperor predicted the outcome of the Allies' council of war in the castle of Brienne: a march on Paris by Schwarzenberg through the Seine valley, and by Blücher through the valley of the Marne. He knew both men. The Austrian, cautious and dilatory, was afraid of Napoleon, while the Prussian hated him and wished to reach Paris first.

In leading his army to Troyes the Emperor left the road clear for Blücher who would doubtless set out for the capital at once, without waiting for the rest of his corps to catch up. By concentrating all available forces around the Guard between the Seine and Marne, Napoleon hoped to defeat his adversaries one by one. They had numbers; he had brains. It was to be mind over matter.

But first he must have twenty days' rations of biscuits prepared, and stock the magazines at Sézanne and Compiègne. He must evacuate the wounded to Nogent via the Seine, and revive Paris whose morale that mollusk Joseph had allowed to flag. He must replace the cowardly prefects who fled with the peasants, instead of organizing them to fight the enemy who was 'eating their food, stealing their livestock, and raping their women'. The ammunition expended at La Rothière must be replaced and Mortier's caissons replenished. Finally, he must have more troops.

On 3 February Drouot wrote Ornano to send to Nogent 1,200 troopers, two battalions of the 2nd Voltigeurs, and 1,000–1,200 voltigeurs and *tirailleurs* each to Curial's and Rottembourg's divisions. In addition, six foot battalions were to be sent out under a major general with around 1,200 draft horses for the train, etc. 'Nothing more is to be sent to Châlons', he concluded.

In the winds of despair blowing over France and its starved and shivering armies the Emperor and the Guard alone stood firm. Though there were many deserters from the army, not one of the lads who had fought so heroically at Brienne dreamed of leaving his post. When you wore the eagle button of the Guard, you stuck.

At Troyes in the imposing mansion of M. Duchâtel-Berthelin in the Rue du Temple the quartermasters were preparing the Emperor's apartments. Cambronne's chasseurs were on duty. The rest of Friant's division had gone with Mortier to conduct the Emperor into the city.

At 10 a.m. on 3 February the horse grenadiers hove in sight. Behind the old walls lining the malodorous streams turned into canals by Thibault de Champagne, the houses were boarded up. At the Pont de Cailles, over which Joan of Arc had ridden, the Emperor dismounted. No one came to greet him. The inhabitants had even sealed their wine cellars, 'as if to reserve them for future requisitions by the enemy'. Did these people think the campaign was over? For Napoleon it was just beginning.

First he would give Schwarzenberg a scare. At eight next morning the whole Guard was drawn up at Sancey near the road to Bar-sur-Seine, with Curial's voltigeurs in front and Meunier's behind them with Rottembourg's *tirailleurs*. Except for Michel's division on outpost duty five miles downstream at Maisons-Blanches, all the Old Guard was in the rear with Nansouty's three cavalry divisions and the artillery.

The Emperor was cheered as he passed down the ranks. Men and horses were muddy but the weapons were clean. The soldiers' freshly shaven faces were pale and drawn, but their hearts were firmly attached to their master.

At 9 p.m. the order to march was given. A vigorous thrust by Michel from Maisons-Blanches knocked out Liechtenstein's division at Saint-Thibaut. Curial occupied Cléry with one brigade and held off a whole division under Bianchi. By evening the offensive reconnaissance had gained its objective and convinced Schwarzenberg that Napoleon was on his way to Langres to cut his communications.

On the 6th the whole army faded back to Nogent behind a screen manipulated by Mortier and the Old Guard. The Emperor breakfasted standing up in the cold grey dawn near the old Carthusian monastery of Croncels with Berthier, Ney, Oudinot, and Grouchy. They spent that night at Grès, while two Guard squadrons lighted numerous camp fires at the destroyed bridge in Maisons-Blanches, and then at 6 a.m. retired at a brisk trot, leaving twenty-five troopers in contact with the Austrian pickets until noon.

Schwarzenberg never knew of the French army's departure until the following day when it loomed out of the void, marching back to Troyes along both banks of the Seine.

The Emperor returned to his headquarters to find nothing but bad news. Murat had turned traitor; Antwerp was besieged; Brussels had been captured by Bülow, and Belgium lost; the Congress of Châtillon was hostile; the Empress and her court, Paris, and the whole nation were in a panic; soldiers were starving, and from four to six thousand had deserted from the army. And from the Guard? Not one! Then all was not lost . . .

Calmly he dictated a long letter to Ornano. 'You inform me you are sending a train company on the 7th . . . Their wagons are probably loaded with flour. If so, order them to unload this at a town along the route and exchange it for bread. If they carry rice, send it here.

'You must have at least twenty battalion cadres . . . When filled up, these will make a fine reserve of 16,000 men . . . By the 10th you will have 10,000 *tirailleurs* and conscripts . . . With these you will form two divisions under Charpentier and Boyer . . . Announce these divisions today and organize them tomorrow. There should be plenty of muskets and cartridge pouches. There are enough shakos in Paris. You will have to scratch for the rest . . . Under present conditions you can dress a soldier with a shako, overcoat, and pouch. The important thing is to give him plenty of target-practice . . .

PLATE 131

PLATE 132

a) Berthier
(*Engr. Cambert*)

b) Exelmans
(*Contemp. lithograph*)

c) Gérard
(*Engr. Bovinet after Vauthier*)

d) Sacken
(*Col. engraving by Velyn after Noireterre*)

e) Yorck von Wartenburg
(*Engr. Jacoby after Woltze*)

PLATE 133

Battle of Brienne
(From a colored engraving by Rahl after Johann Adam Klein)

PLATE 134

Scout-lancer (*Éclaireur, 3ᵉ Régiment*), 1814
(*From an original watercolor by Victor Adam*)

PLATE 135

a) Marmont
(*Engr. Joly after Meyer*)

b) Macdonald
(*Portrait by David: Collection Duc de Massa*)

c) Zieten
(*After contemp. portrait*)

d) Defrance
(*Contemp. lithograph*)

e) Wintzingerode
(*After G. Dawe*)

PLATE 136

Young Guard chasseurs on picket, 1814
(From an original drawing by Carle Vernet)

'As for cavalry, you have 2,400 men and 1,500 horses. A reserve of at least 1,200 can be organized with these.

'Your two divisions can be increased daily by 1,000–2,000 recruits until, together with your 12 squadrons and 22 guns, you have an army of 20,000 men . . . Counting the Line reserve of 10,000 and 6,000 national guards, we can hope to have a reserve of 40,000 men at Meaux by the 10th or 12th . . .

'The four marine batteries at Cherbourg, and those served by the Polytechnicians and the Invalids, will provide between 60 and 80 guns for this army. Send me a detailed report.

'Your returns list 700 Old Guard grenadiers and chasseurs. No more than 200 should ever be unattached. With the surplus you can form a provisional Old Guard battalion to lead your reserve column . . .'

Never had the Emperor been more precise. He was counting more and more on this reserve of 40,000 men, framed by officers and NCO's of the Guard.

Now Napoleon prepared to tackle Blücher.

On 8 February Gérard was barely holding the bridge over the Seine at Méry which he had been defending for two days against Wittgenstein's 6th Corps. Now he was nervous because the Württemberg cavalry – the vanguard of Schwarzenberg's 5th Corps – was approaching.

Meanwhile Yorck, chasing Macdonald up the Marne valley, had reached Épernay. Blücher was taking the shortest route to Paris through Montmirail and La Ferté-sous-Jouarre. This news from Marmont at Sézanne led Berthier to wake His Majesty from a sound sleep.

The Emperor bent over his maps while Ney, Mortier, Nansouty, and Oudinot looked on in silence, their hats under their arms. Napoleon, compass in hand, reread Marmont's dispatch. Sacken was in the van of Blücher's army, and Olsuviev a day's march behind. Blücher was in the rear at Vertus, waiting for Kleist and Kapzevitch to catch up.

Alert everybody! The Emperor dictated feverishly to Joseph: 'I am going to Sézanne with whatever is necessary to beat whomever shows up on the line of communications between La Ferté-sous-Jouarre and Vertus'.

The 'whatever necessary' consisted of Marmont, Doumerc's 1st Cavalry Corps, Bordessoule's, Piré's, and Defrance's horse, and the foot and horse Guard, totaling 20,000 foot and 10,000 horse with 120 guns. Victor, Gérard, and Pajol were left to watch Schwarzenburg on the Seine and Yonne while Macdonald, with Exelmann's and Arrighi's cavalry, opposed the Prussians on the Marne. Oudinot was left in reserve at Provins with Boyer's and Leval's divisions from Spain. In a few days he would also have Rottembourg's division, reinforced by General Charrière's detachment which was now escorting the household, headquarters, and park.

The maneuver had to be prepared from information supplied by Marmont, the general staff, the mayors, and spies. It had been raining steadily for five days, transforming into quagmires the roads from Nogent up to Sézanne, which wound through the Traconne forest and the Barbonne swamps, and also the one Blücher was traveling from Vertus to Montmirail.

'Collect all the bread you can', the Emperor wrote Marmont. 'We are famished.' But there was no more in the villages, for Biren's Cossacks had swept them clean.

Napoleon was playing his trump card. If Blücher escaped him now all was lost. In case of final disaster, he sent the following instructions to Joseph:

'Send a battalion of the Guard to Compiègne and another to Fontainebleau. Order Desmazis to remove the silver and family portraits – but discreetly. Beware of Talleyrand. Never let the Empress or the King of Rome fall into enemy hands. I would rather have my son's throat cut than see him brought up in Vienna as an Austrian prince . . .'

Having put his affairs in order and urged Macdonald 'not to retreat so precipitately', he left for Sézanne on 9 February, escorted by the service squadrons. Mortier remained at Nogent with Michel's Old Guard division in a state of alert, and Rottembourg and the convoy went to Provins.

Meanwhile, Ney had crossed the Seine at Nogent the evening before with his two Young Guard and Friant's Old Guard divisions and Nansouty's three cavalry divisions, and was marching to Sézanne. The road from Villenauxe to Sézanne was a foot deep in mud. The Grumblers and voltigeurs left their shoes behind at every step. The dragoons and grenadiers traveled afoot, pulling their mounts out of the mire by their muzzles. As for the artillery, Dulauloy, Griois, and Leroy used all the horses in Barbonne to pull their guns and caissons through the Traconne forest and up the Brie plateau by night, under the lashes of the carters and the oaths of the NCO's.

At last the foot and horse Guard reached Sézanne and camped in miserable bivouacs, and on the fairground where the Emperor was lodged in the house of the notary Benoit.

Marmont, whose vanguard was down in the Saint-Gond marshes, reported that the Emperor was twenty-four hours too late. Sacken had left Champaubert at 8.30 that morning.

Who cared about Sacken? Neither Marmont, Ney, Victor, nor Joseph understood the Emperor's strategy. Nor did the Grumblers, for that matter; but since he was God the Father to them he was surely not mistaken. The Grumblers were right.

At dawn on the 10th Major Sachon of the dragoons was sent with 100 troopers to take prisoners. Galloping into the village of Bannay he forced 500 Russians to lay down their arms.

Climbing the slopes of Baye, Marmont's infantry collided with Olsuviev's corps on the plateau of Champaubert. The Young Guard kept them covered between Bannay and the forest while Doumerc's horse and the horse Guard surrounded them. By evening the Russian corps had ceased to exist. All Olsuviev's generals, together with 40 guns and 200 wagons, were captured. Brigadier Verjus and two Guard chasseurs captured a howitzer. The French losses were minimal; however, the Guard's artillery was bogged down in the Saint-Gond marshes.

'I shall march to Montmirail tomorrow to attack Sacken', the Emperor wrote that night from the little house in Champaubert that still stands opposite his monument.

Blücher's army was marching in two sections twenty miles apart. While Marmont faced east with one division and a cavalry corps to engage Kleist and Kapzevitch, the Emperor faced west to crush Sacken, and possibly Yorck as he marched from Château-Thierry, between his army and Macdonald's. Orders for this maneuver were issued before the guns of Champaubert were silent.

Nansouty left Champaubert that evening with Colbert's horse, reaching Montmirail at midnight where he surprised Karpov's Cossacks in their sleep and threw them out of town. One of Ricard's brigades from Marmont's corps joined him during the night, and the other next morning.

Mortier left at dawn on the 11th for Montmirail with the Old Guard and the rest of the troops at Sézanne. Rottembourg's division, with a division from the 7th Corps, went to La Ferté-Gaucher, ready to march at the first shot from a cannon.

The Young Guard watched over the Emperor that night. They left Champaubert at six the next morning, an hour after the Emperor, escorted by Laferrière's cavalry. Their commander Ney, as well as Lefebvre and the general staff, rode with the Emperor as usual.

11 February, 10 a.m. At the Château of Montmirail Napoleon swallowed his breakfast in fifteen minutes. Then he climbed the Marchais plateau and halted at the Dogeaterie farm, near the junction of the roads to Meaux and Chateau-Thierry. The weather was fine and clear.

Nansouty, whose tired squadrons were resting at the Montcoupot farm, reported that his outposts had announced the approach of Sacken's corps. Vassilitchikov's hussars and dragoons and Karpov's Cossacks were between Vieils-Maisons and La Haute-Épine, and Yorck's cavalry had reached Viffort. From this intelligence the Emperor concluded that both the Russian and Prussian corps were converging on Montmirail.

Napoleon sent Krasinski's light-horse and the chasseurs ahead with Nansouty, keeping with him Guyot and Dautancourt with the horse grenadiers and dragoons. Shot and shell began to fall on the staff and the brigade drawn up beside the Fontenelle road. Presently the Emperor sent the old chasseurs and grenadiers to the hamlet of Coulais, and Ricard's second brigade to Tremblaye. His whole force numbered 5,000 foot and 4,500 horse with 24 guns of the Old Guard, not including Ricard's 1,800 Line conscripts with their 12 guns.

Napoleon was anxious. The Russian cavalry and artillery were already in sight on the plain north of La Meulière. On the left, Sacken's infantry had reached l'Épine-aux-bois from where it attacked and occupied Marchais around 11 a.m.

At 2 p.m., during a bloody combat, 7,000 Russians pushed Ricard's heroic lads, supported by a battalion of 'old moustaches', back to La Tremblaye. Friant deployed several companies opposite the farms of La Chaise and Les Gréneaux to support Nansouty whose horse was drawn up between Coulais and the Plenois farm. The situation became still more critical when Yorck's infantry appeared at Fontenelle. Where was Mortier?

At 3 o'clock the Duke of Treviso arrived with Defrance's guards of honor. Now assured of a reserve, the Emperor sent Ney with six Old Guard battalions to attack the

353

Russians who were entrenched to their chins in Les Gréneaux and supported by artillery. Thirty guns of the guard went into action, firing at top speed. Carrying their muskets with priming-pans open, the grenadiers marched off at the double by battalions, 100 paces apart, behind the Prince of the Moskva. They attacked the farm and overwhelmed the infantry and gunners who fled, leaving their guns and soup kettles behind them. Then Henrion formed the 2nd Chasseurs in squares, as if at a drill, and threw back the cavalry charges. In front, Heuillet's company seized several guns and the baggage train. Capturing one position after another, Friant's division reached the ridge of La Meulière.

The Emperor supported this magnificent action with the cavalry of the Guard. Dautancourt formed Letort's dragoons in column on the road and took off at a brisk trot. They galloped up to the enemy lines and knocked out the Russian squares. Guyot followed with the horse grenadiers and a company of Mameluks and chased the fugitives on the right of the road back to the La Borde woods, while Dautancourt rallied his dragoons on the left, opposite L'Épine.

The Emperor then sent two battalions of chasseurs under Marshal Lefebvre to attack Marchais from north to south while the rest of Ricard's division marched from La Tremblaye crying 'Vive l'Empereur!' and attacked it from east to west. The Russians poured out of the village towards their own artillery and L'Épine-aux-bois. Noting their disorder, Dautancourt and his dragoons wrought havoc among them and took several prisoners.

In the fighting, which continued until nightfall, the Poles advanced as far as Vieils-Maisons. Deaf to Sacken's frantic appeals for help, Yorck had blindly followed Blücher's order to proceed to Étoge, and engaged only one brigade. This Mortier attacked furiously as it debouched from Fontenelle and pushed it back to the village. That night Yorck returned to Château-Thierry.

The enemy had lost 4,000 men, and Napoleon 2,000. General Michel was wounded in the arm. Lt. Colonel Mallet of the 2nd Chasseurs was mortally wounded and died the 28th. Major Rouillard de Bauval of the flankers, severely wounded, raised his good arm in salute, crying 'Vive l'Empereur!' as his stretcher was carried past Napoleon. His other arm should have been amputated; but, being a bridegroom, he refused. Nursed back to health by his young bride, he was made a baron and recovered to fight again in 1815.

The flanker-chasseurs had 80 officers, including Lt. Colonel Pompéjac and one of its majors, put out of action as well as 22 men killed and 200 wounded. The Italian vélites lost 9 officers. A captain and lieutenant of the horse grenadiers were killed.

On this day a drummer of the Guard was among the killed. He was the legal spouse of the vivandière Marie Tête-du-bois, famous in the battalion for her tart tongue and her bravery and kindness. They had been married in Verona. During the Marengo campaign she had borne him a son who was now drumming in the pupilles. She had nothing left in the world but him. Perhaps the Emperor would make him a sergeant – if God permitted . . .

Since the Young Guard had remained behind with its mired artillery, Montmirail was a victory of the Old Guard, and of Ricard's brave lads who had left half their number on the field. Before the battle the Grumblers had made fun of them; but now they cheered these youngsters, covered with mud and blood, who had faced the Russian colossus without flinching. The survivors, full of enthusiasm, were comforted, fed, and adopted by the grenadiers who could henceforth count on *them*.

Towards 11 p.m. Curial's division, laden with wounded, entered Montmirail and was ordered to guard the prisoners who shouted 'Death to Alexander!' Meunier's division followed and bivouacked behind the Old Guard. Christiani relieved the wounded Michel. The campfires were lighted in the combat positions. Men and horses were too tired to pursue the enemy.

In an attic in Les Gréneaux the Emperor worked, surrounded by his staff who fought for the privilege of sleeping on the staircase. The walls were scarred by cannon balls and there were no windowpanes left. The other rooms were filled with dead and wounded. Grenadiers carried out the former while the surgeons performed amputations on the latter by candlelight.

'My foot Guard, dragoons, and grenadiers performed miracles', the Emperor wrote Joseph.

CHAPTER 5

Château-Thierry

DAWN on 12 February found the Emperor, Mortier, and the staff on the road to Château-Thierry with Christiani's division and the artillery reserve. The guards of honor galloped ahead towards Fontenelle while Ney splashed along the byroads with the horse Guard, Meunier's division, and four battalions of Friant's Grumblers.

Ney had marched all night towards the Marne, looking for the enemy. Two miles beyond Fontenelle the vanguard came upon his outposts which promptly fell back upon their reserves. These were attacked by the duty squadrons with two chasseur battalions and a battery.

Towards 1 p.m. the French spied the Prussian army in position on the slopes of the Caqueret hills, barring the route to Château-Thierry. Soon a cannonade began. Two hundred grenadiers seized the only breach the gunners were neglecting. Then the six Old Guard battalions charged up the hills, supported by the rest of the infantry.

Under a hail of shot, in the midst of the *tirailleurs*, the Emperor watched through his spyglass for the cavalry of the Guard which he had summoned to attack the enemy's right flank. The squadrons loomed out of the mist at a jog trot, led by Letort's Young Guard dragoons. The Prussians quickly formed squares.

Breaking into a gallop under ever increasing fire, they headed straight for the enemy. The troopers dashed upon the first square and sent it flying; then they charged the second and third, knocking the soldiers down and running over them. They ended by cutting off the enemy's retreat to Épernay.

'It was one of the handsomest feats I ever saw performed by cavalry', wrote General Griois.

On the far side of the Caquerets, Jürgass' horse and Sacken's infantry fled to Château-Thierry, pursued by General Belliard and the duty squadrons, while General Petit and two battalions of grenadiers drove Prince William of Prussia and his reinforcements off the Nesle plateau and into the city.

The enemy fled across the Marne bridge in disorder, under fire from Griois' artillery, leaving 1,800 prisoners, their guns, and part of their baggage behind. Yorck retreated to Fismes and Sacken to Rheims, via La Fère-en-Tardenois.

The French bivouacked in the Marne valley, on the left back of the river.

'My foot and horse Guard covered themselves with glory', the Emperor wrote Savary. 'The dragoons distinguished themselves with a performance comparable to those romances of the Age of Chivalry in which a single knight in armor with a well-schooled horse would take on three or four hundred adversaries at once. The enemy seemed struck by a singular terror . . .'

That evening the Emperor awarded a third star of the Legion to General Letort.

The Marne bridge had been destroyed. The marines and sappers repaired it while the jubilant inhabitants thrashed the Prussians and Russians they found hiding in their cellars and threw them into the river.

The following day the Emperor was at the Lumeront farm planning his next move when word came that Victor was retreating from Schwarzenberg who had crossed the Seine. The marshals did not seem to understand that the bridges must be held at all costs! With those at Bray and Nogent lost, now only one remained where Napoleon might stop Schwarzenberg, after he had finished off the Prussians. This was the bridge at Montereau.

Mortier set out for Soissons in pursuit of Yorck and Sacken, taking Christiani, Colbert, the guards of honor, artillery, and sappers, while the Emperor and the rest of the Guard returned to Montmirail to support Marmont against Blücher.

The Guard had dwindled. On the muster roll signed on 15 February by General Delapointe, Mortier's chief of staff, Christiani listed one general (Gros), 1,013 fusiliers, 968 flankers, and 201 *vélites*. With the gunners and service troops, his division numbered a meager 2,385. Its skeleton regiments averaged barely 50 men to a company.

Colbert's 1st Cavalry Division listed 155 Poles of the Line, 253 2nd Scouts, 262 2nd Lancers, and 322 chasseurs and Mameluks, totaling 992 officers and men. Though constantly reinforced, its casualties had been heavy. The 2nd Lancers alone had lost 139 men and 174 horses. Their horse artillery had been reduced to two six-pounders, one howitzer, and two officers! However, Defrance still had 1,000 guards of honor.

Mortier's ammunition was low. On 20 February he wrote the Minister: 'I have sent for infantry cartridges, having but a single caisson left. General d'Aboville wrote Major Noury, who commands my half-battery, that it would be "ridiculous to send cartridges to a guerrilla corps". . . . One is hardly a "guerrilla" when he must contain the corps of Sacken and Wintzengerode who will attack him the moment they find him . . .'

On the night of 13–14 February the whole Guard was alerted to proceed to Montmirail under Ney, with Friant, Meunier, four Old Guard battalions, the cavalry of Laferrière and Guyot, and Drouot's artillery. They were to pick up Curial's division en route. Posts were established every $7\frac{1}{2}$ miles to maintain liaison with Mortier.

Next morning the *Diane* was beaten at 3.30. Word came from Marmont that he was evacuating Champaubert under pressure from Blücher.

A battle was joined at Vauchamps around 9 a.m. The cheers of the troops announced the Emperor's arrival with the Guard who formed in columns of attack behind their artillery, ranged in front. At a given signal they stormed the trenches of Zieten's vanguard, then attacked the corps of Kleist and Kapzevitch. Laferrière's cavalry, south of the highroad, and Grouchy's on the north completed the rout of the enemy.

One lone Prussian battalion held out in the farm of Bouc-aux-pierres in the face of well-directed fire from the French artillery, and succeeded in halting a charge by

Guyot's 'big heels'. A company of foot grenadiers went in at the double and scaled the walls under a hail of bullets. The grenadiers forced their way into the building and bayoneted the occupants, taking the few survivors prisoner. The action was performed with such speed that their losses were insignificant.

The Emperor was jubilant. Standing by the fire at the roadside he watched 8,000 prisoners file past. He himself had lost less than 500 men.

'My duty squadrons covered themselves with glory', he wrote, 'and took 3,000 prisoners.' Their commander General Lion was wounded. Major Labiffe of the *chasseurs à cheval* had particularly distinguished himself. The Guard's enthusiasm ran high. Perhaps tomorrow the Parisians would take heart again . . .

That evening the whole Guard, minus Mortier's detachment, bivouacked at Montmirail. The 1st Old Guard Division camped around the beautiful château of the Duc de la Rochefoucauld where the Emperor was lost in meditation over his maps.

'Napoleon lived in a dream world as well as in the real one', wrote Philippe Gonnard. When his dreams came true he believed in his star and led France and Europe in an orgy of political and military romanticism. 'It is the privilege of great creators to fascinate men.'

'Only the man whom the marshals are accustomed to obey can win a victory', Clarke wrote him on the 14th. So it seemed, since Oudinot and Victor had now retreated to the Yères, and the Austrians had reached Nangis.

The next day Meunier, Friant, and Curial, with the cavalry and artillery of the Guard, were strung out in echelon along the road to Meaux. After swallowing a hasty breakfast on the way to La Ferté-sous-Jouarre, the Emperor lost his temper with General Guyot, who had accomplished prodigies in the last four days, for having lost a gun to the Cossacks at Vauchamps. In the heat of anger Napoleon relieved this brave and loyal officer of his command, giving his division to Exelmans. However, he put Guyot in command of the horse grenadiers of the Guard.

Five days later the Emperor sent for Guyot and made amends by giving him command of his escort, the supreme position of trust in the Guard.

On 16 February Napoleon was at Guignes with the Old Guard and his army, poised to pounce upon Schwarzenberg. With drums beating and flags flying, he prepared to wage war with the corps of Victor, Oudinot, Macdonald, and Pajol, and the cavalry of Saint-Germain, Milhaud, Bordessoule, and Kellermann. Rottembourg's division of 4,000 men, which had escorted the park to Provins, was attached to Oudinot's corps. Meanwhile, the rest of the Guard was given a well-earned respite.

When the army attacked the vanguard of the Austrian army next day at Nangis the Guard remained in reserve. The Young Guard held the rear of the army at Guignes while the Old surrounded the château where the Emperor slept. During their unaccustomed idleness the Grumblers wore a perpetual scowl. Passing a chasseur of the 2nd Regiment, who was bandaging his leg in the middle of the road, the Emperor asked:

'Don't you see me?'

'The road belongs to everyone', was the reply.

'What do you want, sorehead? You have your cross, your musket, your pipe, a full canteen, and plenty of *Kaiserliks* and Russians to fight. You see your Emperor every day. But still you are not satisfied . . .'

'My canteen is as hollow as my guts', replied the old-timer. 'With the 5 sous you pay me – when I get it – a man can't exactly feast . . .'

'Do you think my affairs are going any better than yours?'

'As to that – no, I don't. We are all in the soup . . .'

'I know what you want', concluded the Emperor. 'A battle. Well, you will get one tomorrow – and a good one!' Then turning to his aide: 'Caraman, put this savage down for 10 *napoléons* tomorrow night – if he is still here!'

'*Sacré Tondu!*' muttered the veteran under his breath. 'So we have to go out again and get killed for *him*!'

On the morning of the 18th at Villeneuve-les-Bordes 4,500 fur bonnets were drawn up in two lines behind the Friants, father and son, their drummers poised to beat. Behind them was Dautancourt on horseback at the head of the duty squadrons. The weather was clear and bracing.

Napoleon was very angry. The night before, instead of capturing the bridges at Montereau from the Prince of Württemberg as he had been ordered, Victor had slept in clean sheets in the Château of Montigny. The Emperor ordered Gérard to relieve the Marshal of his command. Then at one o'clock he galloped to Montereau, followed by the Guard.

Within a few hours the Prince's battalions were soundly defeated at the bridgehead north of the town while the foot Guard remained in reserve on the heights above. At the Château of Surville, overlooking Montereau and the bridges over the Seine and Yonne, the Emperor watched the rout of the enemy. A magnificent charge by Pajol was supported by Dautancourt with the Emperor's escort, and even his staff, led by Marshal Lefebvre. They galloped to the bridges, sabered the laggards, and filed through the suburbs and on to the road to Bray. There they ran headlong into a mass of enemy cavalry who brought Lefebvre's squadrons up short.

The Emperor sent a battalion of foot chasseurs to their rescue. Meanwhile, the Württembergers streamed down the Fossard road under fire from two Guard batteries whose leading gun was aimed by the Emperor in person. Eventually Boulart's whole reserve joined in, breaking every window in the château (see Plate 139a).

The victory was complete. Schwarzenberg was appalled to see his army fleeing to Troyes.

Early next morning in the court of the château the Emperor severely reprimanded Marshal Victor. Though deprived of his command, the Marshal refused to go home, requesting to serve as a simple grenadier in the Guard. When he tearfully recalled his twenty-two years of campaigning, the siege of Toulon, and the death in battle of his son-in-law General Châtaux, the Emperor relented and invited him to dinner that evening with General Pajol.

On the 21st Victor wrote the Emperor from Nogent as follows:

'It would be both painful to me and injurious to my reputation to leave the army at this time when it is the duty of every Frenchman devoted to Your Majesty . . . to do his utmost to drive the enemy from our soil . . .'

Napoleon forgave him. 'I cannot give you back your army corps, which I have already given to Gérard, but go take command of my two Young Guard divisions.' These were Charpentier's and Boyer de Rebeval's, numbering over 10,000 men plus artillery.

On the evening of the battle of Montereau the Emperor wrote Joseph from Surville: 'The Tsar of Russia and the King of Prussia are fleeing before me . . .'

He wanted to pursue them, but the bridges over the Yonne and the Seine were destroyed and he had no pontoons.

CHAPTER 6

Mind over Matter

AFTER the battle of Château-Thierry on 13 February Mortier had gone to Rocourt, then Ouchy, where Colbert joined him on 15 February with his 900 troopers. The latter had burned a Prussian baggage train en route and taken 400 prisoners, after which the enemy had retired to Fismes and Rheims.

In spite of his precarious situation, Mortier had attacked the enemy outposts at Ouchy on the 15th, then established his headquarters at Villiers-Cotteret. There news came that Soissons had been captured the day before by Wintzingerode on his way from Belgium. When Wintzingerode left Soissons for Rheims, Mortier sent Major Ciceron to Soissons with 300 infantry and 150 troopers. It was rumored that one of Bülow's divisions was approaching the city in the wake of Wintzingerode. Mortier warned the Emperor that it would require at least 6,000 men with 40 guns to defend Soissons from attack.

On 20 February, as he was leaving the Château of Surville for Nogent-sur-Seine with the Guard, the Emperor received from Marmont a dispatch that caused him anxiety. It appeared that Blücher had retired to Châlons to 'reorganize his army'.

'If he joins forces with the Allied armies', Napoleon wrote Marmont, 'then you must join forces with me.'

From this time on the Emperor began to regroup his forces. On 22 February he recalled Mortier to Château-Thierry, instructing him to leave one battalion and 100 horse under an able commander at Soissons, which must be held at all costs. Then he ordered Oudinot to secure the bridges over the Seine at Méry, and over the Aube at Anglure. (Alas, unknown to the Emperor, both were already in Prussian hands!)

On that day Napoleon fought an action near Nogent. Being Mardi Gras, his young Guardsmen raided a costumer's shop and fought in masks and fancy dress. The fight was rough; however, the presence of the Emperor and the *Kaisergarde* caused Schwarzenberg to retreat beyond Troyes, and the Prussian corps of Yorck and Sacken beyond Anglure. Then Napoleon set out in triumph for Troyes at the head of the Guard, in the wake of Schwarzenberg's army.

The Prince of Wrede, commanding the Troyes garrison, threatened to burn the city unless Napoleon called off his pursuit. Towards noon on the 23rd the French army reached Montgueux on the outskirts. The Emperor occupied the Milliard farm nearby where the mayor of Troyes arrived with Wrede's ultimatum giving the French until 4 a.m. next morning to decamp.

Napoleon was not perturbed. Before going to sleep he allocated four millions from his privy purse to the Guard and granted a clothing allotment to the company of artisans, promoting its lieutenant.

At 5 a.m. on the 25th he set out for Troyes where, after the precipitate departure of the enemy, an immense crowd gathered at the belfry gate to welcome their liberator. The Emperor made a triumphal entry into the city behind the 1st Grenadiers as their band played *Let Us Watch Over the Empire*.

Napoleon ordered Victor's Young Guard corps to Méry, 'by easy stages, without unduly tiring the conscripts', and directed Daru to send bread, beef, and brandy there since 'the region was a desert'. With Ney's two voltigeur divisions at Arcis and Victor's two at Méry, Napoleon hoped to mount an offensive against the Prussians, now contained on the route to Paris by Mortier and Marmont. Having ostensibly driven Schwarzenberg's armies back to Bar-sur-Seine and Bar-sur-Aube, he planned to repeat the Montmirail maneuver against Blücher with his Guard divisions and the best of the Line troops. Meanwhile, he left with Macdonald the troops of Oudinot, Gérard, Kellermann, and Milhaud, and Rottembourg's Young Guard division to defend the Aube around Bar, giving instructions to have the troops cry *'Vive l'Empereur!'* from time to time as though he were present.

On 27 February Napoleon marched by stealth towards Arcis with Friant, the horse Guard, and the artillery reserve, picking up Ney's and Victor's Young Guard divisions en route. After a march of twenty-five miles he halted at Herbisse, evacuated by the Prussians only the day before.

The large artillery park was set up east of the town on the old camp site of Attila the Hun. When the *curé* at Herbisse apologized for the inadequacy of his quarters, the Emperor replied: 'We shall make ourselves very small'. Fifteen thousand Guardsmen bivouacked around the village and in the plain of Champagne, swept by the north wind.

From its outposts Curial's division spotted campfires in the direction of Sézanne. These were the fires of Tettenborn's Cossacks who attacked Exelmans' cavalry next day at Vertus. Their vanguard was already seventy kilometers farther west, near La Ferté-sous-Jouarre. Blücher's Prussians and Russians were racing towards Paris . . .

Meanwhile Mortier, informed of the Prussian movements which threatened to isolate him, had left Château-Thierry the morning before for La Ferté. He had sent an officer of his staff to warn Marmont of his move. Captured en route by Russian cavalry, the interrogation of this officer had led Blücher to believe that Marmont's and Mortier's forces were much larger than they actually were. Were they to unite, Blücher was afraid to cross the Marne in their vicinity.

Next day, the 27th, Mortier and Marmont joined forces conspicuously before La Ferté where they burned the bridge over the Jouarre and set out for Meaux. They crossed the Marne at Trilport by a shaky pontoon bridge at water level. The cavalry and artillery took so long to cross that the last battalions of the Guard came under fire from the Russian horse artillery.

Finally the crossing was completed and the bridge destroyed. Mortier congratulated himself upon preserving his force intact. After three more miles he and Marmont could relax in Meaux . . .

But no – it was full of Russians!

Meaux was divided by the Marne and its canal into three sections connected by stone bridges: the Châlons road ran through the main section on the right bank: the second was an island; and the third, a peninsula from which a road, dominated by the suburb of Cornillon, led to Coulommiers.

As soon as Christiani's division entered the city by the Châlons road, cannon balls began falling in the marketplace. Meanwhile, Marmont was attacked by Sacken's troops from Cornillon. Fortunately, the enemy was only a flank-guard and was soon repulsed. The main force was at La Ferté-sous-Jouarre with Kleist and Blücher.

Aware that Napoleon was at his heels, the old Marshal had halted his march to Paris. That evening at Sammeron his sappers threw a pontoon bridge across the Marne which Kleist crossed during the night, sending his cavalry ahead to Lizy. Sacken camped north of the river where he expected Kapzevitch to join him next day.

With a scant 10,000 men, Mortier and Marmont were in a grave predicament. Though they did not know of Blücher's decision, they knew that 10,000 foot and 1,000 horse of the Guard were approaching from Paris, on their way to join the Emperor. While waiting for the reinforcements to arrive the Marshals decided to hold the line of the Ourcq.

Kleist's cavalry was already five miles beyond Meaux at Gué-a-Tremmes, on the road to La Ferté-Milon.

Early on the 28th Colbert mounted his squadrons, and Christiani's divisions scrambled down the banks of the Therouanne river – a branch of the Ourcq – under well-directed fire from the Russian horse artillery. Reaching Gué, Pompéjac's flankers and Léglise's fusiliers edged their way through the main street while their artillery silenced the Russian guns. After hours of stubborn fighting, ending in hand-to-hand combat, the Russians were obliged to give up the left bank of the river to the flankers and Italian *vélites* and retire to the plateau beyond. Colbert's horse pushed the enemy cavalry back to Étrépilly. By afternoon their infantry was retreating to Lizy.

The French had had nothing to eat since the night before. They rifled the packs of the Russian corpses to find bread. Meanwhile, Marmont pursued Kleist and threw him back to the Neufchelles marshes.

That evening, as Lizy was burning, the firing was resumed and the bridge was blown up. A memorable windfall in the form of a flock of sheep belonging to a Paris banker gave promise of roast mutton for dinner next day. Alas, many fusiliers would not be there to enjoy it! Six officers, as well as Major Cicéron and two lieutenants of the Italian *vélites*, had been wounded, and an artillery captain killed.

That night Sacken at Lizy, and Kapzevitch and Yorck nearby on the left bank of the Ourcq, heard cries and a ceaseless rumble of wagons, muffled by the new-fallen snow. The Guard reinforcements were marching from Paris. They included the 3rd Provisional Young Guard Division under Poret de Morvan containing 5,200 conscripts, and some mixed cavalry with 48 guns. One brigade was commanded by General Guye, a veteran of Austerlitz and of King Joseph's Spanish Guard who was sound on horseback but less so on foot, having been wounded on the Bidassoa in 1813. The cavalry contained around 500 scouts and 500 assorted horse Guards under General Boulnois. The scouts had excellent horses, but the conscripts hung onto them 'by the fifth rein' and were generally green.

At daybreak on 1 March an incredible rumor spread through the enemy camps – already much impressed by the arrival of what they termed the 'Army of Rescue' – to the effect that Napoleon was approaching with the 'Kaisergarde', and that its cavalry had already reached Jouarre.

This was true. Exelman's cavalry division marched out of La Ferté with its horse battery that morning at 10 a.m. Soon French cannon balls were falling on the Prussian and Russian stragglers retreating to the right bank of the Marne. Then the bridge was blown up and the French captured 300 laggards and the baggage train that the enemy had abandoned outside Sammeron.

Laferrière's squadrons followed, then Ney and Friant who entered La Ferté that afternoon while Victor guarded their flank, supported by a reserve corps under Arrighi. But the French were too late. Blücher had escaped from the trap.

Things were going badly.

The day before, at the Château of Esternay, Napoleon had learned that Oudinot and Gérard had been dislodged from Bar-sur-Aube the previous night; and that Caulaincourt was urging the French to accept the Allies' terms at the council of Châtillon.

'Of course he wants peace!' stormed Napoleon. 'And does he think that I do not? But I want an honorable peace, worthy of the French people and of me . . .'

Meanwhile, the Regency Council was sending urgent supplications to make peace, or else . . . because Paris was 'at the end of its tether'.

What about the Young and Old Guards who had marched over sixty miles in rain and snow since Herbisse, and the troopers chasing the Cossacks? And the gunners and train soldiers, soaked to the marrow, who had had to pull their guns and caissons by brute force out of the Rebais mud to get them to the battlefield in time? Were these men at the end of theirs? They grumbled, but they still hoped to win. Victory, duty, the Emperor – these were what counted to the men of the Guard.

While Belcourt's grenadiers set up the 'palace' at La Ferté in the house of Monsieur Huet, the Emperor wrote Joseph: 'I must greatly increase the cavalry of my Guard as these forced marches are causing heavy losses.'

Where were Mortier, Marmont, Blücher? What reinforcements had been sent from Paris? Napoleon sent for the marines and sappers to rebuild the bridge over the Marne 'at once and at all costs'. It was a matter of hours if he were to 'catch up with the canaille that is ruining the country'.

On 2 March cannon thundered all day along the Ourcq, moving steadily northward. A stunning blow dealt Mortier and Marmont by the forces of Zieten and Kleist was repulsed. By midnight the Prussians were retreating toward La Ferté-Milon.

At nine that night the Emperor's cavalry was crossing the Marne by the new bridge at La Ferté-sous-Jouarre, followed at 2 a.m. by Curial's and Meunier's divisions with Dulauloy's artillery.

At daybreak on the 3rd the Old Guard left Jouarre with its cavalry and crossed the river. Meanwhile, Charpentier's and Boyer's Young Guard divisions marched to Château-Thierry.

At 5 p.m. an officer of the guards of honor brought Mortier Napoleon's congratulations on his victory of 28 February, with the following postscript:

'The peasants tell me that all the enemy's baggage is bogged down in the Cocherel marshes and that the escort is weeping and wringing its hands . . . My cavalry is at his heels. At dawn you will hear guns. I shall be at their head with the Old Guard . . . Keep marching . . .'

The situation was in hand and Paris was saved. Blücher was fleeing to Soissons where General Moreau[1] would halt him with his garrison of 700 good Poles, 140 gunners of the Old Guard, some scouts, and the city guard. Then Mortier and Marmont on the left, the Emperor in the centre, and Victor on the right would crush him against its walls.

That night Napoleon wrote Joseph: 'I plan to carry the war into Lorraine. Form a fourth provisional Young Guard division immediately.'

And to the Minister of War: 'I learn with pain that General Maison is still dispersing his troops . . . Let him concentrate them and fall upon the enemy piecemeal . . . A bold move on Antwerp with all available forces to free the troops of that garrison would serve to isolate Brussels and threaten the enemy's line of communications.'

Finally to Mortier: 'I hope we shall have a good day tomorrow.'

On 3 March the Emperor led his Guard to Montreuil, Château-Thierry, and Fismes in an effort to cut off Blücher's line of retreat. Frequently bogged down, the disorganized Prussian columns were fleeing towards Soissons and Bülow's corps, en route from Belgium. Captain Parquin surprised their outposts at Ouchy with his chasseurs of the Guard, rode through the village, and returned with a hundred prisoners including two colonels.

Meanwhile Mortier fell upon Kleist, who was waiting to be reinforced by Yorck and Sacken, at Neuilly-Saint-Front. The latter had halted at Ouchy and Rocourt, too tired after marching night and day over rough terrain to go further. Shelled by Mortier's guns and fiercely attacked by Christiani's fusiliers and flankers, Kleist was forced to retreat. Had Marmont joined forces with Mortier in this attack the Prussian corps would have been annihilated.

Next day Kleist started out in the van of Blücher's army; but today, the 3rd, he found himself leading the rear-guard, since Blücher had turned and fled before Napoleon. Left alone, Kleist retreated towards the Aisne.

In the courtyard of a house in the village of Bézu-Saint-Germain, north of Château-Thierry, the grenadiers of the Guard dried themselves by their fires and watched over

[1] The garrison commander installed by Mortier. – Ed.

the Emperor as he slept. They had had a good day. The Old and Young Guards were there with Guyot's escort. Ahead, Nansouty had entered Rocourt on the heels of the retreating Prussians. Behind them, Charpentier's and Boyer's youngsters marching on the left bank of the Seine had not bothered to wait for the bridge to be rebuilt, but had crossed the river in boats and camped on the right bank.

The vise was tightening on Blücher. Tomorrow its jaws would close and he would be crushed from Fismes to Soissons. Already the cavalry had picked up many stragglers crying with exhaustion.

The morning of 4 March the Guard marched to Fismes, via La Fère-en-Tardenois, chasing Cossacks all the way. At noon a convoy escorting Sacken's baggage was reported to have left Fismes and taken the road to Soissons. Guyot and the duty squadrons captured the convoy, but were fiercely repulsed by the Cossacks of the escort who continued their march towards Soissons.

That evening the Guard was at Fismes with its cavalry and artillery. The Emperor slept in the Heurtevin mansion where the kings had stopped on their way to be crowned at Rheims. Only Curial's division was left at La Fère to wait for Victor.

The enemy had been pursued in all directions and was in the greatest confusion, after having fought three battles and marched three nights in the past sixty-two hours.

The Emperor planned to beat Blücher, then assemble fresh forces at Soissons and Laon and maneuver via Vitry, Saint-Dizier, and Joinville to free the eastern garrisons. Then he would call for a great peasant uprising, and cut off Schwarzenberg from the rear.

But first he must secure Braine to prevent the enemy from crossing the Aisne, and Rheims which Saint-Priest's[2] Russians were approaching from the east.

That evening Laferrière's cavalry mounted their horses and two Line battalions shouldered their packs. They set out for Rheims under General Corbineau, the Emperor's aide.

At Fismes Napoleon began to wonder why Sacken's baggage train had headed for Soissons after Guyot's attack that morning. He asked Berthier to send to General Moreau for news of the Soissons garrison and also to give him news of Marmont and Mortier.

At 11.30 p.m. a courier arrived from Corbineau. 'Two peasants who were driving enemy wagons today assure me that the Soissons garrison has surrendered, and that the enemy has occupied the city and crossed the Aisne.' This was shortly confirmed by Marmont and Mortier. Actually, Moreau had surrendered Soissons on 3 March to Wintzingerode and Bülow.

Now Blücher was not only saved, but reinforced!

By 5 March Blücher had an army of 114,000 Russians and Prussians, including 30,000 cavalry, beyond the Aisne. Napoleon had 39,307, including 8,374 cavalry. Twelve thousand of these were the Line troops of Marmont and Grouchy. The rest – including 4,250 horse – were the Guard.

Where the Guard was not, the army was defeated, since there 'there was no soul'. But where the Guard was, there was victory – even against overwhelming odds. As the Emperor expressed it: 'Faced with disaster, the soul can subsist . . .'

[2] French *émigré* who had been commissioned a general in the Russian army. – Ed.

The Emperor refused to be downed. Of what use was it to curse misfortune? It was better to try and remedy it. Moreau would be summoned before the War Council to explain his surrender and the campaign would continue.

Blücher now held all the Aisne bridges from the right bank. Napoleon must force this barrier through an enemy vastly superior in numbers.

CHAPTER 7

Craonne

SOME good news arrived for a change. On 5 March 600 Poles from the Paris depot dismounted before the 'palace' at Fismes. 'They are superb . . .' the Emperor wrote. Brand new, well dressed, armed, and mounted, they were commanded by General Pac, an Alsatian who had entered the Guard in 1806 and had served in the army of the Grand Duchy of Warsaw. The Emperor reviewed them and attached them to his Guard. He directed Clarke to send along the rest, about 200 left in Paris, with 1,200 newly-organized Polish Cossacks.

Then Corbineau's aide arrived to announce the occupation of Rheims at dawn. Laferrière had stormed the north gate, and the infantry the west. They had taken 1,000 prisoners. Major François and his dragoons had pursued the fugitives to Laon. This was a fine feat of arms. François was decorated and Corbineau, appointed governor of the city, was assigned two battalion cadres of Young Guardsmen to command his national guards. Other cadres were sent to Château-Thierry and Laon to support and train the garrisons.

Many former NCO's of the Old Guard had been brought back to serve as officers in the new regiments. These were old warriors, tanned and wrinkled, some lacking an arm, others striped like zebras with saber cuts. Wearing their old regimentals and their Legion of Honor, they fell easily into their old habits of drinking a drop or two, obeying orders, and getting themselves killed. They never complained, and their men respected their bravery and returned their affection. They went where the Emperor ordered without trying to understand why. What was the use? He knew better than they.

'So you're miserable?' they asked the conscripts. 'Don't worry, the *Tondu* will get us out of this.'

They had the robust faith that moves mountains. They marched, and wherever they went they saw the same sights as before – sacked villages, rutted roads, bivouacs in which one shivered and starved.

'Conscripts', they said, 'you must learn to bear the bad times patiently, seeing as you aren't responsible and can do nothing about it. As for the good times, you owe them to your Heavenly Father and the Emperor.'

While waiting for news from the troopers sent to probe the Aisne crossings, the Emperor made new plans.

'I shall push the enemy back to Laon', he wrote, 'then march to Arcis via Châlons. If Macdonald can hold the Seine for five or six days that will be sufficient.'

Outside the Grumblers smoked their pipes in silence. The couriers returned one by one. Everywhere, and in force, the enemy held the bridges over the Aisne; at Vailly, Maizy, etc. Finally, at 11 a.m. a dragoon officer arrived to report that the stone bridge at Berry-au-Bac was intact and was held by only two regiments of Cossacks with two guns.

To horse! Shoulder packs! Nansouty and Exelmans set off at a gallop with Griois' horse artillery. Pac's Poles at Maizy marched up the river to join them. Laferrière was on his way back from Rheims; Ney and Friant marched across country through the steep wooded ravines around Bouffignereux. Curial had to march all day and part of the night, and Victor even longer. Mortier could join them at Braine or Fismes.

From the top of a hill on the road from Berry to Bouffignereux the whole valley of the Aisne was visible. While his escort chased off the Cossacks the Emperor dismounted and watched Pac's Poles capture the bridge, closely supported by Nansouty and Exelmans. They charged the Cossacks deployed on the left bank and sent them flying, then galloped across the bridge.

Major Skarzynski performed prodigies of valor. Snatching a lance from a Cossack, he created a void around him by knocking over the fugitives in his path and running the rest through with his lance. The other officers followed suit, sweeping Dautancourt's lancers along with them in their mad dash to Corbény. Kalmucks, Bashkirs, and Cossacks fled across the plain, crisscrossed with ditches, leaving behind two guns, 200 men, and their baggage.

That night at Corbény the Poles drank to victory and the Emperor. Nansouty reported: 'Exelmans' division and Pac's Poles have driven the enemy four miles beyond Corbény, fighting all the way. I estimate that the force opposed us was 2,000 horse . . . I am sending 100 troopers to Craonne where enemy wagons and a corps of between six and eight thousand men have been reported.'

The night was cold and snow was falling. The foot Guard lit fires on the right bank of the Aisne beside a brook, while Meunier, Friant, and Boyer's line troops camped on both sides of the road. Guyot's squadrons and the 2nd Grenadiers guarded the presbytery where the Emperor decorated Captain Despierres and his dragoons, including a brigadier who had captured Colonel Count Gagarin of the Borovski Hussars.

Meanwhile, Christiani's battalions made a fruitless attempt to recapture Soissons from 8,000 Russians under Rudzevitch, left there by Wintzingerode to garrison the city. Collecting their wounded, the French retired to the village of Saint-Germain. After marching all day on 6 March they reached Cormicy, south of Berry, where Curial and Victor joined them. Now Napoleon must beat Blücher to Laon.

Rising north of Cormicy, the wooded ridge of Craonne formed the eastern end of a steep plateau dominating the Aisne valley, which was visible for miles. With its joint opportunities for observation and concealment this ridge might harbor some rude surprises for an army marching to Laon. Nansouty's patrols reported enemy columns marching north via the Abbey of Vauclerc and Bouconville, and that the ridge of Craonne was occupied.

The postmaster of Berry and Mayor Belly de Bussy of Beaurieux – an old comrade of Napoleon's in the La Fère Artillery – reported that Blücher had spent the night at Chavignon on the Chemin des Dames,[1] and that his whole army had been marching north since the previous night. Since Bussy's return from exile in 1802 he had gained what he termed a 'colossal reputation' as a hunter in the woods around Beaurieux. He gave the Emperor the following topographical information:

The ridge of Craonne, about two and a half miles long, descended steeply through the woods on the north side to the narrow, marshy valley of the Ailette, and on the south to the Aisne. On the west it was connected to the large plateau by a saddleback about 150 yards wide occupied by the farm of Heurtebise, beyond which was a hill called the 'Cave of the Winds'. The road from Corbény skirted the crest of the ridge to Heurtebise where it joined the Chemin des Dames. The latter road started at the château of Bove north of Craonne, then turned west and ran along the plateau to Chavignon and the Inn of the Guardian Angel on the Soissons-Laon road. Heurtebise was dominated by both plateaus.

The large plateau was accessible only by steep, rocky roads which were slippery at this season. On the north side one road ascended from the Ailette, past the Abbey of Vauclerc, to Heurtebise, while the other ran through the village of Ailles and its adjacent woods to the so-called 'Maiden's Gap'. On the south side was a road running past the Foulon mill, and also paths leading to the Ouche mills and the village of Vassogne.

It was evident that if the enemy were on the ridge a march to Laon was impracticable.

'Bussy, I appreciate the great service you have done me', the Emperor said. 'I shall attach you to my person with the rank of colonel, and appoint you an officer in the Legion of Honor.' Thus Belly de Bussy, an old *mousquetaire du Roi*, ended up in the Guard.

Early next morning two reconnaissance parties were sent out. The aide Caraman led a battalion of grenadiers through the woods past the Pontois mill to the ridge. Farther north, Ney and Meunier's division beat the woods around Corbény in the valley of the Ailette. Meanwhile Pac and his Poles, supported by infantry, scouted towards Laon.

At noon the crackle of musketry burst forth from all sides. Caraman's grenadiers fell upon the Russian regiments posted on the ridge. Lieutenant Viaux and several grenadiers fell in the action which became so lively that the Emperor sent Cambronne with two battalions of chasseurs to their support. Then the Russians, reinforced in their turn, began to advance.

'Stay where you are and don't move', Cambronne ordered Captain Heuillet. Grabbing a musket, Heuillet knocked down the commander of a Russian column, then fell, pierced by two balls. General Cambronne was hit four times. Major Angelet, already wounded ten times, and several officers and Grumblers were put out of action. A handful of braves reached the outskirts of Heurtebise.

The Russians held on until Ney's voltigeurs, after chasing a whole brigade from the Abbey of Vauclerc, pushed them back to Heurtebise. The farm changed hands several

[1] Road running between the Aisne and the Ailette named after the royal princesses, or 'Mesdames de France'.

times; however, that night it was held by the Russians while Meunier camped on the slopes, and Ney spent the night at the château of Bove, near General Boyer's division.

The Emperor was in a fix and so was Blücher. When he heard that the French were marching from Berry to Laon, the Marshal had planned to attack them in flank on the plain with his whole army. But when they suddenly appeared on the plateau he decided to let them attack him, using all his artillery but little infantry, since the terrain was narrow; then to maneuver through the woods on their right and surround them.

At the same time Napoleon decided to climb the plateau and attack whatever he found there (which he estimated to be only a rear-guard) and then continue his march to Laon via the Inn of the Guardian Angel.

The night was cold. It rained and froze as part of the Guard artillery crossed the bridge at Berry with Charpentier's division, Laferrière's cavalry, and Arrighi's corps. Men and horses fell on the icy road. The artillery had to double and triple its teams. Mortier waited at Cormicy until the bridge was clear.

At 8 a.m. the Emperor climbed the ridge and joined the 2nd Grenadiers at the mill of Craonne. Half a mile beyond Heurtebise they could see a strong line of Russian infantry whose flanks dominated the Foulon valley. Behind these were other lines facing Ailles. The saddleback between the plateaus was barred by cannon placed wheel-to-wheel, and Heurtebise was occupied.

Blücher had ordered Vorontzov to hold on at all costs with his 16,000 infantry, 2,000 cavalry, and 96 guns until Wintzingerode – 'the first warrior in Europe' – arrived to lead the enveloping movement, supported if necessary by Sacken.

The Guard ascended the plateau slowly and with difficulty from Craonne. First came Friant's division, surrounding the artillery, then Victor with Boyer's division, still some distance behind.

On the left the lancers, scouts, and dragoons of Exelmans and Colbert mounted the steep paths to Vassogne in single file, with Bussy as guide, but made little progress. On the right Ney climbed through the woods towards Ailles with Meunier's division, while on his left Curial advanced from the Abbey of Vauclerc towards the Maiden's Gap until he was pinned down by fire from the Russian artillery. And the Emperor had promised a frontal attack on those guns!

It was promptly delivered by Drouot's four batteries posted near the mill of Craonne. Swab and range finder in hand, the General went from gun to gun, coaching his green and ill-clad gunners who were being pounded with shot by the enemy. Standing nearby, the Emperor committed two battalions of his chasseurs to the action. Heurtebise was captured.

Victor with Boyer's division skirted the ravine of Vauclerc and debouched from the Chemin des Dames, following the Old Guard. He joined forces with Curial and together they pushed back the Russians.

Heurtebise was on fire and had to be evacuated. Veiled in smoke, Bigarré's and Le Capitaine's brigades emerged in close columns, taking refuge behind the Cave of the Winds to recover their breath; then they advanced behind Ney who reached the plateau. A withering fire decimated the voltigeurs. Colonel Bouvard and his 14th

Voltigeurs held on for an hour under canister shot that felled 28 of his 33 officers, and 300 men. Victor was severely wounded. Bigarré and Le Capitaine were both hit, as were Boyer de Rebeval and General Guye. The French could neither advance nor retreat.

Finally Exelmans and Colbert reached the plateau in the rear of the Russian infantry and routed the Cossacks and hussars in great disorder. Laferrière led his horse grenadiers and chasseurs from the Craonne mill across the saddleback and charged the enemy line, then fell, his leg taken off by a shell. Under cover of the old squadrons, Charpentier's division entered the line with 72 guns of the artillery reserve, amid cheers from the survivors.

Finally Blücher ordered Vorontzov to retreat, covered by Sacken, and the whole Imperial Guard swept forward. Grouchy's Line cavalry, led by Colbert's, thrashed the enemy all the way to the Laon road. As night fell Pac's lancers and Mortier's infantry at Corbény halted the vanguard of Wintzingerode whose maneuver had failed.

Craonne was a costly victory. 'I have beaten Wintzingerode, Langeron, and Vorontozov', the Emperor wrote Joseph on his arrival at the Inn of the Guardian Angel. 'I have lost between 700 and 800 men . . .' Was this true?

Actually, the Guard, Line cavalry, and Boyer's division had lost more than 5,500. In the de La Noue house at Braye, surrounded by Friant's 5,900 Grumblers and Letort's horse Guards, whose old commander Laferrière had just lost his leg, the Emperor examined the returns.

In the divisions of Christiani, Poret de Morvan, and Boulnois, Mortier had about 6,000 men left. Lieutenant Lacrosse of the 2nd Chasseurs – a future cabinet minister – had received fifteen wounds. Meunier's division had lost Colonel de Contamine of the 1st Voltigeurs, six of eight majors, 40 officers, and 500 men. Boyer's divisions had only 56 officers left of 119, and 1,683 men of 3,265. Charpentier's division had lost Major Prelier, a second major, and 20 officers.

The cavalry of the Guard had also suffered. Their horses were foundered and would not eat. Majors Delaporte and d'Harembert of the 'big heels', eight officers, and several veteran troopers were wounded. The dragoons mourned Major Bellot, who was shot through the forehead, and ten of their officers were wounded. In the chasseurs, ten lieutenants, including Marshal Oudinot's son, were wounded and a captain of the Mameluks killed. The surgeon major of the Polish lancers was severely wounded. 'The Young Guard cavalry had melted like snow.'

Sad and anxious among the dead and dying, Napoleon had no illusions about his victory. He had deliberately lied to Joseph, as all heads of government have in similar circumstances, to reassure the public. Reading the bulletin, the Guard veterans chewed their moustaches. They had read such things before.

News came from the two congresses. The Allies had rejected both peace and armistice. The Emperor was furious. Yesterday he had pitted almost his whole army against a small fraction of Blücher's. There was no hope of crushing him. But he was not yet ready to admit defeat.

Meanwhile, Ornano reported the recruiting in Paris a brilliant success. Of 50,000 men reporting for the Guard from the last three levies 43,000 had been accepted. Fewer than a hundred of these 'Marie-Louises' had deserted. Eight new infantry divisions had been raised during the past two months. A ninth under General Henrion would be ready in a few days. Every soldier who could stick on the back of a horse was mounted – some on nags resembling the 'four horses of the Apocalypse'.

Laon, a town of 7,000 inhabitants perched three hundred feet above the Ardon River, was surrounded by a wall 5,000 yards in perimeter. All eleven gates were open and no outer works were visible. The surrounding country was cut up with swamps, willow groves, and marshes. An assault launched in a mist might succeed, since the city was defended by no more than a rear-guard. So said the experts . . .

In reality, Laon was a veritable fortress. Blücher's artillery covered the roads to Rheims and Soissons, and those leading to the suburbs of Sémilly and Ardon, south of the town. All points were held by his infantry. Wintzingerode was on the west with the cavalry, and Kleist and Yorck were on the east. Sacken and Langeron had 90,000 men in reserve. However, the latter were jittery, their chief was ill, and their generals uneasy. What was "Napoleounn" up to? He was rumored to be approaching with 90,000 men. Actually, he had a scant 27,500.

On the misty morning of 8 March the whole Guard, led by Colbert, marched down the Chemin des Dames to the Soissons road, heading for Laon. Ney and the vanguard chased Tchernitchev's Cossacks from Urcel, but could not penetrate Étouvelles where the pass was held in force. Consequently they retired to Urcel while the cavalry occupied Nouvion and Friant camped at Chavignon, near the Emperor, Mortier in the Ailette valley, and Charpentier along the Chemin des Dames.

General Charpentier was a native of these parts. He informed Napoleon that the pass of Étouvelles could be bypassed on the west by a road leading through wooded ravines to Chivy.

At 9 p.m. Gourgaud set out with two battalions of grenadiers, ordered to signal their arrival at Chivy by lighting flares. Boyer chose 400 elite from his skeleton division and took along the sappers. At Gourgaud's signal Boyer's men were to attack the defile with bayonets.

Offering good rewards to the 'little rabbits' who returned alive, Boyer split his force into small columns with peasant guides. Meunier's sparse division and a Line brigade followed in support. Once their objective was reached, Belliard would force an entry into Laon with his cavalry.

Four hundred elite – a quarter of Boyer's whole force! These were flankers and *tirailleurs*, including many NCO's. In the darkness and falling snow the little column climbed in silence and crossed the woods. Crouching on the outskirts of Chivy, they waited for Gourgaud's signal. The minutes ticked away . . . Gourgaud had lost his way and had made a long detour through Anizy-le-château where he fought a skirmish.

2 a.m. They must do without Gourgaud. Entering Chivy with fixed bayonets they captured the large guard post and fought an action in the snow. They did not count

their foes, but at least three Russian regiments fled before them. The French losses were negligible.

Now Meunier entered the pass, joined by Gourgaud – who had finally arrived – at the far end. Meanwhile, Belliard chased the fugitives to Sémilly where he received a warm welcome from the Russian infantry and artillery; but he could not enter Laon. His patrols sent to left and right were everywhere repulsed.

It was now about 5.30 a.m. It had stopped snowing and a heavy mist rose from the Ardon marshes. Under cover of the mist Ney advanced. Mortier sent Poret de Morvan to the village of Ardon which was seized by the 15th Voltigeurs who lost two captains in the process. Bacot, a Saint-Cyrian of the Class of 1804, led his battalion to Saint-Vincent, and one company up to the garden gate. Then the fog lifted, revealing his real strength, and his fifty brats had to beat a hasty retreat.

Since up to that point the attack had been an incredible success, Napoleon persisted in his plan. Still believing he had only a rear-guard before him, he wrote Marmont at 8 a.m.: 'The Emperor has defeated the enemy at Chivy and we believe our vanguard to be at Laon . . .' Another courier took a more reserved message at eleven: 'They are still fighting . . .'

But his troops were no longer there. Blücher had given orders to drive the French away from the city. The attacks on Sémilly and Ardon by Wintzingerode and Blücher were very bloody. The voltigeurs in Ardon fought desperately. The colonel of the 15th was hit; a major of the 16th and General Poret de Morvan were severely wounded. Many officers and men were put out of action. While forced to abandon both villages, the French, though much reduced, halted the enemy.

Meanwhile, another battle was raging to the west. The Emperor sent Charpentier's two small divisions to attack Clacy. Led by General Montmarie, the *tirailleurs* entered the village and took 250 prisoners, but could not hold it. Four majors, 20 officers, and 250 men were put out of action. The survivors retreated to the outskirts and camped nearby.

Night fell. With the wind blowing in the opposite direction, no one had heard Marmont's guns east of the city.

That day Marmont, marching from Berry via Corbény, had attacked the Prussians before Athies and captured the village but was unable to make further progress. Without stopping to find out the result of the Emperor's attack, the Marshal went on to the Château of Eppes for the night, leaving his weak battalions in contact with a formidable enemy. Between 6 and 7 p.m. four Prussian columns launched a full scale attack in the dark on his corps, driving it back to Berry-au-Bac with a loss of 3,500 men, 45 guns, and 120 caissons.

The Emperor at Chavignon knew nothing of this. Next morning he ordered Mortier to attack Ardon with Pac's Poles and the Line dragoons while Ney and Charpentier, with the Old Guard, the cavalry, and the artillery reserve, attacked Clacy. Just as Napoleon was mounting his horse two dismounted dragoons arrived with the news of Marmont's disaster. 'Marmont behaved like a subaltern', was the Emperor's comment. Nevertheless he still persisted in his notion that Blücher intended to evacuate

Laon, interpreting the attack on Marmont as a rear-guard action designed to cover the Prussians' retreat.

But Blücher had no such idea. The old Marshal was ill. He turned over his command to Gneisenau who, fearing to compromise himself, made a few halfhearted attacks which were all repulsed. Tired and diminished, the Guard lacked the means to counterattack. They held on until night. Then Ney lighted numerous campfires and, leaving a detachment of chasseurs and dragoons with two voltigeur battalions to guard the rear, he retired with his 1,000 survivors and joined the army in its retreat to Soissons.[2]

The Emperor arrived at Soissons the afternoon of the 11th with the Old Guard and stayed at the Episcopal Palace. The snow had melted, transforming the manure-covered streets into sewers. The ramparts were full of half-drowned corpses and the horses were up to their hocks in muck and filth. The houses of Saint-Waaste were filled with wounded.

Mortier barricaded himself in Crouy and Cuffies with his two divisions plus those of Charpentier and Boyer, now transferred to his command. He established strong outposts in the vicinity, while Pac's lancers and the Line dragoons scouted on the Soissons-Laon road, and Colbert occupied the suburbs of Rheims; for obviously Blücher would pursue the Emperor.

The Guard had lost 3,000 men. Some of its divisions were no bigger than regiments. Since most of their generals had been wounded the Emperor consolidated the four Young Guard divisions, plus that of Poret de Morvan, into two under Curial and Charpentier. Curial's 1st Young Guard Division was divided into two brigades under Rousseau and Le Capitaine and filled up with *tirailleurs*. Charpentier's 2nd Division was assigned the voltigeurs, with Jamin and La Grange as brigade commanders. (Bigarré relieved Charpentier in command of the division on 17 March.) Each division was assigned two batteries. Finally, Boyer's fusiliers and flankers were turned over to Christiani. Mortier's corps consisted of these three divisions plus 1,800 Line cavalry, aggregating 9,000 men.

The reorganization was made quickly but carefully. As far as possible individual units were kept together under their own commanders. The battalions, varying in strength from 67 to 563, and their officers, varying in number from 5 to 25, had to be equalized; however, the new appointments were made with the same care as the old. General Montmarie was attached to the 1st Old Guard Division. General Sebastiani replaced Nansouty, who was ill, in command of the cavalry of the Guard.

The Grumblers had ceased to grumble. The misfortunes of their country and their desire to save it, combined with the Emperor's energy and intelligence, had given the Guard a new soul. It would conquer or die. The Old Guard had no deserters. The old discipline, strict and eternal, prevailed in its ranks. The grenadiers paraded before the Episcopal Palace at Soissons as if at the Tuileries, in the presence of Mortier, Friant, Petit, and the generals and commandants.

[2] A French army had succeeded in entering Soissons on 8 March. – Ed.

The Emperor prepared to resume the campaign in two days' time. Meanwhile, Marmont held Berry and Fismes and guarded the Aisne.

A reinforcement of Line cavalry under General Berckheim known as the 'united squadrons' arrived with two batteries and some reinforcements for the escort squadrons. Sixty cripples of the Old Guard and 300 of the Young were left at Soissons under the extraordinary Major Gérard, of whom we shall hear more later.

So long as Gérard held Soissons and Corbineau held Rheims the forces of Blücher and Schwarzenberg must remain divided.

CHAPTER 8

Rheims

At 3 p.m. on 12 March an officer of the horse Guard galloped into Soissons with the news that Rheims had fallen. A Russian corps of 15,000 men under the *émigré* Saint-Priest had stormed the city at dawn that morning. The faithful Corbineau had resisted with a garrison of half-armed national guards plus two Young Guard battalions, a few companies of horse Guards and guards of honor, and some old Veteran-Cannoneers who had served under Lafayette and Dumouriez.

The voltigeurs had put up a heroic defense at the Porte Cérès and the Porte de Mars. The commander of the Veteran-Cannoneers and an Old Guard lieutenant had been killed at the Porte de Paris. A major of the voltigeurs was wounded, and General Corbineau was missing.

At Soissons the soldiers' rest came to an end. Taking leave of the bishop, the Emperor set out for Rheims at 2 a.m. on the 13th, escorted by the duty squadrons. He assigned two Young Guard battalions, some Grumblers under Captain Bellanger, and some Polish lancers and scouts to garrison Laon, and left Mortier's corps with Pac's lancers and the 'united squadrons' to hold the Aisne, watch Blücher, and maintain liaison with Imperial Headquarters.

Marmont's corps at Fisme took the vanguard and Ney followed the Emperor with a small Line brigade, Friant's Old Guard, the sappers and marines, and the artillery reserve under Drouot, totaling 13,500 men. The weather was misty and overcast but spring was in the air.

At two that afternoon the Emperor and his escort joined Marmont at Mont Saint-Pierre, a hill about two miles from the suburb of Vesle. On their left rose the towers of Rheims Cathedral where the kings of France were crowned. Marmont's troops had already cleared the enemy from their trenches in the western villages and was waiting for Ney, Friant, and the artillery to arrive before storming the city gates.

At 4 p.m. Drouot's guns thundered in front of Mont Saint-Pierre as the cavalry of Colbert and Exelmans flanked Marmont's attack in the valley of the Vesle. The traitor Saint-Preist was mortally wounded by a shell. Bereft of their leader, the Russians slackened their defense; nevertheless, successive attacks by Marmont and brave charges by the guards of honor were repulsed before the Porte de Vesle was opened to them at eleven that night.

Meanwhile the Emperor, who was very tired, lay on his bearskin rug before a big fire, guarded by Petit's grenadiers. By 9.30 p.m. the suburb of Saint-Brice was occupied, and the Polish lancers and scouts and Exelmans' dragoons entered the flaming city.

Krasinski pursued the Prussians to Berry-au-Bac, followed by Colbert who camped at Neuvillette.

Rheims was brilliantly illuminated to celebrate the victory. 'It was so light', Coigniet reported, 'you could have picked up a needle . . .' The bells of the Cathedral pealed, warming the heart of General Boulart whose father was one of its cantors. The populace cheered the Emperor wildly as he rode into Rheims at the head of the guards of honor who had played a gallant part in liberating the city.

Corbineau emerged from his hiding place of the past thirty-six hours. Laferrière breathed easier on his sickbed in the Rue de l'Oignon, for the Russians had carried off Adjutant General Lacoste who, like himself, had been wounded at Craonne and he had expected a similar fate.

At Monsieur Ponsardin's residence the Emperor received news from Mortier who had been attacked by Sacken on the latter's march from Berry-au-Bac. Christiani's flankers had halted the Prussians at Crouy. Major Deblais and a *tirailleur* lieutenant were killed, and six officers and 40 men wounded. 'The enemy appears to be in full retreat', Mortier reported.

Indeed, when informed that Rheims had fallen, Blücher had recalled all troops pursuing Napoleon to Laon. Meanwhile, Bernadotte halted his drive against General Maison in the north, and Schwarzenberg called off an attack on Macdonald and retired to Provins.

The Emperor was so full of confidence at this moment that he considered attacking Schwarzenberg's right flank while Macdonald stormed his front; but he was deterred by the pitifully small size of his forces.

Rheims, 15 March. 3 p.m. The Emperor mounted his horse, followed by Marshal Lefebvre, Generals Bertrand, Drouot, Dejean, Belliard, and Flahaut in full dress. The garrison commander Corbineau took his place in the suite as aide-de-camp, and the horse grenadiers, in dress coats and plumes, formed the escort. In the market square the trumpets of the chasseurs sounded 'To the Emperor!' Lion presented his squadrons.

This was the first review of the Guard since the beginning of the campaign. The uniforms were not brilliant, but the mud had been scraped from breeches and boots, the wrinkled old mugs were shaven, and the horses groomed.

How many men were present? This agonizing question was asked each company. Colbert's 1st Cavalry Division reported Pac's 600 Poles and 180 2nd Lancers with 6 guns; Exelman's division, 1,500 light-horse, scouts, and dragoons; Letort's Old Guard cavalry, 800 chasseurs, 800 grenadiers, and 200 1st Scouts. Counting 1,500 Poles and chasseurs en route from Paris under Lefebvre-Desnoëttes, the horse Guard mustered around 7,000.

In the Place de la Couture the Veteran-Cannoneers were drawn up on the right of Friant's grenadiers and chasseurs. The bands played *Let Us Watch Over the Empire* and *The Victory Is Ours*. Never had the Guard campaigned so hard nor marched so far with so little rest. 'If we succeed in ridding her of the enemy', wrote the adjutant major of the 2nd Grenadiers, 'we shall have deserved well of our country'.

The men had been rejuvenated by their thirty-six-hour rest and the good wine the mayor provided. Their coats were worn and their bonnets mangy but their belts were white as snow. On the Place Impériale the voltigeur cadres, and the Line framed with veterans, looked gaunt but there was a light in their eye as they presented arms.

The artillery was minutely inspected. Its ammunition would be replenished. Where was the fourteenth Young Guard battery? It had been captured the night before. No matter, it would be re-formed with six French howitzers taken from the enemy, and gunners and train soldiers uniformed in Rheims.

The crowd cheered their liberators and a march-past closed the parade, amid shouts of '*Vive l'Empereur!*' In the general enthusiasm no one suspected that this was the Guard's last review . . .

The march to the Aube began. Ney with 6,000 men captured Châlons from the Russians on 15 March.

The day before, Colbert's cavalry and Pac's Poles, followed by a battalion of voltigeurs and a sapper company to rebuild the bridge in case it were destroyed, had gone to 'open communications with Épernay'. Next morning the vanguard was surprised by Tettenborn, and a captain of the scouts was killed; but the arrival of Colbert's main force restored the situation. In the face of a stubborn defense the stone bridge at Épernay was captured intact that afternoon, and the men taken prisoner in the morning set free. Mayor Jean Moët of Épernay regaled the victors with quantities of champagne which they drank to the Emperor.

Napoleon remained in Rheims until the 17th. He decided to march to Troyes with the Old Guard, leaving Mortier's Young Guard with Belliard's cavalry and Marmont's corps – 22,000 men in all – to try to contain the Prussians and Russians on the Aisne, and retire step by step to Paris if they failed. Mortier, as the senior marshal, was given command of this force; however, Berthier wrote Marmont: 'The Emperor has faith in your talents. Direct the movements, but keep up the appearance of acting in concert with the Duke of Treviso rather than tell him what to do.'

The Emperor left Rheims on the 17th for Épernay with the Old Guard and the artillery. The cavalry marched ahead with Sebastiani, Exelmans, and Letort. Next day Napoleon slept at La Fère-Champenoise while Sebastiani swept the plain of Champagne with Griois' horse batteries as far as Herbisse where swarms of Cossacks were buzzing on Schwarzenberg's right flank.

On his return from scouting around Montmirail Colbert took the vanguard. The enemy made no stand before his squadrons. Even the boldest were halted by a few volleys of canister shot; then they wavered and the Cossacks galloped off, leaving their lame horses and wounded behind.

'This little war is quite amusing', wrote Griois. Sometimes General Exelmans so far forgot himself as to play subaltern and charge, saber in hand, with the scouts while Letort led his dragoons as though they were the 'wingèd light horse'.[1]

[1] During the 16th century the Turkish and Polish light cavalry actually wore wings.—Ed.

On the morning of the 18th Mortier arrived in Rheims with Christiani, Curial, and Belliard's cavalry. The latter had made contact with Marmont's troops at the bridges of Berry and Pontavert. The two Guard divisions were posted north of the city; for Yorck, Kleist, and Sacken were reported to be marching south. Corbineau left Rheims to join the Emperor while Charpentier's division remained at Soissons.

Meanwhile, Schwarzenberg was warned that the Emperor and the Guard, fresh from their victory at Rheims, were marching against him. On the 18th he ordered his army to retire to Troyes under cover of Wrede's 5th Corps which was ordered to hold the left bank of the Aube as far as Arcis. On the 20th Schwarzenberg was due in Bar-sur-Aube, and Wrede in Brienne.

This was bad news for the Emperor. Sheer terror was forcing the Allies to concentrate the scattered army of Bohemia and accelerate its eastward march.

Sebastiani chose this moment to make a swift thrust at Boulages where he met more cavalry than usual. He defeated a large Cossack contingent on the heights of Champfleury and took many prisoners.

At Plancy, where the bridge was down, the enemy defended the Aube crossing with artillery which was soon muzzled by the Guard horse battery. Under cover of an Old Guard battalion, the sappers and pontooneers repaired the bridge with the aid of the inhabitants. Then Exelmans and Colbert chased the Cossacks across the vast plain while Letort's horse Guards and Berckheim's squadrons led the Emperor to Méry.

Here in the rubble the Württembergers marching to Troyes at the rear of the Army of Bohemia paused to defend themselves. When hard pressed, they burned the bridge and streamed across to the left bank of the Seine. The Emperor sent Letort to a ford above the bridge where Lieutenant Allimant and seventeen chasseurs captured 13 pontoons, 3 vehicles, and 98 horses from Schwarzenberg's rear-guard.

By the evening of the 19th the foot Guard had covered more than fifty miles in forty hours, and the artillery had unlimbered their guns twenty times. Had they arrived only six hours earlier, they could have stopped Schwarzenberg.

That evening Letort's cavalry remained at Méry. Macdonald's vanguard was at Villenauxe. The Army of Bohemia was left free either to retreat to Bar, or join forces with the Army of Silesia at Châlons and mass for battle. That night it chose the latter course.

On the night of 18 March, harassed by Blücher and informed of the Emperor's departure, Marmont had retreated to Fismes and summoned Mortier to join him. Annoyed but composed, the Duke of Treviso recalled his cavalry and moved back his two Guard divisions, holding Roussel's dragoons in Rheims until morning. Then, leaving Curial in command, he went with a small escort to meet Marmont.

The interview took place next morning at Jonchéry about 9.30 a.m. The discussion was heated. When Mortier insisted upon carrying out the Emperor's orders to the letter, Marmont finally agreed to his returning to Rheims.

The order to turn back reached Curial a short distance east of Jonchéry, and Roussel farther back. Meanwhile, part of Wintzingerode's army had entered Rheims shortly before noon. Neither the fusilier battalion nor Roussel's dragoons could dislodge them, so Mortier was obliged to spend that night near Fismes where Marmont's small corps was camped.

Here Mortier was surprised to learn that that very morning Marmont had ordered Charpentier to evacuate Soissons, leaving as a garrison Bellanger's 227 Old Guardsmen, two voltigeur battalions, 100 scouts and lancers, and the national guards, under a twenty-nine-year-old commander named Gérard.

How could Mortier obey the Emperor's order that he held in his hand? This read: 'If Blücher takes the offensive, retire to Châlons and Épernay so we can join forces . . .

The Emperor was counting on him. Napoleon had just passed through Plancy where the *curé* had received him in mufti because the Cossacks had stolen his cassock. The whole foot Guard was there with Ney. Sebastiani and the cavalry were near Pouan, occupied by Cossacks. In view of the concentration of the Army of Bohemia, the Emperor had called off his march to Troyes for fear he might face overwhelming odds there. He had decided to turn east instead and cut the enemy's communications.

He planned to march to Vitry via Arcis and fall upon the rear-guards with Macdonald, Oudinot, Ney, the cavalry, and the Guard, reinforced by Desnoëttes who was due momentarily. He expected Marmont and Mortier to join him in this maneuver.

At noon on the 20th Berthier wrote Marmont: 'The Emperor orders you and the Marshal Duke of Treviso to march with your cavalry and artillery from wherever you are to Châlons by way of Rheims: or, if this is impossible, via Épernay . . . with all possible speed.'

Sebastiani and Ney had arrived at Arcis just an hour before. Ordered to proceed to Vitry, Ney hesitated. Some enemy squadrons were patrolling in the direction of Sompuis. On the left bank of the Aube Colbert's and Exelmans' cavalry had captured several Württembergers and soldiers of Gyulay's corps who had come from Troyes and spent the night at Charmont. A patrol of Polish lancers had been unable to scout beyond Aubeterre where the villagers reported masses of enemy troops in the region. Were they mistaken?

They were not.

CHAPTER 9

Arcis-sur-Aube

WORD had reached Schwarzenberg at Troyes that Tettenborn had occupied Châlons and Napoleon had crossed the Aube at Plancy. From the former he concluded that his army had made contact with Blücher; from the latter, that Napoleon had given up marching to Troyes in order to attack his left flank.

He found himself in a dangerous position with a river at his back. Hence, regardless of advice, he decided to halt his retreat, call up his reserves, and march to Arcis on the 20th with all the forces at his command.

By 11 p.m. Wrede on the right, Württemberg in the center, and Gyulay on the left were en route to Arcis, and Barclay de Tolly had reached the Aube from the east.

Meanwhile, in Arcis Ney made contact with Sebastiani who shared his anxiety. Ney occupied the town, set up his artillery, and put Torcy – evacuated twelve hours before by the Bavarians – into a state of defense. Saizieu's 300 marines and Fournier's sappers rebuilt the bridge. Sebastiani deployed his divisions in two lines before Arcis, facing south. Behind Colbert, the Guard horse artillery was divided between the wings. Colbert's patrols were in contact with the Cossacks. An enemy attack was imminent.

At 1.30 p.m. the Emperor, escorted by a single squadron, appeared with his staff on the left bank of the river. The rest of the escort was following with Letort and the dragoons. The horse grenadiers and chasseurs had been left near Méry that morning with Curely's light brigade to escort the captured pontoons.

The Emperor heard Sebastiani's report at the château of his chamberlain Labiffe. Why all the alarm? Did the General believe in ghosts? Schwarzenberg was retreating! An aide sent on reconnaissance with the duty squadron saw nothing but Cossacks. The order to march to Vitry stood. Sebastiani was to watch the road to Troyes. The marines were ordered to Sompuis, to be followed shortly by the Old Guard and the artillery reserve which had left Plancy around 11 p.m. Then, followed by Guyot, the Emperor trotted off to Torcy to confer with Ney, and Sebastiani rejoined his squadrons.

Alert! Warned that enemy cavalry was approaching, Colbert mounted his horse and Griois emplaced his guns. Colbert's scouts and lancers advanced and were promptly met by a volley of shot and shell from the crest of the plateau east of the town, which was more indented than it appeared from below. Charged simultaneously by clouds of yelling Cossacks and Frimont's light cavalry, Colbert's horsemen were thrown into sudden panic and turned tail, colliding with Exelmans' division which promptly headed back to Arcis, pursued full tilt by the Russians.

Upsetting a horse battery of the Guard en route, the Russians gave chase as the motley horde dashed like a whirlwind to the outskirts of Arcis. There they scattered, slowed down, and sought entrance to the town by every avenue of approach. Colbert's cavalry, scrambled together with Exelmans', the dragoons of the Guard, and the Cossacks, reached the bridge to find the Emperor there, sword in hand. (He had just returned from Torcy where his small escort had been mauled by Frimont's hussars. Throwing himself into the middle of one of Ney's Polish squares until the danger was past, he had managed to escape and hurried to the bridge.)

'Will you cross before me?' he cried to the stampeded horsemen heading for the bridge.

Order was quickly restored when the terrified troopers regained control of themselves. Their squadrons rallied and advanced.

At this point the marines of the Guard arrived on the double, out of breath. Short of infantry, Exelmans had alerted them on the road to Sompuis. By well-directed fire they turned back the Cossacks.

By now shells were falling on the town and around the bridge and a lively action was in progress at Torcy. A force of 5,000 Line troops and 2,500 horse Guards was facing 14,000 Allied soldiers, including 8,000 infantry.

Friant's fur bonnets appeared on the winding road through the marshes on the right bank, led by two battalions of Gendarmes of Spain who had been admitted to the Guard because of their bravery at Montereau. The Emperor sent the gendarmes to rescue Ney. Then, as the Guard battalions approached under heavy fire, he posted them on the outskirts of Arcis to block the road to Troyes.

The foot chasseurs crossed the town behind their new commander General Pelet under a rain of shot and opened fire. Drouot's artillery raked the Allied guns and infantry. At one point during the devastating cannonade, which lasted until sunset, the Emperor was knocked off his horse by a bursting shell and disappeared in the smoke. Then he got up – unhurt.

The enemy was being continually reinforced. By evening, 24,500 were holding the line against 13,000 French. Adjutant Sémery, chief of staff of the 1st Young Guard Division, was killed.

Now firing could be heard in the west. It came from the horse grenadiers and chasseurs of the Guard and Curely's brigade, at grips with 4,000 horse of Pahlen, Nostitz, and Bismarck. The latter belonged to the Prince of Württemberg's army which had been en route since morning and had lost its way. Towards evening the enemy cavalry had spied a party of 1,600 horse marching at a walk from Méry, escorting a convoy.

Attacked on front and flanks, the chasseurs of Lion, Bellebaux, and Cayre and the horse grenadiers of Jamin, Venières, and Delaporte put up a heroic fight. When Curely's troopers and horse battery came to their aid they sent word of their predicament to the Emperor. Then they retired slowly to Méry where 100 dismounted chasseurs fooled the enemy into believing the village was held by infantry.

What, the 'gods' and 'cherished children' in danger! At the height of the battle Berthier wrote them the following note and sent it by Rottembourg's soldiers:

383

'Arcis-sur-Aube, 20 March 1814. 4.30 p.m.

'It seems that the horse grenadiers and chasseurs of the Guard have been cut off on the road to Arcis and have retired to Méry . . . All the Guard is ordered to rendezvous at Arcis, via Boulages.'

Under cover of darkness the elite of the horse Guard joined the Emperor at 11 p.m. The fighting continued in the inferno of Torcy where a battalion of the 2nd Grenadiers had been sent to reinforce Ney's infantry.

Before Arcis all combat ceased around 8 p.m., though firing continued amid the flames. Sebastiani, who had fought all day on the right flank, maneuvering from side to side of the Barbuisse valley, ordered half his exhausted troopers to rest while the other half went in search of food and forage.

Alert! A suspicious body of horse appeared, trotting down the road from Plancy. After alarming both Sebastiani and the Emperor, Lefebvre-Desnoëttes and his 1,500 troopers were warmly welcomed. Desnoëttes had brought with him Henrion's division, containing the 8th and 9th Voltigeurs, and three route battalions with six guns and two howitzers under Lt. Colonel Beurmann; however, the conscripts, too tired to fight, had been left at Plancy.

Desnoëttes' arrival determined Sebastiani to avenge his defeat of the morning. His men could eat later. Led to the attack, his three divisions crushed the Cossacks and hussars on the enemy left and advanced to the Russian infantry lines. That night Sebastiani's troopers bivouacked nearby at Nozay, half of them with their bridles over their arms.

The enemy was leaving the field, confirming the Emperor in the belief that today's action had been a diversion to cover Schwarzenberg's retreat. Therefore at dawn he resumed his march to Vitry with Henrion's division and four of Rottembourg's *tirailleur* regiments, keeping the infantry on his right to fend off any attack by the enemy's flank guard.

It was no flank guard, but over 100,000 men with 370 guns that Sebastiani saw at 9 a.m. Surrounded by masses of cavalry, they were drawn up in three lines on the plain where his troopers had fought the day before. At the sight of the French squadrons their drums beat and their artillery opened fire. Sebastiani stood his ground and maneuvered. Griois set up his batteries and fired into the mass. Meanwhile, the Emperor returned at a gallop and ordered a retreat.

This was so skillfully conducted that the enemy did not pursue – at first. 'Ordered to hold his position until dark', Sebastiani maneuvered slowly out of range of the enemy guns and retired his units in echelon, checkerwise. The artillery reserve and Henrion's division crossed the bridge at Arcis, and a second hastily built above it; then Ney retired fighting. Finally, the cavalry, under cover of Rottembourg's and Leval's divisions, returned to Arcis where the *tirailleurs* and veterans of Spain had barricaded the streets, put the houses into a state of defense, and prepared to sell their carcasses high.

Then came the onslaught. The cavalry of the Guard managed to reach Arcis in safety, except for the 2nd and 3rd Scouts who were badly mauled, suffering heavy losses and leaving prisoners behind. At their heels the Russians, Bavarians, Austrians, and Württembergers launched their attack.

A desperate struggle ensued in Arcis. There was hand-to-hand fighting in the market place where the 5th Voltigeurs were hard pressed, and the 8th lost a major, four field officers, and 33 men. The sappers blew up the bridge under cover of Rottembourg's *tirailleurs*, during which operation Captain Fournier and several sappers were killed.

Where was the army? Where was the Emperor? Were they marching to Paris or to the east?

Though Napoleon knew it would be politic to defend Paris, it would mean certain defeat; whereas marching east would force the Allies to retreat. He took the road to the east and left Paris to its fate. From now on the capital of the Empire was no longer Paris, but the errant and precarious Imperial Headquarters, surrounded and defended by the faithful and indomitable Guard.

But why did the Emperor now choose as its next location Sompuis, the humblest village in Champagne, desolate and vermin-ridden? And why did he occupy its poorest house, the deserted and pillaged dwelling of Professor Royer-Collard? The grenadiers set up housekeeping, kindling fires with difficulty. 'It is forbidden to burn the wagons, doors, or windows', they read in the orders. 'The corps must pay for whatever wood it burns.'

Letort's dragoons were quartered in the village. Outside, Henrion's conscripts shivered in the chalky mud, exposed to wind and rain. The cellars and attics of the houses were as empty as the conscripts' bellies. For these lads who still played with tops in their bivouacs real misery was now beginning. The Young and Old Guard troopers of Colbert, Exelmans, and Lefebvre-Desnoëttes occupied the next village while Ney and the Line cavalry camped somewhere ahead along the road. Anxiety reigned in these miserable bivouacs in the midst of a foggy desert surrounded by isolated villages, all pillaged and destroyed.

Meanwhile, to the west, the corps of Oudinot and Macdonald dragged wearily through the night. Where was 'he' leading them?

The enemy had occupied Vitry.

Fifty miles northwest, beyond Fismes, Mortier and his three Young Guard divisions received the urgent order, relayed by Marmont, to join the Emperor. On reading it Mortier thought sadly that if only Marmont had followed him to Rheims, instead of retiring to Fismes, the Russians would not now be drinking champagne and the Allies occupying Chalons and Épernay.

The Soissons garrison had been attacked by Bülow, and 600 *tirailleurs* were isolated at Compiègne. The Guard, once a compact reserve, was now dispersed and was bearing the brunt of the war. The Emperor was far removed from some of its units, and liaison was made difficult by the frequent capture of his couriers.

At dawn next day, 22 March, Sebastiani rode back towards Arcis and the enemy. Soon Exelmans' light troopers collided in the fog with Russian and Württemberg squadrons who seemed remarkably shy. The French were unable to catch a single Cossack. They skirmished during part of the day 'without any result beyond tiring the horses and men', according to Exelmans who refused to go farther west since the

Emperor was marching east. A lively altercation broke out between him and Sebastiani in front of the troops. Finally the latter gave in. That evening the troopers dismounted near the Old Guard bivouacs. Reconnaissances reported strong enemy columns marching east.

This was confirmed by Sebastiani next day. As far as Frignicourt, where his squadrons forded the river, and on the bridge held by Ney, he chased off flankers of Bavarian and Russian columns marching in the same direction as himself. Rottembourg, Oudinot, and Macdonald, whose battalions were strung out between the Aube and the Marne, gave the same information.

Napoleon began receiving these reports the evening of the 22nd at the Château of Plessis, ten miles from Saint-Dizier. He rubbed his hands.[1] The strategists were delighted. The foot Guard feasted, thanks to the generosity of the owner and her cook who emptied the larder for them. For two weeks they had been running and fighting day and night without taking time to eat or even to answer the calls of nature. Now they enjoyed plucking chickens and eating them, drying their shirts, scraping the mud off their gaiters, and emptying the water out of their shoes.

Sacré Tondu! So his father-in-law was after him![2] Now those devils of soft Parisians could stop trembling, and the good-for-nothings who had started grumbling the moment the Guard turned east the day before could shut their traps. 'I tell you, my boy, the *Tondu* is stronger than God!'

The cavalry was at Joinville, en route to Montier-en-Der and Châlons, and communications with Troyes had been restored. The army was occupying Lesmont and was marching to Saint-Dizier next day. The French would win another battle of Brienne where the *Kaiserliks* and Cossacks were congregating, according to the peasants who came to warm themselves and drink a drop with the Grumblers.

That evening the Grumblers were full of enthusiasm and white wine. As they dried their pants and filled their bellies, their gaiety and confidence returned.

---

[1] Schwarzenberg's eastward march, away from Paris, would give Napoleon his only chance of damaging the Austrians; and also, freeing the French garrisons blockaded in Metz, Thionville, Luxembourg, etc., and combining with them to beat Blücher and the Russians. This growing obsession of Napoleon's may help to explain his conduct during the next few days. – Ed.

[2] Emperor Francis had recently joined the Allied Headquarters. – *Ibid.*

CHAPTER 10

The Eleventh Hour

ON the afternoon of 23 March at Pougy the Allied sovereigns and generals concluded that their communications with the Rhine were threatened. The Austrian Emperor proposed to retire and reopen them via Switzerland. Learning from an intercepted dispatch that Napoleon was marching to Saint-Dizier, the rest preferred to join Blücher at Châlons. This course was agreed upon, and the Emperor Francis was persuaded to go to Lyons.

'Twenty-four hours can bring a vast change in a military situation', Napoleon was writing Clarke at that moment. That night his whole army was on the right bank of the Marne except the large artillery park, escorted by Amey's small division, which had missed the road but turned up eventually. Within a few hours he would be surrounded by his Guard as well.

Only Sebastiani was missing. The General berated Macdonald for detaining him ('invoking supposed orders from the Emperor', the General wrote Berthier). Sebastiani joined Napoleon next day.

Installed at the *mairie* at Saint-Dizier, the Emperor read the dispatches. The enemy was evacuating Bar-sur-Aube, Troyes, Chaumont, and Langres, and marching to Vitry. Schwarzenberg was following in the footsteps of the French. At 11.30 p.m. an order was issued to spread the word that the Emperor was marching to Metz; however, another went to the parks of the artillery and engineers to hitch up their teams and leave for Wassy at 4 a.m. Henrion's division would form the vanguard, led by 100 horse of Desnoëttes' division. The Old Guard would leave at 5.30 a.m., followed by the headquarters staff and Desnoëttes himself at 6.30.

They were going to the Aube. From there they could either attack Schwarzenberg's communications, or block his retreat if he turned around.

The Emperor spent the next night at Doulevant-le-Château in the house of the notary Jeausson, whose cook Marie-Jeanne Didier related that the Emperor gave her 5 *napoléons* which she kept as a souvenir, and that 'soldiers were all over the house, and some guarded his room and one, his bed'. The park stayed at Dommartin. Henrion watched the Brienne road. The roads to Chaumont and Bar were guarded by the horse grenadiers and chasseurs. Sebastiani's cavalry was at Wassy. Next day the Emperor hoped to make contact with Marmont and Mortier who should be approaching.

That night Mortier was at Vatry, thirty kilometers northwest of Vitry, with the three Young Guard divisions. They had marched from Fismes through miserable byroads and chalk bogs bordering the river Soude. Marching over 100 kilometers in sixty hours, on the alert against Cossacks, groping their way, bending their backs to the downpours and icy winds, they had cursed the sodden packs that weighed them down and the stiff belts that strangled them. All this to find the *Tondu!* And would they ever find him?

No. Never – never again.

Now, on the night of 24 March, sleeping in the same white mud, Christiani's, Curial's, and Charpentier's *tirailleurs* and voltigeurs saw lights on the eastern horizon. They looked to north and south and everywhere they saw the campfires of the Armies of Silesia and Bohemia which had joined forces behind the Army of Napoleon.

Ten kilometers to the south Marmont was sleeping at the Château of Soudé-Saint-Croix. Next morning, while Mortier and his staff were having breakfast with him, two enemy balls burst through the roof of their headquarters. They were fired by the vanguard of the Allied armies marching to Paris.

Two days before, on the 23rd, Tettenborn's Cossacks had intercepted a packet of dispatches from the Duke of Rovigo (Savary) in Paris, and brought it to the Tsar. Savary wrote: 'There are influential personages in Paris, hostile to the Emperor, whom we have cause to fear if the enemy approaches the capital . . .' This confirmed a letter to Nesselrode,[1] inspired by Talleyrand, with a postscript in invisible ink: 'You are marching on crutches . . . Use your legs . . . March straight to Paris . . . They are waiting for you.'

'Without those bloody traitors and bastards of aristocrats, the *Tondu* would have licked them', the Grumblers said later.

Next morning, 24 March, in the little hamlet of Blacy between Vitry and Sompuis where Schwarzenberg found the Tsar, the King of Prussia, and the Allied general staff, the fate of France and the Emperor was sealed. Since Paris was waiting for them, the Armies of Silesia and Bohemia would set out at dawn next day. In five days they would be in the Tuileries. Meanwhile, Wintzingerode would march to Saint-Dizier with 10,000 cavalry, the light artillery, and several battalions to take care of Napoleon.

Only the last piece of news was brought the Emperor on the 25th by one of Ney's officers. Napoleon had heard nothing from Paris for two days. Why was Schwarzenberg's army marching to Saint-Dizier? Where was he now?

He sent patrols to Brienne, Bar, Joinville, Chaumont, Langres, Troyes, and questioned gendarmes, peasants, and spies. Then he sent Henrion's division to Bar with 100 troopers to hold the city and the bridge at Dolancourt while he attacked the enemy at Saint-Dizier with the foot Guard, the cavalry, and Oudinot. 'All signs indicate that we shall have a good day tomorrow', he dictated at seven that evening.

At 2 a.m. he left Doulevant with the Guard, reaching Wassy at dawn. There he picked up Sebastiani who had whipped Tettenborn's Cossacks at Eclaron. From the heights of Valcour the Emperor saw the enemy drawn up along the Marne from Saint-Dizier to Perthes with several light batteries, some infantry, and masses of cavalry. Catching sight of the Guard squadrons, they formed in columns to retire to Vitry.

[1] Russian diplomat accompanying the Allied armies. – Ed.

Sebastiani promptly crossed the river by a ford, followed by the Old Guard and Macdonald who arrived too late to help Colbert's chasseurs and lancers capture 18 Russian guns. Then the dragoons and horse grenadiers and Trelliard's Dragoons of Spain charged the flank of the enemy horde which they sabered and hacked and sent flying towards Vitry and Bar-sur-Ornain. The Emperor, sword in hand, joined in the pursuit at the head of several squadrons of horse Guards.

'I have served twenty years as a cavalry officer', Sebastiani wrote the Emperor in his report, 'and I cannot recall, Sire, ever having seen a more brilliant charge than that of the leading squadron today.' These were Major Kirmann's Young Guard chasseurs, including the celebrated Captain Parquin (see Plate 136).[2]

Though Lefebvre-Desnoëttes missed the battle, his Mameluks – with Roustam among them – took a crack at some Cossacks whom 'they sabered in their accustomed style', he reported.

The French losses were minimal, but Wintzingerode left 500 dead and wounded and 18 guns on the field. It was a fine victory and a magnificent display of swordsmanship by men full of ardor and in no way discouraged. If only the 'big hats' were as ardent!

Caulaincourt was heard to murmur: 'What are we doing here anyway? If "he" falls shall we not fall with him?'

Most of the 2,000 prisoners taken at Saint-Dizier declared that the Allies were marching to Paris. Next day Henrion's troopers captured a dispatch ordering the parks of the Army of Bohemia to join Schwarzenberg at Chaumont the next evening. It ended: 'Wintzingerode's light troops are our rear-guard'.

The truth dawned on the Emperor on the 27th – and only then! He was transfixed. Shut up in his headquarters in Saint-Dizier, he thought over the situation. His throne was tottering. Yet Oudinot and Rottembourg sent word of harassed convoys being attacked by peasants in Alsace and Lorraine, crying '*Vive l'Empereur!*' From Sainte-Menehoulde the sub-prefect wrote on the 25th: 'Seven hundred and fifty determined partisans are holding the passes through the Argonne and six thousand peasants have answered the tocsin's call'. It was the same in Burgundy, Franche-Comté, Auvergne, the Midi . . . 'The people's ardor should not be allowed to cool', protested Oudinot; and Piré wrote: 'They are waiting for a proclamation from the Emperor at Chaumont'.

'Peasants armed with scythes and fowling pieces are taking thousands of prisoners, cattle, guns . . .' General Henrion reported, adding: 'The Young Guard is full of enthusiasm'. The Old Guard was, too. 'The fact is', they said, 'one must forget about Paris.'

In a house at Marolles on the road to Vitry the Emperor, surrounded by Berthier, Lefebvre, Ney, Caulaincourt, and Maret, decided to march to Paris by way of Troyes. His army must reach the capital in order to utilize its large resources before the enemy.

---

[2] The *Souvenirs du Capitaine Parquin* is one of the military classics of the Empire. – Ed.

At dawn on the 28th he left for Wassy with the foot Guard, the artillery, and Ney. The horse Guard marched via Brienne, followed by Macdonald and Oudinot. Rottembourg was still at Bar-sur-Ornain. The Line cavalry was summoned from Chaumont to Troyes.

The weather was frightful. The cavalry made slow progress on the rutted roads, and the artillery had to burn twenty caissons to release enough horses to move the rest. Detachments went ahead to Troyes to arrange for bread, provisions, and supplies. The army was famished. It had marched clean through the soles of its shoes.

At 2 p.m, having covered thirty kilometers, the army was an hour from Doulevant when a courier arrived from Lavalette, the director of posts in Paris, a veteran of Egypt and loyal, with a message in code: 'The Emperor's presence is imperative if he wishes to prevent his capital from being handed over to the enemy . . . There is not a moment to lose . . .'

Was it so urgent? Was the enemy traveling so fast? What were Marmont and Mortier and the Young Guard doing? And the Guard detachments in Champagne and Brie?

The Emperor halted at Doulevant. At 2 a.m. on the 29th he said goodbye to the notary, who was shot by the Cossacks a few days later, and to Marie-Jeanne and her daughters who wept. What would become of them with these bandits about? Bah! In such times one ceased to be a man. He must march day and night to save Paris.

'We shall cross the Aube at Dolancourt', wrote Berthier.

Friant reached the river at 9 a.m. The Emperor was there with Sebastiani, Lefebvre-Desnoëttes, Henrion, and some couriers from Paris. He was eating a piece of chicken and drinking a glass of wine while reading the dispatches. Lamentations from Joseph. Paris was prostrate . . . the old story. Then the returns from the Guard depots: 5,500 men, plus 1,200 Old Guard foot and horse guarding the Empress and the King of Rome, 500 elite gendarmes, and 500 Veteran-Cannoneers. With the Line depots, etc. there were 26,400 men on hand.

At 11 p.m. a harassed officer arrived from Mortier at Nangis. The previous afternoon the Marshal had received a letter from Clarke, dispatched at 10 a.m. that morning. Twelve copies had been made and given to twelve officers who had left full speed for the Emperor. The bearer of this one had traveled 140 kilometers in less than 18 hours. The message was desperate. Meaux had fallen. The enemy was marching on Claye. 'I dare not hope it can hold out', concluded Clarke. But where was Mortier? And the Guard?

On 25 March, about twelve miles from Vitry, Mortier and Marmont had been attacked near Soudé-Saint-Croix by the whole Army of Bohemia.

Alerted at breakfast, the Marshals had hurried to the banks of the Soude. From there they saw a mass of motley cavalry and artillery – Russian, Prussian, Württemberger – followed by infantry columns that stretched as far as the eye could see. It was Schwarzenberg's whole army!

There was no longer any question of joining the Emperor, but only of defending themselves and delaying the Allies' march on Paris. Captain Bourgoing, sent to warn the Guard bivouacs, owed his life to the speed of his horse. Surrounded by hussars, uhlans, and Cossacks, General Charpentier got his three divisions under way. The flankers, fusiliers, and Italian *vélites* of the rear-guard were already battered by the time they joined Mortier at Sommesous around 8 a.m.

At this moment the great battle began. The Guard was at Sommesous, and the 6th Corps south of the Vitry road, with their sixty guns in front. Since their position was a strong one they hoped to defend it.

'Now, my young friends', shouted Taillan, a former Old Guard grenadier, to his conscripts, 'keep together like sheep and don't fire until they come near, and they won't touch you.'

However, Belliard's cavalry was soon engulfed and thrown into a panic. In their headlong flight the troopers collided with the foot battalions which streamed back towards Connantre. In Charpentier's division, Jamin's entire brigade was captured and the General taken prisoner; in Curial's, Le Capitaine's brigade lost all its artillery. Christiani's solid battalions held firm in the defile at Esternay; but the rest got mixed with the enemy in the rout and poured into La Fère-Champenoise in the greatest disorder.

By 4 p.m. when Charpentier had lost 20 officers and 300 men, and Curial's 3rd Voltigeurs had suffered heavy losses, they suddenly heard guns on their left in the enemy's rear. It must be the Emperor, they thought – it could be no one else! The troops took heart and some cavalry reinforced the unfortunate squadrons of General Belliard and gave them new courage.

They never knew the truth until later. Under Pacthod and Delort, 4,500 national guards, encumbered with a heavy convoy escorted by General Amey, were on their way to join the Emperor when they ran into the flank of the Army of Silesia. Riddled with grapeshot and surrounded by innumerable cavalry, all these brave fellows had been killed or captured except a handful who managed to hide among the reeds in the Saint-Gond marshes. After this the Guard joked no more about the national guards in their funny round hats and blue smocks.

That night Mortier's divisions retired to Allemant. On the 26th they went to Sézanne which Count Compans had succeeded in defending with a handful of men. When the Marshals paused later at Esternay to let their conscripts eat, they found the road to La Ferté-Gaucher barred by the troops of Prince William of Prussia, supported by cavalry and artillery. After a hard fight they marched during the night through roads and byroads to Provins.

On the 27th they bivouacked at Maison-Rouge. The next day they were at Nangis, surrounded by Seslavin's Cossacks, when Clarke's messenger arrived. By now Mortier and Marmont were on their way to Paris.

Forward! The old foot Guard was strung out along the road to Troyes where it arrived on the 29th after a march of over forty-five miles. Exhausted and famished, the men devoured the last bread in town or put it in their packs.

The Emperor reached the Château of Pouilly at the same moment, escorted by Guyot with 1,000 hand-picked troopers. Somehow a mounted foot grenadier had been included. The troopers found hay, bread, and provisions, thanks to the men sent ahead. They were in a hurry for they had to mount their horses again in three hours.

The Empress and the King of Rome had left the Tuileries for Rambouillet with a procession of carriages loaded with an immense quantity of belongings, including the library, regalia, etc. Even the coronation coach was included.

On 30 March the Emperor left Berthier in command of the army with orders to march to Paris, via Villeneuve-l'Archevêque and Fontainebleau, as quickly as possible, and to speed the cavalry on ahead. He left Ney in command of the Old Guard.

That morning, as the bells of the Cathedral struck four, Napoleon left Troyes in the dark, escorted by Guyot, to gallop the eighty-seven miles to Paris. He was followed by Lefebvre, Drouot, Caulaincourt, and Flahaut.

At Villeneuve Napoleon decided to continue the journey by carriage, without escort. He left at 10 a.m. followed by two light carriages carrying Oudinot, Flahaut, Gourgaud, Lefebvre, and the foot grenadier of the escort on the box. Napoleon lunched at Sens, passed through Essones at 9 p.m. and reached Juvisy at eleven that night. At the relay inn *Cour de France* the postmaster changed the horses at top speed. Napoleon was now just two and a quarter relays from Paris . . .

Suddenly he heard horses' hoofs on the road. It was Belliard with the news that Paris had just surrendered. He was too late.

In Paris only one unit still held out. In the park of the Legion of Honor at Saint-Denis Major Savarin and 400 voltigeurs had refused to surrender to Kapzevitch's emissaries.

In the court of the Invalides, 1,417 flags captured from the enemy were burned in the presence of weeping veterans of the Guard and army. Marshal Sérurier had ordered this *auto-da-fé*.

Where was Dejean who had been sent ahead to announce the Emperor's arrival? Was he still en route?

No – he was in Paris where he had met the Duke of Treviso in the midst of the battle.

'But they must hold out until night!' the Emperor cried. 'Everyone has lost his head. Joseph is an ass . . . Clarke an old woman . . . Where is my wife? My son? The enemy? The army? . .'

And the Guard?

It was approaching at full speed. The vanguard of Curial's division was marching to Fontainebleau.

BOOK VIII

THE GUARD STAGGERS

CHAPTER 1

The Fall of Paris

ON Sunday, 27 March, General d'Ornano had paraded the Guard in Paris at the Tuileries in bright sunshine. Dériot was there with his depot troops, also d'Aboville with the batteries from La Fère and the national guard. The King of Rome was wearing a military cap. There were cries of '*Vive l'Empereur!*' when d'Ornano announced that the Emperor was on his way with the army to 'crush the enemy against the gates of Paris'.

Next day Joseph persuaded the Regency Council to order the Empress to leave Paris, against the advice of Talleyrand, Champagny, Savary, and Marie-Louise herself.

'Everyone has lost his head but me', she wrote Napoleon. 'I hope that in a few days you shall tell me I was right not to be stampeded from the capital by the specter of 15,000 cavalry who couldn't even get through its streets.'[1]

On the morning of the 28th ten green carriages blazoned with the Imperial arms, surrounding the coronation coach covered with a tarpaulin, left the Place de la Carrousel. They were escorted by 1,200 Guardsmen from the depot under General Caffarelli, and a detachment of elite gendarmes under Colonel Janin. The Empress left for Rambouillet with the King of Rome, Madame Mère, King Jerome and Queen Catherine of Westphalia, Joseph's consort Queen Julie, the ministers and their staffs, and the Council of State. Joseph remained in Paris to command the army. The roads were full of refugees and the enemy was approaching.

The defenders of Paris consisted of 30,000 national guards under Marshal Moncey, half of whom had no muskets. With these he had to defend its fifty-six gates, not to mention the Tuileries and the *mairies*. In addition, there were 20,000 Line conscripts with 40 fortress guns in fixed emplacements, Marmont's corps, and around 12,000 miscellaneous Guardsmen.

The latter included Mortier's 4,600 tired but indomitable men, quartered at Charenton, Bercy, etc., with 30 guns from the park at Meaux. D'Ornano had formed a mixed division of flankers, *tirailleurs*, voltigeurs, and *pupilles* from the depots which Boyer de Rebeval got out of bed to command. Michel, also suffering from wounds, assisted by Colonels Robert and Sécrétan, took command of another division composed of 4,000 troops from the Guard depots, including 1,000 brand new conscripts who were issued muskets just before the battle.

---

[1] The Empress was right. In the districts where the fighting took place the Paris streets were not more than 30 feet wide.

Major Pion des Loches' six batteries were commanded by the clothing officer, paymaster, bakery officer, etc. Their 20 guns were installed on the outskirts of La Villette and Pantin and near the Barrière du Combat.

Some sapper-firemen and miscellaneous Young Guardsmen were sent to Charenton, Vincennes, and Saint-Denis.

There were also 500 Veterans, some gendarmes, and about 500 mixed horse Guards under General Dautancourt who had been invalided home from Rheims. The night before the battle these troopers chased off the Cossacks harassing the refugees on the road to Le Bourget. They camped near La Chapelle, to the left of La Villette. On the right were Roussel's dragoons. Behind them, d'Aboville and his artillery officers were having supper. The discipline was much relaxed. Looting had begun and one saw soldiers with torches carrying off furniture to their bivouacs.

During the evening King Joseph reconnoitered the area with the Marshals and General Hulin, and organized the defence between the Marne and Saint Ouen according to the terrain. On the right, the park and fort of Vincennes, the plateau of Romainville, and the hills of Belleville and Saint-Chaumont with the neighboring villages of Charonne, Ménilmontant, and Pré-Saint-Gervais, were assigned to Marmont. On the left, the hills of Cinq-Moulins and Montmartre, with the advance posts at Aubervilliers, Saint-Denis, Saint-Ouen, Clignancourt, La Villette, and La Chapelle, were assigned to Mortier and the cavalry. The territory between, including the Ourcq canal and the roads from Germany, Pantin, and Les Maisonettes, were assigned to Ornano whose force consisted of Boyer's and Michel's divisions with one fortress battery in support. This force was entirely inadequate to block these important approaches without help from the Guard.

The Tsar spent the night at the Château of Bondy. Despite his 200,000 troops he seemed afraid of Paris – and especially of the Emperor's arrival.

At 4 a.m. on the 30th the drums beat the *Générale*.[2] In the faubourgs the NCO'S cried 'To Arms!' The Polytechnicians arrived with General Evain and the Veteran-Cannoneers at the Barrière du Trône to man the 28 guns of the artillery reserve.

Mortier took up his position very early before La Villette in a redoubt whose twenty-four-pounder commanded the highroad. He said to his staff: 'We have not enough troops to resist these large armies for long; but today, more than ever before, we are fighting for our honor. We must think first of Paris, and hold our advance positions as long as we can . . .' Then, looking down the Le Bourget road through his telescope, he saw twenty Cossacks approaching. 'Gunners', he said, 'let us see if your big piece caught cold last night . . .'

They fired. 'And that', wrote Captain de Bourgoing, 'was the first cannon fired at a foreigner in defense of Paris since the reign of Charles VII!'

At daybreak the battle began. General Ornano came to report that Joseph had set up his command post on top of Montmartre. Boyer's and Michel's divisions were camped near their combat positions, and Robert's brigade occupied Aubervilliers. As

[2] General Alarm. – Ed.

Marmont's troops began to climb the plateau of Romainville they were attacked by Barclay de Tolly's Russians.

It was then 6.30 a.m. A sharp combat took place around Romainville. Boyer's division marched to Pantin and occupied the first group of houses, but was soon dislodged by the reinforced Russians. A part retired to Pré-Saint-Gervais and another to Les Maisonettes, held by Secrétan's brigade. Meanwhile, with the help of the artillery, the French held on to the plateau.

Delayed by Marmont's columns filing through the narrow streets, Mortier's troops did not reach their positions until 8 a.m. When he spotted the fierce fight in progress on the plateau and before Pantin, Mortier sent Curial to support Secrétan's brigade, Charpentier to the foot of Saint-Chaumont, and Christiani to the outskirts of La Chapelle and La Villette to bar the road from Senlis and support Robert.

The Guard batteries in La Villette were firing continuously. They sent for more ammunition. On their left, Dautancourt's and Belliard's cavalry pounded the plain of Saint-Denis between Clignancourt and La Hutte-aux-gardes. From his new headquarters in the Château of Brouillard on Cinq-Moulins, King Joseph saw Langeron's and Vorontzov's Russian corps approaching from Aubervilliers, followed by the Prussians of Blücher, Yorck, and Kleist.

Surrounded at St. Denis by these forces and under fire from all directions, Major Savarin's voltigeurs ran out of ammunition. The depot battalion of *tirailleurs*, with 80 Polish scouts under Kozietulski, tried to take them cartridges but were halted at the top of Aubervilliers and obliged to retire step by step to La Chapelle.

In the east another battle was raging, but there the situation was still in hand. The 11th Voltigeurs made a handsome charge to rescue one of Marmont's divisions, hard pressed in the woods of Romainville. Together they cleared the Russians from the outskirts of Pantin and Boyer's and Secrétan's troops entered the village on the heels of the Russian cuirassiers.

At this point Joseph sent word to the Marshals to 'surrender if they could no longer hold their positions', and left for Rambouillet. Thus, by 2 p.m. there was no longer commander in chief nor headquarters though, according to Marmont, the situation was not yet critical.

Too weak to attack, the cavalry on the left maneuvered parallel to the enemy, in front of the ancient redoubts below Clignancourt. The Mameluks, scouts, and a few chasseurs charged the enemy skirmishers, driving them into a quarry in front of the Clichy road, and took up a position in the vineyards along the road to Batignolles. There the horse grenadiers came under fire from a battery posted near the fork of the road to La Révolte. This was soon silenced by one of Roussel's horse batteries.

At this point an enemy attack on the right was halted by Evain's artillery, drawn by barge and hack horses and supported by Marmont's cavalry. Then the Russians launched an offensive on the plateau and plain of Romainville.

Boyer's division and Curial's first brigade were hard pressed at Pré-Saint-Gervais. The 2nd Voltigeurs met the Russian grenadiers head on and inflicted heavy losses, but were recalled by Curial to reinforce Mortier's troops between the canal and Montmartre. Secrétan was left alone at Les Maisonettes and on the flanks of Belleville. Michel was seriously wounded. Surrounded in Belleville with part of Boyer's division, Colonel Suisse led his 10th Voltigeurs out at bayonet point, and had his jaw smashed in the process.

Marmont retired to Telegraph Hill from where he personally led a series of counterattacks, then posted his infantry in the Rue de Ménilmontant. Though wounded and bleeding, he refused to surrender.

At La Villette Christiani's division performed prodigies. Desalons' flanker-grenadiers recaptured the bridge over the canal from which fifty Veterans had been dislodged. To inspire the flankers their leaders had only to point to Paris.

Some ammunition caissons eventually reached the Guard batteries which fired full speed until the Prussian Guard appeared in their rear. Then they hurled two guns into the canal and abandoned the other two as they retired before the advancing enemy. Meanwhile, the other two batteries enfiladed La Chapelle and the city gate.

The remnants of Charpentier's, Christiani's, and Curial's divisions retired slowly, unit by unit, fighting all the way. General Le Capitaine, one of the ablest tacticians in the army, brought off his *tirailleur* brigade with admirable precision.

Count Dejean made his way to Mortier's headquarters with an order from the Emperor not to persist in defending the capital, but to seek guarantees from Schwarzenberg based on certain peace proposals Napoleon had made to his father-in-law, the Austrian Emperor. This seemed a bit late, after the battle was lost; however, the Marshal sent his chief of staff General Delapointe to the Prince. The General returned with a copy of the Allied declaration after the breaking off of negotiations at Châtillon.

Then Dejean pursued Joseph and told him of the Emperor's imminent arrival. But nothing would induce Joseph to return to Paris.

By this time the enemy was shelling the city. Langeron's hordes poured into the plain of Saint-Denis and advanced towards Batignolles by a flank march which would have been costly had there been more squadrons to oppose them. In the vine-covered triangle between the roads to Clichy, Saint-Ouen, and La Révolte the Mameluks, scouts, and chasseurs fought with an energy born of desperation; but the charges led by Lafitte and Kozietulski were fruitless. They were soon ordered to retreat by Marshal Moncey who was at the Clichy gate with his national guard.

Falling back towards La Platrière, the Guard squadrons charged the flank of the advancing columns. Major La Tourette of the guards of honor, with a handful of heroes, delivered a final attack. Then the brigade climbed Montmartre on a sunken road, under fire from the Russian guns. It entered Paris by the Martyr's Gate and bivouacked at midnight in Villejuif.

By now the only defenders left in the surrounding hills were 60 gunners with seven pieces at the mill of Lancette and two at Moulin-Neuf, and 250 sapper-firemen of the Guard. Beyond the hills some *pupilles* were still firing at the Russian chasseurs. These lads, between thirteen and sixteen, were well trained in musketry and did not want to stop. '*Nog een Scheut, Capitein!*' (Just one more shot, Captain!) a little Dutchman begged.

PLATE 137

PLATE 138

a) Pac
(*Contemp. lithograph*)

b) Guye
(*After portrait by Goya; Musée de Saint-Dié*)

c) Blücher
(*Original watercolor by W. Heath*)

d) Kleist
(*Contemp. engraving*)

e) Kapzevitch
(*After contemp. portrait*)

PLATE 139

a) Napoleon at Montereau
(From an original wash attributed to E. Lami)

b) Polytechnicians helping a wounded Grumbler at Clichy
(From an original drawing by R. K. Porter)

PLATE 140

Don Cossack and Crimean Tartar
(*From an original watercolor by Ludwig Wolf*)

PLATE 141

a) Talleyrand
(*Contemp. engraving*)

b) Belly de Bussy
(*After portrait by Germain: Collection Col. Tugny*)

c) Langeron
(*Contemp. engraving*)

d) Schwarzenberg
(*Col. engraving after Denis Dighton*)

e) Sebastiani
(*Col. mezzotint by Dickenson after Gérard*)

PLATE 142

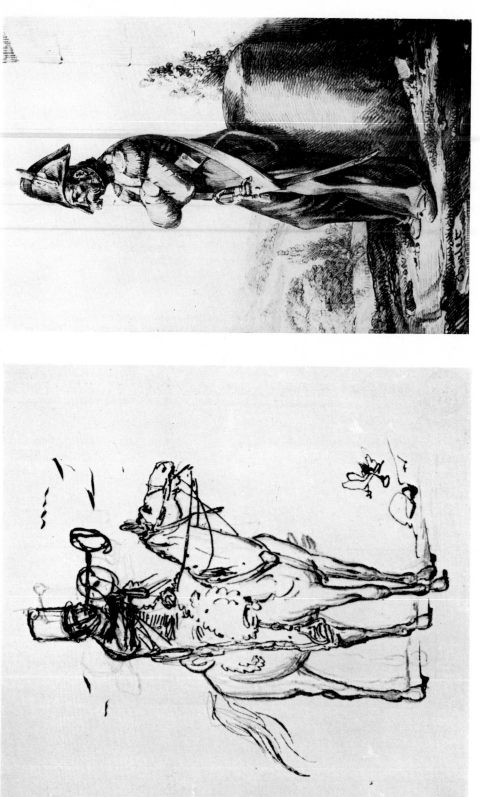

b) Old Guard NCO in walking-our dress
(Lithograph by Charlet)

a) Trumpeter of the 2nd Chasseurs à cheval, Young Guard
(From an original drawing by Géricault)

Everyone was expecting the Emperor. When the troops spied an officer galloping through the suburbs on a grey horse they cried 'Here he comes!'

Major Taillan of the 5th *Tirailleurs*, who had fought all day between Aubervilliers and Montmartre, reached the top of Montmartre with seventy survivors. A group of 400 Old Guardsmen, national guards, etc., held out at the Clichy Gate until Moncey ordered their retreat (see Plate 139b). Lieutenant Viaux of the 2nd Grenadiers, convalescing from wounds, left his bed and collected twenty stray soldiers before Montmartre where his body was found under a tree that night, sword in hand, surrounded by Prussian corpses.

From their barracks at Courbevoie the Old Guard Invalids had to go only a few yards to occupy the bridge at Neuilly. About fifty defended it courageously, replying when called upon to surrender: 'The Old Guard has never laid down its arms'. It was learned next day that they had been granted honorable terms in the surrender, and had been allowed to keep the contents of their magazine.

Meanwhile, Mortier and Marmont met the Allied commissioners in the *Petit Jardinet* café near the gate of La Villette to discuss the surrender terms. 'I shall defend Paris street by street', Marmont declared. After half an hour, Mortier left.

Though the boulevards around Paris were congested, the city streets were empty and forlorn. The gates of the Tuileries were shut. General Dériot had ordered all the Guard stores evacuated during the day.

Before dining with his aides that evening Marshal Mortier ordered the Guard to leave Paris by the Fontainebleau Gate. Led by Curial's division, the troops filed through the city and over the Pont d'Austerlitz, crossing the Fontainebleau road ahead of the Emperor on their march to Villejuif where they spent the night.

General d'Aboville had evacuated artillery stores, and Captain Maziaux, those of the chasseurs. However, during the day work had gone on as usual in the Guard barracks. Conscripts entered the city from the south and west and, to the booming of guns, were received and clothed by the NCO's at the École Militaire.

The Guard suffered heavy losses. In the artillery Major Bitsch was severely wounded, and Captain Raoul and four majors put out of action. The cavalry lost a dozen officers. General Guye; five colonels, including Secrétan, Desalons, and Suisse; 6 Old Guard officers; 50 of the Young, and 1,000 men were wounded. Boyer's division had only 1,122 survivors; Secrétan's brigade, 331. The son of Marie Tête-du-Bois was killed.

In all there were 18,000 casualties. The doctors, military and civilian, were on the go all day. Next day they had to tend the enemy as well.

At 4 a.m., seated at the postmaster's table at the *Cour de France* in Juvisy with his head in his hands, the Emperor looked up as Caulaincourt's groom returned from Paris and announced that all was over. The capitulation had been signed at Marmont's house at 2 a.m. The Allies would enter Paris that morning. It was a disaster.

The Emperor reached Fontainebleau as dawn was breaking. The Guard Veterans presented arms before the château and an old drummer beat '*Aux Champs*' . . .

CHAPTER 2

Fontainebleau

WHEN the fighting was over Marmont's troops marched to Essones and camped along the river. Mortier's divisions were behind at Mennecy. That evening the cavalry of the Guard arrived at Moret from Troyes and Sebastiani went on to Fontainebleau. The foot Guard and army followed by forced marches, the first units arriving on 1 and 2 April.

By this time Talleyrand had presented the keys of Paris to the Tsar, and a few white cockades had appeared on the streets. But the Emperor's army fought on in the provinces.

At Soissons Major Gérard, with a handful of Grumblers under Captain Bellanger, 1,160 voltigeurs and *tirailleurs* under Major Braun, 100 scout-lancers, a few Line infantry and national guards, and 150 gunners, had been besieged since 20 March by 20,000 Prussians with 60 guns. Notwithstanding bombardment, mines, and repeated ultimatums the French refused every summons to surrender, and were still resisting. The Grumblers never left the Place d'Armes.

On 28 March the enemy was drawn up along the moat on the front of attack. Gérard ordered a sortie. Braun stormed their trenches with 500 elite troops, supported by scouts crying *'Vive l'Empereur!'* while the national guards attacked the trenches in Saint-Christophe. Braun was twice wounded and Lieutenant Spies of the scouts was unhorsed during a charge. The Grumblers and national guards surprised the Prussian riflemen in the Château of Breuvery, disarmed them on the battlements, and pinned them down in the gardens below. The enemy fell back to their reserves; but they were numerous and kept up a heavy fire on their assailants.

Finally Gérard recalled his troops within the walls where he marshaled them on the Place d'Armes. With a flag in his arms, he said: 'The eyes of the whole army are upon us as we guard this approach to the capital . . . Let us swear once more by this flag to justify the Emperor's faith in us by defending it to the death . . .'

Every man present cheered and repeated the oath. From then on they held the city, repairing under the enemy's nose the breaches opened by his artillery during the dark nights of 29 and 30 March. Every salvo they fired in response was accompanied by shouts of *'Vive l'Empereur!'*

On 30 March Gérard decided to concentrate his forces at the Saint-Waaste bastion where the Aisne bridge was mined. The Grumblers prepared to sell their lives as high as possible. That evening they set fire to the enemy works at the base of the escarpment and waited for dawn, their fingers on their triggers.

The sun rose amid a hushed silence. The scouts, sent on reconnaissance with a Guard battalion, reported that the enemy had vanished and that their batteries were deserted. What had happened?

Gérard paid no attention. He repaired the fortifications, kept order among the inhabitants and troops with a firm hand, imprisoned General Vézu for announcing some sort of revolution in Paris, and waited. He did not have to wait long.

On 3 April General von Borstell arrived from Holland and posted a brigade close to the city gates – unhealthily close. Despite his wounds, Braun led 500 voltigeurs and *tirailleurs* with two guns down the Crouy road and attacked the Prussian outposts as they were making their soup. The Young Guard brought the half-cooked meat back to Soissons, but left one of its captains dead on the field.

On the 7th a peasant bringing letters from the Prussian general was run out of town without ceremony. Next day a truce envoy was turned back. No one was allowed to leave the town. An aide-de-camp of the war minister wearing a white cockade was greeted with cries of '*Vive l'Empereur!*' and obliged to retreat in the face of furious threats from the soldiers whose officers had the greatest difficulty in controlling them. On Easter Sunday, the 10th, the *Domine salvum fac Imperatorem*[1] was sung in the Cathedral, and the tricolor flag floated from its tower.

What could be done with these madmen? Letters, threats, and courtesies from the Russian and Prussian generals were all unavailing. Even a letter from the new prefect of the Aisne addressed to 'General Gérard' went unanswered.

Finally, on 14 April General d'Aboville of the Guard artillery arrived, prudently wearing a tricolor cockade, and was greeted on the Place d'Armes by Gérard, the garrison, and the inhabitants with cries of '*Vive l'Empereur!*' Was he coming to announce the Emperor's triumphal entry into Soissons?

This time they were obliged to surrender to the evidence if not to the enemy. On the 15th an armistice was concluded. Next day Gérard offered his allegiance to d'Aboville, and that of his troops to the new government. Gérard signed an agreement with General von Borstell granting a safe conduct across the city to the Allied troops, but forbade them to linger or make requisitions from the inhabitants.

Finally, on 4 May Gérard notified the municipal council that the state of siege was lifted. On that day the Emperor arrived at Elba. Unfortunately, the twenty-six stars of the Legion of Honor that the heroic commander requested for his men could not be awarded until a year later, during the Hundred Days.

Meanwhile, there had also been fighting at Compiègne. Major Lecomte had been sent there from Paris on 12 March with 500 voltigeurs and 24 gunners of the Guard to help the little garrison resist the attacks of Bülow's corps. When called upon to surrender Lecomte sent word that the place would capitulate 'when the Emperor so ordered'.

Lt. Colonel Ottentin, the garrison commander, resisted a violent attack on the Pierrefonds gate on 1 April and fell with a ball in the forehead before the gate of the Place d'Armes. The voltigeurs put up a gallant defense, losing 4 officers and 150 men killed and wounded. That evening Lecomte, an old grenadier of the Consular Guard,

[1] Lord save the Emperor. – Ed.

refused to surrender, rejecting all the War Council's pleas. Not until the 3rd, when he learned of the fall of Paris, did he capitulate.

The war in the north was still in progress and all the fortresses were intact. General Maison finally succeeded in conducting a joint operation with the Guard. Marching from Lille with Barrois' Young Guard division, 900 horse Guards under General Castex, and a Line division, he was joined at Courtrai by Roguet who forced his way out of the Antwerp garrison with his cavalry and artillery at a cost of 500 casualties. Together they defeated two enemy corps under Thielmann and the Prince of Saxe-Weimar at Schwegehem, near Courtrai, on 31 March, taking 1,000 prisoners and three guns.

Then they marched back to Lille which they found in chaos. The provisional government had ordered the new conscripts discharged, resulting in many desertions from the army. Very few left the Guard. On 15 April Roguet's division mustered 6,400 men, and Barrois' 3,600.

The Emperor still had an army of 60,000 men in and around Fontainebleau. On 1 April its vanguard was in contact with the Russian outposts who were drinking and singing and offering little protection to the motley soldiery carousing in the capital. A sudden thrust at Paris might have tremendous results. The Emperor believed that the citizens would rise.

After reconnoitering the banks of the Essone and visiting Marmont and Mortier, that evening he wrote a detailed order in his own hand to Berthier for the disposition and reinforcement of his troops. Mortier was ordered to take his headquarters to Mennecy, and the general of the artillery to provide him and Marmont 'with at least 60 guns'. General Sebastiani was ordered to bring Piré's brigade, the three Guard divisions, and the cavalry to Fontainebleau next day 'so I may review them from ten to eleven in the court of Le Cheval Blanc'. Ornano was ordered to relieve Colbert who had been wounded. Marmont was assigned the two battalions of Guard Veterans. A battalion of foot and a regiment of mounted gendarmes were ordered formed and attached to Friant and Lefebvre-Desnoëttes respectively. Napoleon announced that he 'would review them tomorrow at whatever hour they are ready'.

All these orders were executed. The battalion of foot gendarmes numbered 600; the mounted regiment, 500. Boyer's division was assigned to Mortier, and the instruction battalion to Henrion's division.

At Moret on 2 April the horse Guard was incensed to learn of the surrender of Paris. General Griois read in the *Journal des Débats* what he termed the 'homage of the French cowards'. Nevertheless, his horse gunners 'did not consider their cause entirely lost'. Neither did the foot Guards who arrived at Fontainebleau that evening.

The Emperor's proclamation was read to the companies: 'Despite the success of the Coalition Army, over which it will not have cause to gloat for long, do not let yourselves be downcast . . . The Emperor is watching over the safety of all . . .'

They did not doubt it. Lieutenant Franconin of the 2nd Grenadiers wrote his parents from Fontainebleau: 'We hope the Empire wins out . . . if the cowardice of the Parisians has not undone all our efforts, as well as the incredible performance of the greatest of men . . .' He added: 'How the French have degenerated! One would think he was in a foreign country. There is no longer any enthusiasm, any heart, any patriotism here . . . Every effort is being made to recapture Paris. In a day or two we shall scold the Parisians for their lack of patriotism, and drink some good wine . . .'

This opinion was general throughout the Guard. From then on the grenadiers and chasseurs participated in the guard mounting, relieving a battalion of Veterans. When they greeted him with the usual cheers the Emperor's face was impassive. 'The Guard at Fontainebleau appeared the same as in its glorious days of prosperity at the Tuileries, Schönbrunn, Potsdam, the Prado, and the Kremlin', wrote Lieutenant Koch of the Polish light-horse who was there at the time.

No one knew that at this moment the Senate, convened by Talleyrand, had ordered an act drawn up to depose the Emperor; and that Caulaincourt had just brought him the news and demanded his abdication on behalf of the Tsar. Alexander had declared that 'they would see about a regency later . . .'

'A regency is our last resource', concluded Caulaincourt, and several 'big hats' concurred.

The Emperor's answer was 'No'. Except for fifty traitors, the country and the army were behind him. They must fight a final battle against the Allies. Ask the Guard . . .

On Palm Sunday, 3 April, the whole Guard was drawn up in the court of Le Cheval Blanc. Friant's division was at the right of the grand staircase in two lines with the chasseurs in front and the grenadiers and gendarmes behind. Opposite was General Henrion's Young Guard, drawn up in columns by battalion. Both Young and Old Guards were exhausted after marching 120 kilometers in sixty hours. Whenever their commanders had ordered a halt the Grumblers had growled: 'March!'

They waited . . .

At noon the Emperor appeared on the landing with Berthier, Ney, Moncey, Bertrand, Drouot, and the aides and orderly officers. 'They noticed the long faces of the Emperor's suite', reported General Pelet, standing with the chasseurs, 'especially the Duke of Vicenza's' (Caulaincourt's).

The troops presented arms. The drums beat *Aux Champs*. Nervous, his hat slightly askew, the Emperor began his inspection which was long and detailed. How many men present?

Chasseurs: 50 officers, 1,246 men; grenadiers: 69 officers, 1,287 men. (Some were still en route.) Sappers: 16 officers, 115 men; artillery: 5 officers, 124 men. Then the ranks opened and, as was his custom, the Emperor began questioning the soldiers. Sapper Rothier, 1st Chasseurs – 21 years' service, 2 wounds; Sergeant Antoine, 1st Chasseurs – wounded at Novi; Stoll, chasseur – 22 years' service, 20 campaigns, mentioned for distinguished conduct at the bridge of Lesmont . . .

Henrion's division mustered 99 officers and 1,496 men; the cavalry, including the gendarmes, 4,600 sabers. Baron Lallemand presented the artillery reserve whose strength was imposing. Horse artillery of the Guard: 211 gunners, 100 train soldiers, 16 guns, 18 caissons; and of the Line, attached to the Guard: 320 gunners, 102 train soldiers, 17 guns, 28 caissons; foot artillery (Guard and Line): 848 gunners, 53 guns, 106 caissons; pontooneers: 9 officers, 120 men.

After the inspection the Emperor ordered the officers, NCO's, and soldiers with the longest service of each unit to advance to the middle of the court, and the drummers to beat the *Ban*. Then he said:

'Officers, noncommissioned officers, and soldiers of my Old Guard! The enemy has stolen three marches on us. He has entered Paris. I have offered the Emperor Alexander a peace at the cost of great sacrifices: a France reduced to its old boundaries, renouncing . . . all we have conquered since the Revolution. He has not only refused this but . . . at the perfidious suggestion of the émigrés whose lives I saved . . . has authorized the white cockade to be worn. Soon he wants to substitute it for our national cockade. Within a few days I shall march on Paris . . . I am counting on you . . .'

The Emperor paused. Then, puzzled by their silence, he added: 'Am I right?'

With a roar they replied: 'On to Paris! *Vive l'Empereur!*'

Pelet wrote later: 'They were silent at first because they believed an answer superfluous'.

The Emperor continued: 'We shall prove to them that the French are masters in their own house – even though they have spent much time in those of other people . . . and that we are still capable of defending our cockade, our independence, and the integrity of our territory. Communicate these sentiments to your men.'

This time there was pandemonium. The officers repeated to their companies the Emperor's words which were greeted with cries of *'Vengeance! Vive l'Empereur!'* The soldiers swore to go and 'end their careers in the ruins of the capital'.

Then the Guard paraded under arms, their cries drowning out the strains of the *Song of Departure* and *Marseillaise* played by the band of the 1st Grenadiers.

At the foot of the staircase the 'big hats' stood in a group, lost in meditation upon the abdication proposal. This offered them an easy way of quitting Napoleon without shame or suspicion of cowardice. 'The abdication actually suited many people's purposes', wrote Baron Fain.

At this moment the Old Guard watching over the Empress and the King of Rome were listening to Marie-Louise's proclamation to the French people from Blois:

'An incident of war has delivered the capital of France into foreign hands. Hastening to her defense, the Emperor is at the head of his armies which have so often been victorious. They now face the enemy under the walls of Paris . . .

'You will be faithful to your oaths. You will listen to the voice of a princess who has been entrusted to you, whose whole glory lies in being French and in being associated with the destiny of the sovereign you have chosen of your own free will . . .'

By 6 p.m. the Guard was en route to Essonnes, marching silently through the forest by moonlight. Not a sound was heard but the tramping of feet, the clinking of sabers, the rumbling of gun carriages, and the beat of horses' hoofs.

Where had twenty years of victory brought these men? They had sworn an oath that morning. Now they were turning it over in their minds before going to die for their country and the Emperor . . .

CHAPTER 3

Betrayal

MACDONALD arrived at last. The 11th Corps went to Chantilly, the 2nd to Pringy, and the 7th to Fontainebleau. The cavalry divisions camped on the wings around Melun and Le Ferté-Alais, 'to keep them separate from the Guard which might be marching to Paris', the Emperor wrote at 4 a.m. on 4 April.

Meanwhile, a crowd of horsemen, couriers, and carriages came and went through the gates of Le Cheval Blanc. No one knew anything but everyone sensed that the situation was grave.

As the Emperor was returning to his study that morning with Berthier, Caulaincourt, Maret, and Bertrand he overheard Ney, who was inside, say: 'Nothing short of abdication can get us out of this mess'. Without revealing his presence, Napoleon recognized Oudinot, Moncey, and Lefebvre in the room as Ney continued in a loud voice: 'The situation is desperate. There is nothing left for him but to abdicate . . .'

Lefebvre joined in at this point: 'See what you got for not taking your friends' advice when they begged you to make peace . . .'

What indeed would they have got without war, these marshals who had suddenly become so pacific? Especially Lefebvre. If Napoleon had mistrusted these men how can one blame him?

Deeply hurt and utterly disgusted, the Emperor outlined to them his plan to march on Paris.

'I don't care about the throne', he said. 'Born a soldier, I can become an ordinary citizen again without regret. I wanted France to be great and powerful . . . I wanted her especially to be happy . . . It is not for my crown I am fighting, but to prove that Frenchmen were not born to be ruled by Cossacks . . . If I lose this battle the poor French must submit to their rule. For myself, I need nothing . . .'

His plea fell upon deaf ears. When he finished, Ney rapped out: 'The army will not march. It will obey its commanders.'

Had he not heard the Guard cheer just now?

At last, after pondering over the specter of civil war and the future of his son, Napoleon took a piece of paper and wrote the following:

'Since the foreign Powers have declared that the Emperor Napoleon is an obstacle to restoring peace and territorial integrity to France, the Emperor, faithful to his principles and mindful of his oath to do his utmost for the happiness and glory of the French people, hereby declares that he is prepared to abdicate in favor of his son, and to deliver such act in due form to the Senate as soon as Napoleon II shall be recognized by the Powers, together with the constitutional regency of the Empress. This condition fulfilled, the Emperor agrees to retire at once to whatever place is agreed upon.

'Given in our palace of Fontainebleau, 4 April 1814.

Signed: Napoleon' (see Plate 145).

Caulaincourt and the marshals took the conditional abdication to Paris that day while the Emperor watched the parade at the changing of the Guard. The duty battalion marched past crying '*Vive l'Empereur!*' Surely this man was happiest in the midst of his soldiers.

A little later the grenadiers of the palace guard heard him storm and rage. Exasperated by his downfall, he left his apartments and went out into the garden. He slapped his boots, decapitated some flowers with his stick, then stuck it into the sand.

The sentry watched three carriages pass through the gate of the Cheval Blanc: those of the Duke of Vicenza (Caulaincourt), the Prince of the Moskva (Ney), and the Duke of Taranto (Macdonald). What if they returned empty-handed? What if the Allies refused to recognize Napoleon II?

The Emperor promptly issued orders to secure Fontainebleau on all sides. He put General Count Krasinski in command of all Polish units in the army. He ordered Lefebvre-Desnoëttes to bring his division to Fontainebleau at once, and General Defrance to take his guards of honor to La Ferté-Alais, sending patrols to Étampes and a brigade to Malesherbes. He ordered Oudinot to leave 500 men with two guns at Moret and deploy the rest of his corps between Ury and La Chapelle.

Finally he called for ten o'clock that night a conference of Marmont, Mortier, Moncey, Oudinot, and all the generals, stipulating that they 'must arrange to return to their units before dawn'. They all arrived except Marmont (whom Napoleon had urged Caulaincourt to take with him to Paris to aid in the negotiations) and General Souham, the senior division commander.

The Emperor explained to his commanders what had happened in Paris. What did the army think? Would it continue the fight if necessary? The Allies, his enemies, the provisional government, the royalists, and Talleyrand all wanted the Bourbons restored to the throne. The corps and division commanders must question their officers immediately, sign a statement, and let him have it before dawn.

Mortier knew what the Guard would say. However, he had driven that evening to Essonnes with his aide Captain de Bourgoing to see Marmont. Before going on to Fontainebleau he said to Bourgoing:

'I am leaving you here at the 6th Corps headquarters as my representative. If the troops make a move you must find out why and come to warn me.'

'The Duke of Treviso left me there alone' Bourgoing wrote in his reminiscences. 'Around two or three in the morning I was awakened by a noise. I found that the troops were getting ready to march, and asked to speak to the Duke of Ragusa (Marmont). "He is gone", they said. I then addressed myself to one general after another . . . The generals' reply left no doubt in my mind as to their intentions. I soon gathered that if I stayed longer they would prevent me from returning to my chief, so I rode full speed to Mennecy . . .'

General Souham not only knew Marmont's plan to desert the Emperor and take his corps over to the enemy, but had approved it and promised to follow. When Berthier had summoned him to Fontainebleau without giving the reason, Souham took fright and went into hiding with the elite gendarmes. Then, after plotting with two other generals,[1] he sent off the 6th corps to Versailles without telling the troops where they were going.

At 5 a.m. that morning Bourgoing dismounted at the little château of Mennecy just as Mortier's carriage arrived from Fontainebleau. Hearing his report, the Marshal said: 'Go at once and tell the Emperor what you have seen. Assure him of my constant loyalty and the devotion of the Young Guard. We shall stick by him to the death.'

An hour and a half later Bourgoing drove through the gates of Le Cheval Blanc. His entrance caused a sensation. 'What is the news?' asked the grenadier officers. They hoped the army was marching to Paris. 'All the Guard wants to', they said.

A few minutes later the Captain reported to the Emperor, who was conversing with Berthier in the Diane gallery, that the 6th Corps had deserted and was marching – to Paris, probably.

'What is Mortier doing?' Napoleon asked.

'Sire', Bourgoing replied, 'he has sent me to assure Your Majesty of his complete devotion. He awaits your orders to march . . .'

'And his troops? Is my Young Guard also thinking of deserting me?'

'Sire, the Young Guard and all the youth of France are ready to die for you.'

'The Emperor came up to me and looked me in the eye', wrote Bourgoing, 'passing his fingers under the fringe of my epaulet to tap me on the shoulder.

' "Go, my friend", he said, "tell your good Marshal that I count on him and thank him for his loyalty, and that I have every confidence in his troops. Tell him to stay on the alert and watch out for himself. For the rest", he added sadly, "they are trying to ruin me by intrigue. Tell him we shall fight no more . . ." '

On the trip back Bourgoing passed Guard columns marching to their posts. The officers and soldiers thought they were going to attack the Allied army. Kozietulski declared that his Poles were in a fighting mood and were completely devoted to the Emperor.

'Be great nobles', the Emperor had told the marshals when he presented their batons. But their insignia had not made them such.

Mortier and the Guard replaced Marmont's 11,000 men on the Essonne. Now it would be difficult to march on Paris, for Allied troops were already marching to Orléans.

On the morning of 5 April the Emperor decided to retire to the Loire with his little army and join forces with the large bodies of troops in the Midi, Lyons, and the Pyrenees. The troops' departure was fixed for the following day. In his own hand he wrote detailed orders to Berthier for the first day's march.

Meanwhile, the enthusiasm in the bivouacs around Fontainebleau gave way to depression. The melancholy silence was broken only by oaths and quarreling.

[1] Souham's accomplices in this plot were Generals Compans and Bordessoulle.

To the Grumblers Marmont was a traitor and a deserter. They believed the French cockade was the tricolor. They had not eaten acorns and horsemeat and drunk putrid water for twenty years, and marched through heat and frost, and had their hides punched full of holes to make it white again. The Bourbons had nothing to do with the case. The *Tondu* was their chief. If he were attacked they would defend him. If he had to go away they would await his return – for he would return! Meanwhile, they would have their memories; his little hat, the triumphal entries into the capitals of Europe, the girls they had loved there, the rheumatism they had caught in the bivouacs . . . They had nothing to lose, since they owned nothing. But they belonged to the Guard, and some wore the Legion of Honor.

Some of the field officers were men accustomed to obeying orders and waiting for pay day. The Emperor had taken them from nothing and had given them gold-trimmed coats. He had kept them near him and made them knights in his new nobility. Proud, silent, patient, tough, and energetic, they were honorable and patriotic men. No one had consulted *them*.

How, they asked, could 'the red-faced fellow', the 'bravest of the brave' who had commanded the foot Guard – and Oudinot, the grenadiers' old chief who had more holes in his carcass then he had years of service – how could these men make the *Tondu* sign a paper that made him half an Emperor? If 'he' should leave them their glorious years would end. They would have nothing left but the burden of keeping alive and the imperishable memory of having served Napoleon.

Others were young, ambitious, well educated, and felt themselves capable of great deeds under a chief they loved and admired. The idea of laying aside their shakos and plumes was hateful to them. Their enthusiasm of yesterday had given way to fury. But they were still young and the future lay before them.

Finally, there were the generals and marshals who owed their rank, estates, and fortunes to the Emperor. These princes, dukes, counts, and barons he had created had grown tired of serving him. Of all human virtues the most noble is loyalty to one's friends and benefactors in their misfortune. But alas, true nobility is not always conferred with titles!

That evening a secret meeting was called by a group of generals. Its purpose can be guessed. The Guard generals refused to attend because their code forbade deliberations of this nature. It was their duty to obey the government.

At that moment Napoleon's government was tottering. Caulaincourt, Ney, and Macdonald returned from Paris with the news that Marmont's desertion had changed the Tsar's mind. Since they could no longer prove that the whole army was behind the Emperor, the conditional abdication had been refused. The Senate had decided to proclaim the Count of Provence King of France and the Allies, to guarantee Napoleon the sovereignty of the Island of Elba.

The Emperor determined to resort to arms with his forces on the Loire plus those of Augureau, Soult, Suchet, Maison, Eugène, the depots, and the people. The orders had been issued. The Guard was to leave the next morning at 6 a.m.

But the Guard was not to leave. At 2 a.m. Friant warned General Pelet, commanding the foot chasseurs, that the corps commanders had refused to budge. Furthermore, Ney, Macdonald, and Caulaincourt had forbidden Berthier to transmit Napoleon's orders to the troops.

Nothing remained but to ask for the Emperor's sword. This was done in his own room on the morning of 6 April.

After a terrible burst of wrath Napoleon said to his marshals:

'You want a rest – go take it!' Then he pulled a small mahogany table towards him and, abandoned, betrayed, plumbing the depths of man's baseness and ingratitude, he wrote a second abdication – this time definitive and unconditional.

'Since the Allied Powers have proclaimed Emperor Napoleon to be the one obstacle to restoring peace in Europe, the Emperor, faithful to his oath, hereby renounces for himself and his heirs the thrones of France and Italy, and declares that there is no sacrifice, including his life, that he is not willing to make for France.'

This he handed to the commissioners[2] with a second document, granting them full powers 'to negotiate, conclude, and sign such articles, treaty, or convention as they see fit, and to stipulate all arrangements concerning our interests and those of our family, the army, ministers, councilors of state, and other of our subjects who have followed in our path.' The latter was signed after the Emperor by Caulaincourt as Minister of Foreign Affairs and Maret as Secretary of State.

Then Napoleon summoned Ney and gave him command of the Imperial Guard, with power to fix the boundaries of the armistice.

[2] Caulaincourt, Ney, and Macdonald.

CHAPTER 4

A Dynasty in Liquidation

ON 7 April the Emperor called for volunteers from the grenadiers, chasseurs, artillery marines, and cavalry of the Guard to serve in his guard at Elba, consisting of around 500 infantry, 120 cavalry, and 120 gunners.

Generals Friant, Petit, and Pelet were soon swamped with requests for admission. They had to make a difficult choice as well as to console the rejected. Everyone wanted to go with the Emperor. Many officers asked to serve as simple grenadiers in his guard.

Meanwhile, in their bivouacs at Chevannes the Polish light-horse of the Guard were still waiting for orders to march on Paris.

Count Vincent Corvin Krasinski, resplendent, perfumed, wearing beautiful boots, his black horse caparisoned like a charger in the *Arabian Nights*, returned from Fontainebleau followed by his suite.

His splendid squadrons were drawn up in two lines of battle. The trumpets sounded a *Ban*. Then the great mogul announced in Polish:

'God has visited misfortune upon the Emperor . . .' As he continued, his troopers began to weep. They 'regretted they had not all been killed' before hearing that anyone had dared demand the Emperor's abdication. War whoops and cries for vengeance greeted the announcement. Then the regiment set out for Fontainebleau.

Passing through Nainville it was halted by Sebastiani's aide-de-camp who was surprised to see a troop movement not ordered by his chief. General Krasinski galloped off to headquarters to protest that his duty, allegiance, and honor all called him to the Emperor's side, since it was not to France but to Napoleon that he and his compatriots had pledged their lives and service.

That night the Polish light-horse-lancers of the Guard bivouacked in the forest of Fontainebleau, beside the Paris road, where one squadron kept continuous watch. On their right, at the end of the Rue de France, were the campfires of the Guard artillery. The forest was all aglow, tinging with red the forlorn faces of the gunners who were either prostrate with grief and shame or choking with rage.

In the shadows lurked spies who offered them discharges signed with unfamiliar names. The roads were swarming with disarmed soldiers who had been sent home. The château, the town, and the Guard barracks were pervaded by a singular agitation. When the Emperor's final abdication had been announced as an order they were disgusted and near revolt. There was mounting tension in the canteens. Some were to go with him, and some were to stay . . . with whom?

That evening the grenadiers and chasseurs, foot and horse, Old and Young, left their quarters armed, carrying torches, and tramped the streets and the grounds around the château shouting '*Vive l'Empereur!*' 'Down with the traitors!' 'On to Paris!'

In contrast, the old palace was as quiet as a tomb. Its salons had gradually emptied. Would Napoleon be left entirely alone? What plots were the European rulers hatching against the Empress and the King of Rome? The latter had retired to Blois with Madame Mère, King Joseph, Queen Hortense,[1] Jerome, the ministers, and the Council of State. Anything might happen . . .

Couriers could move freely again, and every other day letters were exchanged between Baron Fain at Fontainebleau and Baron Méneval, the Empress' private secretary, at Blois. But Allied troops had been dispatched to Pithiviers, Orléans, Melun, and Montereau and the blockade was tightening around Fontainebleau whose forest was the last Imperial fortress, defended by the Guard. It must remain calm to avoid repressive measures by the provisional government and Metternich. The Emperor's safety – perhaps his very life – was in danger.

'So I have no more generals nor friends nor comrades-in-arms', Napoleon said to Marshal Ney.

'Sire, we are all your friends', the Marshal protested.

'Ah – Caesar's friends were also his murderers . . .'

The grenadiers posted in the court of Le Cheval Blanc let the 'big hats' depart one by one without ceremony. The generals and marshals hastened to bargain with the new government for posts which they finally obtained. Though none wished to be the first to leave the Emperor, they all sought pretexts – and found them. Some, as a last resort, sent messengers to him and others wrote him letters which, alas, are still in their files at the War Ministry. Since Louis-Stanislas-Xavier had been proclaimed king, they had to hurry so as not to be too late.

Mortier wrote his sister on 9 April:

'Emperor Napoleon must go to the island of Elba. I believe Empress Marie-Louise will go, too. I shall probably accompany him. If I can be of any use I shall go with pleasure.

'We hope the peace will last. Having done my duty as an honorable man, I have no anxiety for myself. As to my future, I have faced death too often to fear it now. So long as my wife and children have bread and are happy, I care little what happens to me.

'For the past few days we have been sitting on top of a volcano. When I was summoned to Fontainebleau my troops came near deserting in a body during my absence. Calm was restored only on my return. Several corps wished to rally to my standard . . .

'I shall . . . abide by the Senate's decision and recognize the new government, since France has done so. Farewell.' In a postscript he added: 'Everyone is trying to feather his own nest. I desire only to preserve my honor and merit the esteem of friends and foes alike. All my colleagues have been pushing themselves forward.'

Which of them won the race to serve the new regime? Perhaps it was Nansouty whose letter was dated 2 April. Lefebvre's was dated the 8th. Berthier left the 13th,

[1] Consort of Louis Bonaparte.

promising to return, but never did. General Dulauloy of the artillery addressed an ambiguous declaration to the new government that none of his officers would sign. The rank and file remained loyal, which consoled the Emperor. He was deeply touched to read the service records of the men who wanted to follow him to exile.

Caulaincourt wrote that Napoleon's request for Tuscany had been denied, so they were going to Elba. What did they care? They would follow him wherever he went. The lists were closed on 9 April. There were rows between Grumblers. 'Why wasn't I chosen? I was decorated with the order of Honor. I have served twenty-two years and have three holes in my hide. If they write me out a passport, it should be written in blood!'

The 'Army of Napoleon' was finally fixed at one infantry battalion containing 3 companies of chasseurs and 3 of grenadiers, an artillery staff, a crew of 21 marines, and a squadron of 120 Polish lancers. That evening each of the officers selected had a long interview with the Emperor who planned to review the battalion next day.

At 10 a.m. on 10 April Sergeant Drummer Carré and his eighteen drummers beat 'To the Emperor', and General Cambronne, still very lame from his wounds, presented his Grumblers. Cambronne had been warmly recommended by Dumoustier to command the battalion. His second in command, Major Malet, had served since 1795 in various regiments including the foot guides of Italy and the chasseurs of the Consular Guard. Wounded at Lodi, Acre, and Essling and an officer of the Legion of Honor, he had followed the Emperor from Italy to Fontainebleau, via Egypt, Marengo, Vienna, Madrid, Moscow, and Dresden, and was truly representative of the Old Guard.

Laborde of the fusiliers was captain and adjutant major; Loubers of the 1st Grenadiers, an officer of the Legion with three wounds, together with Combes and Hurault de Sorbée, were among the captains. Among the lieutenants were Noisot of the 1st, and Franconin and Bacheville of the 2nd Grenadiers. Sergeant Major Benigni headed the marines. In all, there were 1,000 stubborn, tough, indomitables whose familiar names had been heard at many a roll call and would doubtless be heard at the last – in eternity.

At assembly the rest of the Grumblers listened to the following words from their chief: 'Your country is eternally grateful to you . . . The war has no longer any purpose or objective . . . You are soldiers of France and must follow the consensus of opinion . . .' Then the Emperor released them from their oath.

General Dupont, the new war minister known in the Guard as 'Dupont of Baylén', published the following notice in the *Monitor:*

'du Plessis-Chenet, 8 April.

'The generals, officers, and soldiers of the 2nd Old Guard Division, the 1st and 2nd Young Guard Divisions of the Imperial Guard, and General Roussel's dragoon division, under the command of His Excellency the Marshal Duke of Treviso, have the honor to beg Your Excellency to present their allegiance to the new Government.

'(Signed) Curial, Charpentier, Bigarré, Boyer de Rebeval, Delapointe, Christiani, Le Capitaine, Bouvard, Guye, Gros, Lavigne, Léglise, etc. etc.'

The marines' declaration, signed by Saizieu, Grivel, etc. was followed by one from the engineers. On 10 April Sebastiani offered allegiance for himself and his troops, though his officers signed nothing. Generals Colbert, Ornano, Lion, and Dériot followed suit for their commands, and Dulauloy, Friant, Boulart, Rottembourg, Laferrière, La Grange, Michel, Flamand, Henrion, Beurmann and their subordinates offered their personal allegiance. Such is the servitude of the military profession.

Meanwhile, documents of a different tenor were widely circulated. One example, headed 'Decree of the French People', began:

'Since the city of Paris was found wanting in the loyalty it had pledged to His Majesty Napoleon I, our august and well-beloved Emperor, and has invited the Empire's enemies within her gates and seen fit to place on the throne the pretender Louis XVIII . . . a kinglet foisted upon the nation by the Erostratus[2] of Russia, the Prussian Nero, the English Childeric, and the Austrian Ogre . . .'

The next day, 8 April, was Good Friday. Napoleon, deserted by his friends, had also been abandoned by his family. Neither Joseph nor Jerome nor Louis found it convenient to travel the 87 miles to Fontainebleau to comfort him with their affection.

The Empress and the King of Rome were surrounded by intrigue. Méneval wrote disquieting letters to Baron Fain, Napoleon's secretary. Many personages, including the Tsar's aide-de-camp Count Shuvalov, one of the Allied commissioners, went to Blois to offer Marie-Louise their services. 'From that moment all means of joining the Emperor were denied the Empress', Méneval wrote in his memoirs.

According to him, the Empress received a letter from Napoleon in code urging her to 'keep in touch with her father so as to seek his protection', and warning her to 'be prepared for anything, including his (Napoleon's) death'.

Accordingly, Marie-Louise sent Champagny, then Beausset and Saint-Aulaire, to her father with letters 'bathed in tears'. Meanwhile, couriers kept her in constant touch with Napoleon.

On 9 April the Emperor wrote her two letters. The first said: 'If you have horses and wish to come here, you may . . .' The second suggested that he meet her 'near Gien'.

Late that afternoon the Empress and the King of Rome arrived in Orléans with their suites, accompanied by Madame Mère, Cardinal Fesch, Joseph and Jerome with their consorts and suites, the ministers, and the Council of State. The city guard lined their route from the Porte Madeleine to the bishop's palace where the bishop welcomed the Empress. The long procession, escorted by horse Guards and Janin's elite gendarmes, was greeted with sporadic cries of '*Vive l'Empereur! Vive l'Impératrice!*'

The treasure wagons and the beautiful court carriages – one of which contained the cradle presented to the King of Rome by the City of Paris – were parked for safe keeping in the courtyard of the Town Hall and in the cloisters of Saint-Croix, watched over by the Guard.

[2] The man who set fire to the temple at Ephesus at the birth of Alexander the Great in 356 B.C. – Ed.

On Easter Sunday, the 10th, Marie-Louise reproached herself for her long delay in joining the Emperor. She planned to leave as soon as de Beausset and Saint-Aulaire brought her father's reply to the letter she had written at Napoleon's suggestion, asking him to grant her Tuscany. That day Champagny brought a letter from the Emperor Francis assuring his daughter of his affection, but warning her that his 'Allies had not the same zeal as himself for defending her interests . . .'

The Emperor was delighted to hear the Empress was coming to Fontainebleau and that she had written her father. Nevertheless, he had Fain write Méneval to ask 'what were the Empress' real intentions'.

On Easter Monday Caulaincourt reported stormy discussions in Paris where Metternich and Castlereagh wished to banish Napoleon from Europe, to which the Tsar had demurred. They hoped the Emperor would get Elba. '. . . But let not Your Majesty be deceived, Austria thinks of nothing but her precious Italy . . .'

However, Napoleon still had illusions about Austria. He believed that Francis' politics and that of his ministers were in conflict. That day he wrote Caulaincourt: 'The Empress wrote me on the 9th that she was going to her father to ask for Tuscany', adding: 'I cannot let her come to Fontainebleau which is now in the front line . . .'

The Guard had been ordered to the Loire where Dupont planned to disperse it. Mortier was summoned to Paris. Leaving Friant in command, the Marshal published this order of the day: 'Since I have the highest esteem for the generals, officers, and soldiers of the Guard, I shall deem it my duty on my arrival in Paris to see that their eminent services, good conduct, and bravery are rewarded, their arrears in pay settled, and their future assured. I shall never forget their constant proofs of affection for me personally, which are a great consolation to me in the present situation.'

On 12 April a courier arrived from Caulaincourt announcing an armistice. 'Arrangements' had been signed that night by which the Emperor and Empress were to keep the rank, titles, and honors of sovereigns. Napoleon was to live at Elba, and Marie-Louise to receive the principalities of Parma, Piacenza, and Guastalla. An income was provided for the Imperial family, also a specified sum which the Emperor might bequeath 'to those he wishes to reward: aides-de-camp, generals, officers of the Guard'. Furthermore: 'The Imperial Guard shall furnish a detachment of 1,200–1,500 men to escort him to Saint-Tropez, the place of embarcation for Elba . . . The Emperor may take 400 volunteers to Elba with him.'

Caulaincourt added in a postscript: 'The Empress will not find her father in a conciliatory mood. I am sad to think that His Majesty may have sacrificed the joy of a reunion with his wife and son to his insistence on Tuscany. May the desired interview not add one more sorrow to his lot . . .'

Nevertheless, that evening Napoleon wrote the Empress telling her of the 'arrangements', particularly in regard to her new principalities, He said that she 'must insist on Tuscany' when she saw her father, or at least on Piombino, Lucca, and the approaches to Elba. 'As soon as everything is finished I shall go to Briare where you shall join me, and we shall travel . . . to Parma and embark at La Spezia . . . I am sending

PLATE 143

Allied Armies entering Paris in March 1814
(From an original gouache miniature by Balthazar Wigand)

PLATE 144

a) King of Rome, 1815
(Watercolor by Isabey: Schatzkammer, Hofburg, Vienna)

b) Joseph
(Contemp. engraving after Vicart)

c) Marie-Louise
(Portrait by Gérard: Musée de Versailles)

d) Alexander I
(Col. engraving, chez Jean)

e) Caulincourt
(Contemp. lithograph)

PLATE 145

First abdication of Napoleon at Fontainebleau
(From an original watercolor by Jules Vernet)

PLATE 146

Cossacks marching through Paris
(*From an original watercolor by Georg Opitz*)

PLATE 147

NAPOLEON'S FAREWELL TO THE GUARD IN THE COURT OF LE CHEVAL BLANC

Central group, left to right: Generals d'Ornano, Belliard, Corbineau, Kossakowski, Baron Fain, Maret, Napoleon, General Petit, Lieutenant Fortin (eagle-bearer), Generals Bertrand, Drouot, the Allied Commissioners (Baron Koller, Col. Campbell, General Shuvalov)

(From the painting by Horace Vernet: Collection of Hugh Bullock, Esq)

PLATE 148

a) Drouot
(*Col. engraving by Meyer*)

b) Cambronne
(*Engr. Boisselman after Mulnier*)

c) Krasinski
(*After contemp. watercolor*)

d) Jerzmanowski
(*Contemp. lithograph*)

e) Louis XVIII
(*Col. aquatint by Levachez after Delaplace*)

Fouler to arrange the equipages.' Count Fouler de Relingue took this letter to Orléans.

The Emperor divided the bequest provided by the treaty as follows: 50,000 francs each to Generals Friant, Cambronne, Petit, Ornano, Curial, Michel, Lefebvre-Desnoëttes, Guyot, Laferrière, Colbert, Marin, Boulart, and Drouot; 170,000 to the thirty officers accompanying him to Elba, and the balance to his household. But in the end, those who signed the treaty and their constituents broke their contract and the legacies were never paid.

Now the Guard began to leave Fontainebleau. Before taking the rest of the artillery to Vendôme, Griois chose from 400 applicants 100 gunners under Captains Cornuel and Raoul for the Elba Battalion. The marines were sent to Le Havre, leaving five NCO's and sixteen men with the Emperor.

The Polish lancers were split into three groups: one squadron under Jerzmanowski remained with the Emperor; a detachment of Frenchmen under Dautancourt was turned over to the chasseurs of the Guard; the rest left for Poland after sending the Emperor the following memorial, signed by all the officers:

'Sire: Released from our obligations, we come with one accord to place at Your Imperial Majesty's feet the arms that no man could take from us by force. If we be presumptuous in addressing Your Majesty directly, our honor will protect us and your great heart will forgive us. As Poles we have served the most amazing man of the century and have quit his service only when he quit us. Sire, accept the homage of our eternal loyalty, maintained under the most trying circumstances, to an unfortunate Prince.'

Then, with trumpets sounding, this fine regiment of 1,384 cavaliers marched past the château into the forest, and on to Paris, Nancy, and Poland, after serving seven years and two months and winning the esteem of Emperor, Guard, and Army.

CHAPTER 5

'Farewell, my children . . .'

As the day of 11 April drew to a close Napoleon received a visit from Baron Beausset, former prefect of the palace, now attached to the Empress' suite. Entrusted with the Empress' letter to her father, Beausset had given it instead to Metternich. The Emperor did not know that this sinister character had promised Metternich to prevent the Empress from joining him.

In a letter Beausset wrote from Rambouillet on 14 April 1814 to Baron Mounier, major-domo of the Court who had been continued in office by the Bourbons, he applied for a post in the royal household. Then he continued:

'We are expecting the Emperor of Austria. I hope the interview will serve to restore the Empress Marie-Louise to her family forever, and erect a perpetual barrier between the Island of Elba and the principalities of Parma and Piacenza.

'For the past few days I have been busy strengthening these hopes in the heart of the Empress, and fighting against the return of any sentimental nonsense. Several hours' conversation with Emperor Napoleon last Monday at Fontainebleau provided me with powerful ammunition with which to sever the bonds of a marriage I consider ended. It proved to me conclusively his irresponsibility and his singular conviction – masquerading as a philosophy – that everything is governed by a fate beyond human control . . . This man has had all the luck of Mahomet, as well as his audacity and charlatanism.'

Surfeited with misfortune, insults, lies; wounded in heart and pride, perhaps Napoleon had allowed himself to blame his misfortunes on fate.

That evening he wrote the Empress and sent the letter by Beausset: 'Tell me if the plan to go to Parma together is agreeable to you. Your letters are full of sentiments that sustain my heart. They touch me deeply and console me.'

Later Napoleon received a letter from Caulaincourt who kept him abreast of events in Paris: 'Orders have been issued for her (the Empress) to go to Rambouillet, if Your Majesty approves, to meet the Emperor of Austria.'

Napoleon was at first surprised, then indignant. Rambouillet? Why make Marie-Louise travel sixty miles when she was tormented and anxious?

In reply to Napoleon's inquiry about the Empress' real sentiments, Méneval assured Baron Fain that she wished to join the Emperor but was no longer free to do so. She relied on the affection of her father who, she said, 'would not let me be separated from my husband and son'. Méneval continued: 'She is reluctant to leave because she fears she will be arrested en route. Also, the idea of flight is repugnant to her . . .'

Meanwhile, Attorney General Dudon of Sceau, who had been cashiered from the Army of Spain for deserting his post, had arrived at Orléans with a government order to seize the Emperor's treasure. This was Napoleon's personal property and included his savings from the civil list, out of which he had paid and clothed the Guard during the last campaign, and also his personal belongings of value. His treasurer-general M. de La Bouillerie had refused to release it.

Only that morning Inspector Peyrusse had left for Orléans with a letter to the Empress and an order to La Bouillerie to send Napoleon the specie, jewels, and accounts of the treasure. That evening the Emperor dispatched to Orléans a detachment of Polish lancers and grenadiers of the Elba Battalion under Captain Laborde to escort Baron Peyrusse and the treasure to Briare. General Cambronne left with the rest of the Battalion at dawn next day.

According to Méneval, when Napoleon learned that Marie-Louise hesitated to join him for fear of being arrested en route, he 'doubtless sent this escort to protect her'. At all events, the Fontainebleau spies warned Paris that a battalion of grenadiers (they said two) with artillery was leaving for Orléans.

On the afternoon of 12 April, Prince Esterhazy and Prince Liechtenstein arrived at Orléans to inform the Empress that her father would meet her at Rambouillet on 14 April. (This was false, since Francis had not yet reached Paris.)

The same day, Fain wrote Méneval: 'It appears that the Empress will gain nothing from the interview at Rambouillet. The Emperor still thinks it best for her to leave with him and travel by easy stages . . .' Six hours later Napoleon wrote Marie-Louise: 'I think we could meet at Briare or Gien'.

Meanwhile, Metternich wrote: 'It would be most suitable for her (the Empress) to go to Austria for the moment, which would be entirely in accordance with her father's wishes.'

Only twenty-two, Marie-Louise was torn between father and husband. Madame Mère had left for Italy; the ministers and councilors, having nothing more to hope for from her, had gone to Paris to bask in the new sun. Despite the baneful influence of Beausset and the Duchess of Montebello, still she hesitated; but she finally gave in to the Austrian princes and agreed to go to Rambouillet before joining her husband.

That day the commandant at Orléans, General de la Hamelinaye, relayed to Caffarelli, the following order: 'The government forbids the Empress to take the road to Fontainebleau under any pretext whatever. If Her Majesty wishes to turn off the Paris road, Captain Cousin, General de la Hamelinaye's aide, . . . must oppose it by all means and remind General Caffarelli of his orders.'

That afternoon the Empress dashed off a note to the Emperor saying she was being pressed from all sides and that, though she deplored a further delay in their reunion, she had been commanded to go at once to Rambouillet.

In the court of the Bishop's palace the King of Rome, wearing a pale blue sailor suit and armed with a wooden sword, was drilling a platoon of pegs the pages had stuck between the paving stones. At 8 p.m. the Count de Ségur, Grand Master of Ceremonies, helped the Empress into her carriage for the last time. The Guard joined the procession at the city gates.

In a loft of the episcopal stables, Inspector Peyrusse, nervous and exhausted, watched anxiously over a pile of manure. Under it reposed all he had been able to salvage of the Emperor's treasure.

The night before, he had left Fontainebleau for Orléans with his servant and a guide. Seeing suspicious campfires along the Pithiviers road, he made a detour and ran headlong into a party of Cossacks. Then he hid in the forest, lost his way, and finally reached Orléans at noon on the 12th.

He was received by the Empress who, with tears in her eyes, plied him with questions about the Emperor. She told Peyrusse that she had been much upset to learn that La Bouillerie had surrendered the Emperor's treasure to Attorney General Dudon, and that Colonel Janin had taken the wagons to Paris, escorted by 80 elite gendarmes.[1]

Fortunately, during the negotiations Champagny and Caffarelli had managed to withdraw six million francs from the coffers parked in the Place de la Cathédrale. Of this sum Peyrusse, 'fighting all opposition', succeeded in salvaging 2,600,000 francs which he packed in thirty cases and hid under the manure in the episcopal stables.

That night the city of Orléans was in an uproar and the people were agitated. Shots rang out. Cries of '*Vive l'Empereur!*' and '*Vive le Roi!*' and the sound of galloping hoofs were heard in every quarter. Peyrusse was entirely alone. After the departure of the Empress and the Guard, he had sent his servant and the guide to Fontainebleau to ask the Grand Marshal (Bertrand) for help. Meanwhile, Cossacks were prowling about.

At dawn next day, from the secret recesses of his stable Peyrusse fixed his eyes on the street below. The hours passed . . . Finally, at 6 p.m. a mail coach arrived bringing Quartermaster Deschamps of the palace. Then Captain Laborde and his vanguard entered the city and, tipped off by a Guard captain in the Empress' escort, found Peyrusse's hiding place. The cases were loaded on a wagon, covered by a canvas 'full of holes', and removed to an inn in the suburbs where Sergeant Delahaye and eight grenadiers were detailed to guard them.

At midnight Cambronne arrived with his grenadiers and artillery. General La Hamelinaye wisely considered Orléans an unhealthy spot for the Grumblers and advised their commander to retire to the village of Ingré. Cambronne informed the Grand Marshal of the whereabouts of himself and the treasure. Then he gave his men a day's rest and, avoiding Orléans entirely, set out with the treasure for Briare to await the Emperor.

---

[1] The *Memoirs* of Méneval states: 'When the Russian general Shuvalov was asked to intervene, he did nothing to prevent this revolting performance.' Lottin's *Recherches historiques sur la ville d'Orléans* says: 'The provisional government ordered Napoleon's treasure seized by commissioners sent for that purpose. The treasure consisted of 23,000,000 francs in gold and 4,500,000 in presents, portraits encrusted with diamonds, etc, gold and silver services and precious objects, including articles in daily use by the Empress and her son. Everything was removed to Paris in the same wagons that had brought them from Blois to Orléans, escorted by the same Imperial Guards. A coffer containing more than 600,000 francs worth of diamonds was deposited with M. Loyré in the rue Mâcheclou, and remained there for two days.'

Meanwhile, at the Pavillon des Rosnières in the forest of Fontainebleau, the quartermasters had been working with Amodru and the stable attendants to put in order the Emperor's horses and carriages, painting out the coats-of-arms, repairing the wagons and harness, and packing the tack. Twenty-three saddle horses, and 78 carriage horses for 15 carriages and 8 wagons were sent under escort to Briare.

The convoy left on the 14th. On the road it passed grenadiers and chasseurs wearing white cockades who envied the marines and lancers of the escort still wearing the tricolor. At Nemours the horse Guards watched with heavy hearts as the procession of familiar carriages, which they would never see again, passed by escorted by Poles who were free to choose their own destiny. Next day many old troopers deserted.

On the convoy's arrival at Briare a Polish officer handed Peyrusse an order to return to Fontainebleau. He set out at once, arriving at the château before nightfall. He found the palace deserted and the Emperor, in the deepest gloom, searching books and maps for information about his new domain.

His servants Roustam and Constant had already left. Besides his aides Flahaut, Montesquiou, and Turenne, only Caulaincourt, Maret, and Drouot had remained with him. Several generals of the Old Guard visited him daily. He was worried about the Empress, the King of Rome, and the treasure.

The night of the 12th Major Jerzmanowski had hurried to Angerville with a letter for the Empress who arrived there from Orléans at 3 a.m. No one knows its contents; however, Caulaincourt reported that Marie-Louise's reply, scrawled in pencil as she sat in her carriage, was 'full of tender and touching sentiments, and expressed in the most positive terms her willingness and desire to join Napoleon after the interview with her father'.

'I shall be firm with my father', she wrote. 'I shall tell him that I insist upon doing what you wish, and shall not permit any violence to restrain me . . .'

This letter, together with an equally affectionate one from Rambouillet on the 13th, revived Napoleon's interest in life. Jerzmanowski reported that the Empress and the King of Rome left Angerville at 5 a.m. escorted by Cossacks.

After this all the news brought Napoleon from Rambouillet was bad. Peyrusse left on the 17th to see the Empress about the balance of the Emperor's funds. Using all his wiles, Peyrusse managed to wheedle 1,500,000 francs out of Marie-Louise who declared that 'in view of her father's financial straits' she had decided to keep a million for herself. Méneval promised he would send this sum to Elba after the Empress reached Vienna.[1]

Since Marie-Louise was leaving for Vienna with the little King 'immediately', according to Metternich, there was nothing to keep Napoleon longer at Fontainebleau.

Madame Bertrand left the Empress to join her husband, and Drouot made his farewells. Having no desire to see Paris again, Drouot wrote a friend:

'My aide-de-camp . . . is going to Paris and I have asked him to go and see you . . . The Emperor is leaving for Elba. Only two officers will accompany him, and I am one. I have loved and served my sovereign well when he was happy. Now I shall follow

[1] He never did. – Ed.

him and lighten his burden in adversity. It is hard for me to renounce my native land, my family, and my dearest friends; but it would be even harder to renounce my gratitude.

'I have said goodbye to my guns which I loved very dearly. Nevertheless, if I am ever called back to . . . France, I shall serve no more but shall consecrate the years it may still please Providence to grant me in this vale of tears to study and the contemplative life. In quitting the military profession I take with me one great consolation – that of having always been guided by honor and honesty.'

Lefebvre-Desnoëttes, originally ordered to escort the Emperor to the port of embarcation, wrote Belliard: 'It seems that I shall be allowed to go no further than Briare'.

On 19 April the remaining Guard generals and the foreign commissioners assigned to accompany the Emperor dined with him at the palace. Next day the traveling carriages were drawn up in the court of Le Cheval Blanc. The 1st Grenadiers lined the route from the grand staircase to the gates.

Followed by Bertrand and Drouot, the Emperor left his apartment and found a group waiting in the vestibule to say goodbye. This included the Duke of Bassano (Maret), General Kossakowski of the Emperor's personal staff, his aides Colonels de Bussy and de Montesquiou, General Belliard, General d'Ornano, the Count de Turenne, the orderly officers Colonel Gourgaud and Baron de La Place, Colonel Athalin of his topographical bureau, his Polish interpreter Colonel Wonsowicz, and his secretaries Barons Fain, Le Lorgne d'Ideville, and Jouanne. Not one marshal of the Empire nor one member of Napoleon's own family was present.

General Petit ordered the troops to present arms. The drummers beat *Aux Champs* as the Emperor appeared on the stairs, wearing the uniform coat of the chasseurs of the Guard with blue breeches, top boots, and his legendary hat. The grooms stood by the carriages. General Lefebvre-Desnoëttes was on horseback at the head of the escort of 1,500 Old Guard troopers. The trumpets sounded 'To the Emperor.'

Napoleon descended the stairs and shook hands with General Petit who came forward to meet him. Then he walked to the center of the court where he said goodbye to the Guard in a firm voice. The speech was not recorded, but those who heard it remembered it in essence as follows:

'Officers, noncommissioned officers, and soldiers of my Old Guard, I bid you farewell. For twenty years I have been pleased with you. I have always found you on the path to glory. The Allied Powers have armed all Europe against me. Part of the army has betrayed its trust – and France. Now that another destiny lies in store for her, I must sacrifice my most cherished interests. With you and the brave men who have remained loyal I could have continued the war for three years; but France would have suffered, which was contrary to my purpose. Be loyal to the new ruler whom France has chosen. Never abandon this dear country that has suffered so long.

'Do not pity my fate. I shall be happy so long as I know that you are happy. I could have ended my life – nothing would have been easier. But no, I shall always keep to the path of honor. Now I shall write the story of what we have done . . .'

At these words General Petit waved his sword in the air and cried '*Vive l'Empereur!*' which was rapturously echoed by the whole Guard. The Emperor continued with feeling:

'I cannot embrace you all, but I shall embrace your general. Approach, General Petit.'

He clasped the general in his arms. 'Let the eagle be brought', he said.

This he kissed three times saying: 'Dear eagle, let my embrace echo in the hearts of these brave men!

'Farewell, my children . . .'

Amid an ovation the Emperor, accompanied by Bertrand, drove off at a brisk trot into exile. Lefebvre-Desnoëttes rode at the right-hand door of his carriage which was surrounded for the last time by *chasseurs à cheval*. Drouot led the procession in his *berline*, followed by the foreign commissioners and the carriages of the suite. Jerzmanowski with the dragoons and horse grenadiers brought up the rear (see Plate 147).

At Montargis the 1st Chasseurs rendered honors as the Emperor descended before the *Hôtel de la Poste* and spoke to General Pelet whose men lined the route with 'tears running down their cheeks', according to Antoine Boivin who was there. 'Not one of these brave men was able to utter a sound, but watched in mournful silence.'

That evening Napoleon arrived at Briare where he was greeted by Cambronne and the Elba battalion, drawn up on the town square. He thanked the officers and Grumblers who had volunteered to accompany him into exile and expressed his pleasure at seeing them again. Meanwhile, the rest beat up some gendarmes who were wearing white cockades, and nailed to a scaffold opposite the bridge a placard inscribed 'Long live Napoleon the Great!'

Next day Napoleon entered his carriage at noon, thanked his escort, wished it bon voyage and disappeared down the road to Nevers, followed only by his suite.

Thus ended the first stage of his journey towards a new destiny.

BOOK IX

THE GUARD FALLS

CHAPTER 1

The Dissolution of the Guard

FROM the beginning the Guard was mistrusted by the new government. 'Discipline must be maintained . . . in the Old Guard', wrote the Minister of War on 21 April. 'In an elite corps the crime of desertion should be unknown.'

True; however, the government had provoked indiscipline by discharging the conscripts at one demagogic stroke of the pen, hamstringing the commanders and flooding the country with a hungry, disorganized mob. This filled the oldest veterans with disgust and caused some to desert.

At Fontainebleau General Friant appealed to the Old Guard in an order of the day that ended: 'Keep faith with your honor and you will reap rewards commensurate with the glory you have truly earned, and obtain honorable discharges which your families and compatriots will respect. Remember, brave Grenadiers and Chasseurs, that you are still the object of everyone's concern. I beg you to keep your reputations intact so that you may also keep your privileges.'

In releasing them from their oath the Emperor himself had told them: 'You are soldiers of France . . . Since I cannot stay, you had best adapt yourself to the Bourbons . . .' However, he said to Caulaincourt: 'The Guard's fidelity to me will prove to the King that it is composed of good men who can be trusted . . . But were I in his place, I should not keep it intact . . . I should grant a number of good pensions . . .'

All men are not heroes, and some become so purely by accident. Actually, the Guard was now a corps without a soul. The Imperial Guard had ceased to exist. With the *Tondu* gone, nothing remained. At once gallant and ferocious, gilded and underpaid, worshiped and envied, drunk with love and glory, these grenadiers, dragoons, and gunners were nomads, indifferent to family ties, who had lived, suffered, and fought for the Emperor alone.

For eight years they had been grenadiers at 23 sous, or corporals for ten years at 34; yet their prestige was greater than a lawyer's or a Line officer's because they belonged to his Guard. They had never left the side of the man whose glance made them quiver and in whose presence their throats felt dry.

On 27 April the Duke of Treviso (Mortier) announced in his order of the day that the King had landed at Calais, and all the fortresses fired salvos. Yet these veterans had got holes in their hides to get rid of him! The white cockade? Those who had served in the *Gardes françaises* – Friant, for example – had thrown it into the moat at the Bastille. Louis-Stanislas-Xavier? Unknown in the battalion.

Well, then? Must they now serve their conqueror? Yes, for France, for their country. But France was him – the Other One. Why go on living? Should they quit the army? What else could they do? They could only shine equipment and march and be killed. They were good for nothing as civilians; besides, they had no families, no homes. Where would they go?

When they got drunk to forget their misery, they regretted that they were not lying in six feet of clay at Montmirail or Craonne. Broken and despondent, the Grumblers of the Imperial Guard had lost their faith in their grandiose destiny. But still they were condemned to live. What would become of them?

Marshal Mortier was in command of the Guard. The Minister, the officers and men had perfect confidence in his honor and integrity.

The Young Guard was licking its wounds in Lille and Orléans. At the beginning of June Mortier's chief of staff General Delapointe undertook to dissolve it by order of the Minister. The *pupilles* were disbanded at the same time, and the flankers later.

The situation in the Guard artillery was confused. Dogureau, its former commander, had been reinstated by the Emperor at the end of 1813 as honorary colonel of the horse artillery and sent to the Northern Army. Now his old rival Drouot was out of the running. The rank and file were devoted to the Emperor, and considered the *Tondu* as one of themselves. After 11 April a great anxiety compounded of wounded pride, dashed hopes, and uncertainty pervaded the corps.

On 15 April General Griois took the artillery of the Guard to Vendôme where the companies were scattered in order to find food and forage for over 1,800 men and 2,400 horses. The officers were split into political cliques, with Pion des Loches, Bitsch, and Leclerc content to serve the King, and Boulart, Marin, Griois, Capelle, and others unhappy with their fate.

When Count d'Osmond was sent to investigate the regiment's loyalty, the gunner took little trouble to hide their sentiments. Madame Boulart wept openly. When a Te Deum of thanksgiving for the Bourbons' return was sung in church, some die-hards heckled the priest who dared to compare 'the virtues of the King with the crimes of the Tyrant'. Before taking the artillery to La Fère on 13 May, Griois tore up a testimonial stating that his gunners' conduct and esprit de corps 'had vastly improved during their stay', and threw it in the face of the mayor.

These incidents, combined with the horse artillery's charge with sabers on the Prussian *Garde du Corps* at Compiègne, and some snide remarks made by Griois and Marin about the King and the Duke of Berry, did not aid Dulauloy's efforts to have the corps admitted to the *Garde Royale*.

On 3 May the General sent the following memorandum to the Minister:

'The services rendered by the Artillery of the Guard during the recent campaigns . . . give it an incontestable right . . . to belong to the *Garde Royale*. If it should have the good fortune to obtain this favor its organization will be modified and reduced . . . The Guard artillery has always been recruited from the elite of the Line. Its officers are choice, and its gunners excellent . . . With such a corps one can be sure of victory . . . Its loss would be irreparable . . .'

Dogureau, whom General Maison had presented to the King at Calais, was appointed major general[1] commanding the artillery. However, his old threat to 'blow out the brains of the first Bourbon who returns to France' had not been entirely forgotten; nor had Lallemand's reference to the Court as 'a canaille of princes and émigrés', nor many other insults.

In the end, discharges and pensions were granted three-fifths of the gunners, and the rest were sent to widely dispersed areas and incorporated into the Royal Corps of Artillery. Bonuses of from 25 to 60 francs, according to rank, were granted them by the King.

Less noisy and more disciplined, the engineers of the Guard disappeared without a scandal, followed by the marines, the sappers' faithful companions in many campaigns. Since the marines had served under Dupont at Baylén in 1808, the Minister asked their commandant Baron Saizieu to file a memorandum pleading their cause, but to no avail. The corps was disbanded on 15 June; its officers were inducted into the navy at an increase in rank and pay, and its men sent to the fleet.

Towards the end of June the wagon train battalion was split into three, and half of its horses lent to the farmers of Angers, Orléans, and Beaugé where the units were stationed. The three artisan companies remained in Orléans until January 1815 when they were abolished.

The commissaries took charge of disbanding the units. Baron Dufour, the Chief Commissary, remained in Paris, while Larrey, Suë, and the medical officers continued their work at the Gros-Caillou.

By 15 June Christiani's 2nd Old Guard Division was already scattered and was scheduled to be disbanded at the end of July.

On 1 May the Minister of War sent a project to His Royal Highness, Monsieur,[2] Lieutenant General of the Realm, for organizing a guard for the king. 'I have tried', he wrote, 'to reconcile what is required to maintain the prestige of the Throne with the present state of France'.

Recalling the fact that in 1791 the *Maison du Roi* had consisted of 1,200 infantry and 600 horse, he recommended forming two infantry regiments aggregating 4,000 men, two cavalry regiments aggregating 1,600, and a regiment of Swiss Guards 'whose loyal conduct in the past would seem to merit this distinction.'

Then he continued: 'The choice of NCO's and men is of paramount importance, and must be made from every corps in the army.' Before being deleted by the Minister, the rest of the paragraph read: '. . . without excluding the men of the Old and Young Guards. The Old Guard, in particular, could furnish specimens valuable for their brilliant valor . . . though one cannot deny that they were famous for their devotion to the head of the late government . . . If one were to exclude the officers and choose individual soldiers from the ranks, one would be sure of obtaining an extremely

---

[1] The old royal rank of *maréchal de camp* was resumed in place of *général de brigade*. – Ed.

[2] The Count of Artois, later Charles X, eldest brother of Louis XVIII. The royal title 'Monsieur' was traditionally borne by the eldest brother of the sovereign. – Ed.

distinguished type; for it is noteworthy that the NCO's and men of the Old Guard infantry are even more remarkable than the officers . . .'

Obviously, the man who drafted this memorandum knew the Old Guard well.

Dupont had other plans for the Old Guard whose present strength was 6,904 grenadiers and chasseurs, including 200 Veterans, and 5,796 horse grenadiers, chasseurs, dragoons, and 2nd Lancers. These corps formed the elite of the French Army. From a military standpoint they left nothing to be desired; however, they were not famous for their devotion to the King. Should the Guard be disbanded, incorporated into the Line, or kept intact under a new name?

Dupont vetoed the first two solutions. If disbanded, 'the best soldiers in the army would go unrewarded', which would be impolitic and even dangerous. If incorporated into the Line, they would be stripped of their privileges and high pay and might mutiny. It was better to keep them intact, give them a new name, and take certain precautions.

The Minister proposed that they be rechristened 'Grenadiers of France' after an elite corps disbanded in 1775. This would flatter the proverbial vanity of old soldiers while their esprit de corps would be weakened by making each battalion autonomous. 'Thus', he concluded, 'they will gradually forget their old chief and devote themselves entirely to the august House of Bourbon, thereby setting an example to the rest of the army in devotion as well as bravery.'

Finally, by retiring some NCO's and promoting others in the Line, the number of irreconcilables would be gradually diminished.

CHAPTER 2

The Royal Grumblers

THE King was at Compiègne preparing his entrance into Paris on 3 May. The marshals of the Empire – now marshals of France – were there to welcome him. Louis' physique was conspicuously unmilitary; he leaned so heavily on the arms of his 'embroidered devotees' that when he asked Lefebvre: 'Well, Marshal, are you one of us?' the Marshal answered: 'Yes'.

The next day 500 grenadiers of the Guard left Fontainebleau for Paris to escort the King into the city, and on to Notre-Dame for a Te Deum.

This was an honor, to be sure; but the day began badly. On the Grumblers' arrival at the Napoleon barracks General Friant deluged them with advice, enumerating everything he expected of them – good discipline, impeccable uniform, etc. But first, they must remove from their bonnets the plaques with the 'cuckoo', since it was no longer in season. In vain had they brushed their bearskins and attached white cockades – the *Tondu*'s insignia was still there, making their disguise incomplete.

In the noon sunshine the Grumblers felt ill at ease among the white-clad girls at Saint-Denis; especially since, for the first time in their existence, they were not at the head of the line. This post was reserved for the Russian guard! Was Louis-Stanislas-Xavier really King of France? The veterans of Tilsit grit their teeth. And Friant wanted them to cry *'Vive le Roi!'*

They recognized the *Tondu*'s green carriages. The arms on the hammer-cloths had been disguised with paper fleur-de-lis which it amused the street urchins to peel off. Half the grooms were still wearing the Emperor's livery. The procession looked like a masquerade – or a funeral. Here and there cries of *'Vive le Roi!'* were stirred up by the police. The crowd was curious and amazed. It applauded the Guard drummers, but discreetly, as if embarrassed to remember something – or someone – else. Nevertheless, they sounded better to Parisian ears than the Prussian, Russian, and Austrian bands.

The French are fickle, frivolous, and forgetful. 'A Frenchman is infatuated the first day, critical the second, and indifferent the third', wrote La Harpe who died in 1803.

'Who is that dressed as an English general?' queried the onlookers.

'The Duc d'Angoulême.'

'Come on, my friends', said Friant, 'you *must* cry "*Vive le Roi!*" '

A wag in the battalion cried: '*Vive* Desnager!' instead.

Who was he? The tavern keeper at La Courtille where they went on Sundays. He had just passed by in national guard uniform.

Soon, fearing a scandal, Friant ordered: 'Right by files!' and marched his Grumblers back to barracks.

Chateaubriand saw them – perhaps through a romantic haze – and wrote: 'I do not believe that human faces have ever worn such threatening and terrible expressions. These grenadiers covered with scars, these conquerors of Europe were forced to salute an old king, a veteran of years and not of war, while an army of Russians, Austrians, and Prussians looked on in the conquered capital of Napoleon. Some puckered their foreheads into a scowl that pulled their enormous fur bonnets down over their eyes, as if they did not want to look; others drew the corners of their mouths into grimaces of scorn and rage. When they presented arms they did it furiously. It must be admitted that no men were ever put to such a test, nor made to suffer greater torture . . .'

On 12 May the King published the following decree:

'The infantry of the Old Guard will form two regiments of three battalions, the first to be known as the Royal Corps of Grenadiers of France; the second, as the Royal Corps of Foot Chasseurs of France. The cavalry of the Old Guard will form four regiments called the Royal Corps of Cuirassiers of France, Royal Corps of Dragoons of France, Royal Corps of *Chasseurs à Cheval* of France, and Royal Corps of Light-horse-Lancers of France . . .

'Officers, noncommissioned officers, and soldiers of these corps will receive higher pay and allowances, in proportion to those fixed for the Old Guard. They will continue to enjoy their former privileges, and a higher rank in the army.'

On 21 October the Veterans' Company of the Old Guard became the 'Royal Company of Veterans of France', keeping its old uniform except that the buttons were stamped with three fleur-de-lis surmounted by a crown and the inscription '*Vétérans royaux de France*'.

The gunners and train soldiers whom Lallemand had not succeeded in transferring to the Royal Guard were sulky; however, Colbert had managed to save his lancers. The silent horse grenadiers protested against wearing helmets like everybody – or nearly everybody – else, and kept the bearskin bonnets, to which their hearts and prestige were attached, for the time being.

The foot chasseurs at Montargis grumbled on the day of the peace celebration when they read this doggerel posted on the Town Hall:

> '*Since to the King and to his crown*
> *We owe our peace and happiness,*
> *We must return his love no less,*
> *And he will never let us down.*'

The fusiliers, who had ranked as Old Guard, complained of their ostracism. On 9 June they, together with the Old Guard NCO's and soldiers in the *tirailleurs* and voltigeurs, were incorporated with the grenadiers and chasseurs. Each corps was given a white flag embroidered with the arms of France and the name of the regiment, and each battalion a guidon. Officers entitled to retirement for seniority or wounds were granted pensions.

The drummers wore the royal livery, but the grenadiers and chasseurs kept their old uniforms with new buttons stamped with fleur-de-lis. Their pay was much lower than before. On 20 May Marshal Oudinot was named 'Colonel General of the Royal Corps of Grenadiers and Chasseurs of France' (see Plate 149).

'The two grenadier regiments will be stationed at Fontainebleau and Nemours, and the two chasseurs regiments at Montargis and Courtenay', wrote the Minister. 'As soon as their organization is completed I shall order them to good garrisons at Metz and Nancy.' Why not Paris?

'Louis-Stanislas-Xavier does not trust the old of the Old', they muttered, 'so he is exiling them to the provinces.'

Oudinot's first task was choosing officers. He proposed Friant and Curial to command the grenadiers and chasseurs, seconded by Roguet and Michel. The roster included familiar names like Petit and Christiani as commandant and vice-commandant of the grenadiers, and Pelet and Poret de Morvan of the chasseurs. Golzio, Martenot, Belcourt, Lafargue, and Guillemin commanded battalions in the grenadiers, and Duuring, Colomban, Angelet, Cardinal, and Agnès in the chasseurs. Some, like Agnès, had served since 1802; others, like Colomban, since *brumaire* and the guides of Egypt. Captain Deleuze had served in the Guard since 1793 and, though only forty-four, was the senior grenadier officer.

They were all honorable men, brave and disciplined, who had worked hard and suffered to get where they were. Their epaulets and crosses had cost them several pints of blood. Though they were not remarkably intelligent, the Emperor, who had chosen each with care, had said ever since the Italian campaign: 'The first qualities of a soldier are steadfastness and discipline; talent is only secondary'. He never even mentioned intelligence, and the future proved him right.

He had left a stamp on them that ten years of suffering and glory had engraved on their souls. They might change their name and the color of their cockade but they could not change their character. If they suffered they suffered in silence.

France had loved them for the glory they won her. Once their swords were sheathed, should they be disdained and discarded? By consoling their sad fate, trusting them, and loving them, the new ruler could have learned to understand these men who, though they preserved the Emperor's image in their hearts and his cockade in the bottom of the caps, were nevertheless prepared to make the king respected because duty and honor demanded it, and because they were the Guard.

On 1 July Marshal Oudinot organized the corps at Fontainebleau and Montargis with identical reports: spirit – excellent; training – good; discipline – severe; type of men – superb; arms – in good condition; appearance – handsome; finances – low; clothing – poor. The corps had no stores of matériel, clothing, or equipment. As for quarters, they were billeted on the inhabitants.

Some 237 grenadiers were retired and placed on half-pay; also 45 officers, including Colonel Léglise, Captain Bernelle, and Lieutenant Sénot. The brave Colonel Robert was promoted general in October. Of the chasseurs, 220 men and 22 officers were discharged, including Lt. Colonel Pompéjac of the flankers for wounds; General Gros for his age, political opinions, and malapropisms; and Lt. Colonel Secrétan, the hero of Paris, because his list of brilliant qualifications ended with the fatal words 'no zeal for the King'.

The men boiled inwardly as the corps finally left for the 'good garrisons' Dupont had promised them. 'It's better to leave Paris', they said, 'since the King considers us brigands and prefers to be guarded by 6,000 Swiss, Chouans, émigrés, armchair soldiers, that traitor Marmont, and Nansouty turned *mousquetaire*'.

The King behaved as though he had been ruling them for the past eighteen years – as if the *Tondu* and his victories could be waved out of existence by a stroke of the pen! It was better to leave Fontainebleau where the new mayor and council thought 'it would be a severe punishment to lodge and feed the Royal Corps of Grenadiers'.

On 25 July His Royal Highness the Duke of Berry reviewed the corps of Grenadiers and Chasseurs of France at Fontainebleau and presented their colors. Had this military amateur been as tactful as he imagined he would have avoided aping the Emperor on this occasion. He had a geniune passion for the army and wished it to love him; but to address the grenadiers as 'thou', pull their ears, taste their soup, and question them brusquely in the manner of the Little Corporal was the royal road to failure.

The response of the troops was glacial. The flags were presented with the usual ceremonial. The newly revived Order of Saint-Louis was awarded to the generals, colonels, and other officers present, as well as to some who had left, like Pompéjac and Léglise, and the Order of the Lily was presented to all. Then, obviously infuriated by his reception and venting his spleen under his breath, His Royal Highness beat a hasty retreat without eliciting any response from the Grumblers beyond a few surreptitious smiles.

Meanwhile, the horse Guard had been given a month's pay from the Emperor's stolen treasure. So Napoleon continued to finance the Guard – even in exile!

Ney experienced difficulties and delays in organizing the royal cavalry corps. The colonels were busy taking inventories of men, horses, and stores. The latter had been evacuated, hidden, or looted and were scattered all over the country.

Before leaving Paris, many quartermasters had stored part of their clothing reserve with private individuals. Many deserters had left with their arms and equipment. All the accounts were in 'frightful disorder'. The inspectors were still writing briefs on the subject five years later.

A white silk standard blazoned with the arms of France was presented to each corps except the dragoons who were given a guidon. All but the cuirassiers retained their old uniforms. The latter wore blue coats without revers, like the Line, trimmed with scarlet, with white cuff flaps, yellow grenades on the skirt flaps, and fleur-de-lis buttons. Marshal Ney ordered the officers to wear moustaches.

On 19 November the officers were appointed: Lt. General Guyot was named colonel in chief of the cuirassiers, with Major General Jamin as vice; Lefebvre-Desnoëttes and Lion held these posts in the chasseurs, and Ornano and Letort in the dragoons.

Naturally Colbert headed the light-horse-lancers. His 2nd Lancers was in a peculiar position. Recruited in 1810 from the Royal Dutch Guard, it had belonged unofficially to the Middle, and some of its officers to the Old, Guard. Later the Emperor added five Young Guard squadrons, ranking the five veteran squadrons as Old Guard without increasing their pay and allowances. At the time of the abdication the regiment had detachments scattered all over.

In short, its only Old Guard elements were a motley collection of Dutchmen (many of them homesick), *vélites* rated as 'bad soldiers' by Colbert, and 'even more worthless' guards of honor. 'However', he wrote the Minister, 'there are many Line NCO's who had entered the Old Guard as privates. During the war the Emperor transferred them as NCO's to my Young Guard squadrons. They do not want to return to the Line and would be useful to the Royal Corps of Lancers . . . If these Young Guardsmen are discharged they will be an incalculable loss.' (He failed to add that without the Young Guard, the Royal Corps of Lancers would cease to exist.)

Colbert, who once said that 'the art of succeeding was simply the art of daring', concluded: 'I should like to know whether I shall be retained.'

He was – and his appointment on 24 August preceded all others.

Marshal Ney organized the new corps on 2 August. There were not enough men, the horses were mediocre, and the clothing was worn and motley, including bits and scraps of uniforms of the guards of honor, scouts, lancers of Berg, etc. The tack and equipment were delapidated. Musketoons, lances, and more than 300 pistols were lacking. The accounts were chaotic, and the magazines as empty as the treasury. The quarters at Orléans were poorly ventilated and the stables inadequate. But the spirit was good, the discipline strict, and the bread and forage of good quality.

Ney had confidence in Colbert whom he termed 'a consummate officer of the greatest distinction'. At thirty-nine, Colbert had a magnificent record.

The vice-commander, Lt. Colonel du Bois de La Ferrière, a Hollander and a charter member of the corps, had to wait until the end of the year for his stars. Among the majors the Dutchman van Ticken and the Corsican Coti were retained. Captain Brack, a graduate of Fontainebleau, we shall meet later on. Fourteen Dutch officers asked to go home and were replaced by Mameluk officers, including Major Renno and Captain Abdallah.

The dragoons were presented by General Ornano. 'The men are very handsome; the horses fine, strong, and well cared for. The officers, NCO's, and soldiers are animated by an excellent spirit, perfect discipline, and have a splendid appearance', the Marshal reported, adding that the clothing and equipment needed repair and the troopers were lacking two pairs of grey overalls, but that the clothing magazines were well stocked. 'The barracks are not much to look at, but are well kept. The stables are ample and sanitary.'

In spite of his rank, Lt. General Letort was named vice commander. How could one separate Letort from the dragoons without causing a mutiny? Majors François, Sachon, and Chamorin were retained, also Captains Ligier, de Montarby and Despierres. Twenty-eight officers were retired, including Lt. Colonel Pinteville for wounds, Lt. Colonel Hoffmayer and Major Pictet for lack of seniority, and General Chouard. The dragoons thought that the King was retaining them only through fear. Why had he lowered their pay? Now, in the Emperor's time . . .

'I beg you, *Monsieur le Comte*, to garrison the Chasseurs of France at Saumur', wrote Marshal Ney to the Minister on 30 July, the day of their organization review. 'The civil authorities have asked this as a favor . . . The spirit of the regiment is excellent. Its discipline and obedience have earned it the admiration and affection of the inhabitants. The soldiers know their business . . . and are handsome in build and appearance. Their clothing is practically new and perfectly maintained. The tack and equipment are complete, in good condition, and very well kept. The barracks and stables are excellent. Only the beds are mediocre. The horses are beautiful and of a good type.'

The regiment still owed the horse dealers at Caen 131,000 francs, dating back to 1813; but thanks to the foresight of their clothing officer, who had hidden the stores, there were plenty of dolmans, colpacks, cloth, and braid, which accounts for the 'practically new' clothing.

The Emperor had created a special esprit de corps in his horse chasseurs and its officers and men were exceptional. The Marshal felt obliged to retain most of them. Major Kirmann, ex-commander of the Mameluks, had been a hussar under Louis XVI, and Major Rabusson had served since 1796. Among the captains were Maziaux, Sève, and Barbanègre. General Dautancourt and Lieutenant Brice were attached without assignments. Major Lafitte transferred to the King's Hussars.

Majors Bellebaux and Cayre, and Captain Chahin' of the Mameluks, as well as some worn-out NCO's and chasseurs were invalided out; 240 foreign[2] NCO's, chasseurs, and Mameluks were retired, and 192 given medical discharges. Since the rest exceeded the specified number, Marshal Ney proposed that 31 be transferred to the *gendarmerie*.

Either the Marshal knew little about the chasseurs, or else he was an optimist. Did he know that during their last review in June on the Champ-de-Mars three-fourths of the troopers had refused to cry '*Vive le Roi*'? Or that their noon assembly ended regularly with '*Vive l'Empereur*'? Had he recommended Saumur as their garrison so these subversive utterances should not reach the royal ear?

When the Duke of Angoulême came to review the chasseurs and award them the Order of the Lily he expressed his satisfaction by raising their pay 5 sous. The chasseurs pocketed the money but were not seduced.

On 4 November, her husband's birthday, Countess Desnoëttes gave a dinner of two hundred which the sub-prefect did not dare attend. The speeches and toasts were so seditious that the squadrons were promptly dispersed through the neighboring villages, and the regiment moved to Cambrai at the beginning of 1815.

Lieutenant Brice was named adjutant major on 14 November, though only last March the Emperor had sent him to Lorraine to raise a guerilla band against the Allies and royalists. Returning to the regiment after fulfilling his mission, Brice became his colonel's devoted assistant in keeping the sacred fire burning in the squadrons.

[2] From former French departments in the Rhineland, Italy, the Low Countries, Switzerland, etc. which had regained their independence. – Ed.

Last came the 'gods', the supreme reserve, whose privileged position the whole army – and even the Guard – had envied. The corps of Royal Cuirassiers was organized at Blois on 23 July by Marshal Ney,who now signed his orders 'Duke of Elchingen' to avoid offending the sensibilities of the Tsar.[3]

Ney's praise of the corps' spirit and conduct was unstinting. Among the officers, Majors Venières, Pernet, and Delaporte had fought in twenty-three or more campaigns. Twenty-three men were invalided out, and 124 foreigners repatriated. The officers put on half-pay included General Castex, and Majors Rémy, d'Harembert, and Testot-Ferry.

Marshal Soult replaced Dupont as Minister of War at the end of the year. In December he decided to send the royal cavalry corps up north to the military district commanded by Mortier, where they would be appreciated. The prefects of police had warned against leaving these regiments too long in one garrison for fear of subverting the inhabitants.

The Cuirassiers of France marched off to Saint-Omer in undress coats and bearskin bonnets, some of which looked rather mangy. For lack of proper accommodations, they were moved to Arras on 15 December.

By now many officers of the ex-Guard were on half-pay, which meant poverty for the captains who had to live on 73 francs a month, and worse for the lieutenants who drew 44. The fortunes of those Guard generals not serving in the Royal Corps, and those of the Young Guard, varied according to their connections, conscience, opinions, and their talent for expressing – or hiding – the latter. Henrion, Sebastiani, Castex, Gros, Dautancourt, Charrière, Bauduin, Le Capitaine, Corbineau, and Chastel were all on half-pay. 'You talk too much', a high official told Boulart who was a member of the artillery committee.

General Meunier, whose division had been disbanded in March, was given command of the 14th Military Division at Caen. Boyer de Rebeval commanded the Aube, but was dismissed in January together with Darriule from the Haute-Pyrénées. Meuziau was made an inspector of cavalry, and Charpentier a commissioner. Audenarde was commissioned lieutenant in the *Garde du Corps*. General Count de la Ferrière was given command of the cavalry school at Saumur.

Nearly all were decorated sooner or later with the Order of Saint-Louis and, from afar, with stars of the Legion of Honor. During the campaign of 1814 the Emperor had created 3,580 chevaliers, but had granted only twenty-six decorations in the higher ranks. The royal government had to depreciate this institution it could not abolish. At the Duke of Berry's suggestion, the profile of its founder was replaced on the insignia by that of Henri IV.

The Guard lived poorly despite the Te Deums and flags, illuminations and processions. The ministry allotted the foot grenadiers 50,000 francs, and the chasseurs 70,000, to 'improve' their clothing and equipment. They no longer rated cloth of the best – or even the second-best – quality. Captains might not issue a pair of pantaloons to their

[3] Ney's title of 'Prince de la Moscowa' commemorated his part in the defeat of the Russian armies at Borodino in 1812. – Ed.

men without an order from the administrative council and a visit from an assistant inspector who alone was credited with enough intelligence to 'decide whether the (old) article was no longer serviceable'.

There was no money except to clothe, mount, and maintain the *Maison du Roi*, which cost 20 millions, and pay 211 new generals who, since the army was much smaller, were only time-servers.

The soldiers of the ex-Guard were not paid. Some asked to be discharged. 'Why do you want to leave when in two years you will have a pension?' the Duke of Berry asked a chasseur with 28 years' service.

'Because we have lost our father', was the reply.

On 15 August Saint Napoleon was fêted in the canteens and his health was drunk, but on the 25th – the King's birthday – the brandy casks were drained in silence.

That winter the people, the army, and the whole scowling Guard thought of the Emperor. The ranks of the new corps dwindled. The grenadiers lost 495 men and the chasseurs 177. The Minister was obliged to fill up the regiments with veterans from the Line and officers who had never been heard of on the battlefield.

While waiting for assignment, Major General Count de Tromelin was attached with the rank of assistant commandant to the grenadiers. He was a conscientious man and a good soldier. A sub-lieutenant in the Limousin regiment in 1791, he had emigrated in the Revolution and campaigned in Egypt with the Turks and English. Then he joined the Emperor, won promotions at Wagram and in Croatia, and was chief of staff to General Morand who had been isolated in Mainz during the last campaign. A royalist by tradition, Tromelin was by conviction a liberal and a patriot.

If his grenadiers did not all prefer the lily to the eagle, what had the regime done to attract these men who owed everything to the Emperor? The Count of Artois played deplorable politics and the nation was becoming exasperated. During an audience with Artois, who had known and decorated him in exile, Tromelin said:

'Monsieur will permit me to tell him respectfully that he is being deceived – that France is irritated. This could lead to catastrophe. Some day the French may again conduct to the frontier all these people who want to return to a past that ceased to exist in 1789 . . .'

'Well – what about me?' replied Artois, laughing heartily. 'If I am one of the party, would you cross the frontier with me?'

'May Your Royal Highness forgive me', replied Tromelin. 'If I could only return with Prussian and Russian armies and Cossacks – no. I would not cross, and I should defend my country again from invasion.'

'Madman!' concluded the future Charles X.

Nevertheless, Tromelin heard the grenadiers talk of 'Jean de l'Epée' and 'Père la Violette'[4] at the beginning of 1815. He would come back . . .

Meanwhile, at Portoferráio the grenadiers of the Elba battalion sat by the sea and smoked their pipes in silence, looking out towards the northwest . . .

---

[4] Underground names for Napoleon after the abdication. – Ed.

CHAPTER 3

The Guard at Elba

AFTER a 750-mile trek via Lyons, the Mont-Cenis pass, and Savona, at last the Elba Battalion joined Napoleon in his island retreat.

Captain Laborde, commanding the vanguard, had arranged for food and lodging with the armies of occupation which were mostly deferential, and the inhabitants who were always friendly. The Battalion entered the villages under arms with drums beating. Sometimes they had disputes with the Austrians but Cambronne settled them peacefully. The Lyonnais cried *'Vive l'Empereur!'* more lustily than ever and the populace was thrilled to see the Grumblers, wearing their tricolor cockades, march by.

'Where are you going?' they asked.

'We are going to join the Emperor.'

On 18 May at Savona the Battalion – now encumbered with the Emperor's horses and carriages – prepared to embark on five English boats which were to take them to Elba. Meanwhile, Cambronne sent Laborde ahead to announce their arrival to the Emperor.

While the English dined the officers, the soldiers danced, sang, and drank the Emperor's health, leaving their companions only at dawn to board the transports.

At Portoferráio Laborde was welcomed by Inspector Peyrusse and presented to the Emperor. Napoleon plied him with questions. When would the rest arrive?

The Emperor scanned the sea anxiously each morning.

Finally, on 26 May 'he trembled with joy', for there were the Grumblers whom he had left thirty-five days before. Accompanied by the Grand Marshal (Bertrand) and General Drouot, he went down to the landing to meet them. At last the gig ferrying Cambronne and his officers reached the shore.

'Cambronne', said Napoleon, holding out his hand, 'I have had some bad moments waiting for you, but now that we are together again all is forgotten.'

Pons de l'Hérault wrote: 'Cambronne was in the seventh heaven', and the old soldiers, their homely mugs 'wet with tears of joy', were in ecstasy. They formed a square on the Place d'Armes and listened with feeling to the Emperor's welcome:

'Officers and soldiers, I have been awaiting you impatiently, and I congratulate myself on your arrival. I thank you for sharing my fate. I find you noble representatives of the Grand Army. We shall make wishes together for our dear France, the mother country, and rejoice in her happiness. Live in harmony with the people of Elba. They have French hearts . . .'

Then they broke ranks and went to their quarters in Fort Étoile, beside the 'palace' at the Moulin bastion, and at the Saint Francis barracks in town.

That evening the officers of the Guard dined with His Majesty while the men amused themselves with the new sights, drank the excellent native wine, and sang, shouted, and danced in the general euphoria of their reunion with the Emperor.

Elba was a place of repose for the Emperor and the Guard. Sixty-five miles in perimeter, it had 12,000 inhabitants. The land was dry, hilly, and rich in iron ore which was exported from the village of Rio. The crops were scanty but the vineyards were lush. From white wine and local herbs was made a vermouth much prized by connoisseurs, of which there were several in the Guard. Good fish was caught in abundance. Though luxury – or even comfort – were unknown to the natives, the seaside towns of Porto-ferráio and Porto Longone were picturesque and hospitable and teeming with olive-skinned maidens in white bodices and bright-colored skirts.

Now that the orphans had found their father again, and the father his children, what else mattered? True, on arrival they had felt a momentary pang at changing their cockade; for the Grumblers now wore the Emperor's, which was white with gold bees in a red circle. 'Bah! they will sting one day', a grenadier observed. Each man kept his old cockade hidden in the bottom of his bonnet and prayed God to let him wear it again one day.

The Napoleon Battalion under Major Malet was composed of a staff and six companies mustering 607 grenadiers and chasseurs. It was given a white flag with on one side a diagonal red stripe emblazoned with three gold bees and on the other a crowned 'N'.

The cavalry, except for five chasseurs and Mameluks with two NCO's and Lieutenant Seraphin, was composed of Polish lancers. Lt. Colonel Jerzmanowski divided it into two companies – a mounted company of 22 troopers under Captain Schultz, a good-natured giant of seven-foot-one, and a dismounted company of 96 light-horsemen under Captain Balinski who had served with the French since 1807. Thirty-five turned over their horses to the Emperor and joined Cornuel's 43 gunners.

The squadron was given a standard with the inscription 'Polish Light-Horse, Napoleon Squadron' embroidered in crimson on a white ground with, on the reverse, a crowned 'N' like that on the shabracks of the Polish lancers of the Guard. Major Roul, an old friend of the Emperor's, commanded the cavalry. He had served in the 13th Hussars in 1793 and had fought the campaigns of Italy and Egypt in the Guides of Bonaparte. Wounded at Malta and Acre, and again severely at Eylau as a chasseur of the Guard, he had been invalided out in 1810.

The 21 marines were attached to the Elba navy, consisting of the brig *Inconstant*, three small boats, and three gigs. Lieutenant Taillade, commanding the brig, lay prostrate with seasickness in his cabin most of the time.

General Cambronne held the posts of commander of the Guard, commandant of the garrisons at Portoferráio and Palmaiola, and president of the Sanitary Commission. General Drouot was governor of the island.

The Emperor made out a budget consonant with his income from the island and the state of his treasury. Strict economy was indicated since the Guard was larger than anticipated. The infantry cost 224,000 francs, including 180,000 francs for wages, 40,000 for clothing, 2,000 for lodging the officers, and 2,000 for bread. The cavalry cost 33,000 francs, the artillery 37,900, and the marines 26,000.

Napoleon found a garrison at Elba consisting of the 35th *Légère* and a battalion of the Italian Colonial Regiment, recruited from the fine flower of the Calabrian streets. Among the officers of the former were Major Guasco, an old Corsican Volunteer of 1792, Captain Arrighi di Corti, a cousin of the General who was now Duke of Padua, and Captain Hivert, a 50-year-old veteran.

Napoleon decided to form a Corsican chasseur battalion under Major Guasco, and offered a captaincy to any man bringing in forty recruits, and a lieutenancy for bringing in thirty. Some young blades produced a few Corsicans (but more Tuscans, Genoese, and Hungarians) and claimed their epaulets.

Three small companies were raised with difficulty. They soon dwindled through desertion, leaving the cadres almost as numerous as the rank and file. In a moment of weakness the Emperor designated one an elite company with higher pay. Another battalion was raised of so-called 'Corsican militia'.

Since the island afforded no resources, a captain of the Guard was sent to Naples for uniforms. He was cordially received by King Murat, loaded with gifts, and given everything necessary. For economy's sake the three battalions had a single clothing depot and magazine. A hospital with two surgeons, two physicians, and two pharmacists was organized.

The Emperor made out the duty schedule himself. There were daily parades on the Place d'Armes before the 'palace', as at the Tuileries. They were attended by the authorities, and many natives came to watch the grenadiers drill.

One hundred grenadiers and 40 volunteer chasseurs were assigned to the guard which posted 35 sentries, including two at the 'palace'. The post at the Porte de Terre was large and well-organized. Major Roul, carrying a brace of loaded pistols, and two mounted lancers escorted the Emperor each day. The cavalry furnished sentries at the stables in Tonara.

The marines, armed with sabers and muskets, manned the Emperor's barge. They were issued straw hats and canvas suits to spare their uniforms.

The Emperor farmed the island of Pianosa, twenty miles south of Elba. A detachment of Poles and gunners, relieved every three months, guarded it against the Barbary pirates. The island was also used as a place of detention.

A small garrison was established at Porto Longone. Several grenadiers worked on the roads and in the gardens at San Martino, the Emperor's little country villa which they called 'Saint-Cloud' and which he visited almost daily. The rest of the troops were drilled under the Emperor's personal supervision.

He saw to everything, distributing rice to keep the vineyards from being harvested prematurely, visiting the barracks where he poked the mattresses, tasted the soup, and inspected the stables. He talked to the Grumblers at parades, asking news of their families and of France to keep up their morale. He was gay, joining in every activity, attending the wedding ball of one of his marines, questioning the soldiers on the gossip of the town, and inviting the officers to dine.

'Wait till they are ripe', he said one day to some Grumblers caught stealing grapes from his vineyard. 'And you ask why we were devoted to him!' Lieutenant Bacheville exclaimed.

Bertrand and Drouot complained of the discipline, but Napoleon knew his grenadiers. If they were bored they would leave. He needed a band to liven the parades and cheer up the garrison. Maestro Gaudiano collected seven or eight virtuosi of the serpent, clarinet, etc, hired a pianist, and formed a small orchestra. His daughter and a companion sang at all the festivities.

The guardroom was very popular. Malet provided fourteen pairs of fencing foils, with gloves and masks. The Emperor attended a shooting competition where a watch worth 36 francs was the first prize. Every important occasion was celebrated. When Madame Mère arrived at the Casa Vantini a reception was given to the officers. The town of Portoferráio entertained the Guard in a large tent on the Place d'Armes, and the Guard gave a party for the notables of both sexes at Fort Étoile. The fêtes always ended with a ball at which the girls, decked with flowers and long earrings, performed Tuscan dances.

The patronal festival of San Cristino was celebrated with great gusto, and the whole town, the Guard, and the Elba national guard celebrated the Emperor's birthday on 15 August. The windows were decorated with draperies and the streets strewn with flowers. The Guard rendered honors in the church for the Te Deum, and salvos were fired by the Poles who had become accomplished gunners. There were horse races in which the cavalry and stable personnel competed against the Elbans on their wild horses.

An evening concert at which *What Better than to Be Home with Your Family?* and the *Marseillaise* were sung was followed by a great ball which warmed up old flirtations and sparked new ones. A hearty supper, at which two British officers got roaring drunk, ended the festivities. By tradition, the gunners of the Guard had prepared fireworks, but the Emperor was afraid of accidents. He asked that they be saved for the Empress' arrival.

She was expected any day.

Captain Hurault de Sorbée was married to one of her ladies in waiting. 'You love your wife', the Emperor said to him one day. 'I offer you the chance to see her again. The *Inconstant* is sailing for Genoa. Drouot will give you a passport. From Genoa you will go to Turin, and on to Aix where you will find the Empress. Your wife is with her.

'Tell her that I have had no letter from her, and that it is cruel to leave me without any news of my son. The Austrian emperor should not be a party to such inhumanity. You will find a sort of jailer with Marie-Louise, Field Marshal Neipperg who calls himself her *'chevalier d'honneur'*. But you will also find Baron de Méneval and the Marquise de Brignole who are trusted friends. You will come back and tell me what sort of reception you had. The brig will wait for you in Genoa.'

The Pavillion Marciano was prepared and the days passed. Finally, at dawn on 22 September the grenadiers were lined up in full dress with ordered arms, and the artillery manned their guns for a salute. But then the orders were countermanded. However, a woman and child were seen at Marciano. After they left it was learned that these were the Countess Walewska and her son.

Meanwhile, Hurault managed to reach Aix. Méneval was away and Madame de Brignole, instead of taking him to the Empress, informed Neipperg who had him arrested and sent to the Ministry of Police in Paris. He was an important prisoner. The King was consulted and forbade him to return to Elba; but he was permitted to visit Vienna where Marie-Louise had gone meanwhile.

Early in 1815 Hurault arrived at Schönbrunn where the Empress received him. He saw the King of Rome who called him 'Papa's soldier'. He spent several days there with his wife, spied on by the police. Meanwhile the *Inconstant* grew tired of waiting and returned to Elba.

The Emperor soon grew bored. He tried to fill up his auxiliary battalions, and Drouot to discipline them, to no avail. The battalions dwindled through desertion and brigandage. The Grumblers kept an eye on these adventurers to see that no traitors or spies bent on assassinating the Emperor infiltrated their ranks.

Towards the year's end the Grumblers' mood changed in the monotony of life in exile. They were haunted by fears of the Emperor's assassination or kidnapping. In passing around his snuffbox, Napoleon told them 'they must take life as it came'; though some claimed to have heard him murmur: 'This won't last forever.'

Strange tales went the rounds of the guardroom at the Porte de Terre. They had never seen so many foreigners landing. The *Auberge Sauvage* was full, and the *Hôtel Bouroux* was as crammed with beds as Dr Eméry's hospital. Everyone wanted to be presented to the Emperor. Over the protests of Cambronne, he received them all. The foreigners brought him news of Vienna, Italy, and Europe. Girls came from Naples, Greece, and Hungary to seek their fortune, or spy, or snare an officer. But few French came because no passports to Elba were being issued in Paris.

Two old foot chasseurs who came from France to join the Battalion reported that at home things were going from bad to worse. People cried *'Vive l'Empereur!'* in the theatre. Twenty thousand officers, covered with scars, were begging their bread while gilded gallants watched over the 'fat pig', as Chouard, the old commandant of the Guard dragoons, called the King.

Vraincourt, a native of Verdun, wrote his family that he 'received 23 sous a day which is *paid*, if you please!' and that the Emperor 'loved them as his eyes'. The reply he received was read and discussed in the guardroom and at the canteen while the Grumblers smoked and drank vermouth:

'I loved you much moor since I knew you were with our fathful Empror. That's the way onest foke should act. I believe you when you say they come from 4 corners of the erth to see him becaus here they came from 4 corners of the town to read your letter, and evryone says you are a man of oner. The bourbons are not the end and we don't like these gentlemen. The Marmont has been killed in a dule. I have no news except that I pray God and make your sister pray for the Empror and King.'

The Emperor needed it. Obsessed with black thoughts at the end of that terrible year, he confided his fears to his suite. Would his enemies try to kill him, to abduct him so they could send him far away? The guns were emplaced, and the men recalled from leave and ordered to remain at their posts with weapons loaded. The atmosphere of fear and despair weighed on the Guard which became ferocious.

The Emperor was in financial straits and was obliged to cut down his standard of living. Impoverished officers arrived from time to time and asked to serve him. Some were attached to the Guard as supernumeraries, but he could no longer afford their pay. These unfortunates agreed to live in the battalion as simple soldiers – some even at their own expense. Napoleon could not reward this devotion 'with what remained'.

In October he wrote Bertrand: 'I intend to distribute the land I own around the salt marshes among my Guard. I shall give the officers . . . two acres freehold for themselves and their children . . .'

Princess Pauline had organized parties and theatrical performances with properties the Battalion had dragged across the Alps, but now the Emperor had to restrain her.[1]

Boinod, former chief comptroller of the Army of Italy, arrived to manage the Emperor's finances. No one had asked him to; but he was a man of 'the old stamp' who had known Napoleon since Toulon and had served him in Italy and Egypt. After the abdication he left for his native Switzerland where he had installed his family and then come to offer his services to Napoleon.

The budget for 1815 was reduced because the two millions of income guaranteed by the treaty of Fontainebleau had not been paid. Talleyrand wrote Bertrand that Louis XVIII did not recognize the treaty. The treasury was dwindling and the future looked dark.

The Guard battalion was reduced to two companies of chasseurs and two of grenadiers. Thirty men who wished to go home were given honorable discharges. 'I recommend that you pay close attention to the service certificates . . . for the grenadiers who are leaving, and see that they are made out to their greatest advantage . . .' the Emperor wrote Drouot, giving him minute instructions as to the wording. 'Those who are dismissed for cause will receive yellow certificates. Have a form printed with my arms . . . omitting the words "Sovereign of the island of Elba" which is ridiculous.'

None of them thought of deserting, but all were somewhat sobered by the monotony of their existence, the poverty of the country, and the Emperor's brooding silences. Some officers and soldiers married Elbans and planned to settle there. Their pay was reduced. The lodging allowance was discontinued. The captains were assigned rooms in the Porte-Neuve barracks; the lieutenants, a room for two.

As the carnival approached 'Jean de l'Epée' – as the Grumblers called Napoleon – cheered up. His boats plied back and forth to the mainland, bringing news, taking messengers, and keeping him informed. Surgeon Eméry received strange messages,

[1] Recent research suggests that she also made a strategic assignation on the mainland with Col. Campbell, the English observer, leading him to quit Elba at the critical moment. – Ed.

hidden in bales of goods consigned to Genoese merchants, from his friend Dumoulin, a glover in Grenoble.

Ney had said to Louis XVIII: 'Change the name of the Imperial Guard to the Royal Guard and your throne will be secure'. But the King did not heed his advice, and Fouché predicted that 'spring would bring back Bonaparte, along with the swallows and violets'.

In the guardroom of the Porte de Terre the Grumblers pricked up their ears at the rumors going round. The sentry at the palace had seen someone, or a lancer of the escort heard something. They were going to Egypt, as before, and on to Constantinople where the Grand Turk was in on the secret. Then they would march up the Danube. Good. The Greeks and a Polish army were joining them, and before they knew it they would be in Vienna. Good. There they would dissolve the Congress and make themselves at home. They would guard Schönbrunn where the *Tondu* would live as before. Then they would leave for France and go to the Tuileries, and all Paris would cry '*Vive l'Empereur!*'

The Grumblers' itinerary was somewhat more circuitous than the Emperor's, but its destination was the same. Actually, whether inspired by his friends who wished to be rid of the Bourbons, his enemies who wished to make an end of him, or his increasing financial straits, Napoleon's real plan was known to no one.

Drouot was thinking of getting married. The Grenadiers, at the first sign of spring, were laying siege to the local girls. For the opening of the carnival Princess Pauline organized a costume ball at which Malet, astride one of the Emperor's horses, appeared as the Sultan and Captain Schultz as Don Quixote, to whom he bore a striking resemblance. When Gaudiano's musicians closed the fête with a rendition of *The Sacred Love of Country*, the spies noticed that the Emperor was annoyed.

He ordered his carriages packed up, since 'we use them so little', and had the flotilla inspected and the crews filled. But this was apparently seasonal, for he also ordered work done on his summer villas at San Martino and Rio.

On 20 February Drouot learned that Peyrusse was having 'coffers made to carry gold', was packing the library, and had stopped paying the troops.

That day Napoleon drilled the Corsican battalion and made a speech. Next day he ordered green uniforms for the first three companies and blue for the fourth, and admitted to the Guard a dozen NCO's and twenty chasseurs with good conduct records.

The Grumblers were issued new coats and two pairs of shoes apiece. The Emperor told the master saddler to 'examine his campaign saddle and put it in order', and gave orders to watch the corvette *Partridge* that had taken Colonel Campbell to Leghorn, and see that it did not return.

A bark called the *Saint-Esprit* from Marseilles arrived to take shelter in a storm. On 25 February Jerzmanowski was ordered to put his lancers on board with their saddles and gear. Peyrusse paid 25,000 francs for their passage. Meanwhile, Pauline gave a ball.

The next day, Sunday, the Guard posts were relieved by a volunteer battalion, and there was a meeting of the commanders at the palace after Mass.

The grenadiers stowed their packs, ate their soup at four o'clock, and waited. Today was the day . . .

To Arms was beaten at 7 p.m. Amid cries of '*Vive l'Empereur!*' and 'Paris or die!' they embarked in the vessels *Inconstant, Étoile, Caroline, Saint-Joseph, and Saint-Esprit* and the feluccas *Fly* and *Bee*, lent by Pons de l'Hérault, director of the Rio mines.

Between decks on the *Inconstant* all the Grumblers who could write painfully copied the following proclamation:

'The generals, officers, and soldiers of the Imperial Guard to the generals, officers, and soldiers of the Army:

'Comrades and soldiers: We have rescued your Emperor from all the traps set for him, and are bringing him back to you from across the sea amid a thousand dangers. We have landed on the sacred soil of France wearing the national cockade and the Imperial eagle. Trample the white one under foot, for the Bourbons' short reign has convinced you that they have forgotten nothing and learned nothing . . . Those who took up arms against their country and against us are now the heroes, and you are the rebels . . . They have deprived us of the political privileges we bought with our blood . . . They have sent to England 400 millions that belonged to us and to the Army as the prize of victory.

'Soldiers, the General Alarm is sounding and we are on the march. To arms! Rally round your Emperor and the eagles with their tricolor flags!'

The proclamation had been signed by all the officers, NCO's, and soldiers of the Elba Guard, and by Drouot as 'Aide-Major General of the Guard'.

Copies were to be circulated when they landed in France, because France could not live without the *Tondu*. When they had followed him 'across the seas' a year ago, they knew that one day they would be asked to come back and free the country from the Tyrant. Now France would owe the Emperor's return to the Old Guard.

The old soldiers were children who still believed in public gratitude. These hard-boiled nomads of glory, unconcerned with everything that did not concern 'him', kept silent, rocked in the cradle of their dreams, proud of their mission, and happy about this new adventure with the Emperor. Six hundred humble men were presuming to dictate their duty to the whole army, because they were the last survivors of the Imperial Guard.

That night the Emperor left a governor on the island with a sum of money and thirty light-horse. Then he bade the Elbans goodbye and boarded his barge. The coxswain shoved off and the marines rowed him out to the *Inconstant*.

Drouot was anxious and Cambronne very worried. Napoleon was greeted by forty officers and officials who had asked to accompany him, and wildly cheered by 400 grenadiers. The other 200 were on the *Étoile*; the 40 gunners with 8 pieces, the horses and carriages, the cavalry, and 300 Corsican chasseurs – now called 'flankers of Elba' – had boarded the other vessels.

The night was luminous, and the moon shone on the harbor. A shot from the *Inconstant* gave the signal for departure. At midnight the Eagle and his eaglets began their flight to Notre-Dame (see Plate 151).

At that moment in Metz, Marshal Oudinot and his Duchess were entertaining the civil and military authorities at the Hôtel de la Princerie. At the height of the party General de Tromelin took the Marshal aside and warned him that a revolt was brewing in Lorraine. Oudinot had other worries at the moment. To silence this bird of ill-omen he asked him for a written report.

This is what Tromelin wrote:

'Metz, 4 March, 1815

'It can no longer be denied that the public shows increasing signs of discontent . . .

'In 1789 the nobility stupidly opposed the will of the vast majority . . . and the results of the ensuing struggle could easily be foreseen. The minority, exiled and despoiled, took its grievances . . . to Europe which engaged in a futile war in its behalf.

'Ten years later the same nobles were only too glad to recognize the victor as their ruler, and accept an amnesty which seemed no hardship . . . after ten years of exile and poverty . . . After 19 *brumaire* the First Consul brought under control a terrible revolution. He suppressed all parties and calmed all hatred by working for the interests of all. By building up a strong public opinion in his favor, he was able to accomplish great things.

'The émigrés owed him their repatriation, the Vendée its pacification, the Church its reconciliation, the revolutionists their political rights, and the nation its glory. Thus the First Consul consolidated his power by following public opinion, and the Emperor Napoleon fell only when he began to disregard it . . .

'The émigrés had already lost their party identity when a new revolution blinded them to their true situation . . . When the Powers permitted the French to choose a new master, all eyes turned to the old dynasty . . .

'The King's declaration of 2 May satisfied all, leading them to believe that misfortune had taught the Bourbons to forget the past and conform to the times and the will of the majority. Supposing, on the contrary, that the recall of the Bourbons confirmed them in their ancient privileges, the émigrés alone complained about the King's declaration and spoke aginst the charter . . .

'At first the King had the strength of character to resist their sad pretensions, but little by little his principles yielded to family affection. How could he refuse when the Comte d'Artois or the Duchesse d'Angoulême demanded posts for persons who had sacrificed all for their noble family? . . . Soon every sub-prefecture was coveted by some self-styled servant of the king. New officials were appointed to pay these debts, casting suspicion upon the King's good faith.

'The men of the Revolution . . . are closing ranks . . . and preparing to fight. The stupidity of their adversaries is strengthening their hand . . . No reasonable man believes that the present situation can last.

'The most gross insults are heaped upon the army . . . and its glory held up to ridicule. As for the administration, it is almost entirely new. The courts are uncertain about their fate. The clergy is divided on the Concordat. The proprietors of lands and businesses are ranged in opposing camps. The nation's glory is tarnished . . .'

The report stops there, unfinished. As Tromelin laid down his pen news came that the Emperor had landed at Golfe-Juan.

PLATE 149

Royal Grenadiers of France
(From a colored lithograph by Charlet)

PLATE 150

Le Printemps de 1815.

THE SPRING OF 1815. The Bonapartists tend their bees while the Royalists water their wilting lilies

(From a contemporary colored caricature)

PLATE 151

Voyage from Elba in the *Inconstant*
(From an original watercolor by Jules Vernet)

PLATE 152

PLATE 153

BOOK X

THE GUARD DIES

CHAPTER 1

The Flight of the Eagle

THE first act of the drama that still astounds the world lasted five days. The voyage was uneventful. Once a French vessel passed close aboard the *Inconstant* and the grenadiers took off their bonnets and lay flat on deck.

At dawn on 1 March Cap d'Antibes loomed to starboard. The Emperor came on deck in his legendary costume, wearing a tricolor cockade, and the grenadiers removed their Elba insignia and followed suit. The flotilla made colors, rounded the cape about 3 p.m. and entered the passage east of Formigue, dropping anchor in the splendid theatre of Golfe-Juan. With the Vallauris mountains and the Vallée d'Or ahead, under the lofty Maritime Alps; the Lerins Islands and La Croisette on the left; and the olive-bordered plain of Ilette on the right, under terraced orange groves dotted with potter's furnaces and an occasional fisherman's dwelling, surely this is the most beautiful spot in the world.

Twenty-one years before, Napoleon had spent a fortnight at Fort Carré in Antibes. Later, while visiting his mother and sister at the Château Salé, the old men of the country recognized him as he trotted through the woods on his grey horse to La Gabelle on the Gulf. He knew that this point was defended by the Foucade battery, between La Gabelle and La Croisette, and that there was a hidden battery near the Gabelous[1] tower; but he also knew that both had been dismantled. However, there might be an over-zealous customs official . . .

Captain Lamouret jumped into a boat with twenty grenadiers and came ashore, to the horror of the customs official who brandished the health regulations in their faces (see Plate 153).

'But it's the Emperor!' said Lamouret. 'He can issue permits . . .'

'Isn't this cockade more becoming to you?' asked a grenadier, attaching the tricolor to the official's hat.

General Drouot arrived in the second load with Captain Bertrand, in civilian clothes, who went off to Antibes to see the commandant, distribute proclamations, and procure blank passports. Meanwhile, Lamouret posted sentries on the roads to Antibes, Vallauris, and Cannes. Then he followed Bertrand with a dozen grenadiers, expecting to pull off a brilliant coup.

At the Porte Royale the Grumblers cried *'Vive l'Empereur!'* and parleyed with the guard, previously alerted by Bertrand's arrival. The colonel gave Lamouret permission

---

[1] *Gabelle* is the French word for salt tax, or storehouse for taxable salt, and *gabelous* for the customs officers who collected the tax. – Ed.

to enter with his men. But then the drawbridge was raised behind them and they faced an armed battalion of the 87th Regiment.

The affair had begun badly. After blows and many words, the grenadiers were marched off to barracks and disarmed, and Lamouret was imprisoned. Later he jumped off the ramparts trying to escape and broke his leg.

By 5 p.m. the landing took place under the Gabelle tower. The guns and horses were brought ashore; Peyrusse's treasure was loaded on a cart bought from a potter for 60 *napoléons*.

Finally, cheered by the Grumblers, the Emperor was rowed from the *Inconstant* in an eight-oared barge, landing from a gangplank put out by the marines in water up to their waists.

The 'palace' had been prepared in a cottage at the end of a sunken road bordered with centenary olives. The road connected the beach with the imperial road from Cannes to Antibes. The Emperor's campaign chair and camp bed were brought to the door, but His Majesty objected to the smoky interior and had them placed outdoors under the olives.[2]

After a nap Napoleon sent a captain of the Guard to the house of a retired Corsican officer to announce his arrival and alert the local partisans. The grenadiers ate their soup. Lieutenant Franconin distributed 15 francs to each and the Emperor gave the signal for departure (see Plate 152).

'Cambronne, you shall command the vanguard in my finest campaign', he said. 'You will go on ahead – always ahead. But remember that I forbid one drop of French blood to be shed to recover my crown.'

Cambronne set out with fifty grenadiers, followed around midnight by the Emperor and his small column, now reinforced by a lieutenant and some soldiers of the 87th Regiment, a staff captain and soldiers from the Antibes garrison, and three half-pay officers of the 11th Cuirassiers. These formed the nucleus of the famous 'Sacred Battalions'.

At 2 a.m. the mayor of Cannes – a prudent man who obeyed the 'Elect of France' – provided 1,700 rations of bread and meat which were brought to the bivouac on the beach, near the present church of Notre-Dame. Here the soldiers lit fires and the peasants, halting at a respectful distance, came to watch. (They had been told that some brigands had landed.)

After the affair at Antibes the grenadiers wondered how it would all end. Then a young optimist, covered with gold braid, rode up. A former postillion of the imperial stables, he was now a courier for the Prince of Monaco. He reported that everyone in Paris was crying '*Vive l'Empereur!*' and that the people and the army were all for Napoleon. 'No one will stop you', he said. 'I can see you in the Tuileries already . . .'

As soon as the moon rose the drums beat the *Diane* and the column set off. Abandoning their cannon en route, the troops took the road to Castellane. It was very bad;

---

[2] A memorial column, whose first stone was laid on 1 March 1815 by the officers of the 87th Regiment, still stands by the roadside. About 30 yards from the olive grove a bust of Napoleon was erected in 1853, destroyed in 1871, and replaced in 1932 by Mr and Mrs Alfred Pardee of Cannes.

snow had fallen and the mud was a foot deep. The light-horse, encumbered with boots, lances, and sabers, carried their saddles on their heads and hung their *czapkas* around their necks. They sounded like itinerant ironmongers as they clanked along. The Emperor fell and there was laughter. But it was cold, and the time had come to get organized.

Cambronne, in the van, sent a message ahead to the sub-prefect at Castellane to procure 5,000 rations, and either 40 four-horse carts or 200 donkeys. The soldiers, with more than fifty kilometers in their legs already, could no longer drag Peyrusse's coffers.

With a blank passport furnished by the mayor of Castellane, Surgeon Eméry hid some proclamations in his boots and left for Grenoble to announce the Emperor's arrival to Dumoulin and his friends. He made slow progress on the tortuous and rocky donkey track to Digne, a walled town clustered about a cathedral, and just missed being captured there by the prefect. Then he struck out for Gap, a scant hour ahead of Cambronne.

Saturday, 4 March, was market day in Digne. The peasants had been coming into town since dawn and the garrison and officials had fled. At noon the beat of drums was heard. Preceded by Polish lancers and followed by officers and grenadiers, who kept back the curious, the Emperor entered by the Rue de la Mère de Dieu which was so narrow that two horsemen could not ride abreast in it.

He had a cool reception. In the crowded market place a few cries of '*Vive l'Empereur!*' were heard, but they came from the grenadiers who occupied the courtyard of the *Arès* tavern while the Emperor went to lunch at the *Hôtel du Petit-Paris*. Neither the mayor nor the prefect showed up; however, several half-pay officers came to pay their respects.

Major Jullien, an Old Guard veteran who had fought in Egypt, had come to his native town to be married. He later rallied his regiment, the 39th Line garrisoned at Embrun, to the Emperor.

After lunch the grenadiers fraternized with the inhabitants and went shopping. The officers had proclamations printed, bought horses for themselves and half the lancers, and rented twenty carts to carry the baggage.

At 8.30 p.m. the Emperor mounted his horse. Followed by detached officers, whose number had now tripled, he set out for Sisteron as the crowd watched in silence. Only the children echoed the grenadiers' cries of '*Vive l'Empereur!*' One lone citizen brought him an eagle for his flag and another kissed his hand.

A few peasants followed the column which was led by the Polish lancers; then came Malet with two companies of Old Guard chasseurs, Captain Loubers and his grenadiers, the detached officers surrounding the Emperor, and the staff with the treasure. Major Guasco and the Elba Flankers brought up the rear (see Plate 154a).

Drouot waited in Digne for the proclamations and the laggards while Cambronne and the vanguard went ahead. So far there was little enthusiasm. Some mountaineers brought provisions and a few bottles of wine, but no one dared commit himself.

The troops expected to find resistance at Sisteron, but thanks to a forced march by Cambronne, who reached the town at 2 a.m. on 5 March, not a shot was fired when the

Emperor passed through and went on to Gap. Next day Drouot left Sisteron with bands of royalists at his heels.

Not until he entered Upaix, on the road to Gap, was the Emperor cheered with fervor. There, surrounded by delegations led by mayors in tricolor scarves, he marched through the town at the head of a gay and picturesque procession. The mayor of Upaix, an old hussar officer, marched at his side, followed by a swarm of detached officers in mufti or partial uniform riding burros and braying donkeys, and the grenadiers, singing.

Next morning the Grumblers split their sides laughing at the nightmare the prefect of the Hautes-Alpes had had on the eve of their arrival. He dreamed he was in bloody combat with enemies who gave no quarter. Bonaparte was with them. 'He flew at me, sword in hand', the prefect related, 'and I had only a dagger. We fell to the ground and rolled over and over, first one on top and then the other. Finally my wife was awakened by my extraordinary gyrations and muffled cries, and woke me. I was in a cold sweat and so paralysed with fear that I never closed my eyes again . . .'

While Napoleon was marching to Gap the prefect departed for an unknown destination.

At eleven on the night of the 5th all the people were at their windows, giving Gap the appearance of being illuminated for Napoleon's arrival. 'There he is!' cried a peasant, comparing his profile with the one on a 5-franc piece. The population was more friendly than the administration. Cambronne had engaged lodgings for the Emperor at the inn. Bonfires were lighted on the Place Saint-Étienne.

With his prefect gone, the secretary-general did not know how to act; but since the municipal council paid the Emperor a visit, the secretary followed suit. He described the scene outside the inn as follows:

'Drawn up in two files to guard the Emperor were the poor, decorated soldiers, their scarred faces as happy as if they had won a great victory. They had such confidence in their master that it never crossed their mind that there could be the slightest obstacle in the path . . . of the man who had just landed in France as an enemy. They laughed at everything and enjoyed everything . . .'

On taking leave of him, Napoleon said: 'I shall be in Paris on 20 March'. Perhaps the Grumblers were right.

By now the proclamation had spread throughout Dauphiné and the authorities were beside themselves. At this moment Louis XVIII was informed by telegraph of Bonaparte's landing. Flahaut, Caulaincourt, and Lavalette feared he would 'not get five miles before being hung'. Fouché notified General Lallemand, brother of the commandant of the Guard artillery, at Laon. Lallemand left on the 6th for Lille whose garrison, in Mortier's district, was commanded by Drouet d'Erlon, and advised Drouet to send his troops to Paris without delay.

On the 8th the Royal Cuirassiers at Arras mounted their horses. From Cambrai Lefebvre-Desnoëttes marched the Royal Chasseurs to La Fère where the other Lallemand donned full dress to break the news to the remnants of the Guard artillery.

At a review in Orléans on the 10th, when Marshal Gouvion-Saint-Cyr and General Dupont exhorted the garrison to side with the King against Napoleon, they were booed, threatened, and chased out of town. Then the Guard lancers, cuirassiers, and infantry rushed to the Porte Saint-Jean, broke the barriers, and started for Paris.

At Vienna the violinists who were playing as the Congress danced stopped the music, their bows in mid-air. He had returned!

Napoleon was approaching Grenoble. Cambronne had been burning up the roads. The day of decision was 7 March.

Generals Marchand, Mouton-Duvernet, etc. had concentrated their forces around Grenoble. They had put the bridges and passes into a state of defense, made speeches, and posted proclamations. The latter had been surcharged by unknown hands with the slogan that Cambronne made famous later on the field of Waterloo.[3]

The Emperor sent Captain Raoul of the Guard artillery ahead to La Mure where he was received by Major Lansard's battalion of the 5th Line Regiment. Laborde proposed in vain that the soldiers of his vanguard and the garrison have a drink together.

Lansard retired with his battalion to Laffrey, the defile guarding the approaches to Grenoble.

The Emperor reached La Mure the morning of the 7th with a crowd which the grenadiers – who had been well wined by the inhabitants – held back with difficulty. Warned by couriers from Cambronne, he decided to go on to Laffrey where he found Lansard's battalion barring the way. An agitated captain began to hurl threats and insults at him.

Leaving the light-horse and chasseurs behind with their weapons at 'secure', the Emperor advanced as the Guard's proclamation was read to the troops. Then, approaching within range of the Line voltigeurs, he said:

'If there is any man among you who wants to kill his Emperor, here I am.'

Captain Randon (who became a marshal of France under Napoleon III) shouted: 'Fire!'

Nothing happened. He overheard a voltigeur say: 'The dumb bastard! If we fired, *he's* not the one we'd shoot.' Then another: 'We would be s-o-b-s to harm a man who has done us nothing but good . . .' (see Plate 154b).

They tossed their white cockades into the air and soldiers and civilians shouted '*Vive l'Empereur!*' Lansard, in tears, offered his sword in surrender while a soldier rattled the ramrod in the barrel of his musket to show the crowd it was not loaded.

At this point Dumoulin, alerted by Surgeon Eméry, galloped out from Grenoble bringing '100,000 francs and his strong right arm' to the Emperor.

'Now all is well', Napoleon told Drouot. 'In ten days we shall be in the Tuileries.'

That evening Cambronne and the vanguard were welcomed at the gates of Grenoble by the 7th Infantry whose young colonel La Bedoyère had preserved his eagle.

'Open in the name of the Emperor!' Raoul called out, but the gunners posted on the ramparts did not stir. 'Are your plums any good?' teased the grenadiers.

'Not for you!' replied the gunners.

[3] '*Merde!*' according to Victor Hugo. – Ed.

The gate was forced by the 'people of Grenoble'. An immense crowd appeared, screaming and shouting. '*We have some apples for the King of Rome*', sang a *cantinière*. The Elba Battalion and the lancers were surrounded and cheered by the 7th and 11th Regiments, the 4th Hussars, the 3rd Engineers, and the 4th Artillery in which Bonaparte had served twenty-five years before.

Saluted by fanfares, Napoleon dismounted at the *Hôtel des Trois Dauphins* whose proprietor was an old guide of Italy. At eleven next morning a grand review of the garrison was held on the Place Grenette before an enthusiastic crowd. The 'adventurer Napoleon' was now Emperor once more.

What could the Count of Artois possibly do at Lyons? Though the Emperor had insisted that 'not a drop of French blood be shed', the Imperial army now contained six regiments numbering 8,000 men, and 30 guns with teams. In addition to the Elba troops, the Guard had been reinforced by nearly 1,000 officers and NCO's whom Drouot attempted to organize into battalions.

The first NCO company mustered 55 sergeants and sergeant majors. The nucleus of the 1st Light Infantry was formed with Young Guard officers. Other units were made up of officers and NCO's of the national guard, medical officers, and inspectors. Some former guards of honor were admitted to the Napoleon Squadron. Meanwhile, recruits from the Midi were forming in the rear.

Hearing that General Brayer was expecting him at Lyons, the Emperor, preceded by Cambronne and the vanguard without ammunition, left Grenoble the afternoon of the 9th.

Next day he entered Lyons amid cheers and illuminations and dismounted before the Archbishop's palace. The whole garrison had come over to his side, and the Count of Artois and the Duke of Taranto (Macdonald) had fled to Paris.

In the north the Emperor's adherents ran into difficulty. On 9 March at La Fère, where Lallemand had been demobilizing the Guard artillery for the past eight months, Lefebvre-Desnoëttes and the Chasseurs of France presented themselves at the gates 'unannounced and without marching papers'.

'Were I in your place, I should refuse to admit them', General d'Aboville advised the perplexed commandant. That was all very well; but no one knew for sure who was ruling, the King or the Emperor! The regiment was traveling on the orders of Count Drouet d'Erlon, the commandant of Lille, and the men were very tired.

The chasseurs spread out over town and Lefebvre-Desnoëttes and his officers went to the post house for supper.

Early next morning Major Bosquet of the ex-Guard artillery entered the barracks and announced that the Emperor had been recognized at Paris, and that the King had been assassinated and a provisional government formed.

But the King of France never dies. What about Monsieur? Dead, too. His sons? All dead. So the Revolution was beginning all over again ... 'Who told you?'

'General Lallemand. He has given orders to re-form the regiment and load the caissons. Count d'Erlon has been summoned to Paris. He has left Lille with 16,000 men and has ordered us to join him at the crossroads at Gonesse, beyond Senlis ...'

At this point Colonel Marin and Captain Charpentier, on half-pay from the Guard artillery, appeared in full dress; then General Lallemand himself. (His brother had already arrived from Laon with an infantry battalion.)

Four batteries were assembled at the city gates. Lallemand tried to take them out but Bosquet called them back, reminding them of their duty to serve the king.

Meanwhile, the trumpeters of the chasseurs sounded Boots and Saddles. At a brisk trot they escaped and headed for the crossroads where all the troops of Mortier's district had been ordered to assemble. En route, Lefebvre-Desnoëttes was joined by an artillery column from Vincennes and a squadron of the King's Dragoons at Chauny. But the Cuirassiers of France did not reach the rendezvous.

There had been a hitch. The inopportune arrival of Marshal Mortier at Lille had frustrated d'Erlon's plans. D'Erlon was shut up in the citadel and his troops sent back to their garrisons.

Nevertheless, Lefebvre-Desnoëttes persisted in his plan to join the Emperor. The Lallemands, Captains Brice, and Colonel Marin agreed; however, General Lion and several officers refused to continue without orders and led the regiment back to Cambrai.

Several days later the Duke of Orléans, accompanied by Marshal Mortier, reviewed the Chasseurs of France at Cambrai. The future Louis-Philippe wrote in his memoirs:

'Finding General Lion outside the city with an escort of Royal Chasseurs, I mounted my horse and went with the Marshal of Treviso to the main square of Cambrai to review the regiment . . . The people's enthusiasm did not alter the temper of the troops who kept silent . . . While almost all had ripped the fleur-de-lis off their sabretaches, I noticed that some still wore them in their buttonholes, and that the officers were wearing them correctly.

'I never saw a finer regiment, nor smarter or better turned-out troops . . . Their uniforms were not new, but I was amazed to find them in such good condition considering . . . that everything I saw had been through the last campaign. The Mameluks, wearing crescents in their turbans, paraded at their head. I asked if there were any Egyptians among them, but was told that they were all French.

'As the regiment marched past I thought of the great mistake the King had made in not having surrounded himself with the Old Guard from the beginning . . . If, instead of alienating them at every opportunity, he had honestly applied himself to winning their devotion, what a difference it would have made! Troops like these devoted to the royal cause would have been far more useful to him than the *Gardes du Corps* and *Mousquetaires*.'

As the popular ovation prevented the Duke from 'calling up the officers', he invited them to meet him at the Archbishop's palace after the review.

'When General Lion presented them to me I began by paying them compliments on the military reputation of their corps . . . I told them I was pleased to find in their fidelity to Napoleon, while he was their chief and the chief of state, a guarantee of the service they would render King Louis XVIII against his enemies at home and abroad, regardless of their personal feelings . . . But they kept silent.'

Notwithstanding the turbulence of their colonel in chief, the chasseurs were disciplined.

Lefebvre-Desnoëttes, Marin, Brice and the two Lallemands had all fled. The last two were arrested and imprisoned at Soissons. Desnoëttes reached Chalons in civilian dress and took refuge with the commandant. After hiding in a garret in Épernay, Brice returned to his corps to find that a warrant had been issued for his arrest; however, his chasseurs cheered him and swore on their naked sabers to defend him. Only Marin succeeded in joining the Emperor at Auxerre. The cavalry of the Guard had missed the bus.

Meanwhile, the infantry made plans to leave its garrisons. Oudinot ordered the Royal Grenadiers and Chasseurs to Paris 'to be near His Majesty'. Which one?

'The King depends upon the fidelity of the soldiers of the Imperial Guard which glories in being the model for every army' said the Duke of Reggio. But no one was fooled by these honeyed words. 'He is laying it on thick today', said the grenadiers.

In the King's name, Oudinot promised promotion to all the officers and a subaltern's epaulet to all the Grumblers. It was too late. The Grumblers at Metz and Nancy replied:

> 'Roll your ball, King Cotillon,
> Give up your crown to Napoléon . . .'

On the 13th they were ordered to Langres, via Pont-à-Mousson, Toul, Colombey, Neufchâteau, Bourmont, and Montigny, to block the usurper's march. But, as a grenadier corporal put it: 'It's not enough to tell 'em, you got to make 'em do it!'

On that day at Lyons the Emperor abolished the *Maison du Roi*, ordered the regiments of grenadiers, chasseurs, and fusiliers re-formed, and dissolved the Royal Corps.

On the night of 15 March the grenadiers stacked arms on the Place d'Armes of Toul where Oudinot was to review them next day. He planned to close the review with a short speech, ending '*Vive le Roi!*'

'You can try it, *Monsieur le Maréchal* . . .' said Old Man Roguet skeptically. At the hotel, which was full of officers, the two discussed the testimony of General Tromelin who had been roaming round town for the past two hours, and reported that the officers and men had decided to join the Emperor by the shortest route.

After trying to dissuade them, Curial asked his officers at lunch if they still recognized him as their colonel. The answer was: 'On condition that you lead us to the Emperor'. When he hesitated, Poret de Morvan took command and Michel followed at a day's march with the third and fourth battalions.

Next day, instead of taking the road to Colombey they marched up the Meuse to Neufchâteau. At Valcouleurs the officers met with the Emperor's emissaries and decided to take the troops to join the Emperor at Sens. This meant doubling their marches, but they were used to that.

Oudinot retired anxiously to his place at Jean d'Heurs while the Guard spent the night of the 17th at Chaumont. Next morning the Grumblers put on tricolor cockades.

Meanwhile, the Emperor had arrived before Auxerre in his calèche, followed by an escort of Polish light-horse. A trooper led Tauris, the Emperor's dapple-grey Persian charger that had campaigned with him in Russia, Germany, and France. Peasants, workmen, women, and children carrying flags and wearing tricolor cockades cheered Napoleon along the route. Beyond Vermanton the party formed a procession led by the prefect's carriage, followed by Drouot's coach. Then came the Emperor with Bertrand and the Polish lancers, wearing their white plumes and carrying crimson and white lance pennants. Jerzmanowski and Duchand, the artillery commander, rode at the carriage doors. Two coaches with the servants and suite ended the parade.

Napoleon wore the sword of Austerlitz on the belt with a diamond buckle that his mother had given him the day he left Elba. Cambronne had left his vanguard to come by water, or by wagon from Lyons, but the detached officers were more numerous than ever. Those attached to the Guard now formed a full platoon.

The Emperor's army comprised three divisions under Generals Jeanin, Brayer, and Girard. The 'Sacred Battalions' were so numerous that Inspector Boinod had not time to enroll them. Companies of NCO's, commissary stewards, medical attendants, and employees of the magazines were mixed helter-skelter; the first contained 177 NCO's; the battalion, thirteen companies in all. Now everyone wanted to join it.

The Emperor received Marshal Ney who had changed sides twice in the past two days. He also reviewed the 14th Infantry under Colonel Bugeaud, the former *vélite*-grenadier, and appointed Captain Coigniet, the Grumbler who had taught Bugeaud the manual of arms at Courbevoie in 1804, quartermaster of the palace and chief wagonmaster of Imperial Headquarters. 'I laughed myself silly', the old soldier recorded.

At the end of this triumphal day the Elba phalanx arrived with drums beating. Moustachioed and wearing queues and gold earrings, the chasseurs and grenadiers paraded in blue overcoats, their sleeves covered with chevrons. Their march was slowed to the pace of the artillery, and brightened by the guidon of honor and victory that the Lyonnais had brought back to the Emperor on 13 March.

The flankers were traveling on foot and did not arrive at Auxerre until 1 April. The Old Guard battalion made only a short stay there, leaving next day by water for Paris.

The evening of 18 March the Emperor entertained the prefect, Drouot, Cambronne, La Bedoyère, Brayer, Jerzmanowski, and Mouton-Duvernet at dinner at Auxerre and the band played *Let Us Watch over the Empire*.

The next day was Palm Sunday. As the bells rang out early that morning the Emperor left the Prefecture, followed by his escort, and disappeared on the road to Sens.

Next morning at Villeneuve-la-Guyard the mayor, who had greeted the Emperor at 2 a.m., was confronted by General Curial who demanded vehicles to transport his 'division'.

Curial had finally decided to take command of the Royal Chasseurs who were leading the Old Guard from Toul. After marching 90 kilometers to Chaumont in thirty-six hours, they traveled 'by post'. Surely this was no novelty to the Grumblers; but this time the transport was operating without official sanction, and most of the prefects were hostile. By charm or persuasion the vanguard had to win over the mayors to obtain wagons and relays. They could pay the drivers nothing but promises.

Nevertheless, beating all records, the chasseurs and grenadiers left Chaumont on 18 March with their indispensable cadres and matériel and arrived at Villeneuve the 20th, having covered 180 kilometers. They were exhausted and famished. Worse, they had missed the Emperor who was hurrying to Paris.

That evening at 9 p.m. the Emperor's carriage passed through the gates of the Carrousel. The troopers of his escort shouted and brandished their sabers. The crowd was so thick that the postillions had to halt at the gateway leading to the Pavillon de Flore. Torn from his carriage and carried on a human palanquin into the Tuileries, Napoleon was greeted respectfully by the courtiers, in full dress, who had deserted and insulted him less than a year before.

The King and his household had fled to the north the night before. Tonight the Emperor was frantically cheered by the people of Paris in a delirium of joy – the same Parisians who only last April had consigned him to the devil. Such are the eternal French!

CHAPTER 2

The Restoration of the Guard

AT noon on 21 March the Elba Grumblers took the right of the line as the troops massed in the court of the Carrousel. At 1 p.m. the Emperor appeared and passed down the ranks. After the review he addressed the regiments formed in a square around him:

'Soldiers, counting on the affection of the people and the memory of the old soldiers, I came to France with 600 men. I was not deceived. Soldiers, I thank you . . .' Then he added: 'We count on you – the people and I. We do not wish to interfere in the affairs of other countries, but woe to those who interfere in ours!'

There were long cheers from the spectators and soldiers; then the Emperor made a sign and Cambronne appeared, followed by the officers of the Elba Battalion 'with the old eagles of the Guard' which they held in front of the grenadiers. Mastering his emotion, Napoleon pointed to the faithful phalanx.

'Here are the officers of the battalion that shared my misfortune', he said. 'They are all my friends. Every time I looked at them my heart was touched because, to me, they symbolized the whole army. These six hundred braves from many regiments reminded me of the great days whose memory is so precious. They all bear honorable scars from . . . those memorable battles. In loving them, I loved all you soldiers of the French Army.

'They have brought you back your eagles. Use them as your rallying point. In presenting the eagles to the Guard, I present them to the whole army. Treason and misfortune have put them into mourning. Swear that they will ever be found where the Fatherland calls them . . .'

'We swear!' shouted the soldiers.

It was urgent to direct this enthusiasm compounded of joy, anger, bitterness, and hate into proper channels. It was just as urgent to gain recognition in three-fourths of the departments where the King still reigned; to restore the tricolor cockade, reassure the men on half-pay, and appease those thirsting for vengeance against the 'traitors' – both real and imaginary.

On 22 March the Emperor decreed: 'The Imperial Guard's functions and privileges are hereby restored: it will no longer be recruited from any source other than men who have served in the armies of France.' Twelve years' service was required for the infantry, eight for other branches, and four for the Young Guard.

This fulfilled the hopes of the veterans herding sheep or tending pigeons; of the gunners buried in the Line, and the train soldiers, marines, and gendarmes.

Marshal Davout, the old colonel in chief of the foot grenadiers, was Minister of War, which was good. The brothers Lallemand were freed, and Lefebvre-Desnoëttes came out of hiding. Marmont had naturally fled; Victor, who had once begged the Emperor to let him serve as a grenadier, had also decamped. But there were no traitors in the grenadiers.

In the confusion no one at the Ministry knew where the Guard regiments were. Neither Dériot at the École Militaire, nor Davout could find the cavalry that had been turned back on its way to Paris. The Emperor wanted the whole Guard to join him immediately. Finally, the Royal Cuirassiers – who had never worn cuirasses – got the word at Ham, and Guyot re-baptized them 'horse grenadiers'. The chasseurs turned up at Saint-Quentin, Colbert's light-horse at Angerville, and the dragoons were eventually located at Tours.

The foot grenadiers removed the fleur-de-lis from the Bonaparte barracks. On their barracks in the Rue Babylone the chasseurs carved eagles that looked like pigeons and traced wobbly 'N's, but their intentions were good.

The Elba Battalion looked down on everybody. Their chant: 'It was *us* who brought him back' closed the mouths of all contenders. While the others were busy replacing their white cockades with the tricolor, the Elbans still wore the 'cuckoo' on their bonnets, pouches, and buttons. This earned them the right to occupy the old barracks of the *Cent-Suisse*, nearest the Emperor, in the Carrousel. These had been completely sacked, but over the door was carved the legend: 'The Home of the Brave'.

In the Célestin barracks Jerzmanowski's light-horse was less grand, but just as uncomfortable, in twelve small rooms 'without beds, tables, or benches'. The troopers slept on straw. Half the horses were jammed into one small stable, and the rest left out.

'But we are the Guard!' stormed Lefebvre-Desnoëttes in whose barracks were neither shelves for gear, racks for arms, 'pegs to hang saddles on', nor accommodations for the 150 chasseurs from the depot who arrived from Saumur.

'The horse grenadiers will post pickets as before; the duty squadron will occupy the Eugène barracks.' When Guyot found it full of lancers and chasseurs – a sacrilege! – Colbert moved his lancers discreetly to Versailles.

During the Emperor's review on 24 March a body of horse, covered with mud, trotted through the gate and raised sabers, crying '*Vive l'Empereur!*' These were Letort's dragoons who had been separated from the *Tondu* for a whole year.

Hurault de Sorbée had returned the previous night from Vienna. Refused a passport by the French Ambassador, he had been arrested, questioned, and released several times en route. That night he had a long interview with the Emperor, bringing him news of Marie-Louise, the King of Rome, and the Congress. All of it was bad. The Empress would remain in Vienna. The sovereigns had signed a treaty of alliance.

Outlawed from Europe and menaced by rulers determined on his downfall, Napoleon had to rebuild the army. But his throne was not yet secure and conscription was unpopular. On 26 March five observation corps were echeloned from Lille to Strasbourg, others posted in the Alps and the Pyrenees, and one held in reserve in Paris. Carnot, the Minister of the Interior, was reorganizing the national guard; and Davout, seven divisions of heavy cavalry, arms factories, remounts, and the home defense.

On the 28th Napoleon recalled all discharged soldiers of the Guard and created twelve regiments of *tirailleurs* and voltigeurs. Immediately, a stream of soldiers, NCO's, and officers swamped the barracks and the ministry.

'All my Old Guard is with me', Napoleon wrote Marie-Louise that night. 'I am waiting for you. Be in Strasbourg with my son between 15 and 20 April.'

The next day Friant wrote Dériot: 'I have ordered all grenadiers who wish to serve in the Old and Young Guards to come to the Courbevoie barracks. When you have some *tirailleur*-grenadiers, I shall send them to Rueil and appoint officers and NCO's to command them.' Curial did the same for the chasseurs at the École Militaire. The surgeons examined the men and Drouot reviewed the NCO's.

The foreign situation grew steadily worse. On 1 April the Emperor wrote each sovereign in turn that he desired peace; yet on the 4th the Duke of Wellington arrived in Brussels to take command of the Anglo-Dutch forces in Belgium, and the Prussian Army of the Lower Rhine set up headquarters at Aix.

On the 8th Napoleon decreed the organization of the Guard as follows: the grenadier corps was to contain three Old Guard regiments and six of *tirailleurs*; the chasseurs, three Old Guard regiments and six of voltigeurs. The 3rd Grenadiers and 3rd Chasseurs replaced the fusiliers. The horse grenadiers, chasseurs, dragoons, and light-horse were each to have four squadrons, and a company of elite gendarmes was formed.

The artillery was fixed at six foot and four horse companies, plus a company of artificers, and eight train companies. The corps was to have 72 guns, including 32 twelve-pounders of the reserve. The Old Guard would also have a company of sappers, four wagon train companies, and a crew of marines.

Drouot was appointed Aide-Major of the Guard. Friant retained command of the grenadiers, with Roguet as vice. Poret de Morvan hoped to replace Curial in command of the chasseurs, but on 13 April the Emperor wrote Drouot: 'Since I cannot permit Curial to command the chasseurs, I have appointed General Morand in his place . . . Had Curial served in the Line, I should have paid no attention to his proclamation against me; but he belonged to the Guard, so I cannot keep him. Ask him what command he would like in the Line and it will be given to him.'[1]

The Emperor expected loyalty and devotion from the commanders of his Guard. These, as well as valor, were present in Morand, a veteran of Egypt who had been cited at Auerstädt and wounded in every battle since. His vice-commander was Michel. His rival Poret was given command of the 3rd Grenadiers.

Guyot, Ornano, Desnoëttes, and Colbert retained their cavalry commands, and Desvaux de Saint-Maurice resumed the command of the Guard artillery that he had held in Russia and Saxony. Colonel Boissonnet commanded the engineers, and Dautancourt the elite gendarmes.

The Old Guard resumed its duty at the palace, 'as before'. It was obsessed with those words. The Grumblers longed to revive the receptions, reviews, and triumphal entries of the old days; to wipe out past humiliations and be glorious – as before. They could

---

[1] He was made governor of Rambouillet and commandant of the military district, under Suchet.

erase the fleur-de-lis; they could recall the tune of an old song and the number of their muskets, but they could not recall the past.

The Emperor knew this and changed the constitution. Though it had taken him only twenty-five days to re-establish his authority in France, he sensed that it was tentative; therefore, despite the threats from abroad and the weakness of the army, he did not dare order a conscription, but confined himself to recalling discharged soldiers and forming elite battalions of the national guard.

As in 1813, he counted on the Young Guard, and as always, on the Old. But infantry was hard to recruit. The decree called for 35,000. Notwithstanding the initial enthusiasm, not all the discharged veterans returned. Some had been spoiled by civil life.

A levy of two officers and twenty men from each Line regiment, added to the Royal Corps and the Elba Battalion, proved inadequate for the Old Guard. The 1st Regiments were filled up with men with twelve years' service from the 2nd; and the 2nd, with old fusiliers and eight-year veterans from the Line. Young Guard veterans and men with four years' service in the Line formed the 3rd Regiments. The Young Guard was recruited with difficulty from retired men, volunteers, and Corsican flankers.

The cavalry was nearly complete. By recalling their old soldiers and making serious inroads into the Line, the artillery, engineers, wagon train, artisans, and medical service could be organized, given enough time.

The situation in Europe spurred the Emperor to feverish activity; but the temper of his men had changed. The Old Guard regiments were no longer homogeneous. An intimacy had grown up at Elba between the Emperor and the Grumblers, and now their gloom of the past months had given way to the pride of triumph. Clinging to their old habits and traditions, the Elba Grumblers were unchanged. They felt a certain scorn for the Royal Corps whose men *had* changed. Once the Emperor had left, those fatalistic veterans would have served the King loyally had he trusted them instead of banishing them to exile and poverty. Their disillusion had left them skeptical and moodily resigned.

The old camaraderie of the Guard was replaced by suspicion. Moreover, the men had seen some of their commanders – Oudinot, Curial, and even Friant – grovel before a throne they had fought to abolish, and this had shaken their faith in their chiefs. But in the end, with the Line soldiers who felt privileged to enter the Guard, their old comrades returned to don a worn cloak and a bald bearskin at the *Tondu's* call. 'Things were better in the old days', they said. Civil life had softened their muscles and changed their ideas; nevertheless, they had had the honor to serve in the Guard, and one did not forget that.

The old spell worked quickly on the patched-up Guard of 1815. The soldiers, who met without recognition in an atmosphere of mistrust, had nevertheless a common passion for the Emperor – a touchy, jealous, violent passion which had increased with age. He should beware of those who now courted him after having betrayed him. He should beware of the marshals who had been shown up at Fontainebleau. On the subject of the *Tondu*, at least, all the Guard was in agreement.

PLATE 154

a) Napoleon's march through the Var
(*Contemp. colored print by Friedrich Campe*)

b) Napoleon before Grenoble
(*From a lithograph by Hippolyte Bellangé*)

PLATE 155

a) Duc d'Orléans
(*Lith. Delpech after Dupré*)

b) Drouet d'Erlon
(*Engr. Réville*)

c) François Lallemand
(*Col. engraving by Legrand after Mullard*)

d) Bugeaud
(*Lith. by A. Bès*)

e) Tromelin
(*After portrait; Collection Comte de Botmiliau*)

PLATE 156

PLATE 157

a) Napoleon in 1815
(*Contemp. engraving*)

b) Pelet
(*Engr. Bouchaudy*)

c) Duhèsme
(*Aquatint by Levachez after Chinard*)

d) Grouchy
(*Engr. Joly*)

e) Poret de Morvan
(*Engr. Forestier*)

PLATE 158

a) Hanoverians at Waterloo: infantry, rifleman, hussar

b) Officer, English light dragoons

(From original wash drawings by Charles Hamilton Smith)

PLATE 159

Wellington
(*From an anonymous drawing c.1811*)

PLATE 160

a) Napoleon with General Haxo   b) Horse gunner of the Guard at Waterloo

(From original watercolors by James Thiriar)

The touchiness, tempered by discipline, of the Old Guard exasperated the Young. Friant complained that the *tirailleurs* 'made noisy demonstrations and went out with girls'. Barrois received a joint petition saying that 1,374 soldiers of the 1st and 2nd Line Regiments who had served in the Guard wanted to return, and had informed their colonel that if in four days their wish were not granted, they would desert.

The officers should restore order – but they were in the same mood as the men. The old half-pay officers were in a feverish hurry to recover their lost privileges and obtain vengeance. Some serving in the Royal Corps had feared the consequences of the Emperor's return. Why had he come back? There had been peace . . .

No, one could not bring back the past!

By the end of April Europe was in arms, France an entrenched camp, Paris a factory, and the war ministry a hell. The Guard was reorganizing slowly. Despite everyone's activity and willingness the days had but twenty-four hours. Clothing was the dominant problem. The magazines were practically empty.

Chief Inspector Boinod was a peerless administrator; nevertheless, he had to clothe 2,456 grenadiers, chasseurs, troopers, and gunners by 1 May. The merchants were swamped with orders, and deliveries were slow.

On the eve of a review the drum major of the grenadiers felt himself dishonored. He had no full dress hat. The hatter was commanded to produce one in twenty-four hours. Pressed for time, the Emperor, colonels, and administrative councils signed contracts without asking for bids, or even knowing what they signed. The Restoration – and even the dead and those who went over to the enemy – were billed for these later.

General van Merlen, vice-commander of the 2nd Lancers, had returned to his native Holland in 1814. He was killed leading a brigade of Belgo-Dutch cavalry at Waterloo. Yet in 1818 he was condemned – in Paradise – to reimburse the French Treasury 1,537.19 francs or be severely punished.

Who could bargain for clothing in April 1815? No one could predict that the Emperor's second reign would last exactly ninety-four days . . .

In Rueil and Paris, where the first five regiments of *tirailleurs* and voltigeurs were being organized, food and clothing were scarce and 'everything was performed in haste and confusion', according to Lt. Colonel Secrétan of the 1st Voltigeurs. When the cadres were appointed on 13 April, many officers failed to show up at the depots.

In the cavalry the chief problem was horses. The chasseurs were allowed 360 francs per mount instead of 600, as in the old days – '100 more than the Line'. Desnoëttes complained bitterly to the Minister. The light-horse, which had had two regiments before the war, was reduced to five squadrons. The first, under Jerzmanowski, was all Polish. The other four wore scarlet like the old 2nd Lancers (see Plate 91).

Desvaux de Saint-Maurice began to organize the foot batteries under Lallemand. Marin rode posthaste from Compiègne, hoping to get command of the horse artillery, but Duchand got ahead of him. With the help of Colonel de Lignim of the park and his old quartermaster, Desvaux scoured the Line for his old personnel and matériel.

They hoped to have at least one battery each of horse and foot and a company of train ready for the Emperor's review on 10 May. Major Leroy returned to command the train.

'We need funds', Desvaux wrote the Minister, 'to dress 802 NCO's, foot gunners, and artificers, 389 horse gunners, 1,076 train soldiers, and to buy 370 saddle horses as well as draft horses, and 400 harnesses.'

Volunteer drivers were enlisted in the wagon train as '3rd class' soldiers, to avoid stripping the Line. Eventually, Gubert located his old officers and requisitioned horses, caissons, and ambulances from the Line. Colonel Boissonnet procured 120 of the required 150 sappers.

Dautancourt was ordered to recruit the elite gendarmes from the gendarmes of the King's Hunt, originally formed by Louis XV to police the king's forests, who wore handsome uniforms with helmets. The new company guarded the Luxembourg barracks, the Palace, and the minister's residence, and provided night patrols. The Emperor hoped their helmets could soon be replaced by the traditional bearskin caps which, he recalled, had been stored in the Vaugirard magazine after the dissolution of the corps in 1814.

At the beginning of May Commander Taillade of the *Inconstant* reported that 100 marines plus two drummers and four NCO's had flooded the depot in response to the Emperor's call. They were from 'Corsica, Piedmont, Baltimore; landlubbers from Paris, Toulouse, Strasbourg, etc – and only one Breton!' Their officers were appointed on the 19th; but the men had no uniforms. And now time was running out . . .

CHAPTER 3

The Last Muster

THE Allies mobilized their forces. On 9 May they agreed on a plan for the invasion of France. This consisted of a joint march on Paris: the left wing via Bâle and Langres, the center via Nancy, and the right wing divided between Blücher's Army of the Lower Rhine, marching via Philippeville and Laon, and the Netherlands Army under Wellington marching via Maubeuge. Their total strength was 850,000 men. The offensive would probably begin in July.

Up to the middle of April the disposition of Napoleon's forces revealed no particular plan. All his preparations seemed purely defensive. On 27 April a series of letters to Davout revealed his fear that the enemy would invade his northern frontier. 'The Northern Army will be the main force', he wrote. He deployed units of the 1st, 2nd, 3rd, and 6th Corps composing this army so that they could concentrate within twenty-four hours. Simultaneously he ordered the Grand Marshal to send his (Napoleon's) camp equipment and horses to Compiègne with 40 elite gendarmes, a squadron of Red Lancers, and one of *chasseurs à cheval*.

On the 30th he organized an Army of the Moselle with the 4th Corps, an Army of the Rhine with the 5th, an Army of the Alps with the 7th (each reinforced with national guards) and Observation Corps in the Jura, the Var, and the Pyrenees.

All during May detachments arrived from the depots to reinforce these corps. The Emperor scoured the countryside for men, calling up sailors for the army, raising volunteer units, putting pressure on the ministry, the arsenals, the district commanders, and the artillery. On 9 May he created the 4th Grenadiers and 4th Chasseurs; and on the 12th, the 7th and 8th Voltigeurs and *Tirailleurs*. These units would give him eight Old and sixteen Young Guard regiments.

'It seems that the Young Guard regiments are very weak and have few means of procuring reinforcements', he wrote the Minister on 12 May. 'Perhaps the conscripts from the north and the Pas-de-Calais should be sent to Paris for the Young Guard; but that would weaken the 1st Corps which must be recruited in these departments.' A second letter of the same date showed his real anxiety: 'The greatest misfortune we have to fear is . . . an initial defeat in the north . . .'

On 16 May Napoleon sent General Barrois, commander of the 1st Young Guard Division, to Compiègne with the 1st Voltigeurs and 1st *Tirailleurs* under General Chartrand, three batteries, four field hospitals, and the artisans and surgeons. 'Prepare the 2nd Voltigeurs and 2nd *Tirailleurs* to leave the 18th', he ordered. With these four regiments he would have a full Young Guard division.

But this was not to be. General Delaborde called for help in the Vendée, where a revolt was brewing, and the Emperor sent him Corbineau with '600 elite gendarmes' (doubtless excellent gendarmes, but certainly not 'elite', since at the moment the Guard contained but 240!). Then, on the 22nd, he sent Delaborde the 2nd Voltigeurs and 2nd *Tirailleurs* by post.

The 2nd Voltigeurs numbered 900 men under Lt. Colonel Suisse; the 2nd *Tirailleurs* under Lt. Colonel Monnier, but 750. Reinforced by units of the 6th Corps, the detachment sent to the Vendée deprived the Northern Army of 10,000 men, and the Guard of a brigade. It was urgent to find means to fill this gap.

On 17 May the Emperor sent the cadres of the 6th Voltigeurs and 6th *Tirailleurs*, 'well-dressed and equipped', to Amiens and Rouen with a commissary ordered to establish 'workrooms to clothe and equip 2,000 men in a hurry'. Pinguern commanded the 6th Voltigeurs and its cadres were sound. De Contamine, severely wounded at Lützen, Brienne, and Craonne, commanded the 6th *Tirailleurs*. His cadres were still incomplete.

'The colonels will send recruiting parties through Picardy and Normandy to enlist volunteers and attract old soldiers . . .' wrote the Emperor. 'They must beat the drums, parade the flags, and display posters. The regiment at Amiens will send men to Saint-Quentin to recruit factory hands.

'The Young Guard officers in Paris must put up posters and bestir themselves to recruit men. Send officers to the *mairies* with bands and drums and . . . do everything possible to arouse enthusiasm in the young.'

On 21 May, the day Pinguern and de Contamine left Paris, Blücher joined Wellington in Brussels where they reviewed their troops and co-ordinated their plans.

On the 25th, considering the weakness of the Northern Army and the Guard, the Emperor alerted the 4th Corps on the Moselle to concentrate between Metz and Thionville. If only he might call up the conscripts of 1815 and assign a third of them to the Young Guard! The order was written, but had not yet been approved by the Council of State.

The approval was granted on 29 May. At the beginning of June the first conscripts arrived at the depots.

On 1 June the ceremony of the Champ de Mai took place. Pavilions were erected at the École Militaire where 200 eagles and 87 flags[1] of the national guard were massed before an altar. One by one, the princes and dignitaries arrived. The Imperial Guard, the Paris garrison, and the national guard legions were drawn up in several lines on the Champ de Mars.

At 11 a.m. the Guard batteries at the Tuileries fired 101 guns, echoed by others at the Pont d'Iéna and the Invalides. The Emperor left the palace.

---

[1] Seventy-two of these are now in the Wellington Museum in London. They are like the army's, except that the embroidery is silver and the eagles are not numbered. Four were graciously presented to the Musée de l'Armée.

At noon the procession appeared, led by Red Lancers and *chasseurs à cheval*. Then came the heralds-of-arms and nineteen coaches. The Emperor's was drawn by eight horses and surrounded by Marshals Soult, Ney, Jourdan and the new marshal, Grouchy. Then followed the aides-de-camp, Savary, Dautancourt and the elite gendarmes, the dragoons, and the horse grenadiers. The route was lined with infantry.

A large crowd cheered the Emperor as he rode onto the Champ de Mai. The magnificent procession, flashing in the brilliant sunshine, reminded the Parisians of the fêtes of the old days, but they had expected to see the Emperor in his green uniform and simple *bicorne*. Instead, he mounted his throne wearing a violet cloak and a plumed hat.

After Mass, celebrated by the Archbishop of Tours to deafening salvos of artillery, delegates of the Electoral Colleges approached, one of whom read a loyal address which was followed by a Te Deum. Then the eagle-bearers and troops closed ranks in a semicircle and the Emperor addressed them:

'I entrust these eagles with the national colors to you. Will you swear to die in their defense?' Then, to the Guard: 'And you, soldiers of the Imperial Guard, do you swear to surpass yourselves in the coming campaign, and die to a man rather than permit foreigners to dictate to the Fatherland?'

These solemn appeals were answered by cheers and cries of 'We swear! and '*Vive l'Empereur!*' which increased during the parade.

It was a fine fête; but the Guard, the army, and the public were disappointed that the Emperor had not taken the time to distribute all the eagles. And why had he worn what the Parisians called his 'fancy dress'? (See Plate 33). Had he hoped to re-create the Federation of 1790 with the pomp of 1810? It was only a makeshift. One can never recover the past . . .

The day before, Napoleon had sent the following order to Drouot: '*Monsieur le Comte*, the Guard must prepare to leave on 5 June. Let me know the strength of the eight regiments of chasseurs and grenadiers, and what artillery they have, and who will command them. Two Young Guard regiments will leave the same day to join the two at Compiègne. Fill them up with all available *tirailleurs*. I count on at least 8,000 Old Guard and 4,000 Young, a total of 12,000 infantry.

'As soon as possible the Red Lancers must be increased to three regiments . . . likewise the chasseurs. There will be two each of dragoons and horse grenadiers. These will be grouped in a light and a heavy cavalry division . . .

'There will probably be a battle soon. I do not need to impress upon you the extreme importance of our batteries of twelve-pounders. You will get together with Evain . . . and see that the four Old Guard batteries leave on 5 June at the latest, and whether it will be possible to have a Young Guard battery as well.'

Let us examine the Guard on the eve of its last campaign.

The Young Guard was still very weak. The 1st Voltigeurs at Compiègne was solidly framed, but numbered only 1,200 men under Colonel Secrétan. Most of the officers, including Majors Laborde, Guasco, and Captains Arrighi and Hivert, came from the Elba Battalion or the Corsican Flankers.

Colonel Hurel commanded the 3rd Voltigeurs which mustered 1,000 men; Colonel Teyssère, the 4th, numbering 700. The 5th at Paris had only its cadres. There had been defections among the officers whom the Emperor could not replace. Major Agnès had been transferred to the 4th Chasseurs.

The *tirailleur* regiments were in approximately the same state. Colonel Trappier commanded the 1st Regiment of 1,000 men. Among his majors was Hurault de Sorbée. Lt. Colonel Pailhès of the 3rd mustered about the same number. In Paris the 4th Regiment under Lt. Colonel Albert had only 400, and the 5th commanded by young Dorsenne, nephew of the General, consisted of cadres alone.

Though few in number, the Young Guard showed excellent spirit. On 2 June Colonel Albert of the 4th *Tirailleurs* wrote the Minister of War that the 'officers, NCO's, and soldiers of the regiment had offered the government three days' pay to help defray the cost of the war'.

By the beginning of June the 1st and 3rd Voltigeurs and *Tirailleurs*, practically clothed and equipped, joined the Northern Army The Young Guard was commanded by General Duhèsme. General Barrois commanded the 1st Division, composed of the 1st Voltigeurs and 1st *Tirailleurs* under General Chartrand and the 3rd Regiments under General Guye. These units aggregated 4,300.

The Young Guard left on campaign wearing blue-grey overcoats with red epaulets for the *tirailleurs* and green for the voltigeurs, and cotton or jersey pantaloons with black or grey gaiters. Their shakos had oilcloth covers and red or green pompons, and they wore swords. Their equipment varied. The officers wore Old or Young Guard uniforms, depending upon their status, and most wore shakos. Neither voltigeurs nor *tirailleurs* carried eagles, but they had drummers and fifers. Both Young Guard brigades had skeleton bands during the campaign, thanks to instruments found in the chasseurs' magazine.

The Old Guard infantry was not in much better shape than the Young. The 1st Grenadiers under General Petit numbered 32 officers and 1,000 'old moustaches', averaging thirty-five years of age and five-foot-eleven in height. A third of its effectives had fought in from twenty to twenty-five campaigns, and four out of five wore the Legion of Honor.

Their uniforms were correct, consisting of half-belted overcoats, blue trousers, bearskin bonnets, and Old Guard packs (see Plate 149). Their brass-mounted muskets and sabers were of the regimental pattern. Their 24 musicians were led by a 'jingling Johnny'[2] and base and snare drums. They included the Grumblers from Elba – led by Loubers and Combes – Assistant Adjutant Major Franconin, and Captain Deleuze, the senior officer of the corps.

The 2nd Grenadiers mustered 34 officers and 1,060 men, dressed nearly alike, under Baron Christiani, assisted by Majors Golzio and Martenot. One of the captains had been at Saint-Cloud on the famous 19th *brumaire* as a grenadier of the Legislature, as had our old friend Lieutenant Sénot.

[2] Chinese bells. – Ed.

The 3rd Regiment numbered 34 officers and 1,146 men under Poret de Morvan. Since there were not enough bearskin bonnets to go round, they wore shakos, hats, or forage caps and carried Line muskets and packs. Some rifle slings were replaced by string. Guillemin and Belcourt were the battalion commanders; the surgeon and many NCO's and grenadiers had been at Elba.

The 4th Regiment, created on 9 May under General Harlet, contained the single battalion numbering 508 men of Major Lafargue. Some of the uniforms resembled those of the provincial national guard.

The four grenadier regiments composed the 1st Old Guard Division commanded by General Count Roguet.

The 1st Chasseurs included men from the Royal Corps of Chasseurs as well as light infantrymen from the Line and veterans discharged in 1814. Though there were a few survivors of the Russian campaign, most of the chasseurs had entered the Guard in 1813; however, the NCO's were old-timers. On 1 June the regiment mustered 1,307 men and 41 officers under Cambronne who had been made a grand officer of the Legion.

'They wanted to please me, and I am pleased', he wrote Dumoustier in Nantes. 'General Drouot wanted to promote me, but I thanked him and said . . . I believed I could serve the Emperor better in the reserve than commanding a division . . .' Such modesty is rare.

Majors Duuring, Lamouret, etc. came from the Royal Chasseurs and the Elba Battalion. Several old NCO's, including Delahaye, had been commissioned subalterns.

The 2nd Chasseurs, numbering 35 officers and 1,200 men under Pelet, included Majors Colomban and Mompez, Surgeon Éméry from Elba, and many old captains such as Heuillet and Anguis. Several lieutenants came from the Corsican chasseurs.

The 3rd Regiment was commanded by Colonel Malet, the old commandant of the Elba battalion, and mustered 38 officers and 1,100 men. Its majors were the veteran Cardinal and Angelet.

The 4th Regiment of General Henrion had a single battalion under Major Agnès. Its surgeon was the famous Maugras, ex-Polish lancers, who had been wounded at Austerlitz. The adjutant major had been a Swiss Guard in 1787 and a corporal in the Consular Guard.

Only the 1st and 2nd Regiments wore bearskin bonnets without plates, and red epaulets with green centers. Not twenty men could be found wearing the same uniform in any company of the 3rd or 4th Chasseurs. Their colonels wanted them to be well dressed, and orders survive for everything to Suvorov boots and felt hats for the band; but these were delivered in July or August – or never. (Thirty-two full dress uniforms for the grenadier band turned up in the depots of the ex-Guard in November, brand-new but without buttons, and were worn by the band of the *Garde Royale*.)

The Grumblers had but one pair of shoes apiece, which alarmed the Emperor. The company commanders were allotted funds for a second pair before they left. Eagles were granted only to the 1st Grenadiers and 1st Chasseurs.

The four chasseur regiments composed the 2nd Old Guard Division under General Michel.

The Emperor did not know the exact strength of the horse Guard. The grenadiers mustered 1,042 magnificent officers and troopers. Guyot commanded the heavy cavalry of the Guard, and General Jamin the regiment. Its old Majors Venières and Delaporte commanded squadrons.

At the beginning of May, 243 old troopers of the Young Guard squadron asked to return. 'Perhaps they are not as perfect as the old grenadiers', wrote Guyot, 'but they hope to be, and take pride in the regiment . . . They gave fine proof of their bravery in 1813 and 1814.' At Waterloo these youngsters charged alongside sixty old horse grenadiers from the *Maison du Roi* who had volunteered to serve.

Once magnificent, the horse grenadiers wore various costumes on this campaign. Most of them wore single-breasted undress coats – some buttons still bore the royal insignia – with orange trefoil shoulder knots and aiguillettes, and either grey overalls or breeches and boots. The majority wore fur bonnets without ornament, but the rest had to wear hats or forage caps. They wore white sword- and pouch-belts over their coats, and their blue-white caped cloaks were rolled on the saddle or across one shoulder. They all wore gauntlets and carried sabers of the regimental pattern, as well as dragoon muskets, butt down, at their hip. A bayonet and brace of pistols completed their armament. The trumpeters wore sky blue uniforms with white bearskin bonnets. The officers wore gold epaulets and aiguillettes and the troopers wore queues and gold earrings.

The dragoons were commanded by General Letort with Lt. Colonel Hoffmayer as vice. Their old chief Ornano had been wounded in a duel and was in a critical condition. The regiment numbered 935 officers and men and had all its old majors – Sachon, François, Chamorin, etc. – as well as Captains Ligier, Montarby, and Despierres from the *Dragons de France*.

They wore green uniforms and brass helmets with a panther skin turban, black horse-hair plume and tuft, and brass eagle-stamped crest. (The latter had caused comment in the king's time, but had survived, see Plate 88.) Considering its touchiness about regimental traditions, it is likely that the regiment still had its sappers in fur bonnets.

The chasseurs had five squadrons numbering 1,267 officers and men. Lefebvre-Desnoëttes was their chief. Because of his conduct at Compiègne, Lion had been replaced as commandant by Lallemand, one of his principal victims. Majors Kirmann, Schmidt, and Lafitte, and Captains Maziaux, Sève, Barbanègre, etc. were at their old posts. Lieutenant Seraphin, a dozen officers, and some Mameluks were attached to the regiment.

The chasseurs' uniforms, once so brilliant, were varied. In May and June the council had ordered green, scarlet, and royal blue cloth. A few chasseurs left for Belgium in dark green undress coats like the Emperor's with scarlet collars and orange shoulder knots and aiguillettes, red waistcoats – either braided in orange or plain – green breeches with Hungarian boots or overalls, and colpacks with red and green cords and plumes. About 500 wore dolmans and pelisses with riding trousers and boots (see Plate 65). Gauntlets, sabers of the regimental pattern, sabretaches blazoned with the Imperial arms, musketoons with bayonets, and a brace of pistols completed their equipment. The trumpeters wore sky blue coats with crimson waistcoats, and the officers' braid was gold.

An Imperial decree of 24 April announced: 'The regiment of *chasseurs à cheval* of our Guard will be augmented by a Mameluk squadron of two companies'. Distinctive Mameluk dress and harness were ordered, including *kaouks*,[3] special braid, silk crescents, and even a small standard[4] costing 38 francs; and, according to the quartermaster's register, many of these items were issued. But since its personnel was listed indiscriminately on the rolls of the chasseurs, and even the lancers, it is not known whether the squadron marched as a unit in 1815 (see Plate 173).

On 21 May the Emperor created a second regiment of Young Guard chasseurs which was inaugurated on the 27th by General Merlin de Douai with four squadrons under Old Guard officers, including the famous Captain Parquin. Its uniform was a green dolman braided in yellow with bright red facings, green trousers with red stripes or Hungarian breeches, and a red pelisse. The shako was red with a green and red cord, and the officers' braid was gold. This regiment, sometimes called the 'Hussars of the Guard', was formed too late to take part in the campaign.

The light-horse-lancers mustered 964 officers and men under General Colbert. Its two commandants were Colonel du Bois de la Ferrière, who was left behind at the depot because of royalist sympathies, and Baron Jerzmanowski. The first squadron under Major Balinski was made up of Poles from the Elba squadron; Captain Schulz commanded one company. The other four squadrons under van Ticken, Coti, etc. came mostly from the Royal Corps or from retirement. A few officers, such as Lieutenant Soufflot, were from the Line.

The Poles wore their old blue uniforms and the rest wore red. The Mameluks Renno, Abdallah, etc. probably wore oriental dress. The English at Waterloo reported that the Polish trumpeters, and even the officers, wore their white full dress uniforms faced with crimson at the battle, and that only the front ranks carried lances. This squadron, which had few new recruits, was well dressed. The Poles' silver trumpets may have sounded the last charge of the Guard (see Plate 114). A Young Guard squadron had been planned but not completed.

The lancers and chasseurs formed the light cavalry division of the Guard under Desnoëttes.

On 1 June the elite gendarmes had taken part in the Champ de Mai ceremony 'in the most uniform dress possible', according to Dautancourt. Two companies left for Belgium, the first under Captain Dyonnet, an old infantryman who turned gunner in 1792.

The Guard artillery had not yet reached the strength desired by the Emperor, through no fault of its officers who had been struggling since 11 April to assemble gunners and matériel from all over France. Desvaux had to take whole batteries from the Line. After the middle of May foot and horse detachments left Paris for Compiègne and Soissons, with and without matériel. Their cadres were very sound. Lallemand, in command of the foot artillery, had his old majors Capelle and Bitsch, and a full complement of officers from the foot artillery of the Guard.

[3] Mameluk headdress.
[4] A Mameluk standard of *c.*1813 reposes today on the 33rd floor of a Wall Street bank as part of the magnificent Napoleonic collection of Hugh Bullock, Esq. – Ed.

The horse artillery was complete. Major Mancel and all his colleagues, as well as most of the company commanders, were from the Old Guard. Lt. Colonel Leroy, once a sergeant in the artillery train of the Consular Guard, stayed at the depot, turning over command of the train to Major Canel. One NCO had served 45 years, and one horse gunner 50 (see Plate 160b).

The gunners' uniforms varied and their equipment was incomplete. (Their magazines were swamped later when vast orders placed during April and May were delivered.) In all, the Guard artillery and train numbered 90 officers and around 3,000 men.

The modest sapper battalion wore grenadier uniforms of blue and black piped with red; whether with burnished iron helmets decorated with eagles and black bearskin crests or with vulgar shakos, no one has recorded (see Plate 76b).

The wagon train, planned at eight companies, had ten by 1 June. The artisan companies were organized at the end of May.

At the École Militaire 46 marines bemoaned their fate. There was no room for them in the Guard. Taillade wrote Drouot on 7 June: '*Mon général*, I beg you to send me orders concerning the forty-six marines I have over my quota. They have the best possible spirit, are trained in the manual of arms, and are burning with the desire to take part in the campaign . . .'

'Are they dressed and ready to leave?' Drouot inquired.

'They will be by Sunday' (11 June), Taillade replied, adding '. . . as well as possible under the circumstances . . .'

CHAPTER 4

The Last Campaign[1]

ACCORDING to his own diary, Marshal Mortier returned to his place at Lalande on 29 May very tired and suffering from an attack of gout, after having inspected 'a garrison a day' for the past month. 'On 8 June', he continues, 'I was ordered to take command of the Guard at Soissons where I arrived next day.' However, the Emperor wrote Davout on the 7th: 'Send Marshal Mortier the order to be in Soissons at noon on the 9th to take command of the cavalry of the Guard . . .'

By this time the conscription had commenced, with the Guard given first priority. Though the enabling act was voted by a large majority, there had been many abstentions. In other respects the elections had gone against the Emperor. The author of the act to depose him in 1814 had been elected president of the Chamber.

Just now General Bonaparte would have preferred to wait for the Young Guard to be filled up before beginning the campaign. But the Emperor Napoleon – whose throne was shaky – needed a quick victory on foreign soil to strengthen his position. On 3 June he decided to precipitate matters.

He ordered the 4th Corps to be at Philippeville on 12 June to reinforce the Northern Army, leaving only the 5th Corps and the national guard with General Rapp 'to guard Alsace and Lorraine'. This was a very grave decision.

'All my Guard will meet in Soissons on 10 June and will "perhaps" go to Avesnes on the 13th', he wrote his new chief of staff.[2] (The quotes are mine.) On the same day, 3 June, he sent detailed orders to Drouot for the departure of the troops.

'You will give orders . . . to have four days' rations of biscuit on hand on the 10th, and all . . . caissons loaded with bread . . . for three infantry and two cavalry divisions and the artillery reserve. Ask the artillery for a pontoon company to be attached to the sappers and marines. Be sure a good officer is in charge.'

Captain Dyonnet took 110 elite gendarmes to Soissons. Did they wear the old visored bearskin caps, buff belts trimmed with white braid, and white epaulets? (see Plate 42a). Recently there was dug up on the Waterloo battlefield a helmet of the Royal Hunt Gendarmes which must certainly have been left there by an elite gendarme.

On 5 June General Desvaux reported that he had sent off six Old Guard foot batteries with 48 guns; four horse batteries with 24; four foot batteries with 32 guns and a horse battery with 6 from the Line, attached to the Guard, making 110 pieces in all. A

---

1 For summary of campaign and map of Waterloo, see pull-out map at end of book.
2 This post was now held by Marshal Soult, Duke of Dalmatia. – Ed.

Young Guard horse battery of eight guns was to leave the 12th, and a second would be ready by the 15th. A second Line horse battery was to join the Guard at Soissons.

This *tour de force*, providing Napoleon with 124 guns of the Guard, had been accomplished in six weeks.

The troops marched as ordered. The marines left Paris dressed in short jackets, trousers, overcoats, and shakos, and armed with dragoon muskets. Each had a forage cap, 40 cartridges, and 4 flints (see Plate 58).

On the 8th the 1st Grenadiers and 1st Chasseurs left for the 'palace' and headquarters in Soissons, arriving the morning of the 10th. Four hundred remained to guard the Emperor until his departure. These were the 'youngest and strongest', since they would have to march day and night. The 4th Voltigeurs and 4th *Tirailleurs*, due to leave the 12th, did not get off until the 18th. They were too late . . .

'Filled with dark forebodings', the Emperor left the Elysée at 4 a.m. on the 12th, lunched at Soissons, and slept at Laon. That day the Guard reached Avesnes.

The Emperor was still free either to take the offensive or wait to be attacked, and to choose his battlefield. Nevertheless, hemmed in by enemies at home and abroad, he felt he must beat the latter to appease the former.

'It would have been better not to call the Chamber into session at this time', General Foy wrote later. This was true; for the Guard, the Emperor, and all France were suffering just then from the malady of makeshift, induced by the effort to bring back the past – the same mistake made by Louis XVIII.

Napoleon's faculties had not diminished; his lucidity, intelligence, and verve were still intact; but now he took longer to make up his mind, and his energy seemed to flag at times. He felt this contest to have begun badly. He had all Europe to fight and, despite superhuman efforts, his resources remained precarious. Like passionate lovers coming together again after a rift, he and France sensed that things were not 'the same as before'. How could he patch up the quarrel? He brooded and hesitated, expressing his state of mind by silences, depression, and torpor. This caused decisions which no one else dared make to be postponed.

Berthier had just died.[3] '*Me quoque fata regunt*' – 'I too am ruled by Fate'. These words Ovid put into the mouth of Jove. The Emperor felt that he and Fate were no longer in accord. He had lost faith in his star.

In the garden of the ex-King's lieutenant in Avesnes, before the 'palace', the grenadiers watched Napoleon walk up and down, deep in meditation and oblivious of the fine view over the valley.

The enemy was posted along 150 kilometers of frontier from Liège to the sea. Today, the 13th, Napoleon decided to attack them. Next day he would concentrate his forces at Beaumont within a rectangle thirty kilometers by eight, and on the 15th make a sudden thrust at Charleroi, the probable point of junction between Wellington and Blücher. He would cross the Sambre and beat them one by one, starting with the Prussians.

[3] Berthier jumped (some say was he pushed) from a window in Bamberg. – Ed.

The next evening, in rain that transformed the ground into a sea of mud, the infantry of the Guard bivouacked half a mile north of Beaumont, with its left wing in advance. The Duke of Treviso, walking with difficulty, chose camps for the artillery, field hospital, and train. The sappers, artisans, marines, and pontooneers camped in front of the infantry behind Lobau's 6th Corps. The vanguard of Vandamme's 3rd Corps camped along the frontier four miles north of Beaumont.

The 1st Grenadiers were quartered in the village around the château of the Prince de Caraman-Chimay where the Emperor slept, while the horse Guard floundered in the muddy valley behind Beaumont. Erlon's 1st and Reille's 2nd Corps were on the left, between Maubeuge and the border; on the right, Gérard's 4th Corps was at Philippeville; the cavalry reserve under Grouchy was near Walcourt.

The troops were forbidden to make a sound or cheer the Emperor, and were ordered to shield their fires. (This was a joke, since the rain had put them all out.) They grumbled.

They were grumbling in Paris, too. 'Yesterday, when I learned of His Majesty's departure', Dautancourt wrote Drouot on the 14th, 'I went to General Dériot for my orders and was sad to learn he had none for me . . . I am strong and vigorous and fit to make war. What am I doing here at the depot? . . . *Mon général* . . . I feel that I am being punished. Have the goodness to send me to Imperial Headquarters where I belong . . .'

Dautancourt received his orders next day and left Paris – June 18th!

At 4.30 a.m. on the 15th the Young Guard drummers beat the *Diane*, followed by those of the chasseurs at 5.00 and the grenadiers at 5.30 – the latter with flourishes whose secret was known only to them. Today was the day.

The Emperor's proclamation was read to the companies under arms beneath the horse chestnut trees on the fairground: 'Soldiers, today is the anniversary of Marengo and Friedland . . . For every true Frenchman the moment has come to conquer or die. . .'

'We will conquer! *Vive l'Empereur!*' they cried.

News came that Mortier was ill and confined to bed. A few scandalmongers have inferred that his illness was diplomatic, which is pure calumny. He wrote in his diary: 'The attacks of gout that began at Strasbourg have increased daily in severity. During the night of the 14th I had violent pains accompanied by chills, and all next day I was confined to bed. M. Percy examined me and warned me that this would continue for forty days. Since I cannot possibly mount a horse, I sent my regrets to the Chief of Staff for my inability, in this condition, to share the glory and dangers of the Army . . . I leave Beaumont the 16th . . .'

One could not command the cavalry of the Guard from a litter.

At dawn on the 15th the Northern Army advanced from Maubeuge to Philippeville. Along the road to Charleroi the Guard marched briskly through the fog in column formation. Suddenly the head of the column halted. The 6th Corps in front was at a standstill. Apparently Vandamme's 3rd Corps had received no order to move and was still in its bivouacs. General Haxo, ordered to march with the sappers and marines behind Vandamme's first regiment, was in a quandary; but since Pajol's cavalry had been galloping ahead all morning, Haxo decided to cross the frontier regardless, and the Guard resumed its march.

The cavalry was reported to have sabered several Prussian companies near Ham-sur-Heure, but in general the enemy was retreating. The Emperor ordered the Guard to the head of the Line. The sun broke through the mist, dried the men's coats, and dispersed the irritation and anxiety caused by the nonappearance of the 3rd Corps. Some men cracked jokes and everyone laughed heartily.

About half an hour's march from Charleroi a fusillade was heard in front and on the left. Domon's horse chasseurs were waiting for the infantry before attacking Zieten's Prussians holding the Sambre bridge. The sappers and marines joined forces on the levee and stormed the arched bridge. They destroyed the barricade erected between the wood railings and threw the debris into the river, clearing a path for the 5th Hussars. Meanwhile, the enemy had disappeared.

The French cavalry could be seen riding up the Rue de la Montagne and down the Fleurus road in pursuit of the Prussians. This battle was getting to be a joke. There had been two enemy battalions in Charleroi. Von Steinmetz's brigade, at grips with Reille's corps before Marchienne, was about to be cut off. The French Army were crossing the Sambre unopposed. The Prussians had fled. On the right bank Zieten quit M. Puissant's house in a hurry, leaving his lunch to the Emperor who dismounted at the gate.

Meanwhile, the foot Guard, followed by Lefebvre-Desnoëttes' cavalry, crossed the narrow bridge over the Sambre very slowly. The sappers and marines, supported by the Young Guard, occupied the houses in the suburbs of Charleroi to organize the defense in case the Prussians should attack.

They were not dreaming of it. At 2.30 p.m. the Emperor occupied the Bellevue tavern at the junction of the roads to Brussels and Fleurus, and watched the Guard pass, cheering. A Young Guard regiment was sent to Lodelinsart to support the 1st Hussars in a skirmish with some Prussian uhlans while the rest of the Guard battalions, arriving one by one, were posted along the Fleurus road, near the crossroads held by the Emperor's escort. They waited . . .

Ahead, the Prussians were building an abatis at the edge of the Fleurus woods. Grouchy's horse batteries lobbed a few balls into their midst.

The *Tondu* was less optimistic than the Guard. Expecting to have 60,000 men on the left bank of the Meuse by noon, at three o'clock he had only 20,000. The 3rd Corps was far behind; the heavy cavalry had not shown up. Where was Gérard?

At 3.30 Ney appeared. Now things would happen! Hurrying from Paris, the Marshal had arrived unexpectedly. The Emperor gave him the 2nd Corps, which had begun to climb the bluffs above the Piéton river north of Charleroi, the 1st Corps which was following, and Kellermann's cavalry which was still out of sight, and ordered him to occupy Gosselies, which was now full of Prussians, and 'push the enemy back'.

When the first squadrons of Desnoëtte's light-horse appeared the Emperor said to Ney: 'I give you also the light cavalry of my Guard – but don't use it.'

Ney attacked the Prussians on the outskirts of Gosselies and pushed them back. He noticed that they retired towards Fleurus. He sent Girard's division in pursuit, and the horse Guards to Frasnes.

Gunfire was heard in the rear and on the left, from Gilly. It was now 6 p.m. and the 3rd Corps had finally arrived. The Emperor sent it to attack the Prussians and push them back to Fleurus. Soon overpowered, Zieten retired and took refuge in the woods. Napoleon was furious to see the Prussians escape from his clutches for the second time that day, and ordered Letort to charge them with the duty squadrons. 'He alone is capable of sweeping up this canaille', he said.

Two squares of the 'canaille' were promptly 'swept up' with cries of '*Vive l'Empereur!*' between Sart-Allet and Farcienne, but Letort received a mortal wound. Taken to the house of Monsieur Delbruyère in Charleroi, he was tended by a Guard surgeon and died during the night of 17 June.

His loss was a great misfortune for the Emperor and a bereavement for the Guard. This brilliant, able, and courageous cavalier, always lighthearted and gay, died like Lasalle at the height of his glory, leading men who adored him, and was spared the final defeat.

Meanwhile, Lefebvre-Desnoëttes' lancers were greeted in Frasnes by musketry. Several companies dismounted while others flanked the village. The enemy fell back to Quatre-Bras. Here is Desnoëttes' report to Ney:

'*Monseigneur:*

Arriving at Frasnes . . . we found it occupied by about 1,500 Nassau infantry with eight guns. When they saw that we were maneuvering to turn their flank they made a sortie from the village where we did in fact surround them. General Colbert advanced up the road to within a musket shot of Quatre-Bras; however, the terrain was difficult and the enemy, with the woods at their back, kept up a lively fire with their eight guns, so we could not get at them. The troops at Frasnes were serving under Lord Wellington. They had not been beaten at Gosselies . . . The troops beaten there this morning marched to Fleurus, and none passed this way. The Belgian army is said to be at Mons.

'We took 15 prisoners and lost 10 men killed and wounded . . .'

General Colbert, two captains, and several lancers were wounded, but the intelligence gathered was very valuable: Blücher was at Fleurus, and Wellington at Quatre-Bras.

The night was hot and the moon was in the first quarter. The French campfires shone in a semicircle from Frasnes to the Sambre. The Guard camped between Gilly and Charleroi while the 1st Chasseurs and 1st Grenadiers went to the headquarters in town in the Puissant house. The Emperor was very tired and went to bed early.

In the Puissant courtyard the grenadiers made their first soup in eighteen hours. They swore as the couriers came and went, knocking over their stacked arms. The 'sudden thrust' the Emperor had planned had netted them a five-mile hike towards Fleurus; but the expected battle had not been fought and the enemy was still intact.

Believing that Blücher was impressed by his sudden appearance and was going to retreat, Napoleon planned to attack him next day with the 3rd and 4th Corps, two cavalry corps, and the Guard. He doubted whether today's skirmish had compromised his Prussian offensive.

'Wellington cannot concentrate his scattered forces before the 17th . . .', he declared.

On the 16th part of Wellington's army halted Ney's forces at Quatre-Bras as the latter's troops arrived in installments towards the end of the day. The horse Guard was not engaged, since the Emperor had instructed Ney to 'cover Lefebvre-Desnoëttes' division with d'Erlon's and Reille's horse in order to spare the Guard'. This made the Guardsmen wince.

Meanwhile, about seven miles to the east at Ligny, the Emperor attacked Blücher.

At 9 a.m. the drums beat. The Guard struck camp at Gilly and, led by the band, marched to Sombreffe behind the 3rd Corps and Milhaud's cuirassiers. It halted at the far end of the Fleurus woods in torrid heat and clouds of dust. The Old Guard took up a position at the right of the road, in close columns by divisions of fifty files. The Young Guard was on their left in the same formation. Some men made parasols by knotting their handkerchiefs together and laying them over the stacked arms.

Amid lusty cheers the Emperor arrived and climbed up to the mill on the outskirts of Fleurus where he had the sappers build him an observation post. On the plateau ahead and to the left, beyond the Line positions between Ligny and Saint-Amand, he saw the Prussians. Grouchy's troopers were right – Blücher was at their head. He must be attacked and destroyed. The 'sudden blow' would be struck today; but first, Napoleon must await the arrival of the 4th Corps whose commander Gérard had not yet recovered from the shock of having one of his division commanders desert with his whole staff.[4]

At noon Gérard arrived and the Emperor ordered the 3rd Corps to attack Saint-Amand on the left; and the 4th Corps, Ligny on the right. The Guard remained in the rear, in reserve.

The *Grenadière* and *Carabinière* were beaten. Within five minutes the twenty-four Guard battalions formed a single column and marched through the fields to Fleurus where the natives lined the main street, more out of curiosity than enthusiasm. At the far end the four chasseur regiments with their battery halted near the mill. The two Young Guard brigades and their artillery took up a position on the left, behind the 3rd Corps, and the grenadiers formed with their battery on the right of the chasseurs. These three large units were echeloned so as to form three defensive squares against cavalry attack in case of need. Surrounded by the heavy cavalry and gendarmes, the artillery halted behind the foot grenadiers.

At 3 p.m. the Line corps were in position. Three shots from a Guard battery gave the signal to advance. The fight was desperate from the start. In suffocating heat, the Prussians and French fought hand to hand under a murderous cannonade. Towards four, the 3rd and 4th Grenadiers were sent with their artillery to support Hulot's division of the 4th Corps, whose right flank was hard pressed by the Prussians. Then Michel led three chasseur regiments with their battery to relieve the Young Guard division

[4] General Bourmont. – Ed.

in reserve when the latter was sent with Duhèsme to rescue the 3rd Corps at Saint-Amand.

The *tirailleurs* and voltigeurs of Barrois, Chartrand, and Guye entered the lines crying '*Vive l'Empereur!*' and, to the music of the *Song of Departure*, captured the village and advanced beyond it, though they could see the enemy being constantly reinforced.

At Fleurus the rest of the foot Guard advanced with the artillery and cavalry. With Friant, Christiani, and Petit leading the 1st and 2nd Grenadiers, 2,000 fur bonnets moved forward in a single column, in close order by battalions. Lallemand and Duchand followed with the artillery, which rolled along with a thunderous roar and deployed its batteries, while 200 yards to the left Cambronne led the 1st Chasseurs, aligned as if at drill, followed by the sappers and marines carrying muskets. Behind them in two columns came Guyot and Hoffmayer with the orphaned dragoons, Jamin's 'giants', rolled cloaks slung across their shoulders, and 1,600 cuirassiers of Delort, well down in their saddles, making 4,000 horse in all.

This was an all-out attack to support the 6th Corps which had been summoned from reserve at Bellevue.

As the drummers limbered up their wrists, the trumpeters moistened their lips, and the musicians' eyes were fixed on the drum major's baton, the Emperor suddenly cried 'Halt!' They were all amazed.

A suspicious column had appeared without warning behind Vandamme. It might be Prussian or English. Malet and the 3rd Chasseurs were sent to investigate. They reported that it was the vanguard of d'Erlon's 1st Corps which by chance had been left idle all day between Quatre-Bras and Ligny.

Seven o'clock struck in the steeple at Fleurus. The Emperor, reassured, placed himself at the head of the Guard. Desvaux saluted the Prussians with all his guns, pounding Ligny and its outskirts and setting up a crossfire with the Young Guard batteries opposite, north of Saint-Amand. The slopes around the Brye mill were literally deluged with balls and shells that pulverized the Prussian battalions.

At 7.30 the heavens added their thunder to that of the guns and it rained in torrents. The old phalanx marched in serried ranks behind the 4th Corps infantry and cuirassiers to the eastern outskirts of Ligny where the men halted to load their muskets. Old Man Roguet said: 'Warn the grenadiers that the first man who brings me a prisoner will be shot!' His threat was superfluous. The last struggle of Europe against Napoleon, of the kings against the Revolution, was a struggle to the death.

The Emperor entered Ligny from the west with the cavalry of the Guard and took up a position on a mound beside a sunken road. From there he watched Delort and the cuirassiers take off, followed by the Old Guard. The drummers beat the Charge. The columns descended the ravine held by the Line and entered the ruined village. The cemetery and the church square were filled with corpses. The avalanche of 6,000 Guardsmen engulfed the remnants of twenty-one battalions led by Henckel, Jagow, Krafft, and Langen, indicating that three Prussian corps had taken the field in succession. These, except for Bülow's corps, comprised Blücher's whole army.

Forming in line of battle at the foot of the slope, then in squares by battalion, the Guard wiped off the uhlans' charges it could not halt, not being echeloned as before. The 4th Grenadiers decimated Lützow's lancers with enfilade fire. (From their motley headgear and shabby coats, the Prussians mistook them for national guards and called on them to surrender!) The grenadiers mowed down the first rank of horse at 20 yards, and the rest were finished off by the duty squadrons of dragoons, grenadiers, and gendarmes.

At 9.30 p.m., by fitful moonlight, the 6th Corps crossed the battlefield and camped at the outposts along the Namur road. The band of the 1st Grenadiers played *The Victory is Ours*, echoed by every member of Guard or Line who could beat or toot. This was a victory, and might have been a second Jena had the French pursued the retreating Prussians who lost 20,000 men as it was.

Unhorsed by a cuirassier charge, Blücher had been heard groaning in the straw as he was taken off the field in a cart. Napoleon's 6th Corps and his Guard were both intact. Pajol's and Exelmans' cavalry had suffered little.

At Quatre-Bras Wellington had stood firm. He and Ney each lost 4,000 men.

That night Napoleon estimated that the campaign was already half-won. 'Every man has done his bit', he said.

The grenadiers, some chasseurs, and Guyot's cavalry bivouacked north of Ligny on the battlefield, behind the 6th Corps. The battalions formed squares in three lines, the first two keeping watch with ordered arms while the third slept. The 4th Corps camped north of Ligny. Vandamme and the Young Guard were ahead at Saint-Amand. The rest of the chasseurs and part of the artillery bivouacked around the Château of Fleurus – known as the 'Peace Castle' – where the Emperor turned in at eleven, too tired to receive Grouchy who came for orders to pursue the Prussians.

All night the sound of firing was heard. Alerted repeatedly by stray horses charging down upon them, by cries, and the roll of drums, the soldiers had little rest. At daybreak they woke to a horrible sight. A whole row of *Landwehr* corpses, crushed by cavalry, lay a hundred yards from the bivouac of the 1st Grenadiers.

The Emperor left his château at 8.30 a.m. and visited the gruesome field. He reviewed the Young Guard as it left Saint-Amand whose outskirts were strewn with dead. It had lost 300 killed, including Captain Hivert of the 1st Voltigeurs, and 500 wounded. The latter were being tended under frightful conditions in the church, presbytery, and neighboring barns where the surgeons worked twenty hours on end without rest. The soldiers, short of food, were obliged to forage in the knapsacks of the dead.

At ten the Old Guard drummers beat 'To the Emperor'. Though wallowing in mud, the veterans had shaved and whitened their belts. One hundred grenadiers and 70 chasseurs were missing at roll call. Of 400 wounded, 200 had dressed their own wounds. A lieutenant of the 2nd Grenadiers, two officers of the 3rd, and two of the 4th were slightly wounded. A captain of dragoons and a gendarme lieutenant had been killed.

The Old Guard had a sixth sense about war and a fear of the inexplicable. What was in store for them?

CHAPTER 5

Waterloo[1]

ABOUT 11 a.m. on the morning of 17 June, at the *Trois Burettes* tavern on the road from Nivelle to Namur, the Emperor detached Marshal Grouchy with two corps and a division of infantry, and two cavalry corps, numbering in all 32,000 men with 96 guns, and sent him to Gembloux. 'You will scout towards Namur and Maestricht, pursue the enemy (meaning the Prussians), and inform me of their movements . . .'

With the rest of the army Napoleon marched towards Wellington at Marblais and Quatre-Bras where Ney had attacked him the day before. But Wellington was no longer there. When he heard of Blücher's retreat to Wavre, the Duke had begun to pull back his forces, under cover of his cavalry, to Mont-Saint-Jean and Hal.

The foot and horse Guard tramped through muddy fields until five that afternoon, looking for the enemy. They found nothing and everything went wrong. On the road from Charleroi to Brussels, in lightning, thunder, and pouring rain, the Emperor galloped ahead with the cavalry of Guard and Line, followed by the 1st, 2nd, and 6th Corps. Since Soult had issued no orders to move, or even to remain where they were, the infantry simply followed the troops in front. Where were they going?

Drenched to the bone, the Guard crossed the river Dyle at Génapp at eight that evening by a narrow, crowded bridge, then set off cross-country to leave the road clear for the artillery and wagons. The men sank to their knees in the Brabant mud, lost their shoes, cursed and swore, and lost their way. Famished, their patience exhausted, the Old Guard units assembled north of Glabais where the men invaded the natives' houses, burnt the furniture, and demanded food, returning to their bivouacs only at daybreak.

The Young Guard was still in the rear. The cavalry troopers spent the night in their wet clothes, propped against their horses, as they had done before at Beaumont, Charleroi, Fleurus . . . Hunger prompted the once disciplined troops to pillage and steal. The bivouacs were turned into political clubs where the hotheads orated, and NCO's and officers joined in the discussion. It was not the Emperor's fault, they said, but he had been betrayed. Powerless to maintain order, the provost marshal sent in his resignation.

Major Duuring's battalion of the 1st Chasseurs, summoned en route by the Emperor, went on duty at the 'palace' in the modest farm of Le Caillou while the Guard bivouacked a mile away. Fireless, the chasseurs watched through the stormy night in a walled garden. On the ridge beyond, crossed by the Brussels road at the tavern of *La Belle-Alliance*, the 1st Corps guarded the outposts facing Mont-Saint-Jean.

[1] See pull-out map at end of book.

At daybreak on Sunday 18 June, 67,000 English, Dutch, German, and Belgian troops under Wellington with 156 guns were holding Mont-Saint-Jean as well as three advance posts: the park and château of Hougoumont on the west, the farm of Papelotte on the east, and the farm of La Haie Sainte in the center. A low plateau with deep valleys on either side, forming dry moats in which troops could be sheltered, protected the front of the position. Here Wellington awaited the French attack.

The three Prussian corps beaten at Ligny had retired with difficulty to Wavre (22 kilometers from Mont-Saint-Jean by a rough and winding road) and behind the Dyle which ran through a deep, wooded gorge cut by ravines. There they joined Bülow's corps which had not been engaged. Though still suffering from his injury at Ligny, Blücher promised Wellington that if Napoleon attacked, he would engage the French right with two – and possibly three – corps.

The Emperor did not know Blücher's whereabouts, and believed his army destroyed. He thought Wellington's of little account, and decided to attack him that day. Meanwhile, Grouchy sent word from Gembloux that he believed part of the Prussian army was at Wavre, towards which he was preparing to march.

By 9 a.m. that morning the French army of 70,000 men with 248 guns had not yet reassembled after a night scattered in miserable bivouacs. The English were 'blue with cold' and the Prussians were in billets. The soldiers of the Grand Army were wet, muddy, and hungry. Their provision caissons, bogged down in the mud, had not stirred from Charleroi.

Early that morning the Emperor had reconnoitered the terrain and the enemy lines, and had sent his engineer general Haxo to study their fortifications. Haxo found only a barricade and some abatis on the road down to La Haie Sainte. Had he looked more closely he would have noticed the weakness of the enemy left, the strength of its center (perceiving from the treetops that the north side of the plateau descended to a pocket where reserves might be hidden – a favorite tactic of Wellington) and the forest of Soignes[2] behind the position. Drouot reported the wet ground precarious for artillery maneuvers.

The foot Guard left Glabais about nine and made a long halt at the Caillou farm, then marched to the Brussels-Charleroi road,[3] past the Callois woods, and halted behind the hill of Rossomme occupied by the Emperor. To the north and northwest they saw through the mist the English on the slopes of Mont-Saint-Jean and Merbraine, the bulbous steeple of Braine-l'Alleud, and the road to Nivelles[4] that joined the Brussels road at Mont-Saint-Jean and ran through the village of Waterloo.

East of the Brussels road the enemy lines were partly hidden by the hill on which *La Belle-Alliance* tavern was situated. On the right was the village of Plancenoît with two roads leading into it, near one of which was the house of the peasant Decoster whom Napoleon had engaged as a guide. East of Plancenoît were thick forests.

[2] Through which there was but one narrow path of retreat. – Ed.
[3] Called hereafter the Brussels road.
[4] Called hereafter the Nivelles road.

The Emperor was roundly cheered by the troops marching to their positions. They were haggard and dirty and their arms had rusted; but the drums beat and the bands played *Let Us Watch Over the Empire*. By 10.30 most of the army had assembled and was drawn up in three lines facing Hougoumont.

In the first line Reille's 2nd Corps, echeloned by divisions, was posted between the Brussels and Nivelles roads; D'Erlon's 1st Corps, east of the Brussels road.

In the second line Kellermann's cavalry was posted 200 yards behind the 2nd Corps; Lobau's 6th Corps, with the cavalry divisions of Domon and Subervie, was in the center; Milhaud's cavalry was behind the 1st Corps.

In the third line was the Guard. Guyot's heavy cavalry was formed in two lines behind Kellermann, its left towards the Nivelles road. From left to right were Hoffmayer's dragoons, Jamin's horse grenadiers, and Dyonnet's gendarmes, with the horse batteries. On the right Lefebvre-Desnoëttes' light cavalry, including Colbert's lancers and Lallemand's chasseurs, was drawn up in two lines to the right of the Brussels road, with the light artillery in the center.

Between the cavalry divisions the foot Guard straddled the Brussels road at Rossomme, with the Old Guard in close columns by division on the left, then Duhèsme's Young Guard, Morand's chasseurs, Bergères' sappers, and Préaux's marines. Batteries were posted to right and left of each division. The artillery reserve was in the rear.

The sun finally pierced through the haze, drying the soldiers' clothes and raising their spirits. It was already high when the English batteries opened fire on Reille's infantry before Hougoumont. Then, for the last time, the Guard artillery fired three shots as the signal for a furious bombardment by 80 guns of the 1st and 2nd Corps and the Guard, posted on the hill of *La Belle-Alliance*.

From Rossomme the Guard saw the gunners sweating like demons in the smoke to deliver their projectiles to the English right flank. The guns of the park were guarded by marines. Soon they saw the cavalry cross the road in front of its positions in the second line and advance towards the enemy right at Hougoumont. It was followed shortly by the 6th Corps.

Around 1 p.m. Bülow's Prussian corps marching from Wavre appeared in the woods beyond Lasnes, heading for Plancenoît.

At 2 p.m. the Guard was suddenly ordered into action. Marching along the Brussels road in close columns by division, it halted when a cry arose from Marie Tête-du-bois, the *cantinière* of the 1st Grenadiers. A ball from Hougoumont had struck the cask she carried around her neck and cut her in two. Grenadier Chactas, who had succeeded her drummer husband in her affections when the latter was killed at Montmirail, was in tears and covered with blood.

The remains of poor Marie – sweetheart, wife, and mother of Guardsmen – were laid in a ditch at the roadside and marked with a cross made of two sticks. Before marching off, a corporal wrote this epitaph:[5] 'Here lies Maria, Cantinière of the 1st Grenadiers of the Old Imperial Guard, dead on the field of honor 18 June 1815. Passerby, whoever you may be, salute Maria.' Poor Marie! No one would ever salute her, as her

[5] Reproduced by Capitaine Mauduit in *Les derniers jours de la Grande Armée*.

grave was soon demolished; or Chactas either, for later in the battle he was killed a few yards away by a Prussian shell.

Between *La Belle-Alliance* and Plancenoît, behind the ridge occupied by the artillery, the foot Guard formed in squares by battalion on the right of the road, echeloned 400 paces apart.

While advancing at the head of his 2nd Chasseurs, General Pelet came upon the debris of the 1st Corps which Ney had led unsuccessfully that morning against the English center at La Haie Sainte. The glen was covered with the jumbled corpses of English and French troopers and their mounts. The surgeons were at work, and the units were in the process of reforming while the gendarmes collected the stragglers. On the right, Domon, Subervie, and Lobau's corps were facing Bülow's Prussians at Plancenoît at right angles to the battle line.

Pelet returned to his chasseurs. While waiting to move he ate a snack and drank a glass of madeira with General Morand. Lying on the wet ground, many soldiers were sleeping, oblivious of the awful din.

Towards 3.30 the Emperor mounted his horse and was riding towards Milhaud's cuirassiers when a shell struck one of his suite. It was General Desvaux de Saint-Maurice, commander of the Guard artillery, who was killed instantly. His command passed to Lallemand who himself was wounded later.

The cuirassiers mounted and rode off to the left. Unwilling to commit his foot Guard to Ney, who had asked for it to help to break the English center, the Emperor sent him a brigade of Milhaud's cuirassiers. Now the other three brigades followed without orders. Then, seized with sudden fury, Kellermann's whole cavalry corps joined in the fray, followed eventually by all the cavalry of the Guard.

After the cuirassiers' departure the horse Guard had been ordered to advance. Formed in a single line of battle, the squadrons halted behind a ridge that hid the lancers on whom they were dressing their line.

Just then Curely, attached to the staff, rode up to greet General Colbert and shake hands with several old comrades. From the top of the ridge the officers watched the charge of the cuirassiers. 'The English are done for! . . Their position is dangerous, with their only line of retreat that narrow road through the woods. Their general is an ignoramus . . . he has lost his head. Hold on – look! They are leaving their guns . . .'[6]

At these words the officers moved forward to see better, and the files on their right followed. A movement to dress the line spread through the squadrons to the chasseurs. The few paces required at the pivot on the right became quite a distance on the left where the last grenadier squadron broke into a gallop. Guyot, awaiting the order to charge, thought it had come and moved off with his squadrons. The light cavalry followed. Was it an accident, or was it mass hysteria?

[6] Wellington was not happy at that moment. With Picton dead, La Haye Saint about to fall, and Hougoumont threatened, his gunners, with or without orders, left their guns when the first wave of French cuirassiers penetrated his center. Had Ney had infantry to follow them up, the French might have been victorious; but Napoleon had learned from a captured hussar of Blücher's approach with 50,000 men on the heels of Bülow's 30,000, and dared not commit his last reserves. – Ed.

Dressing by the left, the light cavalry crossed the road on the bias, following Milhaud's cuirassiers. The four regiments ascended the plateau on which the English were drawn up. They advanced at a trot with clanking bits and creaking leathers, their scabbards knocking against their spurs. The horses stumbled over the rye stalks already trampled in the mud. Through the smoke the troopers saw the red coats of the English and the green coats of the Hanoverian riflemen. On their right, cuirassiers were toppling over, raked by fire from La Haie Sainte. Balls whistled overhead and rockets zigzagged through the air, frightening the horses (see Plate 161).

Threading their way around wrecked gun carriages and through debris of every sort, the units became separated. As they reached the plateau they fell upon the English squares which opened fire.

Those who survived were unable to breach the enemy lines with saber or lance. In desperation, the troopers hurled their lances like javelins into the midst of the enemy. Coming under fire from the artillery in the second line, the squadrons wheeled about and rallied at the foot of the slope. Five times, supported by a Guard battery whose guns skidded out of position on the muddy slope and mowed down a whole file of lancers with their first shell, they tried without success to break this iron front.

The troopers retired slowly as the English light dragoons attacked Colbert's lancers. The horse grenadiers abandoned them to their fate only after half their squadrons were unhorsed.

By now, the number of performers in this bloody circus, whose box seats were held by the English, had singularly diminished. No one can estimate what the result would have been had the cavalry attack been supported by the infantry of Bachelu and Foy, whose path the dragoons and grenadiers had crossed en route, and the twenty-two battalions of the Guard. But by now, the Guard reserve had only fourteen battalions left . . .

North of Plancenoît and in the village itself, the Young Guard with its artillery was engaged in hand to hand combat with the vanguard of Bülow's corps of 30,000 men. Marching through the woods, the Prussian units deployed at the edge, then dashed down into the valley below.

As General Poret de Morvan was forming his 3rd Grenadiers in squares on the hilltop east of *La Belle-Alliance*, he suddenly saw on his right the troops of the 6th Corps and Domon's horse engulfed by Prussians, and retreating towards Plancenoît. The Old Guard, already under fire from the English guns in front, began to be shelled on the right by the Prussians. This did not stop them from cheering the Emperor, nor singing, laughing, and teasing the gunners on the hill above, who now had to point their guns alternately north and east. For the French right flank was cracking.

After a violent struggle with the 15th Prussian Line and the Silesian *Landwehr*, the Young Guard division was obliged to give way before a counterattack by General Hiller with 9,000 men. The French were in the Plancenoît cemetery and around the church where they fought desperately, and where the Prussians – less sheltered than they – were decimated. Taken in flank, the enemy were chased out and charged by

Subervie's lancers. However, as more and more Prussians arrived the tide of battle ebbed and flowed (see Plate 162b).

At each recoil Barrois called for help from the Old Guard. Finally, between six and seven that evening, General Morand sent Pelet the following order: 'Take your first battalion to Plancenoît where the Young Guard is being beaten. Support it and hold the position . . . Keep your troops together and well in hand. If you attack the enemy, employ a single division (two platoons) with bayonets.'

Formed in close columns by platoons, Major Colomban's battalion of the 2nd Chasseurs marched to Plancenoît. En route it passed the dying Duhèsme who was being held on his horse by *tirailleurs* and voltigeurs in rotation.

Chartrand told Pelet the situation had got completely out of hand. Colonel Hurel, commanding the 3rd Voltigeurs, was running after his retreating troops. These were now ordered to turn round and follow the chasseurs. Captain Peschot's company was ordered to fix bayonets and attack the enemy who were coming down the street.

Sergeant Granges stopped the Prussians with the first platoon; but then some men began to fire their muskets and he lost control of the situation. Peschot, following with the second platoon, was also thrown back. Captain Anguis was sent to the street below to halt the *Landwehr* who were trying to outflank the village. Heuillet's company defended themselves in and around the church, then rushed forward to the edge of the woods.

The French cut the throats of their prisoners. Pelet stopped the massacre as best he could and detailed his sappers, who 'complied with reluctance', to guard them. Stripped to his shirt, galloping from group to group on his mare Isabelle, Pelet was trying vainly to rally the voltigeurs to charge with his last platoon when a small column of grenadiers appeared. His chasseurs formed up with the newcomers and stood firm amid the bursting shells and the fires raging in the village. They ran past the burning houses and joined the rest of the grenadier battalion that the Emperor had sent under Golzio to support Pelet, and together they threw back Hiller's Prussians.

'I held on amid a hail of grapeshot, fires that broke out in several houses at once, and a continuous fusillade', Pelet wrote in his journal. 'I held on like a demon. Though I could not collect my men, they were all under cover and kept up a murderous fire which contained the enemy . . .'

Meanwhile, to the south, several platoons of the 1st Grenadiers were sent to a hill above the river Lasnes, opposite the woods of Virère and Hubermont, to cover the French right flank. Major Duuring and a detachment of the 1st Chasseurs forced their way into the Chantelet woods.

Since the French were now in possession of La Haie Sainte and the English seemed to be yielding before their artillery and infantry, the troops believed they would end up victorious in the twilight of that momentous day. All that remained was to administer the coup de grâce.

What forces were left to the Emperor? Of the Guard, only nine battalions, one battery, the service squadrons, and the company of gendarmes. Should he leave Lobau, Barrois, and Pelet to shoot it out with the Prussians and take everything on the field still able to move, group it around the Old Guard, and storm the English lines? The decision must be made at once.

As the sun sank low over Braine-l'Alleud, Zieten's artillery came into action on the right, near Ohain.[7] Napoleon was already on the march at the head of the Guard. To hearten his troops, he announced that Grouchy had arrived.

Six battalions of the 3rd and 4th Chasseurs, numbering less than 3,000, advanced west of the road. Duchand himself placed two guns between each two battalions. Three battalions, numbering 1,500, followed in the second line. These were the second battalions of the 1st and 2nd Chasseurs under Lamouret and Mompez, and the first of the 2nd Grenadiers under Major Martenot. Generals Cambronne, Roguet, and Christiani rode at their head.

On either side of Decoster's house General Petit formed squares with Loubers' and Combes' battalions of the 1st Grenadiers and the sappers and marines. These 1,200 men were the last reserve.

Seeing the foot Guard on the march, the fugitives halted and columns formed up behind it: a meager brigade of cuirassiers, some horse chasseurs, and on the left, the horse Guard, a foot battery, and more cuirassiers. The skeleton battalions were made up of desperate men ready to pass through the breach opened by the Guard and fight. The drums beat, the trumpets sounded, the flags fluttered in the breeze. On the ridge the guns of the Guard and Line blazed away with all their might.

'The Guard is going into action!'

At the sight of their blue overcoats behind the legendary silhouette, the demoralized men took heart, the wounded got up, the still valid men rallied their battalions with cries of 'Vive l'Empereur!' loud enough to waken the dead.

Accompanied by Colonel Bernard, the Emperor himself posted Major Belcourt with a battalion of 3rd Grenadiers on the ridge between La Haie Sainte and Hougoumont to cover the retreat in case the attack should fail. Then he returned to the road. Why were Duchand's guns firing so slowly? Because half the gunners had fallen.

At 8 p.m. the Guard and the remnant of the Imperial Army prepared to make the final attack. The sparse battalions marched down the slope in echelon, with the right-hand column taking the head of the line. The fire from the grand battery gradually diminished as the English artillery opened fire along a thousand-yard arc. Between the road and the top of Hougoumont were ranged eight solid battalions of Germans and Hanoverians, and two of terrified Brunswickers. Lying flat in the rye fields behind them were four ranks of English guards under Maitland, and Adam's foot brigade. At the top of the ridge were more units, looking like phantoms in the dusk. On the down slope, behind the guards, Chassé joined six squares of his Belgo-Dutch division and, supported by the remains of 20 regiments and 40 squadrons, posted batteries.

This mass was waiting to be attacked by 15,000 French of whom 6,500 (including 1,500 horse) were the Guard.

'Bah!' said the grenadiers, 'victory is a trollop we've taken more than once!'

[7] Heralding Blücher's arrival at the head of 50,000 men. About 21,000 of these were in action by 7 p.m. according to Captain Siborne of the English Army. – Ed.

Without a single skirmisher to scout ahead, Ney, Friant, and Poret marched at the head of Guillemin's battalion of the 3rd Grenadiers. At the exit of the 'bloody angle' they came under fire from the English guns just as General Harlet appeared on their left with the lone battalion of the 4th Grenadiers. They joined forces and, climbing over the dead, the debris, and the remains of a hedge, pushed back four of the Duke of Brunswick's and Sir Colin Halkett's battalions. Though wounded in the hand, Friant went to tell the Emperor that all was well.

At that moment Napoleon was forming up the last three Old Guard battalions which had reached the valley in front of La Haie Sainte. Just then Chassé opened fire with one battery and 'launched six battalions with fixed bayonets' against the two French grenadier battalions whose remnants were pushed back down the slope.

Then the battalion of the 1st Chasseurs deployed and the cuirassiers halted. 'The Guard is falling back!' cried the soldiers at La Haie Sainte. Like a powder keg, the sinister words exploded all the way to the village of Papelotte.

The attack on the left ended in catastrophe.[8] Marching to attack the center of the English line, the two battalions of the 3rd Chasseurs, also without skirmishers, advanced in column under a heavy cannonade, but the terrain was easy and clear of obstacles. They knocked out a battery on their right. As General Michel marched at their head with Malet, Cardinal, and Angelet, their battery poured canister shot into the midst of the English 30th and 73rd Foot who recoiled.

Suddenly the command rang out: 'Stand up, Guards!' At 30 paces, 1,500 English Guards under Maitland and 1,200 infantry of Adam's brigade sprang up before them in the rye (see Plate 163). At 'Fire!' Michel, Cardinal, and Angelet fell with 20 officers and 200 men. The rest wavered, hesitated, and then fell back to Hougoumont under cover of Belcourt's small rear-guard, the solitary battalion of the 4th Chasseurs under Henrion, and a few cavalry.

A murderous fight took place before the orchard at Hougoumont; then, attacked in front by Adam and Maitland, on the flank by the King's German Legion, and behind by more Hanoverians, the chasseurs were crushed and practically annihilated. Malet and Agnès were both killed. The action did not last twenty minutes.

The three sparse Old Guard battalions opened fire in a vain effort to cover the retreat. The service squadrons charged. But just then Wellington, on horseback, took off *his* legendary hat and the whole English line advanced (see Plate 164).

With an immense clamor, drums beating, bands playing, pipers piping, and flags unfurled, the English, though much diminished and near exhaustion, came on as the remains of the French artillery blasted away, answered by English and Prussian guns. The French scrambled up to *La Belle-Alliance*, pursued by the whole howling pack.

[8] The last charge of the Guard at Waterloo was complicated by the fact that on Blücher's arrival his vanguard fell upon the troops of the Prince of Saxe-Weimar, who were still wearing their French uniforms, leading the French to believe that these were Grouchy's troops come to their aid. When the French tried to join them in the dusk and were fired on, they panicked and cried 'Treason!' thinking their own comrades had turned against them. Thus, when Blücher attacked its rear and Vivian's fresh hussar brigade dispersed the spent horse Guards coming to its support, the Guard found itself alone. (Achille de Vaulabelle, *Campagne et Bataille de Waterloo*.) – Ed.

Neither the stoic horse grenadiers nor the skeleton battalions of Cambronne, Roguet, Christiani, and Belcourt were able to halt the enemy whose cries of 'Hurrah!' 'Scotland Forever!' and '*Vorwaerts!*' were answered by French cries of 'Treason!' and '*Sauve qui peut!*'[9] – the counterpart of the dirge: 'The Gods have departed!' that froze ancient Rome with terror. The same cry has been heard at the end of all worlds.

The light brigade of the Guard was reduced to three squadrons; Lefebvre-Desnoëttes, Lallemand, and Colbert were all wounded. The artillery above was silenced when the gunners were overwhelmed and forced to abandon their guns. Ten minutes later the Highlanders, drunk with victory, turned the same cannon on Lobau, the Young Guard, the Old, the Prussians – in fact on everyone still crawling on the plain below.

Night fell. In flaming Plancenoît, Pelet, Golzio, and Colomban with their 600 fur bonnets – 'all very pale' according to the General – and the *tirailleurs* and voltigeurs still held out. In the cemetery and the church the 2nd Westphalian Landwehr and the Pomeranians were shooting it out with the French at point-blank range when the units, suddenly outflanked, took to their heels. Pelet rallied his chasseurs around him, but it was so dark they could no longer recognize one another at ten paces. The confusion was complete. On the right, Duuring's chasseur battalion, its back to the Caillou farm, kept the Prussians at bay while the rest deployed on both sides of the road and tried to stop the fugitives.

What could be done to stop this rout, this pursuit in the dark along a front two miles long and a mile deep that lasted for an hour?

Nothing. All was finished: France, the Empire, the Emperor, and the Guard.

Much has been written about mass hysteria. These men gone berserk, drunk with fear, rage, enthusiasm, blood; killing one another regardless of nationality; shouting with joy, cursing, crying for vengeance in five languages, were victims of an emotion neatly summed up in the imprecation[10] attributed to Cambronne on the evening of 18 June 1815.

The Old Guard battalions no longer existed. Emaciated squares, measuring barely fifty yards on a side and numbering less than 400 men, gathered up a few fugitives and fired a few volleys at the English. Then engulfed, sabered, shot, they retreated. 'They no longer recognized the voices of their officers', wrote Christiani (which was not strange, considering two-thirds of them were casualties). Captain Prax of the 3rd Chasseurs, also wounded, reported: 'First our two battalions held the English in checks then night fell, we found ourselves surrounded, and we followed the tide, alas! alas!' Twenty-five of their 30 officers were killed or wounded.

The remnant of the 4th Chasseurs, all of whose officers were out of action, joined up with the 3rd after the fight at Hougoumont. Mompez's battalion of the 2nd Chasseurs, supported by cavalry, defended itself for some time and retired in good order to *La Belle-Alliance*. This was the last Guard battalion to disperse; however, it had had many fewer casualties than the rest.

[9] Every man for himself!

[10] '*Merde!*' according to Victor Hugo. '*La Garde meurt et ne se rendent pas*' (The Guard dies but does not surrender) according to Cambronne's monument. The reader may take his choice. – Ed.

By this time Cambronne's battalion of the 1st Chasseurs had vanished completely. Sent to the left flank by Morand when the English attacked, it fell upon Colonel Hugh Halkett's Hanoverians ('Hano*vorians*' to the Guard) and, after a fierce combat, repelled a charge by the 10th Hussars. Then it retreated towards *La Belle-Alliance*.

Before being shot in the head near there, Cambronne probably uttered his famous remark to Colonel Halkett. The battalion left Cambronne for dead, then scattered after losing seven of its officers. So few of the chasseurs arrived at *La Belle-Alliance* that the eagle-bearer Lieutenant Martin took refuge with Mompez's battalion for protection. Eventually, Martin managed to reach Rossomme where General Pelet found him, gathered several chasseurs around him, lost them in the crush, and never found him again until Laon.

The first battalion of the 3rd Grenadiers was thrown back down the slope after both Poret and Guillemin were wounded. Then Hurault de Sorbée, on horseback in the middle of a square, took command and stopped a charge by the English cavalry. Later he gathered up the marines of Lieutenant Préaux whose horse had just been shot under him. Joined momentarily by Cambronne's chasseur battalion, then decimated by gunfire, the grenadiers dispersed after Hurault's jaw was shattered by a shell. Streaming with blood and accompanied by several survivors, Hurault took refuge after the battle in an isolated house where he found Marshal Ney alone with Poret de Morvan and together made their way to Maubeuge.

The only battalion of the 4th Grenadiers disappeared almost entirely. General Harlet and all its captains and lieutenants were casualties. Roguet met Harlet in the midst of Major Belcourt's square where he had been carried during the retreat by his men.

The glory won by Belcourt's handful of grenadiers has redounded to the credit of the whole corps. Attacked by English cavalry and infantry from Hougoumont, surrounded, and charged, Belcourt's square was then shelled with grapeshot and reduced to a triangle; whereupon the men fired a final salvo crying *'Vive l'Empereur!'* then split into groups and made their way up to Rossomme.

There they heard the drummers of the 1st Grenadiers beat the *Grenadière* to call in the stray Guardsmen returning from *La Belle-Alliance* and Plancenoît. The two battalions of the 1st Regiment under Combes and Loubers had not budged from their positions on either side of the road. The sappers and marines were with them. Filled to bursting with generals, officers, and refugee soldiers, the squares were at least ten rows deep. A Guard battery was firing methodically, but it stopped neither the enemy nor the fugitives.

Marshal Ney, in tatters, appeared with a lone grenadier, then Drouot, who had foundered fifteen horses in four days; then Soult, Bertrand, and the Emperor. Tears were streaming down their faces.

It was 9.30 p.m. The trap was springing shut on the Grand Army. On the right cries were heard from some lost Hanoverians. The French column kept on marching. The Guard battery had just ceased firing. On the left, 500 horse Guards, saber in hand, awaited their commander's decision. Lefebvre-Desnoëttes wanted to stay and be killed on the field. Lallemand proposed going to Maubeuge. The Emperor was still trying to stop the rout . . . But it was time he left the field to avoid capture.

He ordered Petit to beat the Retreat. Bülow's infantry heard it and emerged from burning Plancenoît carrying their shakos on their musket barrels and singing Luther's hymn *A mighty Fortress is our God*. Wellington and Blücher met near *La Belle-Alliance* and congratulated one another on their victory.

The battlefield quieted down. Through the smoke the moon shone down on the pitiless scene of soldiers robbing the wounded, and finishing off those who belonged to the Guard.

The retreat towards Génapp gathered momentum. The road was so cluttered with abandoned vehicles that the 1st Grenadiers, marines, sappers, and Duuring's battalion bypassed the village, while the chasseurs of the escort cleared a passage for the Emperor with the flat of their sabers. En route they passed the *Hôtel d'Espagne* where Duhèsme lay dying.

As midnight struck, the pursuit began to flag. Several Prussian squadrons trampled the stragglers but did not disturb the units that remained together. Escorting the eagle of the grenadiers, Duuring marched through byroads, guided by the natives, and reached Fleurus at dawn. Still guarding those sheltered in its squares, the 1st Grenadiers entered Charleroi after the Emperor had left.

Napoleon crossed the Sambre at 2 a.m. with Bertrand, Drouot, and an escort of Red Lancers and went on to Philippeville.[11]

In the outskirts of Charleroi the wounded, perched on horses or afoot, threaded their way among abandoned caissons, loaves of bread floating in rivers of spilled wine and brandy, and scattered gold pieces from the pillaged treasure.

One by one the foot Guard crossed the Sambre bridge. General Roguet held an impromptu assembly in the field on the right bank, and the units re-formed while waiting for the Line to cross.

[11] See Appendix 'E'.

CHAPTER 6

The Death of the Guard

ORDER was finally restored in the Guard and the Line. The army, though weakened, was still imposing as it marched into Laon on 21 June. Marshal Soult had arrived the previous night. The Guard bivouacked around the main square where it had fought the year before.

Over 6,000 men answered the roll in the foot Guard on the 24th, including around 5,000 grenadiers and chasseurs and about 1,100 *tirailleurs* and voltigeurs. The artillery had lost a third of its effectives. Driving the stragglers before them, the troops marched to Soissons, the 1st Chasseurs forming the rear-guard. The horse Guard had left 1,700 men on the fields of Belgium. There were between 2,000 and 2,500 survivors.

The troops were marching at a good pace when beyond Etouvelles, they were ordered to halt and assemble in columns by regiment at the roadside. Two guns were set up on the road. What had happened? When they had left Laon two hours before there was no sign of the enemy.

The Duke of Dalmatia (Soult) dismounted. In civilian clothes, he nevertheless wore his grand eagle of the Legion and his white-plumed marshal's hat. A hundred paces from the grenadiers he began walking up and down with his hands behind his back, like the Emperor. After an hour had passed he drew from his pocket a paper which his aides copied and read to the battalions:

'Frenchmen! In going to war to preserve our national independence I counted upon the combined effort and co-operation of the nation and the government. On this basis I hoped for success in the face of the declarations made by the Powers against me personally. The situation seems to have changed. Therefore I am sacrificing myself to propitiate the hatred of France's enemies. Let us hope they are sincere in claiming that it is only my person they want! My political life is ended. I proclaim my son Emperor of the French with the title of Napoleon II. The present ministers will form a provisional council. In my son's interest I shall ask the two Chambers to establish a lawful regency without delay. I beg you to unite in the cause of public safety and national independence.

'Given at the Elysée-Bourbon, 22 June 1815,
'(Signed) Napoleon.'

The last words were lost in the din of a great roar of protest. Crying 'Treason!' the soldiers broke ranks, shouting and hurling imprecations. It was not true – not a second abdication! They would believe it only when they saw the Emperor. They jeered at their officers and booed the generals. 'Say that again and you're dead!' cried a grenadier, pointing his musket at a general who had threatened to have him shot.

Some broke their weapons and tore their uniforms. Others knocked down their officers and NCO's and set out forthwith for Soissons and Paris. Still others – the passive type who followed the line of least resistance[1] – were indifferent. They played cards on the drumheads with their noses in the air and smugly contemplated their enraged comrades.

General Petit ordered the 1st Grenadiers back to Étouvelles to relieve the 1st Chasseurs in the rear-guard; but he was wasting his breath.

'All right', he said, 'since the grenadiers wish to dishonor themselves in the presence of the enemy, let the eagle be brought. I myself shall plant it at the rear and stand guard . . .'

At this, Major Loubers accused Petit of planning to deliver the eagle to the enemy. A lively altercation followed during which Loubers worked himself into a towering rage and the Elba veterans joined in.

When calm was finally restored three-fourths of the regiment followed their commander. A few took to the woods, fearing arrest by 'traitors', and 1,000 Guardsmen, with and without arms, set out on their own for Paris to see the Emperor, to hear him speak, and to save him. Beyond Soissons they were arrested by gendarmes.

Mouton-Duvernet, sent by Davout to investigate the morale of the troops, urged them to return to duty.

'To fight for whom?' they asked. 'We have no more Emperor . . .'

Finally, General Roguet took command of the foot Guard and restored discipline.

Marshal Grouchy also knew how to talk to soldiers. Learning the morning of the 19th of the disaster at Waterloo, he had managed to break through the Prussian lines and escape to Namur from where he led his troops back to France with their artillery and wounded. He was now in command of the army.

'Soldiers', he said, 'the Emperor has abdicated his throne. He wished to make this sacrifice in the interest of France . . . The Chambers have recognized his son as Napoleon II. What is now your duty? To be faithful to the new head of the Empire, as you have been to his august father; to close ranks around your eagles and assume the heroic attitude that will make the foreigner respect your independence. Show him that you are the same men today that you were in the past. Be true to the sacred cause of country and liberty in which you have triumphed. Your conduct and efforts at this great moment will secure the Empire's peace and happiness. This will finish your task . . . and put a seal to your glory.'

The Guard at Soissons numbered 6,000 foot, over 2,000 horse, and 30 guns. Its discipline and esprit de corps had been restored and the men had returned to their ranks. Besides, there was fighting in prospect. Hordes of Prussians, crossing the bridges over the Oise at Pont-Saint-Maxence, had reached the junction of the roads to Soissons and Compiègne, leading the French to make a wide detour to the south.

On 27 June the Guard camped along the Claye-Paris road. The soldiers had been marching steadily for a fortnight, often without bread or forage for their horses. The

[1] '*Suivent leur placque de ceinturon*' – literally 'follow their belt-buckles'. – Ed.

houses in Claye had been ransacked and the taverns were filled to overflowing. Wine and politics kept the pressure high under the bearskin bonnets, and the discourse degenerated into a free-for-all that lasted until the beating of the *Grenadière* and *Carabinière* at 2 a.m.

On 29 June the Guard bivouacked under the heights of Charonne and Saint-Chaumont. There the Old Guard under Drouot and Lefebvre-Desnoëttes mustered 458 officers and 9,200 men,[2] including 3,392 cavalry, 1,401 artillery and train, and 460 sappers, marines, and artisans. The Young Guard numbered 200 officers and 2,800 men plus 50 officers and 800 men in the depots. Counting the Guard, France had south of Paris an army of 70,000 (including 15,000 cavalry) and 500 guns with which to oppose the 62,000 Prussians who appeared on her flank, followed by 30,000 English two days' march behind. If only the Emperor were there!

Alas, these men of the Imperial Guard would never see him again. He was at Malmaison, guarded by 300 Grumblers from Rueil, and 50 dragoons and 25 Red Lancers under Major de Brack. He was preparing to leave France. Fouché, Davout, and the government were urging haste for fear Louis XVIII would have him arrested. An unfortunate speech by Ney,[3] the sessions of the Legislature, and his abdication had combined to end Napoleon's career. He offered his sword to the government which refused to accept it.

Fifty marshals and generals met in a war council on 1 July and posed the question: 'For whom are we fighting, for the Emperor or the King? . . .' As if politics were in their province! None of them thought of singing '*Allons enfants de la Patrie!*'[4] their battle cry for the past twenty years, outlining a course of action on which they could all agree.

Old Bugeaud wrote later: 'They feared further crises and they wanted to escape from their enemies. It was cowardice, but it was a fact.'

Nevertheless, Colonel Dorsenne tried to stop the Prussians at Vertus on 30 June with 200 *tirailleurs* of the 5th Regiment. 'This time there were too many', murmured a lad whose arm had been shot off as he fell at the feet of his chief.

A few cannon were fired west and south of Paris on 1 July, and the dragoons and hussars sabered some Prussian hussars near Versailles.

Reassembled at the École Militaire and Montrouge, the foot Guard waited for orders. Lefebvre-Desnoëttes hurried from La Chapelle with 3,000 horse. In Paris Dériot alerted the voltigeurs and *tirailleurs*, together with the depots and the 4,000 Guardsmen unfit for active service, but in vain.

The deputies, the government, and the military chiefs preferred to capitulate so as not to offend the Duke of Wellington. The surrender was signed on 3 July. On that day at Muron, a village between Niort and Rochefort, two old grenadiers went to salute the Emperor on his way to exile while the ostlers changed relays and the crowd

---

[2] The actual losses at Waterloo were fewer than legend would lead one to suppose.

[3] In which the Marshal denied in the Chamber that France had an army left with which to resist invasion. – Ed.

[4] 'Go forward, children of the Fatherland', the beginning of the *Marseillaise*. – Ed.

PLATE 161

Charge of the French cavalry on Mont–Saint-Jean
(*From an original watercolor by William Heath*)

PLATE 162

a) Bülow at Waterloo

b) Prussian infantry at Plancenoît
(*From original drawings by Paul Duncker*)

PLATE 163

'Stand up, Guards!'

(From a contemporary colored lithograph by J. A. Atkinson)

PLATE 164

Wellington raises his hat as a signal for the general advance
(From an engraving by J. Burnett after Atkinson and Devis)

PLATE 165

The last stand of the Old Guard
(*From a colored lithograph by Hippolyte Bellangé*)

PLATE 166

THE FLIGHT OF NAPOLEON. See Appendix 'E'
(From an original drawing by V. G. Kininger, 1817)

PLATE 167

'Courage. Resignation'
(*From a lithograph by Delpech*)

PLATE 168

THE EMPEROR IN A BOTTLE

Left to right: Wittgenstein, Wellington, Blücher, Schwarzenberg, Napoleon, the Prince Regent, Francis I., Alexander I., Frederick William III., and (kneeling) Louis XVIII

PLATE 169

PLATE 170

Aigleville, the Guard colony of refuge in Texas, U.S.A.

(From a colored aquatint by Yerenrag)

PLATE 171

Sargeant Taria, Grenadiers of the Guard 1809–1815
(*From an original photograph taken during the Second Empire*)

PLATE 172

Lancer Dreux, 2nd Light-Horse-Lancers of the Guard 1813–14
(*From an original photograph taken during the Second Empire*)

PLATE 173

Mameluk Ducel, Mameluks of the Guard 1813–15
(*From an original photograph taken during the Second Empire*)

cheered. The game was up in Paris. Run to earth, Napoleon was driven into the arms of the English who were preparing for him the prison of Saint Helena. Meanwhile, Louis XVIII had been journeying to Paris since 20 June in the baggage train of the victor of Waterloo.

The following clause was inserted in the final articles of capitulation:

'The ex-Imperial Guard, taking with it its arms and baggage and its campaign equipment, will retire immediately behind the Loire where it will be disbanded. The wounded may stay in Paris, pending further orders, . . . where they will be under the protection of the English and Prussian generals. The employees of the military administration of the ex-Guard, with their wives and children, may follow the troops . . . In future no unit commanders, generals, staff officers, officers, or NCO's of the ex-Guard who fought against the Allied powers on 16, 17, or 18 June may serve in any capacity in the new army . . .'

These decrees of Wellington and Blücher were approved by Fouché and Davout, among others.

The initial fury that had caused the Guardsmen to revolt, desert, and even commit suicide was followed by a mournful resignation. With Drouot's help, military discipline prevailed in the long run over personal feelings.

On 4 July the army was ordered to retire 'behind the Loire'. It was to march in two columns the following day.

The old veterans wept. These rough warriors were nomads, indifferent to comfort and ephemeral relationships. They had been united by duty and self-denial in a military family whose father was the Emperor. Now they felt orphaned and abandoned. Accustomed as they were to sudden strokes of fate, still they had been wafted by their dreams to the pinnacle of glory. They had believed that 'he' would remain to guide the King of Rome. Now the traitors had recalled the Bourbons and condemned the Guard to poverty and humiliation. Yet an unshakable – if unreasoned – faith in the grandiose destiny of the Emperor still animated the Old Guard. Having braved death a hundred times, it did not want to die.

'He' was cleverer than the others. He had also retired to the Loire. They were going there to meet him. He would return . . .

Actually, Napoleon had thought of it only the day before at Niort when the elder General Lallemand had arrived and the 2nd Hussars had cried 'Vive l'Empereur!' and 'On to the Loire!' But the specter of civil war had deterred him.

On 9 July the foot Guard reached Orléans with 7,700 men, crossed the Loire, and halted next day at the present La Ferté-Saint-Aubin. The cavalry, with 3,800 horse, joined them at Orléans and went on to Saint-Mesmin. The artillery and train were in the second column, marching to Bourges.

The next problem was to secure these men's allegiance to the King, which many generals had refused to offer. Davout proposed the following proclamation as a guarantee: 'No Frenchman will be proscribed or deprived of his rank or employment. The army will be retained in its present status so long as foreign troops are on French soil.'

'I have told you twenty times', replied Marshal Gouvion-Saint-Cyr, the new Minister of War, 'and I repeat for the twenty-first that I have been forbidden to accept anything from the army but submission, pure and simple . . .'

'Count on the King to do more . . .'

On 14 July at the Château de la Source near Orléans, the Prince of Eckmühl (Davout), surrounded by his generals, tried to convince the officers that only the King could prevent the devastation of France, and that he was awaiting a pledge of allegiance from the army. Though not unanimous, most of it pledged its allegiance on the 15th.

On that day at the island of Aix the Emperor, wearing the uniform of the *chasseurs à cheval* with his little hat, boarded the *Bellerophon* to go to England. General Lallemand and Quartermaster Joannis[5] of the marines accompanied him.

At the same moment in Paris Commander Rigny and a lieutenant of the marines of the Guard left for Rochefort with dispatches from the Minister of Marine, addressed to the commander of the frigate *La Saale*, and from Marshal Gouvion-Saint-Cyr to the commandant of Aix, ordering them to deliver Napoleon to the English. Fortunately, the Emperor had already surrendered to Captain Maitland and had thus spared these officers, as well as France and the King, the shame of such an infamy.

Rigny was shortly promoted captain, and later admiral, and the incriminating documents were removed from his file in the naval archives.

On the Loire the moment had arrived for the troops to surrender their flags and change their cockades. Lt. Colonel Duchand of the horse artillery resigned his command in the following order of the day:

'Officers, NCO's, and gunners of the Imperial Guard, I bid you farewell. Since I have had the honor to command you, you have been my whole glory. But all our efforts and courage have come to naught. My comrades, until this dreadful day I have suffered at seeing our dear country sullied by foreigners without being able to avenge her with my blood. Now new conditions have been imposed to which I cannot subscribe. My principles, my honor, my whole soul are opposed to them. No, I shall never address you in any other language than that in which I addressed you at Waterloo. I will not be the one who orders you to defend another standard!'

In times of revolution it is hard to determine where one's duty lies. On his return from Elba Napoleon had solved all questions of conscience when he said: 'The country comes first. Then one can be sure of not making a mistake . . .'

The Paris government promised that no one would be molested for his opinions. But after 25 July the police rounded up their victims: Ney, the younger Lallemand Barrois, Bertrand, Arrighi, Colbert, Ornano, Merlin de Douai, Hulin, etc. Within three months 12,371 officers, NCO's, and soldiers were exiled from Paris, and 7,371 put under police surveillance. Some Guardsmen who had deserted on impulse were picked up by gendarmes and turned over to His Majesty's palace guards who held them prisoner in their barracks. Though the palace guards testified that their prisoners' conduct was exemplary, no one knew what to do with them, since the

[5] Joannis was born in Baltimore, Md. – Ed.

barracks of the Friars-Minor – the only one not occupied by Allied troops – was filled to bursting with retired soldiers.

On 1 August the Duke of Taranto (Macdonald) succeeded Davout in command of the Army of the Loire. There the gendarmes operated in the same manner as in Paris. *Gardes du corps* in mufti brought in lists that permitted Davout to warn those in the greatest danger. Lefebvre-Desnoëttes shaved off his moustache and became a commercial traveler. Delaborde, crippled with gout, hid on a farm where the mistress of the house introduced him to inquisitive gendarmes as her 'poor old invalid grandfather'. For the moment the elder Lallemand was on the *Bellerophon* with the Emperor, together with Savary and Quartermaster Joannis and his wife who had volunteered to follow Napoleon wherever he went. Mouton-Duvernet hid near Montbrison. On their release from English prisons, Drouot and Cambronne gave themselves up to the authorities.

The Guard was closely watched by Macdonald. Dériot was chief of staff, Morand commanded the infantry, and Guyot the cavalry. The artillery was without a commander. The meticulous Boinod and Commissary Dufour put the accounts in order. The survivors of the 4th Grenadiers and 4th Chasseurs had been turned over to the 3rd Regiments.

The 1st Young Guard Division had no chief, but Generals Guye and Chartrand still commanded its brigades. The second brigade had absorbed the volunteer battalions formed at Lyons and Bordeaux during the march from Golfe-Juan. The 2nd Division was commanded by General Meunier, now recovered from his wounds, with Generals Aymard and Girard as brigade commanders.

The infantry was widely scattered, with each regiment in a different town. To facilitate feeding the men and horses and avoid riots, Macdonald broke up the cavalry into squadrons and some infantry into detachments of 25–30 men. Furthermore, since idleness was supposed to breed bad counsel, the troops changed quarters every ten days.

What could they do? The young looked forward to their release, and the old feared it. They knew their days were numbered, and that it was better so. Now that the Emperor had been betrayed and was on his way to Saint Helena, they had better disappear and leave the eagles, now perched on flags they had not seen on any battlefield. Facing poverty, they would still have memories of the father who had taught them to see through his eyes. At the lowest rung of the rank ladder, though often first in the breach, they had shed their blood for the honor of France and the glory of the Emperor. Now they awaited their fate with resignation. But, then, with the *Tondu*, one never knew . . . Perhaps he would return . . .

On 3 August the King decreed the dissolution of the Guard, and Macdonald issued orders for its execution. This was the end.

Chief Inspector Boinod, in charge of liquidating the Guard, kept in his heart the image of the master he had served so faithfully. Only the Veteran's Company under Charpentier was retained to care for a few old soldiers.

The Young Guard regiments were disbanded at the beginning of September by Generals Meunier and Guye whose influence prevented serious incidents. The units were sparse as many officers and men had 'remained in the rear', according to a euphemism of the quartermasters.

On 11 September Old Man Roguet, with death in his soul, reviewed the 1st Grenadiers for the last time. 'Without a murmur', according to the Inspector, General Petit, and Majors Combes and Loubers, 23 officers, 95 NCO's, 24 sappers, and 707 grenadiers listened impassively as seventeen drummers beat 'To the Colors'; then their flag was delivered to the Inspector. Tears were rolling down the moustaches of the grenadiers. For three-quarters of them life was over.

Roguet and Petit would retire to Paris if the King permitted. Thirty-one NCO's and grenadiers would receive a pension of between 115 and 200 francs a year. Fifty agreed to serve in the *Garde Royale* or the departmental legions. The rest were discharged with a certificate.

On the 16th the 2nd Grenadiers was dissolved. Christiani went to Paris where he was turned over to the police. Though Golzio and Martenot were carried on the army list as 'eligible for the departmental legions', places were rare – especially for ex-Guardsmen. Most of the captains, five lieutenants, the drum major, and 13 NCO's were retired on pensions ranging from 200 to 1,200 francs.

On the 24th Porvet de Morvan presented for the last time 403 grenadiers and 37 officers of the 3rd and 4th Regiments. Since their cadres were younger and more adaptable, most of the officers asked to join the new army. One must eat, after all – though the Minister did not always recognize this necessity.

The case of the 3rd Chasseurs was different. On 1 October Lt. Colonel Henrion presented 41 officers, all of whom did not belong to the corps, and only 143 chasseurs. The rest had been lost in the campaign. The other two regiments, disbanded on the 11th, were in better shape. Several of the 1st Chasseurs joined the Royal Guard and the rest were retired or discharged. The Corsicans from Elba finished out their term of enlistment in the Line.

General Noury disbanded the artillery at the end of the month. The horse artillery was dissolved 'without any disorder or a single complaint', followed by the foot companies, train, and depot. In each of the latter from 30 to 80 men, including the trumpet major of the train, transferred to the Royal Guard, and from 20 to 60 to the Line. The rest were discharged, though many had already deserted.

The sappers were disbanded on 16 October. A number of the wagon train transferred to the Line.

The cavalry took several months to liquidate. Of all the Guard, these regiments were most mistrusted by the regime. 'The officers must be employed according to their talents and services; as for their opinions and political acts – that's another matter', wrote the inspectors.

'These gentlemen belonged to a corps afflicted with troublesome prejudices', General Count Founier-Sarlovèze wrote on disbanding a squadron of Red Lancers. Had he forgotten that his brother had been killed at Leipzig as a *chasseur à cheval* of the Guard? Since General Colbert was in prison, General Briche had dissolved the staff and first two squadrons in September. The treasury was empty and the prefect had to advance the money for the men's back pay. 'We disbanded crying *"Vive le Roi!"'* the General reported.

Major Kirmann presented the first two squadrons and staff of the chasseurs to Count Fournier on 2 December. This, being the anniversary of the Emperor's coronation, was an unfortunate date to choose. Moreover, though they had gone unpaid in the Emperor's time without complaint, today the chasseurs rendered their account and demanded full payment, without which they refused to leave.

The rest of the regiment was dissolved without a struggle. Generals Lion and de Castries reported – perhaps optimistically – 'The regiment of ex-*chasseurs à cheval* of the Old Guard, including the Mameluks, was disbanded in perfect tranquillity. Some of the men desiring to join the *Garde Royale* are being formed into companies.'

Presented by Hoffmayer, the dragoons were dissolved in November and December. Several officers were 'absent without permission'; two-thirds of the effectives were discharged and the rest placed on half-pay or retired. Fifteen officers and eleven men asked to join the new army.

Finally, on 25 November, on the mall at Preuilly in Touraine, Generals Dumas and d'Audenarde presided at the death of the 'gods'. The staff and first squadron of horse grenadiers – taking precedence over the whole horse Guard – were disbanded. Nearly all these giants were survivors of Waterloo and were covered with scars and decorations. This had been the Emperor's last reserve.

Today, for the last time, their trumpeters opened the *Ban*. The standard-bearer and guard advanced to the Inspector and presented the standard. Guyot and the ten officers present were unable to look. The Imperial Guard was no more.

CHAPTER 7

The Aftermath

OVER muddy roads, in rain and snow, without arms or bread, the Grumblers marched, wearing military cloaks and forage caps and carrying knapsacks or portmanteaux on their backs. Some also carried a pouch slung over their shoulder, and a scooped-out coconut serving as canteen. Thus they finally reached their native villages.

Like prisoners, soldiers can march for hours without saying a word. The gendarmes insulted them en route, and the inhabitants closed their doors against these 'brigands of the Loire' and 'supporters of the Usurper'. Out of indifference or cowardice, the men whom the French had fêted, cheered, and idolized for fifteen years were now rejected.

Nothing is more stable than that which has ceased to exist. Some of the veterans found a home, a field, and a wardrobe where they could hang the old regimentals that they tearfully brushed each 15 August and 2 December because – who knows – they might wear them again when 'he' returned. Some even found frames for their patents of nobility – their service certificate and cross of the Legion – which they hung under the Emperor's portrait.

They sought some boys whom they might teach to drill, some friends to listen to their tales of Schönbrunn and the retreat from Russia, and some veterans with whom they might drink on market days to 'the other one' and 'his Guard'. They saluted the gendarme corporal because he was a soldier, but they never talked politics. They kept all that inside.

Others, less stable, were watched by the police. They occupied barrack-like rooms in poor lodging houses, and lived by their wits or a few odd jobs. Touchy, embittered, quick-tempered, they wooed the cashier at the café, knocked down the fanatic royalists, killed them in duels, then crossed the frontiers and disappeared, or committed suicide. Balzac knew these men.

Some had no talents beyond the manual of arms. They had overrun Europe, content with a pinch on the ear or a quid of tobacco. They wore on their breasts a piece of 'his' grey cloak, in place of the cross that they believed – not unreasonably – that they had earned. These could think of nothing beyond winning battles and dying for 'him'.

To earn a living, some men served the king. Men who had served in 'his' Guard for the honor of serving ought to set an example to others and show the king's officers, whose gold epaulets were too shiny, what a grenadier of the Emperor was like. These were the 'puritans of honor'. 'Self-abnegation is easier and more common than one would suppose', wrote Alfred de Vigny.

Some were victims of politics and hate, and were struck down by bandits who killed in the king's name. Marshals, generals, captains, and soldiers were imprisoned and tried by the politicians and shot. Others were struck down by gendarmes, police, or a café quarrel-picker. Mameluks crying '*Vive l'Empereur!*' were massacred at Marseille, and thrown into a common grave under the royal ensign. 'These unfortunates had counted on France's good faith and the honor of a generous people, and had expected to find asylum in a hospitable land. They had loved a great captain, attached themselves to his person, and had never received anything but kindness from him whom they had first met as a conquerer at the foot of the Pyramids.'

Some conspired, with or without hope. This was the moment to talk of the 'other one', and to prepare quarters for the 'little one' who had stripped the feathers off Grenadier Coigniet's plume on the banks of the Seine. They would go seek him at Schönbrunn where he played in the Glorietta in the park of '*Beau-père*'. They knew the way!

Some, obsessed with their anger, left France. They were welcomed as brothers-in-arms in the Rhineland where Napoleon's name was a symbol of lost liberties. They found the innkeeper at Zweibrücken who had been a corporal in the *pupilles* and had transferred to the grenadiers and been wounded at Waterloo; and the ex-adjutant NCO of the 2nd Lancers at Oppenheim who had won the Legion of Honor.

Krettly, the old trumpet major of the chasseurs whose mare Fanny had saluted the Emperor with her elegant hindquarters, escaped to Belgium to avoid prison. 'Make yourself at home here', he was told by a brother-in-arms, now colonel of a Belgian regiment. 'Don't speak to me of those men who betrayed their country and their Emperor. All honor to the exiles who are unhappy in France today!'

Some, like the elder Lallemand, went as far afield as Hungary and Turkey; others, like the Bacheville brothers, went to Persia; still others, like Grouchy and Lefebvre-Desnoëttes went to America, the land of Liberty, where they met Joseph Bonaparte as the 'Count of Survilliers'. François Lallemand crossed the seas and tried to organize the colony of Champ d'Asyle in Texas where fugitives from the Bourbons worked to clear ground on which they might live together as before, sleep in their cloaks, wake to the sound of drums, and defend themselves against wild beasts and savages. When the camp of Eagleville, with its Austerlitz Place, Eylau and Wagram Streets, was completed they would go and free the Emperor on Saint Helena. Unfortunately, in a few months yellow fever and cannibals[1] got the better of these pioneers (see Plate 170).

But whether before a firing-squad, or at a tavern, or on sentry-go, or watching the *Mousquetaires* parade, or in Texas, or standing below the column from which 'he' had vanished, or standing in the Carrousel with ordered arms, they thought of 'him' – always of 'him'. They could bear privation, poverty, exile, and death because on his rock he was suffering, too.

[1] Though contemporary Texans may object to this statement, according to Lt. Colonel John R. Elting of the faculty of West Point, 'The Indian tribes along the Texas coast included cannibals; one, the Tonkawas, continued the practice as a ritual act, at least, up to the period of the Mexican War – if not later'. – Ed.

And 'he' never ceased to think of them. When at last death knocked at his door he remembered them in his will: Bessières' son, Duroc's daughter, Letort's children, and the orphans of Mouton-Duvernet and Chartrand who had been shot. To Lefebvre-Desnoëttes, Cambronne, Lallemand, Éméry, Boinod, Drouot, Larrey, he left a sum of money. He left 100,000 francs to be divided among the 'proscribed men wandering in foreign lands'; 200,000 to be divided among the amputees of Ligny and Waterloo, 'with double to the Guard, and quadruple to the men of the Elba Battalion'; '300,000 francs to be distributed among the officers and soldiers of my Guard who served in the Elba battalion and are still living, or to their widows or children, the shares of amputees or severely wounded to be double'.

They knew that he 'was very ill'; but, like him, Prometheus had been chained to a rock and had become immortal. Well, then . . . he, too, perhaps?

From far out in the Atlantic the shadow of the grey cloak and little hat became a legend. Many oppressed peoples of Europe looked to him who had launched a program for ages to come.

One morning in July 1821 the newsboys of the boulevards and the country postmen announced the death of 'Napoleon Buonaparte'. The Guard raged and wept. Some were skeptical. 'Dead, like other people? What are you saying? Some more crackbrained nonsense!' However, by August the novelty shops and peddlers' stands were hawking strange pamphlets entitled: 'Napoleon on the Champs-Elysées, by an Old Soldier'; 'Thoughts of a Warrior on the High Spots of Napoleon's Career'; 'Military Dialogue on the Death of Napoleon, by a Company of Braves of the ex-Guard.' (All spurious and all anonymous, to evade the law.)

Then the *Memorial* of Las Cases appeared; the *History of Napoleon* 'as he never existed', by the ex-*gendarme d'ordonnance* Norvins. Then news of his escape. He had landed at Ostende . . . 'Where are you going?' the wife of a Belgian veteran asked him as he was putting on his grenadier's coat.

'To "him"!'

'Always Him – everywhere Him', wrote Victor Hugo. And Béranger wrote:
They will talk of his glory
Under the thatch for a long time . . .'

Fifteen years passed. Lefebvre-Desnoëttes had died at sea in 1822, shipwrecked on his way home from America. Curial died after a fall from his horse returning from the coronation of Charles X. Other officers and men had gone to join the Emperor, because they were tired and the idleness of peace is often fatal to old soldiers. Fifteen years – the time some brave men had spent winning a marshal's baton and a fortune and turning traitor; the time it took others to work up from grenadier to sergeant major, provided they could read; the time it took to draw up the Code and deliver it to Europe with each new victory.

In Berlin they crammed the University for eighteen months to hear Gans lecture on Napoleon. At Corfu candles burned before his picture. Gobineau found him in Persia, and in Patagonia the Incas welcomed the naturalist d'Orbigny with the words: 'Let me embrace you, since you have seen the demigod'. The natives of New Zealand named their chief 'Napoulo Ponapati' because one of them had seen 'him' at Saint Helena. Lady Stanhope, Pitt's niece, wrote: 'Only one man was worthy to command the Arabs and the world, and the kings of Europe exiled him. They will be punished for it.'

And so they were, in 1830 and 1848, with revolutions in France and Europe and cries of '*Vive la liberté!*' and '*Vive l'Empereur Napoléon!*' The Duke of Orléans, King of the French, gave them back their tricolor flag under which he had served at Valmy and Jemappes, and the cockade he had worn. He also remembered the 'finest regiment he had ever seen' on the square at Cambrai in March 1815.

One cannot recover the past, but one can right its reparable wrongs. Louis-Philippe recalled to the army those veterans of the Guard still able to serve such as Guyot, Lallemand, Petit, Meuziau, Roguet, Guye, Henrion, Barrois, Harlet, Dumoustier, Dautancourt, Poret de Morvan, Schramm, etc.; he conferred the grand cordon of the Legion on Drouot, and generals' stars on Lignim, Duchand, Pailhès, and Trappier, and a marshal's baton on Mouton, Count of Lobau. He revised the pensions of the humble men, authorized an association of the former officers of the Imperial Guard, and put the Emperor back on his column. Then he brought back Napoleon's ashes 'to the banks of the Seine'.

For this ceremony on 15 December 1840 the surviving Grumblers took out of their wardrobes whatever the moths had spared of their old regimentals. The poorest ones were uniformed by General Flahaut. Tottering, lame, shuffling their feet, the Grumblers took their places behind the hearse. The crowd saw them and saluted. Among the Mameluks they looked for Roustam. 'Loyalty may only be displayed at funerals', wrote *Le Temps*. Two marines in full dress, General Duchand, Loubers in his uniform of a lieutenant colonel of the Elba grenadiers, and some Polish lancers were there. All wore in their buttonholes a sprig of laurel from the wreaths on the Emperor's coffin. Veterans came from Belgium and the Rhineland. They marched down the Champs-Elysées to the booming of guns under tricolor flags and eagles. Now they knew he had returned! At the Invalides General Petit saluted them, and the governor Marshal Moncey, the army, the national guard, and all Paris welcomed them.

In Boulogne on 15 August 1841 the marines of the Guard in uniform dedicated a column surmounted by Bosio's statue of Napoleon. General Corbineau presided.

Each year on 29 May, the anniversary of Josephine's death, the old dragoons of the Guard went to pay their respects to the tomb of their gracious patron. Four hundred Guard veterans, led by Arrighi, Jerzmanowski, and others, attended the funeral of Louis Bonaparte, ex-King of Holland, at the church of Saint-Leu in 1846.

On 15 December 1845, at a reunion banquet of the former officers of the Imperial Guard, their president General Schramm eulogized Drouot who had died that year. Then he congratulated Grenadier Noisot who at Fixin, near Dijon, had 'erected at his own expense a very beautiful bronze monument' to the Emperor by the sculptor Rude. (When Noisot died he had himself buried in a standing position a few yards away so he might continue to mount guard on the Emperor throughout eternity!)

But by now the ranks of the Guard were thinning. Hurault de Sorbée, a general in 1839, died in 1850. That year General Petit was made honorary president of the Association which decided that the 'NCO's of the Guard who at the time of its disbanding ranked as officers in the Line should be admitted'.

Ten years later the survivors received from the hands of 'his' nephew, now Emperor, the 'Saint Helena medal' in memory of his 'last bequests to his old companions in glory'. The old horse chasseurs were still jaunty when they paid homage to Napoleon each 15 August and 2 December. They were led by two trumpeters in scarlet pelisses who sounded 'To the Emperor' at the foot of his column.

At the close of the Second Empire about twenty of the last survivors marched in a parade before the column where an old drummer of the foot Grenadiers, a bit shrunk in his uniform, beat the *Grenadière*. Then they visited the Emperor's tomb, stopping on the way to visit their comrades at the Invalides.

Some lived to a great age. In 1872 the marine Jean Leroux died at Treport at the age of eighty-six. He had been cited for bravery at Arcis, and had followed the Emperor to Elba and Waterloo. Returning to the fleet in 1815, he retired on half-pay in 1837. 'Uncle John', as he was called, used to fish on the river bank. In 1847 he presented to the church of Saint-Jacques a jeweled monstrance holding the cross he was awarded on the *Inconstant*; and in 1859, a stained glass window portraying the donor in full dress kneeling on one knee, sword in hand, before the Archangel Michael.

Captain Soufflot, a lieutenant in the Red Lancers at Waterloo, died in 1893 in his 100th year. The year before, chasseur Vivien died in Lyons at 106. But one veteran lived in three centuries. Lieutenant Markiewicz of the Polish light-horse was born in Cracow in 1794, fought in the Russian campaign, was decorated in 1813, charged at Waterloo, and was still living in 1902. By that time the cemeteries held the last survivor of the Guard. But their memory lived on, thanks to Chateaubriand, Heine, Schumann, the Vernets, Béranger, Victor Hugo, Thiers, etc.

An old adage runs: 'There is no temple without a God, and no throne without a Guard'. But there are guards and Guards. There were the Pretorians who sold Galba's head to Otto and put the Empire up for auction; the Strelitz of Ivan the Terrible who revolted and were liquidated by Peter the Great; the Janissaries who were massacred by Mahmoud II; the Mameluks, a troop of infidel slaves who revolted against the Ayoubite Sultans, were defeated by Napoleon, and liquidated by Mohammed Ali. There were the guards of the king of Prussia, the tsar, the Austrian emperor, the English king; the guards of the king of France, and the *Maison du Roy*. But there was never an Emperor's Guard – only the Imperial Guard.

This was no palace troop or political instrument, but a corps of carefully chosen soldiers who won their privileges by distinguished service in the army. The Imperial Guard was analogous to the reserves of 'chosen men' who, according to Xenophon, were 'held in the rear to watch the front lines and support them if they should be intimidated'; to Caesar's reserve to which he owed his victory over Pompey at Pharsalia; to the Swiss at the battle of Dreux; to the solid reserves of Gustavus Adolphus,

Maurice of Nassau, and Turenne. The Imperial Guard was the elite reserve of Napoleon who fashioned it by his spirit and his will and gave it a soul.

His comrades of the Italian campaigns formed its nucleus. They were rough soldiers who owed him their jobs, their prestige, their honor and glory, which they paid for in devotion and loyalty. From this reciprocity was born the spirit of the Guard.

It was the highest expression of the military spirit, which is less a desire to fight than the desire to fight well, the willingness to prepare one's self for war and to learn each day how to die.

In his *Principles of the Art of War* de Billon wrote in 1622: 'The humblest soldier has his honor to recommend him'. The spirit of the Guard was the cult of honor.

'You must love soldiers in order to understand them, and understand them in order to lead them', said Turenne. Those who have had the honor to command Frenchmen have never ignored the role of the heart. By playing it to perfection, Napoleon created the finest army in the world.

Because he loved his men, he was good to them; because he was simple and just in his dealings with them, they loved him in return; because he was brave, they admired him; because he was a Latin, and hence a bit of an actor, he fascinated and awed them.

The Old Guard breathed its spirit into the Young Guard, and both breathed it into the Line, until the spirit of the Guard animated the whole Imperial army and continued to inspire those that came after it in 1845, 1870, and 1914.

So long as the windows of truth are kept open, this spirit will return to clear away the poisonous miasmas of our time. Only mediocre men are embarrassed by the presence of an elite.

Napoleon, a citizen of France, was a universal genius. From the Frenchmen of his day he fashioned the Imperial Guard and led it to immortality.

APPENDIX 'A'
Units of the Guard in Order of their Creation*

GRENADIERS (*Grenadiers à pied*. Nicknames: gaiter-straps; grumblers)

1st Regiment created 2 December 1799; disbanded 11 September 1815.

2nd Regiment created 15 April 1806; merged with 1st Regiment 1809; re-formed 18 May 1811; disbanded 24 September 1815.

2nd (Dutch) Regiment created 13 September 1810; became 3rd Grenadiers 18 May 1811.

3rd (Dutch) Regiment created 18 May 1811; disbanded 15 February 1813.

3rd (French) Regiment created 8 April 1815; disbanded 24 September 1815.

4th Regiment created 9 May 1815; disbanded 24 September 1815.

CHASSEURS (*Chasseurs à pied*. Nickname: grumblers)

1st Regiment created 2 December 1799 as 'light infantry'; became chasseurs 1801; disbanded 11 October 1815.

2nd Regiment created 15 April 1806; merged with 1st Regiment 1809; re-formed 18 May 1811; disbanded 11 October 1815.

3rd Regiment created 8 April 1815; disbanded 1 October 1815.

4th Regiment created 9 May 1815; disbanded 1 October 1815.

HORSE GRENADIERS (*Grenadiers à cheval*. Nicknames: big heels, gods, giants)

Created 2 December 1799 as 'light cavalry'; became horse grenadiers December 1800; disbanded 23 July 1814; re-formed 8 April 1815; disbanded 25 November 1815.

CHASSEURS à CHEVAL (Nicknames: invincibles, cherished children, comrades)

Created 2 December 1799; disbanded 28 July 1814; re-formed 8 April 1815; disbanded 26 October 1815.

LIGHT ARTILLERY (*Artillerie légère*)

Created 2 December 1799 with one mounted squadron; became horse artillery 15 April 1806.

TRAIN OF ARTILLERY (*Train d'artillerie*)

Created 8 September 1800; disbanded 1814; re-formed 8 April 1815; disbanded 1 December 1815.

Young Guard Regiment created February 1813.

COMPANY OF VETERANS (*Compagnie des Vétérans*)

Created 12 July 1801. Continued under the Monarchy.

MAMELUKS

Created 13 October 1801, attached to *chasseurs à cheval*; disbanded 1814.

ELITE GENDARMES (*Gendarmes d'élite*. Nickname: immortals)

Created 19 March 1802; disbanded 23 April 1814; re-formed 8 April 1815.

MARINES (*Marins*)

Created 17 September 1803; disbanded 23 April 1814 (one company went to Elba with Napoleon); re-formed 8 April 1815; disbanded 4 September 1815.

VÉLITE GRENADIERS

Created 29 July 1804.

VÉLITE CHASSEURS

Created 29 July 1804.

VÉLITE HORSE GRENADIERS (*Vélite grenadiers à cheval*)

Created 17 September 1805.

VÉLITE HORSE CHASSEURS (*Vélite chasseurs à cheval*)

Created 17 September 1805.

VÉLITE ARTILLERY (*Vélite canonniers*)

Created 15 April 1806.

HORSE ARTILLERY (*Artillerie à cheval*. Nickname: horse gunners)

Created 15 April 1806 from horse companies of light artillery; reorganized 8 April 1815; disbanded 3 October 1815.

DRAGOONS (*Dragons*)

Created 15 April 1806; became 'Empress' Dragoons' (*Dragons de l'Impératrice*) 1807; disbanded 12 May 1814; re-formed 8 April 1815; disbanded 15 December 1815.

* Dates of creation, disbandment etc. from Sauzey, *Iconographie du costume militaire, Révolution et Empire.* – Ed.

WORK, or ARTISAN BATTALION
(*Ouvriers d'Administration*)
Created 15 April 1806.

FUSILIER-GRENADIERS
Created 19 September 1806; disbanded 12 May 1814.

FUSILIER-CHASSEURS
Created 15 December 1806; disbanded 12 May 1814.

GENDARMES D'ORDONNANCE
Created 23 September 1806; disbanded 23 October 1807.

POLISH LIGHT-HORSE (*Chevau-légers polonais*)
1st Regiment created 2 March 1807; became 1st Light-Horse-Lancers (*Chevau-légers-Lanciers*) 1809; sent squadron to Elba; disbanded voluntarily 1 October 1815.
3rd Regiment created 5 July 1812; practically wiped out in Russian campaign; merged with 1st Regiment 22 March 1813.

FOOT ARTILLERY (*Artillerie à pied.* Nickname: foot gunners)
Created 17 April 1808 as independent organization; re-formed 8 April 1815; disbanded 29 October 1815.

PONTOONEERS (*Pontonniers*)
Attached to foot artillery 1808.

TIRAILLEUR-GRENADIERS
1st Regiment created 16 January 1809; became 1st *Tirailleurs* 30 December 1810.
2nd Regiment created 25 April 1809; became 2nd *Tirailleurs* 30 December 1810.

TIRAILLEUR-CHASSEURS
1st Regiment created 16 January 1809; became 1st Voltigeurs 30 December 1810.
2nd Regiment created 25 April 1809; became 2nd Voltigeurs 30 December 1810.

CONSCRIPT-GRENADIERS (*Conscrits-grenadiers*)
1st Regiment created 29 March 1809; became 3rd *Tirailleurs* 10 February 1811.
2nd Regiment created 31 March 1809; became 4th *Tirailleurs* 10 February 1811.

CONSCRIPT-CHASSEURS (*Conscrits-chasseurs*)
1st Regiment created 31 March 1809; became 3rd Voltigeurs 10 February 1811.
2nd Regiment created 31 March 1809; became 4th Voltigeurs 10 February 1811.

VÉLITES OF TURIN
Created April 1809.

VÉLITES OF FLORENCE
Created April 1809.

LANCERS OF BERG (*Lanciers de Berg*)
Admitted to Guard 17 December 1809; passed into Prussian service on dissolution of Confederation of the Rhine October 1813.

NATIONAL GUARDS (*Gardes nationales de la Garde*)
Created 1 January 1810; became 7th Voltigeurs 15 February 1813.

SAPPERS (*Sapeurs du Génie*)
Created 16 July 1810; disbanded 1814; re-formed 8 April 1815.

2ND LIGHT-HORSE, or 'RED' LANCERS (*Chevau-légers-Lanciers, 'Lanciers rouges'*)
2nd Regiment created September 1810; disbanded 1814; re-formed 8 April 1815; disbanded 20 September 1815.

TIRAILLEURS
1st Regiment created from 1 *Tirailleur*-grenadiers 30 December 1810; re-formed 8 April 1815.
2nd Regiment created from 2 *Tirailleur*-grenadiers 30 December 1810: re-formed 8 April 1815.
3rd Regiment created from 1 Conscript-grenadiers 10 February 1811; re-formed 8 April 1815.
3rd *bis* Regiment created from *pupilles* 17 January 1813; disbanded March 1813.
4th Regiment created from 4 Conscript-grenadiers 10 February 1811; re-formed 8 April 1815.
4th *bis* Regiment created from *pupilles* 17 January 1813; disbanded March 1813.
5th Regiment created 18 May 1811; re-formed 8 April 1815.
5th *bis* Regiment created from *pupilles* 17 January 1813; disbanded March 1813.
6th Regiment created 28 August 1811; re-formed 8 April 1815.
6th *bis* Regiment created 10 January 1813; disbanded March 1813.
7th Regiment created 17 January 1813; re-formed 12 May 1815.
8th Regiment created 23 March 1813; re-formed 12 May 1815.
9th–13th Regiments created 6 April 1813; disbanded 1814.
14th–16th Regiments created 11 January 1813; disbanded 1814.
17th–19th Regiments created 21 January 1814; disbanded 1814.

VOLTIGEURS

1st Regiment created from 1 *Tirailleur*-chasseurs 30 December 1810; re-formed 8 April 1815.

2nd Regiment created from 2 *Tirailleur*-chasseurs 30 December 1810; re-formed 8 April 1815.

3rd Regiment created from 1 Conscript-chasseurs 10 February 1811; re-formed 8 April 1815.

3rd *bis* Regiment created from *pupilles* 17 January 1813; disbanded March 1813.

4th Regiment created from 2 Conscript-chasseurs 10 February 1811; re-formed 8 April 1815.

4th *bis* Regiment created 17 January 1813; disbanded March 1813.

5th Regiment created 18 May 1811; re-formed 8 April 1815.

5th *bis* Regiment created 17 January 1813; disbanded March 1813.

6th Regiment created 28 August 1811; re-formed 8 April 1815.

6th *bis* Regiment created 10 January 1813; disbanded March 1813.

7th Regiment created from national guards of the Guard 15 February 1813; re-formed 12 May 1815.

8th Regiment created 23 March 1813; re-formed 12 May 1815.

9th–13th Regiments created 6 April 1813; disbanded 1814.

14th–16th Regiments created 11 January 1814; disbanded 1814.

17th–19th Regiments created 21 January 1814; disbanded 1814.

PUPILLES (Minors)

Created 30 March 1811; disbanded 1814.

WAGON TRAIN (*Train des Équipages*)

Created 24 August 1811; disbanded 1814; re-formed 8 April 1815.

FLANKER-GRENADIERS (*Flanqueur-grenadiers*)

Created 4 September 1811; disbanded 1814.

VETERAN-CANNONEERS (*Canonniers-vétérans*)

Created 12 January 1812.

LITHUANIAN TARTARS (*Tartares Lithuaniens*)

Created 24 August 1812; incorporated with scout-lancers 1813.

FLANKER-CHASSEURS (*Flanqueur-chasseurs*)

Created 23 March 1813; disbanded 1814.

GUARDS OF HONOR (*Gardes d'honneur*)

1st–4th Regiments created 3 April 1813; disbanded 14–22 July 1814.

SCOUT-GRENADIERS (*Éclaireurs, 1er Régiment*)

Created 29 December 1813; disbanded 1814.

SCOUT-DRAGOONS (*Éclaireurs, 2e Régiment*)

Created 29 December 1813; disbanded 1814.

SCOUT-LANCERS (*Éclaireurs, 3e Régiment*)

Created 29 December 1813; disbanded 1814.

APPENDIX 'B'

Levies ordered by Napoleon from 1800 to 1815

Date	Class	Number of Men	Particulars
26 February 1800	1800	33,000	For the Reserve
18 May 1802	1801	60,000	(30,000 for the Reserve)
6 August 1802	1802	60,000	(30,000 for the Reserve)
26 April 1803	1803	60,000	(30,000 for the Reserve)
16 September 1803	1804	60,000	(30,000 for the Reserve)
24 March 1804	1805⎫	60,000	(30,000 for the Reserve)
29 December 1804	1805⎭		
17 January 1805	1805⎫	60,000	(30,000 for the Reserve)
26 August 1805	1805⎭		
3 August 1806	1806	80,000	(30,000 for the Reserve)
15 December 1806	1807	80,000	(30,000 for the Reserve)
12 April 1807	1808	80,000	(20,000 for the Reserve)
7 February 1808	1809	80,000	(20,000 for the Reserve)
2 September 1809	1806–8	60,000	Extraordinary levy
31 January 1810	1809–10	28,000	Extraordinary levy
12 February 1809	1809–10	1,550	In Tuscan departments
25 April 1809	1806–9	10,000	Supplementary levy for the Guard
12 October 1809	1810	36,000	Complementary levy
20 March 1810	1809	500	In Rome and Trasimena
8 February 1811	1811	120,000	(90,000 for the Reserve)
3 February 1811	1808–10	6,965	In Belgium, Holland, Rhineland, Italy
1 July 1811	1809–11	25,641	In Lippe, Holland, and 24,619 for the Reserve
4 August 1811	1810	3,500	In German departments
11 August 1811	1809, 1811	8,501	In Belgium, Holland, Rhineland, Italy
		1,700	15-year-old foundlings for *pupilles*
20 December 1811	1812	120,000	(7,751 for the Reserve)
14 March 1812	1807–12	108,000	For 100 cohorts of 1st *Ban* of national guard (Only 88 called up)
22 September 1812	1813	137,000	(17,000 to complete cohorts)
11, 20 January 1813	1st *Ban*, national guard	100,000	
	1809–12	100,000	
	1814	150,000	(9,569 for the Reserve)
3 March 1813		10,000	(for guards of honor)
14 March 1813	1st *Ban*, national guard	80,000	
	1814	90,000	
23 July 1813	1813	25,000	Extraordinary levy of deferred conscripts for the Reserve
28 August 1813	1812–14	30,000	In Pyrenees departments, for Army of Spain
9 October 1813	1812–13⎫	120,000	First 75,000 called up at start of invasion
7 January 1814	1812–13⎭		
16 November 1813	1805–14	300,000	(150,000 for Reserve)
6 March 1814	1814⎫	160,000	Continued during Hundred Days
28 March 1815	1815⎭		

TOTAL 2,545,357 men (of whom 1,350,000* were actually called up)

*From January 1791 to July 1799 the Republic conscripted 1,570,000 men.

APPENDIX 'C'

Principal Events of Consulate and Empire

Fall of the Directory, 10 November 1799

Battle of Marengo, 14 June 1800

Treaty of Morfontaine (between United States and France) 1 October 1800

Battle of Hohenlinden (General Moreau defeated Archduke John) 5 December 1800

Attempted assassination of Bonaparte ('infernal machine' incident) 24 December 1800

Treaty of Lunéville (between France and Austria) 9 February 1801

Treaty of Paris (between France and Russia) 18 October 1801

Treaty of Amiens (General Peace) 25 March 1802

Creation of the Legion of Honor, 19 May 1802

Plebiscite electing Bonaparte Consul for life, 2 August 1802

Santo Domingo expedition, January 1802–October 1804

Louisiana Purchase, 30 April 1803

First German Confederation formed (alliance of principalities to counterbalance Prussia and Austria) 1803

Civil Code adopted, 21 March 1804

Execution of the Duc d'Enghien, 21 March 1804

Imperial Constitution, 18 May 1804

Coronation of Napoleon as Emperor of the French, 2 December 1804

Coronation of Napoleon as King of Italy, 26 May 1805

Third Coalition formed against France (England, Russia, Austria, Naples, Sweden) 9 August 1805

Battle of Trafalgar (Lord Nelson defeated Admiral Villeneuve) 20 October 1805

Capitulation of Ulm, 20 October 1805

Treaty of Potsdam (between Russia and Prussia) 3 November 1805

Entry of Napoleon into Vienna, 14 November 1805

Battle of Austerlitz, 2 December 1805

Treaty of Pressburg (between France and Austria) 26 December 1805

Confederation of the Rhine (16 members) 12 July 1806

Fourth Coalition formed against France (Prussia, England, Russia, Sweden) 1 October 1806

Battles of Jena and Auerstadt, 14 October 1806

Napoleon's entry into Berlin, 27 October 1806

Napoleon's entry into Warsaw, 19 December 1806

Battle of Eylau, 8 February 1807

Battle of Friedland, 14 June 1807

Treaty of Tilsit (between France, Russia, and Prussia) 9 July 1807

Grand Duchy of Warsaw instituted at Dresden, 19 July 1807

Jerome Bonaparte named King of Westphalia, 8 August 1807

Abdication of Charles IV and Ferdinand VII of Spain, 10 May 1808

Joseph Bonaparte named King of Spain, 6 June 1808

Capitulation of Baylén, 23 July 1808

Interview at Erfurt between Napoleon and Alexander I, 24 September 1808

Fifth Coalition formed against France (Austria, England, Spain, Portugal) spring, 1809

Battle of Essling (Aspern), 21 May 1809

Battle of Wagram, 6 July 1809

Treaty of Vienna (between France and Austria) 14 October 1809

Divorce of Napoleon and Josephine, 14 December 1809

Marriage of Napoleon to Archduchess Marie-Louise of Austria, 1 April 1810

Birth of the King of Rome, 20 March 1811

French Army crossed the Niemen, 24 June 1812

Rupture of alliance between France and Russia, 15 August 1812

Battle of Borodino, 7 September 1812

Entry of Napoleon into Moscow, 15 September 1812

Departure of French Army from Moscow, 19 October 1812

Battle of Krasny, 16 November 1812

Crossing of the Berezina, 28–29 November 1812

Sixth Coalition formed against France (Austria, Prussia, England, Russia) 14 June 1813

Battle of Vitoria (Duke of Wellington defeated Joseph) 21 June 1813

Joseph evacuated Madrid, 3 August 1813

Battle of Dresden, 26 August 1813

Battle of Leipzig, 16–19 October 1813

Ferdinand VII restored to Spanish throne, 11 December 1813

Allied Armies crossed the Rhine, 21 December 1813–1 January 1814

Treaty of Chaumont (between Russia, Austria, Prussia, and England) 1 March 1814

Fall of Paris, 30 March 1814

First abdication of Napoleon, 6 April 1814

Battle of Toulouse (Wellington defeated Marshal Soult) 10 April 1814

Napoleon arrived at Elba, 3 May 1814

Entry of Louis XVIII into Paris, 3 May 1814

Treaty of Paris (between France and Allies) 30 May 1814

Opening of Congress of Vienna, 1 November 1814

Landing of Napoleon at Golfe-Juan, 1 March 1815

Battles of Ligny and Quatre-Bras, 16 June 1815

Battle of Waterloo, 18 June 1815

Second abdication of Napoleon, 22 June 1815

Return of Louis XVIII to Paris, 28 June 1815

Embarkation of Napoleon on *Bellerophon* for England, 15 July 1815

Napoleon arrived at St Helena, 16 October 1815

Death of Napoleon, 5 May 1821

Second funeral of Napoleon, Paris, 15 December 1840

Final burial of Napoleon in tomb at Invalides 2 August 1861

APPENDIX 'D'

Armament and Tactics of the Imperial Guard

1. *Infantry Small Arms and Bayonets*

AT the beginning of the 18th century matchlock muskets were replaced by flintlocks. The new musket's firing sequence was as follows: when the trigger was pulled, releasing the cock, a small lead-encased flint held in the jaws of the cock struck the steel, or frizzen, producing sparks which ignited the powder in the pan. The fire was transmitted through a small channel, or priming-hole, drilled in the barrel, to the main charge.

Simultaneously, bayonets fixed in the musket barrels replaced the long pikes used for defense by the infantry. Later Vauban devised a method of fixing bayonets in sockets outside the barrels, allowing the piece to be fired with the bayonet in place.

In 1777 portable firearms were classified as infantry, dragoon, artillery, and marine muskets; musketoons and carbines for light and heavy cavalry; and pistols. All had the same caliber of 17·1 mm, the same firing mechanism, and used the same cartridge. These weapons with but slight modifications were used in all wars up to 1840.

The Republic found the ex-royal arms factories inadequate. Consequently, in September 1794 the Convention opened workshops 'on the Great Common of the Château of Versailles'. Confided to the 'enterprise of Master Boutet', whose family for generations had furnished arms to the Royal Household, this became the celebrated Versailles Arms Factory.

As modified in 1801, the 1777 infantry musket was 1·529 meters (about 55 inches) long and weighed 4·4 kilograms (about 9¾ pounds). It had a point-blank range of 234 meters and, fired at an angle of 45°, a trajectory of 980 meters. Its aim was accurate up to 150 meters, and approximate to 250. A musket was designed to fire 25,000 shots.

Infantry muskets were issued to the foot artillery. The marines had brass-mounted muskets 1·41 meters long, like those of the dragoons. Sappers, drummers, and musicians carried light cavalry musketoons 1·11 meters (44 inches) long.

The projectile was a spherical lead ball weighing 25 grams (0·8 ounces). It was placed in a cartridge of thin, tough paper and covered with a charge of 12·5 grams of powder. The cartridge was then sealed and the paper twisted at both ends.

A soldier carried three or four packets containing 10–15 cartridges, wrapped and tied with string, in his pouch together with 3 spare flints, a screwdriver, and a small phial of oil. About 15 per cent. of the cartridges misfired.

Soldiers often whittled down the wood under the mounts of their muskets, or enlarged the ramrod channels to produce a certain rattle and click, which their officers admired, in performing the manual of arms. Needless to say, the arms inspectors did not appreciate these mutilations.

The infantryman carried his bayonet, which had a triangular blade 38 cm long, in a sheath on his left hip, next to his saber. The latter was carried on a belt worn on his right shoulder which was crossed with the pouch belt.

To load his musket the soldier opened the lock by releasing the hammer, or frizzen; tore off the top of the cartridge with his teeth and poured a little powder in the pan; lowered the frizzen; poured the remaining powder into the barrel and inserted the ball; then rammed them home with his ramrod, using the cartridge paper as a wad. The operation was executed in twelve counts.

The highest firing speed obtained was four shots in three minutes. During prolonged firing the soldier had often to clear the vent with a pin carried on his pouch belt, and clean the barrel which fouled after 50 or 60 shots. Cartridges were spoiled by humidity. In wet weather men who failed to keep them dry, or to cap or wrap up their lock plates, were incapable of firing a shot.

The Consular Guard originally inherited the muskets of the Guards of the Directory and Legislature. These were de luxe models similar to those of the Swiss Guards. In 1795 the minister Aubert-Dubayet ordered special weapons for the Guards and for presentation to men distinguished on the battlefield (the original 'weapons of honor') from the Versailles factory.

These were highly-finished models of 1777 with the 1781 'improvement' of an overlapping pan on the lock plate which, though inconvenient and quickly fouled, had been previously adopted by the *Maison du Roy*. This 'improvement' was soon abolished by the First Consul.

The stocks of these weapons, of handsome wood and highly varnished, were arched, with a prominent cheek hollow and a curved butt. They had brass mounts, and the sling fittings on the middle band swivel and trigger guard were rectangular with rounded corners and a square mid-section. The heel of the butt plate was shaped like a grenade, and the lock was stamped 'Manufacture de Versailles'.

In 1800 Boutet began to manufacture two models varying only in length, listed in his catalogue of 1801 as 'infantry' and 'vélite' muskets. Between then and 1813, 10,000 were delivered to the grenadiers and chasseurs of the Old Guard.

2. Infantry Sabers

A majority of the foot Guard used a special saber made in Versailles from 1801 on and often bearing its stamp. This had a slightly curved blade 65 cm long, a single-branch brass guard and quillon, wood grip, and brass-mounted leather scabbard. Similar sabers were made in several factories for the foot artillery and train. The back edge of the sappers' saber was saw-toothed, and its hilt surmounted by a brass eagle head.

The blades of infantry officers' swords ranged in length from 70 to 77 cm, and their gilded bronze hilts had richly carved single-branch guards. The black leather scabbards had gilt mounts. Many swords had the Emperor's profile inlaid in silver in the thumb piece. Some NCO's briquets had similar ornaments. The officers' blades were inscribed 'Garde impériale' and either 'Grenadiers à pied' or 'Chasseurs à pied'.

The saber of the marines of the Guard had a curved blade 65 cm long with a flaring single-branch hilt. Its black leather scabbard had three brass bands and two rings. Most of the blades were inscribed 'Garde impériale'.

3. Cavalry Weapons

THE 1777 musketoon, differing from the infantry musket only in its length of 1·11 meters, was used by the light cavalry, train, gendarmes and, after 1812, the carabineers and cuirassiers of the Line. The musketoons issued after 1803 were fitted with bayonets. These were worn sheathed on a frog at the left side of the sword belt. Three types of pistol were used, the newer models being issued to the Guard.

During the Consulate Bonaparte specified for the horse grenadiers a musketoon of a 'distinguished model, as handsome as possible, the length of a dragoon musket, with a bayonet, enabling

the troopers to maneuver in three ranks'. The rifled carbines issued to them later were probably not all made at Versailles.

Between 1801 and 1813 the Versailles catalogue cites the delivery to the Mameluks of 73 blunderbuses (firearms with large flared muzzles) which were eventually replaced by musketoons, and 503 special pistols. Boutet's archives also note a 'rifled carbine for the dragoons of the Guard' which was doubtless a trial model. In his monograph on the Versailles factory, Captain Bottet shows a photograph of a 'musketoon of the chasseurs of the Guard' without any particulars.

Few specimens of special firearms made for the Guard survive, supporting the testimony of General Gassendi who wrote in 1809: 'The firearms of the Guard are identical with those of the Line except that they are more highly finished at an extra cost of 10 francs'. However, this was not the case with edged weapons.

The horse grenadiers' saber had a slightly curved blade à la Montmorency 97·5 cm long with a flared brass hilt decorated with a flaming grenade. The beechwood grip was covered with parchment, and the wooden scabbard with laminated strips of leather and brass. The rings and shoe, or drag, were iron. The chasseur saber had a curved blade 84 cm long with a single-branch brass hilt and a similar grip and scabbard.

According to Captain Bottet, the Polish lighthorse probably used a light cavalry saber of the universal 1801 pattern with a scabbard trimmed with three brass mounts. Most lancer officers carried chasseur sabers of this model with triplebranch basket hilts. Unfortunately, none survives.

The Mameluks used Turkish scimitars with a single-curved blade 77·2 cm long, wood grip, and brass oriental style quillon. The leather scabbard had four brass mounts. The Mameluk dagger had a blade 35·5 centimeters long with a wooden handle (ivory for officers) and brass sheath.

Old Guard cavalry officers possessed de luxe weapons, which were more ornate the higher the rank, in addition to campaign sabers similar to those of the rank and file except that the hilts and mounts were gilt. The blades of blued steel were inscribed with imperial emblems and the words 'Garde impériale', 'Grenadiers à cheval', 'Chasseurs à cheval', etc. Dragoon officers' sabers had either straight or Montmorency blades and gilded hilts ornamented with fan-shaped trophies of arms. Silver-mounted sabers of this or the horse grenadier model were used by the elite gendarmes. Artillery officers' sabers were decorated with crossed cannon surmounted by an eagle or grenade. All these weapons were well designed and perfectly balanced for attack by point or edge.

The dress swords of Guard officers were richly decorated and the head of the pommels reversed. Several Polish lancer officer's swords with *czapka*-shaped pommels survive.

4. Artillery Weapons

UNDER the Empire the artillery was greatly increased. In 1805 the park contained 4,506 heavy pieces, 7,366 of small caliber, 8,320 howitzers, and 1,746 mortars.

The Guard artillery included 12-, 8-, and 4-pounders (so-called from the weight of the projectile) and 6-inch (166mm) Gribeauval howitzers. Its bronze cannon were mounted on two-wheeled wood carriages, those of the 12- and 8-pounders being fitted with trunnion beds fore and aft on the brackets for the firing and traveling trunions. The simple two-wheeled wood limbers were attached to the carriages by a pintle bolt fitting into a ring on the trail transom of the latter.

The cannon fired a solid ball and two types of canister: one containing 42 large lead bullets; the other 60–100 small ones, depending on the gun caliber. For round shot Gassendi's artillery manual gives 800–900 meters as the effective range for the 12-, 800 meters for the 8-, and 700 for the 4-pounder; for canister shot, 600, 550, and 400 meters respectively.

The projectiles were actually effective at longer ranges where the dispersal was greater if the aim less precise. At the limit of gun elevation the ranges were 1,800, 1,500, and 1,200 meters for the pieces of 12, 8, and 4; however, rolling and ricocheting projectiles were dangerous at much greater distances.

Howitzers fired a spherical shell filled with powder and equipped with a fuse for explosion at distances of 700–1200 meters, whose burst was dangerous within a radius of 20 meters. (They also fired canister shot at point-blank range.) The fuse, which burned for 3–4 seconds during a trajectory of 600–800 meters, was a hollow reed about 8 cm long filled with strands of match impregnated with a compound of powder, saltpeter, sulphur, and pitch.

The cannon balls were cast iron spheres about 2 mm less in diameter than the caliber of the gun. This difference, known as the 'windage' of the ball,

was kept at a minimum, since the less the windage the greater the range and precision of the projectile. The ball was placed on a 'sabot', or round-bottomed shoe of lime or beechwood scooped out to enclose about a quarter of the projectile. Two tin straps nailed to the sabot crossed over the ball, holding it firmly in place.

The ball cartridge consisted of a serge bag into which the powder charge was introduced by hand, then the ball, held in place by tying the bag with string around a groove in the sabot; finally the mouth of the bag was folded over the charge and a second ligature made underneath the sabot.

The canister shot was a tin cylinder, in which the balls were stacked, covered with an iron lid and attached to a sabot.

The double ammunition provision of the Guard amounted to 350 projectiles per gun, distributed between the caissons, park vehicles, and trail chests in the carriage brackets. Each 4-pounder was allotted two caissons, each 8-pounder three, and each 12-pounder and howitzer five. Besides ammunition, the caissons carried portfires, length of match, and sacks of powder.

The table on page 515 gives statistics of each piece of Guard ordnance.

A cannon was loaded in the following manner: first the vent (round hole in the breech-block about 5 mm in diameter) was stopped. Next the gun was pointed, either directly or by means of the rear sight and elevator screw. The barrel was then swabbed out with the sponge, a long-handled brush, and the cartridge and wad (usually of hay) inserted and rammed home with the rammer, a long-handled wooden cylinder. The vent was then unstopped and cleared with the priming wire, a pole with a pointed iron tip, and the cartridge pierced. Into the vent went the firing tube, or primer, a cone-shaped reed containing cotton strands impregnated with an inflammable substance, through which the powder in the cartridge was ignited with either a portfire or linstock. The former, used in rapid firing, was an instrument made of a composition designed to burn for 10 minutes. The latter, a long stick, was stuck into the ground. A clamp at the top held the lighted end of the match wound round the upper part of the linstock. The match had to be tough, fairly rigid, resistant to dampness, and burn continuously at an even rate.

Though the firing rate of the 4- and 8-pounders averaged two shots a minute, it took a full minute to fire the 12-pounder. It required 8 men, including

	12-pounder	8-pounder	4-pounder	6-inch howitzer
Length	230 cm	200 cm	160 cm	70 cm
Weight	986 kg	584 kg	289 kg	318 kg
Caliber	121 mm	100 mm	84 mm	166 mm
Carriage Weight	995 kg	840 kg	660 kg	860 kg

Projectile Capacity

Trail chest (ball cartridges)	9	15	18	4
Caisson (ball cartridges)	48	62	100	49
Caisson (canister shells)	20	20	50	11

5 specialists, to serve a 4-pounder; 13, with 8 specialists, to serve an 8-pounder or 6-inch howitzer; 15, with 8 specialists, to serve the 12-pounder.

The artillery matériel included spare carriages; caissons carrying around 15,000 infantry cartridges as well as projectiles; park wagons loaded with artificers' tools; division wagons with spare axles, wheels, etc.; pontoon equipment, and forges. All vehicles were drawn by horses of the artillery train and driven by its men except the park wagons which were drawn by contract teams. The Guard teams consisted of six horses harnessed in pairs with the near horse saddled after a fashion for the driver.

5. Tactics

THE foot Guard was drilled by the 1782 regulations based on Guibert and the Prussian School, as modified in 1791. After 1804 the drill was simplified and made less formal.

The infantry platoon of 150 men, of which there were four to a battalion, formed in three ranks (two after 1813) occupying roughly 44 yards of front. It was trained to form rapidly into columns of attack, using skirmishers to maximum effect, or into defensive squares.

On route marches the Guard formed in sections (half-platoons), in flank by threes, or in columns of four. The marching rate was 3 to 4 kilometers an hour, depending on road conditions. Though no regular halts were scheduled, the columns usually halted from three to five minutes each hour, and from one to two hours at the half or three-quarter mark. The drums beat during the march and the bands played during rest periods.

The normal combat formation was the 'line of battle'. The firing 'in two ranks' theoretically commenced with a 'fire by files' rolling from right to left and continued 'at will', with the first rank kneeling and the third passing their muskets to the second rank and loading the latter's. In practice, however, every man fired 'at will', naturally including the skirmishers who were considered the best marksmen.

The 'column by divisions' of two platoons was the typical formation for rallying troops and battalion attack. This was a flexible and convenient group, forming a square of 90-100 yards on a side, or a compact mass, as desired. Troops were deployed in several lines, echeloned to attack in succession during an advance, or to re-form easily in case of retreat. Columns spaced by divisions quickly formed squares as cavalry approached.

In 1804 the cavalry drill regulations of 1788 were replaced by a simplified system whose primary tactic was the cohesion of the four platoons of a squadron of two companies, forming 18-20 files. A squadron of 250 men occupied approximately 165 yards of front.

Cavalry route marches were made in columns of four at an average speed of 6-7 kilometers an hour. For combat the cavalry formed in line of battle, in column by platoons spaced one platoon apart, or in close column, sending skirmishers ahead to scout the terrain and harass the enemy. These often shot from horseback.

In battle the troopers slung their cloaks over one shoulder to free their bridle hands and protect their chests. Charges were made at the gallop by echeloned squadrons, regiments, or brigades, and often in column between lines of infantry.

At this epoch nearly all recruits knew how to ride. The horses were of a rather heavy type and were easily schooled. The troopers' training was chiefly confined to practical horsemanship.

The Guard artillery was highly maneuverable, and its gunnery generally excellent, thanks to the annual shooting competitions at La Fère. It was organized in companies and battalions of foot, and squadrons of horse artillery. (The term 'battery' was first used in 1829.)

A Guard foot company served a division of 8 pieces, including 2 howitzers; a horse company 6, including 2 howitzers. Two guns formed a section under the command of an NCO. The gun pointer was captain of the gun.

Custom and experience, rather than regulations, determined the artillery maneuvers of the Guard which were not published until 1812, and then unofficially.

Divisional artillery usually tried to occupy high ground, protected whenever possible by small breastworks. In taking up a position, guides staked out the lines and fixed the interval (about 20 yards) between guns. The caissons were posted in the rear or on the flanks about 50 yards away and given every protection. The gun teams were picketed near the guns.

The batteries opened fire with solid shot on enemy troops or obstacles, either by direct, ricochet, or random fire (the latter with maximum elevation and charge). They seldom fired at enemy artillery, such fire being rarely effective.

Infantry attacks were usually led by artillery firing canister shot. The guns were drawn by horses on a 'prolonge', or long lashing, permitting them to maneuver over rough terrain, or by men using bricoles (drag-ropes).

Meanwhile, foot batteries operated on the wings of the army and attacked the enemy obliquely or in flank. Their changes of position were lengthy and difficult. The horse batteries, on the contrary, were highly maneuverable. Drawn by superior teams, those of the Guard supported the cavalry movements.

Count Sorbier, who succeeded Lariboisière in command of the Guard artillery, massed his artillery in the battles of Raab, Wagram, and Borodino. In principle, most of the artillery was attached to infantry and cavalry divisions and the remainder to the reserve; but the Emperor increased the Guard's reserve so as to open his battles with a massive bombardment.

'In most battles the Guard artillery is the deciding factor', Napoleon wrote Clarke, the Minister of War, on 2 June 1813, 'since, having it always at hand, I can take it wherever it is needed.'

The battles of the Empire were trials of strength lasting several hours, fought on a narrow terrain. Infantry and artillery fire quickly shrouded the field in smoke, blinding the combatants to leeward or, when there was no wind, enveloping the low ground. Since the guns were wadded with hay, their fire created conflagrations that made observation difficult and liaison precarious. Blinded by smoke, the men in reserve were constantly threatened by sudden cavalry attacks.

The charges exploding in their bronze barrels produced a deafening roar of cannon as soldiers marched, ran, fired shoulder to shoulder, collided with their foes, and attacked them with bayonets. Under galling fire they had to repeat the tedious operations of loading and firing and suffer the anguish of misfires. They must obey their sergeants' shouted commands to close ranks and fill the gaps left by fallen comrades, for at the least sign of disorder squadrons of cavalry were waiting to swoop down upon them, dealing death and destruction in their ranks.

A battle at this period was a fearsome spectacle. No longer a contest of honor, as in the 17th and 18th centuries, with its rules of elegance and its somber beauty, this was a struggle to the death, often without quarter, a veritable hell . . .

APPENDIX 'E'

Description of the Military Carriage of the late Emperor Napoleon taken at the Battle of Waterloo, with an Account of its Capture

(From *Waterloo Memoirs*, London, 1817, Vol. II, pp.32-37)

'THE exterior of the carriage is... very like the modern English travelling chariots. The colour is a dark blue, with a handsome border ornamented in gold, but the Imperial arms are emblazoned on the pannels of the doors. It has a lamp at each corner of the roof, and there is one lamp fixed at the back, which can throw a strong light into the interior.

'In the front there is a great projection, the utility of which is very considerable. Beyond this projection, and nearer to the horses, is a seat for the coachman: this is ingeniously contrived, so as to prevent the driver from viewing the interior of the carriage; and ... to afford those who are within, a clear sight of the horses, and of the surrounding country: there are two sabre cuts which were aimed at the coachman when the carriage was taken.

'The pannels of the carriage are bullet proof: at the hinder part is a projecting sword case, and the pannel of the lower part of the back is so contrived, that it may be let down, and thereby facilitate the addition or removal of conveniences, without disturbing the traveller.

'The under carriage, which has sedan-neck iron cranes, is of prodigious strength: the springs are semi-circular, and each of them seems capable of bearing half a ton; the wheels, and more particularly the tires, are also of very great strength. The pole is contrived to act as a lever, by which the carriage is kept level in every kind of road. The under carriage and wheels are painted in vermillion, edged with the colour of the body, and heightened with gold. The harness is very little worthy an imperial equipage; it bears strong marks of its service in the Russian campaign, and its former uses are to be recognized only by the bees which are to be seen in several places.

'The interior deserves particular attention, for it is adapted to the various purposes of a kitchen, a bed room, a dressing room, an office, and an eating room.

'The seat has a separation, but whether for pride or convenience can only be conjectured.

'In front of the seat are compartments for every utensil of probable utility: of some there are two sets, one of gold, the other of silver. Among the gold articles are a tea pot, coffee pot, sugar basin, candlesticks, wash-hand basin, plates for breakfast, etc. Each article is superbly embossed with the imperial arms, and engraved with his favourite N, and by the aid of a lamp, any thing could be heated in the carriage.

Beneath the coachman's seat is a small box, about two feet and a half long ... this contains a bedstead of polished steel, which could be fitted up within one or two minutes: the carriage contained mattresses and other requisites for bedding, of very extensive quality, all of them commodiously arranged. There are also articles for strict personal convenience, made of silver, fitted into the carriage.

'A small mahogany case, about ten inches square by eighteen long, contains the peculiar *nécessaire* of the Ex-Emperor. It is somewhat in appearance like an English writing desk, having the imperial arms most beautifully engraved on the cover. It contains nearly one hundred articles, almost all ... of solid gold.

'The liquor case, like the necessaire, is made of mahogany; it contains two bottles, one of them still has the rum which was found in it at the time, the other contains some extremely fine old Malaga wine.

'Various articles of perfumery are among the luxuries which remain; and notwithstanding Napoleon's wish to discourage British manufactures, there are nevertheless some Windsor soap, and English court plaister; of *eau de Cologne, eau de lavender*, salt spirit, etc. there are sufficient to show that perfumeries are not disregarded.

'There is a *writing desk*, which may be drawn out so as to write while the carriage is proceeding; an inkstand, pens, &c. were found in it, and here was found the Ex-Emperor's celebrated portfolio ...

'In the front there are also many smaller compartments, for maps and telescopes; on the ceiling of the carriage is a net work for carrying small travelling requisites.

'On one of the doors of the carriage there are two pistol holsters, in which were found pistols that had been manufactured at Versailles; and in a holster, close to the seats, a double barrelled pistol also was found. All the pistols were found loaded. On the side there hung a large silver chronometer, with a silver chain; it is of the most elaborate workmanship.

'The doors of the carriage have locks and bolts; blinds behind the windows shut and open by means of a spring, and may be closed so as to form a barrier almost impenetrable.

'On the outside of the front windows is a roller blind, made of strong painted canvass; when pulled down this will exclude rain or snow, and therefore secure the windows and blinds from being blocked up, as well as prevent the damp from penetrating.

'All the articles which have been enumerated still remain with the carriage; but when it was taken there were a great number of diamonds, and a great treasure in money, etc. of immense value.

'Four of the horses which drew the Ex-Emperor, remain with the carriage; they are of Norman breed; of a brown colour, of good size, and each appears to combine more strength, speed, and spirit than are generally found together in one animal.

'The veteran and illustrious Blücher was foremost in the pursuit. Various commands were deputed to different officers, so that no retreat should be left for the convenient escape of the enemy. Among these was a small corps . . . under the direction of Major Von Keller: this excellent and able officer, in pursuance of his instructions, arrived at the town of Genappe, at eleven o'clock at night on the 18th of June. The town was blocked up and barricadoed to prevent the intrusion of the pursuing victors; it was also filled with French military, who maintained a constant firing of artillery and musketry against the Prussian soldiers. The troops were not to be intimidated, but immediately took the place by storm; near to the entrance they met with the travelling carriage of Napoleon, (that is now exhibited)[1] having six horses, and the coachman and postilion ready mounted: the major, full of expectation that Buonaparte was now in his possession, ordered the coachman and postilion to stop, but as they did not obey, the latter was immediately killed, together with the two foremost horses, and the coachman was cut down by the major himself. The marks of the sabre still remain upon one of the carriage springs; the gallant Prussian then forced open one of the doors of the carriage, but in the interval, Napoleon had escaped by the opposite door; and thus disappointed the triumphant hopes of that gallant officer. Such, however, was the haste of the Ex-Emperor, that he dropped his hat, his sword, and his mantle, and they were afterwards picked up on the road.'

[1] The carriage was exhibited for many years at Madame Tussaud's waxwork museum in London, where it was destroyed by fire shortly after World War I. – Ed.

EDITOR'S NOTES ON THE ILLUSTRATIONS

(Except as otherwise noted, all illustrations are from the Anne S. K. Brown Military Collection in Providence, Rhode Island.)

The illustrations in this volume have been selected as far as possible from contemporary documents. The rest are from the work of artists like Raffet, Bellangé, and Lami who, though working after the fall of the Empire, nevertheless spent their childhood amid its panoply and their manhood in its shadow; or else of later artists like Detaille, Huen, and Rousselot who made a profound study of the period. About one-third of the illustrations have not to my knowledge been published before in the form in which they appear. Others are sufficiently rare as to be inaccessible to any but the most importunate researcher.

1. Colored Plates

The jacket illustration, reproduced in Plate 40, is from the painting by Gérard made for General Rapp, now in the collection of Hugh Bullock, Esq. in New York. It is noteworthy that the large canvas of the same subject at Versailles, commissioned by Napoleon, shows Rapp without a moustache. The Bullock painting, though undated, was presumably painted before Rapp's death in 1817, and has been engraved by an anonymous artist.

The frontispiece and plates 29a, 42b, 43a and b, 46a, 47b, 56, 58, 65, 88, 94, 95, 100–1, 104, 111–14, 123, 126, 131, 137, 143, 146, 156, 161, and 169 are from original watercolors not heretofore published or engraved, as far as I know.

Plate 2 (as well as uncolored plates 48e and 61d) is from a series of colored engravings published *chez* Basset; plates 6b, 19a and b, and 25a and b (also uncolored plate 144d) are from a similar series by Chataignier and Poisson, published in Paris during the Republic and Empire *chez* Chataignier and *chez* Jean. The originals are bound in volumes with Napoleon's bookplate.

Plates 5, 6a, 10, 13, 16, 22, 26, 28, 32, and 85–7 are from a collection of unpublished engravings and original drawings in gouache by Nicolaus Hoffmann showing costumes and uniforms of the Consulate and early Empire. Similar collections, with variations, exist in the Cabinet des Estampes of the Bibliothèque Nationale, and in the library of the Sabretache in Paris.

Plate 7 is from a series of colored aquatints by Bartsch, Geissler, and Mansfeld after Wilhelm Kobell, dated 1799–1804 and published by Artaria in Mannheim in 1800–1806, showing French, Russian, Austrian, and German troops on campaign.

Plate 29b is from the original volume of lithographs *Uniformen aller in Hamburg ... 1806/15 einquartirt gewesener Truppen* by Cornelius Suhr after Suhr, Hamburg, n.d. of which only five copies are known. Plate 153 is from an original watercolor for this work.

Plates 29a, 42b, 43a and b, 46a, 47b, and 58 are from a collection of 98 contemporary watercolors of the Grand Army and Guard by an anonymous artist (possibly C.-F. Weiland) reputedly made for Major Otto in Wiesbaden *c.*1808.

Plate 33 is from F. Masson, *Livre du Sacre de l'Empereur Napoléon Ier*, Paris, 1908.

Plates 34–5 are from *Cérémonies et fêtes du sacre et couronnement*, Paris, 1806. (Bound volume from the library of Prince Napoleon.)

Plates 46b, 57b, and 82a and b are from C.-F. Weiland, *Characteristische Darstellung der K. K. französischen Armee und ihrer Allirten*, Weimar, *c.*1807–12. (82a and b are from facsimile copies.)

Plate 42a is from C. and H. Vernet, *Recueil de chevaux de tout genre*, engraved by Levachez, Paris, *c.*1805–10.

Plate 47a is from *L'Armée française, représentée en 18 feuilles* by J. Berka, Prague, *c.*1810.

Plate 50 is from a collection of aquatints of battles, etc. of the Consulate and Empire by J. L. Rugendas, Augsburg, *c.*1800–20. (Uncolored plate 59 reproduces a drawing probably made for this collection but never engraved.)

Plate 57a is from a suite of 4 (?) colored engravings by Frey of the Polish light-horse, Warsaw, *c.*1808.

Plate 60a reproduces a print from *Galerie militaire, Troupes étrangères*, Paris, *chez* Martinet, *c.*1810–14, from the collection of Raoul et Jean Brunon, Marseilles.

Plate 60b is from Martinet, *Galerie militaire, Troupes étrangères*, Paris *c.*1810–14.

Plates 68a and b are from a volume of watercolors attributed to William Heath for Goddard and Booth, *The Military Costume of Europe*, London, 1812.

Plate 73 is from Cte. Alex. André de Laborde, *Précis historique de la guerre entre la France et l'Autriche*, Paris, 1822, Vol.I.

Plates 76, 84, and 117 are from Martinet, *Galerie des enfans de Mars*, Paris, c.1813, dedicated to Empress Marie-Louise.

Plate 78 is from a collection of views of European capitals aquatinted by J. A. Klein after Ferdinand Runk, published in Vienna during the Empire.

Plate 91 is from *Carnet de la Sabretache*, Paris, April, 1904.

Plate 98 is from an original watercolor for Richard Knötel, *Uniformenkunde*, *Lose Blätter*, Rathenow, 1890–1914.

Plates 105 and 152 are from *Campagnes de l'Empire*, a series of colored engravings by Rahl, Bartsch, Beyer, etc. after von Habermann, Klein, Kobell, and Reinhold, published in Vienna by Artaria, c.1812–15. (Uncolored plates 99 and 133 are from the same series.)

Plate 108 is from *Blätter aus meinem Portefeuille im Laufe des Feldzuges* 1812, published in Stuttgart by Ch. F. Autenrieth, 1831–43 and exceedingly rare in colored state. (Uncolored plates 110a and b reproduce original sketches for this series.)

Plate 120 is from an original watercolor for the aquatint published by Beger in Dresden, 1813.

Plate 126 (and uncolored plate 127) are from original watercolors drawn for R. Bowyer, *Important Events in the Annals of Europe*, London, 1815, but never published.

Plate 128 is from an original watercolor for the caricature engraved by Buchhorn c.1813.

Plate 134 is from an original watercolor by V. Adam for *La Grande Armée, Collection desuniformes de l'Empire*, Paris, c.1840.

Plate 140 is from an original watercolor for *Kaiserl. Russ. Soldaten*, Wien, Johann Cappi, c.1815.

Plate 149 is from Charlet, *Costumes militaires*, Paris, de Lasteyrie, 1817–18.

Plate 153 – see note on Plate 29b.

2. *Uncolored Plates*

Plates 3a, 135a, and 157d are from Raphael Morghen, *Collection des Portraits*, Paris, c.1814.

Plate 9 is from an original drawing for Jubé, *Le Temple de la Gloire*, Paris (1818).

Plates 11b and d, 41a and b, 54b, 90d, 118b, and 155b are from A. Hugo, *La France militaire*, Paris, 1836–8.

Plates 11e, 52, 90c, 92b, and 132c are from F. Rouillon-Petit, *Campagnes mémorables des français*, Paris, 1817.

Plate 12 is from *Galerie des militaires français*, Paris, G. Engelmann (1818–20).

Plates 14b, 83b, and 142b are from Charlet, *Recueil de costumes de l'ex-Garde*, Paris (1819).

Plates 18c, 39a, b and e, 44d, 48c, 80b, 90a, 138b, 141b, 157b are from *Carnet de la Sabretache*, Paris, 1893: Annuaires 1913, 1904, 1897, 1927, 1904, 1908, 1948, 1933, 1907, 1914, and 1905 respectively.

Plates 18d, 54d, 55b, 61b, 63d, 71c, 80a, and d, 92a, 103c, 106b, 124a, 132a, and 157a and e are from Dupin *et al*, *Monumens des victoires et conquêtes des français*, Paris, 1819.

Plates 18e, 20d, 63c, 71d, 106e, and 155a are from *Iconographie des contemporains*, Paris, Delpech (1826–40).

Plates 20b, 39d, 54c are from Ternisien d'Haudricourt, *Fastes de la nation française*, Paris (1807).

Plates 20c, 48d, 80e, 138d, 141a and c are from A. de Beauchamp, *Histoire des campagnes de 1814 et de 1815*, Paris, 1816.

Plate 21 shows a mannequin in the famous Brunon Collection in Marseilles. Though the marine wears the uniform of the Consular Guard, his insignia is that of the Imperial Guard.

Plate 23 is from Bellangé; *Album militaire*, Paris, Gihaut (1827).

Plates 24, 83a, and 89 are from Charlet, *Costumes de corps . . . faisant partie de l'armée française avant et pendant la Révolution*, Paris, c.1842.

Plates 27, 30, 37, 45, 51b, 59, 62a and b, 67a and b, 70, 74, 79a and b, 93a and b, 96, 97a, 102a, 107, 110a and b, 116b, 122a and b, 125, 127, 129a, 130, 136, 139a and b, 142a, 145, 151, 158, 159, 160a and b, 162a and b, and 166 are from original drawings and watercolors which to my knowledge have not heretofore been engraved or reproduced in the form in which they appear here.

Plates 39c and 157c are from *Tableaux historiques de la Révolution française*, Paris, Auber, 1804.

Plate 44a is from *Campagnes des armées françaises en Prusse, etc.*, Paris, 1807.

Plate 44c is from Guérin, *Généraux de la République*, Paris, c.1800.

Plate 45 is from an original wash sketch for the painting engraved by Allais and aquatinted by Cotteau.

Plates 48b, 90e, 106c, 124c, 135e and 138e are from *Russkie portrety XVIII i XIX stolieti*, St Petersburg, 1909.

Plates 48e and 61d – see note on colored plate 2.

Plate 49 is from *Scènes de la vie des soldats*, Paris, Gihaut (1836).

Plates 54a, 55d, 106d, 132d, 148a, and 155c are from Meyer, *Collection des portraits de tous les souverains . . . et des hommes illustres*, Paris, 1820.

Plates 55a and c, 118c, and 148d are from Rembowski, *Zrodta do historyi pulka polskiego lekkokonnego gwardi Napoleon I*, Warsaw, 1899.

Plate 61a is from Lomier, *Le bataillon des marins de la Garde 1805–15*, St Valéry-sur-Somme, 1905.

Plate 61c is from *Entrada de los Reyes y Real Familia en la ciudad de Barcelona*, Barcelona, J. Roca y Gaspar, 1802.

Plates 61e and 92c are from a series of aquatints of marshals and generals published in Paris, *chez* Jean, c.1805-13.

Plates 63a and b, 138a and 148c are from Luníski, *Napoleon legiony i ksiestwo Warsawskie*, Warsaw, n.d.

Plate 71b is from *Historique du 2ième régiment d'artillerie*, Grenoble, 1899.

Plate 75 is from a series of 14 *tableaux* of various armies aquatinted by Mansfeld, Rahl, etc. after Wilhelm Kobell, published Vienna, Artaria, c.1809-10.

Plate 90b, after a contemporary portrait in the Musée de l'Armée, is from Bucquoy, *Les uniformes du Premier Empire*, Nancy, 1911-47.

Plate 93a is from an original drawing for A. Adam, *Voyage pittoresque et militaire de Willenburg en Prusse jusqu'à Moscou en 1812*, Munich, 1828. (In the published lithograph the guard of honor has been unaccountably altered to a hussar.)

Plates 99 and 133 – see note on colored plate 105.

Plate 102a is from a personal album and sketchbook of the artist.

Plate 103a is from Général Thoumas, *Les anciennes armées françaises*, Paris, 1890.

Plate 107 is from an original detail drawing for the painting lithographed by Wölfle, n.p.n.d.

Plate 109 is from V. Adam, *Batailles de l'Empereur*, Paris, n.d.

Plates 110a and b are from the field sketchbook carried by the artist in the Russian campaign.

Plate 116a is from L. Fallou, *La Garde impériale*, Paris, 1901.

Plate 118a is from L. Bonneville de Marsagny, *La Légion d'Honneur 1802–1900*, Paris, 1900.

Plate 124d is from Gavard, *Galerie des maréchaux de France*, Paris, 1839.

Plate 127 – see note on colored plate 126.

Plate 135d is from Lomier, *Histoire des régiments de gardes d'honneur*, Amiens, 1924.

Plate 138c is from an original watercolor for a series of portraits of Allied leaders, published London, J. Jenkins, 1814-16.

Plate 139a is probably an original sketch for A.-V. Arnaut, *La Vie politique et militaire de Napoléon*, Paris, 1822-61.

Plate 141d is from a series of portraits of Allied leaders published London by T. Palser, 1814-15.

Plate 144d – see note on colored plate 2.

Plate 147 is from the original painting by Horace Vernet, dated 1824, in the collection of Hugh Bullock, Esq., New York. The painting at Fontainebleau is a later copy by Montholon.

Plate 154b is from Bellangé, *Souvenirs militaires de la République, du Consulat, et de l'Empire*, Paris (1832).

Plate 155e is from *La Revue historique de l'armée*, November, 1943.

Plates 158a and b are from original drawings for Charles Hamilton Smith, *Costume of the army of the British Empire according to the last regulations*, London, 1815.

Plate 159 is from an anonymous drawing probably made in Portugal c.1811.

Plates 160a and b are from a collection of 98 original crayon and watercolor drawings of Waterloo figures made in Belgium c.1943-53.

Plate 163 is from Atkinson's *Military Incidents*, London, 1817, one of the first lithographed books published in England.

Plate 168 is from an aquatint advertisement for Jenkins' *Martial Achievements of Great Britain and her Allies*, first published London, 1814.

Plates 171-3 are from a collection of original photographs of veterans of the Guard and *Grande Armée* made in Paris during the Second Empire. Though some of the uniforms have obviously been recut by Second Empire tailors, the insignia is original.

NOTES ON ARTISTS

(§ Denotes artists whose original works are reproduced from the Editor's collection)

§ADAM, Albrecht, 1786–1862. Bavarian military painter, engraver, and lithographer. Took part in campaigns of 1802 and 1812. Author and illustrator of *Voyage de Willenberg en Prusse jusqu'à Moscou en 1812*, Munich, 1828. Principal paintings: *Battle of the Moskva* (Hamburg mus.); *Napoleon at Ratisbonne* (Hanover mus.).

§ADAM, Victor, 1801–1866. French painter and lithographer, pupil of Regnault. Graduated from Beaux-Arts 1819. Won medals Salons of 1824 and 1836. Painted four canvases for Versailles, including *Entry of French Army into Mainz*. Published albums of lithographs of uniforms and military subjects from Empire to Louis Philippe, of which Empire subjects were considered his best work.

§ATKINSON, John Augustus, 1775–c.1833. English painter and aquatint engraver. Went to Russia to work with his uncle, James Walker, in service of Catherine II, with whom he collaborated on *Picturesque Representation of the Russians*, London, 1803–4. On return to London, published *Picturesque Representation of the Naval, Military, and Miscellaneous Costumes of Great Britain*, London, 1807. In 1813, published set of 7 aquatints on Russian campaign, engraved by Dubourg. In 1815 went to Waterloo with A. W. Devis. Their 'eye-witness sketch' (original draft now in Bibliothèque Nationale) engraved by J. Burnett. Collaborated 1815 in illustrating Bowyer's *Important Events* and Orme's *Historic Military and Naval Anecdotes*. Published *Military Incidents*, London, 1817. Exhibited Royal Academy 1803–33. Watercolors in mus. of Dublin, Manchester, London, etc.

§AUVREST (dates unknown). French calligrapher and portrait painter, specializing in 18th century subjects, including Voltaire, Rousseau, Frederick the Great, etc.

BELLANGÉ, Hippolyte, 1800–1866. French painter and lithographer, pupil of Gros and friend of Charlet. Made early reputation for his lithographs of Empire subjects and battle paintings at Versailles. Most famous picture, *La Garde meurt* . . . exhibited posthumously at World Exposition of 1867. Principal publications: *Uniformes de l'armée française depuis 1815* (116 col. plates) Villain, c.1831; *Cavalerie de l'ex-Garde* (8 col. pl.) lith. by Engelmann, n.d.; *Collection des uniformes de la République et de l'Empire* (50 col. pl.) Dubochet, 1844. Most famous works were fugitive lithographs and caricatures of Imperial Guard. Paintings in Louvre; Wallace Coll. London; Leipzig, etc.

BERKA, Johann, 1758–1815. Bohemian engraver, pupil of Salzer. Worked in Prague. Engraved portraits of Dombrowski, Prince Fürstenburg, etc. Illustrated *L'Armée française* (18 col. pl.) Prague, F. Zimmer, c.1810.

BONNEVILLE (dates unknown). French portrait painter, engraver, and publisher. Published 4 vols. of portraits, *Personnages célèbres de la Révolution*, 1793–1802, also *Costumes des états-majors de la 1er République* (15 col. pl.)

BREE, Mathieu Ignace van, 1773–1839. Belgian painter and aquatint engraver. Born in Antwerp, pupil of van Regemorter, also of Vincent in Paris. Won renown during lifetime. Pictures in mus. of Amsterdam, Antwerp, Brussels, Leyden, and Versailles (*Entry of Bonaparte into Antwerp; Napoleon and Josephine visiting squadron at Antwerp, etc.*)

BUCQUOY, Commandant E.-L., French army officer, author, illustrator, and publisher. Lived at Nancy. Published 1911–47 *Les Uniformes du Premier Empire*, series of over 3,000 colored uniform cards with text. Founder and editor of illustrated periodical *Le Passepoile*, 1921–49. Author of memoirs, unit histories, etc.

§CALLIANO, Antonio Raffaele, 1785–1824. Italian painter, born in Muzzio, died in Spain.

§CHARLET, Nicolas-Toussaint, 1792–1845. French painter, engraver, lithographer, and caricaturist. Fought at Clichy Gate in defense of Paris 1814. Lost job in *mairie* for Bonapartist sympaties. Entered studio of Gros 1817. Glorified Napoleon in painting and lithography throughout Restoration. Professor of drawing at École Polytechnique. Influenced Bellangé and Raffet. Won fame as lithographer and humorist, and as supreme exponent of Old Guard of Napoleon. Published *Costumes militaires* (17 col. pl.) de Lasteyrie,

1817; *La veille armée française* (13 pl. of *Grande Armée*, lith. by C. Motte) n.d.; *Costumes de l'ex-Garde* (30 lith.) Delpech, n.d.; *Costumes militaires françaises* (28 lith.) Delpech, 1818; *Costumes des corps de l'armée française avant et pendant la Révolution*, unfinished series reissued several times between 1842 and 1886 with up to 50 pl. Paintings in Louvre, Versailles (*Passage du Rhin*), Geneva mus. etc.

CHARON, Louis-François, 1783–*c*.1831. French engraver, pupil of Chataignier. Said to have 'brought steel engravings to perfection in France'. Engraved series of portraits of Empire marshals and generals after Aubry, Martinet, etc.

CHATAIGNIER, Alexis, 1772–1817. French engraver and publisher. Principal work was large series of colored engravings of military and civil costumes, portraits, scenes, of Consulate and Empire in collaboration with Poisson. (Napoleon had several bound volumes of these in his library.)

§CROFTS, Ernest, 1847–1911. English battle painter, pupil of Clay in London and Hünten in Düsseldorf. Curator of Royal Academy. Won medal at World Exposition of 1889. Series of Waterloo paintings in mus. of Koenigsberg, Bristol, Liverpool, Sheffield, etc. Drawings in Victoria and Albert Mus. London.

DÄHLING, Heinrich Anton, 1773–1850. German historical and portrait painter. Went to Paris 1802. Returned to Berlin 1811 where he was admitted to Academy, becoming professor there in 1814. Painted portraits and conversation pieces of Prussian royal family.

DAVID, Jacques-Louis, 1748–1825. Most influential painter in France during Consulate and Empire. Most famous work, *Coronation of Napoleon*, in Louvre. Pupil of Boucher. Won Prix de Rome 1771. Returned to Paris 1783 and entered French Academy. Became ardent revolutionist and voted for execution of King and dissolution of French Academy in Rome, yet was imprisoned 7 months by regime. Member of Institute under Directory. Invited to Egypt by Bonaparte, but declined. Exiled to Brussels after Restoration where he died and was buried with great pomp. Paintings in Louvre, Versailles; Hermitage, Leningrad, and Natl. Portrait Gallery, London, etc.

§DEBRET, Jean-Baptiste, 1768–1848. French historical painter, pupil of David. Won 2nd Prix de Rome 1791. Invited to Rio 1815 to establish Fine Arts Institute. Became court painter to Emperor of Brazil. Exhibited at Salon 1799–1814. Painted military scenes at Versailles (*Napoleon decorating Russian soldier; Napoleon addressing Bavarian troops, etc.*)

DEBUCOURT, Philibert-Louis, 1755–1835. French painter and aquatint engraver. Began as genre painter, then took up aquatint and became supreme master of the art in France. From designs of Carle Vernet, aquatinted series of Mameluks *c*.1802; *Napoleon and Alexander meeting on the Niemen*, 1807; *Death of Poniatowski* and *Somo-Sierra*, 1816, after Horace Vernet. Most famous work: *Costumes dessinés d'après nature*, after C. Vernet, 1814–15.

§DETAILLE, Edouard, 1845–1912. French military and historical painter, pupil of Meissonier. Made debut at Salon 1867. Went to Spain and Algeria and returned at outbreak of war of 1870. Joined *Gardes Mobiles* with de Neuville and painted battle scenes of war. Later decorated Hôtel de Ville and Panthéon. Won medals Salons of 1870, 1872, and 1888. Member of Institute, Commander of Legion of Honor. In 1885–9 published *Types et uniformes de l'armée française*, 2 folio volumes, handsomely illustrated.

§DIGHTON, Denis, 1792–1827. English military and portrait painter. Son of caricaturist Richard D. Studied at Royal Academy. Commissioned in army by Prince Regent. Resigned commission 1811 and settled in London as painter. Exhibited Royal Academy 1811–25 and painted many military subjects for Prince Regent. Sudden loss of royal favor unhinged his mind. Retired to Saint-Servan and died there. Pictures in Victoria and Albert Mus. and Windsor Castle.

§DUNCKER, Philip Heinrich, 1780–1836. Swiss painter and engraver, son of painter Balthazar D. Went to Nürnberg and specialized in drawing. Engraved works of Kobell, Roos, Weenix, etc.

DUTERTRE, André, 1753–1842. French painter and engraver. Member of Bonaparte's Institute of Egypt. Exhibited portrait of Desaix at Salon of 1804. Many portraits at Versailles (Desaix, Davout, Friant, etc.).

§FABER DU FAUR, Christian G. von, 1780–1857. German army officer and military painter. Lieutenant in *Grande Armée* during campaign of 1812 of which he made numerous sketches, eventually lithographed in 100 folio plates published by

Autenrieth in Stuttgart 1831–43. In 1831 collaborated with Major F. von Kaussler on campaign memoirs, published in many editions and illustrated after lithograph plates. Ended as general in Württemberg Army.

FREY, Johann Zacharias, 1769–1829. Austrian painter and engraver. Studied at School of Fine Arts in Vienna and later with Benjamin West in London. Moved to Warsaw 1804 and worked with Prince Czartoryski, becoming professor of painting and engraving there.

GÉRARD, François-Paschal-Simon, 1770–1837. French historical and portrait painter. Born in Rome, son of servants in French embassy. Studied in Paris with David. Member of Revolutionary Tribunal. Painting *Belisarius* created sensation at Salon 1795. Commissioned 1805 to paint portrait of Bonaparte, also battle of Austerlitz. During Empire painted whole Imperial family, then, through Talleyrand, became court painter to Bourbons and was created Baron 1819. Employed to decorate Panthéon by Louis-Philippe. Many large canvases in collaboration with Guérin and Steuben in Louvre and Versailles.

§GERICAULT, Jean-Louis-André-Théodore, 1791–1824. French historical and horse painter, also sculptor. Born in Rouen, son of a lawyer. Schoolmate in Paris of Delacroix. Spent afternoons at circus and around stables, studying horses. Studied with Carle Vernet who advised him to give up painting; nevertheless his portrait of Lt. Dieudonné of the '*Guides de l'Empereur*' (now in Louvre) won gold medal at the Salon of 1812, and was followed by *Charging Hussar* and *Exercise à Feu* in 1814. Enlisted in *Mousquetaires du Roi* during Restoration, but returned to painting during Hundred Days. Went to Italy in 1815. Returned in 1818 to paint controversial *Raft of the Medusa*, his most famous canvas. Later went with Charlet to England and died there after a fall from a horse. Paintings in Louvre, National Gallery, Washington, etc.

GIRODET DE RONCY TROISON, Aimé-Louis, 1767–1824. French historical painter and sculptor. David's favorite pupil. Ordered in 1801 by Napoleon to paint picture for Malmaison showing shades of French heroes being transported by Victory to Valhalla. Painted *Revolt of Cairo* and *Napoleon Receiving Keys to Vienna* at Versailles. Masterpiece is 9-foot equestrian statue of Napoleon commissioned by private collector in São Paolo, Brazil.

GOYA Y LUCIENTES, Francisco de, 1746–1828. Spanish portrait painter, etcher, and lithographer. Son of a master gilder. Pupil of Raphael Mengs. As protégé of a minister of Charles III, became play-boy, got into a brawl, and fled to Italy, arriving in rags. There he became intimate with David and painted Pope Benedict XIV (portrait in Vatican). Fell in love with a nun and tried to abduct her. Returned to Madrid, married daughter of painter Bayeu, and had 20 children. Elected to San Fernando Academy 1780. Banished from court because of amours. Sympathized with French Revolution. In 1796, published 84 *Caprices*, ridiculing vices and follies of the day, followed by *Tauromachie* (33 plates). Later, published *Les Malheurs de la Guerre*, series of etchings showing French atrocities in Spain. Died in Bordeaux. Portraits his most famous work. Many in National Gallery and British Museum, London; Metropolitan, New York; Munich Pinacothek; Louvre, etc. Finest work is in Prado, Madrid.

§HABERMANN, Franz von, 1788–? Austrian battle painter, born in Prague. Moved to Vienna where he painted battle scenes (Kulm, Leipzig, Waterloo, etc.) for royal and noble patrons. Collaborated 1812–15 with Kobell, Klein, etc. in designing plates for *Campagnes de l'Empire*, pub. by Artaria. Named Councilor of Plastic Arts in Vienna 1834. In 1838 exhibited battle paintings of Leipzig and Bar-sur-Aube at Berlin Academy. Drawings of Aspern (Essling), aquatinted by Pucherna, and series of *Kriegsscenen*, lith. by Klein, pub. by Trentsensky, c.1840. Paintings in Heeresgeschichtliches Museum, Vienna.

§HEATH, William, c.1785–1840. English military artist, illustrator, etcher, caricaturist and publisher. In 1812 probably designed plates for Goddard and Booth, *Military Costume of Europe*, and in 1814 illustrated Jenkins' *Martial Achievements*, designing series of military portraits for same publisher 1814–16. Published battle-scenes (Pyrenees, Orthès, Salamanca and 5 of Waterloo) 1815–18. In 1818 designed 24 plates engraved by Duplessi-Bertaux for *Campaigns of Wellington*, Paris, n.d. In 1819 illustrated *The Wars of Wellington by Dr Syntax*, designed large colored aquatint plate *The Grand Quintuple Alliance*, and collaborated with Dighton, Atkinson, Scharf etc. in illustrating Orme's *Historic Military and Naval Anecdotes*. In 1820–27 published 5 series of military costume plates, chiefly of British cavalry and Guards; in 1823, *The Life of a Soldier* (satirical poem illustrated with 18 col. plates) and *c.*1825, a miscellany entitled *Collection of Interesting Subjects, Military Occurrences, etc.*, published by McLean. Was a prolific caricaturist from 1808 on, using pseudonym Paul Pry in later years. *Monstrosities* of various years poked fun at military dandies of day. Last work, published posthumously, was 6 plates for Ackermann's *Costumes of the British Army*, 1840–54, lithographed by Giles and Driscoll, for which the original drawings are equal to his best work.

HENNE, Eberhard Siegfried, 1759–1828. German painter and engraver. Worked with Chodowiecki in Berlin, also in Leipzig. Illustrated *Seven Years' War* in collaboration with Archenholz.

§HESS, Johann Michael, 1768–1830. German historical painter, pupil of Maurer. Professor at Vienna art school.

§HESS, Peter, 1792–1871. German battle painter and engraver. Took part in campaigns of 1813–15 in Prince of Wrede's army. Commissioned by Tsar to paint battles of 1812. Later went to Greece with Otto. Painted Greek liberation murals on arcades of Munich Hofgarten. Member of Academies of St Petersburg, Vienna, Munich, and Berlin. Paintings in mus. of Berlin and Munich. Notable drawing of Cossacks escorting French prisoners in Munich Historical Museum.

§HÖCHLE(HOECHLE), Johann Baptiste, 1754–1832. Swiss historical and landscape painter. Worked from 1780 in Munich as court painter to Elector Karl Theodor. In 1800 moved to Vienna where he became court painter to Francis II in 1802. Designed suite of camp scenes at Traiskirchen, engraved by Gurk and pub. by Mollo 1828. Watercolor *Volksfest in Wiener Prater* in Albertina, and *Austrian Army crossing the Vosges* in Heeresgeschichtliches Museum, Vienna.

HOFFMANN, Nicolaus, 1740–1823. Hessian military painter, miniaturist, and engraver. Born in Darmstadt. Lived in Paris 1775–1808 recording French uniforms and court costumes for Landgrave of Hesse. Engraved plates in outline which he painted in gouache for royal patrons, adapting same plates to the uniforms of successive regimes. Later had them colored commercially and published in small editions. Both types are exceedingly rare. Much of his best work burned in Louvre during Commune of 1871. Several collections showing uniforms of Louis XVI, Consulate, and Empire survive in Bibliothèque Nationale.

§HUEN, Victor, 1874–1939. French military painter, illustrator, and lithographer born in Alsace. Pupil of Bouguereau, Gérôme, and of Anton Hoffmann in Munich. Published suite of 16 lithographs *Cavaliers célèbres* in Colmar 1908; illustrated Girodié, *Généraux d'Alsace at Lorraine*, Mulhouse, 1912; *Soldats alsaciens sous Napoléon I*, Colmar, 1911; collaborated with J. Waltz (Hansi) in illustrating *L'histoire d'Alsace racontée aux petits enfants*. After World War I designed *Napoléon et son état-major* for the Imageries Réunies de Jarville-Nancy, also collaborated with Bucquoy in illustrating *Les uniformes du Premier Empire* and *Le Passepoile*. Illustrated Field, *History of the Royal Marines*, London, 1924. Painting *Régiment d'Alsace à la bataille d'Heylissen*, 1705 in Colmar mus.

ISABEY, Jean-Baptiste, 1767–1855. French court painter, miniaturist, and lithographer. Pupil of David. Intimate of Bonaparte and Josephine. Arranged fêtes at Saint-Cloud and Tuileries and designed coronation costumes. Talleyrand took him to Vienna in 1814 to paint Congress; on return became court painter to Louis XVIII, Charles X, and Louis-Philippe in succession. Notable draftsman as well as pioneer lithographer. Paintings in Versailles (*Napoleon visiting factories at Rouen and Jouy*); Louvre; Wallace Coll. London; Windsor Castle (*Congress of Vienna*); Berlin; Dresden; Zurich; and Albertina, Vienna.

§KININGER, Vincenz Georg, 1767–1851. Austrian painter and aquatint engraver, pupil of Schmutzer. Won prize Vienna Academy 1784. Took up aquatint 1786. Designed 44 uniform plates engr. by Mansfeld 1796–8; 15 plates *Corps des österr. allgemeinen Aufgebothes* 1797; *Schema aller Uniformen der K. K. Armee* (130 pl. engr. by Bartsch) 1798; 3 plates of *Bürgermilitair*, 8 *Lagerszenen* and 12 *Heroic Exploits* 1800.

KINSON (KINSOEN), François-Joseph, 1771–1839. Belgian historical and portrait painter. Studied at Bruges Academy. Became court painter to King Jerome of Westphalia. Married daughter of architect Leprince. Moved to Paris and became naturalized Frenchman. Was protégé of Duc d'Angoulême after Restoration. Portraits in museums of Bordeaux, Bruges, and the Hague.

§KLEIN, Johann Adam, 1792–1875. Bavarian military and horse painter, etcher, and engraver. Pupil of Zwingen. Studied Vienna Academy 1811–15. Worked in Frankfurt, Vienna, and Nürnberg. Designed and engr. battle scenes for *Campagnes de l'Empire* pub. by Artaria, Vienna, 1812–15; also engraved views of European capitals after Ferdinand Runk. In 1812–18 published 6 suites of etchings (6 *Blatt Pferde*, 1er, 2e, 3e suites de sujets militaires, etc.) of Allied troops on campaign. Many original watercolors for these now in State Library, Nürnberg.

§KNÖTEL, Richard, 1857–1914. German military and historical painter and illustrator. Painted battle scenes and illustrated regimental histories and works on foreign armies, uniform books (*Die Türkische Armee und Marine*, 1897) etc. Major work *Uniformenkunde*, *Lose Blätter*, Rathenow, 1890–1914, an encyclopedia of world uniforms with over 1,000 colored plates, was continued after his death by his son Herbert who also revised and republished his *Handbuch der Uniformenkunde*, Leipzig, 1896 in Hamburg in 1936 and 1953.

§KOBELL, Wilhelm von, 1766–1855. Bavarian landscape and military painter. Pupil of his father. In 1799–1902 designed series of plates of armies engaged in wars of the Republic, aquatinted by Bartsch and superbly colored. Professor at Munich Academy 1808. In 1809–10 designed series of large tableaux of French, Russian, Prussian, Austrian, and English infantry and cavalry, engraved by Rahl, published Vienna by Artaria; followed later by Chinese, Persian, and Turkish armies. Collaborated 1812–15 with Klein, Habermann, etc. in Artaria series *Campagnes de l'Empire*. Decorated by King of Bavaria 1816. Pictures in mus. of Berlin, Frankfurt, Hamburg, Munich (*Battles of Hanau*, *Bar-sur-Aube*) and drawings and watercolors in Albertina, Vienna.

LAGRÉNÉE, Jean-Jacques, 1739–1821. French historical and portrait painter. Worked at Sèvres porcelain factory. Member of Academy 1775, professor 1781. Exhibited at Salons 1771–1804. Decorated Salle des Spectacles in Trianon, Versailles. Portrait of Rapp in museum at Colmar.

§LAMI, Eugène, 1800–1890. French painter, watercolorist, and lithographer. Pupil of Gros and Horace Vernet. Exhibited Salons of 1824–78. Legion of Honor 1837. Won medal Salon of 1875. Best known works were lithographs in the style of Raffet, but more elegant in execution.

Collaborated with Horace Vernet in *Collection des uniformes 1791–1814*, and *1814–24*. Published 10 cavalry plates 1831, and 20 c.1835. During 1829–30 published *Quadrille de Marie Stuart*, *Voyage à Londres* (in collaboration with H. Monnier), *Voitures* (12 pl.) and *Souvenirs du camp de Lunéville*. His battle pictures among best in Versailles (*Siège d'Anvers*, etc.) Founded Société des Aquarellistes Français. Watercolors in Louvre and Wallace Coll. London, and paintings in Louvre, Chantilly, Strasbourg, etc.

LE CŒUR, Louis (dates unknown). French painter and aquatint engraver. Worked in Paris at end of 18th and beginning of 19th centuries. Pupil of Debucourt. Engraved Watteau's *Folies*, also *Vues de Saint-Petersbourg*, and Swebach's *Bal de la Bastille*. Designed and aquatinted *Sacre et Couronnement de LL. MM. c.1805.*

§LECOMTE, Hippolyte, 1781–1857. French painter and lithographer, pupil of Regnault. Married daughter of Carle Vernet. Designed 380 plates of French costume published 1820–30. Exhibited at Salon 1804–47. Many paintings in Versailles (*Battle of Hochstett*, *Interview with Prisoners at Astorga*, *Napoleon at Würzburg*, and battles of Mantua, Hollabrunn, Corunna).

LE DRU, Hilaire, 1769–1840. French portrait painter and engraver. Exhibited at Salon 1795–1824. Best known work was collection of portraits of Revolution generals, engraved by Lefebvre, Bourgeois, etc., published by Potrelle c.1797–1800. Several, engraved by Bock, were published in Munich in 1797.

LEJEUNE, General Baron Louis-François, 1775–1848. French officer, amateur painter and lithographer, born in Strasbourg. Studied painting in Paris. Volunteered 1792 in Compagnie des Arts recruited among Paris students; then transferred to topographical engineers. Sketched many battlefields, including Austerlitz. As a colonel of engineers, became aide de camp to Murat; captured by partisans in Spain; promoted major general at Borodino; wounded while saving the life of Marshal Oudinot during campaign of 1813. Sent in 1830 as department commander to Toulouse where he remained as mayor and director of the School of Fine Arts and Art Museum. Executed renowned self-portrait and many battle paintings, most famous being those of Marengo and Borodino. The former, as well as *Aboukir* and *Battlefield of Eylau*, were engraved; also a suite of soldiers of the Consular

Guard from painting of Marengo, published in Paris by the Sabretache 1910. Paintings in Versailles include: battles of Lodi, Mont-Thabor, Aboukir, Pyramids, Marengo, Somo-Sierra, Borodino, *Siege of Saragossa, Napoleon's Bivouac at Austerlitz, Crossing of the Rhine*, etc.

§MARTINET, Pierre, 1781–*c*.1845, French historical and military painter, engraver, and publisher. Pupil of Swebach. Exhibited at Salon 1808, 1810, and 1812. Best known works *Galerie des enfans de Mars*, Paris, *c*.1813 (uniforms of Imperial Guard) and *Troupes françaises, 1er Empire* (*c*.250 col. plates of *Grande Armée* and Allies). (Many of his drawings of uniforms now in De Ridder Coll. at the Bibliothèque Nationale.) Designed and published suites on Army, *Garde Royale*, and *Maison du Roi* during Restoration. Designed many fugitive military and battle plates aquatinted by Charon, etc. Illustrated Jubé, *Le Temple de la Gloire*, *c*.1818, and collaborated with Swebach, Lafitte and others in illustrating Ternisien d'Haudricourt's *Fastes de la Nation française*, *c*.1820. Illustrated A. Hugo, *La France Militaire*, Paris, 1836–8, and Laugier de Bellecœur, *Fastes Militaires*, Paris and Milan, 1842–5. House of Martinet continued publishing through Second Empire, latterly in conjunction with Hautecœur.

§MOLTZHEIM, Auguste-Louis-Victor, *c*.1828–189? French artillery officer, military artist, and watercolorist. Son of officer in artillery train. Commissioned in father's regiment 1848. In same year[1] published *Collection des uniformes actuels de l'artillerie européenne 1832*, in Metz with 29 colored plates lithographed by Dupuy. At outbreak of Crimean War transferred to the 1st Regiment of Artillery (Bonaparte's old regiment) and saw service in the Crimea, returning to the train as captain in 1860. In 1868–70 published *Esquisse historique de l'artillerie française depuis le moyen age* in Strasbourg with 64 colored plates, followed in 1875 by *La nouvelle armée française* (32 col. pl.) in Paris, to which he retired as a colonel after the war of 1870. Left many watercolors in private collections, also beautiful copies of Hoffmann, Adolph Menzel, etc. and voluminous note-books with drawings from life and from published works.

[1] Since the title-page of this work describes Moltzheim as 'lieutenant, 3e Escadron du Train d'artillerie', in which he was commissioned in 1848, this work could not have been published prior to that year. – Ed.

§MONTEN, Dietrich, 1799–1843. German historical and military painter, lithographer, and aquatint engraver. Graduated in science from U. of Bonn. Studied at Düsseldorf Academy with Peter Hess. Worked in Munich, also in Austria, Saxony, Prussia, Holland, and Italy. Designed several suites of Bavarian uniforms, including *Die Bayerische Armee nach der Ordonnanz 1825*, lithographed by Troendlin. Best known work was *Sämmtliche Truppen von Europa*, Würzburg, 1838–43 (650 col. pl.) in collaboration with H. A. Eckert and F. Schelver, left unfinished at Monten's death. Also left unfinished was series of folio equestrian portraits *Galerie sämmtlicher Fürsten von Europa*, published Würzburg 1840–4. Paintings in Munich Pinacothek (*Napoleon and his Suite*) as well as Residenz and Armee mus.; also mus. of Berlin, Nürnberg, Wiesbaden (*Death of Brunswick at Quatre-Bras*) Leipzig (*Transport of Wounded, 1813*) and Hanover (*Russian Camp Scene*).

MULLER, Henri-Charles, 1784–1846. French military painter and engraver, born in Alsace. Pupil of Guérin and David. Won medals for engravings. Chevalier of Legion of Honor.

§NAUDET, Thomas-Charles, 1778–1810. French military and landscape painter and engraver, pupil of Hubert Robert. Exhibited at Salon 1795–1808. Official artist of Consulate and Empire. Collaborated with Chataignier and Poisson on series of portraits and costumes published *chez* Jean, etc. *c*.1799–1808, and designed battles of Italian, Egyptian, and Austrian campaigns for same publisher 1792–1807. Painting of Lützen in Volksmuseum, Leipzig.

NOIRETERRE, Marie-Thérèse (dates unknown). French miniaturist working in Paris in late 18th and early 19th centuries. Exhibited at Salon 1785–7. Miniatures in Louvre and Carnavalet.

§OPITZ (OPIZ), Georg Emanuel, 1775–1841. German portrait and genre painter, miniaturist, and engraver. Born in Prague. Studied in Dresden with Casanova. Began with portraits and miniatures, but after 1807 concentrated on genre and caricatures. Went to Paris 1813 in suite of Duchess of Kurland and witnessed arrival of Allied armies. Left many watercolor scenes of Paris and of Leipzig Fair. Designed *Wiener Kaufrufe* (52 col. pl.) aquatinted by Ponheimer and Pieringer, also series of uniform plates of various armies for *Russlands und Deutschlands Befreiungskriege*, engraved by Volz, publ. Leipzig 1816–19. In

1840 designed series of large tableaux of European armies published in Dresden by Louis Kleist. Painting *Napoleon Erecting Column on the Place Vendôme* in Leipzig mus.

ORANGE, Maurice, 1868–1916. French historical and military painter and illustrator. Pupil of Gérôme, Detaille, and Flameng. Regular exhibitor at Salon. Won Prix de Paris 1900. Illustrated Fallou, *La Garde impériale*, Paris, 1901, and designed many uniform plates for *La Giberne*, Paris, 1899–1914. Most famous painting *Les Défenseurs de Saragosse* in Cherbourg mus.

§PORTER, Sir Robert Ker, 1777–1842. English historical painter, author, soldier, and diplomat. Born in Durham, son of an army doctor. Pupil of Benjamin West in London. At age of 15 produced sensation with painting *Storming of Seringapatam*, 120 feet long, at Royal Academy. (Engraved later by Vendramini.) Appointed historical painter to Tsar 1804. Traveled in Finland and knighted in Sweden. Accompanied Sir John Moore to Penninsula and was with him at Corunna when he died. Returned to Russia and married Russian princess. On return to England published account of campaign of 1812, also illustrated accounts of travels in Russia, Sweden, the Orient, and America. In 1826 knighted by Prince Regent and appointed consul in Venezuela where he painted many pictures, including portrait of Simon Bolivar. Returned to Russia 1841 where he decorated Admiralty in Petersburg and where he eventually died.

§RAFFET, Auguste, 1804–1860. French military painter, engraver, and lithographer. Orphaned by assassination of his father in the Bois de Boulogne in 1813. Started as china decorator. Later studied with Charlet and Gros and won fame for lithographs of Napoleon and his soldiers. Most famous (*Midnight Review*; '*Ils grognaient . . .*') unsurpassed in portraying spirit of Old Guard. Tried for Prix de Rome 1831 but lost to Chopin's brother. Developed personal style and excelled in portraying scenes he never saw of Revolution, Empire, and North Africa. Published several military costume suites 1825–33. In 1837 accompanied Prince Demidoff to Crimea, Balkans, and Constantinople, subsequently publishing *Voyage en Crimée*, illustrated with superb lithographs. In 1859 illustrated Fieffé, *Napoléon et la Garde impériale*, and accompanied French army to Italy. Published *Un an à Rome*, illustrated with many lithographs. Traveled continuously in later years and died in Genoa. Paintings in Versailles (battle scenes); Louvre; Metropolitan, New York, and Edinburgh Mus.

REINHOLD. Friedrich Philip, 1779–1840. German portrait, landscape, and military painter and engraver. Studied at Vienna Academy in Dresden. Painted curtain of State Theatre in Prague. Moved to Vienna 1813. Collaborated with Kobell, Klein, von Habermann, etc. on *Campagnes de l'Empire*, published by Artaria 1812–15.

RIESENER, Henri-François, 1767–1828. French portrait and historical painter. Son of famous *ébéniste* of Louis XVI and uncle of Delacroix. Entered Academy 1788. Pupil of Vincent. Debut at Salon of 1793. Became soldier during Revolution. When family ruined, returned to painting and exhibited at Salons of 1799–1814. Painted portrait of Napoleon. Left for Russia 1816 and became protégé of Grand Duke Constantin. Painted Tsar and many notables in Russia. Returned to Paris 1823 and exhibited at Salons of 1824–7. Pictures at Versailles, Louvre, Carnavalet; Hermitage, and Rumiantsev in Moscow, also Krasinski Library, Warsaw.

§ROUSSELOT, Lucien, 1900–. Contemporary military artist and illustrator, now living in Paris. Born in Brie, son of a schoolmaster. Taught himself to draw and achieved high degree of excellence in watercolor. Designed uniform cards for Bucquoy, *Les uniformes du Premier Empire*, Nancy, 1911–47, and *Le Passepoile*, 1921–49. In 1941 illustrated Dépréaux, *Uniformes des troupes coloniales* (16 col. pl.) and collaborated in illustrating *Uniformes de la marine et des troupes coloniales et nord africaines*, Paris, 1931; Dupont, *Nos vieux houzards*, Paris, 1934. Illustrated Saurel, *L'Armée française*, Paris, 1939–40. In 1943 began major work, *L'Armée française, ses uniformes, son armament, son équipement*, folio fascicules in color still being issued, a model of military research and illustration. In 1943–7 contributed illustrations to Bucquoy, *Fanfares et musiques de troupes à cheval*; Brunon and Guignard, *Au service de la France*, Baden-Baden, 1947. Illustrated Montergon, *La cavalerie de la Maison du Roy*, 1947. Collaborated in illustrating Brunon, *Livre d'or de la Légion étrangère*, 1958. His uniform watercolors most prized of any being produced in France today.

§ROWLANDSON, Thomas, 1756–1827. English painter, watercolorist, caricaturist, and engraver.

Born of well-to-do parents. Studied at Royal Academy and in Paris with Pigalle. On return to London exhibited classical paintings at Royal Academy. Inherited fortune from French aunt. Ruined himself gambling, and took up caricature for a living, winning fame and displaying great individuality. Military publications include: *Hungarian and Highland Broadsword*, 1798; *Loyal Volunteers of London* and *Costume of Royal Navy and Marines*, 1799; satirical works *Military Adventures of Johnny Newcome*, 1815, and *Johnny Newcome in the Navy*, 1818. Published many military caricatures, also suites of military genre scenes. Pictures in Victoria and Albert and other London museums.

§RUGENDAS, Johann Lorenz, 1775–1826. German battle painter, aquatint engraver, and publisher, pupil of father, George Lorenz R, and grandson of George Philipp R. Engraved and published suite of Russian uniforms, several military genre scenes, and battle-scenes of Austro-Turkish wars towards close of 18th century. In 1805 designed suite of colored aquatints of Napoleon's French and Italian Guards, published in Augsburg. Chief work was large series (Plates I–XXXIX, plus 2 unnumbered) of colored aquatints of Empire battles, etc. which he designed, aquatinted in collaboration with Steinlein, and published in Augsburg c.1809–20. In 1821 he engraved Captain Marryat's drawing of Napoleon's funeral at St Helena; in 1824, designed *Das Volksfest zu Augsburg*, and in 1825, two plates on Greek War of Independence. Noted as portrait painter. Director of Augsburg art school.

RUNK, Ferdinand, 1764–1834. German landscape painter and aquatint engraver. Born in Freiburg, studied at Vienna Academy. Won fame for views of Tyrol, etc. commissioned by noble patrons, including Archduke John, Princes Schwarzenberg and Liechtenstein. Published series of views in capitals of Europe engraved by J. A. Klein.

SAINT-AUBIN, Louis (dates unknown). French painter, nephew of Augustin. Went to Russia in early 19th century and painted many portraits now in Winter Palace library, Leningrad.

§SAUERWEID, Alexander Ivanovitch, 1783–1844. Russian battle painter and aquatint engraver. Born in Kurland, studied at Dresden Academy. Worked in Dresden until 1814. Published colored uniform suites: *Armée Russe* (12 pl.) Paris, Nepveu, n.d. (1814); *Uniformes de la Garde de*

S.M. le Roi de Westphalie (19 pl.) c.1810; *L'Armée saxonne* (30 pl.) Dresden, 1810; *Costumes de l'armée polonaise* (12 pl.) Dresden, 1813. Designed series of etchings *Dresdener Kriegsscenen* 1813 and 26 etchings of soldiers, later aquatinted in England by E. Hull. Summoned to Petersburg by Tsar 1814 to paint battle pictures now in Tretyakov and Rumiantsev Galleries in Leningrad and Moscow. Many watercolors executed for Prince Regent in Royal Library, Windsor.

§SCHADOW, Gottfried, 1764–1850. Prussian painter, sculptor, caricaturist, and aquatint engraver, pupil of Tassaert. Director of Berlin Academy 1816. Engraved portraits, genre, and military scenes. During 'War of Liberation' designed numerous patriotic caricatures.

§SCHARF, Georg, 1788–1860. German watercolorist and lithographer. Born in Bavaria. Went to London as draftsman to Royal Geological Society. In 1815 was attached to British Army in Paris. Introduced art of lithography into England. Collaborated in illustrating Orme's *Historic Military and Naval Anecdotes*, London, 1818. Watercolors in Victoria and Albert and British Mus., also Dublin Mus.

§SMITH, Charles Hamilton, 1776–1859. English military artist and illustrator, reputedly of Swiss origin. Infantry officer in British Army 1806–21 when he retired as a major. In 1812–14 designed 54 plates and 6 schemes for *Costume of the Army of the British Empire*, followed by *Ancient Costume of Great Britain and Ireland in 1814*. Many watercolors of uniforms, arms, and costume now in Victoria and Albert mus. London.

§SUHR, Christoph, 1771–1842. German portrait and genre painter. In 1808–15 drew 158 watercolors of soldiers quartered in Hamburg, lithographed by his brother Cornelius in an extremely small edition and later republished in Paris 1899 and Leipzig 1902 as '*Manuscrit du Bourgeois de Hambourg*', accounted one of the most interesting documents of the epoch. Published *Hamburgische Trachten*, *Der Ausruf in Hamburg*, and *Spanische National-Trachten*, the latter in collaboration with his brother Cornelius. Later was professor at the Berlin Academy.

SWEBACH-DESFONTAINES, Jacques-François, 1769–1823. Military painter and engraver, pupil of Duplessis. Made debut at 14 at Salon of 1783. Regular exhibitor 1791–1824. In 1800 painted equestrian portrait of Joseph Bonaparte for Malmaison. Chief painter of Sèvres porcelain factory

1802–13. Designed battle scenes for *Tableaux historiques de la Révolution*, 1804, and *Campagnes des français sous le Consulate et l'Empire*. Won Grand Prix at Salon of 1810 for painting of Napoleon crossing the Danube. Pictures in Versailles and Musée Carnavalet.

TAUNAY, Nicolas-Antoine, 1755–1830. French landscape and battle painter, pupil of Casanova. Son of enamelist at Sèvres factory. Went to Switzerland to study landscape. Returned to Paris and won Prix de Rome 1784. Exhibited at Salon 1787 and won renown for pictures engraved by Descourtis. Painted military scenes 1808–14, including *Passage of the Guadarramas*, *Entry of the Guard into Paris*, *Napoleon in Munich*, and Battles of Lodi and Ebersberg. Later went to Rio from where he continued to send canvases back to Paris. Pictures in Hermitage, Leningrad; Victoria and Albert, London; Versailles, and Carnavalet.

§THIRIAR, James, 1889–. Contemporary Belgian painter, watercolorist, and caricaturist. Born in Brussels. Has painted uniforms, historical scenes, and African landscapes. Spent years reconstructing Waterloo uniforms, painting a series of 98 watercolors on this subject. In 1930 designed series of uniform lithographs, published in a special issue entitled *Les uniformes de notre armée* for the Belgian review *Psyche*.

TREZEL, Félix, 1782–1855. French historical and portrait painter. Pupil of Lemire and Prud'hon. Made debut at Salon 1806. Pictures in Versailles and Bordeaux mus.

VAUTHIER, Jules-Antoine, 1774–1832. French historical painter, illustrator, and lithographer, pupil of Regnault. Son-in-law of famous medal engraver, André Galle. Exhibited at Salons of 1802–22. Won second Prix de Rome 1801. Designed military portraits in *Campagnes mémorables des français*, Paris, 1817.

§VERNET, Carle, 1758–1836. French horse, battle, and historical painter, caricaturist, and lithographer. Born in Bordeaux, son of famous marine painter Joseph V, and father of Horace. Visited Rome as child. Entered French Academy 1788. Sister guillotined in Revolution. During Consulate began painting battle scenes (25 engraved by Duplessi-Bertaux for *Tableaux Historiques*, Paris, 1806); but chiefly renowned for pictures of horses and caricatures. With son Horace designed *Recueil de chevaux de tout genre* at beginning of Empire (60 plates of Guard and

Line cavalry, Mameluks, hunters, and race horses) aquatinted in color by Levachez. Most famous series *Collection de costumes dessinés d'après nature*, aquatinted in color by Debucourt 1814–15, shows street types, occupation troops, and the *Garde Royale*. *Collection de chevaux de tous pays montés*, 57 plates showing cavalry of the *Garde Royale* lithographed by de Lasteryie, was followed by series of Cossacks lithographed by Engelmann, and several giant folio plates of Cossacks and Mameluks engraved by Debucourt. Many, crudely copied by Purcell, Addiscombe, etc. were published in London by Dickinson. Recently Vernet's beautiful watercolors of uniforms of the *Grande Armée* in the Ministère de la Guerre have been published by Raoul and Jean Brunon in Marseilles. Paintings at Versailles include *Eve of Austerlitz*, *Napoleon before Madrid*, and battles of Arcole and Marengo. Others in Louvre and mus. of Königsberg, Clamecy, and Neuchâtel.

§VERNET, Horace, 1789–1863. French battle painter and caricaturist, son of Carle V. Born in Louvre which family had to evacuate hurriedly during Revolution. Enthusiastic admirer of Napoleon. Served in national guard during Empire. Exhibited first battle painting at Salon of 1810 and won 1st prize 1812 with portrait of King Jerôme. Collaborated with father in *Recueil de chevaux de tout genre*. In 1815 designed best known work, *Incroyables et Merveilleuses*, satirizing fashions of day and occupation troops, with 35 colored plates engraved by Lanté and Gatine. Remained faithful to Empire during Restoration. Collaborated with Eugène Lami in designing *Collection des uniformes de 1791–1814* and *de 1814–1824* (148 col. lithographs). Famous painting *Barrière de Clichy*, showing defense of Paris in 1814, refused by Salon of 1822 for political reasons. In collaboration with Lami published *Manejo del sable*, Madrid, 1819; designed 10 giant folio plates of *Cossacks*, *Garde Royale*, etc. engraved by Jazet and Coqueret, also lithographs of Empire scenes, military genre pieces, and caricatures. In 1828 appointed director of French Academy in Rome where he was virtual ambassador during Revolution of 1830. Succeeded by Ingres 1835 and returned to Paris. Commissioned by Louis-Philippe to paint numerous battles for Versailles, including Jemappes, Valmy, Hanau, Montmirail, and entire 'Salle de Constantine'. Collaborated in illustrating Arnaut,

Vie politique et militaire de Napoléon, 1822–61: also histories of Napoleon by Laurent l'Ardèche, Bussey, and Horne. Official painter of Second Empire. Paintings also in Louvre; Wallace Coll. London; Palace of Compiègne; mus. of Amsterdam, Genoa, Hamburg, Leipzig, Algiers, Amiens, Chantilly, etc.

§VERNET, Jules, 1792–1843. French portrait painter and miniaturist. Exhibited at Salon 1812–42. Won medal 1834. Painted many celebrities of Empire and Restoration.

WEILAND, C.-F. (dates unknown). German military illustrator and publisher. Officer in Württemberg army, later Prussian artillery. Editor of Geographical Institute in Weimar. Designed and probably engraved *Darstellung der K. K. Französischen Armee und ihrer Allirten*, Weimar, 1807, with 148 col. plates of Imperial Guard and Grand Army. Second edition with text published 1812. Foreword states information for text and plates required 3 years to assemble.

§WEST, Benjamin, 1738–1820. American portrait and battle painter, born in Springfield, Mass. Moved to Philadelphia, and later New York where he painted many successful portraits. Went to Rome 1760 and visited London 1765 where success was so phenomenal he sent for his fiancée in America, married, and settled there. Chosen one of 3 commissioners to organize Royal Academy of which he became president in 1792. In 1766 illustrated Col. Bouquet's *Expedition against the Ohio Indians*, Philadelphia and London, 1766 and Amsterdam, 1769. Many military paintings engraved, including *Death of Epaminondas*, *Mort de Turenne*, *Death of Wolfe at Quebec*, *King Charles II landing at Dover*, and battles of the Boyne, La Hogue, and New Orleans. Painted many portraits of royal family.

Refused knighthood, being a Quaker. Buried in St Paul's Cathedral, London. Pictures in mus. of Boston, Cleveland, Kansas City, Glasgow, and Liverpool (Death of Nelson), and Victoria and Albert, London.

§WIGAND, Balthazar, 1771–1846. Austrian miniature painter. Born in Vienna. Paintings in gouache include popular scenes, military parades, fêtes, etc, and are much admired for their delicacy of color and execution. Miniatures in Liechtenstein Gallery and Belvedere, Vienna.

§WOLF (WOLFF), Ulrich Ludwig, 1776–1832. German historical and military painter and draftsman. Born in Berlin, pupil of Thiele. Member of Berlin Academy. In 1810 designed 10 plates of Berlin *Bürgermilitair* aquatinted by Jügel, followed by *Abbildung der neuen Königl. Preuss Armee Uniformen*, 1812–15, with 71 col. plates aquatinted by Meyer, Jügel, and Leopold, one of the handsomest works of epoch and excessively rare complete. In 1815, designed series of Russian military types published in Vienna by Johann Cappi. Watercolors: *Triumphal Entry into Berlin of King Fred. Wilhelm III*, *Russian Cavalry*, *Allied armies entering Paris*, in National Gallery, Berlin.

ZIEGLER, Johann, 1750–1812. Austrian painter and engraver. Studied at Vienna Academy. Collaborated with Carl Schütz in designing famous *Aussichten der Residenzstadt Wien* published by Artaria at end of 18th century and beginning of 19th, with 50 views of Vienna and its environs engraved by Mansfeld and Ziegler, and beautifully colored. In two subsequent editions both buildings and costumes were brought up to date. Ziegler was in Vienna at time of Napoleon's entry in 1805 and designed a plate showing the vanguard of the *Grand Armée* entering the city.

BIBLIOGRAPHY

Author's Note: The present work, largely compiled from documents in the archives of the Historical Service of the Army, would require a tedious array of notes and references to make it absolutely complete. I shall therefore limit myself to indicating the principal sources of the texts employed.

A) MANUSCRIPTS

National Archives, A. F. N. 1670, etc.
Archives of the Army Historical Service (Archives Historiques):

> Series Xab 1 to 98. Government Guards, Guard of the Consuls, Imperial Guard.
> Series Xac 1, 2, 3, 4. General and specific documents relating to each corps.

C^2 287	Notes sur les opérations de la 2me division de la Jeune Garde (général Roguet).
C^2 308	Ordres du jour de la Garde impériale (général Friant) du 8 janvier 1813 au 14 janvier 1814.
C^2 309	Registre de correspondance du général Roguet, commandant une division de la Garde du 10 juillet au 18 août 1813.
C^2 310	Dépôt de la Jeune Garde, du 1er février au 28 avril 1813.
C^2 320	Correspondance du général Roguet à Anvers, du 7 décembre 1813 au 27 mars 1814.
C^2 169–188	Grande Armée (campagne de France) 1814. Correspondance.
C^2 469	Situations de la Garde impériale 1804-5
C^2 470	„ „ „ „ 1806
C^2 471	„ „ „ „ 1807
C^2 505	„ „ „ „ 1809
C^2 523	„ „ „ „ 1812
C^2 537	„ „ „ „ 1813
C^2 554	„ „ „ „ 1814
C^{15} 20	Livre d'ordres du 2me Régiment des Chasseurs à pied de la Garde impériale du 22 avril au 27 août 1815.
C^{15} 34	Situation de la Garde impériale 1815.
C^{15} 37	„ „ „ „ „
C^8 365	Situation de la Garde impériale en Espagne 1810-13.
C^{17} 538	Correspondance de l'Empereur avec le maréchal Bessières.

The researcher will consult with great interest the inventory compiled by Messrs. Marc-André Fabre, chief archivist; Jean-Claude Devos, archive librarian; André Cambier, curator of administrative archives; and Louis Garros, librarian.

ADMINISTRATIVE ARCHIVES

> Muster rolls of officers and men of the Guard of the Consuls and Imperial Guard 1800-1815.
> Dossiers of the officers of the Imperial Guard (classified alphabetically).

ARCHIVES OF THE DEPARTMENT OF LOIRET
MUNICIPAL ARCHIVES OF MONTARGIS
> Boivin Ms.

Bibliothèque du Ministère de la Guerre
> Service de MM. les officiers de la Gendarmerie d'élite de la Garde impériale.

Archives of Mgr. le duc de Guise at the library of the Musée de l'Armée
Soldiers' letters, field note-books, unpublished documents belonging to the author or lent by historians and collectors

B) PRINTED TEXTS

In addition to Napoleon's correspondence and the contemporary newspapers, we have consulted the National and Imperial Almanachs; Annuaires nationaux et impériaux de l'an VII à 1815; Bulletin of the Société des collectionneurs de figurines historiques and the following books:

Aerts, Winand, and Wilmet, Léon. 1815–18 juin. Brussels, 1904. Campagne de 1815 en Belgique.

Alleaume, Charles. Les gardes d'honneur du Var sous le 1er Empire. Draguignan, 1933.

Aster, Heinrich. Schilderung der Kriegsenreignise in und vor Dresden von 7 März bis 28 August 1813. Dresden and Leipzig, 1844.

Bac (Bach), Ferdinand Sigismund. Vienne au temps de Napoléon. (Translation) Paris, 1933.

Barante, Amable-Guillaume-Prosper Bruguière, Baron de. Souvenirs du baron de Barante . . . 1782–1866 . . . Paris, 1890–1901.

Barbillon, L. Soldats d'autrefois. Quelques mots d'histoire sur les troupes d'Afrique, de la marine, et des colonies. Grenoble, 1941.

Barrès, Jean-Baptiste-Auguste. Souvenirs d'un officier de la Grande Armée . . . Paris (1923).

Bartel, Paul. Napoléon à l'île d'Elbe. Paris, 1947.

Beler, Guy de. Baylen. Paris, 1955.

Belhomme, Victor-Louis-Jean-François, Lieutenant-colonel. Histoire de l'infanterie en France. Paris and Limoges, 1893–1899.

Bertaut, Jules. L'argot dans la Grande Armée. (In *Miroir de l'Histoire*, December, 1952).

Berthezène, Pierre, Baron. Souvenirs militaires de la République et de l'Empire. Paris, 1855.

Berthier, Alexandre, Maréchal. Rapports à l'Empereur pendant la campagne de 1813. Paris, 1909.

Bertrand, Emil. Les marins de la Garde, 1803–1816. Paris, 1895.

Bessières, Albert. Le maréchal Bessières, duc d'Istrie, 1768–1813, le Bayard de la Grande Armée. Paris, 1941.

Bigarré, Auguste, Baron. Memoirs du gal. Bigarré, aide de camp du roi Joseph: 1775–1813. Paris (1893).

Billon, François-Frédéric. Souvenirs d'un vélite de la Garde sous Napoléon Ier. Paris, 1905.

Blayney, Andrew Thomas, General Lord. Relation d'un voyage forcé en Espagne et en France . . . 1810–1814. (Translation) Paris, 1815.

Blaze, E., Capitaine. Souvenirs d'un officier de la Grande Armée. La vie militaire sous le Premier Empire. Paris, c.1890.

Bottet, Maurice, Capitaine. L'arme blanche de guerre française au XVIIIe siècle. Paris, 1910.
— La manufacture de Versailles. Paris, c.1900–1910.
— Monographie de l'arme à feu des armées françaises. Paris, c.1900–1910.

Bouchot, Henri. L'épopée du costume militaire français. Paris, 1898.

Boulart, Jean-François, Général baron. Mémoires militaires sur les guerres de la République et de l'Empire. Paris (1892).

Bourgeois, Henri. L'abbé Barbottin, premier aumônier de la Grande Armée: 1762–1848. Fontenay-le-Comte, 1908.

Bourgogne, Adrien-Jean-Baptiste-François, Sergent. Mémoires du sergent Bourgogne (1812–1813) . . . Paris, 1909.

Bourgoing, Paul, Baron de. Souvenirs d'histoire contemporaine. Épisodes militaires et politiques. Paris, 1864.

Bourgoing, Pierre, Baron de. Souvenirs militaires 1791–1815. Paris, 1897.

Bourguignon, Jean. Mémoires de Marchand. N.p., n.d.

Bouvier, Félix. Les premiers combats de 1814. Paris, 1895.

Bricard, Louis-Joseph. Journal du canonnier Bricard. Paris, 1891.

Brice, Raoul. Une carrière aventureuse. Le général Brice, chef français de partisans lorrains 1783–1851. Nancy, 1923.

Brunon, Jean. Des Tatars au service de Napoléon. Marseilles, c.1938.

Brunon, Raoul and Jean. La revue de décadi. (In *Revue de la Société des amis du musée de la figurine historique*, May, 1952.)

Buat, Edmond-Alphonse-Léon, Général. Étude critique d'histoire militaire; 1809, de Ratisbonne à Znaïm. Paris, 1909.

Bucquoy, E.-L., Commandant, ed. Les uniformes du Premier Empire. Vol. 1, Chap. 6; Les guides de l'état-major. Vol.2, Chap.9: Les chasseurs à cheval de la Garde; La gendarmerie d'élite. Evreux, 1917–c.1945.

Calmon-Maison, Jean-Joseph-Robert. Le général Maison et le 1er Corps de la Grande Armée. Paris, 1914.

Campana, J, Chef d'escadron. La campagne de France, 1814. Paris, 1922.

Carnet de la Sabretache. Vols.1–. Paris, 1893–. Numerous articles published by this magnificent review. Printed index to the year 1902. Repertory compiled by Marc-André Fabre at the Bibliothèque du Ministère de la Guerre.

Caulaincourt, Armand-Augustin-Louis, Général marquis de, duc de Vicence. Recollections of Caulaincourt, Duke of Vicenza. (Translation.) London, 1838.

Chambray, Georges, Marquis de. Histoire de l'expédition de Russie. Paris, 1823.

Chardigny, Louis. Les maréchaux de Napoléon. Paris, 1946.

Chlapowski, Désiré, Général baron. Mémoires sur les guerres de Napoléon, 1806–1813. Paris, 1908.

Chuquet, Arthur. L'année 1814. Lettres et mémoires. Paris, 1914.
— La guerre en Russie. Notes et documents. Paris, 1912.

Cotty, Gaspard-Herman, Colonel. Dictionnaire de l'artillerie. Paris, 1822.

Delhaize, Jules. La domination française en Belgique à la fin du XVIIIe et au commencement du XIX siècle. Brussels, 1908–1912.

Denniée, Baron. Itinéraire de l'empereur Napoléon pendant la campagne de 1812. Paris, 1842.

Douare, Georges. Napoléon au printemps de 1807. Translated by Count Hannibal zu Dohna. Nice, 1908.

Driault, Edouard. L'immortelle épopée du drapeau tricolore; Napoléon-le-Grand, 1769–1821. Versailles, 1930.

— Napoléon à Finkenstein (avril-mai 1807). Paris, 1899.

Druène, Bernard, Lieutenant-colonel. Les Français à Berlin. Berlin, 1949.

— Régiments parisiens des Gardes françaises et la Garde impériale. (In *Revue historique de l'Armée*, Vol.8, No.7, March, 1952.)

du Casse, Albert, Baron. Le général Arrighi de Casanova, duc de Padoue. Paris, 1866.

— Mémoires pour servir à la campagne de 1812 en Russie, suivies des lettres de Napoléon au roi de Westphalie pendant la campagne de 1813. Paris, 1852.

Dubois, A. Les ambulances versaillaises en 1814. Aperçu des évacuations de la Grande Armée. Versailles, 1914.

Ducéré, Edouard. Napoléon à Bayonne d'après les contemporains et des documents inédits. Bayonne, 1897.

Ducor, Henri. Aventures d'un marin de la Garde impériale... Edited by Louis-François L'heritier. (Paris), 1883.

Dumoulin, Maurice. Précis d'histoire militaire. Révolution et Empire. Paris, 1901.

Dupont, Marcel (pseudonym of Marcel-Ernest Béchu). Napoléon et la trahison des maréchaux, 1814. (Paris, 1939.)

— Napoléon et ses grognards. Paris, 1945.

Durand, Alexis. Napoléon à Fontainebleau; choix d'épisodes. (2nd?) ed. Versailles (1912).

Espinchal, Joseph-Thomas-Anne, Comte d'. Journal of the Comte d'Espinchal during the Emigration. Edited by Ernest d'Hauterive, translated by Mrs Rodolph Stawell. London, 1912.

Fain, Agathon-Jean-François. Manuscrit de mil huit cent douze... Paris, 1827.
Manuscrit de mil huit cent quartorze... (Paris, 1823).

Manuscrit de mil huit cent treize... 2nd ed. Paris, 1825.
Mémoires du baron Fain, premier secrétaire du cabinet de l'empereur... Paris, 1909.

Fairon, Emile, and Heuse, Henri. Lettres de grognards. Liège and Paris, 1936.

Fallou, L. La Garde impériale (1804–1815)... Paris, 1901.

Fantin des Odoards, Louis-Florimond, Général. Journal du général Fantin des Odoards; étapes d'un officier de la Grande Armée, 1800–1830. Paris, 1895.

Fay, Charles-Alexandre, Général. Étude des marches (Iéna-Sedan). (2nd?) ed. Paris, 1899.

Fezensac, Raymond-Eyméry-Philippe-Joseph, Général duc de. Journal de la campagne de Russie en 1812. Tours, 1849.

Fieffé, Eugène. Napoléon Ier et la Garde impériale. Paris, 1859.

Friant, Jean-François, Comte. Vie militaire du lieutenant-général comte Friant. Paris, 1857.

Froger, Pierre. Panaches et culottes de peau. Angers, 1946.

Fugier, André. Napoléon et l'Espagne, 1799–1808. Paris, 1910.

Fusil, Louise, Madame. L'incendie de Moscou... London, 1817.

Galli, H. (pseudonym of H. Gallichet). 1806. L'armée française en Allemagne. Paris, 1888.

Garros, Louis. Le général Cambronne. Paris, 1949.

— Quel roman que ma vie! Itinéraire de Napoléon Bonaparte (1769–1821). Paris, 1947.

Gassendi, Jean-Jacques-Basilien de, Général. Aide-mémoire à l'usage des officiers d'artillerie de France attachés au service de terre. 3rd ed. Paris, 1801.

Gastey, Général. Le transport en poste de la Garde impériale, 1806. (In *Revue historique de l'Armée*, Vol.3, No.4, 1947.)

Geisendorf-des-Gouttes, Théophile. Les archipels enchanteurs et farouches; Baléares et Canaries. Geneva (1937.)
Geôles et pontons d'Espagne; l'expédition et la captivité d'Andalousie. Geneva (1932).

Gourgaud, Gaspard, Général baron. Napoléon et la Grande Armée en Russie, ou examen critique de l'ouvrage du comte Ph. de Ségur. 2nd ed. Paris, 1825.

Grabowski, Joseph. Mémoires militaires de Joseph Grabowski. 1812. 1813. 1814. Translated by N. Jean W. Chelminski and Comdt. A. Malibran. Paris, 1907.

Grandin, F. Souvenirs historiques du capitaine Krettly, ancien trompette-major des guides d'Italie . . . devant fournir quelques documents importants aux écrivains qui feront l'histoire du Midi, pendant les Cent Jours. Paris, 1838.

Grasset, Alphonse-Louis, Capitaine. La guerre d'Espagne (1807–1813). Paris and Nancy, 1914–1932.

Griois, Charles-Pierre-Lubin, Général. Mémoires du général Griois, 1792–1822. Paris, 1909.

Gruyer, Paul. Napoléon roi de l'île d'Elbe. Paris, 1906.

Guitard, Joseph-Esprit-Florentin. Souvenirs militaires du Premier Empire; mémoires du grenadier de la Garde Joseph-Esprit-Florentin Guitard (1809–1815) . . . Paris, 1934.

Guitry, Paul-Georges-Marcel, Commandant. L'armée de Bonaparte en Egypte, 1798–1799. Paris, 1897.

Hadengue, Antoine. Les gardes rouges de l'an II . . . Paris, 1930.

Hillairet, Jacques. Évocation du vieux Paris. (2nd?) ed. (Paris, 1952.)

Hollander. Guidons-étendards-tabliers de trompettes et de timbales des chasseurs à cheval de la Garde: Consulat et Empire. Strasbourg, 1926.

Houssaye, Henry. 1814. 63rd ed. Paris, 1909.
—1815. Waterloo. 67th ed. Paris, 1910.
—1815. La première Restauration – Le retour de l'île d'Elbe – Les Cent Jours. 65th ed. Paris, 1912.

Joachim, Erich. Napoleon in Finckenstein. Berlin, 1906.

Job (pseudonym of Jacques Onfroy de Bréville), illustrator. La Vieille Garde Impériale. Tours (1902).

Jolyet, Jean Baptiste, Lieutenant. Souvenirs de 1815. (In Revue de Paris, Vol.5, 1903.)

Jomini, Henri, Baron. La vie politique et militaire de Napoléon, raconté par lui-même, au tribunal de César, d'Alexandre et de Frédéric. Brussels, 1841.

Jouvin, Colonel, and Gillet, Capitaine. Marches et chansons des soldats de France. Paris, n.d.

Kastner, Georges. Les chants de l'armée française . . . précédés d'un essai historique sur les chants militaires des Français. Paris and London, 1855.

Koch, Jean-Baptiste-Frédéric, Général. Mémoires pour servir à l'histoire de la campagne de 1814. Paris, 1819.

Kovatchévitch. Michel. Le sort des artistes français et russes en 1812 et le décret de Moscou . . . Clermont-Ferrand, 1941.

Labeaume. Campagne de Russie en 1812. 5th ed. Paris and London, 1816.

Lachouque, Henry, Commandant. Le secret de Waterloo. Paris (1952).
Terres héroïques; Waterloo, champs de bataille de 1815. Paris (1953).

Larchey, Lorédan, ed. Les cahiers du capitaine Coignet (1776–1850). Paris, 1888.
—Les suites d'une capitulation; relations des captifs de Baylen et de la retraite du 116e régiment. Paris, 1884.

Lavalette, Antoine-Marie-Chamant, Comte de. Mémoires et souvenirs du comte Lavallette [sic], aide-de-camp du général Bonaparte . . . Paris, 1831.

Lebarbier, Notes sur la campagne de Russie en 1812, par un officier de la Grande Armée, le comdt. Michel de la Horie. Paris, 1908.

Lecestre, Léon, ed. Lettres inédites de Napoléon I (an VII–1815). Paris, 1897.

Lefebvre-Pigneaux de Béhaine, François-Armand-Edouard, Commandant. La campagne de France. Paris, 1913–1935.

Lefol. Souvenirs sur le Prytanée de Saint-Cyr . . . Versailles, 1854.

Lejeune, Louis-François, Général baron. De Valmy à Wagram. Près de Napoléon. Paris, 1895.

Lemaître, Paul. Le passage de Napoléon Ier à Gap en 1815. (In Bulletin de la Société des études des Hautes-Alpes, 1903.)

Lenôtre, G. (pseudonym of Luis-Léon-Théodore Gosselin) . . . Napoléon, croquis de l'épopée. Paris (1932).

Leroy, Gabriel. Histoire de Melun depuis les temps les plus reculés jusqu'à nos jours. Melun, 1887.

L'héritier. Napoléon à Schoenbrunn. (In Revue des études napoléoniennes, Vol.19, No.2. September-October, 1922.)

Lignières, Marie-Henry de Bourbon-Busset, Comte de. Souvenirs de la Grande Armée et de la Vieille Garde impériale. Paris (1933).

Lomier. Le bataillon des marins de la Garde, 1803–1815 . . . St-Valéry-sur-Somme, 1905.
—Histoire des régiments des gardes d'honneur, 1813–1814. Amiens and Paris, 1924.

Lottin, Denis. Recherches historiques sur la ville d'Orléans. Orléans, 1836–1845.

Lucas-Dubreton, Jean. Napoléon devant l'Espagne; ce qu'a vu Goya. Paris (1948).
—Soldats de Napoléon. Paris, 1948.

M, A. D. B., Lieutenant (pseudonym of A. D. B. Monier). Une année de la vie de l'empereur Napoléon, ou précis historique de tout ce qui s'est passé depuis le 1er avril 1814 jusqu'au 20 mars 1815 etc. Paris, 1815.

Madelin, Louis. Histoire du Consulat et de l'Empire. (Paris, 1937–1954.)

Manteyer, de. La fin de l'Empire dans les Alpes (19 mai 1813–30 juin 1815). Gap, 1942.

Marco de Saint Hilaire, Emile. Histoire anecdotique, politique et militaire de la Garde impériale. Paris, 1847.

Margerand, J. Les aides de camp de Bonaparte, 1793–1804. Paris, 1931.

Margueron, Louis Joseph, Colonel . . . Campagne de Russie . . . Paris (1897–1906).

Maringoné, Louis-Joseph Vionnet, Général vicomte de. Souvenirs. Edited by André Lévi. Paris, 1913.

Marmont, Auguste-Frédéric-Louis Viesse de, Maréchal duc de Raguse. Mémoires du duc de Raguse de 1792 à 1832 . . . Paris, 1857.

Martinien, Aristide. Tableaux par corps et par batailles des officiers tués et blessés pendant les guerres de l'Empire (1805–1815). Paris, (1899).

Masson, Frédéric. L'affaire Maubreuil. Paris, 1907.
—Cavaliers de Napoléon. Paris, 1895.
—Napoléon chez lui; la journée de l'empereur aux Tuileries. Paris (1894).
—Napoléon et sa famille. Paris, 1904, 1903–1919.

Mauduit, Hippolyte de. Histoire des derniers jours de la Grande Armée, ou souvenirs, documents et correspondance inédite de Napoléon en 1814 et 1815. 2nd ed. Paris, 1854.

Mauguin, Georges. Napoléon et la superstition; anecdotes et curiosités. Rodez, 1946.

Méneval, Claude-François, Baron de. Napoléon et Marie-Louise; souvenirs historiques de M. le baron Méneval . . . Paris, 1843–1845.

Millard, Eugène. Le Golfe-Juan, station d'hiver. Débarquement de l'empereur Napoléon Ier au Golfe-Juan. Cannes, 1867.

Miroir de l'Histoire, Le. Vols. 1–. Paris, 1950–.

Morvan, Jean. Le soldat impérial (1800–1814). Paris, 1904.

Niegolewski, André de. Les polonais à Somo-Sierra en 1808, en Espagne. Paris, 1854.

Odeleben, Ernst, Freiherr von. A Circumstantial Narrative of the Campaign in Saxony, in the Year 1813. Translated by Alfred John Kempe. London, 1820.

Orléans, Louis Philippe, Duc d'. Extrait de mon journal du mois de mars, 1815. Twickenham, 1816.

Pajol, Comte. Pajol, général en chef. 1772. 1796. 1797, 1811, 1812. 1844. Paris, 1874.

Pardée, Marie Antoinette, Mme. Route Napoléon; Golfe-Juan, 1er mars 1815 – 1er juillet 1932. Cannes, 1932.

Parquin, C, Capitaine. Récits de guerre; souvenirs du capitaine Parquin, 1803–1814. Paris (1893).

Paulin Ruelle, Capitaine, ed. Souvenirs du général bon. Paulin (1782–1876) . . . Paris, 1895.

Pelet, Jean-Jacques-Germain, Général. Mémoires sur les guerres de Napoléon depuis 1796 jusqu'en 1815. N.p, n.d.
—Des principales opérations de la campagne de 1813. (In Le Spectateur militaire, Vols.1–4. 1826–1828.)

Pélissier, Léon-Gabriel. Napoléon, souverain de l'île d'Elbe; mémoires de Pons de l'Hérault. (2nd) ed. Paris, 1934.

Perrot, A, and Amoudru, C. Histoire de l'ex-Garde depuis sa formation . . . comprenant les faits généraux des campagnes de 1806 à 1815. Paris, 1821.

Peyrusse, Guillaume-Joseph Roux, Baron. 1809–1815. Mémorial et archives de M. le baron Peyrusse . . . Vienne–Moscou–île d'Elbe. Carcassonne, 1869.

Pils, François. Journal de marche du grenadier Pils (1804–1814). Paris, 1895.

Pion des Loches, Antoine-Augustin-Flavien, Colonel. Mes campagnes, 1792–1815; notes et correspondance du colonel d'artillerie Pion des Loches . . . Paris, 1889.

Plancy, Adrien Godard-d'Aucour, Comte de. Souvenirs (1798–1816) . . . Paris, 1904.

Poumiès de la Siboutie, François-Louis. Souvenirs d'un médecin de Paris . . . Paris, 1910.

Réal, Pierre-François, Comte. Essai sur mes journées des 13 et 14 vendémiaire. Paris (1795).

Reboul, Antoine-Joseph, Colonel. Mes souvenirs de 1814 et 1815, par M. XXX. Paris, 1824.

Regnault, Jean, Commandant. La campagne de 1815; mobilisation et concentration. Paris, 1935.

Rembowski, Aleksander, ed. Sources documentaires concernant l'histoire du régiment des chevaulégers-lanciers de la Garde de Napoléon I. Warsaw, 1899.

Recueil des marches et fanfares de la Garde impériale de Napoléon Ier. (Archives Nationales.)

Revue des études napoléoniennes. Vols. 1–46. Paris and Versailles, 1912–1940.

Revue historique de l'Armée. Vols.2–3. Paris, 1946–1947.

Rossigneux, André. Une étape de Napoléon Ier, Auxerre 17–19 mars 1815. Auxerre, 1911.

—Une étape de Napoléon Ier, Avallon (16–17 mars 1815). Auxerre, 1913.

—Napoléon Ier à Joigny, Sens et Pont-sur-Yonne, 19–20 mars 1815. (In Bulletin de la Société des sciences historiques et naturelles de l'Yonne, 1911, II.)

Rousselot, L. Les grenadiers de la Garde. Les marins de la Garde. (In L'Armée Française: ses uniformes, son armement, son équipement. Paris, 1943–.)

Saski, Charles-Gaspard-Louis, Lieutenant-colonel. Campagne de 1809 en Allemagne et en Autriche. Paris, etc, 1899–1902

Savant, Jean. Les mamelouks de Napoléon. Paris (1949).

Schlumberger, Gustave-Léon. Soldats de Napoléon. Journal de route du capitaine Robineaux (1803–1832). Paris, 1908.

—Vieux soldats de Napoléon. Paris, 1904.

Serieyx, W. Cambronne. Paris, 1931.

Simond, Charles (pseudonym of Adolphe van Cleemputte). La vie parisienne à travers le XIXe siècle. Paris de 1800 à 1900 . . . Paris, 1900–1901.

Six, Georges. Dictionnaire biographique des généraux et amiraux français de la Révolution et de l'Empire (1792–1814). Paris, 1934.

Spectateur militaire, Le. Series 3, Vols.(24–25). Paris, 1884.

Tartary, Madeleine. Épisode de la campagne de France. Nogent-sur-Seine en 1814. Paris, 1939.

Thiard, Auxonne-Théodore-Marie, général Comte de Bissy. Souvenirs diplomatiques et militaires du général Thiard, chambellan de Napoléon Ier. Edited by Léonce Lex. Paris (1900).

Thiébault, Paul, Lieutenant-général baron. Mémoires du général bon. Thiébault. Paris, 1893–1895.

Thiry, Jean. Le vol de l'aigle; le retour de Napoléon de l'île d'Elbe aux Tuileries, Paris, 1942.

Vachée, Jean-Baptiste-Modeste-Eugène, Colonel. Napoléon en campagne. Paris and Nancy, 1913.

Vaudoncourt, Frédéric-Guillaume, Baron de. Critical situation of Bonaparte in his retreat out of Russia, or a faithful narrative of the repassing of the Beresina by the French Army in 1812; by an Eye-Witness. (Translation.) London, 1815.

—Mémoires pour servir à l'histoire de la guerre entre la France et la Russie en 1812. Par un officier de l'état-major de l'Armée française. Paris, 1817.

Vigny, Alfred de. Servitude et grandeur militaires. Paris, 1930.

Wirth, Joseph. Le maréchal Lefébvre, duc de Dantzig (1755–1820). Paris, 1904.

INDEX OF NAMES OF PERSONS

A

B

H

K

L

N

PREFECT OF HAUTES-ALPES, 452

PRELIER, Maj, lt, chass, Cons Gd; lt col cdt 13 Volt; killed at Craonne, 25, 342, 372

PRINCE OF PEACE, see GODOY

PRIVÉ (PRYVÉ), Gen Baron, comm Line drag at Baylén, 125

PROMETHEUS, Greek god who gave fire to man and was chained to rock in punishment, 502

PROPHET, THE, see MAHOMET

PROVENCE, Count of, see LOUIS XVIII

PRUSSIA, King of, see FREDERICK, FREDERICK WILLIAM

PRUSSIA, Pr William of, bro of Fred Wm III, gen comm brig 1814; 356, 391

PUCHEU, Maj, lt, drag of Gd; prom capt at Friedland; maj 1813; 113, 284

PUISSANT, M, citizen of Charleroi, 476–7

PULLY, Gen Randon de Malboissière, Count de, col in ch, 1 Gds of Hon, 286

R

RABUSSON, Maj, lt, *chass à chev*, Cons Gd; capt, Imp Gd; wounded at Eylau; nom to Ord of 3 Golden Fleeces; maj, Chass of France, 26, 88, 167, 434

RADZIWILL, Lt Col Prince, lt-h-lanc; killed at Hanau, 284, 323

RAGOIS, Maj, capt, gren Cons Gd; maj, adjt of Palace, 10, 24

RAGUSA, Duke of, see MARMONT

RANCHON, Capt, 2 Gren, 289

RANDON, Capt, 5 Inf at Grenoble, later mar of France, 453

RAOUL, Capt, Gd art, wounded in defense of Paris; capt, art, Elba Bn; on march from Golfe–Juan; 399, 415, 453

RAPP, Gen Count Jean, col, adc to 1st Consul; adc to Desaix at Marengo; organ Mameluk sqdr; vice-com h gren, Imp Gd; adc to Emp; dist, wounded at Austerlitz; painted by Gérard; helped organize Polish lt-h; dist at Essling; in Russian campaign; at Gorodnia; face frozen during retreat; comm 5 Corps in Alsace 1815; 28, 30–1, 44, 64–5, 70, 86, 156, 250, 269, 473

RAYNAL, Abbé, editor and historian, 209

REDING, Col, Swiss off in Spanish service, 127

REGGIO, Duke of, see OUDINOT

REGGIO, Duchess of, 445

REICHEL (RÜCHEL), von, Prussian gen at Jena, 76

REILLE, Gen Count, later mar of France, adc to Emp; charged at Wagram; comm 2 Corps at Fleurus, Quatre-Bras, Waterloo, 163, 475–6, 478, 483

RÉMUSAT, Count de, 28

RÉMY, Maj Baron de, comm sqdr of h gren in Spain, 187, 435

RENIER, Conscr-Chasseur, 2 Rgt in Spain, 188

RENNO, Maj, capt, maj, Mameluks, dist at Eylau; wounded at Madrid; maj, Lanc of France; att to lt-h-lanc 1815; 95, 104, 113, 121, 433, 471

REPNIN, Prince, cdt Russian *Chevalier Gardes*, adc to Tsar, captured at Austerlitz, 65, 70

REQUIN, marines of Gd, dec Leg of Hon, 182

REYNAUD, Maj, Cons Gd, adjt of palace, 24

REYNIER, Gen Count, comm 7 (Saxon) Corps in Russia, at Bautzen; captured at Leipzig, 253, 299, 313, 318, 320

RICARD, Gen Baron, later Count, comm Line div in Russia; comm Line div 1814; dist at Montmirail, 261, 353–4

RIGNON, Maj, lt, chass, Cons Gd; maj, 2 Chass Imp Gd, 25, 200

RIGNY, Commander de, marines of Gd, later vice-adm; ensign at Boulogne; carried dispatches 1815 ordering Nap surrendered to English, 49, 496

RIMMEL, Corp, volt 1809; conscr-chass 1810; company clerk, 5 Volt 1812; 146, 175, 201

RIVOLI, Duke of, see MASSÉNA

ROBESPIERRE, French revolutionary extremist, 7

ROBERT, Lt Col, cdt 2 Conscr-chass in Spain; comm *tirailleur* depot 1813, Y Gd brig at defense of Paris; gen 1814; 150, 165, 172, 189, 282, 395–7, 431

ROBERT, Capt qm, Gd art, expelled from corps, 124

ROCHAMBEAU, Marshal Count de Vimeur de, comm French exped force in America 1780–3; 90

ROGER-DUCOS, Consul of Rep, xvii

ROGÉRY, Maj, capt, gren; wounded at Eylau; maj, 2 Conscr-gren, 89, 150

ROGUET, Gen Count, comm Y Gd brig at Essling; 2 Gd Div in Spain and Russia; at Borodino, dist at Krasnoye, the Berezina; comm O Gd Div in Germany 1813; at Lützen, Bautzen; comm 4 Y Gd Div, wounded, at Dresden; dist at Dresden, Leipzig; comm provis Y Gd Div 1814 in Belgium; fought way out of Antwerp; vice-com Gren of France, Gd gren 1815; 1 O Gd Div at Ligny; charged at Waterloo; comm ft Gd after abdication; recalled to army by Louis-Philippe, 151–2, 165, 172–4, 186, 188, 192, 198–9, 220, 225, 231–2, 234, 238–9, 245–6, 248–9, 252–3, 258–60, 263–4, 266, 269, 271–2, 275, 277, 281–3, 287–8, 292, 296, 304, 308–9, 311, 315, 321, 326–9, 333–5, 402, 431, 456, 461, 469, 479, 487, 489–91, 493, 498, 503

ROMAÑA, Marquis de la, Spanish gen, 173

ROME, King of, son of Napoleon and Marie-Louise (Napoleon II) later Duke of Reichstadt, 67, 176, 194, 197, 200, 208, 212–13, 218, 224, 237, 252, 277, 342, 352, 390, 392, 395, 404–6, 411, 417, 419, 440–1, 454, 460–1, 492–3, 495

ROQUE, Maj, Royal Dutch Gd; att to gren, Imp Gd; maj, 3 Volt, killed at Wurschen, 190, 300

ROQUEBERT, Commander, marines of Gd; at Danzig; in Spain; transferred to Line 1809; 34, 51, 93, 112, 148

ROSEY, Col Baron, lt, fus-chass; lt col cdt 1 *Tir*-chass in Spain; 2 Chass in Russia, 76, 146, 200, 246

ROSILY-MESROS, Vice-Adm Count de, comm French sqdr at Trafalgar, 125–6, 223

T

ACKNOWLEDGMENTS

I wish to express my gratitude to the following persons:

Rear Admiral Richard W. Bates USN (Ret.), professor emeritus of the U.S. Naval War College, Newport, for reading the manuscript and giving helpful advice.

Mr N. R. Belmont-Maitland of London for reading the manuscript.

Baron Louis de Beaufort of Paris for many hours of research in checking the bibliography.

Captain Harrison K. Bird, of Hulett's Landing, N.Y., military historian, for reading the manuscript.

Monsieur Jean Brunon of Marseilles, member of the Conseil d'Administration, Musée de l'Armée, scholar, and collector, for his advice in preparing the illustrations, and for providing those of the marine of the Guard and the lancer of Berg from his incomparable archives.

Mr Hugh Bullock of New York for permission to reproduce his celebrated paintings of Austerlitz by Gérard and the *Farewell at Fontainebleau* by Horace Vernet.

Captain Ross V. Collins USN (Ret.) of Annapolis for reading the manuscript.

Mr Joseph A. Domingoes, cartographer of the U.S. Naval War College, Newport, for drawing the maps.

Colonel John R. Elting USA of the faculty of the U.S. Military Academy, West Point, for reading the proofs, and for giving much helpful advice on the text and the maps.

Brigadier General Robert G. Fergusson USA, chief military advisor on the staff of the U.S. Naval War College, Newport, for reading the manuscript, for preparing the battle and campaign abstracts, and for providing material for the maps.

Colonel Edward M. Flanagan, Jr USA, military historian, of the faculty of the U.S. Naval War College, Newport, for editing the manuscript.

Professor Robert H. George, professor emeritus of European History at Brown University, for reading the first draft of the manuscript and giving encouragement.

Vicomte Robert Grouvel of Paris, vice president of the Sabretache, for granting permission to reproduce many precious documents from the *Carnet de la Sabretache*.

Madame la Vicomtesse Grouvel of the curatorial staff, Musée de Versailles, for research on several illustrations.

Mr Richard B. Harrington of Providence, my librarian, for his assistance in checking and preparing the bibliography, and for preparing the illustrations for reproduction.

Mr David A. Jonah, librarian of Brown University and director of the University Press, for his indispensable advice and encouragement; and to the staff of the John Hay Library for their efficient help in making available the rich resources of the library.

Commandant Henry Lachouque of Montmartre, the author, for his gracious permission to translate, condense, and adapt his work for English-speaking readers, and for his courtesy and assistance during the process.

ACKNOWLEDGMENTS

Herrn Christian Nebehay of Vienna for his tireless efforts in supervising the manufacture of the blocks for the colored plates; and to Fräulein Gelbmann of his staff.

Monsieur Pierre Ordonneau of Paris, Conseiller d'État, scholar, and collector, for his advice on the illustrations.

Mr Paul Perkins of Ropes, Gray, Best, Coolidge, and Rugg, Boston, for his research and advice on copyrights.

Mr Harold Peterson of Washington, president of the Company of Military Collectors and Historians, eminent scholar and historian of weapons, for reading the manuscript, and for editing the appendix on the weapons of the Guard and making helpful suggestions.

Mrs Mary A. Ryan of Providence, my faithful secretary, for many arduous hours of typing corrections and correspondence in connection with the book.

Dr Bruno Schindler of Percy Lund, Humphries & Co. Ltd, London, for his unfailing courtesy and cooperation and his labors 'beyond the call of duty' in the production of the book.

Monsieur A. Vervaet, director of Bloud & Gay, publishers of the original text, for ceding the rights to the American edition.

Finally, to my long-suffering husband for reading innumerable drafts and proofs and providing fastidious criticism; to my children for bearing with a detached and negligent parent; and to my household for covering up my many derelictions in domestic duties over the past four years.

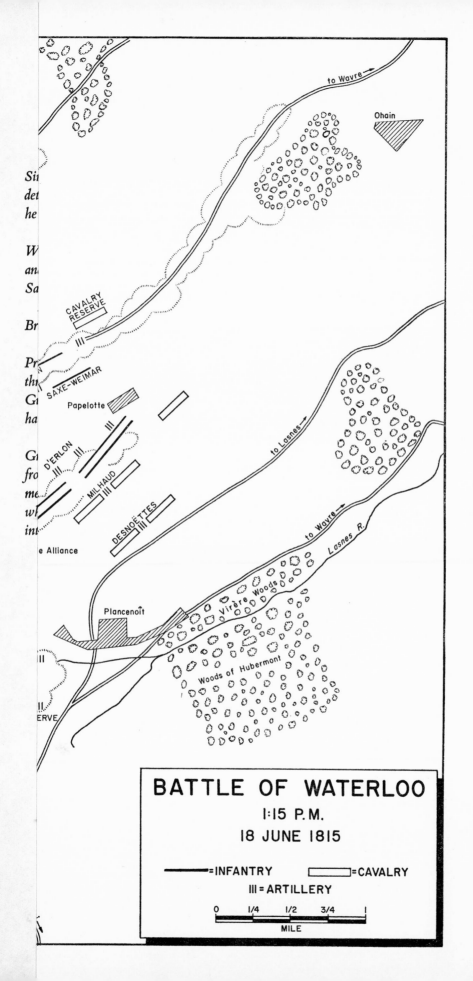

to Wavre

Ohain

Si
det
he

W
an
Sa

Br

Pr
th
G
ha

G
fro
me
wh
int

CAVALRY RESERVE

III

SAXE-WEIMAR

Papelotte

III

D'ERLON

III   III

III

MILHAUD

III

to Lasnes →

DESNOËTTES

III

e Alliance

to Wavre →

Lasnes R.

Virère Woods

Plancenoît

II

II
ERVE

Woods of Hubermont

BATTLE OF WATERLOO
1:15 P.M.
18 JUNE 1815

━━━ = INFANTRY   ▭ = CAVALRY

III = ARTILLERY

0   1/4   1/2   3/4   1

MILE

THE LAST CAMPAIGN

Since the Allies turned down Napoleon's request for peace, and mobilized their armies, Napoleon determined to take the offensive. Believing the Allies could not invade France before mid-July, he would strike their armies in Belgium in June.

Wellington was near Brussels with 90,000 men; Blücher near Namur with over 120,000. With an army of over 120,000, Napoleon planned to strike between the two armies, divide them, and defeat them in turn. On 15 June Napoleon struck Blücher at Charleroi and crossed the Sambre, temporarily preventing the Allies from joining forces.

Blücher concentrated his forces at Sombreffe while Wellington centered his near Quatre-Bras. Ney failed in an attempt to take Quatre-Bras, while Napoleon attacked Blücher.

The French and Prussians met head on at Ligny where Napoleon found practically the whole Prussian Army facing him. When the Guard made a fierce attack across Ligny Brook and through the town, Blücher, with his main strength at Saint-Amand, could not contain it. The Guard's attack smashed the Prussian center. Immediate pursuit of the retreating Prussians would have sealed the French victory.

Thinking Blücher had given up his plan to join Wellington, Napoleon belatedly sent Grouchy with 30,000 troops to follow up the Prussians. On the 17th Wellington withdrew from Quatre Bras, followed by Ney and the rest of the French. That night Napoleon's 72,000 men were deployed facing Wellington's 67,000 Anglo-Dutch near Mont-Saint-Jean. Meanwhile, Blücher reached Wavre, followed by Grouchy who disastrously failed to march on an intercept course so as to prevent him from joining Wellington.